MW01285073

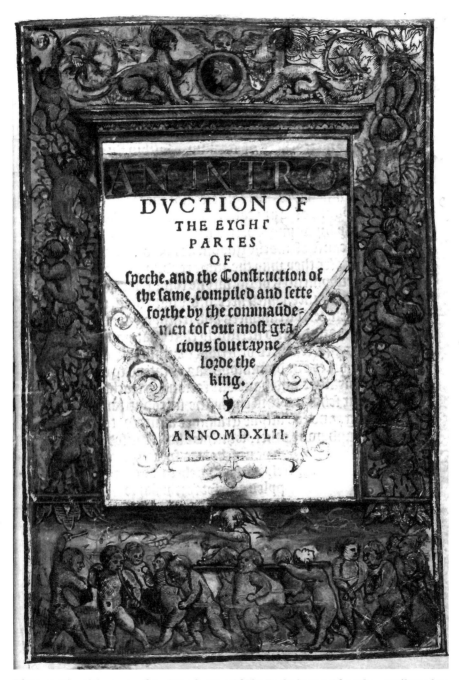

AN INTRO
DVCTION OF
THE EYGHT
PARTES
OF
ſpeche, and the Conſtruction of
the ſame, compiled and ſette
foꝛthe by the commaūde=
ment of our moſt gra
cious ſoueꝛayne
loꝛde the
king.

ANNO. M D. XLII.

Plate 1. The title-page of *An Introduction Of The Eyght Partes Of speche*, attributed to William Lily. London: Thomas Berthelet, 1542. (BL, C.21.b.4.(2).)

Dem Andenken meiner Mutter gewidmet

Lily's Grammar of Latin in English

*An Introduction of the Eyght Partes of Speche,
and the Construction of the Same*

Edited and introduced by

HEDWIG GWOSDEK

OXFORD
UNIVERSITY PRESS

OXFORD
UNIVERSITY PRESS

Great Clarendon Street, Oxford OX2 6DP,
United Kingdom

Oxford University Press is a department of the University of Oxford.
It furthers the University's objective of excellence in research, scholarship,
and education by publishing worldwide. Oxford is a registered trade mark of
Oxford University Press in the UK and in certain other countries.

© Hedwig Gwosdek 2013

The moral rights of the author have been asserted

First published in 2013

Impression: 1

All rights reserved. No part of this publication may be reproduced, stored in
a retrieval system, or transmitted, in any form or by any means, without the
prior permission in writing of Oxford University Press, or as expressly permitted
by law, by licence, or under terms agreed with the appropriate reprographics
rights organization. Enquiries concerning reproduction outside the scope of the
above should be sent to the Rights Department, Oxford University Press, at the
address above

You must not circulate this work in any other form
and you must impose this same condition on any acquirer

British Library Cataloguing in Publication Data

Data available

ISBN 978–0–19–966811–3

Printed in Great Britain by
CPI Group (UK) Ltd, Croydon, CR0 4YY

CONTENTS

Preface   vii
Acknowledgements   xi
List of plates   xiii
Abbreviations and short titles   xiv

1. Introduction   1
   1.1 'Lily's Grammar': the authorized school grammar in England   1
   1.2 Earlier linguistic research   15
   1.3 Bibliographical information since the eighteenth century   24

2. The grammatical tradition   28
   2.1 Elementary Latin grammar and its teaching   28
   2.2 Late Anglo-Saxon vernacular grammar: Ælfric's *Grammar*   32
   2.3 Towards grammar writing in English in the late Middle Ages 41
   2.4 The English grammatical manuscripts   47
   2.5 The early printed grammars in English   58

3. The grammar attributed to William Lily   75
   3.1 Form and contents of the different sections of 'Lily's
       Grammar', London, British Library, C.21.b.4.   75
   3.2 The date and composition of the earliest copy of the
       Introduction   83
   3.3 Biographical background: Lily and the authorship of the
       Introduction   88
   3.4 The *Introduction* and its sources   99

4. Towards a uniform school grammar and its teaching   110
   4.1 Grammatical manuscripts and the teaching of Latin in
       English   110
   4.2 Early printed grammars and the diversity in teaching   116
   4.3 From the diversity of grammars towards a uniform grammar 118

5. 'Lily's Grammar' and the first grammar of English   123
   5.1 Latin and the role of the vernacular in the late Tudor period 123
   5.2 William Bullokar's *Pamphlet for Grammar* (1586)   128
   5.3 'Lily's Grammar' as the model for the first grammar of
       English   133

6. Physical description and editorial principles 140
  6.1 Bibliographical description of the *Introduction* 140
  6.2 The present edition 146

7. The Text of 'Lily's Latin Grammar' in English (1542) 150
  AN INTRODVCTION OF THE EYGHT PARTES OF speche 156
  [The Royal Proclamation by Henry VIII] 157
  TO THE REDER 158
  AD PVBEM ANGLICAM. HEXASTICON 160
  AN INTRODVCTION of the eighte partes of speche 161
  GODLY LESSONS for Chyldren 189
  THE CONCORDES of latyne speche 192
  *GVILIELMI Lilii ad suos discipulos monita pædagogica, seu carmen de
    moribus* 204
  CHRISTIANI HOMINIS INSTITVTVM PER ERASMVM ROTERODAMVM 210

8. Commentary 220
  Title-page 220
  Royal Proclamation 221
  To the Reader 222
  Ad Pubem Anglicam. Hexasticon 224
  The Parts of Speech 224
  Godly Lessons for Children 242
  Construction of the Parts of Speech 243
  Carmen de Moribus 252
  Christiani Hominis Institutum 253

Appendix I: Structure and contents of *AN INTRODUCTION of the
  eighte partes of speche* and *THE CONCORDES of latyne speche* 256
Appendix II: The Oxford proof leaf 263
Appendix III: Editions of the Latin grammar attributed to William
  Lily, 1540–1603 265
Appendix IV: Works by, or attributed to, William Lily 284
Appendix V: Definitions of the parts of speech in Latin grammars
  in English (including some Latin grammars in Latin) 289

Bibliography 309
  Primary Works 309
  Secondary Works 318
Index 337

PREFACE

'Lily's Grammar' is the most famous Latin grammar to have appeared in England and represents a landmark in the country's educational history: it deserves the attention of scholars for a number of reasons. A proclamation of 1542 issued by Henry VIII established its two parts as the only authorized grammar to be used by schoolmasters and teachers of grammar. As the authorized and obligatory text in English schools it dominated the teaching of Latin for more than three centuries and thus became a major component of every schoolchild's education until well into the 1800s. Largely by reason of its unique position, 'Lily's Grammar' exerted great influence, both on Latin grammatical studies and on many of the pupils taught with it. Moreover, it became the basis of the first grammar of the English language and enjoyed continuing influence on English grammar writing. As an elementary didactic grammar of Latin, the first part comprises a basic-level accidence and syntax written in English. The second part, not treated here, taking children into the more advanced stages of grammar, is written in Latin.

The grammar, which has generally been attributed to William Lily, is remarkable both as a contemporary grammar and for the influence it exerted. As a school textbook it can be approached in a variety of ways. Its aim was to provide children with a practical knowledge of Latin grammar—the gateway to all the liberal arts and the essential prerequisite for the later acquisition of professional knowledge in theology, law, commerce, and medicine—and, at the same time, to educate them in Christian principles. It introduces the elementary grammatical rules of Latin by means of the children's own language. In this way it offers extensive material for the study of Latin and at the same time of the English used as the language of explanation. The different grammatical rules and explanations it comprises reflect an attempt to set out clearly and systematically what were thought at that time to be basic principles, tenets, and methods for this stage of learning and what was thought best to be used by all teachers in the country. It contains comprehensive statements about the major categories and structures of Latin and of their functions. As the explanatory language was their mother tongue, the children also studied its own forms and structures and must probably have realized what English had in common with Latin and also where it had its own distinct characteristics. This textbook was thus used as a basis for a complete course of the study of elementary Latin explained in the vernacular.

The first part of 'Lily's Grammar', written in English, was not the starting point itself of a new elementary school grammar but has a longer historical perspective. It is part of a tradition of grammatical manuscripts and early printed grammars written in English, as well as the Latin tradition of teaching grammars and the influences of the New Learning. It necessarily drew on earlier material that was considered appropriate for a description of the language in question and suitable for the assumed needs of children. Moreover, from its status as the school grammar authorized by the king, this manual became important in that it set an example for future school grammars and the teaching of Latin. Finally, the first part of 'Lily's Grammar' was to become an inspirational example when Englishmen sat down to compile the rules for their own language. Aiming to teach children to write English more correctly and express themselves more elegantly and to use their knowledge as a stepping stone to learning Latin and foreign languages, the grammarians also sought to benefit foreigners seeking to learn English. It set the example for William Bullokar's *Pamphlet for Grammar* (1586), generally regarded as the earliest extant grammar of the English language. Bullokar's grammar is, to a very large extent indeed, based on the elementary part of 'Lily's Grammar'. Thus, this elementary Latin grammar in English is of central importance in the development of English grammar. Further studies will certainly show that the foundations of the grammar of English have their origin in the tradition of that part of 'Lily's Grammar' that is explained in the vernacular. The beginnings of the study of English grammar, then in the guise of Latin, can in this way be antedated.

Apart from its function as an important linguistic document, this text also has a general value as an historical and cultural document of mid-sixteenth-century teaching, education, and conditions of schooling, and sheds some light on aspects of the daily life of early Tudor England. It exemplifies the status of elementary Latin grammar and the aims of its teaching shortly after the Reformation. It was compiled in keeping with its own historical moment. However, there is a dimension to such school texts and particularly to this grammatical textbook over and above its purely historical importance: it did not remain in the fixed form of an original and was open to much scrutiny and change, as it was used by many teachers for more than three centuries. The authorized text, modified and revised by various grammarians, appeared in many printed versions, and functioned as an adaptable companion for teachers and pupils in changing times and circumstances. And, like most educational books, it aimed at perfection in its subject.

The text of the earliest recorded edition of 'Lily's' elementary Latin grammar is presented here, as printed by the King's Printer, Thomas Berthelet, in 1542. My aim is to provide the first scholarly edition of this important text in the history of linguistics and language teaching, and in the history of grammar writing in English, as a step towards narrowing the prevailing gap in scholarship. Accordingly, I have provided a detailed apparatus with five appendices that present the text in its bibliographical and grammatical context, together with an introduction. The text of the English part of 'Lily's Grammar' deserves to be edited for a number of reasons. First, the 1542 edition, represented by the complete British Library copy, provides the text that was used as a basis for all subsequent editions, excerpts, and reworkings of this grammar. Second, this text came to epitomize the tradition of the elementary Latin grammar in English of which treatises are extant from c.1400 and thus embraces the results of the efforts of generations of grammar masters since the second half of the fourteenth century. Third, it represents an official document that brought the teaching of Latin under the authority of the king. Fourth, known as 'Lily's Grammar', 'The King's Grammar', and in some later versions as 'The Eton Latin Grammar', this grammar was used in the teaching of Latin in English schools up to the second half of the nineteenth century and thus influenced the learning of most pupils over a very extended period. Finally, an edition of this work fills a gap in scholarship, since 'Lily's Grammar' has continued to occupy the attention of bibliographers for more than 250 years and of scholars of linguistics and language for about 150 years, without their having had access to the text of the first extant edition. An edition of the Latin part would, without any doubt, complement the grammar written in English. However, as the grammar in Latin is also an outcome of many sources of a long tradition of grammar writing, we have not yet reached a stage where a more comprehensive and ambitious edition would be possible. The Latin elementary grammars in England that are derived from Donatus's *Ars minor* and also the later treatises dealing with syntax, other than those listed in David Thomson's *Catalogue* (1979), have not even yet been catalogued.

My aim is to examine the grammar in English and its constituent parts from a number of different aspects. By bringing together areas of scholarship that are usually kept apart, I hope to enable students of different disciplines to gain an understanding of the whole work and to obtain a broader, more comprehensive view of it and thus appreciate its unusual status. Later editions and also the earlier sources of this grammar have often been referred to in scholarly works. However, an attempt has been made here to draw attention to the volume as a whole and to its individual texts, and to consider how 'Lily's' grammars on accidence and construction emerged from the grammatical tradition and how they were transmitted after 1542. The educational and cultural status of the book is also discussed.

I have attempted to present the different texts as far as possible in their original form. I have quoted from those sources of the grammatical tradition that were available to me, mostly in the original, and have presented the later grammatical, educational, and historical evidence. Spelling and punctuation have been retained in references and in quotations from fifteenth- and sixteenth-century documents, but I have expanded all abbreviations. Quotations in foreign languages are given in English translation; where possible, I have used existing translations into English and have indicated the source. However, where these fail I have had recourse to my own translations, without giving an extra reference. I am aware that my contribution can do little more than open the door to the study of grammar in sixteenth-century England. Much source material that remains unstudied will certainly eventually bring to light more details of fact and argument. An edition of the Latin part of 'Lily's Grammar' is urgently needed, and most of its source material in manuscript and early printed books awaits study. Only after that shall we have a more complete picture of the entire grammar attributed to William Lily, of the study of grammar in the Tudor period, and of its general setting within its European context. My study represents but one step in that direction.

Acknowledgements

This work could not have been accomplished without the help and support of many people. I should like to acknowledge my indebtedness to the librarians and archivists who provided me with microfilms and photocopies of the material that forms the basis of this book. They have also been unfailing in answering queries during my visits and in correspondence. I owe thanks to the following libraries, archives, and institutions: University Library, Aberdeen; National Library of Wales, Aberystwyth; Cambridge University Library; Clare College, Cambridge; Corpus Christi College, Cambridge; King's College, Cambridge; Pembroke College, Cambridge; St John's College, Cambridge; Trinity College, Dublin; The National Library of Scotland, Edinburgh; Eton College Library; Glasgow University Library; Leeds University Library; The British Library, London; Guildhall Library, London; Mercers' Hall, London; The National Archives of the United Kingdom, Public Record Office, London; St Paul's Cathedral Library, London; St Paul's School, London; Westminster Abbey, London; Westminster School, London; John Rylands University Library, Manchester; Bavarian State Library, Munich; Northamptonshire County Council Record Office, Northampton; University Library, Nottingham; Bodleian Library, Oxford; Christ Church, Oxford; Corpus Christi College, Oxford; Magdalen College, Oxford; New College, Oxford; St John's College, Oxford; The Venerable English College, Rome; King Edward VI School, Stratford-upon-Avon; Henry E. Huntington Library, San Marino, California; Royal Library, The Hague; Town Library, Ulm; University of Illinois at Urbana-Champaign Library, Urbana, Illinois; Folger Shakespeare Library, Washington, D.C.; and Winchester College, Winchester. I also owe thanks to Bernard Quaritch Ltd., London, for information about catalogues and to University Microfilm International, Ann Arbor, Michigan, regarding microfilms. Most of the work was done at Tübingen University Library, where I owe particular thanks to the staff on catalogue information, the librarians in the reading rooms, the interlibrary loan section, and the photographic section for having been most co-operative and helpful in every way. The book has also profited from the kind help of Susan Bollinger, University of Munich, and Astrid Schröder, MA, University of Bonn.

I am indebted to scholars and colleagues who gave me the initial stimulus to start this project and helped me very generously on various points on its way: to the late Professor Dr Werner Hüllen, University of

Duisburg-Essen; Dr Alfred Hüttemann, Essen; Professor Dr Markus Janka, University of Munich; Professor Louis Kelly, Darwin College, Cambridge; Dr Elisabeth Leedham-Green, University of Cambridge; Professor Nicholas Orme, University of Exeter; Dr Gale Owen-Crocker, University of Manchester; the late Mrs Vivian Salmon, London; Dr Chris Stray, University of Wales, Swansea; the Revd Dr David Thomson, Ely; the late Professor Joseph Trapp, Warburg Institute, University of London; Professor Dr Hildegard L. C. Tristram, University of Freiburg; and Professor Dr Konrad Vollmann, University of Munich. I should like to thank Dr Oliver Pickering, Brotherton Library, University of Leeds, for offering expert advice on many points. I would like to acknowledge the advice and many helpful suggestions I received from the late Mr David Mackenzie, Biddestone, Wiltshire, while I prepared this work. He shared with me his wide knowledge on Lily and the copies of editions of the grammars attributed to him and also read drafts of the manuscript. I owe particular thanks to Professor Dr Hans Sauer, University of Munich, for his continued help, encouragement, and support in many ways. I would also like to thank the two anonymous Oxford University Press readers for their useful suggestions. I am grateful to Mr John Davey, Consultant Editor for Linguistics at Oxford University Press, for unstinting support by him throughout the production of this book, and I am particularly indebted to Mr Adrian Stenton for his painstaking work in preparing the manuscript for printing. All errors and shortcomings of this work are my own responsibility.

My work on this topic was supported by a grant from the Bibliographical Society, London, for which I would like to express my sincere thanks. I should also like to acknowledge the assistance afforded by a travel grant from the Fritz Thyssen Stiftung, Cologne. Moreover, I am most grateful to the Salmon-Verburg Memorial Fund for the award of a grant for the purpose of attending the Henry Sweet Society Colloquium in Oxford, September 2004, which also enabled me to carry out further research in English libraries.

The English translation of the poem *Christiani Hominis Institutum per Erasmum Roterodamum* has been taken from *Collected Works of Erasmus: Poems*, ed. Harry Vredeveld, Vol. 85: 93, 95, 97, 99, 101, 103, 105, and 107. (c) University of Toronto Press, 1993. Reprinted with permission of the publisher.

Hedwig Gwosdek
Spring 2013

List of Plates

1. Frontispiece: The title-page of *An Introduction Of The Eyght Partes Of speche*, attributed to William Lily. London: Thomas Berthelet, 1542. (BL, C.21.b.4.(2).)   i

2. Engraved portrait of William Lily. Anonymous. Modern impression. (The British Museum, Portraits Section, Class 7, Period I. Register No. 1850–6–12–119.)   97

3. Portrait of William Lily in a panel of the south window of the Hall of Christ Church, Oxford. (XIX century.)   98

4. Royal proclamation. (BL, C.21.b.4.(2), leaf A1^v.)   150

5. The beginning of the text on the parts of speech. (BL, C.21.b.4.(2), leaf A4^r.)   151

6. The conjugation of the verbs. (BL, C.21.b.4.(2), leaf C4^r.)   152

7. *Godly Lessons for Chyldren.* (BL, C.21.b.4.(2), leaf F2^v.)   153

8. The end of *Godly Lessons for Chyldren* and the beginning of *The Concordes of latyne speche*. (BL, C.21.b.4.(2), leaf F4^r.)   154

9. The end of *The Concordes of latyne speche*. (BL, C.21.b.4.(2), leaf H4^r.)   155

10. Fragment of a proof leaf of *An Introduction Of The Eyght Partes Of speche*. [London: Thomas Berthelet, c.1540]. (Bodl. Lib., Vet.A1.a.4(1).)   262

Plates 1 and 4–9 are reproduced by permission of The British Library, London; plate 2 by permission of The British Museum, London; plate 3 by permission of the Governing Body of Christ Church, Oxford; plate 10 by permission of the Bodleian Library, University of Oxford.

Abbreviations and Short Titles

1 *References*

Adams	H. M. Adams (1967). *Catalogue of Books Printed on the Continent of Europe, 1501–1600, in Cambridge Libraries.*
Alston	R. C. Alston (1965–). *A Bibliography of the English Language from the Invention of Printing to the Year 1800.*
Alston-Hill	R. C. Alston and Brad Sabin Hill (1996). *Books Printed on Vellum in the Collections of The British Library.*
Ames	Joseph Ames (1749). *Typographical Antiquities.*
BBKL	Friedrich Wilhelm Bautz (Hrsg.) (1975–2010). *Biographisch-Bibliographisches Kirchenlexikon.*
Beale	Joseph Henry Beale (1926). *A Bibliography of Early English Law Books.*
Bland	Cynthia Renée Bland (1991). *The Teaching of Grammar in Late Medieval England.*
BLC	*The British Library General Catalogue of Printed Books to 1975* (1979–1988).
BM Catalogue	George Bullen and Gregory W. Eccles (1884). *Catalogue of Books in the Library of the British Museum [. . .] to the Year 1640.*
BM STC (Netherlands)	*Short-Title Catalogue of Books Printed in the Netherlands and Belgium [. . .] from 1470 to 1600 [. . .]* (1965).
BMC	*Catalogue of Books Printed in the XVth Century Now in the British Museum [British Library]* (1908–2007).
Bodleian Library Exhibition Catalogue	*Bodleian Library Records. Unpublished Papers for Erasmus and his Friends* (1969).
Botfield	Beriah Botfield (1855–1856). *Bibliotheca Membranacea Britannica.*
Britwell Handlist	Sydney Richardson Christie-Miller (1933). *The Britwell Handlist, or Short-Title Catalogue of the Principal Volumes from the Time of Caxton to the Year 1800.*
BRUC	A. B. Emden (1963). *A Biographical Register of the University of Cambridge to 1500.*
BRUO	A. B. Emden (1957–1959). *A Biographical Register of the University of Oxford to A.D. 1500.*
BRUO, 1501–1540	A. B. Emden (1974). *A Biographical Register of the University of Oxford, A.D. 1501 to 1540.*

Certayne Briefe Rules	*Certayne Briefe Rules of the regiment or construction of the eyght partes of speche, in englishe and latine* (1537).
Checklist	Hedwig Gwosdek (2000). *A Checklist of Middle English Grammatical Manuscripts and Early Printed Grammars, c. 1400–1540.*
Colet, *Aeditio* (1527)	John Colet. *Aeditio.* Antwerp: Christopher van Ruremond?
Contemporaries of Erasmus	Peter G. Bietenholz and Thomas B. Deutscher (eds.) (1985–1987). *Contemporaries of Erasmus.*
CWE	Desiderius Erasmus (1974–). *Collected Works of Erasmus.*
Davies	Hugh W. Davies (1962). *Catalogue of a Collection of Early German Books in the Library of C. Fairfax Murray.*
Dibdin, *Decameron*	Thomas Frognall Dibdin (1817). *The Bibliographical Decameron.*
Dibdin, *Library Companion*	Thomas Frognall Dibdin (1825). *The Library Companion.*
Dibdin, *Typographical Antiquities*	Thomas Frognall Dibdin (ed.) (1810–1819). *Typographical Antiquities or The History of Printing in England.*
Dictionary of British Classicists	Robert B. Todd (ed.) (2004). *The Dictionary of British Classicists.*
DNB	Leslie Stephen and Sidney Lee (eds.) (1908–1909). *Dictionary of National Biography.*
Duff, *Handlists*	E. Gordon Duff *et al.* (1895–1913). *Handlists of Books Printed by London Printers, 1501–1556.*
Duff, *Vellum*	E. Gordon Duff (1902). 'English Printing on Vellum to the End of the Year 1600.'
Early Printed Editions	Hedwig Gwosdek (ed.) (1991). *Early Printed Editions of the Long Accidence and Short Accidence Grammars.*
EL	R. C. Alston (ed.) (1967–1972). *English Linguistics, 1500–1800.*
Ferguson	Mungo Ferguson (1930). *The Printed Books in the Library of the Hunterian Museum of the University of Glasgow.*
Gibson	R. W. Gibson (1961). *St. Thomas More: A Preliminary Bibliography of His Works and of Moreana to the Year 1750.*
GL	Heinrich Keil (ed.) (1855–1880). *Grammatici Latini.*
Gneuss, *Handlist*	Helmut Gneuss (2001). *Handlist of Anglo-Saxon Manuscripts.*
Goff	Frederick R. Goff (ed.) (1964). *Incunabula in American Libraries.*
Gray	G. J. Gray (1893). *A General Index to Hazlitt's Handbook and his Bibliographical Collections (1867–1889).*
Greg	W. W. Greg (1904–1906). 'Notes on the Types, Borders, etc., Used by Thomas Berthelet.'

Hain	Ludwig Hain (1826–1838). *Repertorium Bibliographicum.*
Hain–Copinger	W. A. Copinger (1895–1902). *Supplement to Hain's Repertorium Bibliographicum.*
Halkett and Laing	John Horden (ed.) (1980). *Halkett and Laing: A Dictionary of Anonymous and Pseudonymous Publications in the English Language, 1475–1640.*
Halliwell	J. O. Halliwell (1860). *A Hand-List of the Early English Literature Preserved in the Douce Collection in the Bodleian Library.*
Hazlitt	W. Carew Hazlitt (1867). *Handbook to the Popular, Poetical, and Dramatic Literature of Great Britain.*
Heckethorn	Charles William Heckethorn (1897). *The Printers of Basle in the XV and XVI Centuries.*
HEL	Bernard Colombat and Elisabeth Lazcano (1998, 2000). *Corpus Représentatif des Grammaires et des Traditions Linguistiques.*
Herbert	William Herbert (ed.) (1785–1790). *Typographical Antiquities.*
HMC	*Historical Manuscripts Commission.*
Holtz	Louis Holtz (ed.) (1981). *Donat et la Tradition de l'Enseignement Grammatical.*
Hughes and Larkin	Paul L. Hughes and James F. Larkin (eds.) (1964–1969). *Tudor Royal Proclamations.*
HWRh	Gert Ueding (ed.) (1992–2011). *Historisches Wörterbuch der Rhetorik.*
IISTC	Martin Davies (gen. ed.) (1998). *The Illustrated Incunabula Short Title Catalogue on CD-ROM.*
Isaac, *Index*	Frank Isaac (1938). *An Index to the Early Printed Books in the British Museum.* Part II: 1501–1520.
Johnston	Stanley Howard Johnston, Jr. (1977). *A Study of the Career and Literary Publications of Richard Pynson.*
Kennedy	Arthur G. Kennedy (1927). *A Bibliography of Writings on the English Language from the Beginning of Printing to the End of 1922.*
Ker, *Catalogue*	N. R. Ker (1957). *Catalogue of Manuscripts Containing Anglo-Saxon.* (Repr. 1990).
Latham, *Catalogue*	Robert Latham (1978). *Catalogue of the Pepys Library at Magdalene College, Cambridge.*
Latham, *Medieval Latin Word-List*	R. E. Latham (1965). *Revised Medieval Latin Word-List from British and Irish Sources.*
LCL	*The Loeb Classical Library* (1912–). Ed. T. E. Page *et al.*
Lewis and Short	Charlton T. Lewis and Charles Short (1969). *A Latin Dictionary.* Rev., enl., and in great part rewritten.

Lexicon Grammaticorum	Harro Stammerjohann (gen. ed.) (2009). *Lexicon Grammaticorum*. 2nd edn., rev. and enl.
Lily, *Libellus de constructione* (1513)	William Lily. *Libellus de constructione Octo partium orationis* [Anon. Ed. D. Erasmus].
Lily, *Rudimenta grammatices* (1527)	William Lily. *Rudimenta grammatices*, in Colet, *Aeditio* (1527).
Lily, *Shorte Introduction* (1567)	William Lily. *A Shorte Introduction of Grammar*. [A facsimile ed.].
Lily and Colet (1548/49)	William Lily and John Colet. *A Short Introduction of Grammar*. [A facsimile ed.].
Maitland, *Index*	S. R. Maitland (1845). *An Index of Such English Books, Printed Before the Year MDC as are Now in the Archiepiscopal Library at Lambeth*.
Maitland, *List*	S. R. Maitland (1843). *A List of Some of the Early Printed Books in the Archiepiscopal Library at Lambeth*.
McK	Ronald B. McKerrow (1913). *Printers' and Publishers' Devices in England and Scotland, 1485–1640*.
McK&F	R. B. McKerrow and F. S. Ferguson (1932 (for 1931)). *Title-Page Borders Used in England and Scotland, 1485–1640*.
MED	Hans Kurath *et al.* (eds.) (1952–2001). *Middle English Dictionary*.
Moore	J. K. Moore (1992). *Primary Materials Relating to Copy and Print in English Books of the Sixteenth and Seventeenth Centuries*.
Nichols (1857)	John Gough Nichols (ed.) (1857). *Literary Remains of King Edward the Sixth*.
Nijhoff-Kronenberg	W. Nijhoff and M. E. Kronenberg (1923–1971). *Nederlandsche Bibliographie van 1500 tot 1540*.
NUC	*The National Union Catalog. Pre-1956 Imprints* (1968–1981).
ODEP	William G. Smith and Frank P. Wilson (1970). *The Oxford Dictionary of English Proverbs*. 3rd rev. edn.
OED	James A. H. Murray *et al.* (eds.) (1933). *The Oxford English Dictionary*. Oxford. 2nd edn.
ODNB	H. C. G. Matthew and Brian Harrison (eds.) (2004). *The Oxford Dictionary of National Biography*. 2nd edn. of the DNB.
Quaritch Catalogue 436	Bernard Quaritch Ltd. (1930). *A Catalogue of Books in English History and Literature from the Earliest Times to the End of the Seventeenth Century*.
Quaritch Catalogue 464	Bernard Quaritch Ltd. (1932). *A Catalogue of Rare and Valuable Early Schoolbooks*.

Quarrie	Paul Quarrie (1990). *Treasures of Eton College Library*.
Renouard, *Imprimeurs*	Philippe Renouard (1964–1995). *Imprimeurs et Libraires Parisiens du XVIe Siècle*.
Sayle	Charles E. Sayle (1900–1907). *Early English Printed Books in the University Library Cambridge (1475–1640)*.
Shaaber	M. A. Shaaber (1975). *Check-list of Works of British Authors Printed Abroad, in Languages Other Than English, to 1641*.
Sharpe	Richard Sharpe (1997). *A Handlist of the Latin Writers of Great Britain and Ireland Before 1540*.
Shaw	David J. Shaw (1984–1998). *The Cathedral Libraries Catalogue*.
Smith	Constance Smith (1981). 'An Updating of R. W. Gibson's "St. Thomas More": A Preliminary Bibliography', *Sixteenth Century Bibliography* 20.
STC	A. W. Pollard and G. R. Redgrave (1926). *A Short-Title Catalogue of Books Printed in England [. . .], 1475–1640*. 1st edn.
STC²	A. W. Pollard and G. R. Redgrave (1976–1991). *A Short-Title Catalogue of Books Printed in England [. . .], 1475–1640*. 2nd edn.
Thomson, *Catalogue*	David Thomson (1979). *A Descriptive Catalogue of Middle English Grammatical Texts*.
Thomson, *Edition*	David Thomson (ed.) (1984). *An Edition of the Middle English Grammatical Texts*.
Tilley	Morris Palmer Tilley (1950). *A Dictionary of the Proverbs in England in the Sixteenth and Seventeenth Centuries*.
Trapp–Schulte Herbrüggen	J. B. Trapp and H. Schulte Herbrüggen (1978). 'The King's Good Servant'. *Sir Thomas More 1477/8–1535*. Catalogue of the Exhibition at the National Portrait Gallery, London.
UMI, *EEB*	University Microfilms International (1938–). *Early English Books, 1475–1640*.
Vancil	David E. Vancil (1993). *Catalog of Dictionaries, Word Books, and Philological Texts, 1400–1900: Inventory of the Cordell Collection, Indiana State University*.
VCH	*The Victoria History of the Counties of England*.
VD 16	*Verzeichnis der im deutschen Sprachbereich erschienenen Drucke des XVI. Jahrhunderts* (1983–2000).
Walther	Hans Walther (1982–1986). *Proverbia Sententiaeque Latinitatis Medii Ac Recentioris Aevi*. Nova series.
Whiting	Bartlett Jere Whiting (1968). *Proverbs, Sentences, and Proverbial Phrases from English Writings Mainly Before 1500*.
Wing	*Short-Title Catalogue of Books Printed in England [. . .], 1641–1700*. 2nd edn.

Wolf	Melvin H. Wolf (1974). *Catalogue and Indexes to the Title-Pages of English Printed Books Preserved in the British Library's Bagford Collection.*
Zupitza	Julius Zupitza (ed.) (1880). *Ælfrics Grammatik und Glossar.*

2 Electronic catalogues

BBKL	*Biographisch-Bibliographisches Kirchenlexikon* (1990–2009). <http://www.bautz.de/bbkl/>
Database of Bookbindings	*Database of Bookbindings.* London: The British Library. <http://www.bl.uk/catalogues/bookbindings/>
EEBO	*Early English Books Online, 1475–1700.* Online database. ProQuest. Subscription service. <http://eebo.chadwyck.com/>
ESTC	*English Short Title Catalogue Online, 1473–1800.* The British Library and *ESTC*/North America. <http://estc.bl.uk/>
HEL	*Corpus des Textes Linguistiques Fondamentaux.* (= Enl. version of *Corpus Représentatif des Grammaires et des Traditions Linguistiques. Histoire Épistémologie Langage.* Hors-sér. nos. 2–3 (1998, 2000). 2 vols.). <http://ctlf.ens-lyon.fr/>
MED	*Middle English Dictionary.* Ann Arbor. 2nd edn. Online. <http://quod.lib.umich.edu/m/med/>
ODNB	*Oxford Dictionary of National Biography* (2004). The Online Edition. Oxford: Oxford University Press. Subscription service. <http://www.oxforddnb.com/>
OED	*Oxford English Dictionary.* Oxford. 3rd edn. Online. Subscription service. <http://www.oed.com/>
PLRE	*Private Libraries in Renaissance England* <http://plre.folger.edu/>

All accessed 22 May 2013

3 Libraries and archives

BL	The British Library, London
BM	British Museum, London
Bodl. Lib.	Bodleian Library, Oxford
CUL	Cambridge University Library
JRUL	John Rylands University Library, University of Manchester
MCA	Magdalen College Archives, Oxford

TNA   The National Archives of the United Kingdom, Public
                           Record Office, London

4 *Other abbreviations*

e.g. Ames, 173   refers to Ames, p. 173
e.g. *BM Catalogue*,   refers to *BM Catalogue*, vol. 2, p. 883
  vol. 2: 883
e.g. Carlson (1993),   refers to Carlson (1993), p. 127, and note 8, pp. 232–33
  127, and note 8:
  232–33
e.g. McK&F 124   refers to McK&F, no. 124
e.g. Thomson,   refers to Thomson, *Edition*, Text K, p. 56, lines 12–14
  Edition, Text K,
  56, 12–14
Bd., Bde.   Band, Bände
EETS, OS   Early English Text Society, Original Series
enl.   enlarged
Ep.   Epistula, Epistulae
Hrsg.   Herausgeber (editor)
ME   Middle English
MS Add.   Additional Manuscript
OE   Old English
OHS   Oxford Historical Society
orn.   ornament
per.   [during the] period
PMLA   *Publications of the Modern Language Association of America*
rev.   revised
Uncat.   Uncatalogued

1. INTRODUCTION

1.1 'Lily's Grammar': the authorized school grammar in England

'Lily's Grammar'[1] represents the culmination of some two centuries' work of teaching Latin grammar in schools in England from the Black Death in 1348/49 until 1540, when it was introduced by King Henry VIII's proclamation as the first officially authorized Latin grammar for use in English schools. From that time onwards it became the most popular school grammar and was enormously influential until the second half of the nineteenth century. On the basis of the large number of editions published it was undoubtedly one of the best-selling schoolbooks in Great Britain. It became the standard approach to teaching Latin and the key text on which the elementary classes of the grammar schools were founded, as no other grammars could lawfully be used. Not only did it set down the 'correct text', but comprised a great part of the children's personal learning and defined their modes of thought. Moreover, it is not surprising that while the authorized grammar was in use, other grammatical treatises that came to be written in the course of time were influenced by it in shaping grammatical rules and terms, and that it equally influenced the methods of language teaching. This introductory survey, touching a few aspects of the development and use of 'Lily's Grammar' which are of particular interest, will attempt to describe the context in which this popular textbook appeared and give some idea of the multiple roles it played in the second half of the Tudor period when its influence was consolidated.

'The grammar attributed to William Lily', like teaching grammars in general and other manuals required in the classrooms for instruction, is categorized as a textbook, *i.e.* it belongs to that class of books that is prepared for the study of a particular subject and usually written specifically for that practical purpose. Textbooks embody subject matter prepared for instruction according to the pedagogical aims and the institutional contexts in which they are to be used and to form part of the process of

---

[1] In this work the terms 'Lily's Grammar' and 'the grammar attributed to William Lily', comprise the two (in some later editions three) parts of the grammar for the teaching of Latin published from 1540 onwards, *i.e.* the Latin grammar written in English (English part) and the Latin grammar in Latin (Latin part). The English part of the 1542 edition alone is hereafter referred to as *Introduction* and the Latin part of the 1540 edition as *Institutio*.

education.[2] Due to the low esteem they were generally accorded, early editions of Latin grammars, as textbooks in general, are extremely rare today. They were the tools that were needed and of value as long as they served to acquire knowledge or the skills that were necessary to achieve some aim in education or career advancement. Afterwards they may have been passed on to subsequent users, or were thumbed to pieces, or were discarded as being too common to be worthy of preservation. This class of books was often not to be found in libraries, or if there, not catalogued, or if catalogued, not entered in the main catalogue, which is the only one available to most readers. Apart from that, some works compiled by William Lily are occasionally catalogued under different authors, such as John Colet or Erasmus. Complete and incomplete copies of the huge number of editions that were printed, in particular of 'Lily's Grammar', are still being discovered from time to time. Accident usually plays a role in the making of such new discoveries. No doubt copies have survived that remain uncatalogued or lie forgotten in storage rooms or are yet to be discovered in unpredictable libraries. It is not possible to give a reliable answer to the question of how many editions, not to mention the number of copies of editions, were printed during the long history of this grammar. Robin Alston put it this way: "Will we ever, I sometimes wonder, know how many times Lily's grammar was *really* reprinted? If the evidence for English spelling books is any guide, I suspect that 50% of all the Lily's have vanished without trace!"[3] On the number of editions of 'Lily's Grammar' that has survived, *STC*[2], *ESTC*, and Alston must be the main guides. In many cases the editions are represented by no more than a single surviving copy or fragment.[4] From its introduction in 1540 this grammar belonged to that class of books which enjoyed the protection of

---

[2] A textbook is essentially a book designed for use in a formal teaching environment and generally, but not absolutely and exclusively, for studying academic subjects. It provides an authoritative pedagogical version of an area of knowledge. In the earlier sixteenth century, as subsequently, textbooks were an essential component of any course in literacy, the most important of them being the primer, consisting of an alphabet and a collection of prayers and used as the initial reading book in all schools. On the definition of textbook see Christopher Stray (1994), '"Paradigms Regained": Towards a Historical Sociology of the Textbook', *Journal of Curriculum Studies* 26: 1–29; and Ian Michael (1993), *Early Textbooks of English. A Guide*, Reading, 1–2.

[3] Robin Alston (1999), 'What Mad Pursuit?', *The Henry Sweet Society Bulletin* 32: 25–30, at 29. According to Alston, 'Lily's Grammar' "went through some 300 editions". He adds that there are also numerous works published before 1800 which are based on it and which also became popular school texts. See Alston (1966), 'Bibliography and Historical Linguistics', *The Library*, 5th ser., 21: 181–91, at 188–89.

[4] Copies of editions are recorded in *STC*[2] 15610.5–15633.8; Wing, vol. 2, nos. L2254–L2304D; Alston, vol. 15, nos. 494–729; and *ESTC*. The text of a large number of copies of editions is accessible in *EEBO*. Most extant copies of 'Lily's Grammar' comprise two parts, its English and its Latin part often belonging to different editions of the respective part.

the king and which only the King's Printer was permitted to publish, in contrast to the variety of printers who competed to meet the demand of grammar schools and ventured to put out editions of other grammars before that date. However, there is no information available about the number and size of editions of 'Lily's Grammar' when Thomas Berthelet, Printer to King Henry VIII from 1530 until Henry's death in 1547, began to publish it.[5] With the accession to the throne of Henry's son, King Edward VI, important groups of books were assigned to individual printers. Reyner (Reginald) Wolfe was the first printer to be appointed to the office of Royal Printer and Typographer for Latin, Greek, and Hebrew and was also to be the King's Bookseller and Stationer.[6] This patent, including the exclusive privilege to print books of grammar, was dominated by the publication of 'Lily's Grammar'. It was granted for life, and all other printers and booksellers were forbidden to print, sell, or bind any of the books included in this grant. It suggests that the prerogative to print the class of books involved was highly valued and was also intended to protect this cheap, popular, and very profitable textbook from being pirated. The number and size of editions of the authorized grammar issued from Wolfe's press must have varied due not only to the demand for copies for schools in the country but probably due to official regulations.[7] Wolfe's patent was first issued on 19 April 1547 but was reconfirmed on 17 July 1558 under Queen Elizabeth, several printers having ignored the prohibition in the first patent. After Wolfe's death, probably at the end of 1573, the grammar patent was granted to Francis Flower on 15 December of the same year. In the same month, however, Flower, who was not a printer or bookseller, transferred the privilege to six assignes on payment of a yearly rent of a hundred pounds, an action which suggests that the right to print the authorized grammar had become a very valuable property, and the granting of this privilege caused discontent among the less favoured printers.[8] Thus, the imprints in the surviving

---

[5] On Berthelet see *ODNB*, vol. 5: 480–81; also Pamela Ayers Neville (1990), *Richard Pynson, King's Printer (1506–1529): Printing and Propaganda in Early Tudor England*, Ph.D. Dissertation. London, 63–64, 185–86; and E. Gordon Duff (1905), *A Century of the English Book Trade*. London; repr. 2011, 11–12. The King's Printer had the sole right to print any work issued or belonging to the king. The works included in this monopoly at first were Acts of Parliament, law books and year books, Bibles and service books, almanacs, and Latin grammars and other educational works.

[6] On Wolfe see *ODNB*, vol. 59: 970–71; also *Contemporaries of Erasmus*, vol. 3: 459–60. On the patent granted to Wolfe see Nancy A. Mace (1993), 'The History of the Grammar Patent, 1547–1620', *The Papers of the Bibliographical Society of America* 87: 419–36, at 420–22.

[7] See Appendix III, which lists copies of editions that are extant of 'Lily's Grammar' to 1603.

[8] See Appendix III, 26.0, for the first extant copy printed by the assignes of Francis Flower. On 'Lily's Grammar' recognized as part of this privilege see *A Companion to Arber*, ed. W. W. Greg (1967), Oxford, no. 91: 26–27, no. 114: 37, no. 121: 39–40, and no. 4: 116–17. On

copies of 'Lily's Grammar' from 1574 to 1593 read "Assignes of Francis Flower".[9]

According to the evidence of the copies of extant editions, the 1574 edition represents the earliest edition in octavo format in which, for the first time, the two parts of the grammar were printed together as one work with continuous pagination and signatures. The separate title-pages, however, were preserved. So profitable did its publication become that in spite of the royal privilege, this grammar was already being pirated with no publisher's name during Queen Mary's reign and continued to be pirated in Queen Elizabeth's reign.[10] On 11 December 1587 the Court of the Stationers' Company set the number of impressions of 'Lily's Grammar' at four of 2,500 copies each in any one year, but were willing to admit other editions in the same year, provided that they were limited to 1,250 copies each. Since the maximum number of copies set for other books was a single impression of 1,500 copies, some notion of the enormous demand and hence the large market for copies of 'Lily's Grammar' can be gathered.[11]

After Flower's death, probably in 1596, the Stationers' Company was planning to claim the authorized grammar for its own benefit. Thomas Dawson, who had already been printing this grammar, had an interest in the patent and he and two other prominent members of the Stationers' Company wanted its sole use. In the meantime, however, the privilege of being the Queen's Printer of Latin, Greek, and Hebrew was granted to Sir Carew Reynell, one of Queen Elizabeth's pensioners. In March 1597 he surrendered it, presumably because he was not a printer and bookseller, and it was purchased from him by John Battersby of Plymouth, probably a bookseller and stationer. He, in turn, assigned it to Thomas Dawson, Edward White, and Cuthbert Burby. The extant copies of editions of 'Lily's Grammar' dated towards the end of the sixteenth century demonstrate

Flower see *STC²*, vol. 3: 65; Ronald B. McKerrow (ed.) (1910), *A Dictionary of Printers and Booksellers in England* [. . .], *1557–1640*. London; repr. 1968, 106; Vincent Joseph Flynn (1943). 'The Grammatical Writings of William Lily, ?1468–?1523', *The Papers of the Bibliographical Society of America* 37: 85–113, at 110–11; and Foster Watson (1908), *The English Grammar Schools to 1660*, Cambridge; repr. 1968, 255–56.

    [9] See Appendix III, 26.0–38.0. The copy dated 1585 and listed here as no. 32.0 reads: [Thomas Dawson for] Assignes of Francis Flower. On Thomas Dawson see Mace (1993), 423, and *STC²*, vol. 3: 51.

    [10] For editions in the Tudor period which were pirated and printed on the Continent during Queen Mary's and Queen Elizabeth's reigns see Appendix III, 11.0, 12.0, 13.0, and 23.0.

    [11] *Records of the Court of the Stationers' Company. Vol. 1: 1576 to 1602 ~ from Register B*, ed. W. W. Greg and E. Boswell (1930). London, 25; also *A Transcript of the Registers of the Company of Stationers of London, 1554–1640 A.D.*, ed. Edward Arber (1875–1894), 5 vols. London, vol. 2: 23, 43, 883. On the number of impressions of the *Grammar* see the comments by Mace (1993), 425; Cyprian Blagden (1960), *The Stationers' Company. A History, 1403–1959*. London, 45; Flynn (1943), 111; Lily, *Shorte Introduction* (1567), Introduction, x; and Watson (1908), 255–56.

that they maintained the privilege successfully.[12] It is striking that in volumes containing earlier editions of the grammar the imprint of the English part usually shows a later date than that of the Latin part. This difference in dates between the two parts of the grammar seems to be typical of editions of this grammar in the seventeenth century. It may be assumed that the grammar in the vernacular was exposed to more frequent revisions in respect to language and subject matter than the part in Latin. It seems that the latest edition that was then at hand was bound together with copies of the less frequently revised Latin part that were available. Moreover, there was certainly a much greater demand for the vernacular part than for the Latin part.

On 21 May 1603, after James I had acceded to the English throne, John Norton, printer and bookseller, was granted the office of King's Printer of Latin, Greek, and Hebrew for life, following disputes that had broken out over the patent in which it was asserted that Battersby's patent was void. The controversy attests to the value of which the grammar patent was perceived to be and, at the same time, demonstrates how fragile was the monopoly granted by the patent during this period.[13] After John Norton's death in 1612, the royal patent was granted on 6 January 1613, to his cousin, Bonham Norton, printer and publisher, for thirty years. However, in December 1619, he sold it to the Stationers' Company, who incorporated it into the Latin Stock set up in 1616 that was organized within the Company. Norton bought it back from the Company in 1624, holding it until his death in 1635.[14] The monopoly for printing 'Lily's Grammar' continued to be attacked as editions were pirated and printed without publishers' names. A Privy Council decree of 16 April 1629 allowed the printers of the University of Cambridge to print up to 3,000 copies of 'Lily's Grammar' a year. In 1636, another decree of the Privy Council

---

[12] For information about the patent after Flower's death see Mace (1993), 425–26; on Sir Carew Reynell see ODNB, under 'Reynell family' (per. 1540–1735), vol. 46: 521–22; on John Battersby see STC², vol. 3: 15–16; on Edward White (referred to under White, Edward 1), STC², vol. 3: 181–82, and on Cuthbert Burby, STC², vol. 3: 32. For the editions of 'Lily's Grammar' printed from 1596 onwards by Thomas Dawson for the assignes of John Battersby see the copies listed as 40.0–43.0 in Appendix III.

[13] For information about John Norton (1556/57–1612) see ODNB, vol. 41: 174–75; also STC², vol. 3: 126–27, where he is referred to as John Norton 1. This patent is listed in Arnold Hunt (1997), 'Book Trade Patents, 1603–1640', in A. Hunt et al. (eds.), The Book Trade and its Customers, 1450–1900, New Castle, Delaware, 27–54, at 41.

[14] For this patent see Records of the Court of the Stationers' Company. Vol. 2: 1602–1640, ed. William A. Jackson (1957). London, Introduction, xi–xii, 117, 164–65 (records); also Arnold Hunt (1997), 44. On Bonham Norton see ODNB, vol. 41: 156–58; also STC², vol. 3: 125–26. The Stationers' Company possessed several stocks, or collections of titles for some of which they claimed the exclusive copyright. There was the English stock, the Latin stock, the Irish stock, the Bible stock, and the ballad stock. One of the purposes of the Latin Stock was the purchase, through factors and agents on the Continent, of books that were printed abroad to be distributed to the trade in England from a shop in London; see Blagden (1960), 106–107.

of 9 March, authorized the Universities of Cambridge and Oxford to print the same number of copies of this grammar each year, though printing it remained a monopoly of the King's Printer of Latin and it continued to be published in London.[15] The first hundred years of the printing history of the authorized grammar not only reflect the important role that was attributed to it by the monarch in the field of education, but also illustrate aspects of the monopoly granted to individuals, the development of the emerging book trade, and the publishing history of one particular best-selling book. Its text did not remain stable; sections of it were subject to revision, their order changed, and some sections were omitted while others were included under changing teaching conditions. Moreover, its presentation evolved at the hands of those who enjoyed the privilege to publish it.[16]

'Lily's Grammar' was compiled by royal command in, or shortly before, 1540. Before its commission by King Henry VIII, there was great diversity in grammars and other complementary textbooks and hence in the teaching of Latin in English schools. Various treatises and different versions of the same treatise in manuscript were in use for the teaching of accidence, comparison, elementary syntax, vocabulary, and translation practice. Printed treatises written in English, which exerted influence in the period after 1510, were John Colet's *Aeditio*, teaching the eight parts of speech, William Lily's *Rudimenta grammatices* on elementary syntax, John Stanbridge's treatises, and Thomas Linacre's *Progymnasmata grammatices vulgaria* and his *Rudimenta grammatices*.[17] At the same time Robert Whittington's grammars written in Latin also became very popular.[18] Another short syntax in Latin, in its earliest extant edition of 1513, entitled *Libellus de constructione Octo partium orationis*, and in some subsequent editions as *Absolutissimus de octo orationis partium constructione libellus*, was reprinted in a multitude of editions. It passed under Lily's name but was

---

[15] See Blagden (1960), 103; and *A Companion to Arber* (1967), no. 232: 76–77, and no. 310: 100.

[16] The history of the grammar was divided into three periods by former scholars: (1) from its first compilation in 1509 until the royal proclamation in 1540; (2) from 1540 until the grammar was appropriated as the Eton grammar in 1758; (3) from that period to 1868. See J. H. Lupton (1880), 'Lily's Grammar', *Notes and Queries*. 6th ser., 2: 441–42, 461–62; also Watson (1908), 243–59.

[17] For editions of the treatises on accidence, comparison, and elementary syntax see *Checklist*; on the *Progymnasmata* cf. also Meraud Grant Ferguson (2001), *A Study of English Book-Trade Privileges during the Reign of Henry VIII*, D.Phil. Thesis, University of Oxford, 53–58.

[18] Editions of Whittington's grammars are listed in *STC²* 25443.4-25579; Alston, vol. 15, nos. 322–401, 405–22, 425–69; and *ESTC*; see also Eloise Pafort (1946). 'A Group of Early Tudor School-Books', *The Library*, 4th ser., 26, no. 4: 227–61, at 242–54. For information on Whittington and his works see *ODNB*, vol. 58: 773–74; and Gwosdek (2004), 'Whittington, Robert (or Whittinton: c.1480-c.1553)', in R. B. Todd (ed.), *The Dictionary of British Classicists, 1500-1960*. 3 vols. Bristol, vol. 3: 1058–59.

often ascribed to Erasmus or even circulated anonymously.[19] Perhaps due to its being ascribed to Erasmus, most of its editions were published and disseminated on the Continent until the end of the sixteenth century. In addition, such treatises as the Latin grammars of the Italian grammarians Nicolaus Perottus (1429–1480) and Joannes Sulpitius Verulanus (c.1440–1506) circulated in England. They made a direct as well as an indirect impact on English grammar masters and also on English treatises compiled in the last decade of the fifteenth and first three or four decades of the sixteenth century.[20]

The *Day-Book of John Dorne* that recorded the sales of books day by day in Oxford in most of the year 1520 and thus provides evidence of their demand in the university town, sheds a light on the variety of grammars and other school texts and works of authors that were available and in use around this period. Though it cannot provide a representative picture of the grammars that were actually used in English grammar schools, it testifies to the variety of texts for teaching purposes that were on the market in a specific area.[21] In a similar way the contents of the account-book of the Cambridge stationer Garrett Godfrey from c.1527 to 1533 bear witness to the variety of grammatical treatises and other school texts that were in demand in educational institutions during this time. Among the entries listing the purchases of his credit customers is a large number of copies of the elementary grammars by John Stanbridge, Robert Whittington, and William Lily, as well as titles which cannot be identified or attributed to any author.[22]

The introduction of a grammar commissioned by royal command was intended to reform the teaching of Latin and to attain uniformity in grammar textbooks for all schools in England. The grammar attributed to William Lily that was authorized by Henry VIII was a very important means to achieve this aim, followed by the authorized *English Primer* in

---

[19] For the first extant copy see Bodl. Lib., 4° C.23.Art.BS; also Appendix IV, 1. The copy of the *Absolutissimus* referred to here and listed under William Lily's name, is located in Bodl. Lib. 4° E 6(4) Art.Seld. It was printed in 1515.

[20] On Perottus see Bernard Colombat (1998b), 'Perotti, Niccolò', in *HEL*, vol. 1, no. 1243: 78–80. On his grammars and the copy of the *Rudimenta grammatices* printed by Wynkyn de Worde in 1512 (*STC*² 19767.3) see Constance Blackwell (1982), 'Niccolò Perotti in England— Part I', *Res Publica Litterarum* 1: 13–28. For information about Sulpitius see Colombat (1998c), 'Sulpitius, Johannes Antonius—Verulanus', in *HEL*, vol. 1, no. 1244: 80–81. For the use of Sulpitius's grammars in the timetable reflecting its use at Winchester College in 1530 see p. 72 below.

[21] John Dorne, 'Day-Book of John Dorne, Bookseller in Oxford, A.D. 1520', ed. F. Madan (1885), in C. R. L. Fletcher (ed.), *Collectanea* I, Part III, Oxford, 71–177; and 'Supplementary Notes to *Collectanea* I. Part III. 'Day-Book of John Dorne', in M. Burrows (ed.), *Collectanea* II, Appendix, 453–78.

[22] *Garrett Godfrey's Accounts, c. 1527-1533*, ed. Elisabeth Leedham-Green, D. E. Rhodes, and F. H. Stubbings (1992), Cambridge, *passim*. Copies of grammars by William Lily are only listed in this account-book and not in Dorne's ledger.

1545 and the authorized *Book of Common Prayer* in 1549 that were intended to achieve uniformity in religious worship, and by which all existing predecessors were superseded. The authorized grammar, as well as the *Primer* and the *Book of Common Prayer*, were imposed by proclamations.[23] The Latin part of 'Lily's Grammar', printed in 1540, entitled *Institutio Compendiaria Totius Grammaticae*, prescribes the exclusive use of the authorized grammar on its title-page: "*ut non alia quam hæc una per totam Angliam pueris prælegeretur.*" The address to all schoolmasters and teachers of grammar in England that precedes the grammar proper provides information about the compilation of this part of the grammar. It is said that the *Institutio* was compiled by a group of experts in the field of grammar on the initiative of and in accordance with the command of the king, who had entrusted them with this task. The value of a uniform grammar and method of teaching is also emphasized. The compilation had to be pedagogically suitable, in other words, easy to learn by the children and appropriately short. This grammar, together with the edict of the king, was then to be introduced in all schools in the kingdom. The "*Sententia edicti*" that is explained in the address to all schoolmasters prescribes the exclusive use of the grammar in all schools in the kingdom. Its usage in class, however, leaves some room for discretion by the teachers as described in the following passage:

Quod tamen optimi et æquissimi principis edictum non ita intelligi debet, quasi iubeat quicquid hic scriptum reperietis eodem etiam, quo scribitur ordine, et sine interuallo, tenellis adhuc ac fastidientibus puerorum stomachis continuo et citra omnem delectum esse obtrudendum: ceterum hoc cuilibet uestrum integrum relinquitur, ut pro captu auditorum suorum, quicquid sibi commodum uidebitur, uel omittat pro arbitrio suo, uel gregi suo proponat ediscendum, modo non aliam quam hanc grammaticam publice aut priuatim profiteatur aut doceat.[24]

---

[23] Based on the royal prerogative, the authority to issue proclamations having the force of law gave the king powers over fields left untouched by statute or common law, in this case education and religious worship. For an edition of the proclamation for the introduction of the authorized grammar see Hughes and Larkin, vol. 1, no. 216: 317. Hughes and Larkin date it before 25 March 1543, so presumably it is dated 1542. This seems to be the only such proclamation for the grammar. An edition of the proclamation introducing the English *Primer* is also given in Hughes and Larkin, vol. 1, no. 248: 349-50. It is dated 6 May 1545. On uniformity in textbooks and teaching see Chapter 4 below.

[24] For the Latin part of 'Lily's Grammar' see Appendix III, 1.0: *Institutio Compendiaria Totius Grammaticae* (1540). London. BL, C.21.b.4.(3), and the Latin address *Totius Angliae Ludimagistris Ac Grammaticae Praeceptoribus*, A2ʳ–A3ᵛ. The excerpt is given at A3ʳ⁻ᵛ and can be translated as follows: "This directive from the most kind and most just King is not to be understood as prescribing that whatever you will find written here is, in the same order it is written and without delay, to be forced upon the delicate and fastidious intellects and tastes of boys continuously and without any discretion. The rest of what remains of this book is left in the hands of each one of you according to the capacity of your listeners. Whatever seems convenient to you, you may omit according to your own judgement, or give to your pupils to learn, with the proviso that you do not privately or in public follow or teach any grammar other than this one."

The teachers are given a certain freedom in explaining the grammatical rules in class in a way that they need not strictly follow the given order of the textbook but are free to select or omit rules according to the intellectual capacities of the pupils. The edict takes into account the peda-gogical abilities and insight of teachers in using the prescribed grammar.

The surviving text of the proclamation, the formal order issued by the king that had to be made public and that is contained in the English part of the 1542 edition, puts the emphasis on the diversity in the teaching of Latin prior to the introduction of a uniform grammar. It continues by saying that this situation has caused great difficulties to pupils as well as to learning and that the king intends to achieve change and improvement by prescribing the exclusive use of a uniform text. It also emphasizes the advantage to pupils in learning Latin more quickly and more easily, saying:

And to the intent that hereafter they [the children] may the more readily and easily attein the rudymentes of the latyne toung, without þe greate hynderaunce, which heretofore hath been, through the diuersitie of grammers and teachynges: we will and commaunde, and streightly charge al you schoolemaisters and teachers of grammer within this our realme, and other our dominions [. . .] to teache and learne your scholars this englysshe introduction here ensuing, and the latyne grammer annexed to the same, and none other.[25]

The earliest extant edition of 'Lily's Grammar' was published by the King's Printer, Thomas Berthelet, who also printed the subsequent editions until Henry VIII's death in 1547.[26] The grammar became part of the centralizing policy of the Tudors and also enjoyed particular attention in the reigns of the succeeding sovereigns. Other grammars were no longer published and virtually disappeared from the market. Injunctions continued to be promulgated by each monarch in the Tudor period and the text was adapted each time to the reign of the king or queen. Under King Edward VI (1547–1553), Henry VIII's son, the title of the English part was changed to *A Shorte Introduction of Grammar* and the Latin part became *Breuissima Institutio seu Ratio Grammatices Cognoscendæ*.[27] The Injunction contained in the 1548 edition of the English part, the earliest edition extant of King Edward's reign, continues to prescribe the grammar as follows:

Wherfore it hath ben confirmed by our noble Father, and now by the aduise of our entierly beloued vncle Edward duke of Somerset, Gouernor of our Roial person, and Protector of al our Realmes and Dominions and subiectes: and other of our priuy counsel, we haue thought good to establish the same, that this one kynd of grammar, printed by our well beloued subiect Reynold Wolfe, our printer of Latin, Greke, and Hebrue, shuld be openly and priuately redde to al kynd of lerners in

---

[25] This passage is contained in the text of the *Introduction*, Proclamation. See p. 157, lines 8–16 below.

[26] See Appendix III for the extant editions of the grammar printed in Berthelet's printing shop. The latest edition which survives from his press is listed there as no. 7.0.

[27] See Appendix III, 8.0, 9.1, and 9.2.

euery grammar schole, and other places of techyng, and the same and none other to bee vsed.[28]

The subject matter of the grammar and its arrangement remained the same for the immediately subsequent editions; only minor textual corrections and revisions occurring in subsequent editions of the *Introduction* printed after 1542.[29] However, a number of substantial changes and modifications that concern the grammatical texts, in particular the treatise on syntax, were made in the editions appearing soon after Edward VI's accession. It was substantially expanded, the educational texts also underwent revision, and some of them were replaced by different ones. Reyner Wolfe continued to print the grammar in Queen Mary's reign (1553–1558) and also following Queen Elizabeth I's accession to the throne in 1558. The Injunction contained in the English part of the grammar, published by Wolfe in 1558, in Queen Mary's reign, shows that she maintained the authorized grammar sanctioned by her brother and her father. This passage reads:

And lyke as the saide vniform Grammar being thus by our sayd Father, to this godly ende and purpose published and sette forth, was by oure late brother of worthy memory Kinge Edward þe vi. confirmed and alowed, So we no lesse minding the continuance and maintenance therof, haue thought good to approue and ratifie the same.[30]

In the reign of Queen Elizabeth I (1558–1603) 'Lily's Grammar' continued to be prescribed. The relevant passage of the Injunction contained in the first extant copy of her reign, printed in 1560, says:

We settinge before oure eyes this godlie acte and example of this oure deere father in this behalfe, not vnconfyrmed by oure dere Brother and Syster, Kynge Edwarde and Queene Mary: And also consydering that by the learned youthe of this saide Realme, infinite and synguler commodities tendeth towardes þe common welth of the same, haue thought good, by oure special auctoritie to approue and ratifye that worthie acte of oure saide deere father, concerning the premisses.[31]

This evidence shows that a change of monarch, even if it brought change in the established religion from Protestantism back to the Catholic faith, as in the case of Queen Mary, had no effect on the continued use of the grammar first authorized by King Henry VIII. With Queen Mary's death in 1558 the old religion was banished once again.

The use of the grammar was further authorized and imposed by Royal Injunctions sent to the clergy by Edward VI in 1547 and by all the succeeding monarchs of the Tudor period at the start of their reigns. The "Injunctions for Religious Reform; Ordering Homilies to be Read

---

[28] This copy is listed in Appendix III, 8.0. The Royal Injunction is printed on a1ᵛ. For 'the aduise' (first line of the quotation) the original reads 'th aduise'.

[29] See Appendix III, 4.1, 6.0, and 7.1.

[30] For this copy see Appendix III, 14.1. The royal injunction is given on A1ᵛ.

[31] See Appendix III, 15.1. For the royal proclamation see A1ᵛ.

from the Pulpit" of King Edward VI of 31 July 1547, and "Announcing Injunctions for Religion" of Queen Elizabeth I, before 19 July 1559, enjoined:

And that none other Grammar shall be taught in any school or other place within the King's realms and dominions, but only that which is set forth by the said authority. *Item*, that every schoolmaster and teacher shall teach the grammar set forth by King Henry VIII, of noble memory, and continued in the time of King Edward VI, and none other.[32]

The Injunctions assume that the proclamation has established the grammar; they are merely reinforcing it in different wording. The proclamation by Henry VIII and the Injunctions endorsed by the succeeding monarchs that were published in the various editions of the authorized grammar reflect the process of establishing uniformity in the teaching of grammar. At the same time they provide evidence of important legal documents the only surviving original texts of which are those preserved in the different editions of 'Lily's Grammar'. Moreover, the legal documents testify to the monarchs' interest in education and their intervention in the teaching of Latin by prescribing the authorized grammar as the definitive form of a text to be adopted for use in all schools in England.

That the use of this grammar in schools was considered a matter of importance by the authorities in the reigns of the Tudor monarchs is also testified by Visitation Articles and Articles of Enquiry from 1547 onwards. The Royal Articles that are parallel with the Injunction of the same year read: "*Item*, Whether there be any other Grammar taught in any school within the realm, than that which is set forth by the King's Majesty."[33] Articles of Enquiry continued to examine whether the grammar introduced by Henry VIII was being used in schools in the reigns of Queen Mary and Queen Elizabeth I.[34] There are also episcopal Injunctions that indicate that there was a continuing intention to enforce the use of the grammar. It was the duty of the diocesan officials to make inquiries and inspections

---

[32] The royal injunctions are cited in *Visitation Articles and Injunctions of the Period of the Reformation, 1536–1575*, ed. Walter Howard Frere and William McClure Kennedy (1910). 3 vols. London. The references to the grammar occur in vol. 2, no. 34: 129 (Edward VI), and vol. 3, no. 39: 21 (Elizabeth I). These injunctions are also given in Hughes and Larkin, vol. 1, no. 287: 402 (Edward VI), and vol. 2, no. 460: 126, paragraph 39 (Elizabeth I); and in *Documentary Annals of the Reformed Church of England*, ed. Edward Cardwell (1844). Oxford; repr. 1966, vol. 1, injunction II: 20, no. 34, lines 17–20, and footnote b (Edward VI), and vol. 1, no. XLIII: 227, paragraph 39, lines 9–12 (Elizabeth I). See also Watson (1908), 258. There is no reference in Frere and Kennedy (1910), in Hughes and Larkin, and in Edward Cardwell's edition to an Injunction by Queen Mary taking account of 'Lily's Grammar'.

[33] For the Royal Articles of Edward VI see Frere and Kennedy (1910), vol. 2, no. 68: 113.

[34] See Frere and Kennedy (1910), for example, for the Injunctions for the London diocese, 1550 (vol. 2, no. 31: 236), Injunctions for the Bangor (Wales) diocese, 1551 (vol. 2, no. 19: 264), the London diocese, 1554 (vol. 2, no. 109: 355), and the Canterbury diocese, 1560 (vol. 3, no. 19: 85).

at regular intervals to ensure that the proper grammar book was being used in schools. Sanctions were taken against those who ignored the regulations. The *Constitutions and Canons Ecclesiastical* of 1571 endorsed the Injunctions of the previous monarchs. Article 79 of the decision of the *Convocatio prælatorum* of 1604, that included the duty of the schoolmaster, established the authorization of 'Lily's Grammar' for the future by saying: "and they shall teach the grammar set forth by King Henry the Eighth, and continued in the times of King Edward the Sixth, and queen Elizabeth of noble memory, and none other."[35] The Injunctions printed in all the early editions of the grammar and the Injunctions by the clergy provide the basis for its imposition and for the inspection of the teaching of Latin in grammar schools in such a way that uniformity should be achieved. How it operated in practice can only be revealed by detailed studies of records that give evidence of the curriculum and teaching in individual schools of the period.

The most famous schoolboy of the Tudor period, William Shakespeare, was enrolled in King Edward VI School at Stratford-upon-Avon, probably in 1571, at about the age of seven, to acquire his formal education. There he learned the rudiments of Latin with this grammar then authorized by Queen Elizabeth I. A number of allusions scattered in his plays attest to his familiarity with this textbook.[36] He probably studied the form of 'Lily's Grammar' that was in use in the late 1560s, but which of the many editions, each of which was printed in a huge number of copies, he might have used at school is difficult to establish.[37]

'Lily's Grammar' played an important role in the writings of Richard Mulcaster (1531/32–1611) who was headmaster of Merchant Taylors' School in London from 1561–1586, and subsequently High Master of St Paul's School, London, from 1596–1608. He was one of the most famous schoolmasters of the sixteenth century and the advocate of educational reforms in elementary teaching. His practice as a teacher made him support emphatically the principle of a uniform grammar and uniformity in teaching which, in his experience, had yet to be achieved. At the same time he argued for a corrected text of the authorized grammar and to have a uniform method established for the whole curriculum, criticizing the

---

[35] For the Canons Ecclesiastical of 1571 see *Synodalia. A Collection of Articles of Religion, Canons* [. . .], ed. Edward Cardwell (1842). Oxford; repr. 1966, vol. 1: 128, lines 19-21. The English version of the 1604 Canon is also given in vol. 1: 292, lines 7–11. See S. Blach (1909), 'Shakespeares Lateingrammatik', *Jahrbuch der Deutschen Shakespeare-Gesellschaft* 45: 90–91.

[36] Cf. Park Honan (1998), *Shakespeare. A Life*. Oxford, 43–50; T. W. Baldwin (1944). *William Shakspere's Small Latine and Lesse Greeke*, Urbana, vol. 1: 561–80, and *passim*; also Blach (1908), 44: 65, and Blach (1909), 45: 94–95 and 98.

[37] Cf. Baldwin (1944), vol. 1: 494. Blach (1908), 44: 65, and Blach (1909), 45: 51, refer to the edition of the English text of 1566 as probably having been used by Shakespeare. (For this copy see Appendix III, 17.0). J. O. Halliwell-Phillipps suggests the 1568 edition (Appendix III, 21.1); see his note complementing Lupton (1880), in *Notes and Queries*, 6th ser., 2: 462.

variety of textbooks and teaching methods which were then used. He ventured to advise Queen Elizabeth I as follows:

That noble Prince king HENRY the eight, your Majesties most renowned father vouchesafed to bring all Grammars into one fourme, the multitude therof being some impediment to schoole learning in his happie time, and thereby both purchased himselfe great honour, and procured his subjectes a marveilous ease. Now if it shall please your Majestie by that Royall example which otherwise you so rarely exceede, to further not onely the helping of that booke to a refining: but also the reducing of all other schoole bookes to some better choice: and all manner of teaching, to some redier fourme: can so great a good but sound to your Majesties most endlesse renowne, whose least part gave such cause of honour, to that famous King, your Majesties father?[38]

Already at the end of the sixteenth century, however, speculation arose about alternative grammars, which is a sign of the nature of the dissatisfaction which grammar masters felt and indicates doubts about enforced uniformity. They often paid lip service to the use of the authorized grammar. Explanation and commentaries were published which developed out of experience in the classroom. Though, strictly speaking, these textbooks were illegal, they aimed to improve on 'Lily's Grammar' after teachers realized that the children had difficulties with the definitions and rules given in this text. For this reason they provided children with additional material, which, in turn, may also have been beyond their understanding. Specific rules, for example on concord, were compiled as adjuncts to the grammar. The textbook written by the headmaster of Tonbridge School, Kent, from 1574–1587, John Stockwood's *A Plaine And Easie Laying open of the meaning and vnderstanding of the Rules of Construction in the English Accidence* (1590), was a commentary in English explaining the rules of the elementary part of 'Lily's Grammar' and the principles behind it.[39] At the same time amended versions of the text of 'Lily's Grammar' were printed and came into use.

After the Tudor period, the use of 'Lily's Grammar' remained at the core of the educational system, and editions continued to be published in large numbers of copies. Numerous amendments testify to its significance in the seventeenth century.[40] Efforts were made not only to revise 'Lily's Grammar', but also to establish alternatives to it, which were influenced

[38] Richard Mulcaster (1581), *Positions Concerning the Training Up of Children*, ed. W. Barker (1994), Toronto, 5, lines 7–18. See Joan Simon (1966), *Education and Society in Tudor England*, Cambridge; repr. in paperback 1979, 378.

[39] John Stockwood's textbook is listed in Alston, vol. 15, no. 810, with Plates CLVII–CLVIII; also in *STC²* 23280; and *ESTC*. The text is available in digitized form in *EEBO*. On Stockwood see *ODNB*, vol. 52: 837–38; also Watson (1908) 266–67. On commentaries of 'Lily's Grammar' see G. A. Padley (1985), *Grammatical Theory in Western Europe, 1500–1700. Trends in Vernacular Grammar I*. Cambridge, 147–48, where also a list of such textbooks is provided. Nils Erik Enkvist (1975), 'English in Latin Guise. A Note on Some Renaissance Textbooks', *Historiographia Linguistica* 2: 283–98, gives a list of authors at 295–96.

[40] See, for example, the lists given in Watson (1908), 265–75.

by it, as the following example illustrates. According to the Calendar of the House of Lords, on 10 July 1641, the petition of Thomas Farnaby, a distinguished schoolteacher and grammarian in the first half of the seventeenth century, "received special command to compose a Latin grammar more brief and useful than that now taught in schools, called Lilie's grammar".[41] His grammar, the *Systema Grammaticum* (1641), was intended to supersede the authorized textbook, appeared only once, however. So despite repeated challenge, 'Lily's Grammar' continued as the only legal grammar text for schools. That its imposition continued to be a serious issue is shown by the fact that, on 26 May 1675, a bill was brought before the House of Lords, but not proceeded with, which made it punishable for schoolmasters throughout the country to use any other Latin grammar in the classroom than the one "commonly called Lilly's Grammar".[42]

In 1732 Dr John Ward, who was professor of rhetoric at Gresham College in London, was employed by those booksellers who were patentees for printing this grammar to restore the defective text and prepare a correct edition of it.[43] However, no copy of an edition printed in that year seems to have come down to us, although a number of other later editions do survive. Ward, who was a former schoolmaster, had been engaged in revising the grammar before that date.[44] He provided an informative retrospective view of its history in his preface to the grammar, which continued to be used and altered by schoolmasters.[45] Editions were produced until very late in the eighteenth century at an average of about three per year. In accordance with new needs and changing conditions in grammar school education, and as if to make amendments for all attacks upon it, a version of this grammar was produced for Eton which was then overtaking Westminster as the most prestigious school in England. This book, which became known as *The Eton Latin Grammar*, first appeared in 1758 under the title *A Short Introduction to the Latin Tongue*. The words *The Eton Latin Grammar*, however, first appear on a title-page only in the

---

[41] *HMC* (1874), Fourth Report, Part I. Report and Appendix, 86. The text of the *Systema Grammaticum* is listed in Wing F464, also in *ESTC*. The copy located in Illinois University Library is available in digitized form in *EEBO*. On Thomas Farnaby see *ODNB*, vol. 19: 68–70.

[42] 'Lilly's and Camden's Grammar Bill', in *HMC* (1884). Ninth Report, Part II. Appendix and Index, no. 260, p. 63. See also Blach (1909), 45: 91; Watson (1908), 259; and J. H. Lupton (1890), 'The Tudor Exhibition', *The Pauline* 8, no. 40: 71.

[43] John Nichols (1812). *Literary Anecdotes of the Eighteenth Century*, London, vol. 5: 520–21. On Ward see *ODNB*, vol. 57: 314–15.

[44] See the remarks by the Revd Thomas Birch of 21 Sept. 1731 and 5 Oct. 1732 on Ward's edition of 'Lily's Grammar' (BL, MS Add. 6212, fols. 9^{r-v} and 11^{r-v}).

[45] I refer to the edition of the grammar *A Short Introduction of Grammar, generally to be used*, ed. J. W. [John Ward], London 1739 (BL, 1607/6049(1), A2^r–A7^r (preface)). This edition is listed in Alston, vol. 15, no. 659. Ward's 'Memoranda, Collections, Fragments, etc.,' (BL, MS Add. 6218, fols. 12^r–13^v) provide alterations and additions to this preface to be made in the 1751 edition of the grammar.

1790s and, even then, not in books published for use at Eton. With much recognition and many challenges it remained the market leader. It was used by small schools to support their social pretensions, and by 1800 was being pirated in several parts of Great Britain. It continued in use until the headmastership of James John Hornby at Eton, who was appointed to that post in 1868.[46] Under the Public Schools Act in the same year and the change in administration it was superseded by Benjamin Hall Kennedy's grammar, *The Public School Latin Primer*, which was compiled by a small committee including Kennedy himself, who was headmaster of Shrewsbury School from 1836 until his retirement in 1866. The *Primer* was based on his earlier *Elementary Latin Grammar* of 1847 and was published in 1866. Although it was greeted with widespread hostile comment, it was adopted as the basis of a new standard Latin grammar in England and lasted for twenty years. It was revised again and appeared in 1888 to general approval, carried Kennedy's name, and was entitled *The Revised Latin Primer*. It was, however, actually written by Kennedy's two daughters, Marion Grace and Julia, with advice from two of his ex-pupils. After revisions in 1909, 1930, and 1962, it remains in use as the standard Latin grammar today.[47]

1.2 *Earlier linguistic research*

Due to the important role and influence which 'Lily's Grammar' exerted in the formal education of children, it has received wide attention in con-temporary works, in various works over the centuries while it was in use, and also in modern studies, e.g. on humanist grammar, in historical linguistics, education, historical and cultural studies, and also in biblio-graphical works. In studies on the historiography of grammar it takes a central role and is listed among the most important works. It was also considered one of the books most influential for the teaching grammars of English. However, if anyone wishes to discover details about its textual

---

[46] However, its use in schools probably did not stop in 1868. An 1869 edition is recorded, so it must have been in use in 1870 and possibly well beyond, and there is no proof that there were no editions of a later date.

[47] On James John Hornby see *ODNB*, vol. 28: 126–27; on Benjamin Hall Kennedy see also *ODNB*, vol. 31: 234–36. On the *Eton Latin Grammar* in the nineteenth century, the introduction of Kennedy's grammar and its revision see Stray (1996), 'Primers, Publishing, and Politics: The Classical Textbook of Benjamin Hall Kennedy', *The Papers of the Bibliographical Society of America* 90: 451–74; also the correspondence following the publication of Kennedy's *Public School Latin Primer* in 1866, in Stray (1995), *Grinders and Grammars. A Victorian Controversy, Reading*; Stray (1994), 8–25; and Stray (1989), 'Paradigms of Social Order: the Politics of Latin Grammar in 19th-Century England', *The Henry Sweet Society Newsletter* 13: 13–24, at 14–15, 20–21; cf. also H. C. Maxwell-Lyte (1899), *A History of Eton College (1440–1898)*. 3rd edn., London, 539, 546–47.

basis, he or she will be confronted with a rather confusing picture. In this connection Ian Michael, in his 1970 standard work on the historiography of English grammar, *English Grammatical Categories and the Tradition to 1800*, indicates the main reasons why difficulties arise when working with this grammar: "The compilation most briefly known as Lily's grammar is of mixed authorship, uncertain origin and varying title."[48] The text of this grammar, its contemporary grammatical context, as well as its tradition, have hitherto escaped serious comprehensive study based on modern scholarly research.

Beginning with its denomination, this grammar, in various forms, is referred to in textbooks, school statutes, inventories of different periods, and in modern scholarly works under a variety of titles, for example, 'William Lily's Latin Grammar', 'Lily's grammar', 'Lily', 'Grammatica Lilij', 'Colet and Lily', 'Lily and Colet', 'King Henry's Grammar', 'King's Grammar', 'The Royal Grammar', 'Grammatica Regis', 'Grammatica Henrici viij', 'King Edward's Grammar', 'Prince's Grammar', 'Grammatica Regia', 'The Common Grammar', 'The Royal Grammar Reformed', 'Oxford Grammar', and in some later versions as 'The Eton Latin Grammar'. Apart from different grammars, different editions of the grammar attributed to William Lily are also referred to. In most cases the two different parts of the grammar, probably compiled in or shortly before 1540, are not explicitly distinguished, but at the same time, different names for each of the two parts did exist. The English part is often known, for example, as the 'English Accidence', 'Accidence', 'Accidence proper', 'Shorte Introduction', 'English Rudiments', or 'the English Lily'. Turning to the grammars themselves, the English part of the 1542 edition entitled "*An Introduction of the eyght partes of speche, and the Construction of the same*", is referred to in the royal proclamation that is printed with it, as "englysshe introduction", and in the address to the reader as "englyshe Introductions".[49] In the same way, the Latin part is known by a number of different names in various works. It is, for example, referred to as '*Latin grammar*', '*Latin accidence*', '*the Grammar*', '*Brevissima Institutio*', or 'the Latin Lily'. In the 1540 edition its title reads *Institutio Compendiaria Totius Grammaticae*. In the royal proclamation printed together with the English part of the 1542 edition, the Latin grammar is referred to as "latyne grammer", whereas in the address to the reader it is called the "latyn rules".[50] In the editions

---

[48] See Ian Michael's (1970) work, Appendix IV, 542. When referring to the English part, Michael emphasizes again "its varied authorship and piecemeal development", 74.

[49] *Introduction*, Proclamation, 157, line 15, and *To the Reder*, 159, line 53.

[50] *Introduction*, Proclamation, 157, line 15–16, and *To the Reder*, 159, line 54. For the new title of the English part in Edward VI's reign see the copy listed as Appendix III, 8.0. This fragment represents the earliest extant edition of the English part entitled *A Shorte Introduction*. For the earliest copy of the Latin part, entitled *Breuissima Institutio*, see Appendix III, 9.2.

from 1549 onwards, however, it is entitled *Breuissima Institutio seu Ratio Grammatices Cognoscendæ*.

Examining the question of which editions of 'Lily's Grammar' were used as a textual basis in modern and earlier scholarly works in the field of the history of linguistics, one is not surprised by the variety of texts that are referred to and the number of denominations that are used. A chronological investigation of earlier treatments of the grammar and influential editions of texts under the name of 'Lily's Grammar' can help to explain the present situation in respect to its textual base. There is evidence that the English part of the 1542 edition was brought to the attention of linguistic scholarship shortly after the middle of the nineteenth century. It was referred to in a contribution in German by Carl E. A. Sachs at the "Sitzungen der Berliner Gesellschaft für das Studium der neueren Sprachen", on 1 June 1858. The relevant passage can be translated as follows:

Grammatical studies have been especially promoted by the so-called *Paul's Accidence*, a compendium of the Latin language for Englishmen compiled in 1510, for which John Colet, Dean of St Paul's, provided the introduction in English [*i.e.* the accidence] and the name, and Lily the part on syntax. They have also been promoted by the handbook on Latin grammar that was used most in those times and also in later periods, *Lily's* or *King Henry's Grammar*, the earliest complete edition of which, according to reliable investigations, has to be considered that of the year 1542.[51]

This evidence, for which no further details are offered in Sachs's contribution, appears not to have been pursued in subsequent scholarly works. The publication of texts of grammars, which served as sources to 'Lily's Grammar', and of later editions of this grammar and their scientific analysis started only at the beginning of the twentieth century.

A decisive and influential step for future linguistic research was made with Samuel Blach's edition of 'Lily's Grammar' (1908; 1909). Blach's work was of great importance in that it made the text of the English part of this grammar and an earlier grammar available for the first time. However, his edition of the texts is inaccurate and their presentation misleading. It cannot be considered an adequate textual basis for scholarship. In addition, in the 1566 text he used, many passages are omitted in an

---

[51] Carl E. A. Sachs (1858). 'Studien zur Geschichte der Englischen Grammatik', *Archiv für das Studium der Neueren Sprachen* 23: 406–14, at 407 (repr. 1967). (The text in German reads: "Grammatische Studien wurden wesentlich gefördert durch die sogenannte *Paul's Accidence*, ein 1510 erschienenes Compendium der lateinischen Sprache für Engländer, zu dem *Colet* dean of St. Paul's die englisch geschriebene Einleitung und den Namen, sowie Lily den syntaktischen Theil lieferte, und durch das am Meisten in jenen und noch in späteren Zeiten gebrauchte Handbuch der lateinischen Grammatik, *Lily's* oder *King Henry's Grammar*, als dessen früheste vollständig zusammengestellte Ausgabe nach zuverlässigen Untersuchungen die vom Jahre 1542 anzusehen ist.") Earlier scholars in education, for example, Watson (1908), lists and briefly describes the 1542 edition of 'Lily's Grammar', 252–53, 255. It is also discussed in John William Adamson (1919), *A Short History of Education*, Cambridge, 124–25, 130–32.

attempt to reach conformity in the layout of subject matter with the text
that was considered by Blach an earlier edition of 'Lily's Grammar'. In fact,
Blach presented different grammars, namely John Colet's *Aeditio* and
William Lily's *Rudimenta grammatices*, both contained in the textbook for St
Paul's School, London, printed in 1527, and the text of an incomplete copy
of the English part of the 1566 edition of 'Lily's Grammar', the missing
pages of which he completed from a copy of the 1572 edition.[52] The 1566
edition was considered the one that was probably used by William Shakespeare when he learned Latin in the grammar school at Stratford-upon-
Avon. In addition to providing two different grammars under the name of
'Lily', the visual presentation of the texts apparently misled users of his
work. Blach printed the pages where corresponding rules from the 1527
and the 1566 grammars are discussed on the same page, the earlier texts
on the top, and the English part of the 1566 copy, completed by the 1572
copy, at the bottom. This way of presenting the texts may, to some extent,
have been responsible for the assumption that the accidence and syntax of
the two grammars represent an earlier and a later revised edition of the
same grammar, especially as the texts on accidence in the *Aeditio* and the
Shorte Introduction often correspond in wording. The erroneous assumption
that Colet's and Lily's grammars on the one hand, and 'Lily's Grammar'
(from 1540 onwards) on the other hand, represent successive stages of
the same work, including revisions in later editions of the authorized
grammar, is an argument that was perpetuated in many successive
scholarly works. A collation of the texts themselves, however, would
have revealed their differences. In his discussion of the history of 'Lily's
Grammar', which follows his editions, Blach mentions the editions of the
English part of 1542 and the Latin part of 1540 of the authorized grammar,
the latter part being extant in two copies.[53]

   Vincent Joseph Flynn's 1939 doctoral dissertation at the University of
Chicago, entitled *The Life and Works of William Lily, the Grammarian*, makes it
clear that 'Lily's Grammar' took shape about the year 1540. At the same
time he states that several other earlier grammatical compilations, which
passed under Lily's name, were used as sources for the English part of 1542
and the Latin part of 1540 of 'Lily's Grammar'. He lists and describes
Colet's *Aeditio*, Lily's *Rudimenta grammatices*, Lily's *Libellus de constructione*,
in subsequent editions entitled *Absolutissimus*, and also Lily's *De generibus
nominum*. Flynn also quotes from Blach's edition of Colet's *Aeditio* and Lily's
Rudimenta grammatices, but correctly criticizes several of Blach's state-

---

[52] Blach (1908; 1909). For Colet's *Aeditio* see *Checklist*, 20.1, and for Lily's *Rudimenta grammatices, Checklist* 51.3. For the copies of 'Lily's Grammar' in English of 1566 and 1572 see
Appendix III, 17.0 and 25.1. For comment on Blach's edition of the texts see this volume,
Commentary: *Carmen de Moribus*, p. 253, note to line 72.
[53] Blach (1909), 82–83.

ments about the earlier grammars and their tradition. His work shows that he had studied the 1540 and 1542 copies of 'Lily's Grammar'.[54]

Flynn's dissertation had not been known to Otto Funke. In his 1941 study on the early English grammarians and their works, entitled *Die Frühzeit der Englischen Grammatik*, which again proved to be influential on subsequent scholarship, Funke based his investigations on Blach's edition of the 1527 grammar as well as on his 1566 edition of 'Lily's Grammar'.[55] He perpetuates the assumption that 'Lily's Grammar' was, from its very beginning, a joint work by John Colet and William Lily and that the English part on accidence is that of Colet's *Aeditio* and that the syntax goes back to Lily's *Rudimenta grammatices*. He states that both texts survived for the first time in the 1527 edition, though they were actually compiled in 1509–1510. He abbreviated this edition of the two grammars as *L*. He regards later editions of the authorized grammar as successive stages of Colet's and Lily's grammars that were only enlarged to differing degrees. Hence the copy of the 1566 edition, as edited by Blach, represents a revision of the 1527 edition by Colet and Lily. He refers to it as L^1. The Latin part, *Institutio Compendiaria*, was, in his view, only compiled during the reign of Henry VIII. However, he realized that the syntax of the English part printed in 1527 shows revisions in later editions, which, in his opinion, reach a certain completion in the edition of 1557.

Flynn's 1943 article, 'The Grammatical Writings of William Lily, ?1468–?1523', includes the essential portion of his 1939 dissertation, mentioned above. He again makes it clear that 'Lily's Grammar' is a new compilation different from Colet's *Aeditio*, Lily's *Rudimenta grammatices*, and other grammatical treatises compiled by Lily, and represents "the final form of the grammar". The copy of its earliest extant edition of the English part is dated 1542, and the two earliest copies of the Latin part are dated 1540.[56] Then, in 1945, Flynn himself provided a facsimile edition of the English and Latin parts of the unique copy of 'Lily's Grammar' printed in 1567, located in the Folger Shakespeare Library, Washington.[57] In his introduction to this edition Flynn presents the results of his research, listing some of "the earlier texts which went into the making of the final product" and states that "about 1540 a new grammar made its appearance" that was based on the previous grammatical texts, *i.e.* Colet's *Aeditio*, Lily's *Rudimenta grammatices*, and other grammatical texts by Lily.

---

[54] Flynn (1939), *The Life and Works of William Lily, the Grammarian*, D.Phil. Thesis. University of Chicago, 108, 118–42.

[55] See Funke (1941), 49–52. The details about the earlier grammars and versions of 'Lily's Grammar' are already given in Funkes's 1938 article 'William Bullokar's *Bref Grammar for English* (1586)', *Anglia* 62, N. F. 50: 116–37, at 118–20. For the 1566 edition of the English part see Appendix III, 17.0.

[56] Flynn (1943), 85–86, 104–109.

[57] Lily, *Shorte Introduction* (1567). See also Appendix III, 19.0.

Finally he lists the first recorded extant copies of the 1542 edition of the English part and the 1540 edition of the Latin part of 'Lily's Grammar'.[58] Flynn broadened this field of research by providing a complete text of a later edition of the authorized grammar. However, it becomes obvious that future linguistic research used only the text of Flynn's facsimile edition; his observations about the earliest recorded copies and the tradition of the grammar were not being pursued.

Flynn's research had not been known to Ivan Poldauf. In his 1948 Prague work on the development of English grammatical studies, entitled *On the History of Some Problems of English Grammar Before 1800*, Poldauf considered Colet and Lily the "co-authors of a Latin grammar" published in 1509, of which the earliest extant edition is dated 1527.[59] He continues to argue that it was reprinted again and again until about 1850. He concludes that "an important edition of Lily's grammar, a sort of final revision, dates from 1566", citing Blach's work. J. P. Tuck's 1951 article, 'The Latin Grammar attributed to William Lily', focuses on the compilation of the earliest extant edition of 'Lily's Grammar' of 1540/1542 and its authorship. In respect to the English part of 1542, Tuck claims that the accidence that it contains represents Colet's *Aeditio* with minor alterations forming the first section of that part. He states that the part of the grammar in English dealing with syntax goes back to Lily's *Rudimenta grammatices* that was considerably revised. Tuck also mentions the 1557 and the 1567 editions that contain elements pointing to revision by new editors. Though Tuck's article indicates that a new start was made with the compilation of the authorized grammar about 1540, he nevertheless implies that the grammatical texts of the English part are based on Colet's and Lily's grammars in English that were compiled about 1510.[60]

C. G. Allen's 1954 article, 'The Sources of "Lily's Latin Grammar": A Review of the Facts and Some Further Suggestions', continues Flynn's research. Allen lists and examines earlier grammars, which have served as source texts for 'Lily's Grammar' and also the two parts of its earliest extant edition of 1540/1542. He also indicates some reasons for its monopoly and provides details about its compilation. Finally he compares earlier grammars that may have served as sources for the Latin part of 1540.[61]

---

[58] Lily, *Shorte Introduction* (1567), Introduction, iv–ix.
[59] See Poldauf (1948), 46–47.
[60] For Tuck's (1951) article see *The Durham Research Review*, Institute of Education, University of Durham 2: 33–39.
[61] For Allen's (1954) article see *The Library*, 5th ser., 9: 85–100, at 86–89, 99–100. A further discussion of a source text and of the later compilation of the grammar is provided by Allen's (1959) article 'Certayne Briefe Rules and "Lily's Latin Grammar"', *The Library*, 5th ser. 14: 49–53.

In the same way as Funke and Poldauf, Shoichi Watanabe's 1958 doctoral dissertation for Münster University generally states that Colet's *Aeditio* and Lily's *Rudimenta grammatices* printed in 1527 form the English part of the grammar attributed to William Lily. Watanabe based his arguments on the texts provided in Blach's editions.[62] G. Scheurwegh's 1961 article, which he continued in the following year with Carline Leroux, traces the influence of 'Lily's Grammar' on early English grammarians in the Netherlands. It starts with a brief introduction of the authorized grammar of 1540 (Latin part) and also mentions the English part printed in 1542. In their study, however, they used the edition of 'Lily's Grammar' of 1567 as their base text of reference, due to the fact that it was available in the facsimile edition provided by Flynn in 1945.[63]

In his series *English Linguistics, 1500–1800*, a collection of facsimile reprints, R. C. Alston provided the texts of the 1548 and 1549 editions of 'Lily's Grammar' in 1970.[64] Alston reprinted the 1549 fragment of the Bodleian Library copy. The corresponding text of the four missing pages is reproduced from the copy of the 1557 edition that is given as Appendix I in his edition. In the same volume he includes the text of the fragment of the 1548 copy as Appendix II. In his introductory note Alston draws attention to the earliest recorded copy of the edition of the English part of 'Lily's Grammar' dated 1542, and also to the earlier proof fragment that is extant of this part.

Though Ian Michael's standard work of 1970 states the main problems, as indicated above, when working from the relevant primary text of 'Lily's Grammar', his book may serve as an example to illustrate the difficulties. In respect to the English part, Michael distinguishes between "early forms [of] Lily's English accidence" and "later forms of the English accidence". In the first case he quotes from the first extant edition of 1527 of John Colet's *Aeditio*, in the second case he provides examples from the copy of the *Shorte Introduction* of 1567, which represents one of its later editions.[65] This means that Michael, in the same way as Blach and Funke and other scholars before him, regards Colet's *Aeditio* and Lily's *Rudimenta grammatices* extant in the editions printed in 1527 as the earliest stage of the first extant edition of 'Lily's Grammar'. Moreover, Michael lists the copy of the 1566 edition of the grammar and cites it as "Lily, 1566", *i.e.*

---

[62] See Shoichi Watanabe (1958), *Studien zur Abhängigkeit der Frühneuenglischen Grammatiken von den Mittelalterlichen Lateingrammatiken*, Münster, 63–69.

[63] G. Scheurweghs (1961). 'The Influence of the Latin Grammar of William Lily on the Early English Grammarians in the Netherlands (I)', *Leuvense Bijdragen* 50: 140–51, at 140; C. Leroux and G. Scheurweghs (1962), (II), *Leuvense Bijdragen* 51: 124–28.

[64] See Lily and Colet (1548/49). For the copies repr. in Alston's facsimile edition see Appendix III, 8.0 (1548 copy), 9.1 (1549 copy), and 12.1.a (1557 copy).

[65] Michael (1970), 96 and his Appendix IV, 542. For the 1567 copy of the English part referred to see Appendix III, 19.1.

one of the later editions of the English part of 'Lily's Grammar' that was edited by Blach. He also refers to this edition in his book as "The Royal Grammar".[66] Quotations illustrating aspects of the Latin part, however, are taken from the copy of the Latin part of the edition of 1567, which is referred to as "Lily, *Brevissima Institutio, 1567*", in other words, the copy that was made available by Flynn's facsimile edition.[67] Flynn's research on the sources of 'Lily's Grammar' is not listed in Michael's bibliography. However, both Tuck's 1951 article and Allen's article are referred to in his book.

R. C. Alston's 1971 facsimile editions of the first extant editions of Colet's *Aeditio* and Lily's *Rudimenta grammatices* printed in 1527 made available the texts of these two important sources for the English part of 'Lily's Grammar' and provide an important step towards the study of source texts, as well as to the English part of the authorized grammar of 1542.[68] Emma Vorlat's 1975 study of *The Development of English Grammatical Theory, 1586–1737*, perpetuates the views of earlier scholars in that she sees Colet's *Aeditio* and Lily's *Rudimenta grammatices* as the beginning of 'Lily's Grammar'. According to Vorlat, it was only after Lily's death that a Latin version was made.[69] However, she based her investigations of the parts of speech on the copy of the 1567 edition, the first of the two parts of 'Lily's Grammar' that was made available in the facsimile edition by Flynn, as "the one used by the English grammarians".[70]

George Arthur Padley's monograph of 1976, *Grammatical Theory in Western Europe, 1500–1700. Vol. 1: The Latin Tradition*, which is devoted to the theoretical trends, reflected in the Latin grammars of the sixteenth and seventeenth centuries, does not quote from the texts under consideration and only makes some mention of the textual differences between the relevant grammars to which he refers.[71] Padley perpetuates Funke, Michael, and others in that he sees the texts of John Colet's *Aeditio* of 1527 as the "editio princeps" of 'Lily's Grammar', and the 1566 text is regarded as a later revised edition. In the same way as Funke, Padley provides titles for these texts: the 1527 text is referred to as "Lily's Latin grammar of 1527" (abbreviated as *L*) and the later edition of 'Lily's Grammar' is referred to as "Lily's Latin grammar of 1566" (*L'*). He considers that the grammar authorized by Henry VIII only represents a new edition of Colet's *Aeditio*

---

[66] Michael's (1970) Appendix IV, 542. For this copy see Appendix III, 17.0.

[67] Michael's (1970) Appendix IV, 542. See the Latin part of Appendix III, 19.2.

[68] See Colet, *Aeditio* (1527). The text of the *Aeditio* is printed on sigs. A6ʳ-D6ᵛ, and William Lily's *Rudimenta grammatices* is printed immediately afterwards on sigs. D7ʳ-E5ᵛ.

[69] See Vorlat (1975), 6–8.

[70] Vorlat (1975), ix. For the copy of the edition referred to in her work see Appendix III, 19.1.

[71] See Padley (1976), xii, and 24–27. Padley states that the 1549 copy presumably represents the first edition that contains the royal injunction, since, in his opinion, there is no real evidence for the 1540 edition posited by Flynn; see Padley (1976) 25, footnote 1. For the copy of the 1574 edition see Appendix III, 26.0.

and Lily's *Rudimenta grammatices* with a royal proclamation. Padley mentions the 1549 edition which is incomplete, and the 1557 edition, both of which had become known by Alston's facsimile edition (1970), and "the definitive edition of 1574".

Nils Erik Enkvist's 1975 article, 'English in Latin Guise. A Note on Some Renaissance Textbooks', provides examples that underline the blurring of the borderline between the grammar of Latin and the grammar of English which already occurs in the grammatical manuscripts written in English up to those grammars used in the seventeenth century. His observations in respect to 'Lily's Grammar' are based on Flynn's facsimile edition of the 1567 copy, but he also lists Alston's facsimile edition of the 1548/49 copy, and quotes from Henry VIII's proclamation contained in the 1542 edition.[72] Finally, in her *Descriptive Adequacy of Early Modern English Grammars* (2004), an earlier version of which was submitted as a doctoral dissertation to Aachen University, Ute Dons based her arguments on 'Lily's Grammar' on the copies of the 1548/49 editions (complemented by the 1557 copy) of Alston's facsimile edition.[73]

Earlier research in the field of linguistics illustrates, from different viewpoints, how an important text in the history of linguistics and education, which has come down to us in a number of different editions, has been dealt with, when its earliest extant edition has not hitherto been available in a critical edition. Moreover, the text has not been studied in relation to its grammatical tradition. An examination of earlier research on 'Lily's Grammar' reveals that the accounts are incoherent inasmuch as successive scholars appear either not always to have been aware of their predecessors' work, or alternatively failed to take it into account. Various reasons have contributed to this situation, especially the inaccessibility of material due to the closure of libraries during the Second World War and shortly afterwards. The contribution of scholarship, especially from the 1970s onwards, consisted mainly of adding an increasing body of reprints of editions of 'Lily's Grammar' and some of its sources. Critical and facsimile editions played an important role in its study and served as textual foundations on which scholarly works were based. However, it is striking that historians of linguistics have confined their attention to edited texts and to a number of later editions. In some cases they have used more than one of the later editions for their work, or the texts most accessible to them, and that meant using Blach's inaccurate editions of the 1566 text and sources for 'Lily's Grammar' that were taken erroneously to be its earliest extant edition. Flynn's comments, in his thorough doctoral dissertation of 1939, his 1943 article, and in his

---

[72] See Enkvist (1975) 287, 295, and 297.
[73] Ute Dons (2004), *Descriptive Adequacy of Early Modern English Grammars*, Berlin and New York, 18–19, 260.

facsimile edition of the 1567 text, in which he also discussed sources of the grammar and its final form, have not been taken adequately into account. The results of Allen's article, based on Flynn's research, also often seem to have been ignored in subsequent research. Since Flynn's facsimile edition of the 1567 text, and Alston's facsimile editions of the 1548/49 text and the grammars which served as source texts for 'Lily's Grammar', *i.e.* Colet's *Aeditio* and Lily's *Rudimenta grammatices* of 1527, recourse has been taken to them in some scholarly works. In the course of time a number of later editions of 'Lily's Grammar' became available in facsimile editions and hence were also referred to. Although the first extant editions of the English part (1542) and of the Latin part (1540) of 'Lily's Grammar' have been known to scholars from about the mid-nineteenth century onwards and were often referred to in linguistic and educational works, apart from the royal proclamation printed in 1542, Flynn is the only scholar who has sought to establish which was the earliest known edition and to study its text. The main reason probably is that it has not hitherto been accessible in published form. Facsimile editions or transcriptions of later reprints, or even different grammars which must be considered sources for the English part of 'Lily's Grammar', were used as a textual basis at the same time as later revised reprints of the authorized text.[74] It can be concluded that the results drawn from the evidence on which earlier work on 'Lily's Grammar' is based are of doubtful value.

The only way to obtain any clarity in this field is to disentangle the elements by inspecting the books themselves to ascertain the facts about them and their relation to each other. This situation in earlier linguistic research explains why it is necessary to make the text of the first extant edition of 'Lily's Grammar' available and to include its tradition from the time from which grammatical manuscripts in English have survived. It is no less necessary to present the transmission of the text from its first appearance in printed form. There remains an overriding need for critical editions, not only of the Latin part of 'Lily', but also of the earlier printed grammars. One can only hope that other scholars will take up this task before too long.

1.3 *Bibliographical information since the eighteenth century*

Bibliographical knowledge and new discoveries in this field had little or no impact on linguistic scholarship up to the first decades of the twentieth century. This is all the more surprising because the existence of the volume containing the earliest extant and complete editions of the English

---

[74] The problem of reliable textual sources on which linguistic works of earlier periods are based is discussed by Alston (1966), 181–91.

and the Latin parts of this grammar has been known to bibliographers at least since the mid-eighteenth century, before it found a permanent home in the British Museum in 1799. This volume is almost certainly the one listed in an entry in Joseph Ames's *Typographical Antiquities* (1749), the description of which was virtually taken over in William Herbert's extended bibliography (1785–1790), which in turn found its way into the bibliography of Thomas Frognall Dibdin (1810–1819).[75] William Thomas Lowndes listed it in his famous work entitled *Bibliographer's Manual of English Literature* (1834) as follows: "Lond. 1542. 4to. On VELLUM. A copy is in the British Museum."[76] John Gough Nichols discovered this volume in the Library of the British Museum where it was available for consultation. In a short article published in 1858 he described the three books which make up the earliest extant edition of 'Lily's Latin Grammar', mentioned some of its former owners, and referred to the descriptions given by Ames, Herbert, and Dibdin. He was also aware that another copy of the Latin part of 'Lily's Grammar' existed, which was located in Lambeth Palace Library, and adds that he "should be glad to know where any other copies of the same Grammar are preserved, whether upon vellum or on paper".[77] In his *Handbook* published in 1867, W. Carew Hazlitt quotes the title of the English part of the grammar of 1542 with some more bibliographical details. He also mentions four later sixteenth-century editions of the grammar and adds that "there were many other editions".[78] The earliest extant edition of 'Lily's Grammar', the copy-text of the present

---

[75] See Ames, 173, where the contents of the three parts of the complete volume are listed under the entry *Alphabetum Latino Anglicum* of the year 1543. The Latin grammar in English is described there as follows: "Also, An introduction to the eight partes of speech, and the construction of the same, compiled and sette forthe by the commaundment of our most gracious soverayne lorde the King, anno 1543. This book is printed on vellum, and curiously illuminated, and hath the following order: [. . .]. To this is added, *Institutio Compendiaria Totius Grammaticae* [. . .]." See also Herbert, vol. 1: 442–43, and Dibdin, *Typographical Antiquities*, vol. 3, no. 1248: 318–19. Biographical information on these bibliographers is given in the *ODNB*; on Ames (1689–1759), vol. 1: 937–39; on Herbert (1718–1795), vol. 26: 748–51; and on Dibdin (1776–1847), vol. 16: 33–34.

[76] William Thomas Lowndes (1834), *The Bibliographer's Manual of English Literature*, 4 vols. London, vol. 3: 1134.

[77] 'The Latin Grammar Issued by Royal Authority in 1540', *Notes and Queries*, 2nd ser., 6, no. 149: 368. For the copy of the Latin part of 'Lily's Grammar' located in Lambeth Palace Library see Appendix III, no. 1.0.

[78] W. Carew Hazlitt (1867), *Handbook to the Popular, Poetical and Dramatic Literature of Great Britain, from the Invention of Printing to the Restoration*, London, 334. Some later editions are listed in his *Bibliographical Collections and Notes*, published from 1876–1903 in four series, with two supplements to the third series. Cf. the reprint of the series of 1893–1903, New York, 1961; also George J. Gray's (1893) *A General Index to Hazlitt's Handbook* and his *Bibliographical Collections (1867–1889)*, London. Hazlitt's *Bibliographical Collections and Notes* are of particular value in that the transcriptions of the titles are based on personal examination of the items themselves.

edition, is listed in well-known catalogues, for example, in the *Catalogue of Books in the Library of the British Museum* (1884) (*BM Catalogue*) and also in the *Short-Title Catalogue* (1926) (*STC*). It has also been available on microfilm since about 1939 as part of the Early English Books series from University Microfilms.[79] It is now also available in digitized electronic format to subscribing libraries.

During the last three decades of the twentieth century in particular, essential bibliographical aids and studies became available which make it possible to study the text of 'Lily's Grammar', its bibliographical context, and trace its tradition. The revised *Short-Title Catalogue* (1976–1991) (*STC²*) in three volumes, a retrospective survey of printed 'English' books from 1475–1640, is an essential aid for the study of 'Lily's Grammar'. It lists all the known editions from this period and also editions of its printed source texts under the name of their author or title, for example editions of the grammars of John Colet and William Lily, as well as anonymous grammatical texts, such as *Certayne Briefe Rules of the regiment or construction of the eyght partes of speche*.[80] Some further editions and corrections of entries are listed in the *Addenda and Corrigenda* of the first two volumes, and in particular in the list of *Addenda and Corrigenda* of volume three. R. C. Alston's *Bibliography of the English Language from the Invention of Printing to the Year 1800* is an invaluable aid for studies of this grammar. Volume 15, *Greek, Latin to 1650* (2001), lists titles which served as sources for 'Lily's Grammar' as well as a large number of editions of the grammar itself, citing the location of copies in a large number of libraries. In addition, it provides some photographic reproductions of title-pages, and other individual pages that are of particular interest, such as the text of the royal proclamation contained in the 1542 copy of 'Lily's Grammar'. It also records some new finds that have not been listed in *STC²* or other printed catalogues.[81] The revised *STC* as well as the revised edition of Wing for the period 1641 to 1700 are now available as part of the *English Short Title Catalogue* (*ESTC*) online database, where each entry is given a unique identifier, in addition to whatever *STC* or Wing number may be appropriate, and it can be searched by author, title, or identifier number. New bibliographical discoveries, corrections of entries, and movements of books are incorporated into this live database that does not have the limiting finality of the printed book. It is always under construction.[82]

---

[79] Reel 59 was filmed about the year 1939, reel 1845 about 1983.

[80] For bibliographical references to editions of 'Lily's Grammar' cf. also p. 2, footnote 4. For bibliographical references to *Certayne Briefe Rules* see *Checklist* 52.1 and 52.2.

[81] See, for example, the copy of the version of the *Long Accidence*, attributed to John Stanbridge, which was probably printed in London in 1530 (Alston, vol. 15, no. 124, and Plates LXXV–LXXVI).

[82] See David McKitterick (2005), ' "Not in STC": Opportunities and Challenges in the ESTC', *The Library*, 7ᵗʰ ser., vol. 6: 178–94, at 182–84.

Early English Books Online (*EEBO*) is another very useful bibliographical aid, which consists of a full-text archive covering printed books from 1473–1700, as well as a number of items printed after 1700. It provides bibliographical descriptions of records of printed grammars and also makes available digitized images of the pages of the original volumes.

With the aid of research in grammatical manuscripts, especially since the 1970s, it can be shown that the tradition of 'Lily's Grammar' begins with the grammatical manuscripts in English. In this connection, David Thomson's *Catalogue* and *Edition* prove indispensible for any research in this field. Thomson's work is augmented by Cynthia Renée Bland's 1991 edition of two grammatical manuscripts for the teaching of Latin written in English. A further grammatical fragment in manuscript remains unedited.[83] My own *Checklist* combines the grammatical manuscripts written in English and the early printed grammars providing the background for the English part of 'Lily's Grammar' in one book, thus facilitating comparison of one type of record with another and following the tradition of the English grammatical treatises back to the earliest treatise that can be dated *c.*1400. Much potential knowledge is offered in catalogues, bibliographies, editions, and electronic media which provide the textual sources that, one may hope, will stimulate further detailed research on 'Lily's Grammar'. There is, however, no doubt that the bibliographical approach needs constant updating in the light of fresh discoveries of texts and new source analyses.

---

[83] For the bibliographical reference see *Checklist* 32.

2. The Grammatical Tradition

2.1 *Elementary Latin grammar and its teaching*

From antiquity to the early modern period and beyond, the term 'grammar' was generally understood to refer to Latin grammar. It goes beyond what we nowadays understand by grammar in a narrow sense, *i.e.* as comprising morphology and syntax. The rudiments of the structure of Latin were the topics which grammarians regarded as part of their domain: the letters, syllables, the parts of speech, their inflection, concord, and government, as well as prosody and metre. These topics also included a fluency of language sufficient to serve all the communicative needs of its users, both written and spoken, together with composition and some knowledge of literature. Grammar had a fundamental place in all medieval education. The study of Latin began in grammar school, where pupils learned the elements of the language. Here they were to be given a general grounding in the Latin tongue, with the focus not only on the structure of the language but also on literature, especially poetry. Many pupils in grammar school, however, were interested only in the practical uses of the language in the administrative and commercial spheres of life, for which their studies were intended to qualify them. Some of them continued their studies at university, where grammar at a more advanced level was the first of the subjects that constituted the Seven Liberal Arts. It thus represented the foundation upon which all further studies were based. The student was given a thorough training in the subjects that constituted the trivium: grammar, rhetoric, and logic. In these subjects his expressive powers were trained. The trivium was followed by the quadrivium comprising arithmetic, geometry, astronomy, and music. This could then lead to higher studies, civil law, canon law, medicine, and finally theology. Grammar was, in fact, what may be called the very bedrock of medieval intellectual culture.

The discipline *grammatica* was a single field which ranged from the preliminaries at the lowest level, the letters of the alphabet, the syllables, and basic prayers such as the *Lord's Prayer*, the *Creed*, and the *Ave Maria*, to the study and interpretation of texts. The knowledge of the elements of Latin enabled the children to participate in the services of the church. Latin was the language of the church and the sacred scriptures. As the church was the centre of learning and education, Latin became the most important subject of all studies. It was the basis of spoken and written scholarship and of international communication in the Middle Ages and well beyond as the *lingua franca*, and it was the traditional language of literacy. The principal textbooks of all the liberal arts, philosophy, the natural sciences, civil and canon law were written in Latin. Moreover, it long remained the medium of administration.

In contrast to the European native languages, Latin had the advantage of a formal written grammar. The vernaculars, for example English, were held in relatively low esteem in the Middle Ages. Thus, given the overriding importance of Latin, a vast amount of energy went into studying Latin and transmitting it to future generations. Consequently, elementary formal instruction in language, the understanding, speaking, reading, and writing of it, started from Latin. It was the duty of the grammar school teacher to provide his pupils with this foundation. Ælfric's *Grammar* and the grammatical manuscripts of the late Middle Ages illustrate the rules of elementary Latin grammar as well as the method of teaching pupils whose mother tongue was English. Considering the surviving texts, Ælfric's *Grammar*, as the outstanding example of a bilingual grammar of the Anglo-Saxon period using English as the explanatory language, remains an isolated though most remarkable example in the tradition of grammar writing in English. Evidence of a new beginning of grammar writing in the vernacular appears only in the middle of the fourteenth century, and this development finally led to the introduction of the authorized grammar in 1540. The monolingual teaching of Latin at the elementary as well as at a more advanced level, however, continued after the Norman Conquest and grammatical texts were adapted and modified according to the needs of the students. These texts provided examples in structure and content from which the elementary grammars in the vernacular could draw.

Grammars are pedagogical works that serve as tools for teaching and learning the rules of a language, at different levels, for explicating existing literary texts, and for guiding pupils in the writing of new texts, as well as in expressing themselves orally. These textbooks for teaching the elements of Latin also serve as repositories, where the rules of the language and the way of teaching that prevailed at different periods are codified. In many cases they are supplemented by other practical pedagogical works such as vocabularies, collections of proverbs, and exercises to facilitate the study of Latin. In addition, they provide material with the side-effect of illustrating the conditions and manners of the time. In these manuals Latin was both the goal and the medium of instruction. Grammars for the teaching of Latin as a second language, which had to be learned as an overlay on the native language, however, needed a different approach to the rules, a fact that was recognized by grammarians and schoolmasters and which is found incorporated in their works. These manuals had to take into account the vernacular background of the pupils and their different needs.[1] A teaching method that was sufficiently effective was necessary to impress the knowledge of Latin upon the memories of children of about the age of seven. A great deal of oral work in the vernacular was necessary to explain the forms and elucidate the structure of Latin. Additional material, such as reference works and glossaries, was also required to facilitate the study of grammar. In the course of time the pedagogical necessities of the students of Latin, and the experience of the teachers, as well as the aims of the curriculum, found their way into the manuals. Latin grammars actually written in the vernacular as the explanatory language represent a further development in this field. They are the means that had enabled the teaching process to produce Latin users from an English-speaking background. The vernacular was stylized according to Latin and appears side by side with it on the written and later on the printed page. At first, English was included as a subsidiary aid to explain the Latin. However, by explaining points of Latin grammar in English, teachers would often refer to differences between the target language and their own language, thus helping pupils to understand the structure of Latin better. Elucidating the structure of the vernacular has to be considered a diversion at first. From a pedagogical point of view, however, the writing of grammars in the vernacular reflects an immediate need in the field of education. Moreover, it also sheds light on the status of English in the late Middle Ages and the early modern period. From the point of view of writers of grammars of the English language, which first appeared with William Bullokar's *Pamphlet for Grammar* in 1586, the grammar of Latin represented 'grammar' as a school discipline. Other languages could therefore best be presented systematically and taught in that way and through that framework.

Considering the mono- and bilingual Latin elementary grammars from a different aspect, it has to be taken into account that all these works can only be considered partial representations of a teaching process that can no longer be fully recovered. They do not mirror the way instruction in the classroom actually took place. However, they do provide evidence that teachers and grammarians strove to produce and adapt the teaching aids to their students' requirements. The number and variety of elementary grammars reflect their continuing efforts to refine their pedagogy. For this reason treatises for teaching the elements of Latin were compiled in the mother tongue of the learners, and the contents and structure of the texts were designed to meet their needs at this level.[2]

---

[1] See the discussion of 'textbook' in Chapter 1, p. 2, also footnote 2.
[2] On elementary Latin grammar cf. Vivien Law (2003). *The History of Linguistics in Europe. From Plato to 1600.* Cambridge, 190–99, and *passim*; Helmut Gneuss (2003), 'The Study of Language in Anglo-Saxon England', in D. Scragg (ed.), *Textual and Material Culture in Anglo-Saxon England*, Cambridge, 75–105, at 78–79; Ekkehard Eggs (1996), 'Grammatik', in *HWRh*, vol. 3,

The study of elementary Latin grammar, with English as its language of exposition, is a phenomenon that reaches back to the first millennium AD. A brief survey will illustrate that grammar writing in the vernacular and its teachings can already be documented at the end of the later Anglo-Saxon period.[3] Although, as will be indicated below, the tradition of grammar writing in the vernacular of this period cannot be linked to that of which we have written evidence from *c.*1400 onwards and that finally culminated in the authorized grammar of 1540 attributed to William Lily, nevertheless, Ælfric's linguistic works must have an important place in the context of the overall development of Latinity in England. In this context it is of interest to consider briefly the achievements of the study of Latin in English, of language instruction and acquisition which had been made about half a millennium before, and to notice similarities in the responses to teaching problems in the classroom which were probably the same in the different periods. The study of language in the Anglo-Saxon period, as well as in the centuries leading up to 'Lily's Grammar', was primarily devoted to Latin. Apart from the subject matter, these teaching manuals provide evidence of the numerous and differing strategies teachers must have used to make pupils learn the rules of Latin grammar and vocabulary and also to give them fluency in that language.

at cols. 1030–90; Gregor Kalivoda (1996), 'Grammatikunterricht', in *HWRh*, vol. 3, at cols. 1112–59; Hedwig Gwosdek (1994), 'Elementarunterricht', in *HWRh*, vol. 2, cols. 1004–13; J. Gruber *et al.* (1989) 'Grammatik, grammatische Literatur', in *Lexikon des Mittelalters* (1980–1999), eds. Liselotte Lutze *et al.*, 10 vols., Munich and Zurich, vol. 4, cols. 1637–43; Jeffrey F. Huntsman (1983), 'Grammar', in D. L. Wagner (ed.), *The Seven Liberal Arts in the Middle Ages.* Bloomington, 58–95; James J. Murphy (1980), 'The Teaching of Latin as a Second Language in the 12th Century', *Historiographia Linguistica* 7: 159–75; G. L. Bursill-Hall (1977). 'Teaching Grammars of the Middle Ages', *Historiographia Linguistica* 4: 1–29, at 1–5; Nicholas Orme (1973), *English Schools in the Middle Ages.* London, 59–115, and *passim*; also Louis John Paetow (1910), *The Arts Course at Medieval Universities with Special Reference to Grammar and Rhetoric.* University of Illinois Studies, vol. 3, no. 7. Urbana-Champaign, 33–66, and *passim*. Changes that took place in grammatical doctrine in the late eleventh and twelfth centuries, *i.e.* grammar, from being a literary discipline becoming a theoretical, speculative one, are not the focus of the present study. However, in the course of time, the developments in this discipline also had an impact on elementary grammar and its pedagogy that was a propaedeutic and practical discipline and continued to be taught as such on a lower level as an equally lively and certainly more widely exercised one, as a language to be learned. It appears that the subject of speculative grammar had engrossed the attention of some grammar masters, and the methods and subject matter, not the philosophical conclusions, of the speculative grammar filtered down into the advanced classes of the grammar schools.

[3] Helmut Gneuss (1996), *English Language Scholarship: A Survey and Bibliography from the Beginnings to the End of the Nineteenth Century*, Binghamton, New York, 8–14; Robert Henry Robins (1997), *A Short History of Linguistics*, 4th ed. London, 84; also Giulio Lepschy (ed.) (1994), *History of Linguistics*, Vol. 2: *Classical and Medieval Linguistics*, London, 185–86, 256.

2.2 *Late Anglo-Saxon vernacular grammar: Ælfric's* Grammar

This chapter on the most important representative of a bilingual grammar in late Old English times is intended to provide some idea of grammar writing in England at a period long before the grammar attributed to William Lily was compiled. It is of great interest to look briefly at its subject matter and its teaching methods in order to discover how elementary Latin grammar was then taught to English-speaking children. Ælfric, the Benedictine monk and abbot, wrote one of the best-known vernacular grammars of the late Old English period and a pioneering work in the history of linguistics and language teaching. Ælfric's *Grammar* is unique in being the first written introduction to Latin of that time to use English as its medium. Moreover, it is the first grammar that is extant in any European vernacular. It has to be viewed against the background of a precise religious and cultural programme promoted by that great generation of reformers—Dunstan, Æthelwold, and Oswald—and principally aimed at the clergy's education.[4] Ælfric was aware of the importance of the study of Latin, of its necessity and of the practical needs that existed. His educational works were compiled in response to this situation. The addressees of his *Grammar* are the *pueruli* of the monastery schools, but it was probably used for teaching other pupils as well.[5] It was meant as an introduction to their linguistic studies and to prepare them for a higher stage of education. It concentrates on the description of Latin at a fairly elementary level, with the emphasis on accidence, illustrating the teaching methods of the time, which supported the intentions of the teachers and took the level of the pupils and their particular needs into account.

Ælfric's *Grammar* was a well-known and influential schoolbook in the Old English period and achieved almost instantaneous popularity. Obviously it completely displaced other grammars at the elementary level soon after its appearance and retained its dominant position into the twelfth century.[6] It was compiled around the year 995, probably at Cerne, a newly founded monastery in Dorset, where Ælfric was a monk

---

[4] Cf. Donald A. Bullough (1991), 'The Educational Tradition in England from Alfred to Ælfric: Teaching *utriusque linguae*', in D. A. Bullough, *Carolingian Renewal: Sources and Heritage*, Manchester, 297–334, at 308–17, 329–34.

[5] The edition of the *Grammar* and *Glossary* used is that by Julius Zupitza (1880). *Aelfrics Grammatik und Glossar. Text und Varianten*. Vierte, unveränderte Auflage mit einer Einleitung von Helmut Gneuss (2003). Cf. Zupitza, Latin preface, 1, 3–5.

[6] The surviving fifteen medieval complete and fragmentary copies of Ælfric's *Grammar* are listed and briefly described by Gneuss in Zupitza, iv–xii. For the manuscripts containing these copies cf. Gneuss, *Handlist*; and Ker, *Catalogue*. See also briefly Malcolm R. Godden (1999), 'Ælfric of Eynsham', in M. Lapidge *et al.* (eds.), *The Blackwell Encyclopaedia of Anglo-Saxon England*, Oxford; repr. in paperback 2001, 8–9.

and mass-priest, before he became abbot of the monastery of Eynsham, near Oxford, in 1005. He apparently compiled most of his educational works at Cerne, amongst them his grammar which bears the title *Excerptiones de Arte Grammatica Anglice*, his *Glossary*, and his *Colloquy*, which are complementary and were designed to assist in the teaching of Latin. From this it can be assumed that his duties at Cerne probably also included the role of a teacher.[7]

The aims and contents of Ælfric's *Grammar* are stated in its Latin preface. After the pupils were made familiar with the basic concepts of grammar, the grammatical categories, the terminology, and sample paradigms, probably from Donatus's *Ars minor*, they could continue with the new grammar with which they began to study Latin morphology by means of their mother tongue.[8] After that they could continue with the *perfectiora studia*, probably Priscian's advanced grammar, the *Institutiones grammaticae*, or perhaps topics not covered in his grammar, e.g. metre, rhetorical figures, and so forth. In the two prefaces it is also stated that his grammar could be of use for the understanding of both languages, Latin and English.[9] Though it is essentially a grammar whose main object was the teaching of Latin, nevertheless, to some extent the familiar system and categories of Latin grammar could also be applied as a model for describing the vernacular. It was thus supposed to enable the pupil to acquire the ability to describe his own language in precise grammatical terms, drawing on the categories used for the Latin. Thus Ælfric expressly notes that English, too, has eight parts of speech (11,5–7). However, he did not provide a grammar of Old English.[10] The teaching of morphology is organized around the eight parts of speech, in accordance with Donatus's grammars. Syntax is not discussed. Ælfric begins with a series of brief explanations of basic terms, 'voice', 'letter', 'syllable' and 'diphthong'. In the *Praefatio de partibus orationis* he gives a brief overview of the subject before he lists the eight parts of speech in Latin in the order of Donatus's grammars, namely, "NOMEN, PRONOMEN, VERBVM, ADVERBIVM, PARTICIPIVM, CONIVNCTIO, PRAEPOSITIO, INTERIECTIO". Finally he

---

[7] For an account on Ælfric's life and his works see *ODNB*, vol. 1: 387–88; Gneuss (2009), *Ælfric of Eynsham. His Life, Times, and Writings*, Old English Newsletter Subsidia, 34, Kalamazoo, 4–6, and *passim*; Godden (1999), in Michael Lapidge *et al.* (eds.), 8–9; Irène Rosier and Vivien Law (1998), 'Ælfric', in *HEL*, vol. 1, no. 1226: 59–60; Sharpe, no. 53: 25–26; Law, rev. Louis Holtz (2009). 'Ælfric', in *Lexicon Grammaticorum*, vol. 1: 14–15; and James Hurt (1972), *Ælfric*, New York, *passim*. On Ælfric's *Grammar* see Orme (2006), *Medieval Schools*, New Haven 42–43; Law (2003), 191–96; Gneuss (2003), 84–88; Gneuss (2002), 'Ælfrics Grammatik und Glossar: Sprachwissenschaft um die Jahrtausendwende in England', in W. Hüllen und F. Klippel (eds.), *Heilige und Profane Sprachen*, Wiesbaden, 77–92; and Law (1997), 'Ælfric's *Excerptiones de Arte Grammatica Anglice*', in Law, *Grammar and Grammarians in the Early Middle Ages*, London, 200–23.
[8] Zupitza, 1, 5–6.
[9] Zupitza, Latin and English prefaces, 1–3.
[10] See Law (1997), 212–13.

goes on to provide definitions of each of them in the vernacular, to illustrate them by example, and to add further information.[11] In the main section, each part of speech, apart from the noun, opens with a definition in Latin of the individual part of speech, which is immediately followed by a rendering into Old English, along with illustrative examples, explanations, and further information in the vernacular, before its accidents are listed and discussed in turn. The Latin definitions are identical with either Donatus's or Priscian's definitions or are close to them in wording.[12] Usually English terms and translations are presented alongside the Latin paradigms that were intended to make plain the meaning of the Latin and reflect Ælfric's immediate concern with comprehensibility.

In the first sentence of the Latin preface to his *Grammar*, Ælfric already shows its derivative nature by saying that he has made an effort to translate these excerpts from Priscian's *Institutiones grammaticae* into English.[13] His grammar is based on the *Excerptiones de Prisciano* as his principal source, but he also incorporates material from Donatus's and other grammars. Apart from shortening his source still further, he modified it in various ways to meet his own pedagogical aims. His efforts resulted in a teaching manual which corresponded to the level and understanding of his pupils and also to their situation as students of a foreign language. To exemplify proper and common names in the discussion of the noun, he uses the names of his teachers, "Êadgâr, Dûnstân", and "cyning, bisceop, *homo* man" (11,17–18). As proper names of the first declension he includes the biblical names ending in *-as*, namely "*hic Andreas apostolus, hic Thomas, hic Matthias, hic Barnabas*" (25,17–18) which supplement the forms of *hic Aeneas* (25,14). He also explains grammatical rules, for example, by referring to domestic tasks, occupations and utensils related to them, as "*illae nent lanam* hîg spinnað wulle" [they are spinning wool] (97,9), "*sui fabri opus*

---

[11] Zupitza, *Praefatio de partibus orationis*, 8–11.

[12] Zupitza, *Praefatio*, 11, which immediately continues with the discussion of the noun in his work. For the definitions of the parts of speech in Ælfric's *Grammar* see Appendix V.

[13] Ælfric refers to his *Grammar* as "*has excerptiones de Prisciano minore uel maiore*" [these excerpts from Priscian minor and maior], *i.e. De constructione* (Books 17 and 18) and *De octo partibus* (Books 1–16) of Priscian's *Institutiones grammaticae* (see Zupitza, 1, 3–4). Priscian's comprehensive grammar served as the major source for the *Excerptiones de Prisciano*, which proved to be a drastically abbreviated version of Priscian's work. The *Excerptiones* were Ælfric's principal source of his *Grammar*. See the edition with translation by David W. Porter (2002), *Excerptiones de Prisciano: The Source for Ælfric's Latin-Old English Grammar*, Woodbridge. The *Excerptiones de Prisciano* is an anonymous work. However, according to Porter there are important clues that also suggest Ælfric as the author of the *Excerptiones de Prisciano*. Cf. the review article on Porter's edition by Gneuss (2005), 'The First Edition of the Source of Ælfric's Grammar', *Anglia* 223: 246–59; also Law (1997), 204–206, 217–19. The text of the prefaces of Ælfric's *Grammar* is given in *Ælfric's Prefaces*, ed. Jonathan Wilcox (1994), Durham Medieval Texts, 9, New Elvet, Durham; corrected repr. 1996, 114–16, 130 (English translation of the Latin preface). A reprint of the Latin preface and excerpts of the text with an English translation are also found in *Educational Charters and Documents, 598 to 1909*, ed. Arthur F. Leach, New York; repr. 1971, 48–51.

his smiþes weorc" [the work of his smith] (105,10), and "*nostri piscatoris rete* ûres fisceres nett" [the net of our fisherman] (105,12–13).

There are only a few examples in which Latin and Old English are contrasted explicitly. See, for instance, the passage dealing with the copulative conjunction 'and' that highlights the distinctive character of Latin as compared to Old English, where Ælfric concludes that these alternative Latin conjunctions were all equivalent to the one English word 'and'. He says:

þâs sind geþêodendlîce: *et, que, ac, ast, at, atque. uir et mulier* wer and wîf. *stetitque* and hê stôd. *cantauitque* and hê sang. *omnis populus uirorum ac mulierum* eall folc wera and wîfa. *ast alii adfirmant* and ôðre sêþað. *at* is ongeânweardlîc: *at Iesus ait* and se hælend cwæð him tôgeânes; *at illi tacuerunt* and hî sûwodon tôgeânes þæs hælendes wordum. *atque aliis est largus* and ôþrum hê is cystig. ealle ðâs habbað ân englisc, þêah ðe hî for fægernysse fela synd on lêdensprǣce.

(Zupitza. 259,4–13)[14]

His purpose, to make plain the meaning of the Latin, also dictates his handling of the essential grammatical terminology.[15] The terms in Old English were to be used as a means for this purpose. They were explanatory and intended to document and interpret the Latin rules and grammatical phenomena in two languages with Latin coming first, not to replace the corresponding Latin ones. It is possible that they may have been common in the teaching of his time, but many of them may also have been his own innovations. In addition, it is important what Ælfric says in the Latin preface to his *Grammar*, namely that words can be translated in various ways, but that he, in his *Grammar*, has decided to translate them in a straightforward way. He adds that he has learned this method at Æthelwold's school at Winchester. He also indicates how difficult it is to render Latin terms into English.[16] Thus a full pattern of grammatical terminology arose, relating to the parts of speech and their accidents, and also signifying general grammatical terms such as "stæfcræfte" for "GRAMMATICA" (2,14), "stæf" for "LITTERA" (4,18), "stæfgefêg" for "SYLLABA" (7,4) and others. The Latin term is given at least

---

[14] Translation of the Old English passages: These are conjunctions: *et, que, ac, ast, at, atque. uir et mulier* man and woman. *stetitque* and he stood. *cantauitque* and he sang. *omnis populus uirorum ac mulierum* all people, men and women. *ast alii adfirmant* and others confirm. *at* is adversative: *at Iesus ait* and the Saviour called them together; *at illi tacuerunt* and they became silent in response to the Saviour's words. *atque aliis est largus* and to others he is virtuous. All these [words] have an English [equivalent], although for beauty many are in Latin.

[15] On Ælfric's terminology see Dieter Kastovsky (2010), 'Translation Techniques in the Terminology of Ælfric's *Grammar*: Semantic Loans, Loan Translations and Word-Formation', in M. Kytö, J. Scahill, and H. Tanabe (eds.), *Language Change and Variation from Old English to Late Modern English*, Bern, 163–74; Lucia Kornexl (2004), ' "For Englisch was it neuere": Grammatical Metalanguage in Medieval England', in L. Moessner and C. M. Schmidt (eds.), *Anglistentag 2004. Aachen. Proceedings*, Trier, 77–87, at 78–81; Law (1997), 213–15; Teresa Pàroli (1968). 'Indice della Terminologia Grammaticale di Aelfric', *Annali dell'Istituto Orientale di Napoli, Sezione Linguistica* 8: 113–38; also Edna Rees Williams (1958), 'Ælfric's Grammatical Terminology', *PMLA* 73, no. 5: 453–62.

[16] See Zupitza, Latin preface, 1,13–17, and 2,1–2.

once with its English equivalent or with either a short or a more detailed explanatory phrase or clause in English, or with both. The following examples may serve to illustrate some of his procedures. The Latin term and its English equivalent are given in "TEMPVS tîd, MODVS gemet, SPE-CIES hiw, FIGVRA gefêgednyss, CONIVGATIO geþêodnyss, PERSONA hâd, NVMERVS getel" (119,14–16). Though lexical variation is rare, there are some instances of a Latin term being rendered by two alternative English terms, for example, *accidentia* is translated by "gelimp" (92,8) or "gelimplîce ðing" (119,12), DECLINATIO by "declinung" (21,7) or "gebîgednysse" (89,4–5), PRIMITIVA by "frumcennede" (11,12) or "fyrmyste" (11,12).

There are also examples of a Latin term being rendered as two English words, e.g. "PRONOMEN ys naman speljend" (92,3–4), also "ADVERBIVM mæg bêon gecweden wordes gefêra" (223,2–3). Latin terms are also rendered as an explanatory phrase, for instance, "MASCVLINVM and FEMININVM, þæt is, werlîc and wîflîc" (18,5–6), also "NEVTRVM is nâðor cynn" (18,14). The cases of the noun are explained in detail. Note, for example, how the vocative case is presented in Ælfric's *Grammar*:

VOCATIVVS ys clypjendlîc oððe gecîgendlîc: mid ðâm CASV wê clypjað tô ǽlcum ðinge: *o homo, ueni huc* êalâ ðû man, cum hider; *o homo, loquere ad me* êalâ ðû man, sprec tô mê; *o magister, doce me aliquid* êalâ ðû lârêow, tǽce mê sum ðing.

(Zupitza 23,2–6)[17]

The Latin name for this and the other cases is used as a telling name whose meaning and function is made clear to the pupils by their corresponding terms in the vernacular. A related derivational form helping to explain the meaning of each case is followed by illustrative examples.

A method very similar to the explanation of the Latin cases is applied to make the meaning and function of the parts of speech and their accidents clear to the pupils. The definition of the interjection and its only accident, *i.e.* signification, may serve as an example for this procedure. The terms *interiectio* and *significatio* are rendered by corresponding nouns in Old English, of which derivational forms are repeated to explain the meaning and function of this part of speech and its accident. The passage reads as follows:

INTERIECTIO mæg bêon gecweden betwuxâlegednys on englisc, forþan ðe hê lîð betwux wordum and geopenað þæs môdes styrunge mid behŷddre stemne. ân þing hê hæfþ: SIGNIFICATIO, þæt is getâcnung, forðan ðe hê getâcnað hwîlon ðæs môdes blîsse, hwîlon sârnysse, hwîlon wundrunge and gehwæt.

(Zupitza 278,1–6)[18]

---

[17] Translation of the Old English: "The vocative is calling or showing: with this case we call to all things: *o homo, ueni huc* oh you man, come here; *o homo, loquere ad me* oh you man, speak to me; *o magister, doce me aliquid* oh you teacher, teach me something."

[18] Translation of the Old English: "The interjection may be called 'betwuxâlegednys' in English because it is placed between words and opens the emotion of the mind with careful

In many instances throughout the grammar, either the Latin or the English term is chosen to the exclusion of the other. However, in the later sections of the grammar an increasing proportion of Old English terms, which appear without their corresponding Latin equivalents, is to be noticed. Ælfric made available a set of English grammatical terms for use in grammar which function as glosses to the technical vocabulary of Latin, and serve as an aid to the pupil to master the terminology that he would need for further studies in Latin. It seems as though Ælfric was expressly teaching not only the principles of grammar, but also the technical terms, the metalanguage, necessary to an understanding of the various topics of grammar.

As the English pupils were learning a foreign language, they were in need of a detailed discussion of Latin inflectional morphology, which is a prerequisite for successful foreign language teaching and which was the most difficult thing for them to learn. This is why paradigms and lists that normally characterize elementary grammars for the learning of a second or foreign language are prominent. In the discussion of the noun, Ælfric provides paradigms of each major type within each declension. After an introductory treatment of grammatical gender, the discussion of the noun includes paradigms of the five declensions. There is a full list of the singulars and plurals of all six cases of "*hic citharista* ðes hearpere" (21,16); the nouns of the second to the fifth declensions are discussed in the same way. Similarly, paradigms of all regular and several irregular verb types are included. The declension of the verb covers basics like conjugation, voice, and tense, before the verb forms are catalogued, beginning with the first person indicative: "*amo* ic lufige, *amas* ðû lufast, *amat* hê lufaþ;" (130,8-9). Its passive forms follow next and the discussion of the first sample verbs ends with syncopated forms "*amaui, amauisti* VEL *amasti* (hêr ys se *ui* awege), *amauistis* VEL *amastis, amauerunt* VEL *amarunt*" (146,18–147,1).[19] The following three conjugations illustrated by *docere, legere*, and *audire* are presented in the same way.

Around this time Ælfric also composed another two educational works to complement the teaching function of his grammar, his *Glossary* and *Colloquy*.[20] The *Glossary*, a classified Latin–Old English vocabulary, is

---

voice. It has one property: signification, *i.e.* meaning, because it signifies either the mind's happiness or suffering or wondering and mildness."

[19] Translation of the Old English passage "hêr ys se *ui* awege": *ui* is missing here.

[20] The text of Ælfric's *Glossary* appended to his *Grammar* is available in Zupitza, 297–322. The *Glossary* is preserved in seven manuscripts, where it is always preceded by the *Grammar*; see Zupitza, iii. It is discussed in Gneuss (2002), 89–92; Werner Hüllen (1999), *English Dictionaries 800–1700. The Topical Tradition*, Oxford, 62–66, 451–52; Patrizia Lendinara (1999), 'The *Colloquy* of Ælfric and the *Colloquy* of Ælfric Bata', in P. Lendinara, *Anglo-Saxon Glosses and Glossaries*, Aldershot, Hampshire, esp. 224–39; and Gneuss (1996), 12–13.

appended to the *Grammar*, which indicates that the two texts together were essential parts of teaching and learning Latin. Its aim is to provide the pupil with a Latin vocabulary, and the English word is but ancillary to that end. After having learned the forms of Latin from the *Grammar*, the pupil was able to concentrate on building up a broad Latin vocabulary with the help of a bilingual glossary. It is part of the tradition of the 'class-glossary' or topical glossary, a type of collection designed for study and teaching in which the words are arranged according to subject. It consists of much basic vocabulary that is suitable for beginners and intermediate students and is divided into various sections. The entries, not always systematically, consist of nouns, including adjectives and a few adverbs. The words, each followed by its Old English equivalent, are grouped into the elements of the universe, the parts of the human body, and society and the family, while later sections list birds, fish, creatures of the earth, planets, trees, and finally, the parts of the house, tools, and various objects. This arrangement was well suited to help the young students to learn the vocabulary. In a few cases the Latin word is followed by a detailed explanation which must certainly have caught the attention of the pupils and helped them to memorize the new words. See, for example, the beginning of the section "NOMINA FERARVM", especially the explanations appended to "*linx*" and to "*unicornis*":

Fera wildêor. *lupus* wulf. *leo* lêo. *linx* gemenged hund and wulf. *unicornis* ânhyrne dêor (þæt dêor hæfð ænne horn bufan ðâm twâm êagum swâ strangne and swâ scearpne, þæt hê fyht wið ðone mycclan ylp and hine oft gewundað on ðære wambe ôð dêad. hê hâtte êac *rinoceron* and *monoceron*).

(Zupitza, 308,12–14, to 309,1–3).[21]

Ælfric's *Colloquy*, written in Latin with glosses in Old English, represents a separate small pedagogical work that is aimed at the same addressees as his *Grammar* and *Glossary*.[22] The three educational works, sharing a remarkable amount of Latin vocabulary, were designed to form an educational sequence. In this way the *Colloquy* extends the function of

---

[21] Translation of the Old English: *Fera*, wild beast. *lupus*, wolf. *leo*, lion. *linx*, a mixture of dog and wolf. *unicornis*, an animal with one horn. (This animal has one horn above its two eyes which is so strong and so sharp, that he fights with the big elephant and often wounds him on his stomach [womb] until he [the elephant] dies. He [the unicorn] is also called *rinoceron* and *monoceron*.)

[22] The Latin version of the *Colloquy* is preserved, either complete or as a fragment, in four manuscripts. However, only one manuscript contains continuous interlinear glosses in Old English. The text in three manuscripts can be associated with Ælfric Bata, a pupil of Ælfric. For an edition of Ælfric's *Colloquy* see G. N. Garmonsway (1978), 2nd rev. edn. Exeter (1st edn. 1939). An excerpt with an English translation is also given in *Educational Charters and Documents, 598 to 1909*, ed. Leach (1911), 36–48. For Ælfric Bata's colloquies see *Anglo-Saxon Conversations. The Colloquies of Ælfric Bata*, ed. Scott Gwara (1997), translated with an Introduction by David W. Porter, Woodbridge, Suffolk. Cf. the discussion by Orme (2006), 44–46; Lendinara (1999), 207–87; and Hüllen (1999), 79–81.

both schoolbooks studied before and aims at giving pupils the ability to communicate naturally in Latin, putting a strong emphasis on vocabulary learning. It provides teachers and pupils with the foreign language as used in everyday situations and reveals details of activities familiar to the pupils in a monastic school. It consists of an exemplary classroom dialogue in which the master asks short and stimulating questions and the students provide plenty of linguistic material in their answers, including many details of everyday life, topics of agricultural background, tasks of various workers, and so forth. In this way the pupils could practise their Latin vocabulary so that they would be able to use it for ordinary communication in a given situation in the monastic community. Consider, for example, the excellent pedagogical device of creating an occasion to make the novice use and display his vocabulary by asking him about his daily routine. The enumeration of his various tasks begins as follows and is not interrupted by the teacher as it continues:

> Þu, cnapa, hpæt dydest todæȝ?
> *Tu, puer, quid fecisti hodie?*
> Maneȝa þinȝ ic dyde. On þisse niht, þa þa cnyll ic
> *Multas res feci. Hac nocte, quando signum*
> ȝehyrde, ic aras on minon bedde ⁊ eode to cyrcean, ⁊ sanȝ
> *audiui, surrexi de lectulo et exiui ad ecclesiam, et cantaui*
> uhtsanȝ mid ȝebroþrum; æfter þa pe sunȝon be eallum
> *nocturnam cum fratribus; deinde cantauimus de omnibus*
> halȝum ⁊ dæȝredlice lofsanȝas; æfter þysum prim ⁊ seofon
> *sanctis et matutinales laudes; post hęc primam et VII*
> seolmas mid letanian ⁊ capitolmæssan; [etc.].
> *psalmos cum letaniis et primam missam; [etc.].*[23]

Apart from acquiring conversational skills in Latin, which they were supposed to speak both in and out of school, new vocabulary could also be learned and that already known could be applied in the dialogues. In this way the general aim of grammar teaching could be fulfilled, which was to enable the pupils to read, write, and converse in Latin. The reputation of the *Colloquy* was no doubt so well established in the eleventh century as to make it an inevitable choice for the syllabuses of monastic schools. It demonstrates that the use of Latin as a spoken language was an integral part of language teaching, systematically pursued up to the Renaissance and beyond.

Ælfric's grammatical works seem to have exerted a considerable influence on grammar writing and teaching in the eleventh and even the

---

[23] *Colloquy*, 2nd rev. edn. Garmonsway (1978), 43,266–44,272. Translation of the lines in Old English: You, boy, what have you done today? I have done many things. In this night, when I heard the bell, I arose from my bed and went to church, and sang the vigils with the brethren; after that we sang the lauds of all saints and the morning song; after the first hour also the seven psalms with the litany and the first mass.

twelfth centuries. In the same way as manuscripts written in Anglo-Saxon, *i.e.* the Late West-Saxon Standard, the copying and use of Ælfric's works did not come to a sudden stop at the Norman Conquest in 1066. That the *Grammar* continued to attract the attention of teachers after the Conquest is testified by Anglo-Norman glosses which were used to elaborate the Anglo-Norman equivalents of various paradigms of the Latin text, especially the verb conjugations, a practice which may have been of help to English as well as to French speakers.[24] The *Grammar* and the *Glossary* were still being copied in the thirteenth century. The last surviving medieval copy which is known to have been made is an important testimony to the continuity of Old English works during the century following the Norman Conquest. It was entirely written by the 'Tremulous Hand of Worcester', a scribe, presumably a monk, who was well known as a glossator of Old English manuscripts, partly in Middle English but mainly in Latin. He apparently worked in Worcester in the first half of the thirteenth century. None of the other surviving copies of the *Grammar* and the *Glossary* was the exemplar of the 'Tremulous Hand', who copied out a source to which he had access. This indicates that copies of Ælfric's works were still accessible and received attention.[25] However, these texts would have been extremely difficult to use in the teaching of Latin since the Old English script, orthography, and language were likely to be as much of a problem as the Latin glosses for both teachers and students. Although the scribe faithfully follows Ælfric's organization of the two texts, words and forms in this copy are considerably updated in early Middle English, which suggests that the language was changing. The copy provides a final date for the understanding of Old English based on the scribe's forms and vocabulary. Inflectional endings in Middle English replace Old English ones and some archaic lexical terms are replaced by Middle English equivalents. These features suggest that the transmission of Old English came to an end shortly after 1200, apart from a few specific categories of documents such as charters. Texts in Old English were copied only very sporadically after the early thirteenth century and only read by those who made a determined effort to understand them. With the copy by the so-called Tremulous Hand we reach the end of the English tradition of language study through the medium of English.

[24] These glosses are printed in Tony Hunt (1991), *Teaching and Learning Latin in the Thirteenth-Century England*, Cambridge, vol. 1: 101–18. See Gneuss (2002), 91.

[25] This copy is described in Zupitza, manuscript siglum W, ix; Ker, *Catalogue*, 398. The text of the *Glossary* is available in *Anglo-Saxon and Old English Vocabularies*, eds. Thomas Wright and Richard Paul Wülcker (1884), 2 vols. 2ⁿᵈ edn. Darmstadt, repr. 1968, vol. 1, no. XIII, cols. 536–53. See Gneuss (2002), 91; and Christine Franzen (1991), *The Tremulous Hand of Worcester*, Oxford, 12–14, 70–71, 88–92, 111, and *passim*.

The vernacular lost its status as an explanatory language to Anglo-Norman and later to French.[26]

2.3 *Towards grammar writing in English in the late Middle Ages*

It took more than three hundred years after the Norman Conquest for evidence of treatises for the teaching of Latin grammar in the vernacular to appear again. Fundamental changes and developments in political, cultural, linguistic, educational, and intellectual life had taken place in England during this period, which, in the course of time, were of consequence to teaching and learning grammar at the elementary level. English gradually lost its function as an explanatory language in grammatical treatises. As a consequence, the variety and different status of the languages that came into use after the Norman Conquest influenced the writing and teaching of elementary grammar. The fact that Ælfric's works continued to be used indicates that the teaching and learning of Latin in schools was not immediately affected by the Conquest. On the other hand, developments that had taken place in the English language as a result of the Conquest did not readily find expression in manuals for the teaching of Latin, a fact that may be due partly to the usually slow response of schools and their curricula to political and social changes. When Anglo-Norman, *i.e.* the variety of French used in speech and writing in England, became the language of government, trade, education, and other important areas of public life, English lost its status as the language of both government and literature, though it remained in the background and exerted an influence which did not become apparent until late in the thirteenth century. Anglo-Norman was the language of the ruling class, and was the native, spoken, language of the relatively small number of people who accompanied William the Conqueror in 1066 and of those who came later from the same areas to settle in England.

It is among the ruling class that one finds the Anglo-Norman, and, at a later date, the Central French speakers. The knowledge of Anglo-Norman was essential for social, cultural, or professional advancement. Though Anglo-Norman enjoyed prestige among the educated and was the key to social and economic success, it remains unknown how far it penetrated the rest of society. Latin, on the other hand, retained its position as the

---

[26] Hans Sauer (1997), 'Knowledge of Old English in the Middle English Period?', in R. Hickey and S. Puppel (eds.), *Language History and Linguistic Modelling. A Festschrift for Jacek Fisiak on his 60th Birthday*, 2 vols. Berlin, vol. 1: 791–814, at 794–98, 800–801, and *passim*; Franzen (1991), 103–10; also Marilyn Sandidge Butler (1981), *An Edition of the Early Middle English Copy of Ælfric's 'Grammar' and 'Glossary' in Worcester Cathedral MS F 174*, Ph.D. Dissertation, Pennsylvania State University, iii–iv, vii–ix, 22–35, 44–81.

language of intellectual and religious life and replaced Anglo-Saxon in the 1070s as the official language of the king's administration, while English as a spoken language fell to a lowly status as the vehicle of everyday life. It was the vernacular tongue spoken by the vast majority of the population, consisting of peasants comprising probably some 85 to 90 per cent of all the inhabitants, who would not have been affected by the introduction of Anglo-Norman, and who would certainly never have learned that language. Although the two languages, Anglo-Norman and English, were spoken in the country, it is doubtful whether England became a truly bilingual country. The Anglo-Norman group within the population was numerically not very large, but in many areas of life it became influential.

In the twelfth and thirteenth centuries the different languages became associated with particular social and intellectual functions. Anglo-Norman and Latin would primarily have been found in those places where the business of government was transacted and would have been used by men for whom these languages constituted a professional qualification. The majority of the population, however, was monolingual and used only English. However, English rapidly made its way into the higher classes of secular society and was frequently used as the everyday vernacular by nobles and knights in less formal circumstances where the cultural prestige of French was irrelevant. Though, in general, the clergy was subject to French ideas and attitudes, English was a very frequent, if not the only means of communication in church communities, in religious instruction, in preaching, praying, and hearing confession. The insular form of French gradually became the language of record and replaced Latin. The law and other documents were written in Anglo-Norman or Latin, while current business was usually the preserve of Anglo-Norman, whereas purely formal matters of record were written in Latin. Local people presumably made their oral replies to legal matters in English and these would then have been converted into Latin documents by clerks, sometimes perhaps through Anglo-Norman. The use of Anglo-Norman in medieval England was confined in very large measure to the southern part of the country. In the later twelfth century even the members of the feudal aristocracy, to whom Anglo-Norman was probably the primary means of communication, made more and more use of English. A larger number of them had already become truly bilingual, adopting English as their second language. The linguistic situation continued as long as England still held its Continental territory and the nobility of England were linked to the Continent through property and family ties. After the separation of Normandy from England in 1204, which resulted in most of the governing class having only English landholdings, and with no interests at stake in France, for them there was no longer a valid reason for the continued use of Anglo-Norman.

Although Anglo-Norman continued to be used and learned in certain fields, e.g. in education and literature, from as early as the thirteenth century onwards it can be seen that it became gradually assimilated with its Continental stock and had become indistinguishable from it, as 'French'. This is also due to the fact that, at this time, the country experienced a new wave of foreigners mostly from the south of France. French gradually became a common written language in England that was used as the medium for all manner of business, administrative, cultural, and practical purposes. It also began to flourish as a literary language. Being able to use it was especially important for those involved in estate management or legal affairs, where it helped to facilitate communication with foreign trade partners and was useful in business transactions. Though it was mastered as a language of writing and reading, it was not a vernacular, and, in the same way as Latin, required formal instruction. In contrast to Latin, which was primarily and essentially learned from books using grammar as its basis, French at that time could often be acquired informally by hearing and then improved by learning systematically from books. About the middle of the thirteenth century, teachers were engaged in preparing manuals of different kinds to promote the teaching of French as a second language to Englishmen, especially since the mother tongue of the children of the nobility was, in many cases, English. The important words were often provided with an interlinear English gloss. Not only was there a need to teach French for purposes of administration, but it was also used for absorbing and consolidating a knowledge of Latin, the language that was taught in the monastery schools and continued to be used as one of the means of oral as well as of written communication by at least the educated members of the regular clergy. Schools responded only slowly to this need. Though the target language which children had to learn at school was Latin, at the elementary level teachers would most probably have had to demand some translation or explanation to the language of the ruling class, *i.e.* French. In this way both the custom of explaining the rules of Latin by reference to French, and the practice of applying the concepts of Latin grammar to French, become obvious. In the classroom this would amount to translation from one foreign language into another foreign language.[27]

---

[27] For an account of the linguistic situation in England after the Norman Conquest see Norman F. Blake (1996), *A History of the English Language*, Houndmills, Basingstoke, 105–31; M. T. Clanchy (1993), *From Memory to Written Record. England 1066–1307*, 2nd edn. Oxford, 65–66, 197–223; Tony Hunt (1991), vol. 1, Introduction, 11–18; William Rothwell (1983), 'Language and Government in Medieval England', *Zeitschrift für Französische Sprache und Literatur* 93: 258–70; Ian Short (1980), 'On Bilingualism in Anglo-Norman England', *Romance Philology* 33: 467–79; Michael Richter (1979), *Sprache und Gesellschaft im Mittelalter. Untersuchungen zur Mündlichen Kommunikation in England von der Mitte des Elften bis zum Beginn des Vierzehnten Jahrhunderts.* Stuttgart, 25–34, 49–104, 132–47, and *passim*; also Rolf Berndt (1965), 'The Linguistic Situation

During the fourteenth century, French was replaced by English in many official documents and other writings. Although the use of English as the spoken medium was widespread, often the official records might be in French or Latin. Before French became the language of oral pleadings in court and the language of writing on legal subjects from the last quarter of the thirteenth century onwards, Latin was used and statutes were framed in that language. At this point in time at least, the use of French for this new purpose is closely associated with the victory of the royal family over the English barons. However, English gradually won its way into parliament. An official attempt to restore English as the language of English law was made in 1362 when parliament was addressed in English for the first time. In the famous 'Statute of Pleading' by King Edward III it was enacted that all proceedings in the courts of common law should, from that time onwards, be conducted in English for the reason that "the French tongue [. . .] is much unknown in the said realm".[28] This statute constitutes the official recognition of English. English lawyers were forced to replace French terms with English ones, although in reality this was without effect. French had become too strongly entrenched as the language of pleading to be affected by legislation. Not only were the lawyers compelled to go on using French because it was impossible to turn their technical terms into exact English equivalents, any change from French to English was still further retarded by the fact that writings on law, tracts, treatises, and Year Books, *i.e.* commercial and unofficial reports whose purpose was to show the technique of successful pleading, continued to be written in French. In the following year, 1363, the chancellor opened parliament in English for the first time.[29] This evidence, in addition to the fact that during the last few decades of the fourteenth century a number of famous literary works were written in the vernacular, culminating in the works of Geoffrey Chaucer, William Langland, John Gower, the Gawain-Poet, and John Wyclif's Bible, testifies to the flourishing of English.

in England from the Norman Conquest to the Loss of Normandy (1066–1204)', in R. Lass (ed.) (1969), *Approaches to English Historical Linguistics. An Anthology*, New York, 369–91; and Berndt (1963), *Die Sprachsituation in England während der ersten dreieinhalb Jahrhunderte nach der normannischen Eroberung*, Habilitationsschrift (summary), Universität Rostock, 5–23. On the educational background see Orme (2006), 73–78.

[28] *The Statutes of the Realm, from Magna Carta to the End of the Reign of Queen Anne. From Original Records (1101–1713)*, eds. Sir T. Edlyn Tomlins *et al.* (1810–1828), vol. 1, 36° Edw. III. *Stat.* I. c. 15, 375–76. The original is in French and is printed together with the English version. The text in English is also found in Albert C. Baugh and Thomas Cable (2002). *A History of the English Language*, 5ᵗʰ edn. London, 149. The petition on which this statute was based is given in *Rotuli Parliamentorum, ut et petitiones et placita in parliamento [1278–1503]*, ed. John Strachey (1767–1777), vol. 2: 273, nos. 38 and 39. See Baugh and Cable (2002), 146, 149–50.

[29] *Rotuli Parliamentorum*, vol. 2: 275.

There is evidence that French was taught in Oxford as part of a course that led not, as in the university, to a bachelor's degree but constituted a practical programme designed to equip a pupil for a career as a clerk, secretary, manager, or administrator in a household or court. The learning of French was a utilitarian undertaking, allied to such subjects as accounting, conveyancing, letter-writing, and the drafting of wills, charters, and other legal documents. Instruction in these subjects was given, for example, by the Oxford business teacher Thomas Sampson in the 1380s, and by William Kingsmill in the early fifteenth century. This tradition goes back to the beginning of the thirteenth century, testifying to the teaching of at least some of those subjects that were taught by the *Oxford dictatores* of the fourteenth and fifteenth centuries. However, when French was no longer used as a means of correspondence between Englishmen from about the middle of the fifteenth century, this kind of business instruction ceased to have any practical value and had disappeared from Oxford by the end of the century.[30]

The most famous testimony to the linguistic situation and the practice of grammar teaching in schools and the changes at the beginning of the fourteenth century is given in Ranulf Higden's *Polychronicon*, a universal history which was divided into seven books and was originally composed about 1327. The first translation of this work into English was made by John Trevisa in 1385–1387.[31] Higden comments on the neglect of English in schools because children were always being taught to construe their lessons in French and, among the noble class, to speak French from infancy. His words imply that English was the mother tongue of the majority of people but, because it was not an acquired language like French, was subject to widespread variation. At the end of this passage Trevisa adds a comment on the great change in teaching since Higden's time. He tells us that, from the time of the Black Death (1348–1349) onwards, Latin was explained in the mother tongue of the pupils in all the grammar schools in England, and no longer in French. He adds that this change was first introduced by John of Cornwall and was continued

---

[30] For treatises on letter-writing see 'Letters of the Oxford *Dictatores*', ed. H. G. Richardson, in H. E. Salter *et al.* (eds.) (1942), *Formularies Which Bear on the History of Oxford, c. 1204–1420*, Vol. II. New Ser. V: 357–450; also *Tractate zur Unterweisung in der Anglo-Normannischen Briefschreibekunst nebst Mitteilungen aus den zugehörigen Musterbriefen*, ed. Wilhelm Uerkvitz (1898), Greifswald. On business skills see Orme (2006), 68–73; H. G. Richardson (1941). 'Business Training in Medieval Oxford', *American Historical Review* 46, at 259–76; Richardson (1939), 'An Oxford Teacher of the Fifteenth Century', *Bulletin of the John Rylands University Library* 23: 436–57, at 452–57; M. Dominica Legge (1939), 'William of Kingsmill – a Fifteenth-Century Teacher of French in Oxford', in *Studies in French Language and Medieval Literature Presented to Professor Mildred K. Pope*, Publications of the University of Manchester 268, Manchester, 241–46; also Ivor D. O. Arnold (1937), 'Thomas Sampson and the *Orthographia Gallica*', *Medium Aevum* 6: 193–209.

[31] On Trevisa (b. *c.*1342, *d.* in or before 1402) see *ODNB*, vol. 55: 353–54.

by Richard Pencrich, another Oxford schoolmaster of the 1360s, who had learned Cornwall's teaching method from him and carried it on, and taught others to do so, too. Cornwall was a master at a grammar school in Oxford between 1344 and his death in 1349. His pupils included the young scholars of Merton College, Oxford.

As Oxford was the main centre for school as well as for university education during the later Middle Ages, Cornwall appears to have been one of the most influential schoolmasters of his period. His *Speculum gramaticale*, dated 1346 in the colophon, is of special interest in that it represents the earliest surviving grammatical treatise in which English was employed, rather than French, as an approach to Latin. Cornwall introduced English equivalents for a number of Latin verb forms and specimen sentences into his grammar.[32] However, glosses in English alongside French can already be found in school texts from the late eleventh to the fourteenth centuries. They testify to the fact that teachers had recourse to English side by side with French in explaining their pupils' difficulties with Latin forms, structures, and vocabulary.[33] Apart from glosses in school texts, where

---

[32] Ranulf Higden, *Polychronicon Ranulphi Higden Monachi Cestrensis; Together with the English Translations of John Trevisa and of an Unknown Writer of the Fifteenth Century*, ed. C. Babington and J. R. Lumby (1865–1886). Rolls Series, 41. 9 vols., London, vol. 2: 158–61. John of Cornwall's treatise is extant only in one manuscript (Bodl. Lib., MS Auct. F.3.9, pp. 1–180) and is still unpublished. Another copy is attested which was owned by John Bracebridge, schoolmaster of Lincoln in 1406, who gave it to Syon Abbey, Middlesex. See Sharpe 651, also *ODNB*, vol. 13: 469–70. Cornwall's grammar is often referred to in scholarly works. See, for example, Orme (2006), 105–106; John Walmsley (2004), 'Latein als Objektsprache, Englisch als Metasprache in Spätmittelalterlichen Grammatischen Texten', in G. Haßler und G. Volkmann (eds.), *History of Linguistics in Texts and Concepts*, 2 vols. Münster, vol. 2: 455–67, at 455–56; Kornexl (2004), 82–83; Kornexl (2003), 'From Ælfric to John of Cornwall: Evidence for Vernacular Grammar Teaching in Pre- and Post-Conquest England', in L. Kornexl and U. Lenker (eds.), *Bookmarks from the Past. Studies in Early English Language and Literature in Honour of Helmut Gneuss*, Frankfurt, 229–59, at 231, 237, 249–55; Thomas Kohnen (2001), 'Creating Counterparts of Latin: The Implicit Vernacular Tradition in Late Middle English and Early Modern English Grammars and Textbooks', in H. Kniffka (ed.), *Indigenous Grammar Across Cultures*, Frankfurt am Main, 507–42; at 510–11, *passim*; *Checklist*, Introduction, 23–24; Gneuss (1996), 17–18, 93–94; Bland, 15–19; John N. Miner (1990), *The Grammar Schools of Medieval England*, Montreal, 138, and *passim*, also Appendix 2, 279–80 (extract of Cornwall's treatise); Thomson, *Edition*, xi–xii; Thomson (1983), 'The Oxford Grammar Masters Revisited', *Mediaeval Studies* 45: 298–310, at 308–10; Thomson (1980), 'Grammar in English in the Late Middle Ages', in A. C. de la Mare and B. C. Barker-Benfield (eds.), *Manuscripts at Oxford: An Exhibition in the Memory of Richard William Hunt (1908–1979)*, Oxford, 79–82; Thomson, *Catalogue*, xi, 38–40; and R. W. Hunt (1980c). 'Oxford Grammar Masters in the Middle Ages', in G. L. Bursill-Hall (ed.), *The History of Grammar in the Middle Ages: Collected Papers*, Amsterdam, 167–97, at 172, 178–91. To the articles by R. W. Hunt have to be added the additions and corrections in M. T. Gibson and S. P. Hall (eds.) (1982–1985), 'R. W. Hunt, The History of Grammar in the Middle Ages', *Bodleian Library Record* 11: 9–19, see the list of emendations to the article on *Oxford Grammar Masters in the Middle Ages* signalled by David Thomson, at 18–19.

[33] See Tony Hunt (1991), vol. 1: vii, 13–14, and 434–35. Cf. also Kornexl (2003), 237–38, 244–49.

they represent the notes of teachers, it can be assumed that English was used orally in the schoolroom alongside French at this level of teaching Latin to beginners.

Cornwall's treatise appears to represent a novelty by providing English explanations for the Latin grammatical rules, but although there must have been a developing trend in this direction over the previous century or more, for which we have no concrete evidence, the position of Latin as the basic language of instruction remained unaffected. Cornwall may have promoted the adoption of English for this level of teaching Latin in schools during the second half of the fifteenth century. His treatise shows that the Latin text no longer serves as a host to the varying types of vernacular glosses. English explanations and examples are integrated into the text and become an intrinsic part of the whole grammar, a move that is particularly pronounced in the English grammatical manuscript treatises that have survived from about half a century later. In other words, in Cornwall's grammar greater impetus is given to the upward thrust of English which took hold in the second half of the fourteenth century and through which elementary Latin grammar was being absorbed. It seems probable that from this time onwards, grammatical treatises at this level of teaching Latin were set out in English as the explanatory language.

2.4 The English grammatical manuscripts

It is only from c.1400 onwards that grammatical manuscripts for the teaching of elementary Latin in Middle English have come down to us. These bilingual treatises represent the earliest direct treatment of language in English that survive from the period after the Norman Conquest and provide documentary proof of a trend towards the replacement of Latin by English, the language of everyday life. In contrast to Cornwall's rather long and detailed treatise on morphology and syntax, which implies a relatively advanced stage of instruction and incorporates only some passages of vernacular explanations of Latin, the grammatical manuscripts are short treatises written more or less completely in English and which, from a pedagogical point of view, are suited to an elementary level. They testify to the fact that the teaching of Latin with texts written in English had become prevalent. In this way the vernacular became the accepted language for this level of teaching in English grammar schools and gained a status in grammar writing. However, at a more advanced level Latin teaching continued to be carried out using Latin as the means of instruction. This method of teaching elementary Latin using short pedagogically suitable treatises with English as their explanatory language reflects a fresh attitude by teachers towards the use of the vernacular in schools since Ælfric's individual achievement in the late tenth century.

The English grammatical manuscripts represent the beginning of a new and continuous tradition of Latin grammar writing in the vernacular. The terminology elaborated by Ælfric was not continued, and did not become established in the Latin grammars written in the English of the late Middle Ages. It remained unknown until the sixteenth century, by which time the grammatical vocabulary of modern English was already fully formed. When English grammar teachers once again began to compile Latin grammatical treatises in English for the benefit of their pupils during the second half of the fourteenth century, they faced afresh the problem of devising a suitable metalanguage. New coinings of grammatical terms had to be made that ultimately became standard. The elementary Latin grammars in English are of wide-ranging significance and influence in that they represent the beginning of a tradition in the vernacular which subsequently continued in early print and eventually leads to the authorized grammar of 1540. Beyond that, they were of importance to the grammar writing of English itself. They form an important body of evidence of instruction and its methods in schools at that time. Indeed, they are the only evidence, since neither do schools provide a fruitful source of documentary information on fifteenth-century practice, nor do written-out timetables, which are extant only from the end of the third decade of the sixteenth century onwards.[34]

Like Ælfric's *Grammar*, for instance, the English grammatical manuscripts derive from Latin sources; their descriptions of the grammatical system rest on Latin models; they attempt to teach children the principles of elementary Latin grammar in the vernacular and are pedagogic in purpose. The new method of explaining Latin in English was practised and disseminated by successive grammar masters after the innovation which becomes evident in John of Cornwall's treatise, though no actual texts explaining Latin in the vernacular survive from the years up to the turn of the fifteenth century. The new treatises can be seen as a reaction to a situation of which there was no previous example. After that time it is striking that those versions of treatises which have survived no longer

[34] There was, in practice, an educational curriculum and an educational timetable by the early sixteenth century. By the 1520s, Winchester, Eton, and St Paul's School, London, had weekly schemes of lessons, and these were followed at other schools (demonstratively Cuckfield Grammar School and Saffron Walden Grammar School). By the fifteenth century, there were timed starts and breaks and ends to the school day. However, the terms 'time-table', "a table showing how the time of a school or other educational institution, for any day, or for a week, is allotted to the various classes and subjects" (see *OED*, timetable, n.d.), and 'curriculum', "a regular course of study or training, as at a school or university" (*OED*, curriculum), did not exist at that time. I am grateful to Professor Nicholas Orme for his comments on this matter.

resemble John of Cornwall's compendious treatise but are short specific texts, perhaps representing the lectures of the grammar masters which led the children from elementary matter to more difficult material. They are basically in English and use the vernacular to explain Latin grammar. Thirty-nine treatises in manuscript, mainly teaching elementary morphology and syntax, are known, of which at present thirty-eight are available in modern editions. David Thomson listed and described thirty-six treatises in his *Catalogue* (1979), which he also made available in his *Edition* (1984). Cynthia Renée Bland (1991) studied and edited another two treatises and their manuscripts. Another manuscript treatise is known but still remains unedited.[35] These treatises can be divided into those on accidence that deal with the parts of speech, denominated by Thomson as the *Accedence* MSS, those on comparison that treat the comparison of adjectives and adverbs, the *Comparacio* MSS, those that discuss elementary syntax, the *Informacio* MSS, and the *Formula* MSS, the last of which are reworkings of the *Informacio* MSS, and finally a group of *Other* MSS that share much material with the earlier groups. Each treatise of these groups represents a different version, for example of the *Accedence* MSS, etc. Subject matter in these treatises also overlaps and some of them were already combined to form longer, composite works. These treatises in the vernacular are directly or indirectly associated with John Leylond, a grammarian with a national reputation who is also connected with a number of elementary grammars in Latin. The short treatises covering the main parts of morphology and syntax reflect the contents of his lectures on grammar. The earliest evidence of his teaching can be dated to *c*.1401. Other treatises mention him as having lectured at Oxford in 1414. The short grammars represent the next step that was taken after Cornwall, using the vernacular as a means of approaching Latin by composing the manuals almost exclusively in English. Leylond's works brought him fame with his contemporaries and successors. He died in 1428.[36] Only a few grammatical manuscripts survive from his lifetime.

The English grammatical treatises in manuscript are rooted in the tradition of the Latin grammars. They have to be seen within the context of a rich tradition of grammar writing both at the elementary level of school grammars and at the more advanced level of grammatical studies which took place at university level. Those treatises discussing accidence represent the earliest evidence that is extant; the first of them can be dated *c*.1400. The *Accedence* grammars are primarily adaptations into

---

[35] See Thomson, *Catalogue*, and Thomson, *Edition*; also Bland. For these manuscripts see also my *Checklist*. Bibliographical details for the newly discovered treatise are given there as no. 32.

[36] On Leylond and his authorship of the grammatical manuscripts see *ODNB*, vol. 33: 708–709; and Thomson, *Catalogue*, 4–9.

English of versions of Donatus's *Ars minor*, a school grammar for teaching the elements of Latin that circulated in England at this time. Donatus's grammars had been written for students whose native tongue was Latin. His primary grammar, the *Ars minor*, had been in continuous use by beginners of Latin studies for more than a millennium. It exerted vast and inescapable influence throughout the Middle Ages and beyond in Europe, to the extent that, for example, in Middle English *Donet* occurs as a word for grammar and could also serve as a synonym for an introduction into any subject. It was the standard grammar in question-and-answer form for all elementary instruction in Latin and was modified and adapted in the course of time to the needs of those who used it. An expanded version circulated in Oxford at the end of the fourteenth century. It provided the model for the English manuscripts on accidence.[37] That the English grammatical manuscripts rely heavily on it is additionally shown by direct references they contain. They provide evidence that a copy of the Latin text then current was present in the classroom as a book of reference that could be consulted when necessary. Parts of it were probably also used for memorization. See, for example, the references to Donatus in the discussion of the conjunction and preposition in *Accedence* manuscript D:

> How many spyces hath the power of coniunccion? Fyue, by the 'Donet': copulatyf, disiunctyf, expletyf, racionel, and causell.
>
> (Thomson, *Edition*, Text D, 42, 495–97)

---

[37] See *OED*, † 'donet', 'donat'. *Obs*. For the text of Donatus's *Ars minor* see Louis Holtz (ed.) (1981), *Donat et la Tradition de l'Enseignement Grammatical*, Paris, 585–602; also *GL* 4, ed. Heinrich Keil (1864); repr. 1981, 355–66. For the text and translation into English see *The Ars Minor of Donatus*, trans. Wayland Johnson Chase (1926), Madison, Wisconsin, 28–55. See also the edition of a printed version 'Die Donat- und Kalender-Type. Nachtrag und Übersicht', ed. Paul Schwenke (1903), *Veröffentlichungen der Gutenberg-Gesellschaft* 2, at 37–49. Some general discussion of the prominence of Donatus's two grammars, the *Ars minor* and *Ars maior*, is given in Louis Holtz (2005), 'Aelius Donatus (um die Mitte des 4. Jahrhunderts n. Chr.)', in W. Ax (ed.), *Lateinische Lehrer Europas*, Köln, 109–31; see also Law (2003), 65–80, and *passim*; Marc Baratin (1998), 'Donat', in *HEL*, vol. 1, no. 1205: 40–42; and Raffaella Petrilli (2009), 'Donatus, Aelius', in *Lexicon Grammaticorum*, vol. 1: 396–97. Particularly on the *Ars minor* see Tony Hunt (1991), vol. 1: 83–84; Bland, 27–29; Wolfgang O. Schmitt (1969), 'Die Ianua (Donatus)—ein Beitrag zur lateinischen Schulgrammatik des Mittelalters und der Renaissance', *Beiträge zur Inkunabelkunde*. Dritte Folge, 4, Berlin, 43–80; also Chase (1926), Introduction, 1–26. The short grammatical treatises in manuscript written exclusively in Latin for the teaching of morphology and elementary syntax which are associated with John Leylond and which were continued and revised by other teachers of grammar, and also the versions of Donatus's *Ars minor* that circulated in England in the late Middle Ages have not yet been studied. Much basic work of identifying texts and charting their history has to be done. Research on the Latin grammatical manuscript treatises would also shed more light on the treatises in English and on the teaching of elementary grammar in general from the late fourteenth century onwards. Cf. the Latin treatises listed in Thomson, *Catalogue*, 25–26, and *passim*; also in Bland, 27–29.

Wheche beth the preposicion that seruyth to accusatyf case? As many as be conteynyd in thys demaunde of the 'Donet': 'Da preposiciones casus accusatiui'. Wheche beth hy that seruyth to the ablatyf case? As many as beth conteynyd in 'Da preposiciones casus ablatiui, et cetera'.

(Thomson, *Edition*, Text D, 42, 524–28)

The English grammatical manuscript treatises were also subject to textual sophistication from the assimilation and interpolation of material taken from other well-known grammars, amongst them Donatus's *Ars maior*, a more advanced work that is divided into three books and is five times the size of his *Ars minor*. They also reflect the presence and influence of grammatical tracts that were used at university. It can be shown that rules from these tracts filtered down to the elementary school grammars, to the treatises in both Latin and English, where the rules have been simplified and different examples have been used to illustrate them. Direct borrowing from copies of some of these tracts and also indirect borrowing from other school manuals containing passages and verses from more advanced grammatical tracts took place in some cases. An important work that was of great influence on the English grammatical treatises in manuscript is Priscian's *Institutiones grammaticae*, written in Constantinople around AD 515 by a grammarian who was teaching Latin as a foreign language to native speakers of Greek. This large and detailed grammar in eighteen books was enormously influential in the Middle Ages, but was only aimed at students with a high level of competence in Latin. It has been shown by David Thomson that Priscian's *Institutiones grammaticae* was only used as an indirect source by the compilers of the English grammatical manuscript treatises.[38]

The grammarian Petrus Helias (*fl. c*.1135–*c*.1160) is mentioned by name in some of the grammatical manuscript treatises in English. He was teaching and writing in Paris in the 1140s, shortly before the advent of the speculative movement. In his widely read *Summa super Priscianum* he pays special attention to the word classes. The number of surviving manuscripts attests the popularity of his work.[39] Another influential treatise,

---

[38] On grammars that exerted influence on the English and Latin grammatical treatises in manuscript see Thomson, *Catalogue*, 30–47. The text of Donatus's *Ars maior* is available in Holtz (ed.) (1981), 603–74; also in *GL* 4, ed. Heinrich Keil (1864); repr. 1981, 367–402. For the text of Priscian's *Institutiones grammaticae* see *GL* 2 (1855); repr. 1981, 1–597, and *GL* 3 (1859); repr. 1981, 1–377. On Priscian and his *Institutiones grammaticae* see Marc Baratin (2005), 'Priscianus Caesariensis (5./6. Jahrhundert n. Chr.)', in *Lateinische Lehrer Europas*, 247–72; also Law (2003), 86–93, and *passim*.

[39] For the text of Petrus Helias's *Summa super Priscianum* see the edition by Leo Reilly (1993), 2 vols. Toronto. Extracts are also given in Charles Thurot (1869), *Extraits de Divers Manuscrits Latins Pour Servir à L'Histoire des Doctrines Grammaticales au Moyen Âge*, Paris; repr. Frankfurt, 1964, 18–24, 96–135; see Law (2003), 172–73, 180, 183; Irène Rosier (1998c), 'Pierre Helie', in *HEL*, vol. 1, no. 1228: 62–63; Margaret Gibson, rev. Corneille Henri Kneepkens (2009), 'Petrus Helias', in *Lexicon Grammaticorum*, vol. 2: 1158; and R. W. Hunt (1980a), 'Studies on Priscian in

probably dating from the third quarter of the twelfth century, was the *Summa 'Absoluta Cuiuslibet'* by Petrus Hispanus (*fl.* late twelfth century) that was often attributed to Petrus Helias. It was current in England and passages of the English grammatical manuscript treatises correspond to it.[40]

Moreover, material was probably borrowed both directly and indirectly from the popular verse grammars of the Middle Ages which are extant in numerous manuscripts and early printed editions. A considerable number of the verses contained in the English grammatical manuscripts can be traced to the *Doctrinale* of Alexander de Villa Dei (b. *c.*1170), which is traditionally dated to 1199. It represents the most famous of all the verse grammars and was used in schools on the Continent and in England for more than three hundred years. Another popular grammatical text in verse, the *Graecismus* of Évrard de Béthune (*fl.* late twelfth to early thirteenth century), exerted influence on the English grammatical manuscripts. Its author came from Flanders and may have been an ecclesiastical grammar teacher. This grammar was written from about 1180 to 1200, and it has been suggested that it remained unfinished at Évrard's death and was completed by his friends. It was a work scarcely less celebrated than the *Doctrinale*. A smaller number of verses from it are incorporated in the English grammatical manuscript treatises, the reason for this being pedagogical or its availability to grammar masters.[41] The English grammatical treatises also include material from other influential grammars of the Middle Ages. Amongst them is John of Garland's (also Johannes de Garlandia) grammatical work, the *Compendium gramatice*, a complete treatment of Latin grammar in hexameters, which he must have completed from *c.*1234 to 1236. Garland (b. *c.*1195, d. in or after 1258) was a

the Eleventh and Twelfth Centuries I. Petrus Helias and his Predecessors', in G. L. Bursill-Hall (ed.), *The History of Grammar in the Middle Ages: Collected Papers*, Amsterdam, 1–38, at 5, 7–13, 21–30, 36–38; also R. W. Hunt (1980b). 'Hugutio and Petrus Helias', in Bursill-Hall (ed.), *The History of Grammar in the Middle Ages: Collected Papers*, Amsterdam, 145–49.

[40] For the text see Petrus Hispanus (non-papa), *Summa 'Absoluta Cuiuslibet'*, ed. C. H. Kneepkens (1987), *Het Iudicium Constructionis*, Deel IV, Nijmegen, 1–84; also Kneepken's (2009) article 'Petrus Hispanus', in *Lexicon Grammaticorum*, vol. 2: 1158; and R. W. Hunt (1980d), '*Absoluta.* The *Summa* of Petrus Hispanus on Priscianus Minor', in G. L. Bursill-Hall (ed.), *History of Grammar in the Middle Ages: Collected Papers*, 95–116.

[41] For the text of the *Doctrinale* see Dietrich Reichling's (1893) edition, *Das Doctrinale des Alexander de Villa-Dei*, Monumenta Germaniae paedagogica, xii, Berlin; repr. New York, 1974. On this grammar see Reinhold F. Glei (2005), 'Alexander de Villa Dei (ca. 1170-1250), *Doctrinale*', in *Lateinische Lehrer Europas*, 291–312; also Irène Rosier's (1998a) article 'Alexandre de Villedieu', in *HEL*, vol. 1, no. 1229: 63–64; and Bursill-Hall (1977), 3–12. Évrard de Béthune's *Graecismus* is available in the edition of Johannes Wrobel (1887), Corpus grammaticorum medii aevi, i. Breslau; repr. Hildesheim, 1987. See Anne Grondeux (1998), 'Évrard de Béthune', in *HEL*, vol. 1, no. 1230: 64–66; and Christine Brousseau (2009), in *Lexicon Grammaticorum*, vol. 1: 443–44; also Bursill-Hall (1977), 3–5, 12–14.

well-known English grammarian who taught at Paris and Toulouse before the middle of the thirteenth century.[42]

Apart from these grammars, it can be shown that the *Compendium grammatice* of *c.*1250 by Petrus de Isolella was also used by English grammarians when they compiled their Latin manuals. Isolella (*fl.* 1250) is known as a didactic grammarian of Italian origin, whose grammar enjoyed great popularity, attested by the large number of manuscripts that have survived.[43] The *Catholicon* of the Dominican friar John of Genoa (Joannes de Balbis Januensis) (d. *c.*1298) was completed in 1286. It is a dictionary preceded by a grammar that exerted influence on the English grammatical treatises and also on the Latin ones associated with John Leylond. It belongs to the same Italian tradition of preceptive grammar as Petrus de Isolella's grammar, covering a range of topics from morphology and syntax to prosody. Evidence exists that these two grammars also exerted an influence on the English grammatical manuscript treatises in shaping rules or updating verses from the *Doctrinale*. It can further be shown that the English grammatical treatises shared material with Thomas Hanney's work entitled *Memoriale iuniorum*, a tract on the four parts of grammar, which he wrote in Toulouse and Lewes, Sussex, in the year 1313.[44]

The grammatical manuscripts, written in English, present most of the rules in catechetical form, a method that was also applied in Donatus's *Ars minor*. Different types of this form can be found in these manuscripts. In this way the pupils could, for example, repeat a rule that they had already learned, defining a part of speech, for instance, and also listing its accidents:

How knowest a preposicion? A party of reson that is not declinyd and seruith to accusatyf case and ablatyf. How many thyngis falleth to a preposicion? On onlych.
(Thomson, *Edition*, Text D, 42, 520–22)

Moreover, by using the form of dialogue in teaching, the pupils learned to apply a rule that they already knew. For example:

---

[42] The text of John of Garland's *Compendium gramatice* is available in the edition by Thomas Haye (1995), Köln. On Garlandia see Garland *ODNB*, vol. 21: 476–78. His works are listed in Sharpe, no. 709: 253–57; see also Susanne Daub (2005), 'Johannes de Garlandia (ca. 1195–nach 1258)', in *Lateinische Lehrer Europas*, 331–52, at 332–33, 342–43; and Bursill-Hall (1976), 'Johannes de Garlandia – Forgotten Grammarian and the Manuscript Tradition', *Historiographia Linguistica* 3: 155–77.

[43] Petrus de Isolella's treatise was published anonymously by Charles Fierville in his (1886) edition, *Une Grammaire Latine Inédite du XIIIe Siècle*, Paris. For information on the author and his work see Irène Rosier-Catach (2009), 'Petrus de Isolella', in *Lexicon Grammaticorum*, vol. 2: 1157–58; also R. W. Hunt (1980*b*), 148, footnote 3.

[44] Cf. Irène Rosier's article (1998*b*) on Johannes de Balbis, in *HEL*, vol. 1, no. 1236: 72–73. On Thomas Hanney (*fl.* 1313) and his work see *ODNB*, vol. 25: 81. Manuscripts, including fragments, of the *Memoriale iuniorum* are listed in Sharpe, no. 1758: 659–60. The copy consulted is Bodl. Lib., MS Auct. F.3.9, pp. 189–340. See R. W. Hunt (1980*c*), 185–88; and Orme (2006), 105.

'A chirche is a place the wheche Crystyn menne bem mecull holdon to loue.'
Wheche ys thy pryncypall uerbe in þis reson? 'Is'. When þis uerbe *sum, es, fui* is
thy pryncypall uerbe, how schall þu knoo wheche ys thy nominatyue case? By
þis Englyche worde 'Whoo or what?', as 'Whoo or what ys? The chirche is.'

(Thomson, Edition, Text U, 93, 33–38).[45]

Learning the rules on morphology and syntax in this way helped the
pupils, who did not usually have their own copy of the text, to analyse,
repeat, and memorize them. The verses of the didactic verse grammars,
the *Doctrinale*, the *Graecismus*, and others, which are frequently embedded
in the grammatical manuscript treatises in English, had a similar function. In general, they helped to illustrate rules and make learning them
easier. In some cases the verses are modified and have additional verse
lines, which may suggest that schoolmasters found it necessary to adapt
the verses in order to elucidate the rules in question better or to add more
detail. The verses are often inserted at the end of a passage to sum up
the contents of the chapter or to repeat a rule, presenting it in a concise
order and giving it a frame and in this way facilitating its retention in
the memory of the pupils. Compared to the rule given in the treatise, the
verses also frequently provide further illustrative examples, as is shown
by *Graecismus*, verse XXV.15, with an additional second verse.

Ad forum videndum populus currunt. This verbe *currunt* is the plurell nombyr, for a
nowne collectyf yn the nominatyf case syngler may haue a verbe plurell, and all
nownes conteyned in thies versis folowyng be nownes collectifis.

> *Sunt collectiua populus, gens, plebs quoque turba,*
> *Turma, phalanx, legio. cuneus sociare memento.*

(Thomson, Edition, Text BB, 148, 19–24)

Given the scarcity and expense of written books, this method of instruction in the schoolroom inevitably came to emphasize the position of the
teacher, who was almost certainly the only person in the classroom to
have access to a copy of the grammatical treatise being studied. The
pupils' comprehension of the subject was thus conditioned by the text
of the particular copy being used and by the teacher's way of presenting
his material. In this respect it is of interest that most of the actual treatises
in English that have come down to us were written by pupils, as was
suggested by David Thomson. The transmission of these texts through
their hands may explain the mistakes and inconsistencies that they
incorporate.[46]

---

[45] Although the English sentence is being analysed at this point, the forms of the Latin
auxiliary verb *esse* suggest that the pupils must also have been familiar with its Latin version,
Ecclesia est locus quem Christiani tenentur multum diligere, which follows towards the end of this
passage (Thomson, *Edition*, Text U, 94, 59).

[46] On scribes of the English grammatical treatises see Thomson, *Catalogue*, 12–13. In this
connection it becomes obvious that philological and didactic considerations have first to be
taken into account before linguistic conclusions can be drawn from the treatises.

The English grammatical treatises in manuscript spread from Oxford, the principal centre of grammatical studies at that time, to other schools in England, a step that is reflected in the earliest copies that survive. They underwent further revision in the schools in which they were used. Their characteristics are that they were not 'written up' but were of a fluid and dynamic nature and represented the personal usage of the grammar master. The different groups of treatises share many rules and also many verses, but they vary so considerably in their treatment of grammar that there seem to have been as many versions of the different groups of treatises as there were masters of grammar, and not one set of texts was widely used. Teaching was a local business, and there was no structured curriculum at this period. The teachers regarded it as legitimate to modify their copies where the texts failed to meet their needs, and they certainly applied their teaching experience gathered over the years, each time they taught the particular parts of grammar. In this way the tracts represent varying degrees of personal revision and adaptation of their own, or their predecessor's, or of someone else's tracts.[47]

This process may be indicative of the way in which most of the grammatical treatises in manuscript were disseminated from Oxford to other schools in the country. The English grammatical manuscript treatises also reflect teaching practices outside Oxford. The surviving treatises increase in number from about 1450 to 1480, when Leylond's pupils and successors started to teach. Some of the English treatises were connected specifically with the most important educational institutions of the time, Winchester College and Eton College. Winchester College, founded by Bishop William Wykeham as a grammar school in 1382 (the statutes are dated 1400), became the largest and most influential school of its day. At Winchester College, which was closely connected to Oxford through its sister foundation New College, which was also established by William Wykeham, the study of grammar became its central purpose.[48] Eton College was founded by Henry VI in 1440 after the example of Winchester. The grammars in English used at Eton were probably adopted after the pattern of Winchester, since grammars in the vernacular had been in use at Winchester before Eton was founded, and they, in turn,

---

[47] Cf. also Appendix V for variations in the definitions of the same part of speech in the grammatical manuscripts, a variety that is continued in copies representing different versions of early printed grammars. It reflects pedagogical expedience at work and sheds light on the diverse ways in which the rules of Latin grammars were taught in different grammar schools at that time.

[48] On William Wykeham see *ODNB*, vol. 60: 636–40. On Winchester College see Virginia Davis (1993), *William Waynflete. Bishop and Educationalist*, Studies in the History of Medieval Religion, 6. Woodbridge, Suffolk, 11–14, and *passim*.

set the standard for treatises used in other schools.[49] The foundation of
the two colleges went hand in hand with other school foundations and
developments in education, as well as the growing literacy of the laity.
The English grammatical manuscript treatises also show connections to
St Anthony's School, the first grammar school in London at that time, as
well as the school of St Albans, and Exeter City Grammar School.
Apart from secular schools, a group of grammatical treatises in English is
also connected with the teaching of Latin in monasteries and other
institutions.[50]

No timetables of grammar schools, monastic schools, and other institutions where elementary Latin was taught are extant for this period when
instruction was primarily oral and based on the teacher's grammatical
treatises. However, the manuscripts that contain the English grammatical
treatises incorporate other material that was used alongside instruction
in Latin, much of which also served educational purposes. These short
treatises and the notes for use in the classroom were probably revised and
adapted in a similar way to the English grammatical treatises by the
schoolmasters for their practical teaching purposes. They were designed
to complement the learning of grammar by teaching vocabulary and providing additional exercises in the speaking of Latin. It may be assumed
that the use of such additional material as was contained in the manuscripts would depend on the particular grammar school.

Apart from the grammatical treatises in English, other items, most of
them used for the teaching of Latin, appear in the same manuscripts.
There are, for example, amplified versions of Donatus's *Ars minor*, Latin
grammatical treatises written in Latin containing rules and exercises for
construction, treatises on orthography, and on *dictamen*, which in this
context refers to the composition of Latin letters according to standard
forms, and also model letters. These various approaches show that the
productive use of language was taught through the writing of letters and
through composition. In addition, the grammatical manuscripts include
versions of Latin model sentences with or without English translations
('Latins' or *Latinitates*), English sentences with their Latin translation
(*Vulgaria*), wordlists in Latin and English arranged according to topics
(*Nominale*), wordlists in alphabetical order, and similar listings of verbs
for all four Latin conjugations (*Verbale*). Moreover, they also contain
mnemonic vocabularies in verse for teaching the words for the parts
of the body, household words, and other familiar terms, and lists of

---

[49] On Eton College see Davis (1993), 35–56; Orme (2006), 234–35, and *passim*; also H. C.
Maxwell Lyte (1899), *A History of Eton College (1440–1898)*, 3rd edn. London, 4–21. The earliest
statutes of Eton College, instituted in December 1443, no longer exist; those now extant date
from the period c.1447–1455. On the grammars used first at Eton see Thomson, *Catalogue*, 17.

[50] On the connection between the various manuscripts containing English grammatical
treatises and different educational institutions see Thomson, *Catalogue*, 14–22.

synonyms. In addition, there are also verses from the *Doctrinale* with prose commentary, didactic poems, selections of—or abbreviated forms of—the moral precepts from the *Distichs of Cato*, treatises concerned with good behaviour, proverbs in Latin and English, psalms, hymns, and prayers, and some other items. Surviving collections of English–Latin sentences, for example, are rich in their references to the classroom and to the teaching of Latin, in topics chosen from the surroundings and the experience of the children, and even in references to political events. An example from one of the collections of the *Vulgaria* may serve to illustrate the instruction in Latin vocabulary that complements the learning of grammatical rules and helps to provide the pupil with vocabulary. A selection of sample sentences reads as follows:

Hyt befallyth þe mayster to bete roberd and me ȝyf we fayle wan we beþ aposyd yn a lyȝt matyr.
> *Interest a magistro vapulare mea et roberti si deficiamus cum in materia facili nobis apponatur.* (No. 19)

A hard latyn to make, my face wexyth blakke.
> *Difficilem latinitatem composituri, facies mea nigrescit.* (43)

Grete wel þy fader at þat tokyn þat we dranke a pot of wyne þet oþer day at þe wyne taverne.
> *Saluta patrem tuum super hoc intersigno quod bibimus altera die vrnam vini in meroteca.* (54)

Y kan ryde to bathe in a day and als for beȝond for nede.
> *Ego scio equitare bathoniam in vna die et eo vltra pro necesse.* (78)

The kyng dwellyth at calyce, a gode toun and famoce.
> *Rex moratur calisius, bone ville et famose / vel sic: bona villa et famosa.* (92)

My gowne ys y-steynyd.
> *Toga mea est detincta.* (95)

Pore scolares schold bysilych tan hede to here bokys, the whyche byth not y-ware of none other help but of here one konnyng.
> *Pauperes scolares suis libris officiosissime insudarent, qui non considerati sunt de aliquo alio auxilio nisi de sua sciencia.* (98)[51]

As these examples show, topics were chosen to catch and maintain the interest of the pupils, a method of teaching already found in Ælfric's *Colloquy*. These collections fulfilled at least a twofold function: to teach Latin vocabulary and sentence structure as well as good behaviour and

---

[51] Printed in Orme (1989c), 'A Grammatical Miscellany from Bristol and Wiltshire', in Orme. *Education and Society in Medieval and Renaissance England.* London, 87–112, at 101, 104, 105, 108, 109, 110. This text is also listed as 'Bristol Vulgaria' [535], in George R. Keiser (1998). *Works on Science and Information. A Manual of the Writings in Middle English*, vol. 10, ed. Albert E. Hartung, New Haven, Conn., 3720. On 'Latins' and *Vulgaria* see Orme (2006), 109–18. 'Calyce' (in sentence no. 92) means 'Calais'.

morality. Apart from that, the material contained in the grammatical manuscripts not only helps to provide an insight into the methods of instruction of Latin by showing how knowledge in the foreign language was structured and could increase by different methods, but can also shed light upon the educational programme. In this way it becomes possible to get some idea of the curriculum of grammar schools and even to reconstruct them, as almost no other evidence has survived from this period.[52]

Though the grammatical manuscripts containing the English grammatical treatises share some of the short tracts that complement the grammars, they nevertheless present a great variety of short items in both their arrangement and content. This fact sheds light on the diversity in teaching methodology and supports the assumption that each school had its own curriculum for language instruction. From this it can be assumed that each schoolmaster compiled his own teaching programme, so that the treatises he used in some way or other represent his personal adaptations that served his own practical teaching purposes. A vocabulary, a *Nominale*, contains a statement by the compiler who put it together for young boys who only knew English. In his treatise he listed nouns, adjectives, and adverbs, which he collected from learned sources and arranged by subjects. The conjugation of the verb *amo* and the others that follow it in Donatus were particularly to be learned. The text starts with synonyms for God "*hic deus, hic creator, pater et filius et spiritus sanctus coniuncti, hic iesus, hic christus, hic redemptor* [etc.]", and continues with synonyms for the Holy Ghost. The Latin words are written in double columns on the page, in such a way that a number of words are summarized by an English term on the right-hand side of each column, signifying an abstract characteristic feature, such as "*god, god hede, holynesse,* [etc.]". By teaching these words the compiler makes clear the double purpose he intended: to make his pupils acquire as much vocabulary as possible and to enable them to come to know and understand what they hear and read, especially that they may know how to speak of God and of issues concerning the Christian faith.[53]

2.5 *The early printed grammars in English*

Teaching with textbooks in manuscript form gradually came to an end when printed copies started becoming available about 1480. From this

---

[52] For the use of Donatus's *Ars minor* in the classroom, cf. pp. 50–51 above. The contents of the grammatical manuscripts are described in Thomson, *Catalogue*, 105–328; see also Miner (1990), 135–51.

[53] This *Nominale* is contained in BL, MS Add. 37075, fols. 276^r–308^v, at 276^{r-v}. See Thomson, *Catalogue*, 219–32, at 229–30; also Miner (1990), 163.

time onwards the number of surviving grammatical manuscripts declined rapidly. The new technology of the printing press, introduced into England by William Caxton when he set up his press in Westminster in 1476 was the means of creating a lucrative market by providing schools and institutions with multiple copies of virtually identical educational texts. As a consequence of the foundation of new grammar schools during the fifteenth and early sixteenth centuries, there was a considerable demand for educational texts. The first evidence of a printed grammar in English is a copy of the *Long Parvula*, probably printed by Theodoric Rood in Oxford in about 1482. It can be shown that its printer had close connections with Magdalen College School, Oxford, where he may have sold his copies to teachers and students, and where he also obtained the manuscripts that served as exemplars for the school texts he printed.[54] The printed copies were relatively cheap and rapidly became available in considerable numbers.[55]

When early printed English grammars first found their way into the classroom, they were, for some time, used side by side with the treatises in manuscript. In the 1480s and 1490s they were obviously used as parallels rather than successors to the grammatical manuscripts and were circulating together with them until printed texts had become the norm in the first decade of the sixteenth century.[56] Teachers could then adopt their pedagogy to take account of the sources now available in the new medium. They were presented with a grammatical text for their courses with which, however, some may not have fully agreed. Consequently they treated the printed copies of the grammatical treatises and other teaching texts in a way similar to the manuscript copies, by annotating them, inserting corrections into the text as well as in the margins, and also

---

[54] See *Checklist* 48.1. Brief information about Theodoric Rood is given in *STC²*, vol. 3: 147. Cf. also Davis (1993), 86.

[55] A valuable source of information about prices of schoolbooks has proved to be booksellers' day-books. The most famous book of this kind is the account-book of the Oxford bookseller John Dorne where he lists the names of the books he had sold and also the price received for each, throughout the year 1520. For example, one copy of a version of Stanbridge's *Accidence*, his *Long Parvula* and his *Sum es fui* costs one or two pennies each on average, compared, for example, with a "*nouum testamentum erasmi ligatum*" for which he received two shillings. See 'Day-Book of John Dorne, Bookseller in Oxford, A.D. 1520', ed. F. Madan (1885), in *Collectanea* I, Part III, Oxford, 71–177; and 'Supplementary Notes to *Collectanea* I. Part III. Day-Book of John Dorne', in *Collectanea* II. Appendix, 453–78; also p. 7 above.

[56] See *BMC* XI, 53–54, 241–42 (bibliographical description of the earliest copy of the *Long Parvula*); *Checklist*, Introduction, 27–28; also Thomson (1980), 'Grammar in the Late Middle Ages', in *Manuscripts at Oxford*, Oxford, 82, where an example of the closeness of a copy of an early printed grammar (*Long Accidence*, Text A; *Early Printed Editions*, 152–64; *Checklist* 14.1) and a grammatical manuscript (*Comparacio*, Text Q; Thomson, *Edition*, 75; *Checklist* 26) is commented on. For the side-by-side existence of manuscripts and early printed books see also Curt F. Bühler (1960), *The Fifteenth-Century Book*, Philadelphia, 47, *passim*.

inserting continuations to the printed text by hand. In this way the printed copy could be prepared by schoolmasters so that it became their individual teaching copy, a practice that continues in education up to the present. However, the new technology of printing brought innovations within the trade. It introduced the possibility of producing a large number of copies of a text in a short time and, as a consequence, making them available on a much wider scale. Thus the text of a grammatical treatise became available in an edition that consisted of a large number of almost identical copies. Consequently, teaching material that had previously been restricted to a local school or remained in the possession of an individual teacher, gradually became accessible in a larger area, and became common property for those who had to or wanted to use it. This implies that teaching became more uniform in grammar schools, as the same or similar grammatical texts became available. It can be shown that pupils possessed copies of these cheap books that could be passed on to successive pupils in turn, as we can tell from inscriptions in the isolated copies that have survived.

The copies of printed grammatical treatises that have come down to us are very rare individual examples of a huge amount of teaching material that once existed; a fact that holds true also for other teaching material in general. This is why the surviving copies do not give a truly representative picture of the various printed versions that were in use in grammar schools, nor of the curriculum. Nevertheless, the earliest surviving copies of these early printed grammars are of significance because they indicate the type of treatise that the grammar masters thought best suited for their teaching. It may be that some teachers took their copy in manuscript to the printer, where it would be set up by the compositor according to the rules and conventions of the printing shop. If more copies were demanded, the printers issued a new edition. The earliest printed grammars in English continue the manuscript tradition. They closely reflect the manuscript treatises and there is little that is original. Those treatises that were printed probably represent treatises originally in manuscript that have survived only in printed form. They provide another version of the treatise in a different medium. The printed *Long Accidence* and *Short Accidence* grammars, also the *Parvula* and *Long Parvula* grammars, show a close dependence on the grammatical manuscripts but none of these is identical to one of the manuscripts. This is not surprising considering the large number of versions of grammatical treatises in manuscript that were once used in schools. Most of them were not continued in the medium of print.

The *Long Accidence*, attributed to the schoolmaster and grammarian John Stanbridge, master of Magdalen College School, Oxford, from 1488 to 1493, may serve as an example of an early printed grammar in English that follows the grammatical manuscripts very closely. The first extant edition, printed by Wynkyn de Worde, the successor to William Caxton's printing house, can be dated 1495. The same text was reprinted by de Worde, most probably in 1499, which indicates a demand for a new edition.[57] This new edition was set from a copy of an earlier printed edition, presumably that of c.1495. Considering the high rate of lost editions, however, it is possible that other intermediate editions of this treatise were printed in the same printing house. The text of the new edition of the *Long Accidence* from de Worde's printing house differed from that of c.1495 in spelling, with typographical errors corrected, others preserved, and new ones made. It can also be shown from the distribution of the text on the pages that the compositor used a printed copy as his exemplar for the new edition: it was obviously easier to set up the text in this way than by going back to a manuscript. Reprints of the same grammatical texts from the same printing house are not frequently met with in the incunabula period in England, in contrast to the output of the first decades of the sixteenth century.

The numerous extant editions of the early printed grammars show that there was a high demand for these texts in grammar schools. The versions of the *Long Accidence* and *Short Accidence* for example, were often printed by different printers in England as well as on the Continent, especially in the Low Countries. Editions of the version of the *Accidence*, the longest of the three extant versions of the treatises dealing with the parts of speech, were also printed in France. This points to the fact that not only were these grammatical treatises held in favour at that time, but also that the high demand for them could not be satisfied by English printers. Printers both in England and abroad used the printed copies that were available to them to produce further editions. An examination of surviving copies of subsequent editions of the same grammatical treatise proves that the transmission of the text was not linear. The text was set up from different exemplars with different spellings and they often also differed to some small extent in subject matter. In this way both teachers and pupils, though supplied with the 'same text', possessed copies of editions of the grammatical treatise which had differences in the layout of the text, in spelling, and sometimes even in wording, a fact which applied to early printed teaching material in general whenever different editions were available. The humanist and schoolmaster Leonard Cox mentions the problems which were caused in the classroom in his tract *De Erudienda Iuventute* (1526), an essay on education and the classical languages written in the form of a letter, as follows:

---

[57] On John Stanbridge see *ODNB*, vol. 52: 91. For the first extant copies of editions of these printed treatises see *Checklist* 14.1 and 14.2.

First of all, he [the teacher] should read the whole text aloud, telling the pupils to correct whatever mistakes they notice in their own copies, to fill in gaps, and rub out what does not appear in the teacher's text.[58]

The variations in spelling reflect, to differing degrees, the spelling of the compositor, his copy, and perhaps also in a few cases that of the proof-reader. Additional smaller changes in wording, which sometimes comprise complete phrases, can be found in subsequent editions of the printed versions. The variations indicate that the text was still in flux and had not, even in later editions, reached a definitive state. In regard to subject matter, however, variation was limited to a few versions that were printed, and often reprinted, in a number of editions, the copies of which would have been widely distributed. From a different point of view it may be argued that not only a great deal of subject matter, but also much of the variation that the grammatical tradition inherited, and possible developments concerning grammatical rules in particular treatises, were not continued in the new medium. Those versions which went into print represent individual versions of grammatical treatises. They are individual examples of the rich tradition of grammatical manuscripts that very possibly owe their continuation in print to accident or the availability of the particular manuscript. The texts of those versions that succeeded in getting into print were multiplied in successive editions irrespective of their inherent merit. It was only due to the multitude of copies in circulation that these versions became dominant: other possibly better texts which did not succeed in getting into print soon went out of use.

The earliest copies of the English printed grammars, like the manuscripts, are written in question-and-answer form and also include verses that can be traced back to the *Doctrinale*, the *Graecismus*, and other grammars that influenced the grammatical treatises in manuscript. In this respect they continue the methods of teaching and learning reflected by the copies in manuscript, in the medium of print. Yet useful though the grammatical treatises in print were to schools, it seems that they satisfied the teachers for only a short time. This may have been due partly to the limitation in subject matter offered by the printed versions, or perhaps to the spelling to which teachers and pupils were not accustomed and also to the printing errors that may have caused problems. Teachers usually had their own concept of grammatical texts. They were familiar with their own material in manuscript form and accustomed to revising their copies continuously. For these reasons they may have found it necessary to

---

[58] On Leonard Cox see *ODNB*, vol. 13: 854–56. For his treatise see Andrew Breeze and Jacqueline Glomski (eds.) (1991), 'An Early British Treatise upon Education: Leonard Cox's *De Erudienda Iuventute* (1526)'. *Humanistica Lovaniensia* 40: 119 (introduction), 143 (English translation by Breeze and Glomski). The text in Latin reads: "Primum itaque lectionem totam pronunciabunt, iubentes ut quae quisque animaduerterit in codice suo minus recte posita castiget, neglecta adiiciat, superflua expungat" (p. 142).

compile different, and perhaps what may have been deemed by them better, versions of the texts on the subject. Hence a number of grammatical treatises that cover the Latin timetable were compiled by different schoolmasters of which only the copies of these editions which found their way into print became available. Their compilations incorporate subject matter that was available and with which they were presumably already familiar from their teaching with the grammatical manuscripts or even from their own former experience of learning grammar. The variety of material of a treatise and its presentation covers one particular part of the timetable and reflects the pedagogical purposes of the grammarian who compiled it.

The first decades of printing in England coincided with the influence of humanism in English schools that caused changes in the curriculum. Schoolmasters began to revise grammatical usages to accord with classical standards rather than those of the medieval period. In the course of time medieval poets were substituted by classical authors as reading texts. The newly compiled printed Latin grammars in English contain a number of names of classical authors and references to their works as well as to Italian humanist grammarians to illustrate grammatical rules. The surviving grammatical manuscripts, however, provide only a few examples of this practice. This can probably be explained by the fact that most of the treatises in manuscript reflect the teaching of local schools in different parts of the country. By the time manuscript texts reflecting influences of the New Learning spread into the different schools, printed texts containing this new material and practice had probably become available and replaced the handwritten manuals.[59]

Within a decade of its foundation Magdalen College School, Oxford, had become one of the leading grammar schools in England and was to become the pioneer centre of grammar teaching on humanistic lines that had developed on the Continent. The school that became attached to Magdalen College was founded by William Waynflete, Bishop of Winchester, also to provide teaching in Latin grammar, free of charge, to members of Magdalen College and also to boys from outside. John Anwykyll (d. 1487) was the first recorded headmaster of the school and is

---

[59] 'New Learning' was used as a term for innovation in the English school curriculum, which was inspired by the Continental Renaissance. It began in the last quarter of the fifteenth century when new educational ideas reached England from Renaissance Italy. For the influence of humanist grammars in the form of additions to English grammatical manuscripts, for example the references to Nicolaus Perottus's grammatical works, see Thomson, *Catalogue*, 94–96, and his *Edition*, Text KK, 210, 82–84. This manuscript can be dated *c*.1501. However, the New Learning only began to play a significant role in teaching represented by the work of John Colet at St Paul's School in London after 1510. Cf. Orme (1973), 106–15.

referred to from 1483 onwards.[60] That Magdalen College appointed a man who was familiar with humanist grammarians, no doubt with Bishop Waynflete's approval, suggests that the college and the bishop were open and receptive to ideas and influences from the New Learning. Anwykyll's writings for the school and his teaching found favour, and the grammatical innovation was continued after Waynflete's death in 1486. The earliest surviving editions of the *Compendium totius grammaticae*, which is credited to Anwykyll, and the *Vulgaria quedam abs Terencio in Anglicam linguam traducta*, a collection of English and Latin sentences for translation purposes taken or adapted from Terence's plays that was intended to follow the *Compendium*, and was probably also compiled by him, were published by Theodoric Rood in partnership with Thomas Hunt in 1483.[61] Anwykyll thus appears to have been the first English schoolmaster both to have his work printed and to publish school texts teaching Latin on humanistic lines. The books were successful, probably because they combined the pursuit of humanistic standards with material from the grammatical manuscripts and teaching methods familiar in English schools. One particular example of a manuscript copy that was said to have been the property of a teacher associated with Magdalen College School, Oxford, *c.*1501, testifies to the influence of humanist learning. It may even have belonged to John Stanbridge who held the mastership at that school until 1493 as successor to John Anwykyll. This treatise, written in English, deals

---

[60] Magdalen College, Oxford, was founded by Bishop William Waynflete as Magdalen Hall in 1448. It was refounded as Magdalen College in 1458. Statutes for Magdalen College were issued by Waynflete in 1480. Magdalen College School as an adjunct to the college was founded in 1481. It was a novel arrangement that a grammar school in close proximity became attached to a college. See Orme (1998), *Education in Early Tudor England, Magdalen College Oxford and Its School*, 1480–1540, Oxford, 2–14, 32–37, 56; also Davis (1993), 79–89; and Robert Spenser Stanier (1958), *Magdalen School. A History of Magdalen College School, Oxford*, 2nd edn. Oxford, 3–25. On Anwykyll see *ODNB*, vol. 2: 294; Orme (1998), 15–17; also Davis (1993), 86–88. The grammar as well as the *Vulgaria* associated with Anwykyll has not been edited yet. On Anwykyll and the New Learning see James Kelsey McConica (1965), *English Humanists and Reformation Politics under Henry VIII and Edward VI*, Oxford, 44, 50; also Roberto Weiss (1967), *Humanism in England*, 3rd edn. Oxford, 169–78.

[61] Copies of editions of the *Compendium grammaticae* are listed in *STC*[2] 695–696.7. For editions of the *Vulgaria* see *STC*[2] 23904–23908. *STC*[2] lists eight editions of the *Compendium* printed between 1483 and *c.*1517, and seven editions of the *Vulgaria* printed between 1483 and 1529. The *Compendium* (*STC*[2] 696) was probably issued together with the edition of the *Vulgaria* (*STC*[2] 23904). See *ESTC* for these copies; also *BMC* XI, 238–39, for this copy of the *Vulgaria*. The text of the *Compendium* was also available in manuscript. It was written by John Edwards the younger of Chirk in the 1480s (Aberystwyth, NLW, MS 423D, fols. 21[v]-31[r]); see Thomson (1982), 'Cistercians and Schools in Late Medieval Wales', *Cambridge Medieval Celtic Studies* 3: 76–81, at 76–77; also Thomson's *Catalogue*, 106. Anwykyll's work is commented on by Orme (1999), 'Schools and School-books', in L. Hellinga and J. B. Trapp (eds.), *The Cambridge History of the Book in Britain*, Vol. III: 1400–1557. Cambridge, 458–59; and Alexander H. Brodie (1974), 'Anwykyll's Vulgaria. A Pre-Erasmian Textbook', *Neuphilologische Mitteilungen* 75: 416–27. Brodie's article, however, does not take into account the preceding manuscript tradition of the *Vulgaria* treatises. On Thomas Hunt see *STC*[2], vol. 3: 87 (Hunt 1).

with the compounds of the substantive verb *esse* and the verb *ferre*. It consists of subject matter known from the grammatical manuscripts in English. According to David Thomson, this treatise was compiled before sections from the work of the contemporary Italian humanist grammarian Nicolaus Perottus were inserted. Quotations derived from classical authors were added to illustrate the grammatical rules. Note the following passage:

> *Subtersum, -es*, þe which is found but seldon, and *subsum*, Englyshede 'to be vndre', be construed wᵗ a datyue case only. Plinius: *Suberat abieginne trabes. Talpa subterest terre, pisces subtersunt aque.*

> *Desum, -es*, Englyshede 'to lacke' or 'want', is construed with a datyue case of þe lackar and wᵗ a nominatyue case of þe thynge þat is lackyd, except þe infinityue mode lete it. Seneca: *Felix est cui nihil deest. Ad bene beateque viuendum dum nihil deesse memini.*

(Thomson, Edition, Text KK, 209, 17–25)[62]

The earliest printed English grammatical treatises that can be connected with teachers from Magdalen College, Oxford, reflect this practice in a similar way. The *Long Parvula*, for example, is one of the three extant versions on elementary syntax descending from the earlier *Informacio* manuscripts by, or in the style of, John Leylond. It is written in question-and-answer form and was perhaps revised and adapted by John Stanbridge, a pupil of William Wykeham's foundation, Winchester College, and a student of New College, Oxford who afterwards became usher and finally master at Magdalen College School, Oxford, after John Anwykyll's death. The early printed editions of the grammatical treatises on morphology and elementary syntax written in English are anonymous, and it is only during the decade of 1500–1510 that some are described as being, or edited, by Stanbridge. It seems he continued the tradition of revising and improving them, each version to a differing degree, in line with early humanist standards. The *Long Parvula* is an example which demonstrates that the practice of adaptation and revision was continued. At the same time it also shows how material from humanist learning was embedded into a traditional text and appeared in early print. The examples adapted from Pliny and Terence to illustrate Latin compounds of the auxiliary verb *esse* are found side by side with explanations in English. The teaching methodology, within which the conventional material was presented, was preserved, but mnemonic verses are included

---

[62] For information on the contents and the provenance of the grammatical manuscripts containing this treatise see Thomson, *Catalogue*, 94–96, 233–38. On the text see Thomson, *Edition*, Notes to Text KK, 278–79. The reference to Pliny contains a misspelling. It should read: "*Suberat abiegna trabes.*" (There was a pine beam underneath.) As many of these grammars show, lines quoted to illustrate a rule may not have been taken from the original classical text, but from other grammars in which they were already used as examples, or even from the memory of the compiler.

to summarize the rules and facilitate memorizing them. The verses, however, are also improved according to humanist lines. Note the following passage on the construction of the *ablativus temporis* and *ablativus mensurae* in the earliest extant copy of an edition of this treatise, printed by Richard Pynson, probably in 1496:

whan I haue a nown that betokeneth tyme mesure of space if it be nat the nominatif case of the verbe or otherwise gouerned of the verbe: it shalbe put in the ablatif case and often sesons it may be put in the accusatif case as in this ensaumple I am xxvii yere old *Ego sum viginti et septem annos natus. Therentius in Eunucho. Dies noctesque me ames. Exemplum de spacio.* London is fro oxford fyfty myle. *Distat londonium ab oxonia quinquaginta milibus passuum. Exemplum de mensura.* This scole is xx fote brode. *Hec scola est pedibus viginti lata.*

> Quod tempus signat quarto sexto ve locetur
> Mobile mensuram designans addito sexto
> Iungitur et quarto/ testis virgilius extat:
> Tris pateat celi spacium non amplius vlnas.
> (Cambridge, Magdalene College, Pepysian Library, PL 1305(4), a6ʳ)[63]

The *Parvulorum institutio* by John Stanbridge, the longest version on elementary syntax that is extant, also illustrates the way in which humanist material was integrated into the early printed Latin grammars in English. At the same time it shows some innovation in respect to the typographic appearance of the rules and their illustrative examples, indicating an increasing importance becoming associated with this aspect and suggesting that teachers used the textual layout as a teaching aid. The rule for the concord of substantive and relative, for example, is given in the following way:

Notwithstandynge whan the substantyue þat cometh after the relatyue is a propre name than the relatyue comynly shall accorde with hym.

[In smaller type:] Salustius. Est locus in carcere quod tullianum appellatur.
(Cambridge, King's College, M.28.432, A3ʳ)[64]

In this treatise many examples from classical authors, especially from Cicero and Terence, are printed in small type in the margins to illustrate the rules of the main text. At the same time it preserves the question-and-answer form, and also incorporates mnemonic verses, a characteristic of both the English grammatical manuscripts and the early printed English grammars. The rules based on traditional material were complemented by passages from grammars representing the New Learning that served to

---

[63] See *Checklist* 48.2. The citation is Terence, *The Eunuch*, I, 193. The last verse corresponds to Virgil, *Eclogues*, III, 105. In this context it is of interest to see that citations from classical authors and Italian humanist grammarians seem to occur frequently in the early printed treatises on syntax which I have examined, in contrast to those treatises discussing accidence.

[64] For the copy of this edition see *Checklist* 50.1. The quotation is Sallust, *The War with Catiline*, LV,3.

illustrate and improve them. The early printed grammatical treatises reflect teaching methods that were used when teaching was more or less oral. However, they also incorporate devices that point to 'visual' teaching when copies were available to the pupils as well as to the teacher. The different teaching methods indicate a transitional stage from oral to visual teaching and learning. Due to the large number of editions of some of these texts that were printed, these rules and the ways of presenting them were multiplied, spread, and preserved in the first four decades of the sixteenth century. In the case of Stanbridge's *Parvulorum institutio*, the latest extant copy of an edition can be dated around 1539, demonstrating the success of this work in grammar schools and its great influence on the teaching of Latin.[65]

However, other grammars that were also compiled in the early years of printing are written in discursive prose and omit verses. Though mnemonic verses did continue to play a part in Latin grammars in the sixteenth century and beyond, a decline of frequency in their use can be observed. A similar tendency applies to the listing of declensions of sample nouns and the conjugations of sample verbs presented in left to right sequence on the page. Early printed grammars make use of the two ways of presenting them, setting them up in the traditional way from left to right on the lines as well as presenting them in tabular form. These two ways of presentation, however, can already be found in grammatical manuscripts from many centuries earlier.[66] The treatises dealing with morphology in particular make much use of visual means to convey information about the forms of Latin nouns and verbs, with plenty of space to enable the relevant forms to leap to the eye. Visual devices, *i.e.* paradigms that were printed in tabular form, were used intensively and comprise a large portion of the whole text. In addition, citations from classical authors, printed in the margins of the text, imply that the pupils were expected to have access to textbooks and have the text before them in the classroom. In the course of time teachers therefore adapted their teaching methodology to make increasing use of such visual devices when compiling their teaching manuals. The result was that teaching with such manuals formed an ever larger part of children's language learning.

In the first decades of the sixteenth century, a number of Latin grammars in English, orientated towards beginners, and also grammars written in Latin for the teaching of more advanced pupils, were compiled in this way, circulated in printed form, and used in grammar schools.

---

[65] See *Checklist* 50.24.
[66] On the use of verb paradigms in grammatical manuscripts as a method of studying morphology see Law (1990), 'The History of Morphology: Expression of a Change in Consciousness', in W. Hüllen (ed.), *Understanding the Historiography of Linguistics*, Münster, 62.

Additional teaching texts and exercises complemented the learning of Latin grammar in a way similar to the time when grammatical manuscripts were used. Due to the multitude of copies that were printed and disseminated, the influence of the New Learning and the changes in teaching method spread. Treatises of the *Vulgaria* and the *Vocabula* were compiled and went into print. In addition, grammatical works in Latin were used for a more advanced stage of the teaching of Latin. John Anwykyll's successor to the post of headmaster of Magdalen College School, Oxford also compiled texts of the *Vulgaria* and *Vocabula* that were used as companion texts to the teaching of Latin grammar and were intended to supply the children with the vocabulary for their conversations and their written work. In addition, these texts were meant to have some topical interest to appeal to schoolboys.[67] The treatise entitled *Vulgaria Stanbrigiana*, printed by Wynkyn de Worde in 1519, which is probably a revision of Stanbridge's work, starts with a *Nominale* listing nouns in Latin and English according to topics for the different parts of the head, face, and the body. It continues with a list of Latin nouns for various kinds of clothes, items in the house, furniture and food, written in Latin, with their vernacular translations printed above in smaller type, and another three texts entitled 'Herbarium nomina', 'Nomina piscium', and 'De pertinentibus ad equum', were all written in hexameters to make committing them to memory easier. The *Vulgaria Stanbrigiana* is followed by a *Vulgaria* "compiled, together with their vernacular equivalents, according to the custom of the school of St Paul's", which suggests that Stanbridge's method had been adopted in the school founded by John Colet during the time when William Lily was teaching as its first High Master.[68] It consists of English sentences together with their Latin translations. Sometimes alternative renderings into Latin are suggested. The phrases reflect the children's learning of grammar, life at school, their experiences, behaviour, and the world around them, as the following examples show:

> Good morowe. Bonum tibi huius diei sit primordium. (Page 13, line 37)
> Good nyght. Bona nox/ tranquilla nox/ optata requies. (13,38)
> I shall bere the company. Commitabor te/ sociabo te. (14,8)
> How doth my fader. Ut pater se habet. (14,11)
> It is a gret helpe for scollars to speke latyn.
>   Non nihil conducit discipulis loqui latine. (14,26–27)

[67] Copies of editions of John Stanbridge's *Vulgaria* are listed *STC²* 23195.5–23199. These editions date in time from *c.*1509–*c.*1534. For copies of editions of the *Vocabula* see *STC²* 23177.5–23193.9. The first printed copy of an edition can be dated *c.*1505, and the last one bears the date 1639.
[68] The heading of this edition of the *Vulgaria* reads: "Vulgaria quedam cum suis vernaculis compilata iuxta consuetudinem ludi litterarij diui pauli." See John Stanbridge (1519), *The Vulgaria of John Stanbridge and the Vulgaria of Robert Whittinton* (1520), ed. B. White (1932 for 1931), EETS, OS, 187, London; repr. 1971, 13. The copy of this edition is listed as *STC²* 23196.8.

I was set to scole whan I was seuen yere olde.
>Datus sum scolis cum septemnis eram. (14,29–30)

Thou stynkest. Male oles. (17,15)

Lende me the copy of thy latyn and I shall gyue it the agayne by and by.
>Comoda mihi exemplar materie latine: illico tibi reddam. (18,13–15)

My heed is full of lyce.
>Caput meum est plenum pediculorum. (19,13–14)

Ryot is the destruccyon of all yonge men.
>Intemperantia adolescentum omnium pernicies est. (22,17–18)

I sate at the table with the mayre and the sheryues.
>Discubui in mensa cum prefecto ac vicecomitibus. (23,18–19)

Chyldren be brought vp with gret cost of þe fader and moder.
>Liberi magno sumptu parentum educantur. (27,6–7)

He hathe all the maners of a gentylman.
>Cunctos mores nobilitatis habet. (29,11–12)

My mynde is not set to my boke. Animus a studio abhoret. (30,9)

In the same way as printed grammatical texts in English, different versions of the *Vulgaria* and *Vocabula* and further exercises for acquiring Latin vocabulary were compiled by grammarians, issued from different printing houses and used in grammar schools in the early Tudor period.[69]

Timetables of grammar schools surviving from the time shortly before the Reformation are very rare records that provide a great deal of information about the organization of teaching at grammar schools. They give evidence of the different grammatical texts that were in use, list complementary treatises, basic religious texts, and the works of authors to be studied in these institutions. They also provide some insight into the daily routine of the schools from Monday to Saturday in the case of the Eton timetables and also for Sunday in the Winchester timetable, and they indicate the order of teaching in the different forms. It can be seen that the same texts and authors could be studied in more than one form of both schools, a fact partly due to the system of teaching several forms together under one master in one classroom. On the other hand, lack of progress in learning may have made it necessary to spend more time on a given text than was intended by the teacher or prescribed by the timetable. Allowance is also made for alternative choices of authors to be studied as well as for taking into account the comparative progress of pupils and their behaviour. The following discussion of three of the earliest surviving timetables of the most influential schools in England at this time will be of some interest: the timetable of Eton of 1528, adopted for Cuckfield Grammar School, Sussex; the Eton and Winchester timetables of 1530, which were followed at Saffron Walden Grammar School,

---

[69] Cf., for example, the version of the *Vulgaria* compiled by Robert Whittington, which was circulating in numerous editions, in a large number of copies each. Extant copies of editions are listed as *STC*[2] 25569.3–25579.

Essex; and Cardinal Thomas Wolsey's timetable for his short-lived foundation of 1528 at Ipswich. As there is no information about teaching in the majority of grammar schools at this time, these records are of great interest, as other schools followed the most famous institutions as models and took their standards from them.

The Eton timetable of 1528 adopted for Cuckfield Grammar School lists grammars and complementary texts and also provides some information about their usage in the regular six forms as well as in the preparatory class that existed below the regular forms.[70] It is laid down that the children begin to learn the parts of speech by a version of Stanbridge's *Accidence* which is followed in form one by Stanbridge's *Parvula*, which treats elementary syntax.[71] At this level they already had to "make small and easy 'Latins', proper and such as the childen may understand and have a delight in". These treatises continued to be used in the second form with additional Latin exercises. Moreover, *Sum es fui*, a summary on irregular verbs, "or some other verb out of rule" and "also some Latin words from Stanbridge's Collection", probably his *Vocabula*, have to be studied. The teaching of Latin is accompanied by learning the basic prayers, for example, the *Pater Noster*, the *Ave Maria*, the *Creed*, *The Ten Commandments*, or some other prayers, alternatively Sulpitius's poem on table manners, entitled *Quos decet in mensa*. The pupils in this form also "shall learn to write and to read Legends, or the Psalter". In this connection the timetable adds that these texts are not used for religious instruction but for enunciation, though their use does not exclude a double purpose. In the second form, instruction in grammar is given by Robert Whittington's grammatical texts in Latin, which discuss gender and heteroclites. The teaching of grammar is complemented by "a lecture of Cato after the new interpretation" (*i.e.* Cato's *Disticha*). Further grammatical works by Whittington, amongst them the treatises on preterites, supines, and defectives, are to be studied in the third form. Form four continues with Whittington's grammar on regimen, the study of which is complemented by works of Terence or Erasmus. In the fifth form, verse making and prose writing are prescribed, as well as texts by Virgil, Sallust, Horace, or Ovid. Finally, form six has to study Erasmus's *Copia verborum* and the authors listed for the previous form.

[70] For the Eton timetable of 1528, adopted for Cuckfield Grammar School, see *VCH, Sussex*, vol. 36,2: 417–19. See the anonymous article (1911), 'An Eton Curriculum of 1528', *Etoniana* 12: 190–92, which also includes this document. All quotations from this timetable are taken from *VCH, Sussex*, above.

[71] As these documents often do not provide precise information about the title of the grammars and complementary texts used in the different forms of grammar schools, and as not all the versions that are listed may have survived, it is not always possible to identify the titles with extant versions.

Children attending Saffron Walden Grammar School were to be taught after the order and use of teaching grammar in the schools of Eton or Winchester in 1530.[72] The timetable for Winchester is incomplete and comprises only the first five forms out of seven. The Eton document lists six forms and is complete. It bears the signature of Richard Cox, who was headmaster of Eton College at that time. Form one of the Eton document starts its Latin with a version of Stanbridge's *Accidence*. It continues with the *Institutiones parvulorum* and his *Vocabula*, probably also the versions of the treatises by Stanbridge, and the study of table manners, *Quos decet in mensa*, by Sulpitius. For the second form the timetable prescribes the reading of Æsop's *Fables*, the making of 'Latins', and Lily's grammar on gender.[73] The study of Lily's treatise is complemented by the reading of Cato's *Disticha* and making 'Latins' and 'vulgars'. Form three continues with Lily's rules on preterits, reading Terence, and learning hymns.[74] The works of Terence continue to be read in form four, where in addition the *Octo partes Lilii* are studied and Virgil's *Buccolica* are read.[75] Form five has to practise prose writing and work with Despauterius's treatise *On versifying*, also Sallust, Cicero's epistles, and Virgil's *Aeneid*.[76] The sixth and seventh forms are required to study Horace, Mosellanus's treatise *On figures*,[77] or, alternatively, Erasmus's *Copia verborum*, as well as the authors listed for

---

[72] For the Eton and Winchester timetables of 1530, adopted for Saffron Walden Grammar School, see Thomas Wright (1852), 'Rules of the Free School at Saffron Walden, in Essex, in the Reign of Henry VIII', *Archaeologia* 34: 37–41. Wright, however, does not inform us that the timetables reflect Eton and Winchester use but attributed these orders and regulations to Saffron Walden School itself. For these documents see also *VCH, Hampshire and the Isle of Wight*, vol. 15,2: 297–300, and *VCH, Essex*, vol. 13,2: 521. Cf. the anonymous article (1907), 'Eton and Winchester in 1530', *Etoniana* 9: 131–36, which includes the two timetables. They are also given in *Educational Charters and Documents, 598 to 1909*, ed. Leach (1911), repr. 1971, 448–51. See the comment in Orme (1973), 114. All quotations from the two timetables in the following are taken from Leach.

[73] For this grammatical text by William Lily see Appendix IV, 8, *De generibus nominum, Ac verborum præteritis et supinis Regulæ pueris apprime vtiles*.

[74] The grammatical rules are contained in a section of Lily's *De generibus nominum*. See previous footnote.

[75] This treatise can be identified with the *Libellus de constructione*, which in many subsequent editions is entitled *Absolutissimus de octo orationis partium constructione libellus*. See also Appendix IV, 1.

[76] Joannes Despauterius (c.1480–1520) is also referred to by his Dutch name Joannes de Spouter. His grammars were very popular, especially in the Low Countries and in France, throughout the sixteenth and the first half of the seventeenth centuries. They include treatises on morphology, syntax, metre, figures, orthography, and epistolary style. On Despauterius see Bernard Colombat and Carole Gascard (1998), in *HEL*, vol. 1, no. 1247: 84–86; also Jan De Clercq, Pierre Swiggers, and Toon Van Hal (2009), in *Lexicon Grammaticorum*, vol. 1: 372–73.

[77] Mosellanus's treatise on the figures of speech is referred to here. On the grammarian Petrus Mosellanus (1493–1524) (with his German name Peter Schade), see *BBKL* (1993), vol. 6, cols. 169–71.

form five. The repeating of 'Latins' and 'vulgars' is explicitly mentioned in this timetable. According to the Winchester timetable, pupils also start their Latin with Stanbridge's *Accidence*, and continue studying "Comparisons, with the verbe *sum. es. fui* to be said", texts probably also taken from Stanbridge. Form two takes their Latin rules and vocabulary from Stanbridge's *Parvula* and his *Vocabula*, accompanied by the reading of Æsop's *Fables* and verses of Cato's *Disticha*. Form three continues their Latin by learning the genders and heteroclites from Sulpitius.[78] The making of "vulgars" and prose writing, the study of Æsop's *Fables* and Lucian's *Dialogues* (both in Latin translations), and "proper verses of meter of lilies makyng" are also prescribed for this form.[79] Form four had "to make Latins" and "vulgars" and study works of Terence, Ovid, or Cicero. For the fifth form the timetable prescribes versifying rules, rules on preterites, and supines, all taken from Sulpitius. Finally, Ovid's *Metamorphoses*, Sallust, Virgil's *Eclogues*, and Cicero's epistles have to be read. Forms six and seven probably continue to study the same authors. Compared to the Eton timetable of 1528 it is remarkable that the Eton and Winchester documents of 1530 abandoned the use of Whittington's very popular grammars studied there in forms two to four, for those of Lily in the Eton timetable and Sulpitius in the Winchester timetable.

Cardinal Thomas Wolsey, himself a former teacher for two terms at Magdalen College School, Oxford, compiled the *Methodus*, a timetable in Latin for the grammar school that he founded in his native town of Ipswich in 1528. His school was intended to be linked to his Oxford foundation, Cardinal College, Oxford (now Christ Church) where pupils were to study afterwards. In contrast to the documents reflecting the practice of Winchester and Eton College, the timetable for Ipswich Grammar School was modelled on that of St Paul's School, London, which was divided into eight forms. However, the *Methodus* shows that pupils were no longer prescribed to read fourth- and fifth-century Christian authors as stated in John Colet's statutes drawn up in 1518 for St Paul's School, but pagan classical authors. In 1529, Wolsey's timetable was issued together with two elementary grammars, John Colet's *Aeditio* and William Lily's *Rudimenta grammatices*, under the main title *Rudimenta grammatices et Docendi methodus*. The book adds on the general title-page, which also bears Wolsey's coat of arms, that the timetable and the grammars should not be taught only at Ipswich school but in all other schools throughout England. Wolsey's *Methodus* prescribed grammatical texts and specified authors to be studied in each form. The grammars that had to be used are

---

[78] These rules were taken from Sulpitius's grammar *Opus insigne grammaticum*. Separate treatises covering these rules must have also circulated.

[79] The rules on verses were probably taken from Lily's treatise *De generibus nominum*, which contains a section entitled *Compendium versificationis*.

those of St Paul's School. Pupils of the first form are to start by learning their parts of speech using John Colet's *Aeditio* in a slightly revised version from that of St Paul's School, and pronunciation also has to be practised.[80] Form two is required to form Latin phrases from the vernacular. The teaching of grammar is accompanied by William Lily's *Carmen de moribus*, a poem on good behaviour.[81] Cato's *Disticha* can be studied alternatively in form two. In form three, pupils have to work with Lily's treatise *De generibus nominum*, which sets out the rules for distinguishing the genders of nouns and for the inflexion of verbs, and read Æsop's *Fables*. Lily's treatise on preterites and supines follows in form four. In form five, the pupils have to study Cicero's epistles. In form six, they continue with a treatise of Lily's syntax (*i.e.* the *Absolutissimus*), also Lily's rules on defective and irregular verbs, and read Sallust or Caesar's commentaries.[82] Horace's *Epistles* or Ovid's *Metamorphoses* follows in form seven. Finally, in form eight they have to study Horace, Ovid, Valla's *Elegantiae*,[83] and Terence's *Comedies*. However, after Wolsey's fall from power in 1530 Ipswich Grammar School was suppressed by King Henry VIII.

These timetables not only provide first-hand information about the grammars and complementary texts that pupils had to learn at the famous schools which exerted influence on other institutions, but at the same time they indicate the direction in which the teaching of grammar was moving shortly before the Reformation in England.

[80] For the earliest extant copy of Wolsey's *Methodus* see Colet and Lily, *Rudimenta Grammatices et Docendi methodus*. [Southwark]: Peter Treveris, 1529 (BL, C.40.c.39, A3^r-A4^v). In this copy the *Methodus* is printed before John Colet's *Aeditio* and William Lily's *Rudimenta grammatices*. See *Checklist*, 20.4 and 51.6. This timetable was reprinted with the *Aeditio* and the *Rudimenta grammatices*, but also circulated as a single copy; cf. *Checklist*, 20.6–20.14, 51.8–51.15. The latest extant copy of the *Methodus* is bound with an edition of Colet's and Lily's grammars printed in Antwerp in 1539 (*Checklist*, 20.12 and 51.15, second copy). The text of the *Methodus* is available in John Strype (1822), *Ecclesiastical Memorials, Relating Chiefly to Religion and the Reformation of it*, Oxford, vol. 1, part 2, no. 35: 139–43. On Wolsey's grammar school at Ipswich and his *Methodus* see also *VCH, Suffolk*, vol. 34,2: 142–44 and 328–32. Cf. the comments by Orme (2006), 240–42, 294–95; Maria Dowling (1986), *Humanism in the Age of Henry VIII*, London, 119–22; also Joan Simon (1966), *Education and Society in Tudor England*, Cambridge, repr. in paperback 1979, 143–45.

[81] Lily's *Carmen de moribus* is included in the *Introduction* of 1542. See pp. 82, and 88 below; also Appendix IV, 5. This poem is contained in the 1529 copy of the *Rudimenta Grammatices et Docendi methodus* (see previous footnote) on sigs. I1^v-I3^r. It is also included in the following extant editions of the *Rudimenta grammatices*; see *Checklist* 20.5–20.13 and 51.7–51.16.

[82] The rules on defective verbs comprise a section in Lily's treatise *De generibus nominum*. Cf. footnotes 73 and 74 of this chapter.

[83] Valla's grammar, *Elegantiarum linguae Latinae libri sex*, is referred to here. See Wolfram Ax (2001), 'Lorenzo Valla (1407-1457), *Elegantiarum linguae Latinae libri sex* (1449)', in W. Ax (ed.), *Von Eleganz und Barbarei*, Mainz, 29–57; also Frank Bezner (2005), 'Lorenzo Valla (1407-1457)', in *Lateinische Lehrer Europas*, Köln, etc., 353–89, at 354–59, 361–65; and Stefano Gensini (2009), in *Lexicon Grammaticorum*, vol. 2: 1552–1553. Orme (2006), 119–20, touches on the influence of Valla's grammar in England.

Considering the use of treatises for teaching elementary Latin, the time-tables not only shed light on the diversity of teaching texts prescribed in the different institutions but also show that Lily's grammatical texts used at St Paul's School, London, where he was High Master, gained popularity as a result of being adopted at Eton College; this is reflected in the time-table of 1530 and by their being prescribed for Cardinal Wolsey's School at Ipswich. The influence of Wolsey's *Methodus* and the texts printed with it, Colet's *Aeditio*, Lily's *Rudimenta grammatices*, and Lily's poem *Carmen de moribus*, which were stated to be set forth for general use in grammar schools throughout England, becomes obvious by the number of copies that were printed. According to present evidence, the grammars, Lily's poem, and the timetable continued to be issued by printing houses in the Low Countries for use in English schools even after the Cardinal's fall. The *Methodus* also circulated independently. In this way the texts exerted influence, so that not only the grammars used at St Paul's but also the name of William Lily became well known and his works gained popularity in grammar schools in England.

These grammars and the complementary texts used at St Paul's School, also those associated with other famous English grammarians from the early decades of the sixteenth century which were used at the famous grammar schools, are part of a long tradition of grammar writing and teaching in England. Together with the works of Italian grammarians and those of Erasmus, they formed the rich reservoir out of which the Latin grammar in English commonly attributed to William Lily was compiled around 1540. Its compilers, as will be seen below, were familiar with the teaching of Latin at different levels, with the grammars, and the complementary exercises and with the well-known authors being used for teaching classical Latin in English grammar schools.

3. The Grammar Attributed to William Lily

3.1 Form and contents of the different sections of 'Lily's Grammar', London, British Library, C.21.b.4.

'Lily's Latin Grammar' is part of a long tradition of elementary Latin grammar writing which consistently follows the line of vernacular Latin grammars dating from *c.*1400 and earlier. Like the printed Latin grammars in the vernacular that preceded it, it concentrates on the description of Latin at a fairly elementary level, with its emphasis on accidence and construction, but including further texts for teaching the Latin language and for moral and religious education.

The composite volume in the British Library with the shelfmark C.21.b.4., in which the Latin grammar written in English is the second item, is made up of three books in quarto format, each with a separate title-page, printed on vellum by the Royal Printer Thomas Berthelet. It is a volume with woodcut borders on the title-pages and with each chapter beginning with an illuminated initial. It was most probably intended to be a presentation copy to Prince Edward, King Henry VIII's son and the later King Edward VI.[1] Each of the three parts is a complete, bibliographically separate entity that was bound in one volume, probably shortly before it was used for teaching.[2] These three books together make up the earliest extant edition of 'Lily's Grammar'. The first part was printed in 1543, the second in 1542, and the third in 1540. The whole volume comprises books for the different stages of learning Latin grammar for beginners as well as for more advanced pupils and was obviously perceived to be a graded sequence of instruction.

The first book entitled *Alphabetum Latino Anglicum* (shelfmark C.21.b.4.(1)) is dated 1543 in the colophon (A4ᵛ) and consists of four leaves (A1ʳ–A4ᵛ). They contain the following texts: the *Latin English alphabet* (A1ʳ); the *Lord's Prayer*, the *Ave Maria*, the *Creed*, and *The Ten Commandments* (A1ᵛ–A3ᵛ), all of them given in Latin and English; a prayer in English beginning *Thou shalte loue the Lorde thy God with all thyne harte* (Matt. 22: 37-40), the 'Golden Rule' beginning *Therfore what so euer ye wyll that men shulde do to you* (Matt. 7: 12) (A3ᵛ) which also appears only in English; a prayer from the second psalm

---

[1] See also Chapter 6, p. 146 below.
[2] Cf. T. W. Baldwin (1944), *William Shakspere's Small Latine and Lesse Greeke*, Urbana, vol. 1: 202.

entitled *Oratio ad Deum pro timore pio*, in Latin and in English (A4^r); and finally, a prayer in Latin and English entitled *Altera pro docilitate pietatis*, and two verses beginning *Omnis donatio bona* (1 James 1: 17) which are also given in Latin and English (A4^{r-v}).[3] This book contains the most elementary texts of instruction in Latin that teach the children reading and the basic prayers and prepare them for the Latin accidence to be taught in English. It combines the teaching of the letters and syllables with religious instruction at an early stage of education in grammar school and thus illustrates a double purpose in that, from the very beginning, it inculcates in the minds of children some knowledge of both Christian attitudes and practices as well as the foundation of literacy that was necessary to be able to move on to Latin grammar taught in the vernacular, especially on the oral level.

The second book, known as the elementary Latin grammar in English (shelfmark C.21.b.4.(2)), is entitled *An Introduction Of The Eyght Partes Of speche, and the Construction of the same*, and is dated 1542 (*i.e.* old style, between 25 March 1542 and 24 March 1543) on both the title-page (A1^r) and in the colophon (I5^r). It incorporates the following eight texts: the Royal Proclamation by Henry VIII; *To the Reder*; *Ad Pubem Anglicam. Hexasticon*; *An Introduction of the eighte partes of speche*; *Godly Lessons for Chyldren*; *The Concordes of latyne speche*; *Guilielmi Lilii ad suos discipulos monita pædagogica, seu carmen de moribus*; and *Christiani Hominis Institutum per Erasmum Rotero-damum*.[4] The aim at this stage of learning is to introduce the children to the elements of Latin grammar, translation practice, and phrases for memorizing in Latin and the vernacular in order to prepare them for the next stage, the study of the *Institutio*, and for written and oral composition.

The following part, the third book, also issued by royal authority in the same way as the second book, comprises a more advanced grammar written in Latin, and is entitled *Institutio Compendiaria Totius Grammaticæ* (shelfmark C.21.b.4.(3)).[5] It is dated on the title-page (A1^r) and also in the colophon (V6^v) 1540. It comprises the following texts, including the four principal parts of grammar: the royal proclamation entitled *Totius Angliae Ludimagistris Ac Grammaticae Praeceptoribus* (A2^r–A3^v); *Ad Lectorem* (A4^{r-v}); *Errata Insigniora* (A5^v–A6^r); *De Grammatica et eius partibus. De Ortho-graphia* (B1^r–B4^v); *De Etymologia* (C1^r–N2^r); *Syntaxis. De Constructione Octo*

---

[3] For the contents of this book see also Maria Dowling (1986), *Humanism in the Age of Henry VIII*, London, 131–32; Alston-Hill, 79; and Baldwin (1943), *William Shakspere's Petty School*, Urbana, 42. The *Alphabetum Latino Anglicum* is listed as *STC*[2] 19.2.

[4] For bibliographical details of this book see Chapter 6; also Appendix III, 3.0.

[5] Bibliographical details of this copy of the edition of 1540 are given in Appendix III, 1.0. The dates on the title-page and in the colophon of this copy were corrected by hand to 1542, probably to match with the dates of the English part. The second extant copy of the Latin part of the 1540 edition, located in Lambeth Palace Library, London, was probably also a presentation copy; see also Appendix III, 1.0.

Partium (N2ᵛ–S4ʳ); and *De Prosodia* (S4ᵛ–V6ʳ).[6] The *Introduction* as well as the *Institutio* comprises the Latin grammar in English and in Latin which are attributed to William Lily as a whole as well as in its parts. Each of the two parts is referred to as 'grammar', though the English part, as shown above, also incorporates other material for pedagogical reasons.

The second book, the *Introduction*, the subject of this work, is a unique record and represents the earliest complete copy of this text that has come down to us from among a number of copies printed on vellum and an unknown number of copies printed on paper of which no trace has been left. Of any earlier editions of the *Introduction* that may have been published, there are no extant copies, apart from a fragment of a proof leaf in the Bodleian Library (shelfmark Vet.A1.a.4(1)), which was printed in *c*.1540, also in Berthelet's printing house. It represents the earliest evidence of the grammar written in English and is the only surviving record of a possible edition.[7]

The items contained in the *Introduction* comprise two texts on elementary Latin grammar, *i.e.* a treatise on morphology and on syntax, with a set of English sentences and their Latin translations coming between them, finally the *Carmen de moribus* on school topics and good behaviour, and Erasmus's *Christiani Hominis Institutum* on Christian education. These texts again represent a sequential development in learning Latin, leading the pupil step by step through an organized sequence of grammatical treatises written in English, supplemented by texts conveying moral and religious instruction in Latin. The book starts, however, with two legal documents that are printed before the grammatical texts and the other treatises. They are also unique. The first text consists of the proclamation by Henry VIII, a legal and authoritative document which is justified by the common-law prerogative of the Crown. This proclamation was issued while the Statute of Proclamations (31 Henry VIII, c. 8.) was in effect. The 1539 Act gave a general statutory basis to all proclamations and encouraged actions to enforce them. The second text, addressed *To the Reder*, represents an accompanying letter to the royal proclamation and provides further explanation of why the proclamation was issued and orders that it be proclaimed and enforced.[8]

The fact that these documents were printed together with the grammatical texts makes the grammar itself an authoritative document, as, of course, was the proclamation. This also applies to later editions of the

---

[6] For its contents see also Alston-Hill, 71.
[7] See Plate 10 and the bibliographical description given in Appendix II; also Appendix III, 2.0.
[8] R. W. Heinze (1976), *The Proclamations of the Tudor Kings*, Cambridge, 24–26.

grammar.[9] At the same time it ensured that these texts would reach all grammar school teachers and pupils to whom they were addressed. The documents establish the circumstances and refer to the authorship of the grammar. They offer explanations about the prevailing situation of teaching Latin and the diversity of textbooks that were used and thus justify its promulgation as the textbook to be used exclusively in all the grammar schools in the country. In this way, the grammar became exceedingly influential and its appearance in print must have gratified the sovereign, enhancing his reputation as a benevolent ruler. It was Thomas Berthelet, the King's Printer, who was solely responsible for publishing it up to 1547.[10] The official documents are followed by the *Hexasticon*, a poem consisting of three distichs that serves as a link between the official documents and the teaching texts that follow. It praises the King's generosity and, at the same time, draws attention to the grammatical and educational texts that follow and encourages the children to work with them.[11]

The following survey of the individual texts of the *Introduction* will draw attention to some of their characteristics and will also illustrate that this volume shows, step by step, the process of learning Latin from the very beginning and could therefore be used as the basis for a complete course. Each of the major parts—the morphology, the set of sentences for translation, and the syntax—covers a curricular area that is complemented by two further texts in Latin that provide additional exercises, and that also teach good behaviour, morals, and religious rules. The first and longest part of this book is a text on accidence. The eight parts of speech are its organizing principle with the declension of nouns and the conjugation of verbs receiving special emphasis and being discussed in most detail. It provides definitions of the parts of speech, lists and discusses their accidents, and presents the declensions of nouns and the conjugation of verbs in paradigms as well as in continuous text. Obviously the text was aimed at beginners in Latin who had to learn the forms, especially of nouns and verbs that were most useful to them. It enabled them to describe the grammatical features of every part of speech and its accidents such as case, number, gender, declension, and so forth. The subject matter is discussed in affirmative sentences.[12]

---

[9] On royal proclamations in Tudor government see Hughes and Larkin, vol. 1, Introduction, xxi–xliii; G. R. Elton (1960), 'Henry VIII's Act of Proclamations', *The English Historical Review* 75, no. 294: 208–22; Elton's review article (1965) of Hughes and Larkin, vol. 1, in *The Historical Journal*, 8, no. 2: 266–71; also Heinze (1976), 1–64, and 153–99.

[10] The latest extant copy of the *Introduction* printed by Berthelet is dated 1546; see Appendix III, 7.0.

[11] See Chapter 8, Commentary: *Ad Pubem Anglicam. Hexasticon*, 224, note to line 1.

[12] For the structure and contents of the texts on accidence and syntax see Appendix I. The individual texts contained in the *Introduction* that are used for instruction are here referred to as *Parts of Speech, Godly Lessons, Construction, Carmen de moribus*, and *Christiani Hominis Institutum*.

The treatise on accidence in this edition is followed by the *Godly Lessons for Chyldren*, a collection of forty rather short English sentences with their Latin translations.[13] Regular practice in translation, which was part of classroom practice from the beginning, was an effective pedagogical strategy. It exposed the children to the language in use and fostered bilingual comparison of Latin and English. The colloquial English sentences or idioms that children were expected to memorize for their day-to-day conversation practice in school were called 'vulgars' (Latin *Vulgaria*), which had to be rendered into 'Latins' (*Latinitates*). These bilingual exercises could also have been arranged after the text on elementary syntax, as is shown by the proof fragment.[14] They consist of a selection and perhaps adaptation of phrases current at that time from textbooks known as *Vulgaria*, or could have been drawn from classical texts that were then in use without assigning them to an author.[15] Alternatively they could either have been taken from earlier grammars, could have been made up by the master for his own teaching purposes, or have been stored in his memory. Some of these sentences, current at that time, were perhaps so widely used as to make identifying their exact source impossible. They also served as examples for illustrating Latin rules in the text on syntax. Compared to sentences for translation in earlier collections, however, this set of exercises is less colloquial and reflects a tendency to provide general moral rules with a focus on religious subject matter. To this end, a number of verses from the Bible in translation as 'Englishes' and their Latin versions are given, which would satisfy this requirement. Apart from assimilating words and phrases in English through pieces of wise advice, popular proverbs, and sentences of biblical origin, and conveying their ideas, these sentences also served as models for construing exercises. As the first step in translating English into Latin, children were instructed to discover the grammatical construction of the

---

[13] See Plate 7 for the beginning of these sentences.

[14] See Plate 10. The arrangement of the individual texts in the *Introduction* also sheds light on the teaching method.

[15] On collections of English and Latin sentences in school notebooks from the early fifteenth century onwards see Nicholas Orme (2006), *Medieval Schools. From Roman Britain to Renaissance England*, New Haven and London, 109–18, and *passim*; also the articles in Nicholas Orme (1989). *Education and Society in Medieval and Renaissance England*, London, 1–22; 73–86; 87–112; 113–21; and 123–52; also *A Fifteenth Century School Book. From a Manuscript in the British Museum (MS. Arundel 249)*, ed. William Nelson (1956). Oxford; William Horman (1519), *Vulgaria*, London, Facsimile Edition (1975), The English Experience, no. 745, Amsterdam; John Stanbridge (1519), *The Vulgaria of John Stanbridge and the Vulgaria of Robert Whittinton* (1520), ed. B. White (1971 repr.), EETS, OS, 187, London. The bookseller John Dorne, for example, sold a substantial number of classical texts in Oxford in 1520, amongst them Cicero and Terence, see 'Day-Book of John Dorne', ed. F. Madan (1885, 1890); also *Garrett Godfrey's Accounts, c. 1527–1533*, ed. E. Leedham-Green, D. E. Rhodes, and F. H. Stubbings (1992), Cambridge, especially Introduction [xix–xx].

sentence in English, to parse it, *i.e.* to recognize and fit it accurately into the eight parts of speech, then take the words in such an order as to show the meaning of the sentence, and finally translate them word for word.[16] This process of using Latin categories for the vernacular was well known in the tradition of teaching elementary grammar and had already been taught when children learned their basic accidence. The text on syntax in this edition states the method of grammatical analysis:

When an englysshe is gyuen to be made in latyn, loke out the pryncipall verbe. If there be mo verbes then one in a sentence, the fyrst is the principall verbe, except it be the infinitiue mode, or haue before it a relatyue, as that, whome, whiche: or a coniunction, as *ut* that, *cum* when, *si* if, or suche other.

When ye haue found the verbe, aske this question whoo, or what, and that worde that answereth to the question, shalbe the nominatiue case to the verbe. Whiche nominatiue case shal in making and construing latyne, be sette before the verbe, excepte in askyng a question, and then the nominatyue is sette after the verbe or after the sygne of the verbe, as *Amas tu?* louest thou? *Venit ne rex?* doeth the kyng come?[17]

By starting from an English sentence, children became aware of the differences of the forms of the words and structures in the context of the same sentence in both languages and learned the application of the rules of elementary Latin syntax. In this way they were taught proper spelling, choice of vocabulary, idiomatic and proverbial expressions, translation and free composition exercises, the principles of rhetoric, and how to speak Latin freely and correctly.

It is striking that the elementary grammar on syntax continues on the same page in the original immediately after the end of the *Godly Lessons*.[18] From the space devoted to it, it becomes clear that, together with the accidence, it was considered the most important text of the English part of the authorized grammar, a fact that is already indicated on the title-page. It deals with concord and government, though syntactic information is scattered through the accidence text as well. Its heading, *The Concordes of latyne speche*, only indicates the rules of agreement, whereas the text also includes a case grammar that sets forth the rules of the construction of the eight parts of speech as it continues. However, it begins by teaching the technique of how to find the main verb in a sentence (see the quotation above), then continues to provide the three traditional instances of concord: between the personal verb and its nominative that agree in number

---

[16] The word 'parse' was part of the teacher's vocabulary of the medieval schoolroom and is still a current term in schools. It originated in the stereotyped question "*Quae pars orationis est?*" To parse a word was, originally, to fit it into the eight parts of speech of Donatus's *Ars minor*. Cf. also footnote 82 of this chapter for 'construe'.

[17] Chapter 7, *Introduction, Construction*, 192, lines 6–17.

[18] Cf. Plate 10 where the text on accidence in the proof leaf is immediately followed by the text on construction. Colet's *Aeditio*, D7ʳ, for example, also indicates this close connection between the parts of speech and their construction.

and person, between noun adjective and its substantive (in case, gender, and number), and between the relative and its antecedent (in gender, number, and person). The rules of construction of the parts of speech are organized according to their order in the accidence text. Then it continues to catalogue the ways in which each part of speech is said to govern the different cases. The construction of the noun, the verb, and the participle and the cases they require is considered the most difficult and hence is discussed in detail, whereas less emphasis is given to the pronoun and the four indeclinable parts of speech. The illustrative sentences inserted in this part are mostly taken from literary works that were read in the higher forms of grammar schools at that time.

The two grammatical texts, as well as the set of sentences for translation, represent new compilations whereas the following two texts circulated independently before copies were printed together with the three treatises above to form the *Introduction*.[19] The poem entitled here as *GVILIELMI Lilii ad suos discipulos monita, pædagogica, seu carmen de moribus*, is commonly known under the name *Carmen de moribus*, as *Praecepta morum*, or *Ad discipulos de moribus*. In later editions of 'Lily's Grammar' it was frequently referred to as *Qui mihi*. It begins with the words '*Qui mihi discipulus*'. It represents the most famous, and at the same time, the longest and most widely circulated, poem by William Lily that he wrote in about 1510 for the boys of St Paul's School. It consists of eighty-six lines written in elegiac verse and was the first lengthy and consecutive passage in Latin included in the *Introduction* that the pupils had to learn. It is addressed to all students of grammar and contains Lily's pedagogical principles, *i.e.* it describes the conduct and the assiduity to their duties expected of each schoolboy and provides principles of learning Latin by somebody with classroom experience.[20] For example, some verses read in their English translation:

When you see me, your schoolmaster, greet me and also your fellow students in turn. And also take your seat where I tell you to sit, and stay in your place, unless you are commanded to leave.

(Verses 11–13)

Let there always be ready for your studies your prepared arms, a pen-knife, pens, ink, paper and books.

(Verses 17–18)

---

[19] Compared to earlier editions of the *Carmen de moribus*, for example to the copy contained in Colet, *Aeditio*, the copy printed in the *Introduction* shows minor changes in the text.

[20] See also Chapter 8, Commentary: *Carmen de Moribus*, 252, note to line 1. A copy of an earlier edition of the *Carmen de moribus* is also contained in the *Epigrammata Lilii* [1522.], see Appendix IV, 5; also in Colet's *Aeditio* (1527), E5^v–E7^r. For further comment on this poem see Kenneth Charlton (1965), *Education in Renaissance England*. London, 125–26; Vincent Joseph Flynn (1939), *The Life and Works of William Lily, the Grammarian*, D.Phil. Thesis, Chicago, 86–91; and Watson (1908), *The English Grammar Schools to 1660*, Cambridge, 106–108.

If you want to know the laws of grammar correctly, if you wish to learn to speak more eloquently, try to learn the most famous writings of the ancient men, and the authors which the crowd of Latinists teach.

(Verses 59–62)

The *Carmen de moribus* was a well-known text used in the most influential schools in the country. For example, it was prescribed for the second form in the *Methodus*, the curriculum that Thomas Wolsey wrote for his newly founded school in Ipswich in 1529.[21] Apart from textbooks on grammar, it has often been printed with other pedagogical works, but as a result of being incorporated into the English part of the authorized grammar it gained general currency and has been memorized by many generations of schoolchildren.[22]

As the final text, the *Introduction* has a copy of *Christiani Hominis Institutum* composed by Desiderius Erasmus, a short catechism written in Latin hexameters, first published in 1514 and reprinted many times.[23] It was one of the texts used to teach the principles of Christian conduct to the children of St Paul's School, London. By learning the basic prayers the children were to absorb the Christian faith and its practices from the very beginning of their education in grammar school. Erasmus's text contains the *Creed*, slightly paraphrased and explained, a brief exposition of *The Seven Sacraments* in an order different from previous editions, reflecting the theological debates that took place shortly after the Reformation in England, and a number of detailed precepts, under the heading *Amor Dei*, *Amor Sui*, and *Amor Proximi*, that correspond in some measure to *The Ten Commandments*. In a letter to John Colet of 1512 Erasmus underlines the aims and practice of education at St Paul's School by saying "that the youth of England, under carefully chosen and highly reputed teachers, might there absorb Christian principles together with an excellent literary education from their earliest years".[24]

Erasmus composed several texts for Colet's school, amongst them the *Christiani Hominis Institutum* that represents a Latin metrical version of Colet's *Cathechyzon*, *i.e.* the religious rudiments, which were prefixed by

---

[21] See *Secundae Classis*, in Wolsey's *Methodus*, a timetable which precedes Colet's *Aeditio* and Lily's *Rudimenta grammatices* in the elementary grammar in English entitled *Rudimenta grammatices et Docendi methodus* (1529). [Southwark]: Peter Treveris (BL, C.40.c.39, A3ʳ); also *Checklist* 20.4.

[22] It follows the grammatical treatises of Colet's *Aeditio* and Lily's *Rudimenta grammatices* in the editions extant from 1527 to 1539. See *Checklist* 20.1–20.14 and 51.3–51.16.

[23] The copy contained in the *Introduction* is referred to in *BM Catalogue*, vol. 1: 594, and vol. 2: 883. See also Chapter 8, Commentary: *Christiani Hominis Institutum*, 253, note to line 1.

[24] *CWE*, vol. 2, Ep. 260, 226, lines 17–20. This passage reads in Latin: "vbi sub electissimis ac probatissimis praeceptoribus Britannica pubes rudibus statim annis simul et Christum et optimas imbiberet litteras." See *Opus Epistolarum Des. Erasmi Roterodami*, ed. P. S. Allen (1906), vol. 1. Oxford, 511, lines 15–17.

the Dean to his *Aeditio*.[25] The genesis of this text is mentioned by its author as well as by Colet. In a letter of 1514, Erasmus describes the *Christiani Hominis Institutum* "expanded by myself, in verse which aims at clarity rather than polish, from an English text written earlier by John Colet".[26] It is also given attention in the statutes of 1518, which Colet drew up for his newly founded St Paul's School. The chapter entitled "What shalbe taughte" reads: "I will the children lerne firste and above all the Catechizone in Inglyshe and after the accydence [. . .] and then Institutum christiani hominis whiche that lernyde Erasmus made at my requeste."[27] The English part of 'Lily's Grammar', incorporating two grammatical treatises, translation exercises, the *Carmen de moribus*, and the *Christiani Hominis Institutum*, comprised a wider body of learning where the teaching of Latin was embedded in a pedagogical and religious context.

3.2 *The date and composition of the earliest copy of the* Introduction

It is difficult to ascertain the exact date on which the English part first appeared in print and also exactly when it and the Latin part together started their long career as the authorized grammar. The principal facts can be summarized as follows: the copy of 'Lily's Grammar' housed in the British Library is, as described in the previous section, bound as a single volume and consists of three independent parts, each of which is printed on vellum and bears a different date. This volume contains the earliest copy of the English part that has come down to us and was printed in 1542. The two earliest extant copies of the Latin part are both dated 1540 on the title-page as well as in the colophon, the Latin part located in the British Library being bound after the 1542 *Introduction*. In this copy, however, the dates on the title-page and in the colophon were corrected to 1542 in pen facsimile, apparently to make it uniform with the date of the English part.[28] The copy located in Lambeth Palace Library, however, consists of the Latin part alone, also printed on vellum. This raises the question whether a missing copy of the English part, probably also printed on

---

[25] See Colet, *Aeditio* (1527), A2^r-A3^v.

[26] *CWE*, vol. 3, Ep. 298, 4, lines 36–38. The passage in Latin reads: "quod nos carmine dilucido magis quam elaborato sumus interpretati, conscriptum antea sermone Britannico a Iohanne Coleto." See *Opus Epistolarum Des. Erasmi Roterodami*, ed. P. S. Allen (1910), vol. 2: 2, lines 31–33.

[27] *Statuta Paulinæ Scholæ* (BL, MS Add. 6274, fol. 7^{r-v}); see W. H. Herendeen (1988). 'Coletus Redivivus: John Colet—Patron or Reformer?', *Renaissance and Reformation*, New Series 12: 163–88, at 182.

[28] These copies are described in Appendix III, 1.0 and 3.0. It was supposed that the addition in the Latin part of the BL copy was made by the printer before the book circulated. See John Palsgrave (1540), *The Comedy of Acolastus. Translated from the Latin of Fullonius*, ed. P. L. Carver (1937), EETS, OS, 202, London, 183–84.

vellum, was intended to go together with the Lambeth Palace copy. In addition, a proof fragment of the English part exists that can reasonably be dated to about 1540, when the earliest extant copies of the Latin part were printed. From this evidence we may speculate that attempts were being made to publish the English part at or about the same time as the Latin part of this grammar. Moreover, internal evidence from the royal proclamation in the English part, which provides information about the order of teaching Latin, makes it clear that the two parts must have been available about the same time. The legal text encourages the schoolmasters "to teache and learne your scholars this englysshe introduction here ensuing, and the latyne grammer annexed to the same, and none other, which we haue caused for your ease". Finally, the elementary stage of learning Latin, denominated as *rudimenta Anglicae*, is explicitly referred to in the *Institutio*, in which it is said that the pupils are supposed already to have mastered that stage and therefore should know the rules of the conjugation of the verb.[29]

External evidence from two literary works, both published by Berthelet, provides some information about the date of the appearance of the English part and helps to draw conclusions as to when the grammars in English as well as in Latin were published. John Palsgrave (d. 1554), a scholar of languages and the French instructor to Princess Mary, the sister of Henry VIII, later Queen of France, and who, in 1525, became tutor to Henry VIII's illegitimate son Henry Fitzroy, Duke of Richmond, gives some further information about this matter in his translation of *Acolastus*.[30] In his position Palsgrave was familiar with school conditions and the plan to introduce a uniform grammar. From the introductory epistle to his translation of William Fullonius's Latin original of *The Comedy of Acolastus*, first printed in 1529, it becomes clear that Palsgrave's translation was submitted to Thomas Cromwell, Lord Chancellor of England, who suggested that it should be dedicated to the king. From this it follows that the translation must have been finished some time before 10 June 1540, the date of Cromwell's arrest. It was probably the recent appearance of the uniform grammar that caused Palsgrave to try to establish a uniform method of translation into English.[31] His translation, published as a bilingual edition, aimed to give pupils practice in the rules of grammar, develop

---

[29] See Chapter 7, *Introduction, Proclamation*, 157, lines 14–17. For the rudiments in English see *Institutio*, H4ʳ. On the question of an elementary part in English being printed around 1540 cf. Vincent Joseph Flynn (1943), 'The Grammatical Writings of William Lily, ?1468–?1523', *The Papers of the Bibliographical Society of America* 37, at 106–108. It may be that a 1540 English part printed on vellum did not appear, for whatever reason. Had there been a 1540 edition it seems unlikely that it would have been necessary to falsify the date on the Latin part.

[30] On Palsgrave see *ODNB*, vol. 42: 554–56.

[31] Palsgrave (1540), *The Comedy of Acolastus*, ed. P. L. Carver (1937), Introduction, lv; also Baldwin (1944), vol. 1: 182–83.

primarily their Latin speech and also their English, and aid the teachers. Consequently the official grammar to which he refers must already have been in existence before that date. At the beginning of his address to the King, Palsgrave says:

It is clerely perceyued, by your most prudent wysedom, how great a damage it hathe heretofore bene, and yet is, vnto the tender wyttes of this your noble realme, to be hyndered and confounded with so many dyuers and sondry sortes of preceptes grammatical: you haue for the redresse thereof, wylled one self and vniforme maner of teachynge of all those Grammaticalle ensygnements, to be vsed through out all your hyghnes domynions, and commytted the dysposyng of that matter vnto suche syngular personages, both of exact iudgement, and therto of excellent lyterature.[32]

Palsgrave's contemporary, Sir Thomas Elyot (1490?–1546), diplomat, clerk of the king's council, and scholar, was also aware of the introduction of the authorized grammar.[33] From the prefatory statements of the 1541 edition of *The Castel of Helth*, an accessible handbook in English suggesting medicines and treatments for a variety of ailments that was very popular and was subsequently often reprinted, it becomes clear that the authorized grammar was available before this edition of Elyot's work was published. In his new preface to this revised edition he defends himself against detractors who claimed that a knight who was not a physician had no business writing a book on medicine. He comments on Henry VIII's recent act by which this grammar was made the official and exclusive Latin grammar of England and also mentions the role it played in the reform of teaching Latin by saying that

His highnes [King Henry VIII] hath not dysdained to be the chief authour and settar fourthe of an Introduction in to grammer, for the childerne of his louing subiectes, wherby, hauing good maisters, they shall moste easely and in shorte tyme appre-hend the vnderstanding and fourme of speaking of true and eloquent latyne. O royall harte, full of very nobility. O noble brest, settynge fourthe vertuouse doc-tryne, and laudable study.[34]

This evidently refers to the *Introduction*, of which an earlier edition must have been available which preceded the publication of the 1541 edition of Elyot's medical treatise.[35] From the textual evidence, from contemporary sources, and also from the order of teaching Latin grammar, it seems clear

---

[32] Palsgrave (1540), 3, lines 17–26.

[33] On Elyot see *ODNB*, vol. 18: 382–84.

[34] Thomas Elyot (1541), *The Castel Of Helth Corrected And in some places augmented*, London. 4° (BL, C.112. b.23, A3ʳ); see also a second copy of the same edition in quarto in the Bodl. Lib., Tanner 272(1). A copy of another edition of this work issued in octavo format and published in the same year also contains this reference (BL, G.10333, A3ʳ). This passage is also incor-porated in later reprints of this book, e.g. in a copy of 1547 (BL, C.124.aaa.13, A3ᵛ). However, it is not contained in the preface to copies of the two editions of 1539 that I consulted (London, Lambeth Palace Library, 1539.3, and BL, C.54.a.18).

[35] For this assumption see also Thomas Elyot (1531), *The Boke Named the Gouernour*, ed. Henry Herbert Stephen Croft (1880), 2 vols. London, vol. 1, Introduction, cxii–cxiii.

that an English part for beginners must have been in existence at least in parallel with the Latin part used as a teaching text for more advanced pupils.

In the same way as the beginning of its publishing history, the composition and authorship of the authorized grammar cannot easily be determined. Apart from the use of the name 'Edouardus' which surely refers to the young prince, no other name is to be found in the *Introduction* that may give any hint to a compiler.[36] According to the royal proclamation in the English part, this grammar represents a collective effort, in other words, the work of a committee that was responsible for the actual formulation of the text. Most probably it included experienced grammar school as well as university teachers of Latin. It says:

For his maiestie consideryng the great encombrance and confusion of the yong and tender wittes, by reason of the diuersity of grammer rules and teachinges [. . .] hath appoynted certein lerned men mete for suche a purpose, to compile one bryef, plaine, and vniforme grammer, [. . .].[37]

The account of Sir Thomas Elyot of Henry VIII "to be the chief authour and settar fourthe of an Introduction in to grammer",[38] can probably be explained as diplomatic deference to the sovereign and by the fact that the book was published by the king's authority as indicated in the royal proclamation, and that it may perhaps have undergone some examination by him. Almost exactly one century after the authorized grammar had been introduced, Thomas Hayne (1581/2–1645), a former schoolmaster of Merchant Taylors' School and at Christ's Hospital, gives an account of the history of the Latin grammar and its teaching since King Henry VIII. In the address "To the judicious Reader" in his *Grammatices Latinæ compendium*, printed in 1640, he says that he had heard that Richard Cox had been on the committee that compiled the authorized grammar.[39] Cox (*c.*1500–1581), later Bishop of Ely, who was headmaster of Eton College from 1528–1534, was put in charge of the education of Prince Edward from 1543 onwards when the young prince began his studies.[40] Cox was most probably responsible for the additions and corrections by hand in the

---

[36] See Chapter 7, *Introduction, Parts of Speech*, 161, line 22; also Chapter 8, Commentary: *Parts of Speech*, 226, note to line 21.

[37] Chapter 7, *Introduction, To the Reder*, 158, lines 28–34.

[38] See above Elyot (1541) *The Castel of Helth* (BL, C.112.b.23, A3ᵛ). Cf. also the information by John Ward in his Memoranda (BL, MS Add. 6218, fols. 12ʳ–13ᵛ).

[39] Thomas Hayne (1640), *Grammatices Latinæ compendium, Anno 1637*, London (Bodl. Lib., Wood.42.[2], A4ᵛ–A5ʳ). On Hayne see *ODNB*, vol. 26: 58–59; on his grammar see Baldwin (1944), vol. 2: 694, and 700–701; also Watson, 253–55.

[40] On Richard Cox see *ODNB*, vol. 13: 861–65; E. S. Leedham-Green (1992), 'Bishop Richard Cox', in *Private Libraries in Renaissance England*, Vol. I, PLRE 1–4, Marlborough, at 3–4; *VCH, Hampshire and the Isle of Wight*, Vol. 15,2: 38–39; also Palsgrave (1540), Introduction, lv–lvi, and 184. On Prince Edward's education and the role Cox played in it see M. L. Clarke (1978), 'The Education of a Prince in the Sixteenth Century: Edward VI and James VI and I', *History of Education* 7,1: 7–19, at 8–13; also Baldwin (1944), vol. 1: 200–218, and 320.

Introduction, which could have been inserted while he was teaching Latin rules to Edward.[41]

Some additional information about another individual who was most probably involved in the compilation of 'Lily's Grammar' can be gained from a grammar of Greek. It is entitled *Progymnasmata Graecae Grammatices* and was written by David Talley (or Tolley, Tavelegus, Taualegus, Taulaeus, and some other forms) (*c*.1506–1558), a classical scholar and a master of arts of St Mary's Hall, Oxford, who also practised medicine.[42] This grammar, printed in 1547 on vellum and illuminated, was written for the use of Prince Edward and is dedicated to him. It also bears Edward's autograph on the verso of the title-page. In the dedication dated 1546 the following reference to the authorized grammar is given:

Eight years have passed, most illustrious Prince, since your most kind father received from me the rudiments of Greek and Latin under the title of your most famous name. Soon a few men, learned in every way, were entrusted with the task of preparing the complete grammar of the Latin language to be read throughout the whole of England and its dominions. Need I say more? Latin teaching materials have recently been edited under the name of your most excellent father for the highest good of the State.[43]

---

[41] The identification of the handwriting as being by Cox helps to establish a firm link between this volume and Prince Edward, as has long been suggested. See Chapter 8, Commentary: *Construction*, 247, note to line 131.

[42] Information on Talley and his works, and also comments on his relationship to the authorized grammar, are given in Katy Hooper (1994), 'David Tolley. Physician (M.A., B.M.): Probate Inventory. 1558', in *Private Libraries in Renaissance England*, Vol. 3, *PLRE* 67–86. Marlborough, 36–44; for his book-list see the *PLRE* database 68; Halkett and Laing L47; *BRUO*, 1501–1540, 570–71, and Appendix B, 740–42; J. P. Tuck (1951), 'The Latin Grammar attributed to William Lily', *Durham Research Review* 2, 33–39, at 34–35; Joseph Foster (1891–1892). *Alumni Oxonienses: The Members of the University of Oxford, 1500–1714*, London; repr. 1968, vol. 4: 1491; Thomas Tanner (1748), *Bibliotheca Britannico-Hibernica*, London, 704–705; Anthony à Wood (1813–1820). *Athenæ Oxonienses*, 4 vols. London, repr. 1967, vol. 1, col. 195, vol. 2 (in *Fasti Oxonienses*: The First Part), cols. 58, 77, and 87; Charles Dodd (pseud.) (1737–1742). *The Church History of England, from the Year 1500, to the Year 1688*, Brussels; repr. 1970, vol. 1: 367; John Pits (1619), *Relationum Historicarum de Rebus Anglicis*, Paris; repr. 1969, tomus 1, no. 980: 738–39; John Bale (1557–1559), *Scriptorum Illustrium Maioris Brytanniae Catalogus*, 2 vols. Basle, repr. 1971, vol. 1: 719, where he says under Talley's name: "Dicitur edidisse quoque Grammaticam regis, ex omnibus alijs."; and Bale (*c*.1549–1557). *Index Britanniae Scriptorum*, ed. Reginald Lane Poole and Mary Bateson (1902), repr. with a new Introduction by Caroline Brett and James P. Carley, Cambridge, 1990, 61, where the authorized grammar is listed under Talley's works. The entry reads: "Grammaticam regis ex multis."

[43] The Latin version reads: "Octauus iam agitur annus (illustriβime Princeps) quod rudimenta Græca pariter atque Latina, sub inclyti nominis tui præfatione, clementiβimus pater tuus à me suscepit. Mox uiris aliquot undiquaque doctis demandata cura fuit, ut integram Latinæ orationis Grammaticen [*sic*] per uniuersam Angliam, aliasque suæ ditionis partes audiendam, absoluerent. Quid plura? Latinæ institutiones ad utilitatem Reipublicæ non uulgarem, sub excellentiβimi patris tui nomine, nuper æditæ sunt." David Tavelegus (1547), *Progymnasmata Graecae Grammatices Authore Davido Tavelego Medico*, Antwerp: Joannes Loëus (BL, C.28.a.14, A2ᵛ). The Greek grammar is listed in Alston-Hill, 167, and in *BM STC (Netherlands)*, 196.

According to his own account it would seem that Talley had been commissioned around 1539 to prepare the rudiments of grammar of both
Greek and Latin for the future use of Prince Edward. The Latin grammar
mentioned here probably refers to the *Introduction*. But the present
evidence does not specify what Talley's share was, and also what role the
other members of the royal committee played in compiling the complete
grammar in two parts. There is also no further information provided here
about the members of this committee.[44]

3.3 Biographical background: Lily and the authorship of the Introduction

The most important single figure connected with this grammar is
undoubtedly William Lily. His name is, however, not explicitly referred to
in the grammatical texts of the *Introduction*. It is only given in the heading
of his *Carmen de moribus* on H4^v in the *Introduction*.[45] The grammar was not
referred to as 'Lily's Grammar' at the time it was compiled nor, as it
appears, in the first decades when it was in use. A biographical account
of Lily is worthwhile for what it can contribute to our knowledge of the
man whose name became synonymous with Latin grammar and of the
role he played at that time, facts that help to explain why the authorized
grammar became attributed to him. Lily, who is commonly known as its
author, had been dead for about eighteen years when it was introduced.
Though not all details about his life are known from contemporary
records of the late fifteenth and early sixteenth centuries and some
remain obscure, definite facts have emerged that shed light on the man,
his education, his work as a scholar and as a teacher of grammar, and
also on the estimation in which he was held. References to Lily by
contemporaries and scholars of the following century both comment on
the person and his work and also emphasize different aspects about him
in the course of time.[46]

---

[44] See T. A. Birrell (1987), *English Monarchs and Their Books: From Henry VII to Charles II*, Panizzi
Lectures 1986, London, 13. Cf. also the headnote to the group of entries of 'Lily's Grammar' in
*STC*², vol. 2: 62–63, where Talley is said to have revised and expanded the three main sections
of Colet's *Aeditio, i.e.* his accidence, Lily's *Rudimenta grammatices*, and Lily's *Carmen de moribus*,
which then became part of the *Introduction*; and Baldwin (1944), vol. 1: 220–21; vol. 2: 691–93.

[45] Lily's name is, however, mentioned in the discussion of the gender of the noun in the
text on accidence contained in the *Institutio*, C3^v and C4^r; also in the conjugation of the verb
on H4^r.

[46] A number of accounts of Lily's life and works are available. See, for example, Hedwig
Gwosdek (2009), 'Lily, William', in *Lexicon Grammaticorum*, vol. 2: 912–14; *ODNB*, vol. 33: 801–
803; Edward A. Malone and Michele Valery Ronnick (2004), 'Lily, William (c.1468-1522)', in
The Dictionary of British Classicists, Bristol, vol. 2: 579–81; Monique Verrac (2000), 'Colet, John,
[and] Lily, William', in *HEL*, vol. 2, no. 3601: 93–95; also Bernard Colombat (1998a), 'Erasme,
Didier, [and] Lily[e], William', in *HEL*, vol. 1, no. 1248: 86–88; A. H. Mead (1990), *A Miraculous*

The name 'Lily' was spelt in a great variety of ways, amongst others: Lillie, Lilly, Lilye, Lyllie, Lylly, Lyly, Lylye, the latinized Christian and surname Gulielmus Lilius is also frequently recorded. For his birth and also for his death no exact dates are known, though we have to deal with a difference of only a few months at either end of his life. He was born at Odiham in Hampshire about 1468. Almost nothing is known of his parents and his early life, except that he was the godson of William Grocyn (c.1446–1519), who was Reader in Divinity at Magdalen College, Oxford, between 1483 and 1488, and was remembered as such in Grocyn's will, proved 20 July 1522.[47] William Lily was admitted as a demy to Magdalen College, Oxford, by November 1486, at the age of seventeen.[48] He presumably studied Latin at Magdalen College School under its earliest known headmaster John Anwykyll.[49] However, no actual records at Magdalen College survive from the late fifteenth century to shed a definite light on Lily's degree. The original biographical reminiscence of Lily's eldest son, George (c.1512–1559), canon of St Paul's, implies that he took no degree at all at Oxford before going on a pilgrimage to Jerusalem.[50]

Draught of Fishes: A History of St Paul's School, London, 21–22; *Contemporaries of Erasmus*, vol. 2: 329–30; Michael F. J. McDonnell (1959), *The Annals of St Paul's School*, London, 58–64; *BRUO*, vol. 2: 1147; J. P. Tuck (1951), 'The Latin Grammar, attributed to William Lily', *The Durham Research Review*, Institute of Education, University of Durham 2: 33–39; *Lily Shorte Introduction*, iii–iv; Cyril M. Picciotto (1939), *St. Paul's School*, London, 6–7, and 14; Flynn (1939), 2–12; Mary Beth Stewart (1937–1938). 'William Lily's Contribution to Classical Study', *The Classical Journal* 33: 217–25, at 217–18; Michael F. J. McDonnell (1909), *A History of St Paul's School*, London, 69–87; J. H. Lupton (1909), *A Life of John Colet, D.D*, London 2nd edn., repr. 1961, 170–72; *DNB*, vol. 11: 1143–45; Robert Barlow Gardiner (ed.) (1884–1906), *The Admission Registers of St Paul's School, from 1748 to 1876; from 1876 to 1905*, vol. 1: 17; vol. 2: 3; and Joseph Foster (1891–1892), *Alumni Oxonienses*, London, repr. 1968, vol. 3: 915.

[47] The entries read: "Item to W. Lyly, M[aister] Grocyn's godson, for hys bequest . . . vs," and "Item sent to Loven by Mr. Lylly for Greeke bookes to gyve . . . xls.", in Montagu Burrows (1890), 'Linacre's Catalogue of Books Belonging to William Grocyn in 1520', in M. Burrows (ed.), *Collectanea*, 2nd ser. Oxford, part V, 325 and 327.

[48] See John Rouse Bloxam (1853–1885), *A Register of the Presidents, Fellows, Demies [. . .] and Other Members of Saint Mary Magdalen College in the University of Oxford*, Oxford, vol. 4 (1873) [= *The Demies*, vol. 1], 19–24. Lily's name is mentioned in two archive references of Magdalen College, Oxford. Ledger A, EL/1, fol. 96[v], is a list of names made on the eve of St James' Day (24 July) 1484, which includes Lily. In Bursary Book, vol. 1 (CP8/49) for the term beginning September 1485, Lily's name first appears in the 11th week (fol. 47[v]), and then appears regularly for the rest of the term, and he is mentioned regularly in the next term. In all cases, he just appears as a name, with no comment of any kind. I owe this information to Robin Darwall-Smith, archivist, Magdalen College, Oxford. A 'demy' is a term for a junior scholar, specifically at Magdalen College, Oxford. On their position in the Statutes of this College see Virginia Davis (1993), *William Waynflete. Bishop and Educationalist*, Woodbridge, 82–83.

[49] See Orme (1998), *Education in Early Tudor England. Magdalen College Oxford and Its School, 1480–1540*, Magdalen College Occasional Paper 4, Oxford, 55.

[50] On George Lily see *ODNB*, vol. 33: 799–800; Jonathan Woolfson (1998), *Padua and the Tudors: English Students in Italy, 1485–1603*, Toronto, Buffalo, 251–52, and *passim*; *BRUO*,

Afterwards Lily spent some considerable time on Rhodes where he studied the rudiments of Latin and Greek, before travelling to Rome. He was there by November 1490 when he attended the lectures of Joannes Sulpitius Verulanus and Julius Pomponius Laetus who were leading classical scholars at that time. Here he met Thomas Linacre (c.1460–1524), the humanist scholar and physician who later became royal physician to Henry VIII, and other English humanists.[51] He may have returned to England in 1492 and was presumably the "William Lilye Scholarem" who was presented to the rectory of Holcot, Northamptonshire, on 24 May 1492. He was incumbent there until 6 November 1495 when he resigned the benefice.[52] He married at an unknown date. His wife, Agnes, died before him, having borne him fifteen children, among whom were his sons George and Peter and his daughter Dionysia.[53] Afterwards Lily was probably engaged in teaching in London where he made the acquaintance of John Colet (1467?–1519) and Thomas More (1478–1535). With the latter he joined in mutual rivalry over the translation of Greek epigrams into Latin elegiacs.

In 1512, John Colet, Dean of St Paul's, London, appointed Lily as the first High Master of St Paul's School, which he had refounded from c.1508–1512 as a non-ecclesiastical establishment.[54] However, it was not until 18 June

1501–1540, 357. See George's account of his father's life, contributed to the *Descriptio Britanniae* (1548) of Paolo Giovio (Paul Jovius), bishop of Nocera, 47ʳ–48ʳ, where he says: "As a boy he was nobly inspired by desire to travel; for piety he travelled to Jerusalem" (47ʳ). Emden's statement (*BRUO*, vol. 2: 1147) is based on the words of Lily's son. But cf. Wood (1813–1820), vol. 1, cols. 32–38, who is quoted by Bloxam, suggests that Lily took one degree in arts at least before making his pilgrimage.

[51] See George B. Parks (1954), *The English Traveler to Italy*, Rome, Vol. 1: 459, 463–66; also Flynn (1938–1939), 'Englishmen in Rome During the Renaissance', *Modern Philology* 36: 121–38, at 136–37. Lily's name appears in the register of the English Hospice in Rome under 4 November 1490.

[52] See "Remains of William Lilye Master of Pauls School who died 5. Cal. March. 1522.3." (BL, Lansdowne MS 979, fol. 32ʳ); John Bridges (1791), *The History and Antiquities of Northamptonshire*, Oxford, vol. 2: 146; also *The Register of John Morton, Archbishop of Canterbury, 1486–1500*, ed. C. Harper-Bill (1991), Woodbridge, vol. 2, no. 186: 45. The presentation was made by John Kendall (d. 1501), one of the camerarii in office in the English Hospice in Rome during Lily's stay and prior Sancti Joannis de Jerusalem extra muros Londonij in Smythfelde, a fraternity with which Lily had become acquainted on Rhodes. See Bloxam (1873), vol. 4: 22–23; and Flynn (1938–1939), 137. On the change in the career of Lily in the light of the social background see Denys Hay (1975), 'England and the Humanities in the Fifteenth Century', in H. A. Oberman and Thomas Brady (eds.), *Itinerarium Italicum*, Leiden, 336–39.

[53] The epitaph on Agnes Lily by her husband, in Latin elegiacs, records the fact that she died on 11 August at the age of thirty-seven, but does not specify the year; see BL, MS Harley 540, fol. 58ᵛ. On Lily's family cf. Edward L. Hirsh (1935), *The Life and Works of George Lily*, Ph.D. Dissertation. New Haven, Conn., xi–xii.

[54] Robert Barlow Gardiner (ed.) (1884–1906), *The Admission Registers of St Paul's School, from 1748 to 1876*, London, vol. 1: 7–8 and 17; vol. 2: 3.

1518 that Colet delivered his Statutes for St Paul's School to Lily.[55] In the conflict which has become known as the 'Grammarians' War' from 1519–1521, Lily took the part of the Vice-Provost of Eton College, the schoolmaster and grammarian William Horman (*c*.1458–1535), in favour of the imitation of good examples as the road to good Latin, against Robert Whittington (*c*.1480–1553?) and John Skelton (*c*.1460–1529), who favoured the inculcation of grammatical rules. Lily's *Antibossicon*, a series of Latin verse letters, is a product of this controversy. However, there was no real substance to the 'war', except the primary concern of the participants for reputation and an opportunity to display their erudition.[56]

Lily may have travelled to Louvain in 1520 to bring back Greek books as gifts in memory of Grocyn. Lily's own library included Pliny's *Historia naturalis*, printed at Brescia by Angelus and Jacobus Britannicus on 20 April 1496.[57] John Rightwise (or Ritwyse) (d. 1532?) was Surmaster (*i.e.* Second Master) under Lily at St Paul's School from 1517 onwards. Lily held the post of the first High Master until 10 December 1522, when the Mercers' Company appointed Rightwise as his successor, and he held this position until 1532.[58] Some sources claim that Lily must have died shortly before the date when Rightwise was appointed; others say that he was dead before 9 March 1523. He probably died from the bubonic plague and

---

[55] The title reads: "Statuta paulinæ scholæ. Hunc Libellum ego Joannes Colet tradidi in manibus Magistrj Lilij xviij° die Junij anno xi m cccccxviij ut eum in scola seruet et obseruet." See BL, MS Add. 6274, fol. 1ʳ. On this MS see Trapp-Schulte Herbrüggen 14. Other copies of the statutes are preserved at Mercers' Hall, London. The earliest of them shows considerable variations in text from BL, MS Add. 6274. Reprints of this Mercers' Hall MS are found in Samuel Knight (1724), *The Life of Dr. John Colet, Dean of S. Paul's*, London, Appendix, no. 5: 356–69; Robert Barlow Gardiner (ed.) (1884), *The Admission Registers of St Paul's School*, vol. 1, Appendix B.-I., 375–87; and Lupton (1909), 271–84. On the manuscripts and the statutes themselves see J. B. Trapp (1991), *Erasmus, Colet and More*, London, 109–113. A further copy of the statutes is found in BL, MS Lansdowne 949, fols. 1ᵛ–10ʳ. Cf. also Herendeen (1988), 169–79, 186–88.

[56] See Jane Griffiths (2002), 'The Grammarian as "Poeta" and "Vates": Self-Presentation in the *Antibossicon*', in T. van Houdt *et al.* (eds.), *Self-Presentation and Social Identification. The Rhetoric and Pragmatics of Letter Writing in Early Modern Times*, Leuven, 317–35; also David R. Carlson (1992), 'The "Grammarians' War" 1519–1521, Humanist Careerism in Early Tudor England, and Printing', *Medievalia et Humanistica*, New Ser., 18: 157–81; cf. the interpretation of didactic concepts suggested by Gabriela Schmidt (2007), '"The variety of teaching is divers": Pluralisierung der Autoritäten und die versuchte Etablierung von "Uniformität" im englischen Lateinunterricht unter Heinrich VIII.' *,Mitteilungen des Sonderforschungsbereichs 573, Pluralisierung und Autorität der Frühen Neuzeit'* 2007/2, 43–53, at 43–45; John Stanbridge (1519), *The Vulgaria of John Stanbridge and the Vulgaria of Robert Whittinton* (1520), ed. Beatrice White (1971 repr.), Introduction, xxiii–xxxii.

[57] This volume is entitled *C. Plynius Secundus De Naturali Hystoria diligentissime Castigatus*, now BL, IC. 31152, imperfect, wanting the last two leaves (one blank) (Hain 13098; Hain-Copinger 13098; *BMC* VII 977; Goff P-797; *IISTC* ip00797000). On the top of the title-page the following note is written: "Georgij Lilij liber, ex Guil. Lilij patris sui Bibliotheca relictus."

[58] Gardiner (1884). vol. 1: 17; also McDonnell (1959), 64–68.

was buried in the Pardon Churchyard, adjoining the cathedral of St Paul's. Two copies of his will are available that present difficulties about the exact date of his death. His first will was made on 2 September 1522 and proved on 9 March 1523. It mentions an unspecified number of children dead, besides four sons and two daughters living.[59] His daughter Dionysia was married to John Rightwise. The writer and playwright John Lyly (or Lily) (1554–1606) was a grandson of William Lily, as was probably the Church of England clergyman Peter Lily (1562/63–1615). George Lily caused the brass plate from his parents' tomb, with the following inscription, to be affixed to the wall of St Paul's Cathedral near the north door.

Sacred to the Memory of William Lily, the first master of Paul's School, and of Agnes, his wife, both buried together, in the consecrated ground of this church-yard that is now destroyed. George Lily, one of the canons of this church, piously consulting the memory of his parents, has placed his memorial preserved by friends, refixed it here. William Lily died the 5 March 1522 [old style] in his 54th year.[60]

Lily was on terms of friendship and esteem with learned men of his age who had influence. The following sources give some idea of his reputation amongst his friends and contemporaries and some that refer to him within a century of his death. Sir Thomas More counted him amongst his closest friends at least from the time Lily returned to England. In a letter of 23 October, probably written in 1504 to John Colet, More refers presumably to their common pursuits, of which their joint translation of Greek epigrams was an example, when he calls Lily "the dearest partner of my endeavours".[61] Lily and More made rival versions in Latin elegiacs of

[59] See TNA, PROB/11/21, fol. 4, pp. 24^v–25^r, and fol. 8, pp. 61^v–62^r, for the two copies of Lily's will. The second copy that was proved on 21 May 1523 is substantially and almost literally the same as the first, but adds the attestation of witnesses, and has a codicil. For an interpretation of the two copies see Flynn (1939), 6–9, who also gives a transcription of the first copy. This copy and excerpts of the second copy are transcribed by Albert Feuillerat (1910), *John Lyly*, Cambridge, 505–506.

[60] William Dugdale (1818), *The History of Saint Paul's Cathedral in London*, 3rd edn. London, 41. (The English translation is by Dugdale. The inscription in Latin reads: "Gulielmo Lilio Paulinæ Scholæ olim præceptori primario, et Agnetæ conjugi, in sacratissimo hujus Templi Cœmeterio, hinc à tergo nunc destructo, consepultis; Georgius Lilius hujus Ecclesiæ Canonicus, Parentum memoriæ piè consulens, Tabellam hanc ab amicis conservatam, hic reponendam curavit. Obiit ille G. L. Anno D. 1522. v. Calend. Martii: Vixit annos LIV.") This inscription (with textual differences) is also found in: Payne Fisher (1684), *The Tombs, Monuments, etc., Visible in S. Paul's Cathedral* [. . .] *Previous to its Destruction by Fire A.D. 1666*, London, repr. 1885, 104; Knight (1823), Appendix, no. 6: 371; and Bloxam (1873), vol. 4: 22. The memorial stone placed by his son was dated 25 February 1522 (old style) in the codicil appended to the second copy of Lily's will.

[61] See the end of More's letter in *The Correspondence of Sir Thomas More*, ed. Elizabeth Frances Rogers (1947), Princeton: "Interea cum Grocino, Linacro, et Lilio nostro tempus transigam, altero (vt tu scis) solo (dum tu abes) vitae meae magistro; altero studiorum praeceptore; tertio charissimo rerum mearum socio." Ep. 3: 8–9.

eighteen short pieces of Greek text, perhaps in the 1490s. At least sixteen were epigrams that were done from the Greek of the *Planudean Anthology*. The Greek text together with the two sets of translations was first printed, with the title *Progymnasmata Thomae Mori et Guilielmi Lilii sodalium*, at Basle in March 1518 with More's other epigrams and his *Utopia*.[62]

In London Lily gained teaching experience prior to his appointment at "the newe schole of Poules" and built up the reputation that made him seem suitable for the post of the first High Master.[63] The qualifications, respecting good health, good character, learning, and personal status required by the man who was selected by Colet are laid down in the first chapter of his statutes for his school:

Of the mercerye a man hole in bodye honeste and vertuouse and lernyde in the good and clene latten literature and also in greke, yf suyche maye be goten. A weddide manne a syngle or a preste that hathe no benefyce with cure nether servyce that maye lett his due bysynes in the scoole.[64]

Lily is already addressed as "qui primus es huius nouæ Pauli scholæ praeceptor"[65] in Colet's dedicatory letter to him, although the building was not complete until 1512 and he seems not to have been formally appointed until then. The High Master received an exceptionally generous salary of 13s. 4d. a week, which was more than £34 annually. It was more than three times the standard £10 thought sufficient in most endowed schools at that time; even his colleague the surmaster, *i.e.* the second master, received £17.[66]

For the school Lily compiled the *Rudimenta grammatices*, an elementary Latin syntax in English, often printed with Colet's *Aeditio*. His *Libellus de constructione Octo partium orationis*, a more advanced syntax in Latin, also written for the school, was revised by Erasmus at Colet's request, so that neither man felt he could own it and it was first published as an anonymous work by Richard Pynson in 1513. Erasmus tells the story in a preliminary letter added to the revised edition entitled *Absolutissimus de octo orationis partium constructione libellus*, praising Lily as a scholar and teacher, "a man uncommonly skilful in both kinds of literature [*i.e.*

[62] On More's and Lily's Latin verse translations see *The Complete Works of St. Thomas More*, Vol. 3, part II: *Latin Poems*, in C. H. Miller *et al.* (eds.) (1984), New Haven, Introduction, 12–19; the edition of the *Progymnasmata*, 78–95, and commentary, 321–26; and J. B. Trapp (1991), 39–40; also Appendix IV, 3.

[63] See Colet, *Aeditio* (1527), A5ᵛ.

[64] BL, MS Add. 6274, fol. 2ᵛ. The "mercerye" is the Company of Mercers who were the governors of St Paul's School and by whom the High Master of St Paul's School was selected.

[65] Letter by "*John Colet. suo Lilio, Salutem*", dated "*Calen. Augu. An. M. CCCCC. IX.*", in Colet, *Aeditio* (1527), A5ʳ.

[66] See Orme (2006), 176; also Mead (1990), 30.

Latin and Greek] and an artist in the well bringing up of youth".[67] His pupils included Thomas Lupset (c.1495–1530), a Greek and Latin scholar, John Clement (d. 1572), appointed court physician, and John Leland (1503?–1552), the 'King's antiquary' and a personal adherent of Henry VIII.

Richard Pace (c.1483–1536), secretary and ambassador of Henry VIII, also John Colet's successor as Dean of St Paul's, praised Lily in the dedicatory letter to Colet in his book *De Fructu Qui Ex Doctrina Percipitur* (1517) by saying:

You have chosen a virtuous and at the same time a skilful man to teach the boys and young men. [. . .] For they have a teacher whose life and character are impeccable. Besides that, his learning is so great that he has driven out almost all the barbarism our boys once spent their youth on, working long to learn nothing, and as a result he seems to have introduced into our Britain a more polished use of Latin, in fact, the Roman tongue itself.[68]

At the close of his prefatory epistle to Willibald Pirckheimer (1470–1530) that prefaced the first edition of Thomas More's epigrams, printed in 1518, the German classical scholar Beatus Rhenanus (1485–1547) provides more details of Lily's learning, his experience abroad, and his then present position:

William Lily, More's companion with whom he contended in the translation from the Greek of the epigrams included in this volume under the title *Progymnasmata*, is an Englishman, learned in every way, intimately familiar not only with the Greek authors, but also with the customs native to that people, in that he spent some years on the island of Rhodes. He now conducts with great success a grammar school founded by Colet in London.[69]

---

[67] See the copy printed by John Froben at Basle, August 1515 (Bodl. Lib., 4° E.6(4) Art.Seld., a2ʳ). The passage reads: "Gulielmus Lilius vir vtriusque literaturæ haud vulgariter peritus et mirus recte instituendæ pubis artifex." The text is also available in *CWE*, vol. 3, Ep. 341: 145–47. Cf. also Appendix IV, 1, footnote 1.

[68] See "Richard Pace to John Colet, the Most Learned of Theologians and the Best of Men: Greetings" in Richard Pace (1517), *De Fructu Qui Ex Doctrina Percipitur (The Benefit of a Liberal Education)*, ed. and trans. Frank Manley and Richard S. Sylvester (1967), New York, 21. The Latin text reads: "Curasti, ut honestissimus simul et peritissimus uir, pueros, adolescentesque erudiat, [. . .] Habent enim praeceptorem, cuius uita, moresque sunt probatissimi. Tanta praeterea eruditio, ut extrusa pene omni barbarie (in qua nostri olim adolescentes solebant fere aetatem consumere, et longissimo tempore, ut nihil boni discerent, laborare), politiorem latinitatem, atque ipsam Romanam linguam, in Britanniam nostram introduxisse uideatur." (p. 20).

[69] For the Latin text see Thomas More (1518), *Utopia, Epigrammata, etc.* Basle (BL, G. 2398.(1), x1ᵛ–x3ᵛ (= pp. 166–70)). An edition and translation of this letter entitled "Beatus Rhenanus Greets Willibald Pirckheimer, Councillor to the Emperor Maximilian and Member of the Nuremberg Senate" is given in *The Complete Works of St. Thomas More* (1984), vol. 3, Part II: *Latin Poems*, 72–77, at 77. The Latin original of this passage on p. 76 reads: "Guil. Lilius, MORI sodalis, cum quo uertendis Graecis epigrammatibus iam olim collusit, quae Progymnasmatum titulo sunt inscripta, Britannus est, uir omnifariam doctus, non modo Graecos autores, sed et eius nationis mores uernaculos domestice notos habens, ut qui in insula Rhodo fuerit aliquot annos commoratus. Is nunc ludum literarium, quem Londini Coletus instituit, magna cum laude exercet."

In the first printed edition of 1534 of his *Anglica Historia* that was commissioned by Henry VII and dedicated to his son Henry VIII, Polydore Vergil (1470–1555), a friend of Lily's who came to England from Italy in 1502 as a deputy papal collector, refers to the first High Master of St Paul's School as follows:

[John Colet] built a magnificent school, and appointed two teachers—William Lily as Headmaster, and John Rightwise to teach the beginners—because they were men of letters, noted for their virtue and diligence. In the words of Horace, Lily was "a man of upright life and free of guilt".[70] Having spent some years in Italy assiduously deepening his learning, he returned home, and, preeminent among his countrymen, taught Classics.[71]

Thomas Stapleton (1535–1598), a Catholic theologian and professor of Scripture at Louvain, refers to the friendship between Lily and More. This source informs us that Lily, like More, at one period of his life contemplated entering the priesthood: "He [More] debated with himself and his friend Lily the question of becoming a priest."[72] Stapleton's comments of 1588 are of particular interest in that they illustrate the attribution of the grammar to William Lily and represent an early testimony of many subsequent accounts of Lily's reputation for the future. It reads: "William Lily, the companion of More's youth, composed a grammar so well arranged and reliable that all English boys have used it from that time until now."[73]

One of the most famous pupils of St Paul's School, William Camden (1551–1623), antiquary and headmaster of Westminster School, who is also known as the author of the popular Greek grammar *Institutio Græcæ Grammatices Compendiaria* (1597), refers to Lily's deep learning when he

---

[70] Horace. *Odes and Epodes*, I.22.1 (*LCL*, vol. 33).

[71] Polydore Vergil (1534), *Polydori Vergilii Vrbinatis Anglicae Historiae Libri XXVI*. Basle, 610, lines 23–33. See *The Anglica Historia of Polydore Vergil A.D. 1485–1537*, ed. with a trans. by Denys Hay (1950), London, 147. The Latin text reads: "Ioannes [Coletus] [. . .] posuit [. . .] magnificam scholam, dedit'que præceptores duos, alterum principem Gulielmum Lilium, alterum Ioannem Ryghtuysum, qui rudiores informaret pueros, quod in eis erat literatura, mores boni, diligentia summa: nam Lilius uir, quemadmodum dicit Horatius, integer uitæ sceleris-'que purus, postquam in Italia aliquot per annos, perfectis literis operam dederat, domum reuersus, Anglorum primus apud suos, eas docuit." This edition, based on the manuscript version of 1512–1513, is the section covering the reigns of Henry VII and Henry VIII. It includes the additions of the first three printed editions. Only the first printed edition of 1534 that shows substantial textual changes to the manuscript version contains the passage on Lily.

[72] Thomas Stapleton (1588), "Vita et Illustre Martyrium Thomæ Mori, Angliæ Quondam Supremi Cancellarii", in Stapleton's *Tres Thomae*, Douai, 18: "Meditabatur adolescens sacerdotium cum suo Lilio." See *The Life and Illustrious Martyrdom of Sir Thomas More by Thomas Stapleton*, ed. E. E. Reynolds (1966), trans. Philip E. Hallett, London, 8.

[73] Stapleton (1588), 24. The Latin text reads: "Gulielmus Lilius adolescentis Mori socius, Grammaticam egregiè methodicam et absolutissimam (quo tota iuuentus Anglicana ex eo tempore semper est vsa) conscripsit." Translation in Reynolds (1966), 13.

mentions in his *Britannia* (English edition of 1610) an inscription too difficult even for him to read. He says:

I have heard that in the time of King Henrie the Eight, there was found neere this place [*i.e.* Stonehenge] a table of mettall, as it had been tinne and lead commixt, inscribed with many letters, but in so strange a Character, that neither Sir Thomas Eliot, nor master Lilye Schoole-maister of Paules, could read it, and therefore neglected it.[74]

The records illustrate Lily's fame and high reputation amongst his friends and contemporaries and provide the picture of an excellent scholar and an outstanding teacher, though to modern minds the references appear rather vague and economical in detail and have the almost formulaic quality of eulogies. It is, nevertheless, obvious that Lily was held in high esteem by his contemporaries for his scholarly attainments. At the same time his successful teaching in St Paul's School was known to and appreciated by his friends and pupils and was the reason why, in turn, St Paul's School itself gained a high rank amongst the schools of the time. His Latin grammars written in English and in Latin as well as his *Carmen de moribus* were used in those schools in England which took their standard from St Paul's School, and taught according to Cardinal Wolsey's *Methodus*, even after the Cardinal's fall. Later biographical accounts of Lily have added only little detail. His lasting fame up to the present period, however, rests upon the authorized grammar connected with his name, a school textbook that gets no precise reference in the contemporary sources gathered here. It became attributed to Lily only gradually. The connection can already be found in records from the end of the sixteenth century onwards and rests on his pedagogic and scholarly qualities, his career and position as the first High Master of St Paul's School, and the reputation his school enjoyed, as well as on the grammatical treatises and verses known to be written by him.[75] In the course of time, Lily's name lent authority to the authorized grammar and came to signify a genre of textbooks: a 'Lily's Grammar' was the standard school Latin grammar.[76]

---

[74] William Camden (1610). *Britannia. Britain, or a Chorographicall Description of the Most Flourishing Kingdomes, England, Scotland, and Ireland*, London, 254.

[75] For bibliographical details of copies of Lily's works see Appendix IV.

[76] No authentic portrait of Lily survives. Those of the nineteenth century indicate the importance of his grammar even at that time. Plate 2, a small engraving, is commonly taken to be a portrait of Lily. It represents him resting his right hand on a closed book, held upright, on the cover of which is a lily. Below is "*Vera G. L. effigies, ætatis suæ 52. 1520*". In the right upper corner one can see a coat of arms, a chevron between three lilies. Plate 3 shows the full-length figure in stained glass designed by Burlison and Grylls Company, which was placed in 1884 in the Hall of Christ Church, Oxford.

Plate 2. Engraved portrait of William Lily. Anonymous. Modern impression. (The British Museum, Portraits Section, Class 7, Period I. Register No. 1850–6–12–119.)

Plate 3. Portrait of William Lily in a panel of the south window of the Hall of Christ Church, Oxford. (XIX century.)

3.4 *The* Introduction *and its sources*

The *Introduction* represents what is essentially a new version of an elementary textbook for the teaching of a complete course for beginners of Latin and illustrates the state of grammatical knowledge for this level at that time. However, the whole volume, as well as each of its individual texts, also reflects the current pedagogical conception and purpose of the grammar. Like its predecessors in early print and manuscripts that circulated on a more local level or exerted influence due to the prestige and influence of the schools in which they were used, the grammatical texts contained in the authorized grammar are based on the subject matter of earlier Latin grammars in English, but also include material from grammatical texts written wholly in Latin. Many rules that had become well established in the early printed grammars and in the grammatical manuscripts found their way into the grammatical texts of the *Introduction* where they were preserved and perpetuated. Which particular passages, rules, and examples were selected for this grammar depended on pedagogical purposes, the level of the pupils, the aim of the course, and perhaps to some degree on the preference of the compilers, principles that were also applied in the selection of sentences for translation. The new compilation surpassed its predecessors only due to the fact that it was proclaimed by Henry VIII as the authorized textbook to be used in all schools in the country and hence dominated the teaching of Latin. At the same time the explanations in English that it contained gained authority in an age when the vernacular was not part of recognized grammar school instruction. Due to its privilege, the grammar as a whole and the rules in both languages gained support and reputation and became a set of prescribed regulations. The new versions for the teaching of the parts of speech, the translation exercises, and the rules on construction that were made compulsory, were intended to bring an end to the then current variety of grammatical texts and diversity of rules for Latin as well as their explanations in the vernacular. Explanations of the rules given orally in the classroom could, no doubt, vary and the apparent need to add comments and explanations of the rules of the texts is illustrated by contemporary manuscript insertions in the 1542 *Introduction*. Further corrections and improvements also found their way into later printed editions.

The royal committee must have started to compile the new texts in similar ways that schoolmasters had previously made use of available material, together with their own knowledge and teaching experience, and taking into account the pedagogical objectives. The texts on the parts of speech as well as on construction contained in the *Introduction* present the rules in a straightforward manner. The rule is put first and discussed at sufficient length to make the meaning clear, and afterwards usually one or more illustrative examples going back to classical authors, or of the compilers' own devising, are added, often with an English translation. The methods employed in putting together the new versions of the text on accidence, the translation exercises, and the text on construction can be observed and judged by comparison with well-known grammars of the early Tudor period that preceded the publication of the authorized grammar and that went out of use after it had been introduced. However, the relationship of the *Introduction* to those grammars written in English and Latin extant at the time of its compilation must be considered tentative and forever remain so, because a comparison cannot be made with all the grammar textbooks then in use, many of which no longer survive. Moreover, one cannot be certain what material was borrowed from which source because a number of the extant treatises show marked similarities or even have identical passages, and we cannot know which rules the compilers took from their memories and modified according to their scheme. Nevertheless, a few examples of parallel passages in well-known grammars of the period direct the attention to the interrelationship of the material as well as to the linguistic and pedagogical interests of the compilers and deserve to be pointed out, although no direct reference can be made to any of the preceding treatises.

It has commonly been said that the English part as a whole represents John Colet's *Aeditio*, a little Latin accidence in English that he compiled for his newly founded school of St Paul's about 1509.[77] Colet's treatise is, however, considered to be only one source, though a very important one, for the new text on accidence. A comparison shows that the compilers were very familiar with the *Aeditio* and it is apparent that they had access to a copy. The two texts share a large number of passages, and many rules from Colet's grammar were thought relevant and significant and hence were taken over, often with the same wording; for example, the order of the parts of speech, the beginning of the two treatises, the rules on the division of nouns into nouns substantive and nouns adjective, and so forth. It becomes obvious that Colet's grammar served the compilers as the basis on which they modelled their new text on the parts of speech. For example, the rules on the noun adjective in the two texts read as follows: "A nowne adiectiue is, that can not stand by hym selfe, but requireth to be ioyned with an other worde, as *Bonus* good, *Pulcher* fayre.

---

[77] No edition is available from Colet's lifetime. The earliest extant edition of the *Aeditio* is dated 1527, to which a letter of dedication to Lily dated 1509 is prefixed. See Colet, *Aeditio* (1527), with the letter printed on A5ʳ; also *Checklist* 20.1. A fuller discussion is given in Gwosdek (1999), 'The First English Grammars of St Paul's School, London, in Their Grammatical Tradition', *The Henry Sweet Society Bulletin* 33: 5–22; see also Flynn (1943), 86–90.

(*Introduction*, *Parts of Speech*, 161, lines 16–17). "A nowne adiectyue is/ that can not stande by hym selfe/ but loketh to be ioyned with another word as *Bonus, Pulcher.*" (*Aeditio*, A6ᵛ).

Frequently, a tendency to shorten the rules can be observed in the text on the parts of speech of the authorized grammar, which not only represents a modification but a deliberate attempt at conciseness and clarification for pedagogic purposes. On the other hand, Colet's *Aeditio* reflects earlier oral practices of teaching elementary grammar that took the form of enumerations to impose an outer, extrinsic order on the property being discussed. Compare the presentation of the three persons of a pronoun in the two grammars: Colet's treatise gives the number of persons and continues to list them in a fixed order, leading to apparently tautologous exchanges. This arrangement reflects a long-standing convention in grammar writing. The same rule in the *Introduction* appears in a modified form where the list of persons was perhaps considered redundant. Compare the different methods of presenting the accident person of the pronoun as illustrated by the two texts:

A pronowne hath thre persones. The fyrst/ þe seconde/ the thyrde. The fyrst is. whan the speker sheweth his owne selfe/ as *Ego*, I. The plurell *Nos*, wee. The seconde persone is/ whan the speker speketh to an other/ as syngulerly/ *Tu*, thou/ plurally/ *Vos*, ye. And also of this persone is euery vocatiue case. The thyrde persone is/ whan the speker speketh of the thyrde thynge from them bothe. as syngulerly/ *Ille*, he. plurally/ *Illi*, they. And therfore al nownes and pronownes and partycyples be of the thyrde persone.

(Aeditio, B4ᵛ)

A pronowne hath thre persons. The fyrste speaketh of hym selffe, as *Ego*, I, *nos*, we. The seconde person is spoken to, as *Tu*, thou, *uos*, ye. And of this person is also euery vocatyue case. The thyrde persone is spoken of, as *Ille*, he, *illi*, they. And therfore all nownes, pronownes, and participles be of the thyrde person.

(Introduction, Parts of Speech, 169, lines 318–24)

Moreover, it can be shown that details were not only added or omitted in the definitions of the parts of speech and in the discussion of the accidents, but subject matter was also rearranged and new material was introduced from various sources. The text provides exhaustive coverage of Latin inflectional morphology with detailed and systematic information being given in response to the perceived needs of pupils.

The most striking difference between the accidence of the *Introduction* and the *Aeditio*, however, occurs in the verb section that is the most elaborate part in the two grammars. The *Introduction* presents the arrangement of the conjugation tables of the verb in a way that is already to be found in John Stanbridge's *Accidence*, a treatise in current use in grammar schools at the time when 'Lily's Grammar' was being compiled.

The text on the parts of speech in the *Introduction* presents the conjugation of the present indicative, for example, as follows:[78]

Indicatiue mode the present tens singular.

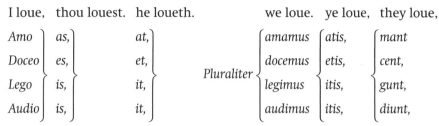

I loue,   thou louest.   he loueth.   we loue.   ye loue,   they loue,

Amo	*as,*	*at,*		*amamus*	*atis,*	*mant*
Doceo	*es,*	*et,*	*Pluraliter*	*docemus*	*etis,*	*cent,*
Lego	*is,*	*it,*		*legimus*	*itis,*	*gunt,*
Audio	*is,*	*it,*		*audimus*	*itis,*	*diunt,*

The preterimperfecte tense singular.

Amabam		I loued or dyd loue.
Docebam	*bas, bat. Pluraliter bamus, batis, bant*	taught.
Legebam		read.
Audiebam		heard.

Compare the paradigm of "The fyrst coniugacyon" illustrated by the verb *amo* in the "Mode indicatyue in tyme" in Colet's *Aeditio*, B6ᵛ–B7ʳ:

present	Singular	*Amo*	*amas*	*amat,*
	Plural	*amamus*	*amatis*	*amant,*
imperfect	Singular	*amabam*	*amabas*	*amabat,*
	Plural	*amabamus*	*amabatis*	*amabant,*
perfect	Singular	*amaui*	*amauisti*	*amauit,*
	Plural	*amauimus*	*amauistis*	*uerunt uel uere.*
pluperfect	Singular	*amaueram*	*amaueras*	*amauerat,*
	Plural	*amaueramus*	*amaueratis*	*amauerant*
future	Singular	*amabo*	*amabis*	*amabit,*
	Plural	*amabimus*	*amabitis*	*amabunt,*

The arrangement of the rules in the authorized grammar indicates a different method of teaching and learning the forms of the Latin verb classes. It starts with the verb in English and provides translations in the vernacular as it continues. The four sample verbs representing the four conjuga-

[78] See Chapter 7, *Introduction*, 171, lines 397–407. For a detailed comparison between the text on the parts of speech of the *Introduction* and Colet's *Aeditio* see Commentary: *Parts of Speech, passim*, also Appendix V for the definitions of the parts of speech. Editions of Stanbridge's *Accidence* are listed in *Checklist* 16.1–16.35. The last extant copy of the version of the *Accidence* printed before 1540 can be dated 1539 (see *Checklist* 16.34). Stanbridge's grammar deserves detailed study, particularly with regard to possible antecedents that may have incorporated the same arrangement of verb conjugation.

tions are discussed together in such a way that corresponding forms are set out vertically. In this way the pupil's attention is drawn to the personal endings of the different verbs, which, for example, he can compare in the same person and tense in the indicative mood. For the following tenses up to the future, only endings of the first person are provided in tabular form. The rest of the personal endings in the singular and plural which are identical for these verbs are only listed and English translations of the first person of the verbs are given. From the point of view of learning the different forms of the verbs, the text avoids setting out at length the conjugation forms of a single verb. Colet's *Aeditio*, on the other hand, shows a different method of approach to conjugation. Verbs are classified here by conjugation where paradigms of each form of the four sample verbs in the active and passive voice and the different moods are displayed separately with the three forms of the singular and the plural in the five tenses being set out, each on a separate line. English translations are not included.[79] The form of each of the four sample verbs is considered in turn so that identical forms of each of the four different verbs have to be pieced together.

The fact that grammatical terms or even passages were probably taken over from other grammars into the new compilation or sometimes applied inconsistently can be illustrated by the use of two different terms for one mood of the verb and probably also by the inconsistent arrangement of some grammatical rules. The rules on the formation of tenses illustrate the way different tenses can be formed in different moods from the first person perfect tense of the verb in the indicative mood according to specified substitution rules, a method which had been previously employed in the English grammatical manuscripts. The passage listing the tenses that can be formed from the preterperfect tense of the indicative mood includes "the Subiunctiue mode" as the last item to be formed in this way. The conjugations of the verbs, however, which are discussed before, are given in the "Coniunctyue mode" of the active and the passive voice.[80] However, this inconsistency of usage of terminology in the authorized grammar may reflect the fact that the distinction between the two terms had already been lost.

A second example of what may be considered an inconsistency is given in the discussion of the tenses of the participle. They are listed in the order of the present participle, the past participle, the future participle ending

---

[79] See Chapter 8, Commentary: *Parts of Speech*, 234, note to line 397.
[80] "Subiunctiue mode", in Chapter 7, *Introduction, Parts of Speech*, 184, line 892. For the discussion of the conjunctive mood of the active verb see the text on p. 173, line 486; of the substantive verb "*sum*" on p. 176, line 588, and also of the passive verb on p. 179, line 694. Cf. Linacre's Latin grammars in English, *Progymnasmata grammatices* and *Rudimenta grammatices*, which make consistent use of the term 'subiunctive' (*Checklist* 54.1 and 55.1).

in –*rus* and that ending in –*dus*. The following discussion, however, varies this order so that the present participle is followed by the future participle in –*rus*, which itself is followed by the past participle and then the future participle ending in –*dus*.[81] This arrangement probably reflects the source from which this passage was taken over or, alternatively, may be due to the personal idiosyncrasies of the compilers of this text. The subsequent variation of a given order of a rule can be found in the grammatical manuscripts where accidents and rules are listed but not always discussed systematically as the text continues. In this way the royal committee did not differ from the schoolmasters in the compiling of grammatical treatises.

The *Godly Lessons for Chyldren* probably also represents a selection of those who were responsible for the compilation of the authorized grammar. The forty sample sentences in English with their model translations into Latin represent common knowledge and advice in teaching that was thought useful to pass on to children in such a way that at the same time they served the purpose to illustrate, apply, and exercise grammatical rules for composition. Sentences like these could also be used for 'double translation', an educational method by which the sentences in the vernacular had to be rendered into Latin. After a suitable interval the same sentences were translated back into English. In the first step the schoolboy had to analyse the grammatical rules of the sentence and construe the passage into Latin, whereas the second step required the same procedure in reverse.[82] Finally the results of this latter exercise were compared with the starting sentence. Improvements in both Latin and English could be achieved by this practice.[83] Additionally, these sentences also served conversational needs in Latin.

Like the text on the parts of speech, the text on construction in the *Introduction* represents the result of the work of the members of the royal committee. This text has often been considered identical with William Lily's *Rudimenta grammatices*, an elementary book on Latin syntax in English written in affirmative sentences with the heading "To make latyn". It was compiled by Lily, probably in 1509, for St Paul's School and circulated independently, although in most cases it was issued together with Colet's *Aeditio*.[84] It shares the character of the *Aeditio* in that simple

---

[81] Chapter 7, *Introduction, Parts of Speech*, 185, lines 906–22.

[82] 'Construe' is another word from the teacher's vocabulary of the medieval schoolroom, when the schoolboy applied the rules of Donatus's *Ars minor* to the sentence and traced the grammatical construction of it. It is still common use in the modern classroom. Cf. also p. 80, footnote 16, for 'parse'.

[83] See William E. Miller (1963), 'Double Translation in English Humanistic Education', *Studies in the Renaissance* 10: 167–74; also Stanbridge (1519), *The Vulgaria of John Stanbridge and the Vulgaria of Robert Whittinton* (1520), ed. B. White (1971 repr.), Introduction, xliv.

[84] For editions of Lily's *Rudimenta grammatices* see *Checklist* 51.1–51.16; for a discussion of this grammar, cf. Flynn (1943), 90–95.

explanations of the rules are given for children with no knowledge of the rudiments. A comparison between Lily's *Rudimenta grammatices* and the syntax of the authorized grammar, however, shows that the new text was not modelled on this treatise, even though they have many rules in common. According to present evidence, the new text on construction exemplifies a blending of material from a number of grammars that were widely current at the time of its compilation, with Lily's short treatise in English being only one amongst many. For example, the rule at the beginning of the royal grammar on how to turn an English sentence into Latin by finding the principal verb first is a commonplace found in the tradition describing a practice familiar in the classroom. It could have been taken from a number of grammars or even drawn from memory. It is included in Lily's *Rudimenta grammatices*, and in the treatises written in question-and-answer form, the *Parvula*, and the *Long Parvula*, both attributed to John Stanbridge, and also in his *Parvulorum Institutio*, a text that was reprinted up to the introduction of the authorized grammar.[85] Compare this rule in the authorized grammar with the passage given in Stanbridge's *Parvulorum Institutio*:

Whan an englysshe is gyuen to be made in latyn, loke out the pryncipall verbe. If there be mo verbes then one in a sentence, the fyrst is the principall verbe, except it be the infinitiue mode, or haue before it a relatyue, as that, whome, whiche: or a coniunction, as *ut* that, *cum* whan, *si* if, or suche other.
    Whan ye haue found the verbe, aske this question whoo, or what, and that worde that answereth to the question, shalbe the nominatiue case to the verbe.
(Introduction, Construction, 192, lines 6–13)

What is to be done whan an englysshe is gyuen to be made in latyn. Fyrst þe verbe must be loked out/ and yf there be mo verbes then one in a reason I must loke out þe pryncypall verbe and aske this questyon who or what/ and þat worde þat answereth to the questyon shal be the nomynatyue case to the verbe.
(Stanbridge, Parvulorum institutio, A2[r])

The same rule can also be found in the short anonymous manual entitled *Certayne Briefe Rules of the regiment or construction of the eyght partes of speche, in englishe and latine*, of which two copies of the 1537 edition and one printed in 1538 are extant and which were also published by the King's Printer, Thomas Berthelet. In this context it is striking that the text on construction in the authorized grammar presents the subject matter, the arrangement of the rules, which are set out systematically under the three concords, as well as the construction of the eight parts of speech, their wording, and examples in a manner which, to a great extent, is similar to that of *Certayne Briefe Rules*. In the latter treatise, however, each

---

[85] See Lily, *Rudimenta grammatices* (1527), D7[r-v] (*Checklist* 51.3); *Long Parvula*, Cambridge, Magdalene College, Pepysian Library, PL, 1305(4), a1[r] (*Checklist* 48.2); *Parvula*, Bodl. Lib., Douce D 238(3), A1[v] (*Checklist* 49.1); and *Parvulorum institutio*, Cambridge, King's College, M.28.43[2] (*Checklist* 50.1).

rule is given in both languages with the rule in English coming first, but only the Latin rule is illustrated by examples.[86] From these parallels it can be assumed that the compilers knew and made use of this treatise, introducing their own modifications. Compare, for example, '*The case of the relatiue*' in the two grammars:

Whan there commeth no nominatiue case betwene the relatyue and the verbe, the relatiue shall be the nominatiue case to the verbe, as, wretched is that person, whiche is in loue with money, *Miser est qui nummos admiratur.*

But whan there commeth a nominatiue case betwene the relatyue and the verbe, the relatyue shall be suche case, as the verbe wyll haue after hym, as Happie is he, whom other mennes harmes do make to beware, *Felix quem faciunt aliena pericula cautum.*

(*Introduction, Construction,* 193–94, lines 73–80)

Whan there cometh no nominatiue case betwene the relatiue and the verbe, the relatiue shall be the nominatyue case to the verbe: But whan there cometh a nominatiue case betwene the relatiue and the verbe, the relatiue shalbe suche case, as the verbe wyll haue after hym.

Cum nullus nominatiuus verbo et relatiuo interponitur, relatiuum erit verbo nominatiuus, vt, Miser est, qui nummos admiratur. At si nominatiuus intercedat, relatiuum regitur a verbo, vt, Fœlix quem faciunt aliena pericula cautum.

(*Certayne Briefe Rules,* A4[v])[87]

Close parallels for a large number of rules and examples can be found between the text on construction of the authorized grammar and the *Libellus de constructione,* which in some later editions is entitled *Absolutis-simus.*[88] This short treatise for more advanced pupils, written throughout in Latin, covers the facts on Latin syntax and sets them out in a concise way. It provides detailed information about the syntactic behaviour of the eight parts of speech beginning with the verb and the nominative case preceding it and then lists, classifies and discusses the verbs that are followed by the genitive, dative, accusative, and ablative cases. The participle and the cases it takes follows next, before the noun and the pronoun are dealt with. Finally the four indeclinable parts of speech are discussed receiving shorter treatment. The rules on the parts of speech are followed by appendices and exceptions that explain and qualify them. Sufficient short examples are provided to illustrate the rule previously stated. Both the rule in its English translation and many examples can often be found in the authorized grammar. Compare, for example, the cases that are taken by the participle:

---

[86] See *Checklist* 52.1 and 52.2. On this treatise see C. G. Allen (1954), 'The Sources of "Lily's Latin Grammar"': A Review of the Facts and Some Further Suggestions', *The Library,* 5th ser., 9: 85–100; also Allen (1959), 'Certayne Briefe Rules and "Lily's Latin Grammar"', *The Library,* 5th ser., 14: 49–53.

[87] See the copy of the edition printed in 1537 (Bodl. Lib, Douce G.359).

[88] See also Appendix IV, 1; Allen (1954), 87–90; and Flynn (1943), 94–95, 99–101.

Participles gouerne suche case as the verbe that they come of, as *Fruiturus amicis,*
Consulens tibi, Diligendus ab omnibus.

        (*Introduction, Construction,* 201, lines 348–49)

> *Participia sequuntur constructionem verborum a quibus deriuantur.*
> *Donaturus tibi vestem. Donaturus te veste.*
> *Consulens tibi. Fruiturus te.*
> *Diligendus ab omnibus: quamquam in his vsitatior est datiuus. Diligendus omnibus.*
>
>   (William Lily, *Libellus de constructione,* C5ᵛ)

The text on construction in the authorized grammar also bears resem-
blances to the extant copies of the two Latin grammars in English, the
Progymnasmata grammatices vulgaria (*c.*1512) and the *Rudimenta grammatices*
(*c.*1525) by Thomas Linacre.[89] That this material represented common
knowledge in the teaching of Latin may be seen by comparing the text on
syntax in the *Introduction* with Linacre's grammars in English. Compare,
for example, the rules on verbs taking the ablative case of the word that
signifies price in the text on construction in the *Introduction* with Linacre's
Progymnasmata and his *Rudimenta grammatices,* the latter treatise adopting
the catechetical method used in the earlier tradition:

> The worde of price is put after verbes in the ablatiue case, as *Vendidi auro, Emptus*
> *sum argento.* except these genitiues, whan they be put alone without substantiues,
> *Tanti, quanti, pluris, minoris, tantiuis, tantidem, quantiuis, quantilibet, quanticunque,* as
> *Quanti mercatus es hunc equum? Certe pluris quam uellem.*
>
>   (*Introduction, Construction,* 198, lines 231–35)

> Also after all maner of verbys: þe word that stondyth as price shall be put in the
> ablatyfe case yf it be a nowne appellatyf. as vendidi auro. emi argento. but of
> adiectyues there be .ix. the whiche yf they stond as pryce: and haue none appel-
> latyf with them they must be putt in the genytyf. and they be these tanti. quanti.
> pluris. minoris. quantiuis. quantilibet et quanticunque. tantiuis et tantidem. [etc.].
>
>   (Thomas Linacre, *Progymnasmata,* e2ʳ)

> *Emi librum decem denarijs, why is denarijs the ablatiue? For after all maner of verbes, the*
> *worde that standeth as price, shalbe put in the ablatiue case, if it be a nowne appellatiue:*
> *as Vendidi auro. Emptus sum argento. Tacet magna mercede. Loquitur paruo. Dormit nullo*
> *precio. Vigilat magno precio.*
>
>   (Thomas Linacre, *Rudimenta grammatices,* I3ʳ)

These few examples show that the grammatical texts of the authorized
grammar must be considered derivative and the compilers' debt to their
predecessors becomes evident. Most of the material of the grammar
on morphology and syntax contained in the *Introduction* can be traced to
treatises that were widely current and used in grammar schools at the
time that the authorized grammar was compiled, amongst them the
grammars of John Colet and William Lily. Moreover, rules and examples,

---

[89] For Linacre's Latin grammars in English see *Checklist* 54.1, 55.1, and 55.2; also Kristian
Jensen, rev. Hedwig Gwosdek (2009), 'Linacre, Thomas', in *Lexicon Grammaticorum,* vol. 2:
914–15.

probably from a number of grammatical textbooks of which no trace has been left, may well have been absorbed into the new texts with or without modification by its compilers. Textual agreements between the *Introduction* and other grammars that were in use before 1540 can demonstrate a direct connection between them, but they are certainly not sufficient to tell the whole story. In most cases definitions and rules reflect common knowledge that can be found in a number of grammars in use at the period. The grammatical treatises that preceded the authorized grammar were themselves derivative and show many parallels with the English grammatical manuscripts. At the same time the tradition was flexible in that it took over material from the New Learning, a fact which had become evident in the manuscript treatises and was continued in the early printed grammars. New treatises which were compiled after the beginning of the sixteenth century and which only circulated in print continued in this way. The royal committee which had been entrusted with the compilation of a new grammar made use of this vast tradition, modelling the grammatical texts according to its own aims, applying its own standards, and introducing pedagogical principles which were themselves indebted to the tradition. The thread, so it seems, which runs through the compilation of these grammars on accidence and syntax, is the desire to assemble the best and most reputed contemporary grammatical texts which were in use into texts which would meet the needs of pupils in the elementary stage of grammatical instruction when the teaching of Latin would take place in the vernacular.

As with the grammatical texts, the sentences for translation, the copies of the *Carmen de moribus* and Erasmus's *Christiani Hominis Institutum*, which were included in this volume, also reflect the principles of the compilers. The fruit of their labours was eventually to become the authorized grammar for the teaching of Latin in English, illustrating the state of grammatical knowledge at that time for that level of instruction, and it remained the best text for pupils in grammar schools for a very long time. King Henry VIII's decree gave the new grammar royal authority and it was prescribed for use in all grammar schools. Its introduction established a new era in Latin teaching in England. In this way the new text has to considered the culmination of the tradition of grammatical teaching. Though revisions of the grammatical texts, rearrangement and exchange of the religious and moral texts which were also included in the volume, took place from time to time due to changing circumstances and influences, the rules for the Latin language as well as for the vernacular as presented in the authorized grammar became fixed in this form, not only in textual terms, but due to its introduction by royal command. It was taught in that way and within that framework, and, in turn, provided the basis for the early grammars of the English language. In referring to its long tradition, the *Introduction* can be considered one element in an unbroken chain of Latin grammars in the vernacular and, in turn, served as a basis and link for future texts for other grammatical instruction. William Bullokar's *Pamphlet for Grammar*, which represents the earliest extant grammar of English written in English, published in 1586, provides ample testimony to that influence.[90]

---

[90] See Chapter 5.

4. Towards a Uniform School Grammar and its Teaching

4.1 *Grammatical manuscripts and the teaching of Latin in English*

The intention behind the introduction of 'Lily's Grammar' in 1540, which carried the king's authority, was to reform the teaching of grammar. The aim was to remedy the imperfections of the current English grammar textbooks by teaching with the new compilation to be imposed by royal decree for use throughout the realm, and at the same time expressly forbidding the use of any other grammar. As a result, this measure virtually put an end to the use and hence also to the publication of other teaching grammars. The English part of the authorized grammar of 1542 contains two legal texts that incorporate the royal proclamation and an address to the reader that supplements the latter.[1] These represent official documents that prescribe the teaching of Latin for future generations of pupils. According to the evidence in the English part of the authorized grammar, the authorities had realized that the diversity of existing grammar textbooks was undesirable and would be a great hindrance to the process of learning. The measures that were taken in about 1540 were a response to this situation, when King Henry VIII appointed "certein lerned men mete for suche a purpose, to compile one bryef, plaine, and vniforme grammer" in order to avoid the harm done to the children's education due to the diversity of grammars and teaching methods.[2] This reference in the preface (*To the Reder*) sheds light on the royal committee that was entrusted with this task by taking into account its objective, and the learning and most probably reputation and teaching experience of the members who were selected for this purpose. It also draws attention to the dependence of Latin elementary grammars on other contemporary grammars that were in use by referring to the new text as a compilation and thereby hinting at its tradition. Finally, it takes into account the capabilities of the children at the elementary level.[3] This measure meant

---

[1] Though the proclamation and the address to the reader do not bear a date, they can probably be assigned to or shortly before 1540. See Foster Watson (1908), *The English Grammar Schools to 1660*, Cambridge; repr. 1968, 252–53.

[2] Chapter 7, *Introduction, To the Reder*, 158, 33–34.

[3] Cf. "A lytell proheme to the boke", in Colet, *Aeditio* (1527): "In whiche lytel boke I haue lefte many thynges out of purpose/ consyderyng the tendernes and small capacyte of lytel myndes" (A5ᵛ).

that every pupil at grammar school had to use the same textbook and learn the same rules that had to be taught according to the same teaching methods, the intention being that children could more readily and easily attain the rudiments of Latin grammar. Henry VIII's diktat that only the authorized grammar be used in schools from 1540 onwards is the outcome of an awareness and a process that can be traced back to a number of complex changes that influenced work within the classrooms. From about the last quarter of the fifteenth century onwards, teaching underwent changes due to the impact of the new technology of printing and the influence of the New Learning. In addition, it was affected by the religious attitudes which led to the Reformation and its influence thereafter.

The period spans about 140 years from the time when the first manuscripts explaining Latin in the vernacular became available, until the introduction of the authorized grammar. To gain a clearer view of the situation, it seems helpful to distinguish a three-stage process, though this certainly implies a drastic oversimplification, especially given that a strict demarcation of these periods, to which no exact dates can be assigned, is not possible. The first stage covers the time when grammatical manuscripts were used for the teaching of elementary Latin. The second stage shows the beginning of the overlap of manuscripts with printed grammars that gradually superseded the handwritten schoolbooks. In the third stage, when the variety of printed grammars was seen to be a hindrance to learning and teaching, attempts by the authorities were made to introduce uniformity, *i.e.* the requirement that children should use the same textbook for the learning of Latin in school. These efforts, in the end, led to the introduction of the grammar attributed to William Lily.

From about 1400 to about 1480, *i.e.* the period from which grammatical manuscripts for the teaching of elementary grammar in English have come down to us, teaching was more or less local. A number of the treatises in use in this period can be connected to John Leylond, the foremost grammarian of the early fifteenth century in Oxford, which was the centre of grammatical teaching at that time.[4] Treatises that teach elementary morphology, *i.e.* the parts of speech, comparison, and also the rules of construction, have survived; the material in the manuscripts also overlaps and some of them had been combined to form longer, composite works.[5] Each manuscript represents a different version of the treatise

---

[4] On biographical details of Leylond and his connection to the English grammatical manuscripts see p. 49 above.

[5] For detailed information about the Latin grammatical manuscripts in English see Thomson, *Catalogue*, 1–47. Valuable additional information is given in Thomson's thesis (1977), *A Study of the Middle English Treatises on Grammar*, D.Phil. Thesis. University of Oxford, Vol. 1, *passim*.

on which it is based. There are also texts in existence that are the only versions now remaining of the original treatises from which they stem. Teaching spread out from Oxford, from where the masters took both their texts and their accumulated teaching skills. The manuals edited or written by John Leylond and other grammarians in Oxford circulated widely and were used to teach basic Latin in the manner and to the standards of the schools in which they were employed. As new grammar schools were founded in one town after another, each teacher compiled his own teaching materials from texts already in existence. Pupils often did not have their own textbook, but were expected to memorize the rules. When they changed school, or if a new teacher took over, they had to go right back to the beginning and start again with different texts and so wasted much time; a situation that was noticed by teachers and by the authorities over the course of time.

The manuscripts reflect the common Latin curriculum, chiefly its lower levels. It also becomes evident that masters adapted the curriculum locally, probably in response to their pedagogical needs and circumstances. They also wrote new versions of grammars. The striking characteristic of these treatises is their instability. Teachers modified what they found in their exemplars, deleting apparently irrelevant or confusing material, or abbreviating it, interpolating material from elsewhere to expand underdeveloped or more relevant subjects and to add new information, and revising and rearranging material to serve perceived needs in the light of their own experience. Some treatises may scarcely have outlived their authors. However, most of them probably passed from one generation to the next, revised by those who used them. In this way the grammatical rules passed through many shaping hands, a fact that increased variation and emendation and resulted in an idiosyncratic text. Moreover, the English grammatical manuscripts have to be seen against the Latin background that was of significant influence. Versions of Donatus's *Ars minor*, then current in England, were present in the classroom as a book of reference, as is indicated in some of the treatises. Moreover, the famous colleges of Winchester and Eton exerted their influence on textbooks and teaching methods from which other teaching institutions took over their own standards, and thus the treatises were adapted once again by their new users. The grammatical manuscripts present the rules for learning the elements of Latin in the vernacular in a variety of ways.

Their characteristics, as has been indicated above, are that they were not 'written up' but were of a fluid and dynamic nature and represent the personal use of the grammar master. Two important rules in these manuscripts may give some idea of this variation as far as the written text is concerned. For example, the identification of the noun adjective that is given in all of the nine surviving manuscripts of the *Accedence* represents one of these main rules, as does the section on the identification of the impersonal verb in the manuscripts of the *Informacio*. The rules of the nine treatises of the *Accedence* are cast in catechetical style with alternating questions and answers, but they differ in respect to the information about the morphological and syntactic features of the noun adjective. Compare the rules, given in chronological order, on how to identify the noun adjective:

How knowest a noun adiectyf? Euery word that is declined by thre articles or by thre diuerse endyngis in o case, as *hic et hec et hoc felix*, other as *bonus, -na, -num*.

(Thomson, Edition, Text D, 32, 14–17)

How knowustow a nown aiectyf? Þat ys clynud wit iii articuls or wit iii diuerse endyngus in on case. Wit iii articuls as how? As *hic et hec et hoc felix*. Wit iii diuerse endyngus, as *bonus –a –vm*.

(Bland, 149)

How knos þu a nowne adiectiue? For hyt ys declynet wᵗ iij artyculs or iij dyuers endyngus in on case. Wych byn þi articuls? *Hic, hec, hoc*. Wych byn þi dyuers endyngus? *–Vs, -a, -vm; -r, -a, -vm*, most comynly.

(Thomson, Edition, Text A, 1, 16–19)

How knowe ȝe a noun adiectyf? For hit may not be vnderstond by hitself wᵗowte helpe of a noder word owte sette or vnderstond, and is declyned in Latyn wᵗ iij articles or wᵗ iij dyuers endynges in on case as 'wys' and 'good': *hic et hec et hoc sapiens, bonus, -na, -num*. And euery noun þat may receyue comparyson is a noun adiectyf, as *senex, senior, iuuenis, iunior*.

(Thomson, Edition, Text B, 9, 16–22)

Qwerby knowyst a nown adiectyf? For he may not stonde alone in a perfyth reson wᵗowtyn help of a noþer wurd, as 'qwyt', 'red', 'blak', and is declyned in Latyn wᵗ iij articulys or iij dyuerse endynggis in o case, as nominatiuo *hic et hec et hoc felix*, or nominatiuo *bonus, bona, bonum*.

(Thomson, Edition, Text C, 17, 18–23)

How knowist a nown adiectif? For he may not stond by hymsilf wᵗout the help of a nother worde and is declyned yn Latyn wᵗ iij articulis in on case as *hic et hec et hoc felix* or hels whith iij diuers endyngys in oon case as nominatiuo *bonus, -a, -um*.

(Thomson, Edition, Text L, 61, 34–38)

How know þu a nown adiectyve? For he may not stonde by hymself wᵗout þe helpe of a noþer worde and is declyned in Laten wᵗ iij artikyllis as *hic et hec et hoc felix*, or wᵗ iij diuerse endyngis as *bonus, -a, -um*.

(Thomson, Edition, Text F, 45, 19–23)

How knowest þu a nowne adiectyf? For he may not stande by hymself wᵗoute help of another word and is declyned wᵗ iij articlys, or wᵗ iij diuerse endyngis in one case: wᵗ iij articlys as nominatiuo *hic, hec, hoc felix*; wᵗ iij diuerse endingis as nominatiuo *bonus, -a, -um*. And also euery nowne that may receyve comparson is a nowne adiectif, as *senex, senior; iuuenis, iunior*.

(Thomson, Edition, Text M, 63, 26–32)

How knowyst a nowne adiectyfe? For he ys declynd wᵗ iij artyculs or wᵗ iij dyuerse yendyngys. Wyche byn þe artyculys? *Hic, hec* and *hoc*. Wyche byn þe iij dyuerse yndyngys? *–Vs, -a* and *–vm*. How? As *bonus, bona, bonum* for 'goode'.

(Thomson, Edition, Text K, 56, 17–21)

All the manuscripts say that the noun adjective is declined with three articles, but one adds "in on case" (Text L), or with three diverse endings, while seven specify them by saying "in o case" (e.g. Text D). Four of them provide syntactic information by saying that it "may not stonde by hymself w^{t}out þe helpe of a noþer worde" (e.g. Text F). One of them describes the adjective semantically by saying that it "may not be vnderstond by hitself w^{t}owte helpe of a noder word owte sette or vnderstond" (Text B). They all share "*hic, hec, hoc*" that are referred to as articles, and some of them illustrate the rule by the adjectives "*sapiens*" or "*felix*" and the endings, e.g., of "*bonus, -a, -um*". However, they differ in providing illustrative examples in Latin, in most cases without their English translation, and also in giving information about the comparison of the noun adjective.

The six manuscripts of the *Informacio* on elementary syntax that are extant contain the rule on the identification of the impersonal verb. They are also cast in catechetical style, but differ in how detailed they present the same rule, a matter in which they resemble the manuscripts treating morphology. The rules given in chronological sequence read as follows:

Qwerby knowes þu a verbe impersonill? For he hase nouther nowmbur ni person ny nominatyf case, and is declinet in þe voyce of the thridde person, and comes in Englissh with one of these sygnes 'hit' or 'me', as 'Hit behose me to lorne', *Oportet* (*me adiscere*). 'Me redes', *Legitur*.

(Thomson, *Edition*, Text W, 109, 191–96)

How knowest a verbe inpersonell? For it hath nother noumber ne person ne nominatife case and is declined in the voice of the thrid person, singler noumber, and comes in Inglish w^t one of this ij signes 'it' or 'me'.

(Thomson, *Edition*, Text Y, 125, 165–68)

Whereby knowyst a verbe inpersonall? For hit hathe nether numburre nether person nether nominatyff case and commythe yn Englyssch w^t one of these iij signes 'hyt', 'me', or 'the'. *Verbum dicitur inpersonale. Quare? Quia non habet suppositum rectitudinis a parte ante.*

(Thomson, *Edition*, Text X, 116, 248–52)

How knawis þu a verbe inpersonyll? For hyt hase nawther nowmbur ne persun ne nomenatyff case to be gowerunde by, and is declinet in the voce of the third persun singuler nowmbur and comys in englisshe whytt onne of theis signes 'hit' or 'me'.

(Woking, Surrey History Centre, MS LM 1327/2, fol. 6^r)[6]

How knous þu a uerbe inpersonell? For hyt hase nothur nowumbur ne person ne no nominatyue case and is declynyd in þe voyce of the iij person singler nowumbor and comys in Englyche w^t one of thes synis 'hyt' or 'me'.

(Thomson, *Edition*, Text U, 99, 297–300)

---

[6] For bibliographical details of this manuscript see *Checklist* 32. The notebook from the Losely collection is now located at Woking, Surrey History Centre.

How knowystow a verbe inpersonall? For hyt hath noþer nowmbur ne person ne nominatif case before hym, but he ys declint in þe voice of the iij person singler and comus in English wᵗ on of these ij synys 'hyt' or 'me'.

(Thomson, *Edition*, Text T, 88, 294–97)

The passages of the treatises of the manuscripts state that the impersonal verb has 'neither number nor person nor nominative case', to which one adds that the nominative case is placed before it (Text T), or is governed by it (Woking MS). Its 'declension' in the third person singular is given next in five manuscripts. Apart from the fact that all of them continue to render the Latin rule into English by making use of the "signes" "it" or "me", one adds "the", they differ in providing illustrative examples in English. The most interesting case is that one manuscript (Text X) adds how to identify an impersonal verb in Latin, namely that it does not have the subject before the verb, *i.e. suppositum* in the terminology of the day. Though the examples of variation that have been chosen here are not necessarily representative, they can give some idea of the manifold ways that rules could be approached and presented in these manuscripts. The most noticeable feature of these manuscripts is their variation in the wording of the rules, but, at the same time, they also vary considerably in subject matter.[7] From this it can be inferred that, in spite of the many rules which the manuscripts share, the changes reflect the ways teachers approached their texts in the classroom, what they regarded as relevant and important, and how the rules were written down either by the schoolmasters or even by pupils.

The treatises, however, do not reflect the actual teaching in the classrooms, *i.e.* how the grammatical rules were explained, or in what detail, nor how often they were repeated. The methods employed amongst individual teachers and schools always varied, a phenomenon that is a characteristic of any work in a classroom. However, only from a later perspective by investigating and comparing the grammatical manuscripts of different schools that were used over several decades does the variation in subject matter as well as the different ways of presenting the rules become obvious. The problems the pupils had to face when they had to change schools and/or masters at the time of the plague or for any other reason then become clear. Only later in the sixteenth century, when moves were made to standardize teaching, would the variation that characterizes the manuscript tradition and which is continued in the printed books give way to the grammar that was introduced by royal authority.

---

[7] Cf. also Appendix V for the presentation of alternative definitions of the same part of speech in the grammatical manuscripts, a fact that is continued in the early printed grammars and most probably reflects pedagogical expedience at work.

4.2 Early printed grammars and the diversity in teaching

From about 1480 to about 1520, printed textbooks gradually replaced handwritten ones and the New Learning entered the grammar schools of England. The first evidence of an early printed Latin grammar in English we have is two leaves extant of an edition of the *Long Parvula*. It deals with elementary syntax and was probably printed by Theodoric Rood in Oxford in 1482.[8] The elementary grammars were frequently reprinted so that shortly after 1500 grammatical manuscripts that were still being compiled can be considered personal compilations of the master and thus outside the mainstream of the tradition. Humanist influence had gradually been gaining ground in educational institutions and in teaching material. Magdalen College School, Oxford, founded by William Waynflete (*c.*1400–1486) in 1480 as part of Magdalen College, became the chief centre of humanistic studies in the country. It was initially established for the purpose of fostering the neglected discipline of grammar and for training undergraduates or 'demies' and other boys for the College; Waynflete may also have wished to train its own future staff.[9] The earliest known grammar master of Magdalen School was John Anwykyll, who died in 1487, and was succeeded by John Stanbridge (1463?–1510), first assistant master or usher and then master of the school from 1488–1493. Treatises on elementary syntax were connected to his name. To a great extent they represent a continuation of versions of the English grammatical manuscripts in early print. In the same way printed grammars on accidence followed the manuscripts, which were presumably revised and used by him.

To mention only one criterion for humanist Latin in school texts, one can see in Stanbridge's *Parvulorum institutio*, for instance, that examples from classical authors were introduced to substantiate the rules, though, at the same time, the traditional practice of invented examples was retained. A passage from a *Vulgaria* text that probably reflects the teaching of Andrew Scarbot (*fl.* 1494–1499), Stanbridge's successor at Magdalen School from 1494–1498, and which was written at the end of the fifteenth century, provides the earliest evidence of the new situation at school, putting it as follows:

Ther is so great diversite of autors of gramer and of eloquence that I cannot tell to whom I may incline, for theis new auctors [*i.e.* modern grammarians] doth rebuke the noble dedes of them that ben before them. therfor oure myndes be plukkyde by ther and thither [hither and thither]. but we be so variable and wandrynge of mynde that we covett the newer thynges and tho thei be worse.[10]

---

[8] See *Checklist* 48.1.
[9] Nicholas Orme (1998), *Education in Early Tudor England. Magdalen College Oxford and its School, 1480–1540*, Magdalen College Occasional Paper 4, Oxford, 5–6.
[10] *A Fifteenth Century School Book*, ed. W. Nelson (1956), Oxford, no. 78: 19–20.

The author seems to have been in conflict over what to learn, but is not ready to discard the traditional grammar books in favour of the new works of the humanists that were already being followed. The influence of their works on the grammatical treatises compiled in English and also their usage in schools, as in the case of Perottus's and Sulpitius's grammars, may be seen as a cultural change in education. At about the same time, the invention of the new technique of printing started to facilitate an evolution of textbooks for the teaching of grammar. When manuscripts were used for teaching, it was normally only the school-masters who possessed or had recourse to manuscript textbooks. Though the impact of printing on school texts was a gradual one, the supply of textbooks enabled pupils as well as the schoolmasters to have recourse to their own copies. They could also recognize that the schoolbooks of different schools were different when compared. At the same time their habit and also their judgement of the different treatises were probably the reasons why masters continued to compile their own versions in the same way as their predecessors had done, but had them printed and multiplied in a number of copies. The attempts of John Colet have to be understood in this way when, in the preface to his *Aeditio*, he points to the fact that other versions of grammar textbooks co-existed at the same time by saying:

Al be it mani haue written/ and haue made certayne introducyons in to latyn speche/ called Donates and Accidens in latyn tongue and in englyshe in suche plenty that it sholde seme to suffyse. Yet neuerthelesse for the loue/ and the zele that I haue vnto the newe schole of Poules/ and to the children of þe same: somewhat I haue also compiled of þe mater/ and of the .viij. partes of grammer haue made this lytel boke. not thynkynge that I could say ony thynge beter than hath be sayd before/ but I toke this besynes hauynge grete pleasure to shewe þe testymony of my good mynde vnto the schole.[11]

Colet's statutes for St Paul's School of 1518 also point to the existence of other versions that were circulating, when he states in the chapter on "What shalbe taughte": "I will the Children lerne firste and above all the Catechizone in Inglyshe and after the accydence that I made or sum oder yf any can be better to the purpose to induce children more spedely to laten speche."[12] When school texts became generally available in print, the multiplicity of versions of the grammatical treatises was reduced to a few versions that became dominant due to the fact that they were avail-able and complete. Chance may have also played a role in this selection process. In addition, the evidence of the treatises shows that even before 1500, a number of versions of elementary grammars co-existed in print. This was when different versions of late medieval Latin grammars in

---

[11] Colet, *Aeditio* (1527), A5ᵛ.
[12] *Statuta Paulinæ Scholæ. John Colet's Statutes for St Paul's School*. Mid-Sixteenth Century (BL, MS Add. 6274, fols. 6ᵛ-7ʳ).

English and humanist grammars were in use at the same time. By about 1510 humanist grammars and reading texts became the preferred choice. Colet's preface in his *Aeditio* and his Statutes of St Paul's School prove that masters were aware of the competing grammatical texts that were current at the time and that these, in his opinion, differed in quality. An adverse judgement is perhaps implied by the fact that he and other masters found it necessary to compose their own textbooks and have them printed rather than use existing ones, a fact which again contributed to the diversity of versions that came into use. Though the diversity of grammars that was available and to which they may have had access offered a wider choice for schoolmasters, there were certainly also complaints that they had to rely on books not written precisely for their requirements. It was not only the number of different textbooks containing different versions of elementary Latin grammar that created difficulties in teaching and learning, but even the use of the same printed treatise in the classroom revealed problems for the teacher and his pupils, a fact that applied to printed teaching material in general when different editions were available.[13]

4.3 *From the diversity of grammars towards a uniform grammar*

In the period from about 1520 to 1540, an increasing awareness of the diversity of grammar textbooks and the desire for uniformity in texts and teaching can be documented. Measures were taken to obtain an improvement in textbooks and in the daily practice of teaching Latin. This period also illustrates the procedures by which more influence and control over teaching was exerted by the ecclesiastical authorities. The earliest evidence that there was some plan to impose one version of grammar, at least across the Province of Canterbury, covering roughly the southern two-thirds of England, is a reference in the revised Statutes of Manchester Grammar School, dated 1 April 1525, that is commonly regarded as its foundation deed. The chapter on the status and education of the headmaster reads:

A syngilman, prest or not preste, [. . .] having sufficient litterature and lernyng to be a Scole maister, and able to teche childeryn gramyer after the Scole use maner and forme of the Scole of Banbury in Oxfordchire nowe there taught, wiche is called Stanbryge gramyer, or after suche Scole use maner as in tyme to cum shalbe ordeyned universally throughe oute all the province of Canterbury.[14]

---

[13] See the reference in Leonard Cox's (1526) treatise, *De Erudienda Iuventute*, in Andrew Breeze and Jacqueline Glomski (eds.) (1991), 'An Early British Treatise upon Education: Leonard Cox's *De Erudienda Iuventute*', with translation and introduction, *Humanistica Lovaniensia* 40, p. 89, chapter 2.

[14] *VCH Lancashire*, vol. II: 583.

These statutes prescribe the use of the grammar of John Stanbridge, who was master of the grammar school of St John at Banbury from 1501 until his death in 1510. Versions of early printed grammars that continue the tradition of the grammatical manuscripts and the teaching of accidence and construction were connected with his name and became very popular. The statutes also suggest that a project to have one pre-scribed form of grammar was under consideration. It becomes evident that the movement towards a uniform grammar was gaining ground.

A further attempt towards achieving uniformity also goes back to the church authorities. When Cardinal Thomas Wolsey began to establish Cardinal College at Oxford in 1525, which subsequently became Christ Church, he also intended to endow a grammar school in his birthplace, Ipswich, to be connected with the Oxford College. Wolsey, who was him-self a master at Magdalen College School, Oxford, for two terms in 1498 to 1499, compiled a basic curriculum for all eight forms of his new school. His *Methodus* of 1529 was printed as prefatory material to the elementary Latin grammars in English that represent slightly adapted versions of John Colet's *Aeditio* and William Lily's *Rudimenta grammatices*. One edition of this grammar, intended for Ipswich School, was printed by Peter Treveris, probably at Southwark, in 1529. Its Latin title-page prescribed the book explicitly and did not merely offer it as a model that might be followed at the schoolmasters' choice. It may be translated as follows:

The rudiments of grammar and the method of teaching, not merely of the school of Ipswich, happily established by the most reverend Lord Thomas, Cardinal of York, but also prescribed for all the other schools of all England.[15]

Wolsey may have been intending to prescribe his Ipswich grammar for all schools in England, but no ordinance or statute is known. Following his fall from power in October 1529, Ipswich School was dissolved by Henry VIII just two years after its inception. The matter of moving towards a uniform grammar and method of teaching was again taken up very soon by the Convocation of the Province of Canterbury which met at St Paul's, London, to consider ecclesiastical reform and to take measures against heresy. The Convocation, representing the clergy of southern England, appointed a commission to decide on a grammar to be authorized. Its decrees in respect to grammar, approved on 22 March 1530, explicitly take

---

[15] BL, C.40.c.39, A1ʳ. The title-page reads: *Rudimenta grammatices Et Docendi methodus, non tam scholæ Gypsuichianæ per reuerendissimum .D. Thomam Cardinalem Eboracensem feliciter institutæ, quam omnibus aliis totius Anglię scholis prescripta.* For bibliographical details see *Checklist* 20.4 and 51.6. Cf. the comments in Gabriela Schmidt (2007), ' "The variety of teaching is divers": Plural-isierung der Autoritäten und die versuchte Etablierung van "Uniformität" im englischen Lateinunterricht unter Heinrich VIII.', *Mitteilungen des Sonderforschungsbereichs 573, Pluralis-ierung und Autorität der Frühen Neuzeit 2007/2*, 43–53, at 46–47; Vincent Joseph Flynn (1943), 'The Grammatical Writings of William Lily, ?1468–?1523', *Papers of the Bibliographical Society of America 37*, at 95–98; and Watson (1908), 250–52.

into consideration the diversity of textbooks for the teaching of Latin and the disadvantages arising for the pupils by saying:

And whereas either through the plague raging in places where public schools are, or through the death of the master, it often happens, that a boy who has begun to learn grammar for a year or two under one teacher, is obliged to leave him and go to a new teacher, who has another method of teaching, so that he is almost laughed at by all; and so it happens that those who are still raw in grammar suffer great loss in the progress of their learning.[16]

As a result of this situation, the Convocation ordained the following measures towards a uniform method of teaching grammar:

For the common benefit, therefore, of the whole province of Canterbury, with the approval of this holy council, we ordain, in order that after a year from the date of the publication of these presents, there shall be one uniform method of teaching throughout the whole province of Canterbury, no author of grammar rules or precepts shall be put before boys being taught grammar, except the one which the archbishop of Canterbury with four other bishops of the province, four abbots and four archdeacons to be named at this synod shall next year prescribe for boys to read.[17]

No outcome of these deliberations is known. Only at the end of the 1530s did King Henry VIII take up the project of moving towards a uniform grammar, the result of which was to become the model for the elementary Latin grammars of the future. His proclamation provides the most detailed account of the state of grammar textbooks and teaching. The title-pages of the first extant copies of the Latin (1540) and English part (1542) of the authorized grammar state the king's authority and the future role of this textbook in the teaching of Latin:

Institutio Compendiaria Totius Grammaticae, Quam Et Eruditissimus atque idem illustrissimus Rex noster hoc nomine euulgari iussit, ut non alia quam hæc una per totam Angliam pueris prælegeretur.[18]

---

[16] *Concilia Magnae Britanniae et Hiberniae, a Synodo Verolamiensi A.D. CCCCXLVI. ad Londinensem A.D. MDCCXVII*, ed. David Wilkins (1737), London, repr. 1964, vol. 3: 723: "Et quoniam vel propter pestem laborantem in locis ubi hujusmodi publicae scholae sunt, aut propter mortem praeceptoris (ut plurimum contingit) quod qui anno aut biennio sub uno praeceptore grammaticam addiscere coepit, illo relicto, cogitur novum adire praeceptorem, apud quem alius est docendi modus (ut pene diversus est apud omnes) atque ita fit, ut rudes adhuc in grammatica magnum ex hoc sentiant in provectione studii detrimentum." See also *Educational Charters and Documents, 598 to 1909*, ed. A. F. Leach (1911), repr. 1971, 446–47, where the above translation into English is given on p. 447.

[17] *Concilia Magnae Britanniae et Hiberniae*, vol. 3: 723: "Ad communem igitur utilitatem totius provinciae Cant. hoc sacro approbante concilio, statuimus, ut post annum a publicatione praesentium unus et uniformis sit docendi grammaticam modus per totam provinciam Cant. nullus auctor regularum seu praeceptionum grammaticalium pueris in grammatica instituendis ediscendus proponatur, nisi quem archiepiscopus Cant. simul cum quatuor aliis suae provinciae episcopis, quatuor abbatibus, quatuor archidiaconis in hac synodo deputandis hoc anno prox. sequen. praescripserint pueris perlegendum." See also *Educational Charters and Documents*, 446–47, with the translation into English, 447.

[18] *Institutio*, A1ʳ. See Appendix III, 1.0.

An Introduction Of The Eyght Partes Of speche, and the Construction of the same, compiled and sette forthe by the commaundement of our most gracious souerayne lorde the king.[19]

The evidence that has come down to us illustrates the gradual development of the concept of uniformity in grammar textbooks and teaching, how it took shape, and how it became a reality shaped by the needs of the pupils and influenced by the new technique of printing and also by the evolving interests in education. The authorities, *i.e.* the king and the Church, had given little consideration to schools when textbooks in manuscript form were the norm. The Church's interest in education took place on a local rather than on a national scale and its attention was focused on educating schoolchildren and the laity in Christian doctrine. Teaching as such and the management of the schools were shaped by local considerations and also by models taken from influential educational institutions such as Eton and Winchester. The authorities had scarcely been aware which textbooks had been used for the teaching of grammar or of the methods and quality of teaching. The problems that must, however, have been caused to pupils and their learning by the diversity of Latin grammars when they had to change schools or when a new teacher was appointed must undoubtedly have existed and caused confusion as well as being a hindrance to learning on a personal level.[20]

When the new technology of printing made it possible to multiply texts, thus continuing the tradition of the English grammatical manuscripts, and when humanist grammars first came to England and exerted influence on grammar writing, textbooks and teaching gradually underwent changes. The advent of the new technique of multiplying books was a decisive factor in the development towards uniformity in textbooks. Printing made it possible to envisage uniformity because the same text could be printed quickly in a large number of copies that could serve as teaching texts in schools all over the country. Their distribution and use in the different schools was, however, a gradual process. It also took the schoolmasters some time to adjust their teaching to the printed textbooks. The new grammars in print and the fact that they became more easily available for use in the classroom did not, however, bring uniformity to the teaching of Latin. Different grammars and different versions of grammars in different editions were on the market and there was great competition amongst the printers to issue school texts because they proved most profitable to their business.[21] Schoolmasters could make comparisons

---

[19] *Introduction*, A1[r]; see p. 156 below; also Appendix III, 3.0, and Plate 1. Frontispiece. Cf. Schmidt (2007), 49–50.

[20] At a time when pupils could afford their own textbooks, the diversity in texts and teaching, which already existed when grammatical manuscripts were in use, becomes even more apparent; cf. pp. 112–15 above.

[21] See Nicholas Orme (2006), *Medieval Schools. From Roman Britain to Renaissance England*, New Haven and London, 126, 288–97, 308–309, and *passim*.

between the different grammars and hence became more and more aware of their diversity and the problems involved for teaching and learning. Some of them did not hesitate to make public their opinions about rival texts. Their insights and also their comments about rival grammars may have drawn public attention to this general problem.

The authorities had already turned their interest to schools in the 1520s, before the Reformation had an impact on schools and teaching. However, it took more than another decade before the responsibility of the king for public instruction became a favourite theme. Due to the Reformation, the ecclesiastical authorities realized the importance of schools and teaching as being crucial to the good of the Church and state. Thus the diversity of grammars became an important matter and actions were taken towards introducing uniformity in textbooks and teaching. A special pronouncement on this subject can be found in the Proclamation and the address to the reader contained in the elementary part of 'Lily's Grammar'. The introduction of a uniform grammar for the teaching of Latin in grammar schools by Henry VIII's decree became part of his educational policy and a means to ensure control over teaching in grammar schools, a privilege once held exclusively by the Church. This measure became an important part of the king's political control of education and reform in the interests of religious uniformity after the Reformation. It can be considered the culmination of a development that reflects the expectations and values of teaching Latin at this level within the educational, cultural, and religious contexts of the time. This response had evolved over several decades, resulting from an insight into the problems of teaching with differing grammatical textbooks and the disadvantages they caused to the children and to education in general. Its introduction brought about an official change in education policy, in that by the sole use of a uniform grammar authorized by the monarch, for the teaching of Latin from 1540 onwards, the framework of the grammar school system was shaped into an authorized form. It is striking that uniformity in the teaching of Latin grammar came before uniformity in religious worship in England, a development that may be explained by the fact that schools and teaching provided the opportunity to educate the rising generation in letters while at the same time establishing their religious beliefs. In 1545 the uniform grammar was followed by the authorized *English Primer*, a uniform primer of prayers for use in school. The compilation that was to become the English part of the authorized Latin grammar must be seen in the light of the technological, educational, and religious developments of the decades preceding its introduction, and, in a wider context, it must be considered the changing-point of a grammatical tradition going back more than two centuries.

5. 'Lily's Grammar' and the First Grammar of English

5.1 *Latin and the role of the vernacular in the late Tudor period*

The introduction of the grammar authorized by Henry VIII and those who succeeded him to the throne continued to set the standard for the teaching of elementary Latin, and its dominant position in the school curriculum remained unchallenged in the following decades. Its use was enforced by regular diocesan inspections, and in this way it became the major component of the education of children of the upper classes and the more fortunate ones of the lower classes of society. It is therefore not surprising that its influence in the fields of learning and education was profound. However, from the last two decades of the sixteenth century onwards comments and criticism by teachers of grammar schools became frequent, and even amendments to 'Lily's Grammar' were published, all of which were the result of practical experience in the classroom.

The rules for writing Latin were learned following the pattern of classical Latin, which continued to be the basis throughout the sixteenth century and beyond. Latin was the second language for all educated people after their native tongue. The ability to write good Latin prose was the passport to official life, to what today would be called the higher civil service and diplomatic service. Even the style of the English used in many formal texts was apparently praised according to how close it came to Latin models. Most of the technical literature of the two lay professions, medicine and law, was written in Latin; and a classical education was the fundamental tool necessary for the comprehension of scientific information and the prime requisite for its practice. At about this time there was some debate about the importance of making practical information on the useful arts, trades, and sciences available, either in translation or in original English texts, for those with no knowledge of Latin. This implies that the use of English had to extend into domains that had hitherto been almost exclusively associated with Latin. The present chapter is intended to sketch the changing status and the increasing self-confidence of English from around the middle of the sixteenth century, together with the linguistic background that helps to explain the attempts by grammar masters in the 1580s to codify the rules of their native language. It will provide some examples of the system, the rules, and the method according to which William Bullokar's *Pamphlet for Grammar* was taught at the time that 'Lily's Grammar' was in use. By comparing some aspects with the authorized grammar, I hope to shed some light on the role the official Latin grammar played in the description of the rules of English, and how individual rules of the vernacular deviated from the framework of Latin.[1]

In the course of the sixteenth century English gained more and more ground and esteem in society and encroached on the domain of Latin. A higher regard for the native language becomes particularly obvious from the middle of the second half of the sixteenth century onwards. The reasons for the educated Englishman's appreciation of his own language are complex. The printing press had made reading matter much more accessible, and, in turn, literacy grew amongst the population. A large number of books on subjects that were hitherto more or less exclusively dealt with in Latin started being written in, or translated into, English. In addition, the Reformation, with its overwhelming insistence on the Bible as a guide to Christian belief and as a source of religious authority, contributed to the rise of the vernacular at the gradual expense of Latin. The word of God had to be made accessible to all individual Christians by translating it into the vernacular, something already initiated by the Wycliffites at the end of the fourteenth century but then proscribed by the Church.[2] It was Erasmus who again expressed the need for translations so that all could be familiar with the Bible. In the prologue to the 1516 edition of his new Latin translation of the New Testament, based on the original Greek texts, he claimed that the Gospel should be translated "into the tongues of all men", so that not only would women be enabled to read the Gospel and St Paul's Epistles, but ploughmen and weavers would be able to sing or recite passages from them while at work.[3] This claim could not fail to have a far-reaching effect on an already existing movement which eventually culminated in the publication of the Authorized Version of the Bible in 1611.

With the development of printing it was obviously desirable to reach the general reader and increase profits and English was the obvious medium in which works had to be published. However, the multitude of books that were printed showed a great variation in word-forms that

---

[1] On the linguistic background see Norman Blake (1996), *A History of the English Language*, Basingstoke, 172–235; Manfred Görlach (1991), *Introduction to Early Modern English*, Cambridge, repr. 1993, 36–60, 136–210; W. Keith Percival (1986), 'Renaissance Linguistics: The Old and the New', in T. Bynon and Palmer, F. R. (eds.), *Studies in the History of Western Linguistics in Honour of R. H. Robins*, Cambridge, 56–68; and Charles Barber (1997), *Early Modern English*, 2nd edn. London, repr. 2001, 42–102.

[2] Those favouring the ideas of John Wyclif (d. 1384). From an early stage they were also known as Lollards. On Wyclif see *ODNB*, vol. 60: 616–30.

[3] See R. R. Williams (1940), *Religion and the English Vernacular*, London, 36–37. On the vernacular as a medium for the Bible see Richard Foster Jones (1953), *The Triumph of the English Language*, London, repr. 1974, 53–65.

caused uncertainty and confusion and compared unfavourably with the regular and standardized spelling of Latin that was looked upon as a model. It was necessary for the early printers to provide the public with books in English that was acceptable and comprehensible to everyone, especially in relation to the orthography. As a consequence, English became the subject of scholarly study and schoolmasters' comments. At the same time this question also occupied the early printers, for example, John Rastell (c.1475–1536), as early as the 1520s onwards. The topic of spelling reform became a subject of serious discussion and different suggestions and concepts began to appear before the middle of the sixteenth century. Amongst the most prominent of those taking an active interest in the subject were Sir Thomas Smith (1513-1577), John Hart (c.1501-1574) and William Bullokar. Apart from the fact that the proposed spelling reforms were never adopted, it is significant that they were based on the spoken language.[4]

However, there was not only experimentation with the orthography of the vernacular in order to fix spelling and punctuation. At the same time severe attempts were made to enrich its vocabulary in order to make English suitable for all purposes. From the beginning of the sixteenth century until the 1570s especially, English was felt to be insufficiently expressive because it lacked the necessary vocabulary in terms of elegance. Many words were borrowed for stylistic and prestige reasons, resulting in the creation of doublets that had the same or similar meanings. It also proved inadequate to express technical and scientific concepts and discoveries. These aspects were a common cause of complaint. Attempts were made to translate Latin works into the vernacular or to compose scientific treatises in the mother tongue by coining new words where none had existed before, some of these attempts being more modest in their approach, others somewhat excessive. A notable original work amongst the skilful scientific writing by trained scholars in English in this period is Sir Thomas Elyot's *The Castel of Helth*, which became very popular from the time it first appeared in print, probably in 1534, throughout the sixteenth and into the early seventeenth centuries. Elyot was careful to advise his readers to have recourse to a physician for the diagnosing of illness, but this was obviously not enough to protect him from attack by the medical profession, for in the 1541 editions of the work he introduced a new preface answering such attacks. He also had to defend the very fact of producing his work in English. He writes:

---

[4] See Vivian Salmon (1989), 'John Rastell and the Normalization of Early Sixteenth-Century Orthography', in L. E. Breivik *et al.* (eds.), *Essays on English Language in Honour of Bertil Sundby. Studia Anglistica Norvegica* 4: 289–301; and Salmon (1999), 'Orthography and Punctuation', in *The Cambridge History of the English Language*, Vol. III, ed. Roger Lass, pp. 13–55, 670–76. On Sir Thomas Smith see *ODNB*, vol. 51: 324–30; on John Hart, *ODNB*, vol. 25: 582–83.

But if phisicions be angry, that I haue wryten phisike in englyshe, let theym remembre, that the grekes wrate in greke, the Romanes in latyne, Auicena, and the other in Arabike, whiche were their owne prope and maternal tonges.[5]

The use of Latin as the language of scholarship persisted in the sixteenth and seventeenth centuries and the books most likely to be written in Latin were works of science and the humanities, especially those aimed at an international audience. However, it becomes noticeable that attempts were made to make scientific knowledge available by using a suitably scientific vocabulary and raise English to a status equal to Latin as a language of scholarly learning. New vocabulary could be borrowed from other languages, principally from Latin and to some extent also from Greek, by devising terminations appropriate to English, or new words could be coined from the language's internal resources. In this way English augmented its already large store of scientific, technical, and general vocabulary.

In the last quarter of the sixteenth century, praise for the English language became more frequent than criticism of its deficiencies. English became increasingly used as a medium to convey scientific and scholarly thought in both original works and translations. In the 1580s especially there is a great deal of evidence that English was praised and patriotic feeling and national pride were taken in the English language. It was considered to be on the same level as Latin. This general appreciation comes to the fore especially in the work of the educational reformer and grammar master Richard Mulcaster, who was convinced that English had developed all its possibilities when, in 1582, he asks the provocative question:

But why not all in English, a tung of it self both depe in conceit, and frank in deliuerie? I do not think that anie language, be it whatsoeuer, is better able to vtter all arguments, either with more pith, or greater planesse, then our English tung is, [. . .]. And tho we vse and must vse manie foren terms, when we deal with such arguments, we do not anie more then the brauest tungs do and euen verie those, which crake of their cunning.[6]

Though Mulcaster certainly pays homage to the classical languages, he claims the use of English in the treatment of subjects which had, with exceptions, until his time been dealt with in Latin or Greek. Finally, he continues to argue that English is not only of equal status to other languages but surpasses them, an argument that overrules his earlier opinion that all languages are of equal value.

[5] See Thomas Elyot (1541a). *The Castel of Helth* (BL, C. 112.b.23, A4ᵛ) (*STC²* 7644). On this work see also pp. 85–86 above. Its earliest surviving edition is dated 1539, but Elyot's statements indicate that an earlier edition of the book was printed. The date 1534 is found on the woodcut title-page border of the BL copy, C.54.a.18 (*STC²* 7643); the colophon gives the actual publication date as 1539. For early extant editions see the Bibliography. On this work and medical treatises in general published in English see Jones (1953), 48–51, 65–66, and 79.

[6] Richard Mulcaster (1582), *Mulcaster's Elementarie*, ed. E. T. Campagnac (1925), Oxford, 274–75.

The general admiration and love for the mother tongue had consequences for language teaching. As the status of English changed, so the desirability and need to have a sound knowledge of the mother tongue and a systematized grammar of the English language grew and became increasingly evident in the last decades of the sixteenth century. An important feature in the field of education in the later Tudor period was the introduction of 'Lily's Grammar' for the instruction of Latin. The elementary part of the authorized grammar offered a system for grammar writing in English that had been known since the vernacular was used in explaining elementary Latin grammar, as exemplified in the Latin grammatical manuscripts written in English in which grammatical rules of English, in combination with Latin, were already, though implicitly, codified. During the process of teaching and explaining Latin grammar in the vernacular, the rules of English were reflected and at the same time written down in the notes of teachers and pupils. In explaining Latin rules, the metalanguage was not strictly confined to English, as a number of passages were also rendered into Latin, a method that may partly have been intended to prepare the pupils for learning Latin monolingually at an advanced level in the upper forms. Though the grammatical manuscripts written in English aimed at teaching Latin, not only was the metalanguage confined to a fixed pattern, in that English was the overall explanatory language, but at the same time the target language was not confined only to Latin. In a large number of cases it was the English that was explained in Latin categories. The explanation of Latin rules as well as those of English can be considered partly a combined process and partly a parallel one in the English grammatical manuscripts. In this way the Latin grammars written in English also encompass the beginnings of the teaching of English. This system was ultimately prescribed by royal decree and popularized in the elementary part of 'Lily's Grammar', and hence extended to the English that was used as the explanatory language. Due to its influence and status it was impossible to overlook or ignore the set of prescribed regulations in this grammar. Though the chief concern there is with Latin, the two languages were, in fact, being treated in close combination and in comparison. Latin was not only taught in English, but the Latin grammatical categories were being expressed in terms of English structure, rules of the vernacular were being explained in the framework of the classical language, and its terminology was also in English and moreover in the English of contemporary usage, as the English grammatical manuscripts illustrate.[7] Consequently it must have

---

[7] See John Walmsley (2004), 'Latein als Objektsprache, Englisch als Metasprache in Spätmittelalterlichen Grammatischen Texten', in G, Haßler and G. Volkmann (eds.), *History of Linguistics in Texts and Concepts*, 2 vols., Müster, vol. 2: 458–66. For the question of how far English as the explanatory language affected the description of elementary Latin grammar in the grammatical manuscripts and early printed grammars in English see also Thomas

seemed a logical step to grammarians in the late Tudor period, when setting out to compile rules of their native language, to have recourse to the elementary part of 'Lily's Grammar' which continued the tradition of the Latin grammars that had been explained in the vernacular for over two hundred years and more and to use it as a point of departure for a grammar of English. The close treatment of the two languages together in 'Lily's Grammar' suggested that English was also subject to the same grammatical system and with the same categories as Latin. In the grammar of English, however, the vernacular no longer had the ancillary function assigned to it to explain rules of the target language Latin, but took over the status of Latin and became itself the target language whilst continuing to remain the metalanguage.

In applying Latin grammatical categories to the vernacular, William Bullokar was backed up by a tradition dating back over two hundred years. However, his *Pamphlet for Grammar* represents the earliest extant example of a grammar in which Latin grammatical categories continued to be applied to English and in which, at the same time, English gained the status of the target language. The process towards this status commenced, however implicitly, at the time that elementary Latin was being explained in English, as the Latin grammatical manuscripts written in the vernacular illustrate.

5.2 *William Bullokar's* Pamphlet for Grammar *(1586)*

William Bullokar (c.1531–1609), a spelling reformer and grammarian, is famous for having compiled a grammar of the English language, the earliest surviving grammar published in English known to exist at present.[8] The *Pamphlet for Grammar* is said to have been Bullokar's major achievement. It has to be considered a pioneer work, in that English acquired a different status from that achieved in the tradition of elementary grammar teaching. It provides the earliest evidence of a set of rules for the English language presented in a systematic and effective way which the student needs to know when studying the language. Grammatical rules and the structures of English are codified and set out, a method for which no earlier evidence exists and which testifies that the

---

Kohnen (2001). 'Creating Conterparts of Latin: The Implicit Vernacular Tradition in Late Middle English and Early Modern English Grammars and Textbooks', in Hannes Kniffka (ed.), *Indigenous Grammar Across Cultures*, Frankfurt am Main, 507-43, at 508, 514-32.

[8] For information about Bullokar's life and works see Emma Vorlat (2009), in *Lexicon Grammaticorum*, vol. 1: 227-28; *ODNB*, vol. 8: 651-52; Monique Verrac (2000*b*), in *HEL*, vol. 2, no. 3603: 97-100; E. J. Dobson (1968), *English Pronunciation, 1500-1700*, 2 vols. 2nd edn, vol. 1: 93-96; also the introduction to William Bullokar (1580-1581), *A Short Introduction or Guiding*, in B. Danielsson and R. C. Alston (eds.) (1966), *The Works of William Bullokar*, Vol. 1, Leeds, x-xlii.

native language itself has come to be the aim of instruction. Moreover, Bullokar's grammar illustrates that English can be taught formally and that its rules and its structures can be explained in the same language. It is intended that the student should learn how to recognize its forms and structures and also learn how to compose it in the same way as he has to learn Latin, or in the case of the foreigner, how he may already have learned Latin.

Only two copies of the *Pamphlet for Grammar* are known to have survived, one in the Bodleian Library, Oxford (Tanner 67(5)), and the other in the library of Christ Church, Oxford. The Bodleian copy is misbound, with the title-leaf at the end, and since the time of its first editor, Max Plessow, this work has been referred to by its running-title *Bref Grammar*. Christ Church Library, Oxford, possesses a perfect copy of the *Pamphlet for Grammar* with its proper title-page in the correct place. The grammar was printed throughout in Bullokar's reformed orthography by Edmund Bollifant, alias Carpenter, in London in 1586. Both copies contain manuscript notes and corrections and a series of numbers added in the margins, all of them in Bullokar's own hand.[9] No further editions are known, though his notes and his practice of revising suggest that he planned a further edition. The grammar may have become unobtainable after some time, which, to a considerable extent, may be due to the spelling that was used. A modern critical edition does not yet exist.

On the title-page of his work Bullokar called his grammar *William Bullokarz Pamphlet for Grammar: Or rather too be saied hiz Abbreuiation of hiz Grammar for English, extracted out-of hiz Grammar at-larg.* It is described in a similar way at the beginning of the section on the parts of speech. At the end of the grammar Bullokar added by hand in the copy in the Bodleian

---

[9] The text of the two copies is made available in J. R. Turner's facsimile edition (1980), William Bullokar (1586), *Pamphlet for Grammar*, in *The Works of William Bullokar*, Vol. II, Leeds, where the text in facsimiles of the corresponding pages has been printed side by side so that a comparison can be made between them with regard to both the printed texts and the manuscript additions. The facsimile of the Bodl. Lib. copy is printed at the top of each page and that of the Christ Church copy is printed below it. The text of the Bodl. Lib. copy is also reproduced in William Bullokar, *Booke at Large* (1580) and *Bref Grammar for English* (1586), Facsimile Reproductions with an Introduction by Diane Bornstein (1977), Delmar, New York. Along with Bullokar's other writings, the grammar contained in the Bodl. Lib. copy was edited by Max Plessow (1906), entitled '*Bref Grammar for English*' by William Bullokar, in *Geschichte der Fabeldichtung in England bis zu John Gay* (1726), Berlin. In Plessow's edition the grammar is given as two separate works, owing to the fact that this copy is misbound, with the title-leaf at the end, and treated as such by subsequent scholars. See Plessow's text, 331–85, 386–88. The work is listed as two grammars in Kennedy, nos. 5700 and 5701: 204. R. C. Alston has proved that the Bodleian copy is wrongly bound and that *Bref Grammar* is the running-title for the work. See Alston (1965–; 1974 repr.), vol. 1, no. 1: 2; Alston (1966), 184; also R. H. Robins (1998b). 'William Bullokar's *Bref Grammar for English: Text and Context*', in V. Law (ed.), *Texts and Contexts. Selected Papers on the History of Linguistics*, Münster, 169–84, at 170. The text of the Bodl. Lib. copy is also available in digitized form in *EEBO*. The grammar is listed *STC*[2] (*STC*) 4087 and *ESTC* S109589. For brief information about its printer, Edmund Bollifant see *STC*[2], vol. 3: 25.

Library: "for this iz the first gramar for english that ever waz: except my gramar at larg."[10] At various points throughout the book Bullokar makes it clear that the *Pamphlet for Grammar* represents an extract of *The Grammar at Large*, a publication for which we have no other evidence.[11] The latter grammar does not seem to have survived, nor is there any evidence of its having been printed. The *Pamphlet for Grammar* was apparently part of an overall plan to provide a complete course for the teaching of literacy. This would include a grammar and a set of readers in the new alphabet, and would make it necessary to accommodate the different symbols that his orthography required, in the various styles of Tudor handwriting. Bullokar planned to compile a dictionary of different spellings for homophones, which he ultimately did not live to complete.

Bullokar's *Pamphlet for Grammar* states three aims and is aimed at both English students and foreigners. First, it is intended as a grammar for English-speaking students to learn how to parse English quickly "for the perfecter wryting thær-of, and vzing of the best phrases thær-in". Second, it aims to introduce native speakers of English to the secrets of the grammar of other languages "ruled or not ruled by Grammar" and of understanding them more readily. Third, his grammar is aimed at foreigners, *i.e.* speakers of other vernaculars, who want to learn English perfectly and quickly.[12] The *Pamphlet for Grammar* comprises eighty pages and begins with a short chapter on phonology and orthography in which Bullokar recognizes forty-four distinct sound units—consonants, vowels, and diphthongs—which he represents by the letters of the alphabet with or without diacritical marks. This section is followed by Bullokar's address to the reader, a lengthy epistle in fifty-one rhyming verses in which he explains and justifies his grammar. This is followed by the treatment of the eight parts of speech, a short treatise on syntax, and a text on prosody. Bullokar's grammar appears to be the first in a line of grammars of English that apply a Latin grammatical framework.

When Bullokar's *Pamphlet for Grammar* was compiled, instruction in schools meant the teaching of the rules found in 'Lily's Grammar'. The authorized grammar occupied the prime and central place in education and hence it was impossible to overlook or avoid its overwhelming influ-

[10] See the *Pamphlet for Grammar*, the text on accidence, heading, 1, also the addition in manuscript at the end of the text on prosody, 68. (All references are to Turner's facsimile edition (1980).)

[11] In verse 37 of the section 'William Bullokar to the Rædor' of his *Pamphlet for Grammar* he compares it to *The Grammar at Large* as follows: "A Twin this volum iz, that hath / a felow of mor fam, / whoo shal in swadling cloths ly stil, / vntil it tak hiz nam." (Apart from the diacritics that have been omitted and the ligatures -oo and -wh that have been reproduced as two letters, Bullokar's spelling has been preserved in all quotations.) There are two further references to *The Grammar at Large* in his *Pamphlet*, on pp. 33 and 38.

[12] *Pamphlet for Grammar*, title-page.

ence, a fact testified to by the number of editions that became available in a multitude of copies and also by the attention it received from the authorities. Bullokar's grammar must also be seen in the context of the high esteem in which Latin was held in late Tudor England and far beyond, as an international language with universally acknowledged rules which served very many purposes in society. Moreover, it has to be viewed in the context of an established tradition of writing and reading the vernacular, a vital prerequisite for Bullokar's vernacular grammar, or else it would have found few users.

The *Pamphlet for Grammar* has usually been studied from the point of view of its contribution to grammatical theory, as a starting point for studies of grammar writing in English and the English grammar tradition, for English word-formation, and for the teaching of English.[13] Since it was published in Bullokar's reformed orthography, it has also been studied from a phonological point of view.[14] It was compiled when 'Lily's Grammar' was in use and at a time when the vernacular was enjoying a rise in esteem. In this way it is interesting to draw attention to the linguistic and intellectual context of its author's own time, and finally to his own appreciation and response in the form of a grammatical treatise.

William Bullokar's grammar serves as a representative of the new evaluation of the vernacular in England and gives a brief assessment of his native language. It may be taken as a response to the needs and the challenge of a new situation and the intellectual context of his time which sought to have the rules of English written down and made available for systematic study. Starting from the text of the *Pamphlet for Grammar* itself, even its title reflects the new view and claim of the vernacular in that the work is actually called a grammar, a term hitherto reserved for the study of Latin and one which embodied its cultural dominance. Bullokar's grammar is called a grammar of English, in the same way as 'Lily's Grammar' is denominated a grammar for the study of Latin, which was a

---

[13] See, for example, Ute Dons (2004), *Descriptive Adequacy of Early Modern English Grammars*, Berlin and New York, v, 7, passim; Lilo Moessner (2000), 'Word-Formation in Early Modern English Grammars', in B. Reitz und S. Rieuwerts (eds.), *Anglistentag 1999. Mainz. Proceedings*, Trier, 21–34; G. A. Padley (1985), *Grammatical Theory in Western Europe, 1500–1700. Trends in Vernacular Grammar*, I, Cambridge, 146–52; Ian Michael (1970), *English Grammatical Categories and the Tradition to 1800*, Cambridge 214, 328, passim; Ivan Poldauf, 45–48; Otto Funke (1941), *Die Frühzeit der Englischen Grammatik*, Bern, 25–27, 52–58. Cf., however, Shoichi Watanabe's analysis of the structure of Bullokar's grammar in his doctoral thesis of 1958, *Studien zur Abhängigkeit der Frühneuenglischen Grammatiken von den Mittelalterlichen Lateingrammatiken*, Münster, 103–50.
[14] Dobson (1968), vol. 1, 97–117; R. E. Zachrisson (1927), *The English Pronunciation at Shakespeare's Time as Taught by William Bullokar*, New York (repr. 1970).

school discipline.[15] The English part of 'Lily's Grammar' was entitled *A Shorte Introduction Of Grammar* according to the evidence of the 1548 edition onwards.[16] This application of the term to a textbook for the study of English implies that the term 'grammar' was on the way to becoming a generic one. No longer is any difference made in the use of 'grammar' that was learned, *i.e.* Latin grammar, and the vernacular which was acquired untaught. In this particular case it was Bullokar's concern to show that English, in the same way as Latin, can be subject to grammatical study. It follows grammatical constraints, exhibits a grammatical structure, and can be taught in that way and through that framework. That it is a perfectly "ruled tongue" Bullokar obviously discovered on his travels abroad, when he observed foreigners trying to learn English. In his auto-biographical remarks he claims to have seen military service abroad in the reign of Queen Mary. He says in the rhymed introduction to his grammar:

> And by my trauel English tryd,
> a perfect ruled tung,
> conferabl in Grammar-art,
> with any ruled long.[17]

English is as orderly and as subject to grammatical rules as any language that has been the object of prolonged teaching. Bullokar's opinion, set out in this verse, makes clear both the principal purpose and the contemporary context of his writing such a grammar book aimed at native speakers of English as well at foreigners. His grammar addresses his students in a form different from the grammar of Latin by stating a number of aims for different purposes:

This being sufficient [*i.e.* Bullokar's extract from his *Grammar at Large*] for the spedi lærning how too parc English spech for the perfecter wryting thær-of, and vzing of the best phrases thær-in, and the æzier entranc intoo the secrets of Grammar for other langages, and the spedier vnderstanding of other langages ruled or not ruled by Grammar: very-profitabl for the English nation that dezyreth too lærn any strang langag: and very-aid-ful-too the strangor too lærn english perfectly and spedily.[18]

---

[15] Cf. *OED*, grammar, *n.* 1.a., in which the first evidence of the extended application of the term 'grammar' to 'English grammar' is said to have been apparently Ben Jonson's book, written *c.*1600. The respective entry in the *OED* is given as: *a*1637 B. JONSON *Eng. Gram.* I.i. in *Wks* (1640) III, "*Grammar* is the art of true, and well speaking a Language: the writing is but an Accident".

[16] See Appendix III, 8.0.

[17] Bullokar, *Pamphlet for Grammar*, To the Rædor, verse 42. Cf. *OED*, ruled, *ppl.* a. where there is no reference to language governed by rules. However, see *OED*, rule, *n.* II. 7. c. Grammar, where the first entry referring to English grammar is 1636 B. JONSON *Eng. Gram.* xiv. Cf. also *OED*, conferrable, *a.*, where the first example is dated 1660. See the comments on Bullokar's grammar in Robins (1998*a*). 'The Evolution of English Grammar Books Since the Renaissance', in V. Law (ed.), *Texts and Contexts. Selected Papers on the History of Linguistics*, Münster, 113–28, at 115, 119.

[18] *Pamphlet for Grammar*, title-page.

Its first aim was to make native speakers take another look at their own language which they had used from the beginning and probably thought they already knew. They are taught to parse English in order to write it perfectly which, in turn, was to enable them to recognize the words and fit them accurately into the framework of the eight parts of speech according to the same method that grammar-school boys applied when analysing Latin. By their daily translation practice from English into Latin and vice versa, students were to be enabled to analyse English vocabulary in the same way as Latin and distribute it according to the Latin framework, a teaching method that indicates that the vernacular can be described in terms of Latin. By equating English words to Latin inflected words, students came to regard them as belonging to the same formal categories and applied the names of Latin forms to English.

Bullokar's aims also indicate that the study of English would provide native speakers of English with a sound basis for learning Latin or any other language. Moreover, learning the rules of English first enables students to learn other foreign languages more easily. These aims reflect a change in the attitude towards the use of the vernacular. Bullokar saw the possibility of using the vernacular as a tool for the learning of Latin, and, at the same time, in connection with learning other vernacular languages. It thus becomes obvious that English should get attention and was deserving of study in its own right. Moreover, its study also has a propaedeutic value for learning Latin and other vernacular languages. In addition, Bullokar's *Pamphlet for Grammar* addresses foreign speakers, *i.e.* speakers of other vernacular languages, to teach them English as a foreign language. Given these aims, his grammar suited different kinds of students in approaching English and presented its rules in the common way like Latin grammar, and in the manner with which some of his students were already familiar. The aims stated in Bullokar's grammar indicate his attempt to demonstrate that the rules of English conform to the long-established rules of Latin grammar.[19] He intends to demonstrate that English is as good and well-furnished a language as any and better than some, even though this was not fully appreciated in his own time.

5.3 *'Lily's Grammar' as the model for the first grammar of English*

William Bullokar's *Pamphlet for Grammar* has not only to be viewed against its historical and cultural background, but has also to be seen in its linguistic and pedagogical context, as one representative of the

---

[19] It was only later, when the rule-governed nature of English was widely accepted, that a subsequent generation of grammarians asked for new categories which described the vernacular as fully as possible.

genre of teaching grammars. In this respect it can be compared with the authorized Latin grammar. It is of interest to examine which rules of English Bullokar documented in his grammar and the way he presented them to achieve his educational aims. Given the enormous impact of the Latin grammar on formal study due to its renown as the official grammar, together with its widespread use and availability, it is not surprising that its influence can be discovered in Bullokar's work. A link between the vernacular grammar and the Latin grammar underlying it has been indicated in several studies, but has not yet been examined in detail. Bullokar's grammar has quite often been dismissed as Latinate, in that it copies or closely imitates 'Lily's Grammar' and was denounced as unoriginal in its descriptive apparatus; for example, in the grammatical categories the definitions of the parts of speech are said to be inadequate for the description and teaching of English. However, this view does not reflect the linguistic interests and assumptions expressed in Bullokar's *Pamphlet for Grammar*. Looked at from the point of view of its conception and purpose, and in the context of the genre of contemporary grammar writing and in its teaching context, his grammar was exactly the kind that his English students needed and with which foreign students were already familiar, where the presentation of the rules according to the Latin pattern was practical and pedagogically effective. In respect to its contents, as Bullokar expresses explicitly in his verses, English was considered worthy of study in its own right, notwithstanding the traditional status of Latin. From that point of view it is of interest to look at the different ways Bullokar attempts to put his grammar on a level equal to Latin, to see how the conceptual framework is taken over from Latin and applied to the vernacular, and also to discover indications of his awareness of the different structure of English.[20]

The chances are that Bullokar was himself taught from 'Lily's Grammar' for the latter part of his schooling and must surely have used it when he was working as a schoolmaster. However, it is not known to which edition of the authorized grammar he had access, nor is it known which other sources, Latin and English, influenced him or were available to him. He certainly received inspiration from his own teaching experience, as he was employed in the 1550s as a schoolmaster, and also from his military service abroad in the reign of Queen Mary.[21] Stating that English, just as

---

[20] See Werner Hüllen (2002), 'Three Properties of Early European Language Teaching and Learning', in W. Hüllen and F. Klippel (eds.), *Heilige und Profane Sprachen*, 211–20, at 215; also Robins (1998*b*), 169.

[21] Funke's argument in his (1938) article, 'William Bullokars Bref Grammar For English (1586)', 118–19, that for the compilation of this grammar Bullokar uses a revision of 'Lily's Grammar' as it is extant in the editions after 1557 and of the copy of the 1566 edition as edited by Blach, denominated by Funke as L^1, requires revision. Cf. also p. 19 above. A critical

Latin, is a rule-governed language, he tries to compare it in terms of being a copy of Latin which had the one and only system of grammatical rules that enjoyed universal acceptance. Consequently, his aim was to show that English conformed to the rules of Latin. This shaping influence and even a family resemblance to 'Lily's Grammar' becomes immediately evident in Bullokar's *Pamphlet for Grammar*.[22] A few examples must be sufficient here to illustrate this connection.

In Bullokar's grammar, morphology is discussed in detail, but only a small section is devoted to syntax. In the discussion of the parts of speech, in the same way as in the English part of 'Lily's Grammar', Bullokar does not begin with a definition of grammar but immediately embarks on listing the eight parts of speech, divided into the group of those which are declinable, the noun (including the adjective), pronoun, and verb and those that are indeclinable: the participle, adverb, conjunction, preposition, and interjection. English vocabulary, like that of Latin, can be classified according to the eight parts of speech. In Bullokar's own words: "So, that ther iz no-on word too be vttered in our spech, but it iz on of the eiht parts befor mentioned."[23] In this way the Latin framework used by Ælfric in his Latin grammar that was explained in Old English and handed down in the English grammatical manuscripts, the early printed grammars in English, and the English part of 'Lily's Grammar' was taken over into the English language of the late sixteenth century when the English words were assigned to each word class. As in 'Lily's Grammar', Bullokar continues to provide a definition of each part of speech, give subdivisions of some of them, include an account of each accident in turn, and provide illustrative examples. The conformity to the Latin grammar becomes especially obvious in the discussion of the adverb, conjunction, and interjection, where the discussion focuses on semantic categories. Bullokar lists the same classes in the same order, with little deviation except in the names given to the classes.

As the standard was set by Latin, it appears that Bullokar wanted to indicate that English is on the same level as Latin. That implies that he had to adjust and integrate English rules to the Latinate tradition that set the standard and provided the model. It was his aim to demonstrate that Latin grammar could be properly and successfully applied to English and that English was, therefore, itself a 'proper ruled tongue'. Once the English language could be shown to have rules then it was demonstrably equal to Latin. Consequently English must have the same *partes orationis* and

---

edition of Bullokar's grammar may shed light on the material that was available to him, in particular on the text of 'Lily's Grammar'. He probably used an edition of the authorized grammar that was available to him around the time he compiled his *Pamphlet for Grammar*.

[22] See Vivien Law (2003), *The History of Linguistics in Europe. From Plato to 1600*, Cambridge, 239.

[23] See *Pamphlet for Grammar*, the beginning of the text on accidence, 1, lines 4–8.

grammatical categories as Latin. Although the order of the parts of speech is that of 'Lily's Grammar', they are no longer divided into two equal groups, as in the Latin grammar, according to the presence or absence of inflections. A few examples, from a large field, which needs further detailed research, may give some idea of the way English was at first adapted to the existing structure of Latin grammar. In Bullokar's grammar there are three word classes characterized by inflections, and five word classes that lack the inflected category; the first of the latter group is represented by the participle. Bullokar's discussion of the participle begins as follows:

A Participl iz a part of spech deryued of a verb, from whoom it taketh hiz significa-tion or mæning: and being of the Present-tenc endeth in, ing, aded too the simpl of the verb: az of too lou, louing: of too tæch, tæching: and may be vzed absolutly without any substantiu gerundially iooined mostly in composition after a prep-osition: az, in-louing goodnes, and by-tæching the sam, vertu iz encræced [etc.].[24]

Compare the beginning of the treatment of the participle in the authorized grammar:

A Participle is a parte of speche, deriued of a verbe, and taketh part of a nowne as gendre and case, parte of a verbe, as tense and signification: and parte of bothe, as number and figure. A participle hath .iiii. tenses, the present, the preter, the future in *rus*, and the future in *dus*.

A participle of the present tense hath his englysshe endyng in yng, as louyng, and his latine in *ans*, or *ens*, as *Amans, docens*: And it is fourmed of the preterimperfect tense, by chaungyng *bam*, into *ens*, as *Amabam, amans, Audiebam audiens*. [etc.].[25]

Only the first part, namely that the participle is derived from a verb, follows verbatim the definition of the participle as given in 'Lily's Grammar'. Formal criteria, for example, the endings of the present and past participles and also illustrative examples, follow the authorized grammar.

The framework of Latin grammar can also be seen in further examples. The English articles *A, An*, or *The*, having no Latin counterpart, are not given full word-class status, but merely referred to as notes or signs of a following noun to identify them as such. Only their usage is briefly described.[26] The Latin tradition is also seen in the retention of the adjective within the noun class. It is defined solely in syntactic terms: "A Nown-Adiectiu iz a word not perfectly vnderstanded except a nown-substantiu be iooyned with it."[27]

Another striking example of English being presented in the Latin framework can be illustrated by the discussion of the accident declension

---

[24] *Pamphlet for Grammar*, 36, lines 24–26, and 37, lines 1–7.
[25] Chapter 7, *Introduction*, 184, lines 901–905, and 185, lines 906–909.
[26] *Pamphlet for Grammar*, within the definition of the noun, 1, lines 12–19, and 2, lines 1–4.
[27] *Pamphlet for Grammar*, within the definition of the noun, 1, lines 16–19, and 2, lines 1–4, 9–15. The quotation is at p. 2, lines 9–11.

of the noun substantive. Bullokar's presentation of English noun paradigms only shows distinct forms in the singular and plural, one for the nominative, accusative, gainative, *i.e.* dative, vocative, and the other for the genitive case. He lists five groups of nouns in his grammar. Cf., for example, the third group of nouns, ending in *-l, -m, -n, -r* and in a consonant before *-l*:

Singularly	bul,			bulz.	
Nominatiu,	ram,			ramz.	
Accusatiu,	pan,		Genitiu	panz.	
Gainatiu and	bar			barz.	
Vocatiu,	trobl,			troblz.	

Plurally	bulz,			bulzes.	
Nominatiu,	ramz,			ramzes.	
Accusatiu,	panz,		Genitiu	panzes.	
Gainatiu and	barz,			barzes.	
Vocatiu,	troblz,			troblzes. [28]	

Bullokar recognized or assumed the six Latin cases. He set out the case paradigm with four cases in English, the nominative, accusative, gainative, and vocative, which cannot be distinguished morphologically, except the genitive which is in part morphologically marked. Each case is distinguished by its place in the sentence or by the preposition that precedes it. The sixth case of the Latin paradigm not listed for English is defined by Bullokar as follows: "The cas caled Ablatiu in Latin or other langag iz in english the accusatiu, thowh gouerned of a preposition signifying ablatiuly."[29] In the Latin grammar this scheme is used to denote the property of inflection, *i.e.* to set out the quantity of Latin noun endings for the different declensions which show a change in the relation of these words. There are five declensions in Latin which are characterized by the final letter of their respective stems. The case-endings in combination with the stem-characteristics give rise to the system of terminations. In Bullokar's grammar, however, this scheme is adopted to a different end, namely to detail the endings of five groups of different nouns themselves.[30]

---

[28] *Pamphlet for Grammar*, 8, lines 6–15.
[29] *Pamphlet for Grammar*, 6, lines 14–16.
[30] See Bullokar's comment in the passage on the declension of adjectives before substantives: "and then [they] folow the declyning of a substantiu according too the ending letter: az befor iz shewed too declyn a substantiu." *Pamphlet for Grammar*, 13, lines 1–2. However, his procedure of stacking different lexical items into the same paradigm and his focusing on the final consonants of the nouns that he chooses to put in the same paradigm have to be discussed.

On the other hand, Bullokar made use of categories that had no counterpart in 'Lily's Grammar', a fact that demonstrates that independent and critical thought had been given to this subject. One can notice only a few of his observations on the structural diversity of English and the phenomena not found in Latin, such as the use of 'do' as a substitute verb as in "how doo you think? az you doo".[31] Another example is the use of 'did' in the preter tense with no function other than to mark tense, as in "I did lou, thu didst lou".[32] Finally, the present tense with future meaning, as in "I ryd ten dayz henc, and my man cometh after me",[33] Bullokar made many other original comments on the peculiarities of English grammar that he integrated into the Latin framework.

Bullokar's aim was to show that English conforms to the rules of Latin. He undertook the task of proving its conformity to Latin, and by doing so he intended to show that English is no longer inferior to Latin. The subjects that are treated in his grammar were determined by the tradition of Latin grammar, and his own grammar does not deviate greatly from these prescribed fields of interest. This does not, however, preclude innovations. 'Lily's Grammar' provides the background against which Bullokar's grammar must be seen. Bullokar's interests and aims and the problems he faced were also partly those of 'Lily's Grammar'. Apart from that, his attitude towards the vernacular must be taken into account. It becomes obvious that his *Pamphlet for Grammar* continued, on the one hand, to utilize the technique of description and the framework from 'Lily's Grammar' in order to use it for his own account of English. In this way he used concepts and methods that had been inherited, in an unbroken tradition, from the time when Ælfric compiled his Latin grammar in Old English and again later, when the Latin grammatical manuscripts were written in English. On the other hand, however, Bullokar was well aware that the English and Latin grammatical structures diverge. In his brief prosody written in verse he remarks that English "should be wrongd if you it ty /vntoo a strang tungs grac".[34] He integrates the peculiarities of his own language into the traditional Latin framework. In this way the first grammar of English represents the beginning of a continuing process of testing and revising the grammatical framework handed down in the Latin-based system of description, in the light of actually observed English forms and structures.

In this context it is possible to indicate a characteristic problem in the history of grammar. The tradition of Latin grammar writing in English that culminated in the elementary part of 'Lily's Grammar' was an overpowering feature. Moreover, this tradition was, in addition, reinforced

---

[31] *Pamphlet for Grammar*, 35, lines 24–26.
[32] *Pamphlet for Grammar*, 24, lines 21–22.
[33] *Pamphlet for Grammar*, 32, lines 17–20.
[34] *Pamphlet for Grammar*, 64, line 25, and 65, line 1.

and prolonged by the authorization of 'Lily's Grammar' by the king. It is Bullokar's *Pamphlet for Grammar* which illustrates that the imitation of the Latin grammatical tradition written in English had a definite place in the development of the vernacular tradition. Though the peculiarities of English were realized, it took a long time and probably much intellectual confidence to introduce any change in a time-honoured system when applying it to the vernacular, and finally to abandon it completely. The extent to which innovation was brought in by the peculiarities of the vernacular and the extent of their impact on the treatment of the material in Bullokar's *Pamphlet for Grammar* have still to be discovered in detail. However, once the step to compile a guide for the rules of the native language within the framework of Latin had been undertaken, the writing of grammars of English developed its own momentum, was copied by others and refined. According to present evidence, William Bullokar's grammar, the earliest extant grammar of English, represents the first step in this direction.

6. PHYSICAL DESCRIPTION AND EDITORIAL PRINCIPLES

6.1 *Bibliographical description of the* Introduction

An appreciation of the physical aspects of the volume in which the 1542 edition of *An Introduction of the eyght partes of speche, and the Construction of the same* is contained is necessary for an understanding of the context in which this important text has come down to us. This quarto volume contains three separate works, printed on vellum and partially illuminated in gold and colours, which have remained together since their production in the mid-sixteenth century. The first piece, of only four leaves, is *Alphabetum Latino Anglicum*, an *ABC* with various prayers in Latin and English, printed in London by Thomas Berthelet and dated 1543. The second, *An Introduction of the eyght partes of speche, and the Construction of the same*, is discussed in more detail below, and the third and most substantial piece is the *Institutio Compendiaria*, also attributed to Lily, printed by Berthelet in 1540. The detailed bibliographical description of the *Introduction* is followed by sections dealing with various aspects of the volume as a whole.

The following bibliographical description is based on a personal examination of the original. The following conventions have been adopted. A superscript numeral after initial letters indicates the equivalent number of lines of adjacent text that the initial occupies. A vertical stroke (|) indicates the end of a line of text in the original. Round *r* and long *s* are given as *r* and *s*; ligatures are given as two letters.

No attempt has been made to differentiate between various forms of black-letter, all of which are transcribed in Times New Roman. Similarly, roman and italic types are not distinguished, both being also transcribed in Times New Roman and are italicized. Varying type sizes have been standardized.

The titles of the different sections and the colophon are given in extenso; of the beginning and end of the individual texts about twenty words are quoted. Abbreviations (e.g. w^t (with), q3 (*-que*)) have been retained. The Latin digraphs æ and œ are reproduced as given. Obvious printers' errors are indicated by [*sic*]. The punctuation and chapter marks of the original have been preserved. Ornaments have been reproduced or described. Only the printed lines, including the headline at the beginning of a new text, have been counted. All sizes are given in millimetres, the vertical measurement stated first.

Contents of *An Introduction of the eyght partes of speche* (1542):

[Title A1ʳ, within title-page border (McK&F 19; Greg, Border B, 198–200, illuminated):] *AN INTRO=|DVCTION OF | THE EYGHT | PARTES | OF |* speche, and the Construction of | the same, compiled and sette | forthe by the commaūde=|men tof [*sic*] our most gra=|cious souerayne | lorde the | king.| [leaf type orn.] | *ANNO.MD.XLII.*

[Begins A1ᵛ, lines 1–4:] *H⁶ENRY THE .VIII. BY | THE GRACE OF GOD KYNG |* of Englād, Fraunce, and Ireland, de=|fendour of the feithe, and of the church | [Ends A1ᵛ, lines 26–32:] bryefely and playnely to be com=|pyled and set forth. Fayle | not to apply your scho|lars in lernynge | and godly e=|ducation.| [A triangle of three asterisks]

[Heading A2ʳ:] [Leaf type orn.] *TO THE REDER* [triangular mark] | [Lines 2–6:] *A⁶LBEIT THIS Realme of* | Englande hath iuste cause to thynke it | selfe moste bounden to the goodnes of | God, for manifolde and sundry bene=|fittes [Ends A3ʳ, lines 27–30:] with you. For whom ye haue great cause to praye that | he may be the soonne of a longe lyuyng father. | [In tabular form, braced to left:] Lerne dylygently. | Loue God entierly.

[Heading A3ᵛ:] [Leaf type orn.] *AD PVBEM ANGLICAM | HEXASTICON.* | [Lines 3–4:] *O² TVA parue puer non parua est gloria, Rex est | Commoda qui studiis prospicit ampla tuis.*| [Ends line 8:] *Hæc hauri, hæc auidis faucibus ebibito.*| [Row of leaf type orn.] | [Greg, *Ornament o*, 212–14; with the legend: *ARMA REGIS ANGLIE ET F.* (= Beale 17)] | [Leaf type orn.] *GOD SAVE THE | KYNG* [triangular mark]

[Heading A4ʳ:] [Leaf type orn.] *AN INTRODVCTION | of the eighte partes of speche.*| [Begins line 3:] *I²N speche be these .viii. partes folovvyng.* [Lines 4–7, in tabular form:] [Left column:] Nowne| Pronowne| Verbe| Participle| [Four lines braced to right] [between lines 5 and 6:] declyned. [Four lines braced to left] [Right column:] Aduerbe| Coniunction| Preposition| Interecition [*sic*].| [Four lines braced to right] [in lines 5 and 6:] vndecly|ned. [Chapter heading, line 8:] [Leaf type orn.] *Of the novvne.* [Begins lines 9–12:] *A⁷ NOVVNE IS the name* | of a thyng that maye bee seen, felt, | heard or vnderstand. As the name | of my hande in latine is *Manus.* | [Ends F2ʳ, lines 27–29:] [Paragraph mark] Some of laughyng, as *Hah, ha, he.* | [paragraph mark] Some of callyng, as *Eho, oh, io,* [added by hand:] *heus, o.* | [paragraph mark] Some of silence, as *Au.* And suche other.

[Heading F2ᵛ:] [Leaf type orn.] *GODLY LESSONS* | for Chyldren. [Begins lines 3–7:] *I⁷T IS THE FYRST* | poynte of wysedome, to knowe | thy selfe. | *Primus est sapientiæ gradus te ipsum | noscere.*| [Ends F4ʳ, lines 17–20:] A lyer is not beleued, though he swere. | *Mendaci non creditur ne iurato quidem.*| Let no daye scape without profitte. | *Nullus prætereat sine linea dies.*

[Heading F4ʳ, lines 21–22:] [Leaf type orn.] *THE CONCORDES | of latyne speche.* [Begins lines 23–25:] F⁶Or the due ioynyng of woordes in con|struction, it is to be vnderstande, that | in latyn speche there be .iii. concordes. [Ends H4ʳ, lines 26–30:] Certaine an accusatyue, as *Heu stirpem inuisam.* Cer=|tayne a vocatyue, as *Proh sancte Iupiter.*| And the same *proh*, wyll haue also an accusatiue, as | *Proh deum atq; hominum fidem.*| *FINIS.*

[Heading H4ᵛ:] *GVLILIELMI Lilii ad suos discipulos monita | pædagogica, seu carmen de moribus.*| [Begins lines 3–5:] *Q⁴VI mihi discipulus puer es, cupis atqȝ doceri,*| *Huc ades, hæc animo concipe dicta tuo.*| *Mane citus lectum fuge, mollem discute somnum:* | [Ends I1ᵛ, lines 24–27:] *Et tecum quoties ís'qȝ, redis'qȝ, feras.*| *Effuge uel causas faciunt quæcun'qȝ nocentem,*| *In quibus & nobis displicuisse potes.*| [Cross type orn.] *FINIS* [cross type orn.]

[Title I2ʳ:] [Leaf type orn.] *CHRISTIANI HOMINIS* | *INSTITVTVM PER ERASMVM* | *ROTERODAMVM.*| [Lines 4–5:] *Ad Galat. 5.*| *Valet in Christo fides quæ per dilec-tionē operatur.*| [Headings, lines 6–7:] *FIDES.*| *CREDO. PRIMVS ARTICVLVS.*| [Begins lines 8–10:] *C⁵Onfiteor primum ore pio, ueneror'qȝ fideli*| *Mente deum patrē, uel nutu cuncta potentē.*| *Hunc, qui stelligeri spaciosa uolumina cœli,*| [Ends I5ʳ, lines 5–8:] *Atqȝ his præsidijs armatus (sic uti dignum est | Christicola) forti ac fidenti pectore, uita* | *Decedam, bonitate dei super omnia fretus.*| *HOC FAC ET VIVES.*| [Colophon lines 9–14:] [Leaf type orn.] *LONDINI* [leaf type orn.] | *IN OFFICINA Thomæ Bertheletity-|pis [sic] impress.*| *Cum priuilegio ad imprimen-|dum solum.*| [Greg, *Ornament 1*, state TBᵇ, 210 (= Beale 16)] | *ANNO.M.D.XLII.* [Device I5ᵛ:] [McK 80].

Collation: 4°: A–H⁴ I⁶ (I6 blank), 38 leaves, unnumbered.

Signatures:
Of gathering A only A2 has a signature, gatherings B and G are signed 1–2, and in gatherings C–F and H–I the first three leaves are signed. On the first leaf of a gathering the signatures consist of a capital letter only, for example B, except for gatherings F and I, where the capital is followed by a lower-case roman numeral enclosed within full stops, for example F.i. All lower case roman numerals occur between two full stops, except Fii, and use the letter i, for example C.iii. Exceptions are *E.ij.*, *I.ij.*, and *I.iij.* where the variant *j* is used. The signatures appear in the direction-line immediately following the text area and are usually set in the same type as the majority of the text on that page. They are placed within the right half of the line leaving a larger space, further to the right, for catch-words, which, in contrast to the signatures, are found on every full text page positioned at the outer right margin of the same line. In most cases the catchwords have the same spelling and are printed in the same type as the word or syllable which is repeated in the first line of text of the next page. Pinholes which are arranged in a small circle in the lower right margins of A3 and A4 show how these pages were backed up on each side of the leaf in perfect register. However, most of the leaves are not in register.

Typography, material, and other physical features:

Printed on vellum, the leaves are arranged as follows: The title-page is printed on a flesh side. In all openings hair side faces hair side and flesh side faces flesh side, except for the facing pages H4^v–I1^r, where flesh side faces hair side; I2^v–I3^r, where hair side faces flesh side; and I4^v–I5^r, where flesh side again faces hair side. The device on I5^v is also printed on a flesh side. The text pages are ruled throughout by hand with faint red ink lines for the right and left margins, and for the beginning and end of the text area at the top and bottom of the pages, with an extra line drawn for the running-title on each page. A full page of printed text contains 28–32 lines, excluding the running-title, e.g. B2^r contains 28 lines, D4^r 30 lines, and F4^v 32 lines. The text on B2^r measures *c.*139 × 96 mm, excluding the running-title. On D4^r it measures *c.*149 × 113 mm, and on F4^v *c.*149 × 95 mm.

Printed lines have been crossed out on A2^r and A2^v, with visible attempts to erase the text and to insert it again by hand. MS additions to the text hand are found on A2^r, A2^v, F2^r, G3^r, and H1^r within the text or margins. On C2^v an illegible word has been erased and the wording reintroduced by hand. An examination under ultraviolet light reveals that two lines of illegible manuscript, which were later scraped off the vellum, occur on A3^v below the royal arms. On H1^v a larger number of lines in manuscript, written within the text and in the right margin, are also no longer visible. The corrections and additions by hand suggest that the book had some use after publication. Some of them probably go back to Richard Cox.[1] However, other additions within the text and in the marginalia which are no longer visible have not been identified.

Two main type families are employed: black-letter and roman, by which the two languages, English and Latin, are distinguished. Three different groups of black-letter in different sizes are used for printing the vernacular, according to the significance of the subject matter: textura, rotunda, and bastarda. These are distributed as follows: textura for the main text in English, for definitions and explanations of the Latin rules; rotunda for additions and notes to accompany the textura type, e.g. for translations of Latin verbs into English; with a small amount of bastarda types, for example, to indicate the tenses in English. In this way the different levels of the vernacular have been distinguished typographically, though not always consistently. Roman characters are also employed in different sizes. They are used for the Latin text, for part of the title, running-titles, and chapter headings. Only one variety of italic type is used for a chapter heading which was set up in the last line of the previous paragraph as there was no separate line left on the page. The different types in their different sizes fulfil a didactic function. They help to structure the printed page for the pupils, distinguish the different languages

---

[1] Cf. pp. 86–87; also Chapter 8, Commentary: *Construction*, p. 247, note to line 131.

and different levels of the vernacular and, moreover, emphasize information not given explicitly in the text.

In the following table the size of each type is indicated by the measurement of twenty lines in millimetres, followed by the different typefaces,
the numbers given to them in Greg's list,[2] and an example of their occurrence in the original.

95b   Textura (Greg 1) (e.g., title-page, A1^v: of England, Fraunce, and
       Ireland);
62   Textura (Greg 8) (e.g. C4^v: Optatyue mode the present tens);
87a   Rotunda (Greg 5) (e.g. D1^v: To haue or had loued.) (With a tail to the
       h-sort which, in most cases, is different from 87b rotunda (Greg 6),
       and only one form of d);
72   Bastard (Greg 4) (e.g. E2^v: Preterperfect and preterpluperfect.);
288   Roman (e.g. title-page, A1^r: AN INTRO=);
109   Roman (Greg 7) (e.g. A3^v: *parue puer non parua est gloria.*);
90   Roman (Greg 12) (e.g. D3^r: *Amor, aris uel are, amatus sum uel fui*);
95   Italic (Greg 15) (H3^r: *A Participle.*)

Decorated initials of different sizes are used to structure the texts. They
are used to mark the beginning of new sections and/or new chapters. All
are illuminated in different colours and most differ in design. Identical
initials of the same size are illuminated differently. Their sizes range from
two to seven lines of text. The title-page border (McK&F 19) measures *c*.172
× 117 mm, enclosing 100 × 70 mm, and is illuminated. Berthelet's device of
the *Lucretia Romana* (McK 80) measures 106 × 73 mm; it is not illuminated.
Greg, Berthelet, *Ornament 1* measures *c*.95 × 19 mm (not illuminated), and
Ornament o measures *c*.87 × 60 mm (illuminated).

Punctuation marks used in different types:
Full stop, comma, colon, question mark, single hyphen, double hyphen,
parentheses have been used. The chapter mark in black-letter and roman
types precedes chapter headings and/or introduces a new passage.

Frequent abbreviations:
Ampersand *⁊* and & (both abbreviations stand for *and* as well as *et*); y^e (þe),
y^t (þat); w^t (with); *i.* (*id est*); *p* (*per*, e.g. *per*); p (-per-, e.g. Preterperfect); *p̄* (*pre-*,
e.g. *preterquam*); ꝑ (pro-, e.g. promis); *q̃* (*quam, quam-, -quam*, e.g. *quam,*
quamuis, quisquam), also Q̇ (*Quam*); q3 (*-que*, e.g. *Vsque*) and also *q;* (-que, e.g.
atque); ꝙ (*quod*); ꝰ (-*us*, e.g. *possumus*); ɫ (*vel*); oῑbus (e.g. *omnibus*); omission of
a following -*m* or -*n*, indicated by a superior stroke, e. g. *amabā* (*amabam*) or
tēder (*tender*); contractions such as *nr̃s* (*nostris*), Ntō (*Nominatiuo*), *Gtō*

---

[2] Greg's list contains fifteen types which were used by Berthelet for printing the actual
text of the works. A larger number of different types which he possessed but only used
occasionally on title-pages, in colophons, etc., and were evidently not complete founts, are
not considered; see Greg, 188.

(*Genitiuo*), Dtō (*Datiuo*), Actō (*Accusatiuo*), Vctō/Voctō (*Vocatiuo*), and Abltō (*Ablatiuo*). Abbreviations are employed indiscriminately and without uniformity and increase in frequency as the text proceeds.

Binding and provenance:
The volume is bound in a late eighteenth-century English binding of red goatskin (includes morocco, turkey, etc.), tooled in Cracherode gold with border fillets and of small floral tools, with arms of the Rev. Clayton Mordaunt (1730–1799), in the centre of each cover, encircled by a wreath of leaves. The spine has been rebacked with the original panels laid down. Although attractively presented it is not of the highest quality. The motifs tooled on the covers are relatively common; many English binders working during Cracherode's lifetime had similar covers but I have not been able to attribute the work to an identified binder.[3]

Cracherode's monogram of entwined Cs and an M followed by the year 1789 is written in his own hand on the second fly-leaf, as is the note: "See Typographical Antiquities by Ames and Herbert, Vol. I, p. 442."[4] Another note here says that he bought it in 1789. Cracherode collected books in fine bindings and also commissioned work from contemporary binders, including Roger Payne, the foremost binder of the day. Cracherode may well have bought this book already bound and had his coat of arms added to the binding; it is difficult to be certain. The volume is now in the Cracherode Collection of the British Library.[5] In 1784 Cracherode was elected a Trustee of the British Museum. At his death in 1799, he left 4,500 volumes, all of which were remarkable either for their rareness or the excellence of the printing or binding. Almost all of his books, together with his prints, coins, and gems were bequeathed by him to the British Museum.[6]

In the preface to his revision of the authorized grammar, John Ward gives valuable information about the provenance of the 1542 volume

---

[3] See the online *Database of Bookbindings* under the shelfmark C21b4.

[4] Information on Cracherode's life and his collections of books is given in *ODNB*, vol. 13: 909–11; P. R. Harris (1998), *A History of the British Museum Library, 1753–1973*, London, 29–30; Antony Griffiths (1996), 'The Reverend Clayton Mordaunt Cracherode (1730–99)', in A. Griffiths (ed.), *Landmarks in Print Collecting*, London, 43–46; also Adina Davis (1974), 'Portrait of a Bibliophile XVIII: Clayton Mordaunt Cracherode I, II', *The Book Collector* 23: 339–54, 489–505. In the handwritten *Catalogue of the Library of the Rev. C. M. Cracherode* only the grammar in Latin is listed for the whole volume: "Lillius, Guilielmus. Institutio Compendiaria Totius Grammaticae. 4°. Exemplar impressum in membranis, auroque et coloribus exornatum. Londini. ex Off. Th. Bertheleti 1542." (BL, MS Add. 11360, fol. 74ʳ; also BL, King's MS 387, fol. 72ʳ).

[5] See Davis (1974), 495.

[6] See *Cracherode's Notebook* (BL, MS Add. 47611, fols. 2ᵛ–41ʳ); *ODNB*, vol. 13: 909–11; Mirjam M. Foot (1978–1983), *A Collection of Bookbindings. The Henry Davis Gift*, 2 vols. London, vol. 1: 102; also B. C. Bloomfield and Karen Potts (eds.) (1997), *A Directory of Rare Book and Special Collections in the United Kingdom and the Republic of Ireland*, London, 138.

by saying: "I am indebted to my worthy friend, Mr. Henry Newcome of Hackney, for the sight of this rare and curious book."[7] In his *Typographical Antiquities* (1749) Joseph Ames says that this book is "In the possession of my learned friend Mr. Henry Newcom".[8] Newcom can be identified as Dr Henry Newcome of Hackney (1689–1756) who must have owned the volume at the time John Ward and Joseph Ames saw it. On the title-page (A1[r]) of the *Alphabetum Latino Anglicum* the autograph "Arthur Maynwaringe" is found. He can probably be identified as Arthur Maynwaring (1668–1712), who may have owned it sometime before Newcome.[9] This volume may have come from Edward VI's library.[10]

Bibliographical references:
Ames, 173; Herbert, vol. 1: 442–43; Dibdin, *Typographical Antiquities*, vol. 3, no. 1248: 318–19; Dibdin, *Decameron*, vol. 2: 370; Dibdin, *Library Companion*, 571–72; Maitland, *List*, 207, Note DD, 385–86; Botfield, 20–21; Nichols (1857), vol. 1: cccxlii; Hazlitt, 334; *BM Catalogue*, vol. 2: 883, 954; Gray (1893), 452; Duff, *Handlists*, part 3, p. 9; Duff, *Vellum*, 14 and 19; Kennedy 2491; *NUC*, vol. 333, no. 0366505; *STC* 15605; *STC*[2] 15610.6 (with incorrect collation; correction in the *Addenda and Corrigenda*, vol. 3: 285); *BLC*, vol. 160: 69; *Halkett and Laing* I47; Alston-Hill, 72; Alston, vol. 15, no. 495 (with Plates CXXVII (reproducing A1[v]) and CXXVIII (A4[r])); *ESTC* S120457; *EEBO*.

6.2 *The present edition*

Most of those grammars of the early modern period printed in England whose text has already been made accessible are available only as

---

[7] See the copy of the (1752) edition of William Lily, *A Short Introduction of Grammar, etc.*, ed. John Ward, London (BL, 1568/3357(1), A4[r–v]); also the "Alterations and Additions to be made in the preface of the Latin Grammar, edited 1751" by Ward where this passage was revised to: "One of those Latin grammars is in the Lambeth library; but the other, with the English introduction [. . .] were communicated to me by my worthy friend, Dr. Henry Newcome of Hackney" (BL, MS Add. 6218, fol. 12[v]). Cf. John Gough Nichols (1858), 'The Latin Grammar Issued by Royal Authority in 1540', *Notes and Queries*, 2nd ser. 6, no. 149: 368; and T. W. Baldwin (1944), *William Shakspere's Small Latine and Lesse Greeke*, vol. 2, Urbana, 693–94.

[8] Ames, 173. The name "Henry Newcome, M.A. of Hackney" is listed under "Subscribers' Names" in Ames's book. Newcome was schoolmaster of the noted school at Hackney. See John Venn and J. A. Venn (1922–1927; 1974–1976 repr.), *Alumni Cantabrigienses*, Part I, Cambridge, Vol. 3: 246; and Sylvanus Urban (1756), 'List of Deaths for the Year 1756', *Gentleman's Magazine* 26: 500, where the date and place of his death are given: "23. [October 1756]. Rev. Mr. Newcomb, at Hackney".

[9] On Arthur Maynwaring see *ODNB*, vol. 37: 610–11. According to A. N. L. Munby and Lenore Coral (eds.) (1977), *British Book Sale Catalogues, 1676–1800. A Union List*, London, 25, his library was sold on 4 February 1713 in London, at D. Brown's Warehouse, Exeter-Exchange, Strand.

[10] T. A. Birrell (1987), *English Monarchs and Their Books: From Henry VII to Charles II*, London, 13 and 19 (footnotes 16 and 18).

facsimile editions.[11] It is therefore of particular interest to prepare a critical edition with commentary of a grammar that was printed in the early 1540s when pupils had been used to learning most of their Latin from printed textbooks. At the same time one has to take into account that the editing of these texts of this period requires special procedures. This is due to their specific nature as teaching texts and also to the multiplicity of editions that were printed. In contrast to texts of other genres, many grammars not only went through more editions because of the great demand for them in schools at that time, but were also put to different uses by contemporaries. They were not just read like a prose text or consulted once for a particular purpose like a medical text, but were used daily in schools for the learning of a foreign language. Although, as in all pre-twentieth century education, much learning went on orally in the classrooms, nevertheless in the first decades of the sixteenth century pupils owned their own textbooks from which they could learn Latin visually from the printed page. Hence the way the subject matter is presented on the printed pages illustrates methods of learning Latin in this period. In 'Lily's Latin Grammar' a number of visual devices for learning were applied in similar ways to those found in previous early printed elementary Latin grammars. Some of these devices are not novel but had already been used in grammatical manuscripts, such as noun and verb forms that are set out in column format.[12] Their visual differentiation from the rest of the chapter helped the pupils to learn the declensions of the nouns and the conjugations of the verbs more easily. Apart from some exceptions found in early printed grammars, the text is usually spaced out and structured by chapter headings, and in most cases a new line indicates the beginning of a new grammatical rule. 'Lily's Latin Grammar' is also no different from other early printed grammars in using different typefaces for Latin and English in order to distinguish the target language from the explanatory language, and in printing the names of the tenses and moods in English in different types in the left margin of the page next to the corresponding paradigm. Due to its authorization by the king, it set an example for the use of pedagogical devices of its time.

In addition to their special way of presenting most of their text, grammars were subject to additional alterations due to their nature as teaching tools. They were always exposed to the critical eyes of schoolmasters who, for pedagogical reasons, included corrections of obvious errors in manuscript in individual copies of editions, changed spelling and wording which they considered incorrect, and introduced longer revisions

---

[11] A considerable number of them is available in the series *English Linguistics, 1500–1800* (EL), ed. R. C. Alston (1967–1972), 365 vols., Menston; and also in the online database *EEBO*. Cf. p. 2 above.

[12] Cf. p. 67 above.

which they regarded as an improvement of the rules. New editions that were printed incorporated corrections which the teachers had noticed, also alterations which they found necessary to include. As the authorized grammar, 'Lily's Latin Grammar' set the norm for the teaching of Latin in that it was the only grammar allowed to be used in schools. The text was additionally subject to change because of the instability of English at that time, with the result that compositors could and did introduce alterations in spelling at the same time as correcting typographical mistakes in their copy-text.

The edition of this grammar aims at presenting the 1542 copy of *An Introduction of The Eyght Partes Of speche* in a way that, as far as possible, tries to preserve the nature of this school text. For this reason the text has been reproduced as faithfully as possible, subject only to a certain amount of standardization and minor rearrangement, partly due to modern printing types but necessary also for the benefit of the modern reader and to make the text more accessible. The following editorial principles have been observed.

Some features have been retained, namely the chapter divisions of the original; the beginnings of new lines within a chapter that are indicated by a paragraph mark; nominal and verbal paradigms; and the lists of words set up in columns. Otherwise adjustments have had to be made to the layout of the text because of the nature of modern printing types. Text printed in the margins of the original has been integrated into the main text in the edition, for example the indication of the tenses and moods given in the paradigms. Following usual sixteenth-century practice, Berthelet employed mostly black-letter types for English vernacular text, with roman and some italic for the Latin. To make the text more easily accessible to the modern reader, whilst at the same time preserving the typographical differentiation between the vernacular and Latin, black-letter typography in the original has here been rendered in Times New Roman, with the roman and italic of the original rendered in Times New Roman, italic. The varying type sizes employed have been standardized, and no attempt has been made to differentiate between the textura, rotunda, and bastarda forms of black-letter. Paragraph marks and ornaments in the original have not been reproduced.

The original editors used diacritical marks to indicate a change in stress caused by an enclitic *-que* (e.g. *manus'q3*), in contrast, for example, to *absque*, where *-que* is part of the word. Accents were used in the original text to distinguish forms with the same spellings, e.g. *eò* for the adverb, in contrast, for example, to *eo*, the form of the ablative singular masculine and neuter of the demonstrative pronoun. These characteristics of the original that helped the pupils to analyse the texts have been retained in the present edition. The two different forms of *r* and *s* are given in only one form, as modern *r* and *s*. Ligatures are transcribed as two letters. However, the Latin digraphs æ [ae] and œ [oe] reproduce those of the original, as is also the case with *e-caudata* [ę]. The spelling and punctuation of the original have been retained. Spelling variations, such as preterimperfect tense versus Preterimperfectens and future tense versus Futuretens are already given in Colet's *Aeditio* and the English grammatical manuscripts. Abbreviations occurring in the text have been expanded silently.

Editorial corrections involve the following circumstances. In the frequent cases of words divided at line endings without a hyphen in the original, such as Con|struction, Eng|lande, par|ticiple, *quan|tiuis*, and *Vergi|lium*, the two parts have silently been joined together. In the case of hym|selfe the word has been given as two words as it occurs in the original. Typographical errors have been corrected and marked in a footnote; they comprise wrong letters (e.g. fyngularly for singularly), inversion of letters (e.g. wihche for whiche), omission of letters (e.g. trstior for *tristior*), and wrong spacing between and within words (e.g. Anowne, *quo d*), as well as omission of letters of a word when it was separated at the end of a line (e.g. Preterim=|fecte for Preterim=|perfecte). Examples of turned letters, which have been corrected silently, are the following: l in *plurima*; m in mayster; n in hygh|nes, n in prepositions; the first *n* in *non* (cf. Plate 7, line 13 of the text); u in singular, the second u in accusatiue, and in *unum*.

Occasions where the compositor has made a more serious mistake, such as substituting preterpluperfect for preterimperfect and ablatyue for accusatiue have been corrected and recorded in a footnote. Partially legible or missing letters in the original, probably the result of imperfect inking, have been supplied conjecturally in angle brackets (cf. Plate 5, lines 22 and 23 of the text). Words added by hand to replace words erased in the original have been included in the edited text, signalled by footnotes, and commented on in the commentary. Longer passages where the text has been crossed out and reinserted by hand in the original have been retained, signalled by footnotes, and explained in the commentary. Smaller corrections by hand, such as single letters inserted above the line, which in most cases are indicated by a caret at the approximate point in the original, are signalled by footnotes alone (cf. Plate 5, line 15 of the text).

7. The Text of 'Lily's Latin Grammar' in English (1542)

ENRY THE. VIII.BY THE GRACE OF GOD KYNG of Englåd, Fraunce, and Jreland, defendour of the feithe, and of the church of England, and alfo of Jrelande, in erth the fupreme hed, to all fchoolemaſters and teachers of grammer within this his realm greetynge. Emong the manyfolde bufines and moſte weyghty affayres, appertaynyng to our regall auctoritee and offyce, we forgette not the tendre babes, and the youth of our realme, whofe good education and godly bryngyng vp, is a greate furniture to the fame and caufe of moche goodneffe. And to the intent that hereafter they may the more readily and eafily attein the rudymentes of the latyne toung, without ỹ greate hynderaunce, which heretofore hath been, through the diuerfitie of grammers and teachynges: we will and commaunde, and ſtreightly charge al you fchoolemaiſters and teachers of grämer within this our realme, and other our dominions, as ye intend to auoyde our difpleafure, and haue our fauour, to teache and learne your fcholars this englyfſhe introduction here enfuing, and the latyne grammer annexed to the fame, and none other, which we haue caufed for your eafe, and your fcholars fpedy preferment bryefely and playnely to be compyled and fet forth. Fayle not to apply your fcho lars in lernynge and godly e= ducation.

Plate 4. Royal proclamation. (BL, C.21.b.4.(2), leaf A1ᵛ.)

✺ AN INTRODVCTION
of the eighte partes of fpeche.

IN fpeche be thefe. viii. partes folovvyng.

Nowne		Aduerbe	
Pzonowne	declyned.	Coniunction	vndecly
Uerbe		Pzepofition	ned.
Particiyle		Interecition.	

✺ Of the novvne.

NOVVNE IS the name of a thyng that maye bee feen, felt, heard oz vnderftand. As the name of my hande in latine is Manus. The name of an howfe , is Do= mus . The name of goodneffe is Bonitas .

Of nownes fome be fubftantiues fome be adiectiues. ❡ A nowe fubftantiue is, that ftandeth by hym felf, and requireth not an other woozde to be ioyned with hym, as Homo a manne, and it is declyned with one article, as hic Magifter, a maifter, oz with twoo, as hic & hęc parens, a father oz mother .

❡ A nowne adiectiue is, that can not ftand by hym felfe, but requireth to be ioyned with an other woozde, is Bonus good, Pulcher fayze . And it is declyned, et= her with thzee terminations, as Bonus, bona, bonum, ozels with thzee articles, as Hic hæc & hoc felix, happy, hic & hæc leuis, & hoc leue, lyght.

❡ A nowne fubftantiue, either is propet to the thyng, that it betokeneth, as Edouardus is my pzoper name,

oz it

Plate 5. The beginning of the text on the parts of speech. (BL, C.21.b.4.(2), leaf A4^r.)

eyght partes of fpeche.

	I loue,	thou louest.	he loueth.	we loue.	ye loue, they loue,
Indicatiue mode the prefent tes fingular.	Amo ⎱ as, ⎰	at,	⎱ amam⁹	⎱ atis, ⎱ mant
	Doceo ⎱ es, ⎱	et, ⎱ Pl.	docem⁹	etis, cent,
	Lego ⎱ is, ⎱	it, ⎱	legimus	itis, gunt,
	Audio ⎰ is, ⎰	it, ⎰	audimus	itis, diunt,

The pre=terimperfecte tenfe fingular.

Amabam ⎫ I loued or dyd loue.
Docebam ⎬ taught.
Legebam ⎱ bas, bat.Plur.bamus, batis,bant.
Audiebam ⎭ read.
          heard.

The pre=terperfecte tenfe fing.

Amaui ⎱ I haue loued.
Docui ⎱ taught.
Legi ⎬ ifti, it.Plu.imus, iftis,erunt uel ere.
Audiui ⎭ read.
      heard.

The pre=terplupers fecte tenfe. Syngular.

Amaueram ⎱ I had loued.
Docueram ⎱ taught.
Legeram ⎬ ras,rat.Plu.ramus, ratis,rant.
Audiueram ⎭ read.
      heard.

The future tenfe fyng.

Amabo ⎱ I fhall or wyll loue.
Docebo ⎰ bis,bit.Plur.bimus,bitis, bunt.
        teache.
Legam ⎱ read.
Audiam ⎰ es,et,Plur.emus, etis, ent.
        heare.

Impera= tiue mode the prefente tenfe fing.	Loue thou.	Loue he,or let hym loue,let vs loue.	Loue we,or	Loue ye	Loue they, or let them loue.
	Ama ⎱ amet ⎱		amemus	⎱ amate	⎱ ament
	Amato ⎰ amato ⎰			⎰ amatote	⎰ amanto
	Teache thou	**Teache he or let vs teach,**	**Teache we,or let vs teache**	**Teache ye**	**Teache they, or let them teache.**
	Doce ⎱ doceat ⎱		doceamus	⎱ docete	⎱ doceant
	Doceto ⎰ doceto ⎰			⎰ docetote	⎰ docento
	Lege ⎱ legat ⎱ Plura.			⎱ legite,	⎱ legant
	Legito ⎰ legito ⎰ legamus			⎰ legitote	⎰ legunto

Audi

Plate 6. The conjugation of the verbs. (BL, C.21.b.4.(2), leaf C4ʳ.)

ꝫ GODLY LESSONS
for Chyldren.

IT IS THE FYRST poynte of wyſedome, to knowe thy ſelfe.

Primus eſt ſapientiæ gradus te ipſum noſcere.

Feare of the Lorde, is the begynnyng of wyſedome.

Initium ſapientiæ timor domini.

There is no manne that ſynneth not.

Non eſt homo qui non peccet.

If we ſaye we be fauteleſſe we decepue our ſelues, and truthe is not in vs.

Si dixerimus peccatum uon habemus, nos ipſos fallimus, & ueritas in nobis non eſt.

So God loued the worlde, that he gaue his only begotten ſoonne, that none whiche beleueth in hym, ſhuld periſſhe, but enioye euerlaſtyng lyfe.

Sic deus dilexit mundũ, ut filium ſuum unigenitũ daret, ut omnis qui credit in eum, non pereat, ſed habeat uitam æternam.

Chriſte is the lambe of God, whiche taketh away the ſynnes of the worlde.

Chriſtus eſt agnus dei, qui tollit peccata mundi.

There is none other name vnder heauen, giuen vnto menne, by the whiche we muſt be ſaued.

Non eſt aliud nomen ſub cœlo datum hominibus, in quo oporteat non ſaluos fieri.

He that hath my commandmentes, and kepeth them, it is he that loueth me.

Qui

Plate 7. *Godly Lessons for Chyldren.* (BL, C.21.b.4.(2), leaf F2ᵛ.)

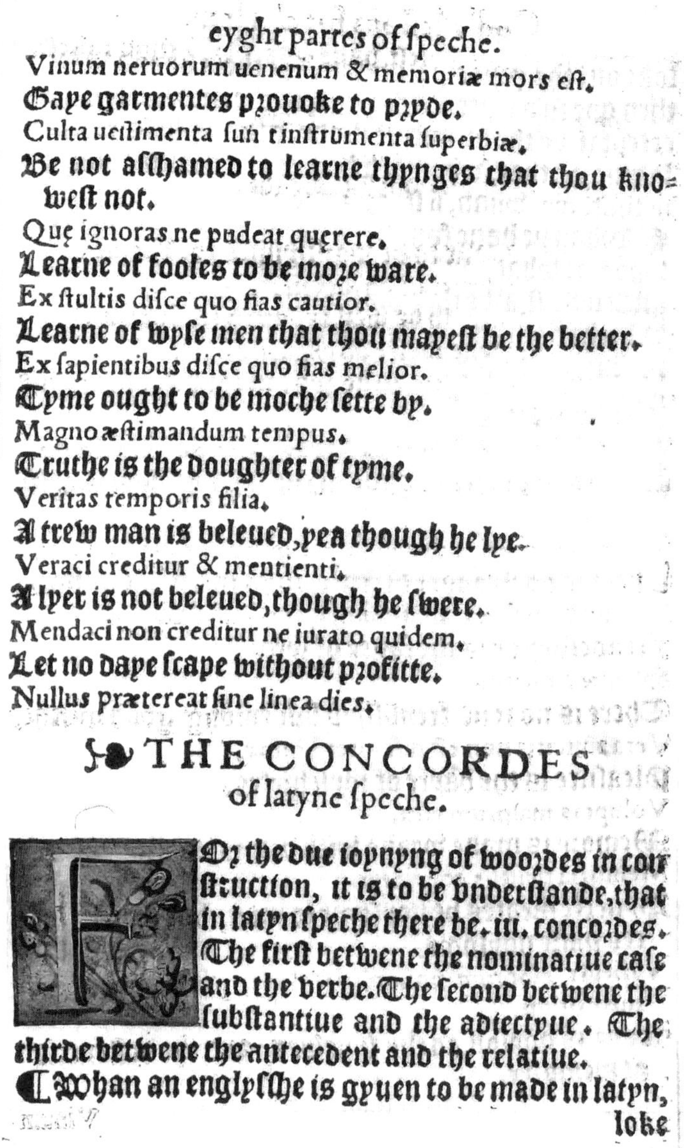

Vinum neruorum uenenum & memoriæ mors eſt.

Gaye garmentes pɀouoke to pɀyde.

Culta ueſtimenta ſun t inſtrumenta ſuperbiæ.

Be not affhameð to learne thynges that thou kno=
weſt not.

Quę ignoras ne pudeat quęrere.

Learne of fooles to be moɀe ware.

Ex ſtultis diſce quo fias cautior.

Learne of wyſe men that thou mayeſt be the better.

Ex ſapientibus diſce quo fias melior.

Tyme ought to be moche ſette by.

Magno æſtimandum tempus.

Truthe is the ðoughter of tyme.

Veritas temporis filia.

A trew man is beleueð, yea though he lye.

Veraci creditur & mentienti.

A lyer is not beleueð, though he ſwere.

Mendaci non creditur ne iurato quidem.

Let no ðaye ſcape without pɀofitte.

Nullus prætereat fine linea dies.

❧ THE CONCORDES
of latyne ſpeche.

Oɀ the ðue ioynyng of wooɀðes in con
ſtruction, it is to be bnðerſtanðe, that
in latyn ſpeche there be. iii. concoɀðes.
The firſt betwene the nominatiue caſe
anð the verbe. The ſeconð betwene the
ſubſtantiue anð the aðiectyue. The
thirðe betwene the anteceðent anð the relatiue.

Whan an englyſſhe is gyuen to be maðe in latyn,
loke

Plate 8. The end of *Godly Lessons for Chyldren* and the beginning of *The Concordes of latyne speche*. (BL, C.21.b.4.(2), leaf F4ʳ.)

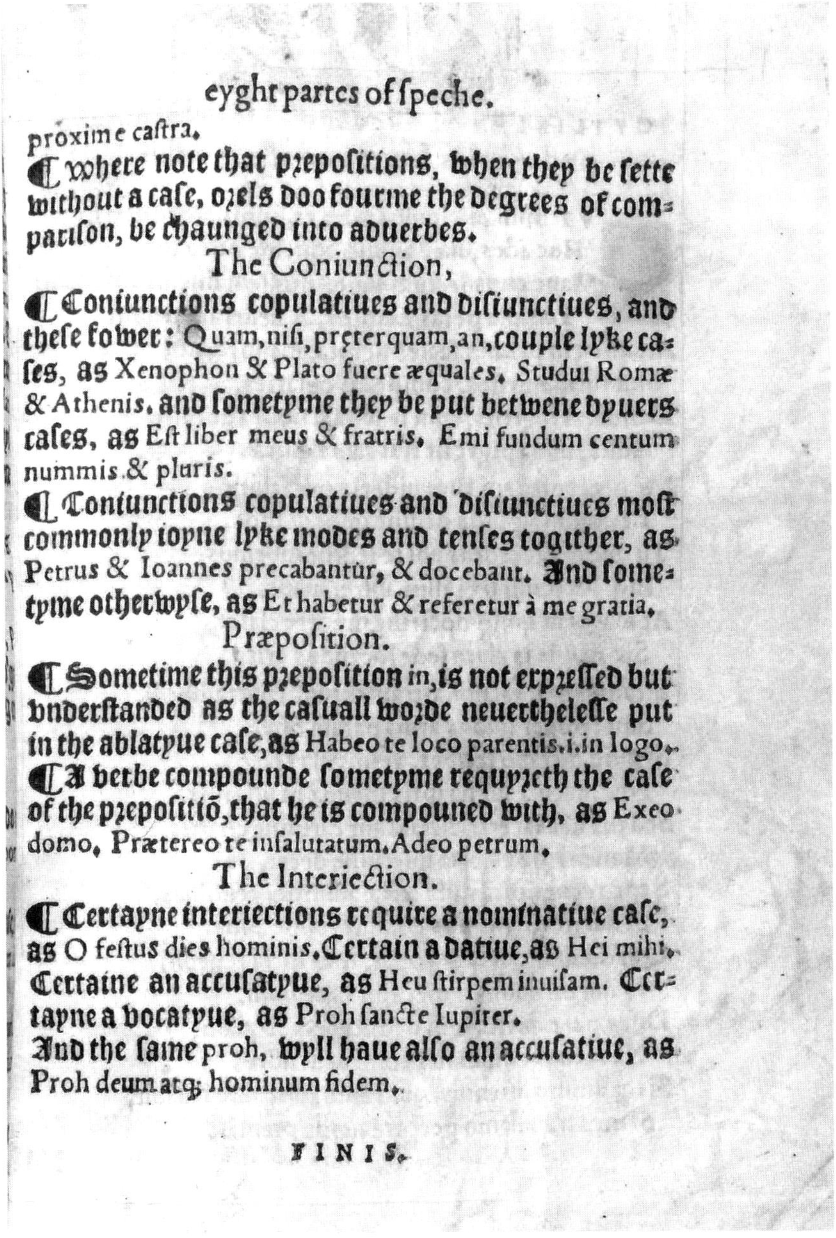

proxime caſtra.

℘ where note that prepoſitions, when they be ſette without a caſe, orels doo fourme the degrees of comparison, be chaunged into aduerbes.

The Coniunction,

℘ Coniunctions copulatiues and diſiunctiues, and theſe fower: Quam, niſi, preterquam, an, couple lyke caſes, as Xenophon & Plato fuere æquales. Studui Romæ & Athenis. and ſometyme they be put betwene dyuers caſes, as Eſt liber meus & fratris. Emi fundum centum nummis & pluris.

℘ Coniunctions copulatiues and diſiunctiues moſt commonly iopne lyke modes and tenſes togither, as Petrus & Ioannes precabantur, & docebant. And ſometyme otherwyſe, as Et habetur & referetur à me gratia.

Præpoſition.

℘ Sometime this prepoſition in, is not expreſſed but bnderſtanded as the caſuall worde neuertheleſſe put in the ablatyue caſe, as Habeo te loco parentis, i, in logo.

℘ A berbe compounde ſometyme requyreth the caſe of the prepoſitiõ, that he is compouned with, as Exeo domo. Prætereo te inſalutatum. Adeo petrum.

The Interiection.

℘ Certayne interiections require a nominatiue caſe, as O feſtus dies hominis. Certain a datiue, as Hei mihi. Certaine an accuſatyue, as Heu ſtirpem inuiſam. Certayne a bocatyue, as Proh ſancte Iupiter.

And the ſame proh, wyll haue alſo an accuſatiue, as Proh deum atꝗ hominum fidem.

FINIS.

Plate 9. The end of *The Concordes of latyne speche*. (BL, C.21.b.4.(2), leaf H4ʳ.)

AN INTRODVCTION OF THE EYGHT PARTES OF

speche, and the Construction of the same, compiled and sette forthe by the commaundement of[1] our most gracious souerayne lorde the king.

ANNO.MD.XLII.

---

[1] commaunde=|men tof

[The Royal Proclamation by Henry VIII]

HENRY THE .VIII. BY THE GRACE OF GOD KYNG of England, Fraunce, and
Ireland, defendour of the feithe, and of the church of England, and also of
Irelande, in erth the supreme hed, to all schoolemaisters and teachers of
grammer within this his realm greetynge. Emong the manyfolde busines
and moste weyghty affayres, appertaynyng to our regall auctoritee and 5
offyce, we forgette not the tendre babes, and the youth of our realme,
whose good education and godly bryngyng vp, is a greate furniture to the
same and cause of moche goodnesse. And to the intent that hereafter they
may the more readily and easily attein the rudymentes of the latyne
toung, without þe greate hynderaunce, which heretofore hath been, 10
through the diuersitie of grammers and teachynges: we will and commaunde, and streightly charge al you schoolemaisters and teachers of
grammer within this our realme, and other our dominions, as ye intend
to auoyde our displeasure, and haue our fauour, to teache and learne
your scholars this englysshe introduction here ensuing, and the latyne 15
grammer annexed to the same, and none other, which we haue caused for
your ease, and your scholars spedy preferment bryefely and playnely to be
compyled and set forth. Fayle not to apply your scholars in lernynge and
godly education.

TO THE REDER

ALBEIT THIS Realme of Englande hath iuste cause to thynke it selfe moste
bounden to the goodness of God, for manifolde and sundry benefittes
receyued of his inestimable bountifulnesse, yet if we wyl wey the iust
valu of thynges in an equall balance, as a certayn wyse Phylosopher dyd,
whiche affirmed that realme to be most happy, where as eyther a wise and
a lerned man had the rule, or the ruler applyed hym selfe to wysedom, and
lernynge: we may perceyue vs englishmen, in nothyng so fortunate, as in
that we haue a kyng and gouernour, both of excellente wysedome,
lernyng and vertu, and also of great study and diligence to encreace the
same, whose kyngly qualities, whan they shal here after by such godly
monumentes, as his maiesty shal leaue behynd hym, appere so playnly to
his posteritie, as we now presently see thynges, many of them alredy don,
som in doing,[1] and mo shal see, which his maiestie by the grace of god,
entendeth hereafter to do: out of questyon al þat haue gone before hym,
may wel appere but shadowes. And to leaue the large fieldes of his
pryncely actes, wherein the wysest and best lerned myght walke tyll wyt
and eloquence were bothe wery, what constant iudgement, and what
profound knowlege hath his maiesty shewed and declared to all the
world, in this varietie of iugementes and lerninges? and what peynes,
study, and trauayle doth he take, to bryng thynges farre out of square to a
conformitie, and to take good heede of Christis churche to lead his flock
into [A2ᵛ] the folde of tru doctrine, þe hurdels of þe same so wel vnderpyght, þat the wolues shal not be able to ouerthrowe them?[2] And as his
maiesty purposeth to establyshe his people in one consent and harmony
of pure and tru relygion: so his tender goodnes toward the youth and
chyldhode of his realme, entendeth to haue it brought vp vnder one
absolute and vniforme sorte of lernynge. For his maiestie consideryng
the great encombrance and confusion of the yong and tender wittes, by
reason of the diuersity of grammer rules and teachinges (For[3] here tofore
euery maister had his grammer, and euery schole dyuers teachynges, and
chaungyng of maisters and scholes dyd many tymes vtterly dull and vndo
good wyttes) hath appoynted certein lerned men mete for suche a purpose, to compile one bryef, plaine, and vniforme grammer, whiche onely
(al other set a part) for the more spedynesse, and lesse trouble of yong
wittes, his hyghnes hath commanded all sholemaysters and teachers of

---

[1] indoing

[2] The text from 'and to take good heede' to 'ouerthrowe them?' has been crossed out and erased and inserted again by hand.

[3] The opening bracket before 'For' has been inserted by hand over the full stop.

grammer within this his realme, and other his dominions, to teache their scholers. Nowe consider you fathers in this realme, howe moche ye be bound to such a gratious kyng, whose care is not onely for you, but for your posterity also, and your tender babes. And you scholemaisters of 40 England, to whome the cure and education of tender youthe is commyt-ted, with what great study and dylygence ought you to folowe the example of our most gratious souerayne? which among the infinite busynes apperteinyng to his regall office, so ernestly mindeth the wel bryngyng vp of youthe, in lernyng and vertue? Howe glad howe desirous ought you 45 to be, not only to do this his gracis commaundment [A3ʳ] but also busylye to applye your selues, to trade and bryng vp your scholers in good maners, in knowlege of tonges, and sciences? And somewhat to declare vnto you the condition and qualitie of this grammer, ye shall vnderstand, that the .viii. partes of spech, and the Construction of the same, be not here set 50 forth in englysshe at large, but compendyously and briefely for the weake capacitie of yong and tender wyttes. And therfore if any thyng semeth here to want in this englyshe Introductions, ye shall vnderstande, it was left ou<t> of purpose, and shall be supplied in the latyn rules made for the same intent, whiche chyldren shalbe apte to lerne, what tyme they shall 55 haue competent vnderstandyng by these former rudimentes. You tender babes of Englande, shake of slouthfulnes, set wantonnes a parte, apply your wyttes holy to lernyng and vertue, wherby you maye doo youre duetye to god and your kyng, make gladde your parentes, profytte your selues, and moche auaunce the common weale of your countrey. Let noble 60 prynce Edwarde encourage your tender hartes, a prynce of greate towardnes, a prynce in whome god hath powred his graces abundantly, a prince framed of suche perfectnes of nature, that he is lyke by the grace of god, to ensue the steppes of his fathers wysedome, lernynge, and vertue, and is nowe almost in a redynesse, to rounne in the same rase of lernyng 65 with you. For whom ye haue great cause to praye that he may be the soonne of a longe lyuyng father.

{ Lerne dylygently.
{ Loue God entierly.

AD PVBEM ANGLICAM.

HEXASTICON.

O TVA parue puer non parua est gloria, Rex est
  Commoda qui studiis prospicit ampla tuis.
5 *Rex magnus tibi parue puer, Rex porrigit ultro*
  Dulcia nectareæ pocula grammaticæ.
Accipe munifici dulcissima pocula regis,
  Hæc hauri, hæc auidis faucibus ebibito.

GOD SAVE THE

10 *KYNG*

[To the English schoolboys
Hexastichon.

Your glory, my little boy, is far from small. It is the King
who provides amply and well for your studies.
To you the great King, my little one, through his generosity grants
the pleasant cups of honeyed grammar.
Accept these most delicious cups from the generous king.
Drain them, greedily drink them dry.]

IN speche be these .viii. partes folovvyng.

Nowne			Aduerbe		
Pronowne	}	declyned.	Coniunction	}	vndeclyned
Verbe			Preposition		
Participle			Interiection[1].		

Of the novvne.

A NOVVNE IS the name of a thyng that maye bee seen, felt, heard or vnder-stand. As the name of my hande in latine is *Manus*. The name of an howse, is *Domus*.The name of goodnesse is *Bonitas*.

Of nownes some be substantiues some be adiectiues.

A nowne[2] substantiue is, that standeth by hym self, and requireth not an other woorde to be ioyned with hym, as *Homo* a manne, and it is declyned with one article, as *hic Magister*, a maister, or with twoo, as *hic et hęc parens*, a father or mother.

A nowne[3] adiectiue is, that can not stand by hym selfe, but requireth to be ioyned with an other worde, <a>s *Bonus* good, *Pulcher* fayre. And it is declyned, ei<t>her with three termynations, as *Bonus, bona, bonum*, orels with three articles, as *Hic hæc et hoc felix*, happy, *hic et hæc leuis, et hoc leue*, lyght.

A nowne substantiue, either is proper to the thyng, that it betokeneth, as *Edouardus* is my proper name, [A4ᵛ] Or it is common to mo, as *Homo* is a common n<a>me[4] to all menne.

Noumbers of novvnes.

In nownes be two numbers, The syngular and the plurall. The syngular numbre speketh of one as *lapis*, a stone. The plurall noumber speaketh of moo than one, as *lapides*, stones.

---

[1] Interecition
[2] nowe. The second n has been inserted by hand above the line; it is indicated by a caret below the line.
[3] Anowne
[4] na me|

Cases of novvnes.

Nownes be declyned with syxe cases syngular<l>y[1] and plurally. The
30 nominatyue, The Genityue, the Datiue, the Accusatyue, the Vocatyue, and
the Ablatiue.

The nominatyue case commeth before the verbe, and answereth to this
question who or what, as *Magister docet*, the maister teacheth.

The genitiue case is knowen by this token of, and answereth to this ques-
35 tion, whose or whereof, as *Doctrina magistri*, the learnyng of the maister.

The datyue case is knowen by this token to, and answereth to this
question, to whome, or to what, as *Do librum magistro*, I gyue[2] a boke to the
maister.

The accusatyue case foloweth the verbe, and aunswereth to this question,
40 whom, or what, as *Amo magistrum*, I loue the mayster.

The vocatyue case is knowen by callynge or speakyng to, as *O magister*,
O maister.

The ablatyue case is commonly knowen by these sygnes, in, with,
through, for, from, by, and than, as *Cum magistro*, With the mayster.

45
Artycles.

Articles be borowed of the pronowne, and be thus declyned. [B1ʳ]

Singulariter
- Nominatiuo hic, hęc, hoc,
- Genitiuo huius,
- Datiuo huic,
- Accusatiuo hunc, hanc, hoc,
- Vocatiuo caret,
- Ablatiuo hoc, hac, hoc,

Pluraliter
- Nominatiuo hi hæ hęc,
- Genitiuo horum harum horum
- Datiuo his,
- Accusatiuo hos has hæc,
- Vocatiuo caret.
- Ablatiuo his.

Genders of novvnes.

Genders of nownes be .vii. the Masculine, the Feminine, the neuter, the
55 common of two, the common of thre, the doubtfull, and the Epicene.

The masculine gender is declyned with this artycle *hic*, as *hic uir*, a manne.

The feminine gender is declyned with this artycle *hæc*, as *hæc mulier*, a
woman.

The neuter is declyned with this article *hoc*, as *hoc saxum*, a stone.
60 The common of two is declyned with *hic* and *hec*, as *hic et hec parens*.

The common of three is declyned with *hic hæc* and *hoc*, as *hic hęc et hoc felix*.

The doubtfull gender is declyned with *hic* or *hæc*, as *hic uel hęc dies*, a daye.

---

[1] fyngularly
[2] gyke

The Epicene gendre is declyned with one artycle, and vnder that one artycle, both kindes be signified, as *hic passer*, a sparowe, *hæc aquila*, an egle, both he and she, 65

The declensons of novvnes,

There be fyue declensons of nownes.

The first is, whan the genitiue and the datyue case syngular ende in *æ* diphthong, the accusatyue in *am*, the vocatiue lyke the nominatyue, the ablatyue in *a*, [B1ᵛ] The nominatiue plural in *æ* diphthong, the genitiue 70 in *arum*, the datiue in *is*, the accusatyue in *as*, the vocatiue lyke the nominatyue, the ablatyue in *is*, as in example

Singulariter {
Nominatiuo hęc musa
Genitiuo huius sæ,
Datiuo huic sæ,
Accusatiuo hanc sam,
Vocatiuo o musa,
Ablatiuo¹ ab hac musa,
}
Pluraliter {
Nominatiuo hæ musæ,
Genitiuo harum musarum,
Datiuo his musis, 75
Accusatiuo has musas,
Vocatiuo o musæ,
Ablatiuo ab his musis.
}

The seconde is, whan the genitiue case syngular endeth in *i*, the datiue in *o*, the accusatyue in *um*, the vocatiue for the moste parte lyke the nomy- 80 natyue, the ablatyue in *o*. The nominatiue plurall in *i*, the genitiue in *orum*, the datyue in *is*, the accusatyue in *os*, the vocatiue lyke the nominatiue, the ablatyue in *is*, as in example.

Singulariter {
Nominatiuo hic magister
Genitiuo huius gistri,
Datiuo huic stro,
Accusatiuo hunc strum,
Vocatiuo o magister,
Ablatiuo ab hoc stro,
}
Pluraliter {
Nominatiuo hi magistri,
Genitiuo horum strorum, 85
Datiuo his magistris,
Accusatiuo hos gistros,
Vocatiuo o magistri,
Ablatiuo ab his gistris.
}

HERE IS TO be noted, that whan the Nominatiue endethe in *us*, the 90 vocatyue shall ende in *e*, as *Nominatiuo hic dominus, uocatiuo o domine.* Except *Filius*, that maketh *o fili*, and *deus*, that maketh *o deus*. Whan the nominatiue endeth in *ius*, if it be a propre name of a manne, the vocatyue shall ende in *i*, as *nominatiuo hic Georgius, uocatiuo o Georgi.* [B2ʳ]

NOTE ALSO that all nownes of the neuter gender, of what declenson so euer 95 they be, haue the nominatyue, the accusatyue, and the vocatiue lyke in bothe numbres. And in the plurall noumbre they ende all in *A*, as in example.

---

¹ *Ablto*

100 *Singulariter* {
Nominatiuo hoc regnum,
Genitiuo huius regni,
Datiuo huic gno,
Accusatiuo hoc regnum,
Vocatiuo o regnum,
Ablatiuo ab hoc regno,
} *Pluraliter* {
Nominatiuo hæc regna,
Genitiuo horum regnorum,
Datiuo his regnis,
Accusatiuo hæc regna,
Vocatiuo o regna,
Ablatiuo ab his regnis.
}

105 Except *ambo* and *duo*, whiche make the neuter gender in *o*, and be thus declyned.

Pluraliter. {
Nominatiuo ambo, ambæ, ambo,
Genitiuo orum, arum, orum,
Datiuo obus, abus, obus,
110 Accusatiuo bos, bas, bo,
Vocatiuo bo, bẹ, bo
Ablatiuo obus, abus, obus.   Lykewyse *duo*.
}

The thyrde is, whan the genitiue case singular endeth in *is*, the datyue in *i*, the accusatyue moste commonly in *em*, and sometyme in *im*, and sometyme
115 in bothe the vocatyue lyke the nominatiue, the ablatiue in *i*, sometyme in *e*, sometyme in bothe. The nomynatiue case pluralle in *es*, the genityue sometyme in *um*, and sometyme in *ium*, the datiue in *bus*, the accusatyue in *es*, the vocatiue lyke the nominatyue, the ablatyue in *bus*, as in example,

120 [B2ᵛ] *Singulariter* {
Nominatiuo hic lapis
Genitiuo huius dis,
Datiuo huic di,
Accusatiuo hunc dem
Vocatiuo o lapis,
Ablatiuo ab hoc de,
} *Pluraliter* {
Nominatiuo hi lapides,
Genitiuo horum lapidum,
Datiuo his lapidibus,
Accusatiuo hos lapides
Vocatiuo o lapides,
Ablatiuo ab his lapidibus.
}

125 *Singulariter* {
Nominatiuo hic et hæc parens,
Genitiuo huius rentis
Datiuo huic parenti,
Accusatiuo hunc et hanc tem,
Vocatiuo o parens
130 Ablatiuo ab hoc et hac parente,
} *Pluraliter* {
Nominatiuo hi et hæ parentes,
Genitiuo horum et harum, tum,
Datiuo his parentibus,
Accusatiuo hos et has rentes,
Vocatiuo o parentes,
Ablatiuo ab his parentibus.
}

The fowerth is, whan the genitiue case syngular endeth in *us*, the datiue in *ui*, the accusatiue in *um*, the vocatiue lyke the nominatiue, the ablatiue in *u*. The nominatyue plurall in *us*, the genitiue in *uum*, the datyue in *ibus*, the accusatiue in *us*, the vocatiue lyke the nominatiue, the ablatiue in *ibus*, as
135 in exaumple,

Singulariter {
Nominatiuo hec manus,
Genitiuo huius, nus,
Datiuo huic ui,
Accusatiuo hanc num,
140 Vocatiuo o nus,
Ablatiuo ab hac nu,
} *Pluraliter* {
Nominatiuo hæ manus,
Genitiuo harum manuum,
Datiuo his manibus,
Accusatiuo has manus,
Vocatiuo o manus,
Ablatiuo ab his manibus.
}

The fifth is whan the genitiue and the datyue case syngular ende in *ei*, the accusatiue in *em*, the vocatiue lyke the nominatiue, the ablatyue in *e*. The nomynatyue plurall in *es*, the genitiue in *erum*, the datyue in *ebus*, the accusatiue in *es*, the vocatyue lyke the no[B3ʳ]minatiue, the ablatiue in 145 *ebus*, as in example.

Singulariter
{
Nominatiuo hic meridies,
Genitiuo huius ei,
Datiuo huic ei,
Accusatiuo hunc em,
Vocatiuo o dies,
Ablatiuo ab hoc die,
}

Pluraliter
{
Nominatiuo hi meridies,
Genitiuo horum meridierum,
Datiuo his meridiebus,
Accusatiuo hos meridies,   150
Vocatiuo o meridies,
Ablatiuo ab his meridiebus.
}

The declinyng of adiectiues.

A nowne adiectiue of .iii. terminatyons is thus declyned.

Singulariter
{
Nominatiuo bonus, na, num,
Genitiuo boni, næ, ni.
Datiuo bono, ę, o,
Accusatiuo bonum, nam, num,
Vocatiuo bone, na, num,
Ablatiuo bono, na, no,
}

Pluraliter
{
Nominatiuo boni, bonæ, bona,   155
Genitiuo bonorum, arum, orum,
Datiuo bonis,
Accusatiuo bonos, bonas, bona,
Vocatiuo boni, bonæ, na,
Ablatiuo bonis.   160
}

There be besides these certayn nownes adiectiues of an other maner of declynyng, whiche make the genitiue case syngular in *ïus* or *ius*, and the datyue in *i*, whiche be these that folowe with theyr compoundes.

Singulariter
{
Nominatiuo unus, a, um,
Genitiuo unius,
Datiuo uni,
Accusatiuo unum, nam, num,
Vocatiuo une, na, num,
Ablatiuo uno, na, no,
}

Pluraliter
{
Nominatiuo uni, unę, una,
Genitiuo unorum, arum, orum,   165
Datiuo unis,
Accusatiuo unos, nas, na,
Vocatiuo uni, unæ, una,
Ablatiuo unis.
}

In lyke maner be declyned *totus*, *solus*, and also *ullus*, *alius*, *alter*, *uter*, and 170 *neuter*, Excepte that these fyue laste rehersed lacke the vocatiue case.

[B3ᵛ] A nowne adiectiue of .iii. articles is thus declined.

Singulariter
{
Nominatiuo hic hæc et hoc felix,
Genitiuo huius felicis
Datiuo huic lici,
Accusatiuo hunc hanc cem
et hoc felix,
Vocatiuo o felix,
Ablatiuo ab hoc hac hoc ce uel ci,
}

Pluraliter
{
Nominatiuo hi et hę ces, et
hęc cia,
Genitiuo horum harum et   175
horum cium.
Datiuo his felicibus,
Accusatiuo hos et has ces et
hec cia,
Vocatiuo o ces et cia,   180
Ablatiuo ab his felicibus.
}

$$\text{Singulariter} \begin{cases} \textit{Nominatiuo hic hęc tristis et hoc te,} \\[6pt] \textit{Genitiuo huius tristis,} \\[6pt] \textit{Datiuo huic sti} \qquad\qquad \textit{Pluraliter} \\ \textit{Accusatiuo hunc hanc tem, et hoc te,} \\[6pt] \textit{Vocatiuo o stis et o ste,} \\ \textit{Ablatiuo ab hoc hac et hoc tristi,} \end{cases}$$

Nominatiuo hi et hæ tristes et hec tristia,	
Genitiuo horum harum et horum tristium,	
Datiuo his tristibus,	
Accusatiuo hos et has stes et hæc tia,	
Vocatiuo o es et o tristia,	
Ablatiuo ab his tristibus.	

Comparisons of novvnes.

Adiectiues, whose sygnification maye encrease, or be diminished, receyue comparison.

There be three degrees of comparisons.

$$\begin{cases} \text{The Positiue} \\ \text{The Comparatyue,} \\ \text{And the Superlatiue.} \end{cases}$$

The Posityue betokeneth the thynge absolutely without excesse as *durus,* harde. [B4ʳ]

The comparatiue excedeth somewhat his positiue in signification, as *durior,* harder: And it is fourmed, of the firste case of his positiue, that endeth in *i,* by puttyng therto *or,* and *us,* as of *duri, hic et hæc durior et hoc durius,* of *Tristi, hic et hæc tristior*[1] *et hoc tristius,* of *Dulci, hic et hæc dulcior et hoc dulcius.*

The superlatyue excedeth his positiue in the highest degree, as *durissimus,* hardest: And it is fourmed of the fyrst case of his positiue that endeth in *i,* by puttyng therto *s,* and *simus,* as *duri durissimus, tristi tristissimus, dulci dulcissimus.*

From these general rules be excepted these that folowe.

$$\begin{cases} \textit{Bonus} \\ \textit{Melior} \\ \textit{Optimus.} \end{cases} \qquad \begin{cases} \textit{Malus} \\ \textit{Peior} \\ \textit{Pessimus} \end{cases}$$

$$\begin{cases} \textit{Magnus} \\ \textit{Maior} \\ \textit{Maximus.} \end{cases} \qquad \begin{cases} \textit{Paruus} \\ \textit{Minor} \\ \textit{Minimus.} \end{cases} \qquad \begin{cases} \textit{Multus plurimus} \\ \textit{Multa plurima} \\ \textit{Multum plus plurimum} \end{cases}$$

And if the positiue ende in *r,* the superlatiue is formed of the nominatiue case, by puttynge to *rimus,* as *pulcher pulcherrimus.*

Also these nownes endyng in *lis,* make the superlatyue by chaungyng *is,* into *limus,* as *humilis humillimus, similis simillimus, facilis facillimus, gracilis gra-* cillimus, agilis agillimus, docilis docillimus,

---

[1] trstior

All other nownes endyng in *lis*, do folowe the generall rule afore goyng.
[B4^v]

A Pronowne is a parte of speche, muche lyke a nowne, whiche is vsed in
shewyng or rehersyng.   225

There be .xv. Pronownes, *Ego, tu, sui, ille, ipse, iste, hic, is, meus, tuus, suus,
noster, uester, nostras, uestras.*

To these may be added their compoundes, as *egomet, tute, idem,* and also *Qui
quę quod.*

These .viii. pronownes, *Ego, tu, sui, ille, ipse, iste, hic,* and *is,* be primitiues, so 230
called for bycause they be not deriued of other. And they be also called
Demonstratiues, bycause they shewe a thyng not spoken of before.

And these .vi. *Hic, ille, iste, is, idem,* and *qui,* be relatiues, because they
reherse a thyng that was spoken of before.

These .vii. *Meus, tuus, suus, noster, uester, nostras,* and *uestras,* be deriuatiues, 235
for they be deriued of their primitiues, *Mei, tui, sui, nostri,* and *uestri.*

There belongeth to a pronowne, these .v. thynges, Number, Case, and
Gender, as are in a Nowne, Declenson, and Person, as here foloweth.

There be foure declensons of pronownes.   240
These .iii. *Ego, Tu, Sui,* be of the fyrste declenson, and be thus declyned. [C1^r]

Singulariter	Nominatiuo Ego, Genitiuo mei, Datiuo mihi, Accusatiuo me, Vocatiuo caret, Ablatiuo a me,	Pluraliter	Nominatiuo nos, Genitiuo nostrum uel nostri, Datiuo nobis, Accusatiuo nos, Vocatiuo caret, Ablatiuo a nobis.
Singulariter	Nominatiuo Tu, Genitiuo tui, Datiuo tibi, Accusatiuo te, Vocatiuo o tu, Ablatiuo a te,	Pluraliter	Nominatiuo uos, Genitiuo uestrum uel uestri, Datiuo uobis, Accusatiuo uos, Vocatiuo o uos, Ablatiuo a uobis.
Singulariter	Nominatiuo caret, Genitiuo sui, Datiuo sibi, Accusatiuo se, Vocatiuo caret, Ablatiuo a se,	Pluraliter	Nominatiuo caret, Genitiuo sui, Datiuo sibi, Accusatiuo se, Vocatiuo caret, Ablatiuo a se.

245
250
255

These .vi. *Ille, ipse, iste, hic, is,* and *qui,* be of the .ii. declenson, and be thus 260
declyned,

Singulariter	Nominatiuo iste ista istud,	Pluraliter	Nominatiuo isti iste ista,
	Genitiuo istius,		Genitiuo istorum istarum istorum,
	Datiuo isti,		Datiuo istis,
	Accusatiuo istum istam istud		Accusatiuo istos istas ista,
	Vocatiuo caret,		Vocatiuo caret,
	Ablatiuo isto ista isto,		Ablatiuo istis.

Ille is declyned lyke *iste*, and also *ipse*, excepte that the neuter gendre in the nomynatyue case, and in the accusatyue case syngular, maketh *ipsum*.

Nominatiuo hic, hęc, hoc, Genitiuo *huius*, as afore in the nowne. [C1ᵛ]

Singulariter	Nominatiuo is ea id,	Pluraliter	Nominatiuo ij eę ea,
	Genitiuo eius,		Genitiuo eorum earum eorum,
	Datiuo ei,		Datiuo ijs uel eis,
	Accusatiuo eum eam id,		Accusatiuo eos eas ea,
	Vocatiuo caret,		Vocatiuo caret,
	Ablatiuo eo ea eo,		Ablatiuo ijs uel eis.

Singulariter
Nominatiuo { qui / quæ / quod [1] }
Genitiuo cuius
Datiuo cui
Accusatiuo { quem / quam / quod }
Vocatiuo caret
Ablatiuo { quo / qua / quo } uel qui

Pluraliter
Nominatiuo { qui / quę / quę }
Genitiuo { quorum / quarum / quorum }
Datiuo quibus uel queis
Accusatiuo { quos / quas / quæ }
Vocatiuo caret
Ablatiuo quibus uel queis

Lykewyse *quis* and *quid*, be declyned, whether they be interrogatiues or indefinites.

Where note that *quid*, is alwayes a substantiue of the neuter gender.

These .v. *Meus, tuus, suus, noster,* and *uester*, be of the .iii. declenson, and be declyned as nownes adiectiues of .iii. terminations, in this wyse.

Singulariter	Nominatiuo meus mea um,	Pluraliter	Nominatiuo mei meæ mea,
	Genitiuo mei meæ mei,		Genitiuo meorum mearum orum,
	Datiuo meo meæ o,		Datiuo meis,[2]
	Accusatiuo meum meam um,		Accusatiuo meos meas mea,
	Vocatiuo mi[3] mea um,		Vocatiuo mei meæ mea,
	Ablatiuo meo a o,		Ablatiuo meis. [C2ʳ]

So is *noster*, declyned, and *tuus, suus, uester*, except that these thre laste, do lacke the vocatyue case.

---

[1] *quo d*   [2] *m eis*   [3] *mei*

Nostras uestras and this nown *cuias*, be of the fourth declenson, and be thus declyned. 305

| Singulariter | { Nominatiuo hic et hæc nostras et hoc te,
Genitiuo huius tis,
Datiuo huic ti¹,
Accusatiuo hunc hanc
tem et hoc te,
Vocatiuo o nostras et o te
Ablatiuo ab hoc hac et hoc
te uel ti, | Pluraliter | { Nominatiuo hi et hæ nostrates,
et hæc nostratia,
Genitiuo horum harum horum tium,
Datiuo his nostratibus,
Accusatiuo hos et has
strates, et hæc nostratia,
Vocatiuo o tes et o tia,
Ablatiuo ab his nostratibus, |

310

Here is to be noted, that *nostras*, *uestras*, and this nowne *cuias*, be called 315 *Gentiles*, bycause they properly betoken perteinyng to countreys or nations, to sectes or factions.

A pronowne hath thre persons.

The fyrste speaketh of hym selffe, as *Ego*, I, *nos*, we.
The seconde person is spoken to, as *Tu*, thou, *uos*, ye. 320
And of this person is also euery vocatyue case.
The thyrde persone is spoken of, as *Ille*, he, *illi*, they.
And therfore all nownes, pronownes, and participles be of the thyrde person.

Of a verbe. 325

A VERBE is a parte of speche, declyned with mode and tense, betokenyng to do, as *Amo*, I loue: to suffer, as *Amor*, I am loued: or to be, as *Sum*, I am.
Of verbes such as haue persons be cal[C2ᵛ]led personalles, as *Ego amo*, *Tu amas*. And suche as haue no persons, be called impersonalles, as *Tædet*, it yrketh, *oportet*, it behoueth. 330
Of verbes personalles there be .v. kyndes. Actyue, Passyue, Neuter, Deponent, and Common.
A verbe actyue endeth in *o*, as *Amo*, and by puttyng to *r*, may be a passiue² as *Amor*.
A verbe passiue endeth in *or*, as *Amor*, and by puttyng away *r*, may be an 335 actyue, as *Amo*.
A verbe neuter endeth in *o*, or *m*, and can not take *r* to make hym a passiue, as *Curro*³ I renne, *Sum* I am.
A verbe deponent endeth in *r*, and yet in sygnification is actyue, as *Loquor uerbum*, I speake a woorde, or neuter, as *Glorior*, I boste. 340

---

¹ *t i*   ² 'passiue' inserted by hand over an illegible erasure.
³ *Curo*. Another *r* has been inserted by hand above the line; it is indicated by a caret below the line.

A verbe common endeth in *r*, and in sygnification is bothe actiue and passiue, as *Osculor te*, I kysse the, *Osculor a te*, I am kyssed of the.

Modes.

There be .vi. Modes. The Indicatyue, the Imperatyue, the Optatyue, the
345 Potencial, the Subiunctyue, and the Infinityue.
The Indycatyue mode sheweth a reason true or false, as *Ego amo*, I loue:
orels asketh a question, as *Amas tu*? Dooest thou loue.
The Imperatyue byddeth, or commaundeth, as *Ama*, loue thou.
The Optatyue wyssheth or desyreth, with these signes, Would God, I praye
350 God, or God graunt, as *Vtinam Amem*, I praye God I loue.
The Potencyall mode is knowen by these sygnes may, can, myght, would,
should, or ought, as *amem*, I can or may loue.
[C3ʳ] T<h>e Subiunctyue[1] ioyneth sentences togyther, as *Cum amarem
eram miser*, Whan I loued I was a wretch.
355 The Infinityue signifieth dooyng, sufferyng, or beyng, and hath neyther
numbre, nor person, nor nominatiue case before hym, and is knowen
commonly by this sygne to, as *Amare*, to loue. Also whan twoo verbes,
come togyther without any nomynatyue case betwene theym, then the
later shall be the Infinitiue mode, as *Cupio discere*, I desyre to lerne.
360 There be moreouer belongynge to the infinityue mode of verbes certayne
voyces, called gerundes endyng in *di, do*, and *dum*, and haue bothe the
actiue and passiue signification, as *amandi*, of louing, or of being loued,
amando, in louyng or in being loued, *amandum*, to loue or to be loued.
There be also perteynyng vnto verbes two Supines, the one endyng in *tum*,
365 whiche is called the firste Supine because it hath the signification of the
verbe actyue, as *Eo amatum*, I goo to loue. And the other in *tu*, whiche is
called the later supine because it hath for the moste parte the sygnification passiue, as *Difficilis amatu*, Harde to be loued.

Tenses.

370 There be .v. Tenses or tymes. The presente tense, the preterimperfect[2]
tense, the preterperfect, the preterplusperfect, and the future tense.
The present tense speaketh of the tyme that now is as *Amo*, I loue.
The preterimperfecte tense speaketh of the tyme not perfectly paste, as
Amabam, I loued or dyd loue.
375 The preterperfect tense speketh of the time perfect[C3ᵛ]ly past, with this
signe haue, as *Amaui*, I haue loued.
The preterplusperfecte tense speketh of the tyme more then perfectely
paste, with this sygne hadde, as *Amaueram*, I had loued.

---

[1] S ubiunctyue
[2] preterpluperfect

The future tense speketh of the tyme to come with this signe, shall or wyll, as *Amabo*, I shall or wyl loue. 380

Persons.

There be also in verbes .iii. persons, in bothe numbres, as Singulariter *Ego amo* I loue, *tu amas* thou louest, *ille amat* he loueth. Pluraliter *Nos amamus* we loue, *uos amatis* ye loue, *illi amant* they loue.

Coniugations. 385

Verbes haue .iiii. Coniugations, whiche be knowen after this maner.
The fyrste coniugation hath *a*, long before *re*, and *ris*, as *Amáre, amáris*.
The seconde coniugation hath *e*, longe before *re*, and *ris*, as *Docére, docéris*.
The third coniugation hath *e*, shorte before *re*, and *ris*, as *Légere, légeris*.
The fourth coniugation hath *i*, long before *re*, and *ris*, as *Audíre, audíris*. 390
Verbes in *o*, of the fower Coniugations, be declyned after these exaumples.
Amo, as, amaui, amare, amandi, do, dum, amatum, tu, amans, amaturus, to loue.
Doceo, doces, docui, cere, docendi, do, dum, doctum, doctu, docens, docturus, to teache.
Lego, legis, legi, gere, legendi, do, dum, lectum, lectu, legens, lecturus, to reade.
Audio, audis, audiui, audire, audiendi, do, dum, auditum, auditu, audiens, auditurus, 395
to here.

[C4ʳ] Indicatiue mode the present tens singular.

I loue	thou louest.	he loueth.		we loue.	ye loue,	they loue,
Amo	as,	at,		amamus	atis,	mant
Doceo	es,	et,	Pluraliter	docemus	etis,	cent,	400
Lego	is,	it,		legimus	itis,	gunt,
Audio	is,	it,		audimus	itis,	diunt,

The preterimperfecte tense singular.

Amabam			I loued or dyd loue.
Docebam			taught.	405
Legebam	*bas, bat. Pluraliter bamus, batis, bant.*	read.
Audiebam			heard.

The preterperfecte tense singular.

Amaui		I haue loued.
Docui		taught.	410
Legi	*isti, it. Pluraliter imus, istis, erunt uel ere*	read.
Audiui		heard.

The preterpluperfecte tense. Syngular.

Amaueram		I had loued.
Docueram		taught.	415
Legeram	*ras, rat. Pluraliter ramus, ratis,*	read.
Audiueram		heard.

The future tense syngular.

Amabo			I shall or wyll loue.
420 Docebo	bis, bit. Pluraliter bimus, bitis, bunt		teache.
Legam			read.
Audiam	es, et, Pluraliter emus, etis, ent.		heare.

Im<p>erat<y>ue mode the presente tense singular.

Loue	Loue he, or	Loue we, or	Loue	Loue they, or
425 thou.	let hym loue,	let vs loue.	ye	let th<e>m loue.
Ama	amet		amate	ament
Amato	amato	amemus	amatote	amanto
Teache	Teache he or	Teache we, or	Teache	Teache they, or
thou	let hym teach,	let vs teache	ye	let them teache.
430 Doce	doceat		docete	doceant
Doceto	doceto	doceamus	docetote	docento
Lege	legat	Pluraliter	legite,	legant
Legito	legito	legamus	legitote,	legunto [C4ᵛ]
Audi	audiat	Pluraliter	audite	audiant
435 Audito	audito	audiamus	auditote	audiunto

Optatyue mode the present tens singular vtinam

Amem, es, et. Pluraliter utinam, amemus, ametis, ament. God graunt I loue.

Doceam		taught.
Legam	as, at. Pluraliter utinam, amus, atis, ant.	reade.
440 Audiam		heare.

Preterimperfectens singular vtinam

Amarem		would god I loued.
Docerem	res, ret. Pluraliter utinam remus, retis,	taught.
Legerem		read.
445 Audirem		heard.

Preterperfecte tense. singular vtinam

Amauerim		I praye god I haue loued.
Docuerim	ris, rit. Pluraliter utinam, rimus, ritis	taught.
Legerim		read.
450 Audiuerim		harde.

Preterpluperfect tense. singular vtinam

Amauissem		would god I had loued.
Docuissem	ses, set. Pluraliter utinam, semus, setis	taught.
Legissem		read.
455 Audiuissem		heard.

Future tens singular vtinam

Amauero		God graunt I loue hereafter.
Docuero	*ris, rit. Pluraliter utinam, rimus, ritis,*	taught.
Legero		reade.
Audiuero		heare. 460

Potential mode present tens Singular.

Amem, ames, amet. *Pluraliter amemus, ametis, ament.* I may or can loue.

Doceam		taught.
Legam	*as, at. Pluraliter amus, atis, ant.*	reade.
Audiam		heare. 465

[D1ʳ] Preterimperfect tens Singular.

Amarem		I myght or coulde lou\<e\>.
Docerem	*res, ret. Pluraliter remus, retis, rent.*	teache.
Legerem		reade.
Audirem		heare. 470

Preterperfecte tense Singular.

Amauerim		I myght, should or ought to haue loued.
Docuerim	*ris, rit. Pluraliter rimus, ritis. rint.*	taught.
Legerim		reade.
Audiuerim		heard. 475

Preterpluperfecttens Singular[1].

Amauissem		I myght, should or ought to had loued.
Docuissem	*ses, set. Pluraliter semus, setis, sent.*	taught.
Legissem		read.
Audiuissem		heard. 480

Futuretens singular

Amauero		I may or can loue hereafter.
Docuero	*ris, rit. Pluraliter rimus, ritis, rint.*	teache.
Legero		reade.
Audiuero		heare. 485

Coniunctyue mode. present singular cum.

Amem, es, et. *Pluraliter amemus, ametis, ament.* when I loue.

Doceam		teache.
Legam	*as, at, Pluraliter amus, atis, ant.*	reade.
Audiam		heare. 490

[1] Singul ar

Preterimperfectetens singular cum.

Amarem		Whan I loued or dyd loue.
Docerem	*res, ret. Pluraliter remus, retis, rent.*	taught or dyd teache.
Legerem		reade or dyd reade.
495 Audirem		heard or dyd heare.

Preterperfecte tense singular cum.

Amauerim		Whan I haue loued.
Docuerim	*ris, rit. Pluraliter rimus, ritis, rint.*	taught.
Legerim		read.
500 Audiuerim		heard.

Preterpluperfect tens singular cum.

Amauissem		Whan I had loued.
Docuissem	*ses, set. Pluraliter semus, setis, sent*	taught.
Legissem		read
505 Audiuissem		heard.

[D1ᵛ] Futuretens singular cum.

Amauero		Whan I shall or wyll loue.
Docuero	*ris, rit. Pluraliter rimus, ritis, rint.*	teache.
Legero		reade.
510 Audiuero		heare.

Infinitiue mode present and preterimperfect tens

Amare		to loue.
Docere		teache.
Legere		reade.
515 Audire		heare.

Preterperf<e>cte and preterpluperfecte tense.

Amauisse		To haue or had loued.
Docuisse		to haue or had taught.
Legisse		to haue or had read.
520 Audiuisse		to haue or had heard.

Future tens

Amaturum esse		To loue hereafter.
Docturum esse		to teache hereafter.
Lecturum esse		to reade hereafter.
525 Auditurum esse		to heare in tyme to come.

Gerundes

Amandi	of louyng.	do	in louyng	dum	to loue[1].
Docendi	of teaching	do	in teachyng	dum	to teache.
Legendi	of readyng	do	in readyng	dum	to reade.
530 Audiendi	of hearyng	do	in hearyng	dum	to heare.

[1] toloue

Supines.

Amatum	To loue.	⌠*Amatu*	To be loued.
Doctum	to teache.	⎪*Doctu*	to be taught.
Lectum	to reade.	⎨*Lectu*	to be read.
Auditum[1]	to heare.	⌡*Auditu*	to be heard. 535

Participle present.

⌠*Amans*	⌠Louyng.
⎪*Docens*	⎪Teachyng.
⎨*Legens*	⎨Readyng.
⌡*Audiens*	⌡Hearyng. 540

[D2ʳ] Participle Future.

⌠*Amaturus*	To loue or about to loue.
⎪*Docturus*	to teache or about to teache.
⎨*Lecturus*	to reade or about to reade.
⌡*Auditurus*	to heare or about to heare. 545

Here before we declyne any verbes in *or*, for supplyeng of many tenses, lackynge in all suche verbes, we muste lerne to declyne this verbe *Sum*, in this wyse.

Indicatiue mode present tense. singular.
SVM, es, fui, esse, futurus. 550
Sum I am, *es, est. Pluraliter sumus, estis, sunt.*

Preterimperfect singular
Eram, I was, *eras, erat. Pluraliter eramus, eratis, erant.*

Preterperfecte tense
Fui, I haue ben, *fuisti, fuit. Pluraliter fuimus, fuistis, fuerunt uel fuere.* 555

Preterpluperfecttens Singular[2].
Fueram, I had ben, *fueras, fuerat. Pluraliter fueramus, fueratis, fuerant.*

Futuretens singular
Ero. I shall or wyll be, *eris, erit. Pluraliter erimus, eritis, erunt.*

Imperatiue mode present tens Singular. 560

Sis ⌉			*sitis* ⌉	*sint* ⌉	
Es ⎬	be thou *sit* ⌉	*Pluraliter Simus*	*este* ⎬	*sunto.*⌡	
Esto⌡	*esto* ⌡		*estote* ⌡		

Optatyue mode present singular vtinam
Sim,   I pray god I be, *sis, sit. Pluraliter simus, sitis, sint.* 565

Preterimperfect singular vtinam
Essem,   I would god I were, *esses, esset. Pluraliter essemus, essetis, essent.*

---

[1] *Amatum*   [2] Singul ar

Preterperfecte tense singular vtinam

Fuerim,　　I pray god I haue ben, *ris, rit. Pluraliter fuerimus, fueritis, fuerint.*

570　Preterpluperfect tens Singular vtinam

Fuissem,　　Wolde god I had bene, *fuisses, ses, set. Pluraliter fuissemus, fuissetis,*
　　　　　　　fuissent.

[D2ᵛ] Futuretens singular vtinam

Fuero,　　God graunt I be hereafter, *fueris, fuerit. Pluraliter fuerimus, fueritis,*
575　　　　　*fuerint.*

Potential mode present tens singular

Sim,　　　I may or can be, *sis, sit. Pluraliter simus, sitis, sint,*

Preterimperfecttens. Singular.

Essem,　　I myght or coulde be, *esses, esset. Pluraliter essemus, essetis, essent.*

580　Preterperfecte tense. singular vtinam

Fuerim,　　I myght shulde or ought to haue ben, *fueris, fuerit. Pluraliter*
　　　　　　　fuerimus, fueritis, fuerint.

Preterpluperfect tense. singular vtinam

Fuissem,　　I myght shulde or ought to had bene, *fuisses, fuisset. Pluraliter*
585　　　　　*fuissemus, fuissetis, fuissent.*

Future tens singular vtinam

Fuero,　　I maye be hereafter, *fueris, fuerit. Pluraliter fuerimus, fueritis, fuerint.*

Coniunctiue mode present singular cum.

Sim,　　　Whan I am, *sis, sit, Pluraliter simus, sitis, sint.*

590　Preterimperfect singular cum.

Essem,　　Whan I was, *ses, set. Pluraliter semus, setis, sent.*

Preterperfecte tense. singular cum

Fuerim,　　Whan I haue ben, *fueris, fuerit. Pluraliter fuerimus, fueritis, fuerint.*

Preterpluperfecte tense singular cum.

595　*Fuissem,*　　Whan I had bene, *fuisses, fuisset. Pluraliter fuissemus, fuissetis, fuissent.*

Future tens singular cum.

Fuero,　　Whan I shall or wyll be, *fueris, fuerit. Pluraliter fuerimus, fueritis,*
　　　　　　　fuerint.

Infinitiue mode ⎫　　　　　Preterperfect　⎫　　　　　⎧to haue
600　present and　　⎬ *Esse,* to be　and　　　　⎬ *Fuisse.* ⎨or had
imperfect tense.⎭　　　　　preterpluperfect. ⎭　　　　　⎩ben.
Future tense, *Fore uel futurum esse,* to be hereafter

[D3ʳ] Verbes in *or* of the foure coniugations be declyned after these examples.

⎧ *Amor, aris uel are, amatus sum uel fui, amari, amatus, amandus.*
⎪ *Doceor, ris uel cere, doctus sum uel fui, doceri, doctus, docendus.*   605
⎨ *L<e>gor, geris, u<e>l gere, lectus sum uel fui, legi, lectus, legendus.*
⎩ *Audior, diris uel ire, auditus sum uel fui, audiri, ditus, audiendus.*

Indicatiue mode present tense. singular.

Amor aris, u<e>l are, atur, ⎤	I am loued.	
Doceor, eris, uel ere, etur. ⎥	I am taught.	*Pluraliter mur, mini, tur.* 610
Legor, eris, uel ere, itur, ⎦	I am read.	
Audior, iris, uel ire, itur.	I am heard.	

The preterimperfecte tense. singular.

Amabar ⎤	I was loued.	
Docebar ⎥	taught.	*baris, uel bare, batur. Pluraliter bamur,* 615
Legebar ⎥	read.	*mini, tur.*
Audiebar[1] ⎦	heard.	

The preterperfecte tense singular

Amatus ⎤		I haue ben loued. ⎤	*tus es uel fuisti, tus est uel fuit.*
Doctus ⎥	*sum uel fui,*	taught. ⎥	*Pluraliter ti sumus uel imus,* 620
Lectus ⎥		read. ⎥	*ti estis uel istis, ti sunt fuerunt*
Auditus ⎦		heard. ⎦	*uel fuere.*

The preterpluperfecte tense. Syngular.

Amatus ⎤		I had ben loued. ⎤	*tus eras uel fueras, tus erat uel fuerat.*
Doctus ⎥	*eram uel fueram*	taught. ⎥	*Pluraliter ti eramus* 625
Lectus ⎥		read. ⎥	*uel fueramus, ti eratis uel*
Auditus ⎦		heard. ⎦	*fueratis, ti erant uel fuerant.*

The future tense. syngular

Amabor ⎤	*beris uel ere, bitur, bimur, bimini, buntur.*	I shall or wyll be loued.
Docebor ⎦		taught. 630
Legar ⎤	*eris uel ere, etur. Pluraliter emur*	read.
Audiar ⎦		heard.

[D3ᵛ] Imperatyue mode present tens Singular.

Be thou loued.	let hym be loued.	let vs be loued.	be ye loued.	let them be loued. 635
Amare ⎤	*ametur* ⎤	*Pluraliter emur*	*amini* ⎤	*entur* ⎤
Amator ⎦	*amator* ⎦		*aminor* ⎦	*antor* ⎦
Docere ⎤	*Doceatur* ⎤	*Pluraliter amur,*	*cemini* ⎤	*ceantur* ⎤
Docetor ⎦	*Docetor* ⎦		*minor* ⎦	*centor* ⎦
Legere ⎤	*legatur* ⎤	*Pluraliter amur,*	*gemini* ⎤	*gantur* ⎤ 640
Legitor ⎦	*legitor* ⎦		*minor* ⎦	*guntor* ⎦

---

[1] *Audibar*

| *Audire* ⎫ | *audiatur* ⎫ | *Pluraliter iamur,* | *imini* ⎫ | *antur* ⎫ |
| *Auditor* ⎭ | *auditor* ⎭ | | *iminor* ⎭ | *untor* ⎭ |

Optatyue mode the present tens singular vtinam

645 *Amer, eris uel ere, etur. Pluraliter emur, emini, entur.* God graunt I be loued.

Docear ⎫		taught.
Legar ⎬	*aris, are, atur. Pluraliter amur, amini, antur.*	read.
Audiar ⎭		heard.

Preterimperfectens Singular.

650 *Amarer* ⎫ Wolde god I were loued.
Docerer ⎟ | | taught.
Legerer ⎬ *eris uel ere, etur. Pluraliter remur, remini, rentur.* read.
Audirer ⎭ | | heard.

Preterperfecte tense. singular vtinam

655 *Amarer* ⎫ wolde god I haue ben loued.
Doctus ⎟ *sim uel fuerim, sis uel fueris, tus sit uel fuerit.*
Lectus ⎬ *Pluraliter ti simus uel fuerimus, ti sitis uel fueritis,*
Auditus ⎭ *ti sint uel fuerint.*

Preterpluperfect tense. singular vtinam

660 *Amatus* ⎫ wolde god I had ben loued.
Doctus ⎟ *essem uel fuissem, tus esses uel fuisses, tus esse<t>*
Lectus ⎬ *uel fuisset. Pluraliter ti essemus uel fuissemus, ti*
Auditus ⎭ *essetis uel fuissetis, ti essent uel fuissent.*

Future tens singular vtinam

665 *Amatus* ⎫ God graunt I be loued hereafter.
Doctus ⎟ *ero uel fuero, tus eris uel fueris, tus erit uel*
Lectus ⎬ *fuerit. Pluraliter ti erimus uel fuerimus, ti eritis*
Auditus ⎭ *uel fueritis, ti erunt uel fuerint.*

[D4ʳ] Potentiall mode present tens singular

670 *Amer, eris uel ere, etur. Pluraliter emur, emini, entur.* I may or can be loued[1].

Docear ⎫		taught.
Legar ⎬	*aris. uel are, atur. Pluraliter amur, amini, antur*[2].	
Audiar ⎭		heard.

Preterimperfect tens singular.

675 *Amarer* ⎫ I wolde should or ought to be loued.
Docerer ⎟ | | taught.
Legerer ⎬ *reris uel rere, retur. Pluraliter emur, emini, entur* read.
Audirer ⎭ | | heard.

---

[1] o ued
[2] *anttur*

Preterperfecte tense Syngular.

Amatus	I wolde shoulde or ought to haue ben loued.	680
Doctus	*sim uel fuerim, tus sis uel fueris, tus sit uel*	
Lectus	*fuerit. Pluraliter ti simus*[1] *uel fuerimus, ti sitis*	
Auditus	*uel fueritis, ti sint uel fuerint*[2].	

Preterpluperfecte tense Singular.

Amatus	I wolde shoulde or ought to had ben loued.	685
Doctus	*essem uel fuissem, tus esses uel fuisses, tus esset*	
Lectus	*uel fuisset. Pluraliter ti essemus uel fuissemus, ti*	
Auditus	*essetis uel fuissetis, ti essent uel fuissent.*	

Futuretens Singular.

Amatus	I may or can be loued hereafter.	690
Doctus	*ero uel fuero, tus eris uel fueris, tus erit uel*	
Lectus	*fuerit. Pluraliter ti erimus uel fuerimus, ti eritis*	
Auditus	*uel fueritis, ti erunt uel fuerint.*	

Coniunctiue mode present singular cum.

Amer, eris uel ere, etur. Pluraliter emur, emini, entur.	whan I am loued.	695
Docear	taught.	
Legar	*aris, uel are, atur. Pluraliter amur, amini, antur,*	read.
Audiar	heard.	

Preterimperfect tens singular cum

Amarer	Whan I was loued.	700
Docerer	*reris uel rere, etur. Pluraliter emur, emini,*	taught.
Legerer	*rentur.*	read.
Audirer	heard.	

[D4^v] Preterperfecte tense. singular cum.

Amatus	whan I haue ben loued.	705
Doctus	*sim uel fuerim, tus sis uel fueris, tus sit uel*	
Lectus	*fuerit. Pluraliter ti simus*[3] *uel fuerimus, ti sitis*	
Auditus	*uel fueritis, ti sint uel fuerint.*	

Preterpluperfect[4] tens singular cum.

Amatus	whan I had ben loued.	710
Doctus	*essem uel fuissem, tus esses uel fuisses, tus esset*	
Lectus	*uel fuisset. Pluraliter ti essemus uel fuissemus, ti*	
Auditus	*essetis uel fuissetis, ti essent uel fuissent.*	

---

[1] *sin us*

[2] *fu erint*

[3] *sin us*

[4] Pteterpluperfect

Future tens singular cum.

715 *Amatus*⎫   whan I shall or wyll be loued.
    Doctus ⎪   *ero uel fuero, tus eris uel fueris, tus erit uel*
    Lectus ⎬   *fuerit. Pluraliter ti erimus uel fuerimus, ti eritis*
    Auditus⎭   *uel fueritis, ti erunt uel fuerint.*

Infinitiue mode present and preterimperfect tens

720 *Amari*⎫   to be loued.
    Doceri⎪   to be taught.
    Legi ⎬   to be read.
    Audiri⎭   to be heard.

Preterperf\<e\>cte and preterpluperfecte tense.

725 *Amatum*⎫   To haue or had ben loued.
    Doctum ⎪   to haue or had ben taught.
    Lectum ⎬ *esse uel fuisse*   to haue or had ben read.
    Auditum⎭   to haue or had ben heard.

Futuretens

730 *Amatum iri uel amandum esse*   to be loued hereafter.
    Doctum iri uel docendum esse   taught hereafter.
    Lectum iri uel legendum esse   read hereafter.
    Auditum iri uel audiendum   heard hereafter.

Participle preterit.

735 ⎧*Amatus* Loued.   ⎧*Amandus* To be loued hereafter
    ⎪*Doctus*   taught. Participle ⎪*Docendus* taught.
    ⎨*Lectus*   read.   future   ⎨*Legendus* read.
    ⎩*Auditus* heard.   ⎩*Audiendus* heard. [E1ʳ]

⎧ *Possum, potes, potui, posse, potens.*   to may or can
740 ⎪ *Volo, uis, uolui, uelle, uolendi, do, dum, supinis caret,*
    ⎪   *uolens.* to wyll.
    ⎪ *Nolo, nonuis, nolui, nolle, nolendi, do, dum, supinis caret,*
    ⎪   *nolens.* to nyll.
    ⎪ *Malo, mauis, malui, malle, malendi, do, dum, supinis caret,*
745 ⎨   *malens.* to haue lyeffer.
    ⎪ *Edo, es uel edis, edi, edere uel esse, edendi, do, dum,*
    ⎪   *esum, esu, edens, esurus.* to eate.
    ⎪ *Fio, fis, factus sum, fieri, factus, faciendus,* to be made.
    ⎪ *Fero, fers, tuli, ferre, ferendi, ferendo, ferendu\<m\>,*
750 ⎪   *latum, latu, ferens, laturus.* to beare or to suffer.
    ⎪ *Feror, ferris, latus sum uel fui, ferri, latus, ferendus.*
    ⎩   to be borne or suffered.

Indicatiue mode present tens.

Singulariter   *Pluraliter*

⎧ *Possum potes potest,*   ⎧ *possumus*[1] *potestis possunt.*   755
⎪ *Volo, uis, uult,*   ⎪ *Volumus, uultis, uolunt.*
⎪ *Nolo nonuis nonuult*   ⎪ *Nolumus nonuultis nolunt.*
⎨ *Malo mauis mauult*   ⎨ *Malumus mauultis malunt.*
⎪ *Edo, edis uel es, edit uel est,*   ⎪ *Edimus, editis uel estis, edunt.*
⎪ *Fio, fis, fit,*   ⎪ *Fimus, fitis, fiunt.*   760
⎪ *Fero, fers, fert,*   ⎪ *Ferimus, fertis, ferunt.*
⎩ *Feror, ferris,* ⎫   *fertur* ⎩ *Ferimur ferimini feruntur*
         uel re ⎭

Preterimperfect tens Singular.

⎧ *Poteram* ⎫   765
⎪ *Volebam* ⎪
⎪ *Nolebam* ⎪
⎨ *Malebam* ⎬   *as, at. Pluraliter amus, atis, ant.*
⎪ *Edebam* ⎪
⎪ *Fiebam* ⎪   770
⎩ *Ferebam* ⎭

                    ⎧ *aris uel*
Ferebar   ⎩ *bare*   ⎰ *batur. Pluraliter bamur, mini, tur.*

[E1ᵛ] Preterperfecte tense. Singular.

⎧ *Potui* ⎫   775
⎪ *Volui* ⎪
⎪ *Nolui* ⎬   *isti, it. Pluraliter imus, istis, erunt uel ere.*
⎨ *Malui* ⎪
⎪ *Edi* ⎪
⎩ *Tuli* ⎭   780

              ⎧ *sum uel fui, tus es uel fuisti, tus est uel fuit.*
⎧ *Factus* ⎫ ⎨ *Pluraliter ti sumus uel fuimus, ti estis uel fuistis,*
⎩ *Latus* ⎭ ⎩ *ti sunt fuerunt uel fuere.*

Preterpluperfect tens singular

⎧ *Potueram* ⎫   785
⎪ *Volueram* ⎪
⎨ *Nolueram* ⎬   *ras, rat. Pluraliter ramus, ratis, rant.*
⎪ *Malueram* ⎪
⎪ *Ederam* ⎪
⎩ *Tuleram* ⎭   790

[1] *p ossumus*

$\left\{\begin{array}{l} \text{Factus} \\ \text{Latus} \end{array}\right.$ $\left\{\begin{array}{l} \text{\textit{eram uel fueram, tus eras uel fueras, tus erat}} \\ \text{\textit{uel fuerat. Pluraliter ti eramus uel fueramus, ti}} \\ \text{\textit{eratis uel fueratis, ti erant uel fuerant.}} \end{array}\right.$

Futuretens singular

795   $\left\{\begin{array}{l} \textit{Potero, ris, rit. Pluraliter rimus, ritis, runt.} \\ \textit{Volam} \\ \textit{Nolam} \\ \textit{Malam} \\ \textit{Edam} \\ \textit{Fiam} \\ \textit{Feram} \end{array}\right.$

800

$\left\{\begin{array}{l} \textit{Volam} \\ \textit{Nolam} \\ \textit{Malam} \\ \textit{Edam} \\ \textit{Fiam} \\ \textit{Feram} \end{array}\right\}$ *es, et. Pluraliter emus, etis, ent.*

Ferar $\left\{\begin{array}{l} \textit{reris uel} \\ \textit{rere} \end{array}\right\}$ *retur. Pluraliter remur, remini, rentur.*

Imperatyue mode

805 *Possum* $\left.\begin{array}{l} \textit{Possum} \\ \textit{Volo} \\ \textit{<Malo>} \end{array}\right\}$ *haue none imperatiue mode.*

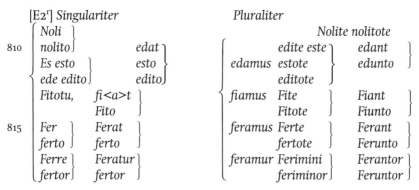

Optatyue mode the present tens singular vtinam

820   $\left\{\begin{array}{l} \textit{Possim} \\ \textit{Velim}^{1} \\ \textit{Nolim} \\ \textit{Malim} \end{array}\right\}$ *is, it. <P>luraliter imus, itis, int.*

825   $\left\{\begin{array}{l} \textit{Edam} \\ \textit{Fiam} \\ \textit{Feram} \end{array}\right\}$ *as, at. Pluraliter amus, atis, ant.*

Ferar, feraris uel ferare feratur. Pluraliter feramur, amini, antur[2].

---

[1] *Volim*
[2] *āntur*

Preterimperfecte[1] tense. singular vtinam

$$\left\{\begin{array}{l} Possem \\ Vellem \\ Nollem \\ Mallem \\ Ederem \\ uel\ Essem \\ Fierem \\ Ferrem \end{array}\right\}\ \text{es, et. Pluraliter emus, etis, ent,}$$

830

835

Ferrer reris uel rere retur. Pluraliter remur, remini, rentur.

Preterperfecte tense. singular

$$\left\{\begin{array}{l} Potuerim \\ Voluerim \\ Noluerim \\ Maluerim \\ Ederim \\ Tulerim \end{array}\right\}\ \text{ris, rit. Pluraliter rimus, ritis, rint.}$$

840

[E2ᵛ]

$$\left\{\begin{array}{l} Factus \\ Latus \end{array}\right.\ \left\{\begin{array}{l} \text{sim uel fuerim, tus sis uel fueris, tus sit uel fuerit.} \\ \text{Pluraliter ti simus uel fuerimus, ti sitis uel fueritis, ti} \\ \text{sint uel fuerint.} \end{array}\right.$$

845

Preterpluperfect tense singular vtinam

$$\left\{\begin{array}{l} Potuissem \\ Voluissem \\ Noluissem \\ Maluissem \\ Edissem \\ Tulissem \end{array}\right\}\ \text{ses, set. Pluraliter semus, se<t>is, sent.}$$

850

$$\left\{\begin{array}{l} Factus \\ Latus \end{array}\right\}\ \left\{\begin{array}{l} \text{essem uel fuissem, tus esses uel fuisses, tus} \\ \text{esset uel fuisset. Pluraliter ti essemus uel} \\ \text{fuissemus, ti essetis uel fuissetis, ti essent} \\ \text{uel fuissent.} \end{array}\right.$$

855

Futuretens singular vtinam

$$\left\{\begin{array}{l} Potuero \\ Voluero \\ Noluero \\ Maluero \\ Edero \\ Tulero \end{array}\right\}\ \text{ris, rit. Pluraliter rimus, ritis, rint.}$$

860

865

---

[1] Preterim=|fecte

$\left\{\begin{array}{l}\textit{Factus}\\\textit{Latus}\end{array}\right\}$ $\left\{\begin{array}{l}\textit{ero uel fuero, tus eris uel fueris, tus erit uel}\\\textit{fuerit. Pluraliter ti erimus uel fuerimus, ti eritis}\\\textit{uel fueritis. ti erunt uel fuerint.}\end{array}\right.$

870 The Potencial and the subiunctiue mode be formed and coniugated or varied lyke the Optatiue.

Infinitiue mode present and preterimperfect tens

$\left\{\begin{array}{l}\textit{Posse}\\\textit{Velle}\\\textit{Nolle}\\\textit{Malle}\\\textit{Edere uel esse}\\\textit{Ferre}\end{array}\right.$	Preterperfect and preterpluperfect.	$\left\{\begin{array}{l}\textit{Potuisse}\\\textit{Voluisse}\\\textit{Noluisse}\\\textit{Maluisse}\\\textit{Edisse}\\\textit{Tulisse}\end{array}\right.$ Future.	$\textit{Esurum}$ $\textit{Laturum esse}$

875 (Malle)

[E3ʳ] Presente and preterimperfecte ten<s>e.

$\left\{\begin{array}{l}\textit{Fieri}\\\textit{Ferri}\end{array}\right.$ $\left\{\begin{array}{l}\textit{Preterperfecte and}\\\textit{preterpluperfect.}\end{array}\right.$ $\left\{\begin{array}{l}\textit{Factum esse uel fuisse.}\\\textit{Latum esse uel fuisse.}\end{array}\right.$

880

Futuretens

$\left\{\begin{array}{l}\textit{Factum iri uel faciendum esse.}\\\textit{Latum iri uel ferendum esse.}\end{array}\right.$

Eo and *queo* make *ibam* and *quibam* in the preterimperfect tense of the
885 indicatiue mode: and *ibo* and *quibo* in the future tense, and in all other modes and tenses are varied lyke verbes in *o*, of the fowerth coniugation, sauynge that they make the gerundes: *Eundi, do, dum. Queundi, do, dum.*
Fourming of tenses.
Of the preterperfect tense of the Indicatyue mode be fourmed the
890 preterpluperfect tens of the same mode. The preterperfecte tense, the preterpluperfecte tense, and the future tense of the optatyue mode, the potencial mode, and the Subiunctiue mode. The preterperfecte and pluperfect tense of the infinitiue mode, as of *Amaui*, are fourmed *amaueram, amauerim, amauissem, amauero, amauisse, ram, rim,* and *ro,* by
895 chaungynge *i,* in to *e, sem,* and *se,* kepyng *i* styll.
Impersonals be declyned in the voyce of the third person through out all modes and tenses, as *Delectat, delectabat. Decet, decebat,* and haue commonly before their englyshe this sygne it, as It deliteth me to rede, *Delectat me legere.*

900   [E3ᵛ] *OF A PARTICIPLE*

A PARTICIPLE is a parte of speche, deriued of a verbe, and taketh part of a nowne as gendre and case, parte of a verbe, as tense and signification: and parte of bothe, as number and figure.
A participle hath .iiii. tenses, the present, the preter, the future in *rus,* and
905 the future in *dus.*

A participle of the present tense hath his englysshe endyng in yng, as louyng, and his latine in *ans*, or *ens*, as *Amans, docens*: And it is fourmed of the preterimperfect tense, by chaungyng *bam*, into *ens*, as *Amabam, amans, Audiebam audiens.*

A participle of the future in *rus*, betokeneth to do lyke the infinitiue mode 910 of the actyue voyce, as *Amaturus* to loue or about to loue. And is fourmed of the later supyne, by puttyng to *rus*, as *Doctu, docturus.*

A participle of the preter tense, hath his englysshe endyng in d, t, or n, as loued, taught, slayne, and his latyn endeth in *tus, sus, xus*, as *Amatus, uisus, nexus*, and one in *uus*, as *mortuus*. And is fourmed of the later supyne, by 915 puttynge to *s*, as *Lectu lectus.*

A participle of the future in *dus*, betokeneth to suffer lyke the infinitiue mode of the passyue voyce, as *Amandus* to be loued. And it is fourmed of the genytyue case of the participle of the present tense, by changyng *tis*, into *dus*, as *Legentis legendus*. And it is also found to haue the signification of 920 the present tense, as *Legendis ueteribus proficis*, In readyng olde aucthours thou dooest profit.

[E4ʳ] Of a verbe actiue, and of a verbe neuter, whiche hath the supines, come .ii. participles, one of the present tense, and an other of the future in *rus*, as of *Amo* commeth *amans, amaturus*, of *Curro, currens, cursurus.* 925

Of a verbe passiue whose actiue hath the supines, come .ii. participles, one of the preter tense, and an other of the future in *dus*, as of *amor*, commeth *amatus, amandus.*

Of a verbe deponent commeth .iii. participles, one of the present tense, one of the preter tense, and an other of the future in *rus*, as of *Auxilior,* 930 *auxilians, auxiliatus, auxiliaturus*. And if the verbe deponent gouern an accusatiue[1] case after him, it may fourme also a participle in *dus*, as of *Loquor, loquendus.*

Of a verbe common commeth .iiii. participles, as of *Largior*, commeth *largiens, largiturus, largitus, largiendus.* 935

Participles of the present tense, be declyned lyke nownes adiectiues with .iii. articles, as *hic hęc et hoc Amans.*

Participles of other tenses be declyned lyke nownes adiectiues of .iii. dyuers endynges, as *Amaturus, Amatus*[2], *Amandus, a, um.*

OF AN ADVERBE 940

AN ADVERBE is a parte of speche, ioyned to the verbes to declare his sygnification.

Aduerbes some be of tyme, as *Hodie, cras, olim, aliquando.*

---

[1] anaccusatiue
[2] *Amas*

Some of place, as *Vbi, ibi, hic, istic, illic, intus, foris.*
945 [E4ᵛ] Some of number, as *Semel, bis, ter, quater.*
Some of order, as *Inde, deinde, denique, postremo.*
Some of askynge or doubtyng, as *Cur, quare, unde, quorsum, num, numquid.*
Some of callyng, as *Heus, o, ehodum.*
Some of affirmyng, as *Certe, næ, profecto, sane, scilicet, licet, esto.*
950 Some of denying, as *Non, haud, minime, nequaquam.*
Some of sweryng, as *Pol, ædepol, hercle, medius fidius.*
Some of exhortyng, as *Eia, age, agedum.*
Some of flateryng, as *Sodes, amábo.*
Some of forbyddyng, as *Ne.*
955 Some of wysshyng, as *Vtinam, si, osi, o.*
Some of gatheryng togither, as *Simul, una, pariter, non modo, non solum.*
Some of partyng, as *Seorsim, sigillatim, uicatim.*
Some of choosyng, as *Potius, imo.*
Some of a thyng not fynisshed, as *Pene, ferè, uix, modo non.*
960 Some of shewyng, as *En, ecce.*
Some of doubtyng, as *Forsan, forsitan, fortassis, fortasse.*
Some of chaunce, as *Forte, fortuito.*
Some of lykenesse, as *Sic, sicut, quasi, ceu, tanquam, uelut.*
Some of quality, as *Bene, malè, doctè, fortiter.*
965 Some of quantity, as *Multum, parum, minimum, paululum.*
Some of comparison, as *Tam, quam, magis, minus, maximé.*
Certayne aduerbes be compared, as *Docte, doctius, doctissime. Fortiter, fortius,*
fortissime. Prope, propius, proxime.

[F1ʳ] OF A CONIVNCTION

970 *A CONIVNCTION* is a parte of speche, that ioynethe woordes, and sentences
together.
Of coniunctions, some be copulatiues, as *Et, que, quoque, atque, nec, neque.*
Some disiunctiues, as *Aut, ue, uel, seu, siue.*
Some discretiues, as *Sed, quidem, autem, uero, at, ast.*
975 Some causales, as *Nam, nanque, enim, etenim, quia, ut, quod, quando, quum.*
Some conditionalles, as *Si, sin, modo, dum, dummodo.*
Some exceptiues, as *Ni, nisi, quin, alioquin, preterquam.*
Some interrogatyues, as *Ne, an, uerum, necne, anne, nonne.*
Some illatiues, as *Ergo, ideo, igitur, quare, itaque, proin.*
980 Some aduersatiues, as *Etsi, quanquam, quamuis, licet.*
Some redditiues to the same, as *Tamen, attamen.*
Some electiues, as *Quam, ac, atque.*
Some diminutiues, as *Saltem, uel.*

OF A PREPOSITION

A *PREPOSITION* is a parte of speche moste commonly sette before other 985
partes in apposition, as *Ad patrem*, or in composition, as *Indoctus*.
These prepositions folowyng serue to the accusatiue case.

[F1ᵛ]					
Ad	to,	*Extra*	without,	*Post*	after
Apud	at,	*Intra*	within,	*Trans*	on the ferther syde. 990
Ante	before	*Inter*	betwene,	*Vltra*	beyond,
Aduersus ⎫ *Aduersum* ⎭	agaynst	*Infra*	beneth	*Pręter*	besyde
		Iuxta	besyde or nygh to,	*Supra*	aboue
Cis ⎫ *Citra* ⎭	on this side	*Ob*	for,	*Circiter*	about 995
		Pone	behynd	*Vsque*	vntyl
Circum ⎫ *Circa* ⎭	about	*Per*	by or thrugh	*Secus*	by
		Prope	nigh	*Versus*	toward
Contra	agaynst	*Propter*	for	*Penes*	⎧ in the
Erga	toward	*Secundum*	after		⎩ power. 1000

Where note that *uersus*, is sette after his casuall worde, as *Londinum uersus*,
Towarde London. And lykewyse may *penes* be set also.

These prepositions folowynge, serue to the ablatiue case.

⎧ *A* ⎫		⎧ *Pro*	for	
⎪ *Ab* ⎬	from or	⎪ *Pre*	before or in comparison 1005	
⎩ *Abs* ⎭	fro	⎬ *Palam*	openly	
⎧ *Cum*	with	⎪ *Sine* ⎫		
⎨ *Coram*	before or in presence	⎪ *Absque* ⎭	without	
⎩ *Clam*	priuily	⎩ *Tenus*	vntyll or vnto.	
⎧ *De* ⎫				1010
⎨ *E* ⎬	of or fro			
⎩ *Ex* ⎭				

Where note that if the casuall woorde ioyned with *tenus*, be the plurall
number, it shal be putte in the genitiue case and be sette before *tenus*, as
Aurium tenus, Vp to the eares. 1015
[F2ʳ] These prepositions folowyng serue to bothe cases, as *In*, with this
signe to, to the accusatiue[1] case, as
In urbem, into the city.
In, without this sygne to, to the ablatyue, as
In te spes est, my hope is in the. 1020
Sub noctem, a lyttell before nyght.
Sub iudice lis est, the matter is before[2] the iudge.
Super lapidem, vpon a stone.

[1] ablatyue
[2] befo re

Super uiridi fronde, vpon grene leaues
1025 *Subter terram*, vnder the earthe.
Subter aqua, vnder the water.

OF AN INTERIECTION

AN INTERIECTION is a parte of speche, which betokeneth a passion of
the mynde, vnder an vnperfect voyce.
1030 Some are of myrth, as *Euax, uah*.
Some of sorowe: as *Heu, hei*.
Some of drede, as *Atat*.
Some of maruailyng, as *Pape*.
Some of disdeinyng, as *Hem, uah*.
1035 Some of shunnyng, as *Apage*.
Some of praysyng, as *Euge*.
Some of scornyng, as *Hui*.
Some of exclamation, as *Proh deum atque hominum fidem*.
Some of cursyng, as * Vȩ, malum*.
1040 Some of laughyng, as *Hah, ha, he*.
Some of callyng, as *Eho, oh, io*.
Some of silence, as *Au*. And suche other.

GODLY LESSONS for Chyldren.

IT IS THE FYRST poynte of wysedome, to knowe thy selfe.
Primus est sapientiæ gradus te ipsum noscere.
Feare of the Lorde, is the begynnyng of wysedome.
Initium sapientiæ timor domini. 5
There is no manne that synneth not.
Non est homo qui non peccet.
If we saye we be fautelesse we deceyue our selues, and truthe is not in vs.
Si dixerimus peccatum non habemus, nos ipsos fallimus, et ueritas in nobis non est.
So God loued the worlde, that he gaue his only begotten soonne, that none 10
whiche beleueth in hym, shuld perisshe, but enioye euerlastyng lyfe.
Sic deus dilexit mundum, ut filium suum unigenitum daret, ut omnis qui credit in
eum, non pereat, sed habeat uitam æternam.
Christe is the lambe of God, whiche taketh away the synnes of the worlde.
Christus est agnus dei, qui tollit peccata mundi. 15
There is none other name vnder heauen, giuen vnto menne, by the
whiche we must be saued.
Non est aliud nomen sub cœlo datum hominibus, in quo oporteat nos[1] *saluos fieri.*
He that hath my commandmentes, and kepeth theim, it is he that loueth me.
[F3^r] *Qui habet precepta mea, et seruat ea, ille est qui diligit me.* 20
Ye be my frendes, if ye do what so euer I command you.
Vos amici mei estis, si feceritis quæcunque ego præcipio uobis.
I gyue you a newe commaundement, to loue eche other, as I haue loued
you.
Preceptum nouum do uobis ut diligatis mutuo, sicut dilexi uos. 25
Not the herers of the lawe be iust before god, but they that expresse the
lawe in theyr workes, shall be counted iuste.
Non qui audiunt legem iusti sunt apud deum, sed qui legem factis exprimunt, iusti
habebuntur.
Honour thy father and mother, that thou mayest doo well, and lyue long 30
vpon the earthe.
Honora patrem et matrem, ut bene tibi sit, et sis longeuus in terra.
Be subiect to the kyng, as to the moste excellent, and to his deputies,
whiche be sent of hym.
Regi subditi estote tanquam precellenti, et præsidibus ut qui ab eo mittantur. 35
Dooe reuerence to age.
Coram cano capite assurge.
Thou shalte not hurte no wydowe, ne none that is fatherlesse.
Viduæ et pupillo non nocebis.
Thou shalt vpbrayed no straungier. 40
Aduene non exprobrabis.

---

[1] *non*

Nothyng is gyuen more truely to Christe, than that that is gyuen to the poore.

Nihil uerius datur Christo, quam quod egenis confertur.

45 [F3ᵛ] Se not whan thou giuest, haue an eie whan thou takest.

Da cęcus, accipe oculatus.

A good conscience, is a sure defence.

Murus ęneus sana conscientia.

Be in dede, as thou dooest pretende.

50 *Quod uideri uis esto.*

It is trewe honour to be worshypped for vertue.

Verus honor est uenerari ob uirtutem,

It is trewe glory, to be well reported for vertue.

Vera gloria est bene audire ob uirtutem.

55 It is trewe nobilytie to be lyke in condityons to the good parentes.

Vera nobilitas est, bonis parentibus esse moribus similis.

It is trewe power to haue many whome thou mayste doo for.

Vera potentia est, habere multos quibus probe consulas.

There is no stronger defence, than faythfull frendes.

60 *Nullum potentius satellitium, quam amici fideles.*

Frendeshyppe is the sauce of lyfe.

Sal uitæ amicitia.

There is no true frendshyp but emong good menne.

Vera amicitia non est nisi inter bonos.

65 Pleasure is the bayte of myschiefes.

Voluptas malorum esca.

Memory is made weake with delycates.

Memoria delitijs eneruatur.

Dyuerse meates be noysome to man, but dyuers sauces more noysome.

70 *Varietas ciborum homini pestilens, pestilentior condimentorum,*

Wyne is poyson to the synewes, and the destruction of memorye.

[F4ʳ] *Vinum neruorum uenenum et memoriæ mors est.*

Gaye garmentes prouoke to pryde.

Culta uestimenta sunt instrumenta¹ superbiæ.

75 Be not asshamed to learne thynges that thou knowest not.

Quę ignoras ne pudeat quęrere.

Learne of fooles to be more ware.

Ex stultis disce quo fias cautior.

Learne of wyse men that thou mayest be the better.

80 *Ex sapientibus disce quo fias melior.*

Tyme ought to be moche sette by.

Magno æstimandum tempus.

Truthe is the doughter of tyme.

---

¹ *sun tinstrumenta*

Veritas temporis filia.
A trew man is beleued, yea though he lye.   85
Veraci creditur et mentienti.
A lyer is not beleued, though he swere.
Mendaci non creditur ne iurato quidem.
Let no daye scape without profitte.
Nullus prætereat sine linea dies.   90

FOr the due ioynyng of woordes in construction, it is to be vnderstande,
that in latyn speche there be .iii. concordes. The first betwene the nominatiue case and the verbe. The second betwene the substantiue and the
adiectyue. The thirde betwene the antecedent and the relatiue.

5 Whan an englysshe is gyuen to be made in latyn, [F4ᵛ] loke out the
pryncipall verbe. If there be mo verbes then one in a sentence, the fyrst is
the principall verbe, except it be the infinitiue mode, or haue before it a
relatyue, as that, whome, whiche: or a coniunction, as *ut* that, *cum* whan, *si*
10 if, or suche other.

Whan ye haue found the verbe, aske this question whoo, or what, and that
worde that answereth to the question, shalbe the nominatiue case to the
verbe.

Whiche nominatiue case shal in making and construing latyne, be sette
15 before the verbe, excepte in askyng a question, and then the nominatyue
is sette after the verbe or after the sygne of the verbe, as *Amas tu?* louest
thou? *Venit ne rex?* doeth the kyng come?

The fyrst concorde.

A verbe personall agreeth with his nomynatyue case, in number and per-
20 son, as The mayster redeth and ye regard not, *Præceptor legit, uos uero
negligitis.*

Where note that the first person is more woorthye then the seconde, and
the seconde more woorthy than the third.

Many nominatyue cases singular with a coniunction[1] copulatyue com-
25 myng betwene them, wyl haue a verbe plurall, whiche[2] verbe plurall,
shall agre in person, with the nominatyue case of the moste worthy person, as I and thou be in sauegarde, *Ego et tu sumus in tuto.* Thou and thy
father are in ieoperdie, *Tu et pater periclitamini.* Thy father and thy maister
haue sent for the, *Pater et præceptor accersunt te.*

30 When a verbe commeth betwene two nominatyue cases of dyuers numbres, the verbe may indifferently accorde with eyther of theym, so that
they be bothe of one persone, as *Amantium irę amoris redintegratio est,* [G1ʳ]
The falling out of louers is a renewyng of loue. *Quid enim nisi uota supersunt?*
For what remayneth sauyng onely prayers.

35 ### *The seconde concorde.*

When ye haue an adiectiue, aske this question who or what, and that that
answereth to the question shall be the substantiue.

---

[1] coniun=|tion
[2] wihche

The nowne adiectyue agreeth with his substantiue, in case, gender, and number, as A sure frende is tried in a doubtfull matter, *Amicus certus in re incerta cernitur.*   40

Lykewyse particyples and pronownes be ioyned with substantyues, as A manne armed, *Homo armatus*, a fielde to be tylled, *ager colendus*, this manne, *hic uir*, it is my mayster, *meus herus est.*

Here note that the masculyne gender, is more worthy then the feminine, and the feminine more worthye than the neuter.   45

Many substantyues singular, with a coniunction copulatiue commyng betwene them, wyll haue an adiectiue plurall, whiche adiectyue shall agree with the substantiue of moste worthy gender, as The king and the quene blessed, *Rex et regina beati.*

The thirde concorde.   50

Whan ye haue a relatyue, aske this question, who or what, and that that answereth to the question, shall be the antecedente, whiche is a woorde that goeth before the relatiue, and is rehersed again of the relatiue.

The relatyue agreeth with his antecedente, in gender, number, and person, as That manne is wyse that speketh fewe, *uir sapit qui pauca loquitur.*   55

[G1ᵛ] Whan this englysshe[1] that, may be turned into this englyshe whiche, it is a relatiue, otherwyse it is a coniunction, whiche in latyne is called *quod*, or *ut*, and it may elegantly be put away by turnynge the nominatiue case into the accusatiue[2], and the verbe into the infinitiue mode, as I am gladde that thou arte in good helth, *Gaudeo quod tu bene uales*,   60 *gaudeo te bene ualere.* I byd the to go hens, *Iubeo ut abeas, Iubeo te abire.*

Many antecedentes syngular, hauyng a coniunction copulatiue betwene theym, wyll haue a relatiue plurall whiche relatyue shal agre with the antecedent of the moste worthy gender, as The rule and dignitie whiche thou haste requyred, *Imperium et dignitas quæ petijsti.* For in thynges not   65 apte to haue life the neuter gender is moste worthy, yea and in suche case though the substantyues or antecedentes be of the masculyne or of the feminine gendre, and none of them of the neuter, yet may the adiectiue or relatiue be put in the neuter gender, as The bowe and arrowes be good, *Arcus et calami sunt bona.* The bowe and arowes which thou hast broken,   70 *Arcus et calami quæ fregisti.*

The case of the relatiue.

Whan there commeth no nominatiue case betwene the relatyue and the verbe, the relatiue shall be the nominatiue case to the verbe, as, wretched is that person, whiche is in loue with money, *Miser est qui nummos*   75 *admiratur.*

---

[1] enlysshe
[2] theaccusatiue

But whan there commeth a nominatiue case betwene the relatyue and the verbe, the relatyue shall be suche case, as the verbe wyll haue after hym, as Happie is he, whom other mennes harmes do make to beware, *Felix quem faciunt aliena pericula cautum*[1]. [G2ʳ] When a relatiue commeth betwene two substantiues of dyuerse genders, it maye indifferent<e>ly accorde with eyther of theym, as The byrde whiche is called a sparowe, *Auis quę passer appellatur*, or *Auis qui passer appellatur*.

Nownes interrogatiues and infinites, folowe the rule of the relatyue, as
85 *Quis, uter, qualis, quantus, quotus. et cetera.* which euer come before the verbe, lyke the relatiue, as *Hei mihi qualis erat, talis erat, qualem numquam uidi.*

Construction of novvnes substantiues.

Whan .ii. substantiues come tegether betokenyng dyuerse thynges, the later shall be the genitiue case, as The eloquence of Cicero, *Facundia*
90 *Ciceronis*, The boke of Vergile, *Codex Vergilij*. A louer of studies, *Amator studiorum*. The opinion of Plato, *Dogma Platonis.*

But if they belonge both to one thyng, they shalbe putte bothe in one case, as My father beyng a manne, loueth me a chylde, *Pater meus uir, amat me puerum.*

95 Whan the englyshe of this worde *res*, is putte with an adiectiue, ye may put away *res*, and put the adiectiue in the neuter gender like a substantiue, as Many thynges haue letted me, *Multa me impedierunt.*

An adiectiue in the neuter gender, put a lone without a substantiue, standeth for a substantiue, and may haue a genitiue case after him, as if it
100 were a substantiue, as Moche gaynes, *Multum lucri.* Howe much businesse, *Quantum negocij.* That werke, *Id operis.*

The prayse or disprayse of a thing is vsed di<u>ersly, but moste commonly in the ablatiue, or in the genitiue case, as A childe of a good towardnesse, *Puer bona indole, puer bonæ indolis.*

105 [G2ᵛ] *Opus* and *usus*, latyne for nede, requyre an ablatyue case, as I haue nede of thy iudgemente, *Opus*[2] *est mihi*[3] *tuo iudicio.* My sonne hath nede of twentie poundes, *Viginti minis usus est filio.*

Construction of adiectiues.
The genitiue case.

110 Adiectiues that sygnifie desyre, knowlege, remembraunce, or contrary wise, and suche lyke, require a genitiue case, as Couetous of money, *Cupidus auri.* Experte of warfare, *Peritus belli.* Ignorant of all thynges, *Ignarus omnium.* Bolde of hearte, *Fidens animi.* Doubtfull of mynde, *Dubius mentis.* Myndefull of that is paste, *Memor pręteriti.* Accused of thefte, *Reus furti.*

---

[1] *cau tum*   [2] *O pus*   [3] *estmihi|*

Nownes partityues, and certayne interrogatiues, with certayn nownes of 115
noumber, requyre a genitiue case, as *Aliquis, uter, neuter*[1], *nemo, nullus,
solus, unus, medius, quisque, quisquis, quicunque, quidam, quis* for *aliquis,* or *quis,*
an interrogatiue, *unus, duo, tres. et cetera. Primus, secundus, tertius. et cetera,* as
Aliquis nostrum. Primus omnium.
Whan a question is asked, I shall answere by the same case and tense, that 120
the question was asked by, as *Cuius est fundus?* uicini. *Quid agitur in ludo
literario?* studetur. Excepte the question be asked by *Cuius, a, um,* as *Cuia est
sententia? Ciceronis.* Or by a woo<r>de that maye gouerne dyuerse cases, as
Quanti emisti librum? paruo. Or excepte I must answere by one of these
possessyues, *Meus, tuus, suus, noster, uester,* as *Cuius est domus? non uestra, sed* 125
nostra.
Nownes of the comparatyue and the superlatyue degre, put partitiuely,
that is to say, with this english [G3ʳ] of, or emong, after them, requyre a
genitiue case, as Of the eares the left is the softer, *Aurium mollior est sinistra.*
Cicero the moste eloquent of oratours, *Cicero oratorum eloquentissimus.* 130
Nownes of the comparatiue degree, hauyng than or by after them, wyll
haue an ablatyue case, as *Frigidior*[2] *glacie,* More coulde than yce. *Doctior
multo,* better learned by a greatte deale. *Vno pede altior,* higher by a foote.

The datiue case.

Adiectiues that betoken profite or disprofitte, lykenesse, vnlykenesse, 135
pleasure, submittyng, or belonging to any thyng, requyre a datiue case, as
Labour is profitable to the bodye, *Labor est utilis corpori.* Equall to Hector,
Aequalis Hectori. Fitte for warre, *Idoneus bello.* Pleasaunt to all persons, *Iucun-
dus omnibus.* Suppliaunt to his father, *Parenti supplex.* Propre to me, *Mihi
proprium.* Lykewyse nownes of the passyue sygnification in *bilis,* and parti- 140
cipialles in *dus,* as *flebilis flendus omnibus,* to be lamented of all menne,
formidabilis formidandus hosti, to be feared of his enemie.

The accusatiue case.

The measure of length, breadth, or thyckenesse of any thynge, is putte
after adiectiues in the accusatiue case, and sometyme in the ablatiue case, 145
as *Turris alta*[3] *centum pedes,* A toure an hundred foote high. *Arbor lata
tres digitos,* A tree three fyngers brode. *Liber crassus tres pollices, uel tribus
pollicibus,* a boke three ynches thicke.

---

[1] *neurer*
[2] *Frigideor*
[3] *alia*

The ablatiue case.

150 Adiectyues sygnifieng fulnesse, emptinesse, plentie [G4ᵛ] or wantyng, require an ablatiue case, and sometyme a genitiue, as *Copiis abundans. Crura thymo plena. Vacuus ira, irę, ab ira. Nulla epistola inanis re aliqua. Ditissimus agri. Stultorum plena sunt omnia. Quis nisi mentis inops oblatum respuat aurum? Integer uitę sceleris'que purus. Non eget Mauri iaculis nec arcu. Expers*
155 *omnium, Corpus inane animæ.*

These adiectiues *Dignus, indignus, præditus, captus, contentus*, with suche other, wil haue an ablatiue case, as *Dignus honore. Captus oculis. Virtute pręditus. Paucis contentus.*

Construction of the pronovvne.

160 These genityue cases of primatiues, *mei, tui, sui, nostri*, and *uestri*, be vsed whan sufferyng is signified, as *Pars tui, Amor mei*: but whan doyng is sygnified, *meus, tuus, suus, noster*, and *uester*, be vsed, as *Ars tua. Imago tua.*
These genityue cases, *Nostrum, uestrum*, be vsed after distributiues, partitiues, comparatyues, and superlatiues, as *Nemo uestrum, aliquis nostrum,*
165 *maior uestrum, maximus natu nostrum.*

Construction of the verbe, and fyrste
vvith the nominatiue case.

Sum, forem, fio, existo, and certayne verbes passiues, as *Vocor, salutor*, and verbes of behauiour or gesture, as *Bibo, cubo, dormio*, wyll haue suche case
170 after them as they haue before them, as *Fama est malum. Malus cultura fit bonus. Cræsus uocatur diues. Horatius salutatur poeta. Virtus clara æterna'que habetur. Dormit securus. Bibit ieiunus. Petrus studet uideri diues. Malo me diuitem esse quam haberi.*

[G5ʳ] The Genitiue case.

175 This verbe *Sum*, betokenyng possession or perteynyng to any thyng, wyll haue a genitiue case, as *hæc uestis est patris. Insipientis est dicere, non putaram.* Except these nominatyue cases, *meum, tuum, suum, nostrum, uestrum*, as *Meum est iniuriam non adferre, tuum est iuxta omnia pati.*
Verbes that betoken to esteme or regarde, require a genitiue case, as *Parui*
180 *ducitur probitas, Maximi penditur nobilitas.*
Verbes of accusyng, condemnyng, or warnyng, and verbes of contrary sygnification, wyl haue a genitiue case, or an ablatiue of the cause, most commonly without a preposition, but sometyme with a preposition, as *Hic furti se alligat uel furto, admonuit me errati uel errato. De pecunijs repetundis*
185 *damnatus est.*
Satago, misereor, miseresco, require a genitiue case, as *Rerum suarum satagit. Miserere mei deus.*

Reminiscor, obliuiscor, memini, wyll haue a genitiue or an accusatiue case, as
Reminiscor historiæ, obliuiscor carminis, Recordor pueritiam, Obliuiscor lectionem.
Memini tui uel de te, I speake of the. *Memini te*, I remembre the.   190
Egeo, indigeo tui uel te. I haue nede of the. *Potior*[1] *urbis*, I conquere the citie.
Potior uoto, I obtayn my desyre.

The datiue case.

All maner of verbes put acquisitiuely, that is to say, with these tokens to,
or for, after them, wyl haue a datiue case, as *Non omnibus dormio*, I slepe not 195
to al menne. *Huic habeo non tibi*, I haue it for this manne, and not for the.
[G5ᵛ] To this rule dothe belong also verbes betokenynge
To profit or disprofit, as To compare, as

⎧ *Commodo*	⎧*Comparo*		
⎨ *Incommodo*	⎨*Compono*		200
⎩ *Noceo*	⎩*Confero.*		

To gyue or restore, as) To promis or to pay, as) To commaund, or shewe, as)

⎧ *Dono*	⎧*Promitto*	⎧*Impero* ⎫
⎨ *Reddo*	⎨*Polliceor*[2]	⎨*Indico* ⎬
⎩ *Refero*	⎩*Soluo*	⎩*Monstro* ⎭ 205

To truste, as) To obey or to be agaynst, as (To thretten or to be angry.

⎧ *Fido* ⎫	⎧*Obedio* ⎫	⎧*Minor* ⎫
⎨ *Confido* ⎬	⎨*Adulor* ⎬	⎨*Indignor* ⎬
⎩ *Fidem habeo* ⎭	⎩*Repugnd* ⎭	⎩*Irascor* ⎭

Sum, with his compoundes, except *possum*, also verbes compounded 210
with *Satis, bene*, and *male*, as *Satisfacio, benefacio, malefacio*: finally certayne
verbes compounded with these prepositions, *Præ, ad, con, sub, ante*[3], *post,
ob, in*, and *inter*, wyll haue a datyue case, as *Præluceo, adiaceo, commigro,
suboleo, antesto, posthabeo, obijcio, insulto, intersero.*
Est, put for *habeo*, wyll haue a datyue case, as *Est tibi mater.* Also *Sum* and 215
many other verbes wyll haue a double datyue case, as *Sum tibi præsidio. Do
tibi uestem pignori. Verto hoc tibi uitio. Hoc tu tibi laudi ducis.*

The accusatiue case.

Verbes transitiues, are all such as haue after them an accusatiue case of
the sufferer, whether they be actiues, common, or deponentes, as *Vsus* 220
promptos facit. Fœminæ ludificantur uiros. Largitur pecuniam.
Also verbes neuters maye haue an accusatiue case of theyr owne signification, as *Endimionis somnum dormis. Gaudeo gaudium. Viuo uitam.*
Verbes of askynge, teachyng, and arrayeng, wyll [H1ʳ] haue two accusatiue
cases, one of the sufferer, and the other of the thinge, as *Rogo te pecuniam,* 225
Doceo te literas, quod te iamdudum[4] *hortor, Exuo me gladium.*

---

¹ *Ptoior*   ² *Pollicior*   ³ *an*   ⁴ *iamdud um*

The ablatiue case.

Al verbes require an ablatiue case of the instrument or of the cause, or
of the maner of doyng, as *Ferit cum*[1] *gladio, Taceo metu, Summa eloquentia*
230 *causam egit.*

The worde of price is put after verbes in the ablatiue case, as *Vendidi auro,
Emptus sum argento.* except these genitiues, whan they be put alone without substantiues, *Tanti, quanti, pluris, minoris, tantiuis, tantidem, quantiuis,
quantilibet, quanticunque,* as *Quanti mercatus es hunc equum? Certe pluris quam*
235 *uellem.*

Verb<e>s of plenty or scarsenes, fylling or emptieng, lodyng or vnlodyng,
wyll haue an ablatyue case, as *Affluis opibus, Cares uirtute, Expleo te fabulis,
Spoliauit me bonis omnibus, Oneras stomachum cibo, Leuabo te hoc onere.*
Lykewise *Fungor, fruor, lętor, gaudeo, dignor, muto, munero, communico, afficio,*
240 *prosequor.*

Verbes that betoken receiuyng, distance, or taking away, wyll haue an
ablatyue case with *a, ab, e, ex,* or *de,* as *Accepi literas à Petro. Audiui à nuncio.
Longe distat a nobis. Eripui te à malis.* And this ablatyue may be turned into the
datiue, as *Subtraxit mihi cingulum.*

245 Verbes of comparison or excedyng, maye haue an ablatyue case of the
word that signifieth the measure of excedyng, as *Prefero hunc multo. Paulo
illum superat.*

A nowne or a pronowne substantyue, ioyned with a participle, expressed
or vnderstand, and hauing none other woorde, wherof it may be
250 gouerned, shall be put in the ablatiue case absolute, as The kyng
commyng, the ennemies fled, *Rege ueniente hostes fugerunt.* I be[H1ᵛ]yng
captayne, thou shalte ouercome, *Me duce uinces.* And it may be resolued by
any of these woordes, *Dum, cum, quando, si, quanquam,* or *postquam,* as *Rege
ueniente. id est dum ueniret rex. Me duce. id est si ego dux fuero.*

255   *Construction of passiues.*

A verbe passyue wyll haue after hym an ablatyue case, with a preposition,
or sometime a datiue, of the doer, as *Vergilius legitur à me. Tibi fama petatur.*
And the same ablatiue or datyue shalbe the nominatiue case to the verbe,
if it be made by the actiue, as *Ego lego Vergilium. Petas tu famam.*

260   *Gerundes.*

Gerundes and Supines wyll haue suche case, as the verbes that they come
of, as *Ocium*[2] *scribendi literas, Ad consulendum tibi. Auditum poetas.*

---

[1] *eum*
[2] *O cium*

Di.

The gerunde in *Di*, is put after certayne substantiues, as *Studium, causa,*
tempus. Ocium[1]*, occasio, libido. Spes, oportunitas, uoluptas. Modus, gestus, satietas.* 265
Potestas, licentia, consuetudo. Consilium, uis, norma. Amor, cupido, locus, And
others lyke.
It commeth also after certayn adiectiues, as *Cupidus uisendi, Certus eundi.*
Peritus medicandi, Gnarus bellandi.

Do.

270

Whan I haue the englysshe of the participle of the present tense with this
sygne of, or with, commyng after a nowne adiectiue, it shal in latyne
makyng, be put in the gerund in *Do*, as *Defessus sum ambulando.*
Also the englysshe of the participle of the presente tense, comming
without a substantiue, with this signe in or by, before hym, shall in latyne 275
makyng be put in [H2ʳ] the gerunde in *Do*, as *Cęser dando, subleuando,*
ignoscendo, gloriam adeptus est. In apparando, totum hunc consumunt diem.
And the gerund in *Do*, is vsed eyther without a preposition, or with one of
these prepositions *A, ab, de, E, ex, cum, in,* as *Deterrent à bibendo, ab amando,*
Cogitat de edendo, Ratio bene scribendi cum loquendo coniuncta est. 280

DVM.

The englishe of the infinitiue mode commyng after a reason, and shewyng
a cause of the reason, maye be put in the gerund in *dum*, as *Dies mihi ut*
satis sit ad agendum, uereor. The gerund in *dum*, is vsed after one of these
prepositions, *Ad, ob, propter, inter, ante,* as *Ad capiendum hostes. ob, uel propter* 285
redimendum captiuos. Inter cœnandum. Ante damnandum.
And whan ye haue this englyshe muste, or ought, in a reason, where it
semeth to be made by this verbe *oportet*, it maye be put in the gerund in
dum, with this verbe *est*. And than the woord that in the englysshe semeth
to be the nominatyue case, shall be put in the datyue case, as I must goo 290
hens, *Abeundum est mihi.*

Supines.

The firste supine hath the actiue signification, and is put after verbes
and participles that betoken mouynge to a place, as *Eo cubitum. Spectatum*
admissi risum teneatis amici? 295
The later supine hath the passiue signification, and is putte after nownes
adiectiues, and suche lyke, as *Dignus, indignus, Turpis, fœdus. Procliuis, facilis.*
Odiosus, mirabilis, optimus. And this supine maye also be turned in to the
infinitiue mode passiue, as It may be [H2ᵛ] indifferentlye, sayde in

---

[1] *O cium*

300 latyne *Facile factu*, or *facile fieri*, Easie to be doone. *Turpe dictu*, or *turpe dici*, unhoneste to be spoken.

The Tyme.

Nownes that betoken parte of tyme, be commonly vsed in the ablatiue case, as *Nocte uigilas, Luce dormis*, but nownes that betoken continual terme
305 of time be vsed commonly in the accusatiue case, as *Sexaginta annos natus. Hyemem totam stertis.*

Space of place.

Nownes that betoken space betwene place and place, be commonly put in the accusatiue case, as *Pedem hinc ne discesseris*, goo thou not a foote from
310 this same place.

A place.

Nownes appellatyues or names of great places, be put with a preposition, if they folowe a verbe that sygnifieth, in a place, to a place, from a place, or by a place, as *Viuo in Anglia. Veni per Galliam in Italiam. Proficiscor ex urbe.*
315 In a place, or at a place, if the place be a proper name of the fyrste declenson, or seconde, and the syngular number, shalbe put in the genitiue case, as *Vixit Londini. Studuit Oxonię.* And these nownes *Humi, domi, militiæ, belli,* be lykewyse vsed, as *Procumbit humi bos. Militię enutritus est. Domi bellique ociosi uiuitis.*
320 But if the place be the thirde declenson or the plurall number, it shall be put in the datyue or in the ablatiue case, as *Militauit Carthagini* or *Carthagine. Athenis natus est.* Lykewyse we say, *Ruri* or *rure educatus est.*
To a place if the place be a proper name, it shall be put in the accusatiue case without a preposition, as *Eo Romam.* Likewyse *Confero me domum.*
325 *Recipio me rus.* [H3ʳ]
From a place, or by a place, if the place be a proper name, it shall be put in the ablatyue case without a preposition, as *Discessit Londino. Profectus est Londino, uel per Londinum, Cantabrigiam. Domus* and *rus,* be vsed lykewyse, as *Abijt domo, Rure reuersus est.*

330 ## *Impersonalles.*

A verbe impersonall hath no nominatiue case before hym, and this worde It, commonly is his sygne. *Interest, refert,* and *est* for *interest,* require a genityue case of all casuall wordes, excepte *Mea, tua, sua, nostra, uestra,* and *cuia,* as *Interest omnium recte agere. Tua refert teipsum nosse.*

Certayne impersonalles requyre a datyue case, as *Libet, licet, patet, liquet,* 335
constat, placet, expedit, prodest, sufficit, uacat, accidit, conuenit, contingit[1], and
other lyke.

Some wyll haue an accusatyue case only, as *Delectat, decet, iuuat, oportet,*
some besyde the accusatiue wil haue also a genitiue, as *pœnitet, tædet,*
miseret, miserescit, pudet, piget, as *Nostri nosmet pœnitet. Me ciuitatis tædet. Pudet* 340
me negligentiæ. Miseret me tui.

A verbe impersonall of the passiue voyce, hath like case, as other verbes
passyues haue, as *Bene fit multis à principe,* yet many tymes the case is not
expressed but vnderstande, as *Maxima ui certatur.*

Whan a dede is sygnified to be done of manye, the verbe beyng a verbe 345
neuter, we may well chaunge the verbe neuter in to the impersonalle in
tur, as *In ignem posita est, fletur. et cetera. A Participle.*

Participles gouerne suche case as the verbe that they come of, as *Fruiturus*
amicis, Consulens tibi, Diligendus ab omnibus.

Here note that participles may fower maner wayes [H3ᵛ] be changed into 350
nownes, The fyrst is, whan the voice of a participle is construed with an
other case then the verbe that it commeth of. as, *Appetens uini,* gredie of
wyne. The seconde, when it is compouned with a preposition, which þe
verbe that it commeth of, can not be compouned withal, as *Indoctus,*
innocens. The third whan it fourmeth all the degrees of comparison, as 355
Amans, amantior, amantissimus. Doctus, doctior, doctissimus. The fowerth when
it hath no respect nor expresse difference of tyme, as *Scripturus,* about to
write, *Homo laudatus,* a man laudable. *Puer amandus, id est amari dignus,* a
chylde woorthye to be loued. And al these are called nownes participiall.

Participles whan they be changed in to nownes, requyre a genitiue case, as 360
Fugitans litium, Indoctus pilæ, Cupientissimus tui, Lactis abundans.

These participiall voyces *Perosus, Exosus, Pertesus,* haue alwayes the actiue
signification, and gouern an accusatiue case, as *Exosus seuitiam,* hatyng
cruelty. *Vitam pertesus,* werie of the life.

The aduerbe. 365

Aduerbes of quantity, tyme, and place, do require a genitiue case, as
Multum lucri. Tunc temporis. Vbique gentium.

Certayn aduerbes[2] wyll haue a datyue case, lyke as the nownes that they
come of, as *Venit obuiam illi. Canit similiter huic.*

These datyues be vsed aduerbially. *Tempori, luci, uesperi,* as *Tempori* 370
surgendum. Vesperi cubandum. Luce laborandum.

Certayne aduerbes wyl haue an accusatiue case, of the prepositions that
they come of, as *Propius urbem,* [H4ʳ] *proxime castra.*

Where note that prepositions, when they be sette without a case, orels
doo fourme the degrees of comparison, be chaunged into aduerbes. 375

---

[1] *contigit*   [2] ad verdes

The Coniunction,

Coniunctions copulatiues and disiunctiues, and these fower: *Quam, nisi, prȩterquam, an,* couple lyke cases, as *Xenophon et Plato fuere æquales. Studui Romæ et Athenis.* and sometyme they be put betwene dyuers cases, as *Est*
380 *liber meus et fratris. Emi fundum centum nummis et pluris.*
Coniunctions copulatiues and disiunctiues most commonly ioyne lyke modes and tenses togither, as *Petrus et Ioannes precabantur, et docebant.* And sometyme otherwyse, as *Et habetur et referetur à me gratia.*

Præposition.

385 Sometime this preposition *in,* is not expressed but vnderstanded and[1] the casuall worde neuerthelesse put in the ablatyue case, as *Habeo te loco parentis. id est in loco*[2].
A verbe compounde sometyme requyreth the case of the preposition, that he is compounded with, as *Exeo domo, Prætereo te insalutatum. Adeo petrum.*

390 ### The Interiection.

Certayne interiections require a nominatiue case, as *O festus dies hominis.* Certain a datiue, as *Hei mihi.* Certaine an accusatyue, as *Heu stirpem inuisam.* Certayne a vocatyue, as *Proh sancte Iupiter.*
And the same *proh,* wyll haue also an accusatiue, as *Proh deum atque*
395 *hominum fidem.*

FINIS.

[1] as
[2] *logo*

GVILIELMI Lilii ad suos discipulos monita pædagogica,
seu carmen de moribus.

QVI mihi discipulus puer es, cupis atque doceri,
 Huc ades, hæc animo concipe dicta tuo.
Mane citus lectum fuge, mollem discute somnum:
 Templa petas supplex, et uenerare deum.
Attamen in primis facies sit lota, manus'que,
 Sint nitidæ uestes, compta'que cæsaries.
Desidiam fugiens, cum te schola nostra uocarit
 Adsis, nulla pigrę sit tibi causa moræ.
Me pręceptorem cum uideris ore saluta,
 Et condiscipulos ordine quos'que tuos.
Tu quoque fac sedeas ubi te sedisse iubemus,
 Inque loco, nisi sis iussus abire, mane.
At magis ut quisquam doctrinę munere claret,
 Sic magis is clara sede locandus erit.
Scalpellum¹, calami, attramentum, charta, libelli,
 Sint semper studijs arma parata tuis.
Si quid dictabo scribes, at singula recte,
 Nec macula aut scriptis menda sit ulla tuis.
Sed tua nec laceris dictata aut carmina chartis,
 Mandes, quæ libris inseruisse decet.
Sępe recognoscas tibi lecta, animo'que reuoluas.
 Si dubites, nunc hos consule, nunc alios.
Qui dubitat, qui sępe rogat, mea dicta tenebit,
 Is qui nil dubitat, nil capit inde boni.
Disce puer quęso, noli dediscere quicquam,
 Ne mens te insimulet conscia desidiæ.
Sis'que animo attentus, quid enim docuisse iuuabit,
 Si mea non firmo pectore uerba premis?
[I1ʳ] Nil tam² difficile est, quod non solertia uincat:
 Inuigila, et parta est gloria militiæ.
Nam ueluti flores tellus nec semina profert,
 Quin sit continuo uicta labore manus
Sic puer ingenium si non exercitet³ ipsum
 Tempus et amittet, spem simul ingenij.

¹ Sscalpellum
² Nilt am
³ excercitet

Child who are my scholar, and you desire to be taught,
come here, grasp firmly these sayings in your mind.
Early in the morning leave your bed, shake off gentle sleep.
Humbly go into the church, and worship God.
But first of all, let your face be washed and your hands,
let your garments be clean and your hair combed.
Avoid idleness when our school calls you.
Have no excuse for lazy dawdling.
When you see me, your schoolmaster, greet me
and also your fellow students in turn.
And also take your seat where I tell you to sit,
and stay in your place, unless you are commanded to leave.
And when somebody is more excellent in the gift of learning,
so he shall sit in a higher place.
Let there always be ready for your studies your prepared arms,
a pen-knife, pens, ink, paper, and books.
If I shall dictate anything, you shall write it down, but everything
correctly, and let there be no blot or fault in your writings.
But neither commit your Latins nor verses to loose papers,
which should be written in books.
Often repeat to yourself the things you have read
and turn them over in your mind.
If you are not sure, ask sometimes these, sometimes others.
The person who is unsure and often asks questions,
will observe my precepts;
he who doubts of nothing, gets thereby no good.
Child, learn, I pray you, do not forget anything,
so that a guilty conscience will not accuse you of laziness.
And be attentive; for what will it profit you that I have taught you,
if you do not print my words in sure memory?
Nothing is so hard which diligence cannot overcome.
Take pains, and you will be rewarded for your struggles.
For as the earth brings forth neither flowers nor seeds,
unless it be tilled with continual labour of the hand.
So a child, unless he often exercises his wit,
will both waste time and not do justice to his ability.

Est etiam semper lex in sermone tenenda,
  Ne nos offendat improba garrulitas.
Incumbens¹ studio submissa uoce loqueris:
40 Nobis dum reddis, uoce canorus eris.
Et quæcunque² mihi reddis, discantur ad unguem³:
  Singula et abiecto uerbula redde libro.
Nec uerbum quisquam dicturo suggerat ullum:
  Quod puero exitium non mediocre parit.
45 Si quicquam rogito, sic respondere⁴ studebis,
  Vt laudem dictis et mereare decus.
Non lingua celeri nimis aut laudabere tarda,
  Est uirtus medium, quod tenuisse iuuat.
Et quoties loqueris, memor esto loquare latine,
50 Et scopulos ueluti barbara uerba fuge.
Pręterea socios quoties te cunque rogabunt,
  Instrue, et ignaros ad mea uota trahe.
Qui docet indoctos, licet indoctissimus esset,
  Ipse breui reliquis doctior esse potest.
55 Sed tu nec stolidos imitabere grammaticastros,
  Ingens Romani dedecus eloquij.
Quorum tam fatuus nemo, aut tam barbarus ore est,
  Quem non autorem barbara turba probet.
Grammaticas recte si uis cognoscere leges,
60 Discere si cupias cultius ore loqui,⁵
Addiscas ueterum clarissima dicta uirorum,
  Et quos autores turba latina docet.
[I1ᵛ] Nunc te Vergilius, nunc ipse Terentius optat,
  Nunc simul amplecti te Ciceronis opus.
65 Quos qui non didicit, nil præter somnia uidit:
  Certat et in tenebris uiuere Cimmerijs.
Sunt quos delectat studio uirtutis honestæ
  Posthabito, nugis tempora conterere.
Sunt quibus est cordi manibus pedibus ue sodales,
70 Aut alio quouis sollicitare modo.
Est alius qui se dum clarum sanguine iactet,
  Insulso reliquis exprobret⁶ore genus.
Te tam praua sequi nolim uestigia morum
  Ne tandem factis præmia digna feras.

¹ In cumbens
² quæqunque
³ unquem
⁴ respondete
⁵ loqui.
⁶ exprobet

Also order is to be observed always in speech,
so that too much talking does not offend us.
As you are mulling over your lesson, you shall speak softly.
When you say it to us, your voice shall be loud.
And whatever you recite to me, must be accurately committed to
memory, and give me every word with the book shut.
And let nobody prompt any word to you to say,
which brings no small hurt to a child.
If I ask anything, you shall endeavour so to answer,
that you may deserve praise and commendation by your words.
You will not be praised for speaking too fast or too slow,
the mean is a virtue which is useful to observe.
And as often as you speak, remember that you speak in Latin,
and avoid barbarous words as rocks.
Besides, teach your fellows as often as they will ask you,
and bring the ignorant up to my standards.
He who teaches the unlearned, although he were most unlearned,
may shortly himself be better learned than the rest.
But you shall not imitate silly pretenders to grammar,
the great disgrace of the Latin tongue.
Of whom there is nobody so foolish, or so barbarous in speech,
whom the barbarous multitude does not accept as an author.
If you want to know the laws of grammar correctly,
if you wish to learn to speak more eloquently,
try to learn the most famous writings of the ancient men,
and the authors which the crowd of Latinists teach.
Sometimes Virgil wishes to embrace you, sometimes Terence
himself, and sometimes the works of Cicero invite you.
When he who has not learnt, has seen nothing but dreams
and strives to live in perpetual darkness.
There are some, after having neglected the study of commendable
virtue, enjoy spending their time in trifles.
There are others who like harassing their fellows
with their hands or feet or any other way.
There is another who boasts about his family, and cruelly teases
others about their ancestry in unsavoury language.
I would not have you to follow such an unseemly example,
so that in the end you do not receive rewards
worthy of what you have done.

75   *Nil dabis aut uendes, nil permutabis, emes ue*
        Ex damno alterius commoda nulla feras.
    Insuper et nummos, irr<i>tamenta malorum,
        Mitte alijs, puerum nil nisi pura decent.
    Clamor, rixa, ioci, mendacia, furta, cachinni,
80   *Sint procul a uobis, Martis et arma procul.*
    Nil pœnitus dices quod turpe aut non sit honestum,
        Est uitæ ac pariter ianua lingua[1] necis.
    Ingens crede nefas cuiquam maledicta referre,
        Iurare aut magni numina sacra dei.
85   *Denique seruabis res omnes atque libellos,*
        Et tecum quoties is'que, redis'que, feras.
    Effuge uel causas faciunt quæcun'que nocentem,
        In quibus et nobis displicuisse potes.
                FINIS

[1] *linguę*

You shall give or sell nothing, you shall exchange or buy nothing,
you shall not profit from another's loss.
And moreover, leave money, the enticements to evil,
to others; nothing but things free from abuse are decent for a child.
Keep away from noise, contention, scoffings, lies, thefts,
scornful laughter, and avoid fights.
Do not say anything filthy or dishonest,
the tongue is the gate to life and also to death.
Take it as a serious sin to curse anybody,
or to swear by the sacred name of Almighty God.
To conclude, you shall keep all your things and books,
and shall carry them with you as often as you come and go.
Avoid even occasions of whatsoever things make you offensive
and in which you may displease me.
          END]

CHRISTIANI HOMINIS INSTITVTVM PER ERASMVM ROTERODAMVM.
Ad Galatas 5.
Valet in Christo fides quæ per dilectionem operatur.

FIDES.
CREDO. PRIMVS ARTICVLVS.

COnfiteor primum ore pio, ueneror'que fideli
Mente deum patrem, uel nutu cuncta potentem.
Hunc, qui stelligeri spaciosa uolumina cœli,
Et solidum omniparę telluris condidit orbem.
         ET IN IESVM.   II.
Eius item gnatum IESVM cognomine CHRISTVM,
Quem dominum nobis agnoscimus ac ueneramur.
         QVI CONCEPTVS.   III.
Hunc Maria afflatu diuini numinis, aluo
Concepit uirgo, peperit purissima uirgo.
         PASSVS SVB PONTIO   IIII.
Et graue supplicium immeritus (damnante Pilato)
Pertulit infami suffixus in arbore, mortem
Oppetijt, tumulatus humo est, clausus'que sepulchro:
Interea penetrat populator ad infera regna.
         TERTIA DIE.   V.
Mox ubi tertia lux mæsto se prompserat orbi,
Emersit tumulo superas rediuiuus in auras.
         ASSENDIT.   VI.
Inde palam ętheream scandit sublimis in arcem.
Illic iam dexter patri assidet omnipotenti.
[I2ʳ]   ITERVM VENTVRVS EST.   VII.
Idem olim rediturus, ut omnem iudicet orbem,
Et uiuos pariter, uita'que ac lumine cassos.
         CREDO IN SPIRITVM.   VIII.
Te quo'que credo fide simili spirabile numen
Halitus, afflatus'que dei sacer, omnia lustrans.
         SANCTAM ECCLESIAM.   IX.
Et te confiteor sanctissima concio, qua gens
Christigena arcano nexu coit omnis in unum

Based on Galatians 5:
What counts is faith in Christ that works through love.

FAITH
THE CREED.   The first article
First of all, I profess with a pious mouth and I venerate with
a faithful mind God the Father, who rules all things at his
slightest nod, the same God who created the vast spheres
of the starry heavens and the solid orb of the all-fruitful earth.
   AND IN JESUS.   The second article
And also his son Jesus, surnamed CHRIST,
whom we acknowledge and venerate as our lord.
   WHO WAS CONCEIVED.   The third article
By the breath of the Divine Spirit Mary conceived
him in her womb, still remaining a virgin,
and brought him forth, still a most pure virgin.
   SUFFERED UNDER PONTIUS.   The fourth article
And, though innocent, he was condemned by Pilate and
suffered a heavy punishment. He underwent his death fixed
to a tree of infamy. He was buried in the earth and shut up
in a sepulchre. In the meantime he invaded and
plundered the kingdom of hell.
   ON THE THIRD DAY.   The fifth article
As soon as the third day dawned on a grieving world,
he rose from the grave, alive once more in the air above.
   HE ASCENDED.   The sixth article
Then he rose in full view high up to the heavenly palace.
There he now sits at the right of his almighty Father.
   HE WILL COME AGAIN.   The seventh article
The same Christ will one day return to judge the whole world,
both the living and those deprived of life and light.
   I BELIEVE IN THE SPIRIT.   The eighth article
With a similar faith I also believe in you, O life-sustaining
divinity, Holy Spirit and Breath of God, illuminating all things.
   IN THE HOLY CHURCH.   The ninth article
And I profess you, most holy assembly, in which the whole
family of Christ comes together by a secret bond into one body

Corpus, et unanimis capiti sociatur IESV.
Hinc proprium nescit sed habeat communia cuncta.
     REMISSIONEM PECCATORVM.   X.
Hoc equidem in cœtu sancto, peccata remitti
40   Credo, uel ijs sacro fuerint[1] qui fonte renati,
Vel qui diluerint ultro sua crimina fletu.
     CARNIS RESVRRECTIONEM.   XI.
Nec dubito, quin[2] exanimata cadauera sursum
In uitam redeant, animas sortita priores.
45   VITAM AETERNAM.   XII.
Vtraque pars nostri corpus'que animus'que deinceps
Iuncta simul, uitam ducent sine fine perennem.
     SACRAMENTA.   VII.
HOC quoque persuasum est, ecclesia mystica septem
50   Munera dispensat, quę sacramenta uocantur.
Hinc uariæ dotes, et gratia plurima menti
Cælitus inseritur, si quis modo sumpserit aptè.
     MATRIMONIVM.   I.
Munere coniugij nati hunc prodimus in orbem,
55   Vsque adeo pulchri, pulcherrima portio mundi.
     [I3ʳ] BAPTISMVS.   II.
Munere baptismi longe felicius ijdem
Quam prius, in te Christe renascimur atque nouamur.
     CONFIRMATIO.   III.
60   Deinde in amore dei nos confirmatio sacra
Constabilit, mentem'que inuicto robore durat.
     EVCHARISTIA.   IIII.
Misticus ille cibus (græci dixere synaxim)
Qui panis uini'que palam sub imagine Christum
65   Ipsum præsentem uere exhibet, intima nostri
Viscera, cælesti saginat et educat esca:
In'que deo reddit uegetos, et reddit adultos.
     POENITENTIA.   V.
Si quem forte deo capitalis reddidit hostem
70   Noxia, continuo metanœa medebitur illi
Restituet[3] lapsum, rescissa'que fœdera[4] rursum
Sarciet[5], offensi placabit numinis iram,

---

[1] fuetint
[2] qui n
[3] Restituit
[4] fœder a
[5] Sartiet

and with one soul is joined to its head, JESUS. Hence it knows
nothing of what is private but holds all things in common.

IN THE FORGIVENESS OF SINS.   The tenth article
In this holy gathering, indeed, I believe that sins are forgiven,
both of those who have been reborn through the holy font or of
those who of their own accord have washed away their offences
with their tears.

IN THE RESURRECTION OF THE FLESH.
The eleventh article
I have no doubt that soulless corpses will arise once more
to life, each being allotted the soul it had before.

IN THE LIFE EVERLASTING.   The twelfth article
Thenceforth both parts of us, body and spirit joined
together, will lead an endless and everlasting life.

THE SEVEN SACRAMENTS
I am also persuaded of this: the church dispenses seven
mystical gifts, which are called sacraments. By them
various gifts and an abundance of grace from heaven are
implanted into the mind, if only they are received fittingly.

MATRIMONY.   The first sacrament[1]
By the gift of marriage we are born and come forth into this
world, ourselves the most beautiful part of a world so beautiful.

BAPTISM.   The second sacrament
By the gift of baptism we become far more blessed than we
were before because in you, Christ, we are reborn and renewed.

CONFIRMATION.   The third sacrament
Then holy confirmation makes us firm in the love of God
and hardens the spirit with invincible strength.

THE EUCHARIST   The fourth sacrament
That mystical food (the Greeks call it 'synaxis'),
which under the outward appearance of bread and
wine clearly tenders to us Christ himself truly present,
fattens and fosters our inmost hearts with heavenly
food and makes us vigorous and mature in God.

PENANCE.   The fifth sacrament
If perhaps a mortal sin makes someone God's enemy,
a change of heart will immediately heal him. It will reinstate
the fallen and restore the broken covenant; it will placate
the anger of the offended Deity, provided that the sinner

---

[1] The order of The Seven Sacraments in the version originally used as a source text for
this translation into English differs from the order in the version presently being used. See
p. 254, note to line 48, of the commentary.

Commissi modo pœniteat, pigeat'que nocentem,
Is'que uolens peragat præscripta piamina culpæ.

75   ORDO.   VI.

Ordine sacrato confertur sacra potestas,
Vt[1] fungare munisterijs (Christo auspice) sanctis.

        VNCTIO.   VII.

Vnguinis[2] extremi munus nos munit, et armat,
80 Migrantem'que animam per summa pericula, tutò
Transmittit patrię, et superis commendat euntem.

        AMOR DEI.

HAEC est indubitata fides, cui pectore certo
Nixus, amabo patrem super omnia cunctipotentem,
85 Qui me condideritque, et in hunc produxerit orbem.
[I3ᵛ] Rursus amore pari dominum complectar Iesum,
Qui nos asseruit, precio'que redemit amico.
Spiritum item sanctum, qui me sine fine benigno
Afflatu fouet, atque animi penetralia ditans
90 Dotibus arcanis, uitali recreat[3] aura.
Atque hic ternio sanctus, et omni laude ferendus,
Toto ex corde mihi, tota de mente supremis
Viribus obsequio, merito'que coletur honore.
Hunc unum reuerebor, et hoc semel omnis in uno,
95 Spes mea figetur, hoc omnia metiar uno,
Hic propter sese mihi semper amabitur unus.

        AMOR SVI.

Post hunc haud alia ratione, ac nomine charus
Ipse <m>ihi fuero, nisi quatenus omnis in illum
100 Ille mei referatur amor, fontem'que reuisat.

        FVGA PECCATI.

Culpam pręterea fugiam pro uiribus omnem.
Præcipue capitale, tamen uitauero crimen,
Quod necat, atque animam letali uulnerat ictu.
105   SVPERBIA, INVIDIA, IRA.

Ne fastu tumeam, ne uel liuore maligno
Torquear, aut bili rapiar feruente, cauebo.

        GVLA, LVXVRIA, PIGRITIA.

Ne uel spurca libido, uel insatiabilis aluus
110 Imperet, enitar, ne turpis inertia uincat.

        AVARITIA.

Ne nunquam saturanda fames me uexet habendi,
Plus satis ut cupiam fallacis munera mundi.

---

[1] Vt
[2] Vnguini s
[3] tecreat

repents and is sorry for his transgression and that he
willingly carries out the prescribed expiation of his guilt.

HOLY ORDERS. The sixth sacrament
For holy orders bestows the holy power to exercise
the sacred ministries under the auspices of Christ.

ANOINTING. The seventh sacrament
The gift of the last oil fortifies and arms us and through the
greatest dangers safely conveys the travelling soul over to its
homeland, and, as it goes, comments it to the powers above.

LOVE OF GOD
This is the undoubted faith. Relying on it with a firm heart,
I will above all love the omnipotent Father,
who has all power over all things, who created me
and brought me forth into this world.
Moreover, I will embrace with an equal love the Lord Jesus,
who set us free and paid our ransom like a friend.
Likewise I will love the Holy Spirit, who warms me endlessly
with his kind breath and, enriching the innermost recesses of
my mind with secret gifts, recreates me with his life-giving spirit.
And this Trinity, holy and worthy to be exalted with all praise,
I will obey and worship and deservedly honour with all my heart,
with all my mind, with my utmost strength.
I will revere only this triune God; on him only
all my hope will be fixed once for all; by him only will I measure
all things. Only him will I always love for his own sake.

LOVE OF SELF
Next to him, I will be dear to my own self, but only
provided that and in so far as all that love of myself
is referred to him and goes back to its source.

FLEEING FROM SIN
Moreover, I will flee all guilt to the best of my
ability; but I will especially avoid mortal sin, which
kills the soul and wounds it with a lethal stroke.

PRIDE. ENVY. ANGER
I will take care not to swell with pride or to be tormented
with malicious envy or to be carried away by seething anger.

GLUTTONY. LUST. SLOTH
I will struggle not to be subject to impure desires or an
insatiable stomach or to be conquered by shameful laziness.

AVARICE
I will try not to be plagued by an insatiable hunger for possessions
so as to desire more than enough of the gifts of this deceiving world.

FVGA MALORVM HOMINVM.

115 Improba pestiferi fugiam commercia cœtus
Omnia, summo animi conatu, pro'que uirili.

[I4ʳ] STVDIVM PIETATIS.

Atque huc incumbam neruis ac pectore toto,
Vt magis atque magis, superet mihi gratia uirtus,
120 Augescat'que piæ diuina scientia menti.

ORATIO.

Orabo superos'que precum libamine puro
Placare adnitar[1] cum tempore sedulus omni,
Tum uero eximie, quoties lux festa recurret.

FRVGALITAS VICTVS.

125 Frugales epulę semper mensæ'que placebit
Sobria mundicies, et auari nescia luxus.

IEIVNIVM.

Seruabo reuerens, quoties ieiunia nobis
130 Indicit certis ecclesia sancta diebus.

MENTIS CVSTODIA.

Sancta uti sint mihi secretæ penetralia mentis,
Ne quid eò subeat fœdum ue, nocens ue, studebo.

LINGVAE CVSTODIA.

135 Ne temere iuret, ne unquam mendacia promat,
Turpia ne dictù dicat mea lingua, cauebo.

MANVS CVSTODIA.

A furto cohibebo manus, nec ad ulla minuta
Viscatos mittam digitos, et si quid ademptum
140 Cuiquám erit, id domino properabo reddere iusto.

RESTITVTIO REI FORTE REPERTAE.

Id quoque restituam, si quid mihi forte repertum est,
Me penes haud patiar prudens aliena morari.

AMOR PROXIMI.

145 Nec secus atque mihi sum charus, amabitur omnis
Proximus, est autem (ni fallor) proximus ille
[I4ᵛ] Quisquis homo est, ac sic ut amor referatur amici
In Christum, uitam'que piam, ueram'que salutem.
Huic igitur (fuerit quoties opus, atque necesse)
150 Sedulus officio corpus'que, animum'que, iuuabo.
Vt mihi succurri cupiam, si forsan egérem.
Id tamen inprimis prestabo utri'que parenti,
Per quos corporeo hoc nasci mihi contigit orbe.
Tum præceptori, qui me erudit, instituit'que
155 Morigerus fuero, ac merito reuerebor honore.

---

[1] adniter

FLEEING FROM EVIL MEN

With the greatest effort of my mind and with all my strength
I will avoid all dealings with wicked and corrupting company.

THE PURSUIT OF HOLINESS

And I will strain every nerve and try with all my heart to be
more and more ruled by grace, by virtue, and to enlarge
the holiness of my mind by the knowledge of God.

PRAYER

I will pray and will strive to win over the powers above by
a pure libation of prayers, zealous in such prayer at all
times, but especially when their holydays recur.

TEMPERANCE IN EATING

My feasts will always be frugal and I will find pleasure in meals
marked by a sober elegance, with no trace of greedy luxury.

FASTING

I will reverently observe fasts on those fixed days
which holy church has indicated to us.

GUARDING THE MIND

I will take pains to keep the secret recesses of my mind holy,
so that nothing filthy or harmful may approach there.

GUARDING THE TONGUE

I will take care to keep my tongue from swearing thoughtlessly,
from ever putting forth lies, from saying what it is shameful to say.

GUARDING THE HANDS

I will restrain my hands from stealing, and I will not lay sticky fingers
on the slightest thing whatsoever; and if anything has been taken away
from someone, I will hasten to return it to its rightful owner.

GIVING BACK SOMETHING FOUND BY CHANCE

I will also give back whatever I might happen to find; I will be too
prudent to allow the property of others to remain in my possession.

LOVE OF NEIGHBOUR

And just as I am dear to myself, I will love all my neighbours
and unless I am mistaken, anyone who is a human being is my
neighbour—and I will do so in such a way that my love for
a friend is referred to Christ and to a holy life and to true salvation.
Therefore, whenever it is needful and necessary,
I will assist him in body and mind, eagerly and dutifully,
just as I would wish to be helped if I should lack for something.
But I will especially do this for both my parents,
through whom I happened to be born into this corporeal world.
Next I will be obedient to my teacher, who instructs and trains me,
and I will give him the obedience and honour he deserves.

Ac rursus dulcis'que scholę, studij'que sodales,
Semper (uti par est) syncero amplectar amore.
ASSIDVA CONFESSIO.
Si quando crimen fuero prolapsus in ullum,
160   Protinus enitar, pura ut confessio lapsum
Erigat, ac iusta tergatur noxia pœna.
SVMPTIO CORPORIS CHRISTI
IN VITA.
Ast ubi sacrati me ad corporis atque cruoris
165   Cælestes ępulas pietas'que dies'que uocabit,
Illotis manibus metuens accedere, pectus
Ante meum, quanta cura studio'que licebit,
Purgabo maculis, uirtutum ornabo nitelis.
MORBVS.
170   Porrò ubi fatalis iam terminus ingruet æui,
Extremumque diem cum morbus adesse monebit,
Mature sacramentis me armare studebo.
Atque his muneribus, quæ[1] ecclesia sancta ministrat
Christigenis, reteget confessio crimina uitæ
175   Sacrifico, sumam Christi uenerabile corpus.
[I5ʳ] MORS.
Quod si uicinæ propius discrimina mortis
Vrgebunt, supplex accersam qui mihi rite
Oblinat, ac signet sacro ceromate corpus.
180   Atque his præsidijs armatus (sic uti dignum est
Christicola) forti ac fidenti pectore, uita
Decedam, bonitate dei super omnia fretus.

HOC FAC ET VIVES.

LONDINI
IN OFFICINA Thomæ Bertheleti
typis[2] impressoris
Cum priuilegio ad imprimendum solum.

ANNO. M. D. XLII.

[1] que
[2] Bertheletity-|pis

Then, too, I will always, as is fitting, embrace with a sincere affection
the companions of my studies in this sweet school.

FREQUENT CONFESSION

If I should ever fall into any sin, I will immediately make
an effort to recover from my fall by a sincere confession and
to wipe away the damage by performing a just penance.

RECEIVING THE BODY OF CHRIST
DURING MY LIFETIME

But when piety and the proper day call me to the
heavenly banquet of the consecrated body and blood,
fearing to approach with unwashed hands,
I will purge my heart beforehand of its stains
with all the care and diligence I can muster, and I will adorn it
with the scintillating brightness of the virtues.

ILLNESS

Then, when the fated limit of my lifetime thrusts itself
upon me and illness warns that my last day is at hand,
I will take care to arm myself betimes with the sacraments
and with those gifts which holy church ministers to the
family of Christ: in confession I will reveal the sins of my life
to a priest, and I will receive the venerable body of Christ.

DEATH

But if the dangers of approaching death draw near
and press upon me, I will humbly summon someone
who will anoint me according to the proper rites
and make the sign of the cross on my body with holy oil.
And armed with these defences, I will depart from this life
in a manner worthy of a Christian, with a strong and trusting
heart, relying above all on the goodness of God.

DO THIS AND YOU WILL LIVE.]

8. COMMENTARY

The commentary provides bibliographical information and comment on different aspects of the individual texts of the *Introduction, i.e.* on typography, layout, language, and grammar. In respect to the two grammatical parts included in the *Introduction*, they also draw attention to subject matter that is derived from earlier grammatical traditions, by starting from the texts of the *Introduction* and going back to earlier English printed grammars. An attempt has also been made to draw attention to distant parallels with the earliest English grammatical manuscripts. References to the present edition are given by line number or by verse of the individual texts. The page numbers refer to the opening line of each passage.

TITLE-PAGE

156,1 See Plate 1. Frontispiece. The printed title-page border is illuminated in colour. In the sill there is a triumphal procession of putti, one is sitting on a litter carried by four putti. The further pole of the litter is not visible owing to the perspective. At the left and right sides putti are climbing from bottom to top, where two sphinxes are sitting left and right holding a portrait medallion. Within the border the title of the book is arranged. The first line of the title is set to the full width of the opening in the title-page border with a division of the word *INTRO=|DVCTION*, over two lines, the second line being in a smaller type size than the first. The title indicates the contents of the book as well as the year of publication. The two major texts, on accidence and construction, are mentioned, indicating that they were considered the two most important treatises. The fact that the texts are compilations is indicated and their authoritative status emphasized. The border is possibly based on a design by Hans Holbein the Younger. It was in use by Berthelet in a number of books from about 1530 to 1549, when it appears to have been acquired by John Wyer (*fl.* 1550–1552, d. 1552), a printer in London, who lived in Fleet Street; see Herbert, vol. 2: 712–13. This copy is probably the only one which has survived, but one must assume that there were other, non-illuminated copies in existence. Any importance derived from the decoration can obviously only refer to this particular copy, not to the edition as a whole. The overall printed presentation is indicative of a book of substance, produced by the King's Printer with the status of royal approbation, and that this particular copy has added significance from the way in which it has been decorated.

ROYAL PROCLAMATION

157,1 See Plate 4, page 150. A facsimile reproduction is also given in Alston, vol. 15, no. 495, Plate CXXVII. For a transcription of this text see Ames, 173, reprinted in Herbert, vol. 1: 442–43, and Dibdin, *Typographical Antiquities*, vol. 3, no. 1248: 318–19. It has also been transcribed in Blach (1909), 45: 85; in John William Adamson (1919), *A Short History of Education*, Cambridge, 124–25; in John Stanbridge (1519), *The Vulgaria of John Stanbridge and the Vulgaria of Robert Whittinton*, ed. White (1971 repr.), xxxviii; in Elizabeth M. Nugent (ed.) (1956), *The Thought and Culture of the English Renaissance*, Cambridge, 111 (excerpt); and in Hughes and Larkin, vol. 1, no. 216: 317, where it is entitled "Establishing One Authorized Grammar [London, before 25 March 1543, 34 Henry VIII]". An excerpt is given Nils Erik Enkvist (1975), 'English in Latin Guise. A Note on Some Renaissance Textbooks', *Historiographia Linguistica* 2: 283–98, at 295. The surviving text of the proclamation contained in the BL copy and the editions printed by Berthelet to 1546 is the only evidence which is extant of the legal document issued by the order of Henry VIII. The only information about its textual provenance and genesis given by Hughes and Larkin is "*STC* 15,605, BM C.21.b.4,2".

157,5 *moste weyghty affayres, appertaynyng to our regall auctoritee and offyce*: See *OED*, appertain, *v.* 3. To belong as a right or privilege *to*. At this point the proclamation states the role and particular care of the king as the head of the Church and his hierarchy for the schools and education. See Foster Watson (1908), *The English Grammar Schools to 1660. Their Curriculum and Practice*, Cambridge University Press, 15–23.

157,7 *whose good education and godly bryngyng vp, is a greate furniture to the same*: *OED*, furniture, 2.a. The condition of being equipped whether in body or mind. *Obs. exc. arch.* The first example provided by the *OED* with this sense is dated to 1594.

157,9 *easily attein the rudymentes of the latyne toung*: *OED*, attein, *v.* †9. To get to know, 'get at', find out. *Obs.*

157,10 *without þe greate hynderaunce*: The letter þ (thorn) in initial position is used in this and the following document *To the Reder*. Except in one or two cases, it does not occur in the two grammars or the *Godly Lessons*. This passage refers to the confusion caused by different grammars and systems as children changed schools and teachers, and therefore underlines the need of a uniform grammar. It presents the royal ordinance as a remedy for the present situation. See also Chapter 4, esp. pp. 120–22.

157,13 *as ye intend to auoyde our displeasure, and haue our fauour*: This sentence includes the enforcement clause of the legislative order by stating the vague threat of the king's displeasure that offenders would suffer who use grammars different from that prescribed. See R. W. Heinze (1976), *The Proclamations of the Tudor Kings*, Cambridge University Press, 60–63.

157,15 The last ten lines of this page beginning [*ensu*=||]*ing, and the latyne grammer annexed to the same*, are arranged in inverted triangular form in the original; see Plate 4, p. 150. The grammar in English is referred to as "this englysshe introduction", the part written in Latin which immediately follows as "the latyne grammer", denominations which may have contributed to the number of different names for 'Lily's Grammar' from that time onwards. See Chapter 1, p. 16. The proclamation says that the grammar represents a new compilation of material already well known, which needed to be revised and standardized for the more uniform and efficient teaching of Latin throughout the land. The words on the title-page "compiled and sette forthe" are taken from the proclamation.

157,18 *compyled*: See *OED*, compile, *v.* I. 2; and *OED*, set forth, 143 d. For the construction of *apply*, in "Fayle not to apply your scholars in lernynge" see *OED*, apply, *v.* 6. "To put to use, to employ", with a quotation from 1534, "[He] hadde applied the moste parte of his lyfe in warre".

To the Reader

158,1 This text addressed *To the Reder* has been transcribed in Blach (1909), 45: 85–87; in John Stanbridge (1519), *The Vulgaria of John Stanbridge and the Vulgaria of Robert Whittinton*. Ed. White (1971 repr.), xxxviii–xxxix; and in Nugent (ed.) (1956), 111–12 (excerpt).

158,4 *if we wyl wey the iust valu of thynges in an equall balance, as a certayn wyse Phylosopher dyd*: This passage refers to the philosopher Plato, not by name but by epithet, and alludes to the commonplace of the ideal of the philosopher-king. The allusion may be seen as a passing reference based on secondary sources. Formulations that are quite near are in Plato's *Republic* V. 473 ff.; VI. 484 D., 498 E.ff., 501, 503 B; 502 A.ff.; cf. also VII. 519 C.ff., 525 B., 540 A.ff.; and VIII.543 A (*LCL*, vols. 237, 276, 123, and 164). On the knowledge of Plato before and during the Tudor period see Sears Jayne (1995), *Plato in Renaissance England*, Dordrecht, 22–59, 83–136. The allusion to Plato is an encomium of Henry VIII, representing the wise ruler.

158,22 *and to take good heede of Christis churche to lead his flock into* [A2ᵛ] *the folde of tru doctrine, þe hurdels of þe same so wel vnderpyght, þat the wolues shal not be able to ouerthrowe them*: The passage on the recto page was crossed out and erased. Finally it was inserted again by hand in an antiquarian attempt at English black-letter. On the verso page the passage was crossed out but not erased, but rather strengthened by manuscript. As the text was probably written after the Act of Supremacy in 1534, it refers to the Church as reformed by Henry VIII. Thereafter, sometime in Mary's reign, the passage was deleted by some person who wished to remove any reference which might possibly be construed as heretical. At some later date, probably in Elizabeth's reign, or maybe even much later, the original, by now quite an acceptable text, was reinstated.

158,23 *folde*: OED, fold, *n.*[2] b. *fig.*, *esp.* in a spiritual sense. See also *vnder-pyght* (same line): OED, †underpight, *pa. tense* and *pa. pple. Obs.* Supported from below; propped up. Also *fig.*

158,24 *wolues*: OED, wolf, *n.* 5.a., in allusion to enemies or persecutors attacking the 'flocks' of the faithful. Cf. Matt. 7,15 and Acts 20.29.

158,29 *the great encombrance and confusion of the yong and tender wittes*: See OED, encumbrance, 2. *concr.* That which encumbers; a burden, impediment [. . .]; in stronger sense, an annoyance, trouble. This passage illustrates the situation in grammar teaching before the royal grammar was introduced. Note the correction by hand in line 30.

158,33 *certein lerned men mete for suche a purpose*: The text refers to the royal committee that probably also compiled the uniform grammar in Latin. No names of the individual members of the committee are given in the text and are not known from other contemporary sources.

159,46 *busylye to applye your selues, to trade and bryng vp your scholers*: See OED, trade, *v.* †4. *trans.* To familiarize with the use, practice, etc. *Obs.*

159,49 The text takes into account the stage of learning of the school-boys in a similar way to John Colet's *Aeditio*, where he says: "In whiche lytel boke I haue lefte many thynges out of purpose/ consyderyng the tendernes and small capacyte of lytel myndes" ("A lytell proheme to the boke", A5ᵛ).

159,57 *shake of slouthfulnes, set wantonnes a parte*: See OED, slothfulness. The state or character of being slothful; sluggishness, laziness. OED, wantonness, †f. Unruliness, naughtiness (of a child). *Obs.* For the verb see OED, set, *v.* 138. set apart, †a. To lay aside, put on one side. *Obs.*

159,60 *Let noble prynce Edwarde encourage your tender hartes*: Henry VIII's son, the later King Edward VI, is held up as a model and example to other young learners to follow his steps.

159,61 *a prynce of greate towardnes*: See OED, towardness. Now *Obs.* or *arch.* 2. *spec.* Willingness and aptness to learn. Prince Edward was born on the 12 October 1537 and was about five years old when this edition was printed. He would have been just about ready to start Latin, and in fact may have already started, since by eight boys were expected to have acquired sufficient knowledge to be able to go on to more serious studies.

The appearance of this volume at this time may have been linked to Edward's requirements. It would have been a politic act on the part of the committee to ingratiate themselves with the king by completing their task in time for the *Introduction* to be used by Edward.

AD PUBEM ANGLICAM. HEXASTICON.

160,1 This text has been transcribed in Blach (1909), 45: 87. The idea surely is that the king, having realized the importance of standardizing the teaching of Latin, had caused to be prepared a grammar which would facilitate learning for the benefit of all pupils. The woodcut below the verses shows the old royal arms (England and France, quartered), crowned, supported by two putti, the whole flanked by a pair of antique columns and surmounted by two swags. It is illuminated in bright colours and gold. The lower margin of the woodcut bears the inscription "*ARMA . REGIS . ANGLIE . ET . F[RANCIE]*". These arms were introduced by Henry IV in 1411 and remained in use until the reign of George III, in the nineteenth century. See A. C. Fox-Davies (1909). *A Complete Guide to Heraldry*, rev. and annotated by J. P. Brooke-Little, London; repr. 1969, 207. Below the wood-cut is printed *GOD SAVE THE KYNG*. This, in turn is followed by two lines in manuscript setting forth the value of the study of grammar. The writing has been erased and is only legible under ultraviolet light where it reads: "*Grammatices labor est paruus, sed fructus in illa est | Non paruus—parua haec discito, parue puer.*" ['The labour in grammar is small, but its fruits are any-thing but small. Learn these little things, little boy.'] These lines represent the first two lines of a four-line epigram entitled '*Studium Grammatices omnibus esse necessarium*' which can be found in later editions of the grammar in English, for example in that of 1548, a4^v. See Appendix III, 8.0.

160,9 *GOD SAVE THE KYNG*: This standard phrase which appears at the bottom of royal proclamations issued by Thomas Berthelet as the King's Printer, follows the royal coat-of-arms, lending authority and authenticity to the text as a whole. See also Pamela Ayers Neville (1990), *Richard Pynson, King's Printer (1506–1529): Printing and Propaganda in Early Tudor England*, Ph.D. Dissertation, London, 85–120.

THE PARTS OF SPEECH

161,1 See Plate 5, p. 151. This page has also been reproduced in Alston, vol. 15, no. 495, Plate CXXVIII. The text presents the eight parts of speech in an order which reflects their importance. They are set up in two inflexionally contrasting groups, each in a column: the inflected or variable and the uninflected or invariable parts of speech. This division is the beginning of grammatical analysis in this treatise and the first classification. The order and arrangement of the word classes are identical to John Colet's *Aeditio* (A6ʳ) (*Checklist* 20.1). This classification is also found in the English grammatical manuscripts; see, for example, Thomson, *Edition*, Text A, 3–7. It reflects Priscian's analysis of the parts of speech into declinables and indeclinables (*GL* III, 24, 2–5). Otto Funke (1941), *Die Frühzeit der Englischen Grammatik*, Bern, 78, refers to the 1566 edition of the English part of 'Lily's Grammar' (Appendix III, 17.0). See also Emma Vorlat (1975), *The Development of English Grammatical Theory, 1586–1737, with Special Reference to the Theory of Parts of Speech*, Leuven: Leuven University Press, 49, whose discussion is based on the 1567 edition (Appendix III, 19.1). In the text the verb is said to be a declinable part of speech (line 5; also p. 169, line 326, and p. 171, line 391), but its groupings are referred to as conjugations (cf. p. 171, line 386).

161,8 Each word class in the text on accidence is introduced by a separate definition, as in the tradition of teaching grammars, which makes their difference quite explicit. Each definition covers the entire membership of the class, and various subdivisions and subclasses within it. The definition of the noun is based on semantic terms, away from strictly formal criteria. It is an almost verbatim repetition of that given in Colet's *Aeditio*, except that the latter adds the substantive verb "to be" in his definition: "A nowne is the name of a thynge that is. and may be seen/ felte/ herde/ or vnderstande" (A6ʳ). Cf. George Arthur Padley (1976), *Grammatical Theory in Western Europe, 1500–1700. Vol. 1: The Latin Tradition*, Cambridge, 56, on the definition; for "*esse*", also Padley, p. 46. Ian Michael (1970), *English Grammatical Categories and the Tradition to 1800*, Cambridge, 55, is correct in saying that in this respect 'Lily's Grammar' (though in fact he refers to Colet's *Aeditio* (1527)) sets a norm for the English grammars that followed, in defining the parts of speech semantically rather than formally. The predecessors in manuscript and early print offer a variety of formal, syntactical and semantic criteria; cf. Appendix V.

161,11 "Noun" is the general term for this part of speech. The noun class is subdivided into nouns substantive and nouns adjective. In the tradition substantive and adjective must therefore have been regarded as subordinate categories within this class; see Michael (1970), 202 and 206. The noun substantive itself comprises proper and common nouns. The division into nouns substantive and nouns adjective is based on the syntactic independence of the former, not shared by the latter. Cf. the brief discussion of the noun substantive by Colet where no illustrating examples are given and declension is not mentioned. Note also his alternative nomenclature on the same page: "A nowne/ or a name substantyue" (A6ᵛ). See Appendix V; also Michael (1970), 89; For the division of the noun into nouns substantive and nouns adjective see also Vorlat (1975), 70–71, 74–75, and Padley (1976), 39–44.

161,16 The adjective is treated as a subclass of the noun, from which its denomination as noun adjective can be explained. It inflected almost identically to the noun and functioned substantively. In its first part it is defined syntactically, in its second part, by reference to formal categories, according to its endings or the three articles it takes. Cf. the detailed explanation in the *Aeditio*: "A nowne adiectyue is/ that can not stande by hym selfe/ but loketh to be ioyned with another word as *Bonus, Pulcher*. whan I say in latyn *Bonus* good/ or *Pulcher* fayre/ it loketh to tell what is good/ or what is fayre. And therfore it must be ioyned with an other worde: as a good childe/ *Bonus puer*. A fayre woman *Pulchra fœmina*. And a nowne adiectyue eyther it hath thre terminacions: as *Bonus, bona, bonum*. or elles it is declyned with thre artycles *Hic, hæc, hoc*. as *hic, hæc, et hoc fœlix*" (A6ᵛ). The forms of the demonstrative pronoun *Hic, hæc, hoc* are referred to as articles. They are used to distinguish the substantive from the adjective. The latter can have any of the three articles before it. A substantive, however, can take only one out of three before it. *Hic* is also classified amongst the fifteen pronouns; see p. 167, line 226. *Hic, hæc, hoc* being denominated and used as articles can be found in the English grammatical manuscripts, e.g. Thomson, *Edition*, Text D, 32, 13–17 (*Accedence* MS; *Checklist* 2). It reflects the practice amongst Latin grammarians of indicating noun gender by means of the appropriate form of *hic, hæc, hoc*, described as the [*pronomen*] *articulare praepositivum vel demonstrativum* in Donatus's *Ars minor* (Holtz, 589, 15; *GL* IV, 357, 35).

161,21 The division of the noun substantive into the two classes of proper and common nouns is based on the alleged semantic distinction between individual quality and common quality. The two classes of the noun are not distinguishable morphologically or syntactically. "Edouardus" is given here as an example for a proper name instead of "*Ioannes*" as in the *Aeditio* (A6ᵛ), the latter possibly referring to Colet's Christian name. The name given in the *Introduction* is most likely an allusion to Prince Edward, later King Edward VI. Cf. the text *To the Reder*, p. 159, lines 60–61, and also the Commentary. On the proper noun see Michael (1970), 85–86. The definition of the common noun is similar to that given in the *Aeditio*, A6ᵛ.

162,29 The text recognizes six Latin cases in the declension of the English noun. As the case definitions refer to the English cases (though the examples in Latin are given before those in English), contrastive classroom definitions are provided which must have made the student aware of the differences between English and Latin word order. For the distinction of the nominative and accusative cases the text gives a definition according to word order and meaning, *i.e.* the nominative precedes the verb, the accusative follows it, which must refer to English word order;

both cases also being identified by different interrogative pronouns. The other four cases are identified according to their meaning. The genitive and dative cases in English are marked by the use of the "tokens", "of" and "to" respectively, the ablative by a number of "signs" before the noun. The *Aeditio* uses almost the same definitions apart from the fact that for the first four cases the pupil is not told by what interrogative pronoun to ask for the particular case. In the present text the ablative is identified by "sygnes" (p. 162, line 43) which are called "preposicions of the ablatyue case" in Colet's grammar (A7^r). Contrastive observations in defining the cases were already well established and can be found in the English grammatical manuscripts, e.g. Thomson, *Edition*, Text D, 34, 105–67 (*Accedence* MS; *Checklist* 2). For the terms "sign" and "token" in their grammatical sense see *MED*, signe, *n.*, 8. (b). A word indicating a grammatical category; also *MED*, token, *n.*, 11. (c). A word or words, indicating a grammatical case. Signs are usually taken to be English words which correspond to a bound morpheme in Latin and the grammatical category marked by it. On the term sign and its use in grammatical texts of the fifteenth and early sixteenth centuries see Kohnen (2001), 518–32; cf. also Enkvist (1975), 287–88; and Vorlat (1975), 149.

162,46 The article is treated within the discussion of the noun, but the text indicates that the article is taken from the word class of the pronoun; see p. 229, note to line 226 below. *Hic, hęc,* and *hoc* are arranged in paradigms for the singular and plural according to the six cases and are only given in Latin, apparently because of the lack of gender and case distinctions in the English articles. The names of the cases are given in Latin. In the *Aeditio*, the discussion of the article is arranged according to its five genders from "the masculyne gendre" to the "comyn of .iij." and follows there after the discussion of the declension and the gender of nouns (B2^r).

162,54 In the discussion of gender only the Latin nouns are treated here, where an English translation of the word in question is added, except for "The common of two" and "The common of three" (lines 60 and 61). The system of gender comprises seven categories which are also found in Colet's grammar. For the list of the seven genders see Michael (1970), 112, where he refers to the 1567 edition of the Latin part of 'Lily's Grammar' (Appendix III, 19.2); also Vorlat (1975), 123. For the categories of gender see the discussion in Thomson, *Edition*, Text D, 34, 74–94 (*Accedence* MS).

163,67 The five declensions of the noun are discussed in detail, which shows the importance given to their analysis in the classroom. They are distinguished in the traditional fashion, *i.e.* in terms of the ending of the genitive singular. The sample paradigms of each declension are exemplified in two different ways: first, the termination of each model noun is the starting-point in the way that the final letters or syllables representing the case-endings in the singular and in the plural of each declension are set out in running text; secondly, each declension is illustrated by a model word displayed in columnar format, which demonstrates visually the different forms of the Latin noun to the English schoolboy. The inflections of the other nouns of this declension are gained by analogy. All forms of the model nouns are preceded by the appropriate forms of *hic, hęc, hoc*, a practice which goes back to the *Ars minor* of Donatus. No vernacular translations are provided. For the same method see Colet's *Aeditio*, A7ʳ–B1ᵛ. Cf. the explanation of the oblique cases in the succeeding text given in the *Aeditio*: "The fyrst is whan from the nominatyue case synguler the genityue falleth in ae. [. . .]" (A7ᵛ). On the two different ways of presenting paradigms, cf. Law (1990), 62.

163,73 Compared to the case-endings of the noun "musa" set out in isolation, it is striking that the endings of the genitive and the dative singular in columnar format read *sæ* instead of *æ* diphthong, and that the accusative singular ends in *sam* instead of *am*. This, at first glance inconsistent presentation of the case-endings of the noun, can be explained by the fact that the word was regarded as the minimal semantic and hence morphological unit, as an organic whole, not as a set of component parts. An apparent exception was the ending. The only concept available was those of "word" and "ending". The latter was conceived as a roughly delimited portion of the whole. Consequently, when it was separated from the rest of the word, the point at which the division was made could vary from one case to the next. On the perception of the word, cf. Law (1990), 63–67.

163,84 Cf. the case-endings in the two ways of presentation of the paradigms of the noun of the *o*-declension. In the columnar format "magister" ends in *gistri* and *strorum* in the genitive singular and plural, in *gistros* (accusative plural) and in *gistris* (ablative plural). See the previous two notes.

163,95 This passage is not found in the *Aeditio*. However, it represents common material which can be found in earlier printed grammars and grammatical manuscripts. See, for example, John Holt's *Lac puerorum*, BL, C.33.b.47, A5ᵛ (*Checklist* 53.2).

164,125 The declension of *parens, parentis* also represents subject matter which is not given in Colet's grammar.

165,155 At this point the *Aeditio* includes the additional paradigm of "A nown adiectyf of al gendres: as *Fœlix*, is thus declyned" (B1ʳ).

165,161 *There be besides these certayn nownes adiectiues of an other maner of declynyng, whiche make the genitiue case synguler in* ïus *or* ius, *and the datyue in* i: The text draws attention to the difference of the adjectives of the *o*- and *a*-declension and the pronominal adjectives. The latter take the genitive ending *ius* and the dative ending *i*. They usually make the genitive singular in *ius* for all genders, but the *i* may be long or short, e.g. the short *i* in the compounds of *uter*, as *utriusque*. The pronominal adjectives are discussed in the second declension of the pronoun in early printed grammars, e.g. in John Stanbridge's *Accidence*, Bodl. Lib., 4° A1.8(2) Art.BS., A6ᵛ (*Checklist* 16.1), and in some grammatical manuscripts. See, for example, Thomson, *Edition*, Text D, 37, 244–49 (*Accedence* MS): "Which is the secunde [declynson]? Of the which the genityf case singuler endyth in -*ius* vel -*ius*, the datyf in -*i* uel in -*c*. How many pronounez hath he? Fyue, videlicet *ille*, *ipse*, *iste*, *hic* and *is*, and viij nounes wyth hure compounez, videlicet *vnus*, *vllus*, *totus*, *solus*, *alter* and *alius*, *quis* and *vter* et eorum composita."

166,192 This explanation on the comparison of adjectives is not found in the *Aeditio*. It only says: "In nownes also be degrees of comparyson/" (B2ʳ).

166,195 For the adjective a paradigm of gradation into positive, comparative, and superlative is given. The definitions of the three degrees are different from those in Colet's grammar where they read: "The posytyue degre betokeneth somwhat of the thynge/ as *Durus*, harde. The comparatyue degre betokeneth more of the thynge/ as *Durior*, harder. The superlatyue degre betokeneth moost of the thynge: as *Durißimus*, hardest" (B2ʳ). In the present text the formation of the three degrees immediately follows after each definition and is illustrated by Latin examples, whereas in the *Aeditio* formation is discussed separately (B2ʳ⁻ᵛ).

167,224 The definition of the pronoun is framed in terms of meaning and function. It is neither further explained nor illustrated. In the *Institutio*, the Latin part of 'Lily's Grammar' printed in 1540, the definition reads: "*Pronomen est pars orationis, qua, in demonstranda, aut repetenda re aliqua, utimur*", p. 22 (listed in Appendix III, 1.0). The second part of this definition renders that of the present text: "whiche is vsed in shewyng or rehersyng". See Michael's (1970) explanation on p. 72, and Vorlat (1975), 186, who refer to the 1567 copy of the Latin part (Appendix III, 19.2). It also provides a comment on the present text. Michael's comment on the English grammar on the same page, however, refers to the definition given in the *Aeditio*: "A Pronowne is moche lyke a nowne/ and in reason standeth for a nowne" (B3ʳ). Padley's explanation (1976) on p. 44 refers to the 1557 edition of 'Lily's Grammar' in English (Appendix III, 12.1.a). For the definition of the pronoun in this tradition see Appendix V.

167,226 The list of fifteen pronouns consisting of personal and demonstrative pronouns can also be found in Colet's *Aeditio*, B3ʳ, and in the English grammatical manuscripts. See, for example, Thomson, *Edition*, Text D, 36, 200–202 (*Accedence* MS). It goes back to Priscian, *Institutiones grammaticae*, *GL* II (1855), 577, 6–12. *Hic* is also discussed within the noun class, where it is referred to as the definite article in the masculine case; see p. 227, note to line 46. At this point it is grouped amongst the pronouns and is said to be a primitive and demonstrative pronoun. Cf. Michael

(1970), 67–68, also his comment on the classification of pronouns, 101; and Vorlat (1975), 199–200. This indicates the instability inherent in the system in Latin. The three compounds of pronouns listed here, which are derived from *ego, tu,* and *is,* are mentioned in the previous list. This represents an example of word-formation expressed by the accident "figure" (shape, simple and compound); cf. p. 240, note to line 985. The compound pronouns and the three relative pronouns "*Qui quę quod*" (line 228) are not mentioned in the *Aeditio,* where the primitive pronouns are called demonstratives.

167,233 The first four of the six relative pronouns "*Hic, ille, iste, is*" have already been included among the primitives. The six relative pronouns are not listed in the *Aeditio.*

167,235 This is another example of how new words can be coined due to the accident "species" (primitives and derivatives).

167,237 Of the five accidents of the pronoun listed at this point only two are given in the *Aeditio* in the following way: "Pronownes also haue nombres/ synguler and plurell: as hath a nowne/ and be declined in to theyr cases syngulerly and plurally" (B3ʳ).

167,260 The pronoun *qui* is not listed in the discussion of the second declension in Colet's grammar, B3ᵛ. A list of five pronouns is already given in the grammatical manuscripts. See Thomson, *Edition,* Text D, 37, 247 (*Accedence* MS).

168,262 The text gives the paradigm of *iste* listed in the third place instead of *ille* with which it begins. The former pronoun is the first item listed in the *Aeditio.*

168,270 The declensions of *hic, hęc, hoc* are arranged in a separate table in the *Aeditio,* B3ᵛ.

168,273 The text lists alternative forms for the dative and ablative cases plural "*ijs uel eis*", whereas the *Aeditio* only gives "*Datiuo eis*" and "*Ablatiuo ab eis*" (B4ʳ) for the demonstrative pronouns. For the alternative forms of the two cases see Stanbridge, *Accidence,* B1ʳ. The two forms for the ablative plural "*ab hijs eis*" are also given in the grammatical manuscripts. See Thomson, *Edition,* Text C, 23, 292 (*Accedence* MS; *Checklist* 7).

168,277 The declensions of the relative pronouns *qui quæ quod,* as well as information about the interrogative pronouns *quis* and *quid* (p. 168, line 291), represent material which is not found in the *Aeditio.* Again it is common subject matter, which, for example, which can be found in Thomson, *Edition,* Text C, 23, 293–98 (*Accedence* MS). The alternative form *qui* in the ablative singular for the three genders is a pre-classical form; see Thomson, *Edition,* Text C, 23, 295. This form is already cited in Donatus, *Ars minor,* in Holtz, 589, 25; 590, 1 = GL IV, 358, 8–12. The alternative form *queis* (lines 283 and 289) in the present text for the dative and ablative plural is also a pre-classical form. On these forms see Gildersleeve and

Lodge (1894), no. 105: 59. The declension of the interrogative pronouns *quid* and *quis* as a whole is included in Thomson, *Edition*, Text C, 23, 293–98 (*Accedence* MS).

168,297 The form *mei* is the genitive singular masculine of the personal pronoun of the first person *ego*. Its use as a vocative of the possessive pronoun *meus* is either an error in the compilation of this text or an error by the compositor. Cf. the *Aeditio* which reads *mi* for the vocative singular masculine on B4ʳ, also the grammatical manuscripts, e.g. Thomson, *Edition*, Text C, 24, 315 (*Accedence* MS).

168,302 The declension of *noster* is given in a separate table in the *Aeditio* on B4ʳ.

169,304 Nostras uestras *and this nown* cuias: These are the gentile adjectives. *Nostras*: 'of our country'; *uestras*: 'of your country', and *cuias*: 'of whose country?' The early printed grammars and grammatical manu-scripts do not provide all forms of the paradigm. For example, the *Aeditio* does not give the neuter forms of *nostras*. For the vocative it lists only one form on B4ᵛ. Thomson, *Edition*, Text C, 24, 343–49, gives only the mascu-line and feminine forms (*Accedence* MS).

169,315 this nowne cuias: It is not listed as a pronoun of the fourth declension of pronouns in Colet's grammar. However, it represents common material in the tradition; see, for example, Thomson, *Edition*, Text C, 22, 251–56 (*Accedence* MS).

169,326 The definition of the verb admits formal as well as semantic criteria. Cf. those given in the definition of the *Aeditio*: "A Verbe is a specyall parte of speche that cometh in euery perfyt reason/ and in eueri sentence. And it is a worde that eyther betokeneth beynge of a thynge/ as *Sum*, I am: or doynge of a thynge/ as *Amo*, I loue: or sufferynge of a thynge/ as *Amor*, I am loued. Verbes/ some haue persones/ as *Amo, amas*, some haue no persones/ as *Tedet, oportet*," (B5ʳ). The definitions, however, given in both grammars agree, though not literally, on the semantic criteria as denoting action and passion and include the substantive verb "to be". On Colet's definition see Michael (1970), p. 60.

169,330 oportet, *it behoueth* See *OED*, behove, behoove, *v.* 4. *quasi-impers.* a. It is incumbent upon or necessary for (a person) *to do* (something). Also 4.b. or 4.c. *arch.*

169,331 The five genders of the personal verb are referred to here as "kyndes"; see *OED*, kind, *sb.* †7.a. gender; sex (L. genus.) *Obs.* The same term for verbal gender is also used in the *Aeditio* on B5ʳ. Inflection is the main criterion in distinguishing the different genders of the Latin verb, but for the deponent and common verb semantic considerations are also included. Definitions based on inflectional and also semantic criteria can be found in the early printed grammars and grammatical manuscripts; cf. Thomson, *Edition*, Text D, 38, 327–40 (*Accedence* MS). See Michael's (1970) comment on p. 96. The substantive verb *sum* is listed as a neuter verb (p. 169, line 338) where it follows after *Curro*. Colet's *Aeditio* gives almost verbatim definitions, but omits the substantive verb in the list of neuter verbs (B5^{r-v}).

170,344 Six modes are given here instead of five in the *Aeditio*: "Indicatyue/ the Imperatyue/ the Optatyue/ the Coniunctyue/ and the Infinitiue" (B5^v). Cf. Linacre, *Rudimenta grammatices* (= *EL*, 312 (1971)) (*Checklist* 55.1) in the section dealing with the definitions of the parts of speech (F4^v): "Modis be .vj. the indicatiue, the imperatiue, the optatiue, the potential, the subiunctiue, and the infinitiue." In the preceding part of Linacre's treatise discussing declension, only five modes without the potential are listed (B2^v). In the same way, his *Progymnasmata*, BL, G.7569 (*Checklist* 54.1) also lists six modes in the section on the definitions of the parts of speech on c3^r, whereas in the section on declension it only provides five modes without the potential (A4^v). On this text cf. Funke (1941), 90 (and footnote 8). John Holt's *Lac puerorum* shares this pattern. In the section on definition it gives six modes and defines the potential as follows: "The potencyall mode betokeneth a thynge as not done/ but that may or myght haue be done and hath as grete strength as one of these verbes *Possum. volo. debeo*" (D4^{r-v}). In his first section dealing with declension he lists seven modes (including the "subiunctyf") on B3^v. See the discussion of "The potencyall mode" on C1^r. John Stanbridge's *Accidence* also lists the potential among the six moods of the verb on B2^r. The grammatical manuscripts only provide the common five moods without the potential. On this mood see Michael (1970), 115–16. The present text reads "Subiunctyue" (line 345), whereas Colet's *Aeditio* uses the term "Coniunctyue" on B5^v for the same mood. On the distinction of these two terms in the tradition see also Michael, 116. In the present text the primary criterion for the identification of the six moods is that of meaning. An additional criterion for recognizing the optative, the potential, and the infinitive mood (p. 170, line 349) is the occurrence of "signes"; the uninflected form of the verb in the infinitive mood is not mentioned. The subjunctive mood is defined according to syntactical criteria. Cf. also Vorlat (1975), 329–30, and 334.

170,360 The discussion of the gerund (verbal noun) and the supine within the infinitive is not found in the *Aeditio*. But see their discussion, for example, in Linacre's, *Rudimenta grammatices*, in the section on declension, B3^v.

170,370 At this point "tense", *i.e.* a feature of words, and "time", a feature of consciousness, are used as synonyms. Cf. Colet's definition: "In modes al verbes vary by reason of tymes/ called tenses/ whiche be .v." (B6^r); cf. Michael (1970), 116. "Preterpluperfect" in the original should read "preterimperfect" in this list see line 370. The *Aeditio* gives the correct reading. This error in the text points to a corruption which could go back to the compositor or it could have been found in his copy. In the same way as in the *Aeditio*, the present text states that there are five tenses in English as in Latin: the present, the past, and the future, with the past subdivided into three tenses. The primary criterion for their recognition is meaning. But the perfect, the pluperfect, and the future in English are also recognized by their construction with "have" or "had", with the past participle for the past tenses and "shall" or "will" with the infinitive for the future tense. Cf. also Michael, 118; and Vorlat (1975), 303–304, 307–308. The imperfect in Latin denoting continuance in the past is rendered in English by "I loued or dyd loue". The construction with "dyd" is given here as an alternative to the simple verb form in the imperfect. The use of "dyd" has no other function than to mark tense. See Rissanen (1999), 240–43. In both grammars the Latin verb and its English equivalent are provided. As with moods, the auxiliary verbs "haue, hadde, shall or wyll" are also called "signs" and are taken as markers of the tenses corresponding to the Latin perfect, pluperfect, and future. In English there is no formal mark of difference between the present and future in the verb itself. The same tense system is found in grammatical manuscripts; see, for example, Thomson, *Edition*, Text D, 39, 352–64 (*Accedence* MS).

171,382 The discussion of the accident "person" as a formal feature of verbs includes the Latin example as well as its English equivalent. In Colet's grammar "person" immediately follows the discussion of the accident "tense" (B6ʳ).

171,391 The text says that verbs "be declyned" (see also p. 161, line 5 at the beginning of the text). The *Aeditio* also speaks of "The declynacyons of verbes" (B5ᵛ) and "How verbes of euery coniugacyon declyned" (B6ᵛ). See also the grammatical manuscripts, e.g. Thomson, *Edition*, Text D, 38, 291–94 (*Accedence* MS). "Decline" in these grammars has a wider meaning than our modern usage. "Declinatio" is an oral explanation of the grammatical forms in a given text. To "decline" then is to produce the "derived" forms of each word which is subject to varying inflections in the different moods, cases, numbers, and tenses. Declination thus includes both what is called today "declension" and "conjugation". Cf. *OED*, decline, *v*. 20. a. *Gram*. The four conjugations in the *Introduction* are distinguished by the thematic vowel characteristics with which the stem of the Latin verb can end, that are á, é, ĕ, í, which may be found by dropping "*re*" from the present infinitive active, or "*ris*" from the second person singular present indicative passive. As an additional mark indicating the long and the short vowels in each of the two forms of the representative verbs, the text shows accents on these vowels. For the same way of identifying the conjugations see the rule of the first coniugation in Stanbridge's *Accidence* in the form of question and answer: "How knowe you a verbe of the fyrste coniugacion? For in declynynge he hath A longe be fore the re in the actyue voyce. or be fore ris in the passyue voyce as amare amaris" (B3ʳ). In the present text and in the *Accidence* the verb can hence be considered to consist of different units: a first part which is not further specified, a thematic vowel which follows, although this term is not used, and the endings "*re*" or "*ris*" for the present infinitive active or the second person singular present indicative passive. Cf. Vorlat's (1975) brief comment based on the 1567 copy of 'Lily's Grammar', 290 (Appendix, III, 19.1).

171,392 The following forms of the four Latin model verbs *amare*, *docere*, *legere*, and *audire*, which represent the four conjugations, are set out in running text, each on a separate line. The full form or the ending of each verb in the active voice of the first and second person singular indicative present tense is provided, the first person perfect, the present infinitive, the genitive, dative, and accusative forms of the gerund, the two forms of the supine, the present and future participle, and also the infinitive form of the English equivalent. This passage is not found in Colet's grammar; but see Stanbridge's *Accidence* for the same list on B3^{r-v}. The concept of the ending of the word as a roughly deliminated portion of the whole is evident in the present text and the *Accidence*. See also p. 227, note to line 67, and p. 228, note to line 73 above.

171,397 The discussion of conjugation is given generous coverage in the text as in the *Aeditio*, reflecting a teaching method which made use of the visual presentation of the verb forms and responded to the level and need of the student to acquire the basic language skills. The English schoolboy should concentrate on studying the inflections of the Latin verbs systematically. See also p. 227, note to line 67. The text, however, shows a different arrangement of the forms from that given in the *Aeditio*. See Plate 6, p. 152. Paradigms are absent. Instead, all four conjugations are discussed together. The forms of the same person of each verb are presented in a table in the singular and plural through all moods and tenses. Each form of the first person of the four model verbs in each of the six moods is given in full, in a way that the same forms of the first person singular can be compared with the endings of the other conjugations. The forms of the first person present indicative are given in detail, but the English equivalent is only provided for *amare*. The endings from the second person singular to the third person plural are listed in a series, and English equivalents of the four verbs are only provided for the first person. From the imperfect indicative onwards only the first person is given in detail. This arrangement is also applied to the gerund, the supine, the present and future participle, and to the substantive verb *esse* (see p. 236, note to line 550). It is repeated for the verbs in the passive voice (pp. 177–80, lines 603–738), and finally for *posse*, *velle*, *nolle*, *malle*, *edere*, *fieri*, and *ferre* (pp. 180–84, lines 739–883). It enables the pupil to compare the same form of the different conjugations at the same time. The same arrangement of the forms of the four representative verbs is found in John Stanbridge's *Accidence*, B3^{v}–C1^{v}. It goes back to Priscian's *Institutiones grammaticae*, Books 9 and 10, but it can also be found in the anonymous *Excerptiones de Prisciano*. See the edition by Porter (2002), 208–43. In Colet's *Aeditio*, on the other hand, the verbs are classified by conjugation. The paradigm of each Latin verb of each conjugation is listed separately, without its English equivalent through all of the five moods listed there and the tenses in the active and in the passive voice (B6ᵛ–C6ʳ). In the present text the emphasis is put on the form of the verbs in the same person, whereas in the *Aeditio* the focus lies on the different conjugations.

171,404 Amabam: *I loued or dyd loue*: See also p. 232, note to line 370. The two English alternative forms are also given in John Stanbridge, *Accidence*, B3ᵛ.

172,419 Amabo: *I shall or wyll loue*: In the English translation two auxiliaries with the first person subject and the infinitive form of the verb are given as alternatives to indicate future tense. See Rissanen (1999), 210–12; also Fridén (1948), 124–207.

172,423 *Imperatyue mode the presente tense singular*: The text includes the forms of the imperative future. The passage is arranged in five columns which start by listing the English equivalents first, which are followed by the corresponding Latin forms of *amare* and *docere* in the two tenses of the imperative mood, before providing only the Latin forms of *legere* and *audire* in the two tenses of this mood. In Stanbridge's *Accidence* the forms of the imperative future are given separately where the Latin forms are also given first (B4ʳ).

172,442 Amarem: *would god I loued*: This rendering of Latin *Amarem* in a formulaic way into English, as the first person singular imperfect optative mood of *amare*, is also found, for example, in Holt's *Lac puerorum* under "The wysshynge mode" (B4ᵛ), and in Stanbridge's *Accidence* as "wolde to god I louyd" (B4ʳ).

173,457 Amauero: *God graunt I loue hereafter*: The first person singular future tense of the optative mood is rendered in a formulaic way with an additional adverb indicating future. Cf. Stanbridge, *Accidence*, "god graunt I shall loue" (C1ʳ).

173,462 Amem: The first person singular present tense of the potential mood of *amare* is rendered periphrastically in English as "*I may or can loue*". Cf. also the alternatives in English given in Holt, *Lac puerorum*, "I may loue. I wolde loue. I shall loue etc." (C1ʳ). On these auxiliaries see Rissanen (1995), 237–38. The text provides the children with the singular and plural forms of the *a*-conjugation to distinguish it from the other conjugations, an arrangement that, on the other hand, allows no space in the original to the compositor to fit the English equivalent of the first person singular into the same line as the Latin form.

173,472 Amauerim: *I myght, should or ought to haue loued*: On the three English equivalents which are given here for the Latin first person singular perfect tense of the potential mood of *amare* see Rissanen (1999), 231–32. The Latin form is also given in Holt's *Lac puerorum* on C1ʳ.

173,487 Amem: The first person singular present tense of the conjunctive mood of *amare* is rendered into English as "*when I loue*". This translation has already been given in Stanbridge's *Accidence*, B5ʳ. The text provides the student with the singular and plural forms of the *a*-conjugation, which is different from the other conjugations, hence the problems of space for the compositor to fit the English version into the corresponding line. See note to line 462 above.

174,517 Amauisse: *To haue or had loued*: The Latin infinitive perfect active is rendered alternatively by the English infinitive perfect and infinitive pluperfect forms with "to" as marker of the infinitive, "have" or "had", and the past participle of the verb. For the same forms see Stanbridge, *Accidence*, B5ᵛ. These forms are commented on in Rissanen (1999), 290.

175,546 *before we declyne any verbes in* or: For the term "declyne" for the inflection of verbs see p. 233, note to line 391 above. The pupil is prepared to form the passive voice by the ending of the verb, in this case of the first person singular present tense indicative. This passage, which interrupts the conjugation of the four model verbs, may be seen as an explicit pedagogical device; an insertion by the teacher for which very little room is left in the grammatical texts due to the nature of these texts which is factual, and their use in the classroom. Cf. Thomas Linacre, *Rudimenta grammatices*, B3ᵛ, where the forms for "*esse*" also come between the conjugation of the active and the passive verbs. They are introduced there in almost identical wording to the present text.

supplyeng of: See *OED*, supply, *v*.¹, 3.c. To add (something that is wanting). The construction with "of", however, is not found in the examples given there.

175,550 The conjugation of the substantive verb "*sum*" and its English translation in all forms of the first person singular is presented here through all moods in all tenses, whereas in the *Aeditio* it is listed as the first in the list of irregular verbs (C6ʳ). The forms of *esse* and its compounds, as well as some other common irregular verbs, are discussed in the printed treatises entitled *Sum, es, fui* which deal with the comparison of adjectives in their first part. Cf. the copies listed in *Checklist* 27.1–27.27. The irregular verbs are also dealt with in the grammatical manuscripts of the *Accedence*. See, for example, Thomson, *Edition*, Text C, 27, 448–73 (*Accedence* MS).

176,602 *Future tense,* Fore uel futurum esse: For the future infinitive forms Colet's *Aeditio* reads: "Futuro caret" on C6ʳ, which indicates a general pedagogical principle of the early Latin grammars in English, namely to select what was thought by the compilers of the texts to be important for the pupils; classroom practice may have been different.

177,604 The base forms of the four model verbs are listed before the text starts to discuss, in tabular form, the four conjugations in the passive voice through all of the six moods and five tenses, in the same way as in the active voice. On the separating of the endings from the rest of the word see p. 228, note to line 73.

177,629 Amabor: *I shall or wyll be loued*: This form is rendered in Stanbridge's *Accidence* by the abbreviated "I shall be louyd" (B6ʳ). See also p. 235, note to line 419, for the active forms.

178,672 Legar: *read* is missing in this table in the original.

180,725 Amatum esse uel fuisse: *To haue or had ben loued*: The Latin infinitive perfect and infinitive pluperfect passive forms are rendered by the English infinitive perfect and pluperfect passive forms, with "to" as marker of the infinitive, "have" or "had", the perfect form of "to be", and the past participle of the verb. Cf. also p. 236, note to line 517, for the active forms.

180,730 Amatum iri uel amandum esse: *to be loued hereafter*: The gerundive (verbal adjective) is given as an alternative form of the future tense infinitive passive. For the same forms and the English rendering "to be louyd" see Stanbridge, *Accidence* (C1ᵛ).

180,733 Auditum iri uel audiendum: The text should be completed as: *Auditum iri uel audiendum esse*. The auxiliary verb *esse* may have been omitted when the text was set by the compositor.

180,739 The text lists the stem forms of the irregular verbs *posse, velle, nolle, malle, edere, fieri, ferre*, and *ferri* with their English translations in the infinitive. Cf. the way these verbs are introduced in Linacre's *Progymnasmata grammatices vulgaria*: "Declination of anomall verbys. There be some verbys that kepe not þe ruel of theyse iiii. verbys in all tens as these that folow with other" (b2ᵛ) (*Checklist* 54.1). They are also discussed after the conjugation of the passive verbs, but only some English translations are given there (b2ᵛ–b4ᵛ). In Linacre's *Rudimenta grammatices* they are introduced in almost the same wording, but no English translations are given (D2ʳ-E4ʳ). The infinitive marker with "to" is striking in the present text. For these non-finite forms of the modal auxiliaries in English see Rissanen (1999), 231–32.

to may or can (line 739) are used as equivalents for Latin *posse*.

to wyll (741) renders Latin *velle* (cf. Linacre, *Progymnasmata*, "volo. I wyl" (b3ʳ)).

to nyll (743) is given for Latin *nolle* (cf. Linacre, *Progymnasmata*, "nolo I wyll not" (b3ʳ)).

to haue lyeffer (745) is an equivalent for Latin *malle* (cf. Linacre, *Progymnasmata*, "malo. I haue leuer" (b3ʳ)). See *OED*, lief, *adv.* d. In various constructions with *have; I had* (*occas.* † *have*) *liefer* (*than*), to express preference or comparative desirability. See have, *v.* 22.a.

to be made (748) translates Latin *fieri*.

to beare or to suffer (750) are given as alternatives for Latin *ferre*.

to be borne or suffered (752) are represented as alternatives for Latin *ferri*.

181,755 The irregular forms of these verbs are listed in this order, in tabular form, through the six moods and five tenses, in the same way as the four model verbs. See p. 234, note to line 397. No English equivalents are provided. In Colet's *Aeditio*, on the other hand, all forms of the irregular verbs *possum, volo, nolo, malo, fero, edo, fio*, and *eo* are given separately for each verb, in the same way as the model verbs are conjugated there (C6ʳ – D1ᵛ).

184,884 Two tense forms and the gerund of each of the irregular verbs *eo* and *queo* are listed continuously from now on in the text. Cf. the *Aeditio*: "Lyke wyse declyne *Queo*, and *Nequeo. Ista uerba præcedentia, uidelicet. Sum, Possum, Volo, Nolo, Malo, Fero, Feror, Edo, Fio, Queo, et Nequeo sunt anomala*" (D1ᵛ).

184,889 Specified substitution rules are applied to convert one complete form of a verb into another by deleting or substituting letters or syllables. This method of studying verb morphology is used in addition to the paradigms. It is also based on the assumption that the word is a unity: one complete word-form generates another. Cf. Law (1990), 62–63, also p. 227, note to line 67 above. This passage can be explained like this: From the perfect tense of the indicative mood (*amaui*) are formed the pluperfect tense of the same mood (*amaueram*); the perfect and pluperfect subjunctive and the future perfect tense of the indicative moods (*amauerim, amauissem, amauero*); and the perfect and pluperfect tenses of the infinitive mood (*amauisse*): *amaueram, amauerim, amauissem, amauero, amauisse; -ram, -rim, -ro* by changing *-i-* into *-e-*; *-sem, -se* keeping *-i-* still. The order of the endings has been changed to fit with the memory hints. The rules on the formation of tenses from the perfect indicative are also found in the *Aeditio* after the discussion of defective verbs on D3ʳ, where "coniunctyue" is listed as a mood. This method of forming tenses by specified substitution rules had already been employed in the English grammatical manuscripts; see, for example, Thomson, *Edition*, Text D, 39, 365–79 (*Accedence* MS): "How many tymes be formed of the furst person of the tyme that is fullych a-goo of the indicatyf mode? Thre. Whych thre? The tyme that is more than a-passed in the same mode, the tyme that is parfetly a-passyd in the coniunctyf mode, and the tyme that is to come of the same mode; as *amaui*, chaungyth the *I* into an *E*, thenne hyt schall be *amaue*, sette ther-to *-ram* and thenne hyt is *amaueram*; or sette ther-to a *-rim* and thenne hyt is *amauerim*; or sette ther-to a *-ro* and thenne hyt is *amauero* [etc.]."

184,896 *Impersonals be declyned in the voyce of the third person*: See *OED*, voice, *sb.* 5. *Gram.* one or other of the modes of inflecting or varying a verb according to the distinctions of *active, passive*, or *middle*. The impersonal verb in English is formed with "this sygne it", whereby a term is employed that is well-known, in the tradition of the elementary Latin grammars in the vernacular, for rendering Latin into English. The declension of impersonal verbs is not given in Colet's grammar. On impersonal verbs see Rissanen (1999), 249–52.

184,901 The participle is defined in terms of form. Its definition refers to the noun and the accidents shared with it, then follow the accidents it has in common with the verb, *i.e.* tense and signification, and finally those accidents follow that it shares with both noun and verb. Colet's definition first lists the accidents it shares with the verb, then follows the accident case that it has in common with the noun. The accidents that are shared by the two parts of speech are missing in his definition: "A Participle cometh deryued of a verbe and hath in sygnificacyon moche the maner of his verbe that he cometh of and is declyned with case as a nowne" (D3^r). See Michael (1970), 76; also Vorlat (1975), 351–52, for the definition given in the copy of the 1567 edition.

184,904 The list of the tenses of the participle is not given in Colet's grammar. But see, for example, Stanbridge's *Accidence*, which distinguishes between "a participul of the fyrste futyr. Another of the latter futyr" (C2$^{r–v}$).

185,906 The four tenses of the participle are identified according to their endings. For the present and past participle the text gives the English and the Latin endings, as well as examples in the two languages. This is followed by the rules on their formation. For the future tenses the Latin endings and their meanings are provided, illustrated in the two languages. Finally the rules on their formation are given. The above order of the tenses (line 904) is not observed: the participle of the first future is discussed before the past participle, an inconsistency which probably goes back to the use of different source texts when this text was compiled (cf. p. 238, note to line 889). See, for example, Colet's *Aeditio*, D3$^{r–v}$, where the active and the passive verb are the starting-point for the formation of two participles of each tense. In the present text the tenses of the participle are formed according to substitution rules; see also note to line 889 above.

185,929 The discussion of the deponent and the common verb is not found in such detail in the *Aeditio* (D3^v).

if the verbe deponent gouern an accusatiue case after him (line 931): That is a deponent verb which takes the accusative case. See also *OED*, govern, *v.* 11. *Grammar*. On government see p. 243 below, note to line 2, on the text on *Construction*.

185,936 The rules on the declension of the participle are not given in Colet's grammar.

185,941 In the definition of the adverb mention is only made of the part of speech of the verb to which the adverb is joined and which it limits. A similar definition in more detail is given in Colet's *Aeditio*: "An aduerbe is a parte that accompanyeth the verbe and declared the maner and the

circunstans of the doynge or of þe suffryng of the verbe: as sayenge. *Amo,
I loue.* This maye I saye that I do it in tyme: as *Amo hodie*" (D5ʳ). See Michael
(1970), 74; cf. also Vorlat (1975) on the 1567 copy, 367–68, and 372.

185,943 The twenty-four different classes of adverbs are listed
according to semantic criteria. Latin examples are provided to illustrate
each class. A list of twenty adverbs is found in the *Aeditio* where they
are discussed seriatim, each illustrated by a short Latin sentence (D5ʳ).
In Stanbridge's *Accidence* they are listed in question-and-answer form, in
most cases in Latin (C3ᵛ–C4ʳ). Lists similar to the present text are given in
Holt's *Lac puerorum* (C6ᵛ–C7ʳ) and Linacre's *Progymnasmata* (b4ᵛ–b5ʳ) and his
Rudimenta grammatices (E4ᵛ–F1ʳ). In the grammatical manuscripts the
adverb is dealt with rather briefly, except for Thomson, *Edition*, Text D, 40,
384–86 (*Accedence* MS), where a reference to the *Donet* (a medieval version
of Donatus's *Ars minor*) is given: "The significacions of the aduerbe be
diuerse for summe be aduerbes of place, and summe of tyme, as the
'Donet' declareth." Schoolmasters probably found the classified lists of
adverbs more useful for teaching purposes than its definition. See Michael
(1970), 66, and his brief comment on the lists of adverbs, 103. Similar lists
can also be found for conjunctions and interjections (see the following
note to line 970, and also p. 241, note to line 1030 below).

186,970 The discussion of the conjunction receives the smallest space of
all the parts of speech in the present text. In the definition the joining
of words and sentences is given equal emphasis. Cf. the almost identical
definition of Colet's grammar: "A Coniunccyon is that byndeth wordes
and sentences togyder" (D5ᵛ). See Michael (1970), 64.

186,972 The twelve classes of conjunctions, for which Latinized terms
are given, are listed according to semantic criteria. They are illustrated
by Latin examples. Cf. also Stanbridge's *Accidence* (C4ᵛ–C5ʳ), Holt's *Lac
puerorum* (C7ᵛ), Linacre's *Progymnasmata* (b5ᵛ) and his *Rudimenta grammatices*
(F1ʳ). Colet's *Aeditio*, on the other hand, presents the conjunctions in a
way which is easier for the schoolboy to learn and to remember. For
copulatives and electives, for example, it says: "Coniunccions some
couple: as *Et, que, atque.* Some betoken choyse: as *quam. Malo diues esse quam
pauper*" (D5ᵛ). Cf. Vorlat's (1975) comment based on the copy of the 1567
edition, 388–89, and 396.

proin (line 979): an abbreviated form for *proinde.*

187,985 The preposition is defined according to syntactic criteria and is
a prefix in word-formation. Part of it is identical to Priscian, *Institutiones
grammaticae, GL* III (1859), 24, 13–14. Cf. Vorlat (1975), 402. The accident
"figure" (shape) identifies simple and compound words. Cf. also
p. 229, note to line 226 above. The distinction between separable and
inseparable forms is a characteristic of the preposition which can already
be found in Donatus's *Ars maior* and *Ars minor;* see the definitions in
Appendix V. The *Aeditio* provides more details: "A Preposicyon is a parte

of speche put before other wordes: other [*sic*] ioyneth to the wordes in compoundes: as *Indoctus*, or a soundre from þe wordes: as *Coram deo*, determining them to the accusatyf case/ or to þe ablatyf case/ or to bothe" (D5ᵛ); see Michael (1970), 67.

187,988 The text lists prepositions taking the accusative or the ablative case in tables and provides their English equivalents. The *Aeditio*, on the other hand, lists a larger number of Latin expressions by using prepositions taking one or the other case, but does not give their English translations (D5ᵛ–D6ʳ).

187,1001 *Londinum uersus*: The text draws attention to the word order of two Latin prepositions. The place name adds some local colour and indicates where the grammar was most probably compiled.

187,1018 Each of the four prepositions is illustrated by two Latin phrases, one indicating the accusative and the other the ablative case. For this rule the *Aeditio* only lists the prepositions "*Sub, Super, Subter*" (D6ʳ) without any examples.

188,1028 The definition of the interjection uses psychological criteria outside the terms of formal grammar. This part of speech lacks the syntactic relation with the rest of the sentence in which it is used. For the expression "*which betokeneth a passion of the mynde*" see *OED*, passion, *sb.*, 6. a. Any kind of feeling by which the mind is powerfully affected or moved. Cf. the different definition using the same criteria in Colet's *Aeditio*: "An interieccyon is a sounde or a voyce that brasteth out in speche betokenynge the affeccyon of the mynde" (D6ᵛ). See Michael (1970), 80–81. Cf. also Vorlat (1975), 410, on the 1567 copy.

188,1030 The text provides a larger number of interjections than the *Aeditio*, cf. D6ᵛ. Additional examples of interjections have been introduced by hand into the text: *0* as an interjection expressing exclamation (line 1038), and *heus, o*, as examples for interjections of calling (line 1041). They provide evidence suggesting that this copy of the grammar was actually used for teaching purposes.

GODLY LESSONS FOR CHILDREN

189,1 See Plate 7, p. 153 for the beginning of this text. The Oxford proof leaf of *c*.1540 (Plate 10, see p. 262) only includes the first fifteen lines of the English and Latin sentences, seven of which are incomplete. The 1542 text has been transcribed in Blach (1909), 45: 87–89. On *Vulgaria* see John Stanbridge (1519), *The Vulgaria of John Stanbridge and the Vulgaria of Robert Whittinton*, ed. White (1971 repr.), xxxvii–lxi; Nelson (1952), 121–23; William E. Miller (1963), 165; and Orme (1973), 98–100. For the first proverb given here see Whiting K100; Tilley K175; and *ODEP*, 435.

189,4 This proverb is recorded in Whiting B194.

189,6 Recorded in Whiting M235.

189,8 This sentence goes back to 1 John 1,8. For the Latin version (line 9) of this and the following sentences from the Bible see *Biblia Sacra iuxta Vulgatam Versionem*. Ed. Robert Weber *et al.* (1969; repr. 1983).

189,10 John 3,16.

189,14 John 1,29.

189,16 Acts 4,12.

189,19 John 14,21.

189,21 John 15,14.

189,23 John 13,34.

189,26 Romans 2,13.

189,30 Exodus 20,12; Deuteronomy 5,16.

189,33 This command shares the general tenor of the royal proclamation, the letter to the reader, and also the hexastichon.

189,38 Exodus 22,22.

189,40 *vpbrayed*: See *OED*, upbraid, *v.* I. 2. To reproach, reprove, censure (a person, etc.). See Exodus 22,21.

190,46 The Latin proverb is recorded in Walther 36062.

190,50 For the Latin proverb see Walther 39912.

190,57 *whome thou mayste doo for*: See *OED*, do, *v.* B. V. 38. do for. a. To act for or in behalf of; to manage or provide for; to attend to. Now *colloq.*

190,62 For the Latin proverb cf. Walther 34706a.

190,66 For the Latin proverb see Walther 44445b.

190,67 *delycates*: See *OED*, delicate, *n.* B. 2. A thing that gives pleasure (usually in *pl.*): †a. *gen.* A luxury, delight. *Obs.*

190,72 See Plate 8, p. 154, for the last part of this text. For the Latin proverb cf. Walther 44296c8.

190,77 *to be more ware*: See *OED*, ware, *v.*[1] †1. *intr.* To give heed, take care, be on one's guard.

190,81 *to be moche sette by*: See *OED*, set, *v.*[1] VII. 91. c. To "esteem or value highly, think or make much of". *Obs.* exc. *arch.* or *dial.* For this proverb see Whiting T322.

190,83 Recorded in Whiting T504; Tilley T580; and *ODEP*, 844.

191,85 For this proverb cf. Tilley L217. *yea*: See *OED*, yea, *adv. (sb.)* Now *dial.* and *arch.* A. †2. Used as an ordinary adverb directly qualifying a clause or word: even, truly, verily. *Obs.*

191,87 The proverb in English is recorded in Whiting L222; Tilley L217; and *ODEP*, 457. For the Latin version, cf. Walther 38206k.

191,89 *scape*: See *OED*, scape, *v.*[1] 1. = Escape *v.*

CONSTRUCTION OF THE PARTS OF SPEECH

192,2 The beginning of this text (see Plate 8, p. 154) is concerned with the grammatical relations between single words in the discussion of the three concords; this also applies for the case grammar that discusses the rules on government which follows next. The rules on concord apply to individual constructions. For example, in the noun adjective relationship, as in *amicus certus*, they deal with the agreement between the adjective and the noun that it modifies according to case, number, and gender. In the early printed grammars and grammatical manuscripts the rules on concord (agreement) are often added at the end of the treatises on accidence; see, for example, the early printed grammars of the *Long Accidence* (*Early Printed Editions*, Text A, 164, 659–75) (*Checklist* 14.1), the *Short Accidence* (*Early Printed Editions*, Text I, 227, 94–100, p. 228, 101–107) (*Checklist* 15.1), also the grammatical manuscripts in Thomson, *Edition*, Text A, 8, 331–45 (*Accedence* MS; *Checklist* 5) and Thomson, *Edition*, Text C, 31, 617–52 (*Accedence* MS; *Checklist* 7). These rules are also found embedded in treatises on accidence see Thomson, *Edition*, Text G, 51, 32–40 (*Accedence* MS), and in Stanbridge's *Accidence* (*Checklist* 16.1), where they are discussed at the end of the section on the verb on C2[r]. In Holt's *Lac puerorum* they are given detailed treatment at the beginning of the part on syntax (E2[v]–E5[r]), and in Lily's *Rudimenta grammatices*, they are discussed after the impersonal verb (E1[r]–E3[r]). In Linacre's English grammars *Progymnasmata* (C4[r]–C5[r]) and *Rudimenta grammatices* (G2[r]–G3[v]) the three concords are denominated in the heading by the syntactic term "Of intransityue construction" (*Progymnasmata*). The grammatical tradition also offers four or even five concords. Four concords are listed in Thomson, *Edition*, Text EE, 178, 26–115 (*Other* MS), where the last reads: "the fourthe bytwene the noune partytyf, the noune dystributyf, the noune of superlatyf degre, and the genityf case that folweth" (lines 29–31) (*Checklist* 41). Five concords are given in Thomson, *Edition*, Text A, 8, 334–36, where the fourth and fifth concords read: "þe iiij betwen þe nowne partytyue and þe genitiue case þat folus, þe v betwene þe superlatyue degre and þe genitiue case þat folus" (*Accedence* MS). On the category of concord see Michael's (1970) comment, 132–33.

192,6 This passage teaching the children how to construe a Latin sentence by starting from "an englysshe", *i.e.* an English sentence that has to be turned into Latin, is included here before the discussion on concord continues. It introduces children to the method of identifying the English constituents and their functions in order to give them their proper Latin forms. It starts from the main verb in the sentence and moves on to the nominative case (we would use the concept of subject as distinct from the case that marks it). This section which refers to the process of translation was present in texts in the grammatical tradition. See *Certayne Briefe Rules* (A2^{r-v}) (*Checklist* 52.1), Lily's *Rudimenta grammatices* (D7^{r-v}) (*Checklist* 51.3), *Long Parvula* (a1^r) (*Checklist* 48.2); *Parvula* (A1^v) (*Checklist* 49.1); *Parvulorum Institutio* (A2^r) (*Checklist* 50.1); also in the grammatical manuscripts, e.g. in Thomson, *Edition*, Text W, 105, 5–18 (*Informacio* MS; *Checklist* 28). Cf. Walmsley (2004), vol. 2: 463.

192,11 Though the children are asked to analyse an English sentence in order to parse it and translate it into Latin, the text lists Latin conjunctions first, as if the children had to analyse the sentence in Latin.

192,14 The relative pronoun "Whiche" is used as an equivalent to a demonstrative pronoun for the purpose of linking this sentence together with the preceding one, which is a characteristic of an English construction modelled on the Latin. The text also comments on word order in interrogative sentences. In the first example it points out that the Latin nominative is set after the verb, which is repeated in the vernacular (line 16). The Latin sentence including the negative particle *ne*, however, is rendered in English with the "sygne of the verbe" "doeth" preceding the nominative and the verb.

192,19 The rule of the first Latin concord is illustrated by an example in English where most of the endings of the verb were lost at that time. The discussion on the hierarchy of "person" in Latin is found in the tradition of the earlier grammars. See, for example, in more detail and with illustrative examples, the discussion of the second rule of Lily's *Rudimenta grammatices* (E2^v). The adjective "worthy" in a grammatical sense is not recorded in either *OED* or *MED*.

192,24 This rule and also the Latin examples are covered in *Certayne Briefe Rules*, under the heading "Conception of persons" (Bodl. Lib., Douce G 359, A2^v–A3^r) (*Checklist* 52.1), and the Latin treatise Lily, *Libellus de constructione* (1513), A2^{r-v}; see Appendix IV, 1.

whiche verbe plurall (line 25): The relative pronoun is used for a demonstrative pronoun. See note to line 14 above.

192,32 Amantium irę amoris redintegratio est: Adapted from Terence, *Andria*, 555. (*LCL, vol. 22*).

Quid enim nisi uota supersunt? (line 33): Ovid, *Tristia*, I.2,1 (*LCL*, vol. 151).

The text shows the then newer practice of citing sentences from classical authors in the same way as some of the other Latin grammatical treatises in English that preceded it. But like them, it also uses many of its own examples that had been made up by its compilers or used those which had been found in their sources.

193,39 *A sure frende is tried in a doubtfull matter,* Amicus certus in re incerta cernitur: The Latin sentence was adapted from Cicero *De amicitia*, XVII.64 (*LCL*, vol. 154).

193,44 For the traditional hierarchy of "gender" see, for example, the explanations in Lily's *Rudimenta grammatices* (E2ʳ). Cf. *Certayne Briefe Rules*, "Conception of genders" (A3ᵛ). In John Holt's *Lac puerorum* these rules are summarized as follows: "For lyke as the fyrst persone is more worthy than the seconde or þe thyrde so is the masculyne more worthy than the feminyne or the neutre" (E3ᵛ).

193,51 *Whan ye haue a relatyue:* i.e. a relative pronoun. This rule is covered in *Certayne Briefe Rules* (A3ᵛ). Cf. Lily's more detailed explanation in *Rudimenta grammatices*: "The antecedent is a worde goynge before þe relatyue/ and answereth to this questyon who/ or what rehersed wᵗ þe verbe. as I loue Edwarde/ whiche techeth me. This worde Edwarde is þe antecedent for it answereth to this questyon. who techeth" (D8ʳ).

193,56 For this passage see *Certayne Briefe Rules* (A3ᵛ–A4ʳ). It is not found in Lily's *Rudimenta grammatices*. On these relative pronouns see Rissanen (1999), 293–96. Before the children are taught the rules on how to form a sentence with the accusative with infinitive construction, which the text says to be more elegant and reflect classical use, they first have to give a literal translation of the English sentence into Latin with the conjunction *quod* with the indicative. However, there are no further remarks about the specific verbs and expressions on which the construction of the accusative with infinitive depends. For this rule see, for example, the grammatical manuscript, Thomson, *Edition*, Text LL, 216, 101–10 (*Other* MS; *Checklist* 47).

193,62 The gender of the relative pronoun and the adjective is determined by the sense and not by the form of the antecedent or noun of the most 'worthy' gender. For this rule and also the Latin example in line 70 see *Certayne Briefe Rules* (A4ʳ). Cf. p. 244, note to line 19.

193,73 The different constructions of the relative case represent familiar subject matter in the grammatical tradition. See *Certayne Briefe Rules* (A4ᵛ), which provides the same Latin examples; Lily's *Rudimenta grammatices* (D8ʳ⁻ᵛ); also the grammatical manuscripts, e.g. Thomson, *Edition*, Text W, 105, 32–39 (*Informacio* MS; *Checklist* 28).

194,79 *Happie is he, whom other mennes harmes do make to beware,* Felix quem faciunt aliena pericula cautum: For the English version see Tilley M612. The Latin proverb is recorded in Walther 36887a.

194,80 The construction of a relative pronoun between two nouns of different gender that refer to the same thing is also found in *Certayne Briefe Rules* (A4ʳ); it can be traced back to the grammatical manuscripts, e.g. Thomson, *Edition*, Text Y, 122, 34–42 (*Informacio* MS; *Checklist* 30).

194,84 On the construction of these interrogative pronouns see *Certayne Briefe Rules* (A4ᵛ); also Lily's *Rudimenta grammatices* (D8ᵛ).

194,88 This section on government comprises the discussion of case grammar, which is organized around the eight parts of speech, beginning with the noun and the specific cases it requires. Government discusses the presence or particular form of a word when it is constructed with another, whereby the governed element is always a noun, a pronoun, or a participle functioning as a noun. A noun, for example, requires the genitive case, as in *Facundia Ciceronis*. The English construction, on the other hand, takes the preposition "of". On the genitive case see also *Certayne Briefe Rules* (A4ᵛ–A5ʳ); and Linacre, *Progymnasmata* (c5ᵛ–c6ʳ), and his *Rudimenta grammatices* (G4ʳ⁻ᵛ).

194,92 The text means that the word in apposition agrees in case with the principal word. This rule is found in *Certayne Briefe Rules* (A5ᵛ). See also Holt's summary in his treatise *Lac puerorum*: "Therfore it is comenly sayd/ that all þat longeth to one thynge shall be putte in one case/ as my fader a man loueth me a chylde. Pater meus vir diligit me puerum" (E3ᵛ–E4ʳ). The text treats apposition as part of the syntax of substantives. See Michael (1970), 136.

194,97 *Many thynges haue letted me*: OED, let, *v.*² arch. 1. *trans.* to hinder, prevent, obstruct, stand in the way (of a person, etc.). This rule and the two Latin examples are also included in *Certayne Briefe Rules* (A5ᵛ). In Lily's *Rudimenta grammatices* the same rule reads as follows: "An adiectyue standyng without a substantiue shal be put in the neutre gendre substantyuate: as It is good. *Bonum est.* Lykewyse yf this worde *Res.* come after an adiectyue: as a delectable thynge. *Delectabile*" (E2ᵛ).

194,98 The noun adjective can also govern oblique cases. When it takes the genitive case the rule in Lily's *Rudimenta grammatices* reads as follows: "Some adiectyues put in the neutre gendre mai turne theyr substantyues into the genityue case. Of his kynde be they that answere to this question. how moche. *Quantum.* as *Multum, plus, plurimum, nihil, parum.* [. . .]" (E2ᵛ).

194,102 The rule on the ablativus qualitatis or genitivus qualitatis had previously appeared in *Certayne Briefe Rules* (A5ʳ). It can be traced back to the grammatical manuscripts, e.g. Thomson, *Edition*, Text BB, 153, 238–43 (*Formula* MS; *Checklist* 35).

towardnesse (line 104): see Commentary: To the Reader, p. 223, note to line 61.

194,105 Cf. *Certayne Briefe Rules*: "Opus et vsus for nede, requireth an ablatiue case" (A5ᵛ).

194,110 This passage on the construction of adjectives that require the genitive case due to their specific meaning also represents traditional material. See, for example, Linacre's *Progynasmata*, c6ʳ, also his *Rudimenta grammatices* (H1ʳ).

195,115 For this rule see *Certayne Briefe Rules* (A5^v–A6^r). The ordinal numbers which take the genitive case are listed in Linacre's *Progymnasmata* (c6^v); see also his *Rudimenta grammatices* (H1^r).

195,131 The rule of comparative nouns taking the ablative case is found in *Certayne Briefe Rules* (A5^v); in Linacre's *Progymnasmata* (d1^r), and also in his *Rudimenta grammatices* (H2^r). In the *Introduction* the rule is continued by hand as follows: "and some tyme two: as, *Doctior mé multo.*" The manuscript addition means that a noun of the comparative degree can take two ablatives: an *ablativus comparationis*, "*mé*", and an *ablativus qualitatis*, "*multo*". The addition suggests that this copy was actually used in teaching and that this particular rule was dealt with in detail. A comparison of hands shows that the addition was probably made by Richard Cox who was appointed tutor to the young Prince Edward. For a specimen of Cox's handwriting see *Autograph Letters of Reformers and Martyrs, 1536–1569*. Letter no. 92, by Richard Cox, 3 Maij 1566 (BL, MS Royal 19,400, G3^r). See also pp. 86–87 above.

195,135 Semantic properties of parts of speech are taken into consideration to classify grammatical relations; e.g. adjectives denoting profit, likeness, pleasure, etc., take the dative case. They are also discussed in this way in *Certayne Briefe Rules* (A6^v); in Linacre's *Progymnasmata* (c6^v), and in his *Rudimenta grammatices* (H1^v).

disprofitte: See *OED*, disprofit, *n. Obs.* or *arch.* The opposite of profit; disadvantage, detriment.

195,144 The rules for adjectives of measure taking the accusative or ablative cases represent traditional material and are found in *Certayne Briefe Rules* (with the last two Latin examples) (A7^r); in Linacre's *Progymnasmata* (c6^v–d1^r); cf. also his *Rudimenta grammatices* (H1^v–H2^r), on examples formed with the accusative case. The rules can be traced back to the grammatical manuscripts, e.g.: "*Tribus pedibus* is the ablatif case, for euery adiectif betokenyng mesure may gouern an ablatif case. [Verses:] *Mobile mensuram designans addito sexto:* | *Lignum sex pedibus longum latumque duobus.*" See Thomson, *Edition*, Text BB, 155, 318–21 (*Formula* MS; *Checklist* 35).

196,152 Crura thymo plena: Adapted from Virgil, *Georgics*, IV.181 (*LCL*, vol. 63).

Stultorum plena sunt omnia (line 153): Cicero, *Ad familiares*, IX.22,4 (*LCL, vol. 216*).

Integer uitẹ sceleris'que purus (line 154): Horace, *Odes*, I.22,1 (*LCL*, vol. 33). See also p. 95 above. The text does not give English translations of the Latin passages at this point. Translations in the vernacular or illustrations of words are not provided systematically, but more or less *ad hoc. Certayne Briefe Rules* (with the first three Latin examples) (A6^r), Linacre's *Progymnasmata* (c6^r), and his *Rudimenta grammatices* (G4^v), cover these rules. They are also found in the grammatical manuscripts; see, for example, Thomson, *Edition*, Text BB, 153, 236–42 (*Formula* MS).

196,160 Compared to preceding grammatical treatises the construction of the pronoun is dealt with very briefly. Cf. this passage in *Certayne Briefe Rules* (A7^{r-v}). Part of it, in almost identical wording, is given in Lily, *Libellus de constructione* (1513) (D4^{r-v}). It is discussed in detail in Linacre's *Progymnasmata* (d1^v–d2^v).

196,169 *verbes of behauiour or gesture:* The text classifies verbs by the cases they govern and labels the resulting classes with semantic epithets. These rules are also covered in *Certayne Briefe Rules* (with most of the Latin examples) (A7^v–A8^r).

196,175 This rule on the auxiliary verb "*Sum*", which governs the genitive case, is given in Lily, *Libellus de constructione* (1513), which also contains the first example (A3^v). It is also found in Linacre's *Progymnasmata* (d5^v).

196,179 For verbs denoting esteem or regard that require the genitive case see the treatise *Certayne Briefe Rules*, where "or an ablatiue seldome" is added (A8^v–B1^r); also Lily, *Libellus de constructione* (1513) (A4^{r-v}). The two Latin examples are also given in the latter grammar.

196,181 The text does not give English translations at this point. For this rule on Latin verbs denoting accusing, condemning, etc., which take the genitive case see also *Certayne Briefe Rules* (A8^v). Cf. also Lily, *Libellus de constructione* (1513) (A5^v).

196,187 Miserere mei deus: Gives the beginning of Psalm 50,3 (Bible, Vulgate version). For "*miseret et cetera*" see Lily, *Libellus de constructione* (1513) (A6^r). The text does not provide English translations of the Latin passages.

197,190 The text goes back to provide English translations for most of the Latin examples. In the treatise *Certayne Briefe Rules* the verbs treated here are listed under the heading "Diuerse casis" (B1^r); see also Lily, *Libellus de constructione* (1513) (A6^v); Linacre's *Progymnasmata* (d6^r) and his *Rudimenta grammatices* (I1^r). The verbs "*egeo*" and "*indigeo*" are discussed in Linacre's *Progymnasmata* (d5^v) and his *Rudimenta grammatices* (H4^v).

197,194 *All maner of verbes put acquisitiuely:* These verbs, which govern the dative case, are neuter verbs and have a descriptive label in that they are called "acquisitive". See also *Certayne Briefe Rules* (B1^r). Cf. the passage "*Datiuus post verbum*" in Lily, *Libellus de constructione* (1513), where the two Latin examples of the present tense are also found (B1^r).

197,198 The text shows eight groups of Latin verbs in the first person singular that are arranged in tabular form. All of them take the dative case in Latin, whereas in English they are rendered with the prepositions "to" or "of". Each group consists of three verbs of which at least two exhibit synonymy; in some cases one of the three verbs gives the contrary meaning. Their English translations are provided in a separate line preceding each group. This arrangement indicates a pedagogical device to make learning these verbs easier for the pupils. Cf. the explanation of "Verbes put acquisitiuely, with to, for [etc.]" and the three columns of verbs in *Certayne Briefe Rules* (B1ʳ⁻ᵛ). Some of the same Latin verbs are used as illustrative examples in the chapter entitled "*Acquisitiua*" in Lily, *Libellus de constructione* (1513) (B1ʳ–B2ʳ).

197,212 The abbreviation for "*ante*" should read "*añ*" in the original. For these prepositions functioning as prefixes to verbs and for illustrative examples see also Lily, *Libellus de constructione* (1513), B3ᵛ–B4ᵛ.

197,219 *Verbes transitiues, are all such as haue after them an accusatiue case of the sufferer*: See *MED*, sufferer(e *n*., (b) one who is acted upon; *gram*. a noun or its substitute denoting that on or toward which the action of the verb is directed. The term 'accusatiue case of the sufferer' is assigned on purely semantic grounds. It can be traced back to the grammatical manuscripts, e.g. Thomson, *Edition*, Text X, 111, 2–7 (*Informacio* MS; *Checklist* 31): "I schall reherse myne Englysche onys, ij or iij, and loke owt my principall verbe and loke whether (he) betoken 'to do' or 'to suffer' or 'to be'; and yf he betokyn 'to do' þe doyr schall be þe nominatiff case to þe verbe and þe sufferer schall be suche case as þe verbe wyll haue after hym."

Endimionis somnum dormis (line 223): Adapted from Cicero, *De finibus*, V.20,55 (*LCL*, vol. 40).

197,224 *Verbes of askynge, teachyng, and arrayeng*: Verbs are allotted to subclasses depending on what case or set of cases they govern to the right. See *MED*, arraien, *v*. 3. (a) To equip (sb.), fit out, provide (with sth.); to arm. The example of the text illustrates the meaning 'disarray'. For this rule see also *Certayne Briefe Rules*, where four of the illustrative verbs are covered (A8ʳ⁻ᵛ), Linacre's *Progymnasmata* (e1ʳ) and his *Rudimenta grammatices* (I2ʳ).

198,228 For verbs constructed with the *ablativus instrumentalis* and *ablativus causae* see *Certayne Briefe Rules* (B2ʳ); Lily, *Libellus de constructione* (1513) (C1ʳ⁻ᵛ), also Linacre's *Progymnasmata* (e1ᵛ–e2ʳ), and his *Rudimenta grammatices* (I2ᵛ–I3ʳ). The latter treatise only discusses the construction with the instrumental ablative.

198,231 For the word denoting price which is put after verbs in the ablative case see Linacre's *Progymnasmata* (e2ʳ), and his *Rudimenta grammatices* (I3ʳ).

198,236 The text also lists the rule on verbs of plenty and want, filling and depriving. The deponent verb "*vescor*" is added by hand to the lists of verbs (line 240). On H1ʳ many additions by hand occur within the text and in the margin that comment on the rules given here. Many of these insertions are only discernible under ultraviolet light. For this rule see also *Certayne Briefe Rules* (B2ʳ⁻ᵛ), and Lily, *Libellus de constructione* (1513) (C2ᵛ), with which it shares some examples.

198,241 For these verbs taking the ablative case cf. *Certayne Briefe Rules* (B2ᵛ), where the same examples are given.

198,245 For the rule on the *ablativus mensurae* see also Lily, *Libellus de constructione* (1513) (C1ᵛ–C2ʳ).

198,248 In Linacre's *Progymnasmata* this rule of the absolute ablative is entitled "The ablatyfe in consequence" (e4ʳ); see also his *Rudimenta grammatices* (I3ᵛ–I4ʳ).

198,256 The rule on the construction of passives is also given in the treatise *Certayne Briefe Rules* (B3ʳ); see also Lily, *Libellus de constructione* (1513), where it reads as follows: "*Passiuis additur ablatiuus agentis: sed accedente prepositione a/ vel ab*" (C3ʳ⁻ᵛ).

198,261 The rule on the cases which are required by the gerund (verbal noun) is also covered in *Certayne Briefe Rules* (B3ʳ), and Lily, *Libellus de constructione* (1513) (C4ʳ).

199,264 For the gerund (verbal noun) taking the genitive case in *-di* see *Certayne Briefe Rules* (B3ʳ⁻ᵛ); Lily, *Libellus de constructione* (1513) (C4ᵛ); also Linacre, *Progymnasmata* (e5ʳ), and his *Rudimenta grammatices* (I4ʳ).

199,271 The text starts from an English sentence to be turned into Latin, but only gives the result in Latin. For this rule see also Lily, *Libellus de constructione* (1513) (C4ᵛ–C5ʳ), Linacre's *Progymnasmata* (e5ᵛ), and his *Rudimenta grammatices* (I4ᵛ). For the gerund in *-do*, used after verbs with or without a preposition (lines 278–80), cf. *Certayne Briefe Rules* (B3ᵛ).

199,282 The text implies that an analysis of an English sentence had taken place before the Latin sentence was construed. Examples are provided illustrating the use of the gerund in *-dum*. See also *Certayne Briefe Rules* (B3ᵛ–B4ʳ); Lily, *Libellus de constructione* (1513) (C4ᵛ); Linacre's *Progymnasmata* (e5ᵛ), and his *Rudimenta grammatices* (I4ʳ⁻ᵛ).

199,293 For the rules on the first and second supines see *Certayne Briefe Rules* (B4ʳ); Lily, *Libellus de constructione* (1513) (C5ʳ⁻ᵛ); Linacre's *Progymnasmata* (e5ᵛ–e6ʳ), and for the supine in *-tu* only, his *Rudimenta grammatices* (I4ᵛ–K1ʳ).

200,303 The rule on the *ablativus temporis* is also found in *Certayne Briefe Rules* (B4ᵛ); Lily, *Libellus de constructione* (1513) (B6ʳ⁻ᵛ); Linacre's *Progymnasmata* (e2ᵛ–e3ʳ), and his *Rudimenta grammatices* (I3ʳ).

For *terme of time* (line 304) see *OED*, term, *sb*. II. 4. *transf*. a. A portion of time having definite limits; a period; duration, length of time.

200,308 For this rule see also *Certayne Briefe Rules* (B5ʳ); also the section entitled "*Spacium loci*" in Lily, *Libellus de constructione* (1513) (B6ᵛ), where the same Latin example is given.

200,312 For the rule on the *ablativus loci* see also *Certayne Briefe Rules*, where some of the rules are explained in the same wording in English. This treatise also covers the examples "*Venio per Galliam in Italiam. Viuo in Italia, proficiscitur ex Italia*, [etc.]" (B5ʳ⁻ᵛ); the rule is also given in Linacre, *Progymnasmata* (e2ᵛ).

200,331 The text starts from the construction of the impersonal verb in English with the word "It", but does not provide any example in the vernacular. Impersonal verbs are those which occur only in the third person singular. They are arranged here according to the cases they require. On the impersonal verb in English see Rissanen (1999), 249–52. For the construction of the impersonal verb with the different cases cf. *Certayne Briefe Rules* (B6ʳ⁻ᵛ); also Linacre, *Progymnasmata* (e3ʳ⁻ᵛ). In Lily's *Rudimenta grammatices* the English impersonal verbs are roughly classified into three different groups, following semantic considerations, with their Latin equivalents (verbs indicating mental processes or states, those indicating events or happenings, and also those relating to the weather) (D8ᵛ–E1ʳ).

201,345 The text shows how to change a neuter verb, which represents one of the five genders into which a personal verb can be divided, into an impersonal verb. A neuter verb is a verb which ends in -*o* but does not form a passive in -*or*, e.g. *fleo*, 'cry', *vivo*, 'I live'. On the construction of neuter verbs see Linacre's *Rudimenta grammatices* (H3ᵛ–H4ᵛ). The Latin example, *In ignem posita est, fletur* (line 347), is adapted from Terence, *Andria*, 129. As the compositor was dependent upon his copy and had to fit a previously allocated body of text onto this page he has saved space by setting the chapter heading, "*A Participle*", at the end of the discussion of "Impersonalles". A chapter mark before this chapter heading should have helped to draw attention to the beginning of the discussion of the construction of the participle.

201,348 The rule for the cases that are taken by participles of different tenses can be found in Lily, *Libellus de constructione* (1513) (C5ᵛ), which also contains two identical examples. See also Linacre's *Progymnasmata* (e3ᵛ), and his *Rudimenta grammatices* (I3ᵛ).

201,350 For the four ways of participles being changed into nouns see also Lily, *Libellus de constructione* (1513) (C5ᵛ–C6ʳ). Cf. Linacre's *Progymnasmata* (e3ᵛ–e4ʳ), where the introductory sentence reads: "Particyples when they lese þe signification of tyme chaynge in to nownes iiii. wayes."

201,360 This rule on participles turned into nouns is also given in Lily, *Libellus de constructione* (1513) (C5ᵛ–C6ʳ), where it reads: "*Cum transeunt in naturam nominum genitiuum postulant.*"

201,366 The text does not include any translations into English, or explanations in the vernacular in the discussion of the construction of the adverb. For adverbs taking the genitive case see also *Certayne Briefe Rules* (B7ʳ); Lily, *Libellus de constructione* (1513) (D5ʳ⁻ᵛ), Linacre's *Progymnasmata* (e6ʳ⁻ᵛ), and his *Rudimenta grammatices* (K2ʳ).

201,368 For adverbs being followed by the dative case see *Certayne Briefe Rules*, where the same examples are listed (B7ᵛ); also Lily, *Libellus de constructione* (1513) (D5ᵛ–D6ʳ).

201,372 For particular adverbs taking the accusative case this rule in Lily, *Libellus de constructione* (1513) reads: "*Sunt que accusandi casum admittunt prepositionis vnde sunt profecta*" (D6ʳ). It is illustrated by the same two examples.

202,377 The text does not provide translations into the vernacular or any explanation of the construction of the conjunction. On the construction of copulative and disiunctive conjunctions see Linacre, *Progymnasmata*, e6ᵛ-f1ʳ, and his *Rudimenta grammatices*, K2ʳ⁻ᵛ.

202,381 For the construction of these conjunctions with verbs in the same as well as in different moods and tenses cf. Linacre, *Progymnasmata*, f1ʳ.

202,385 The text does not offer any vernacular equivalents in the discussion of the construction of the preposition. This rule discusses the *ablativus loci*; in this case "*loco*" illustrates the use of the ablative without "*in*".

vnderstanded (line 385): See *OED*, understand, *v*. The form used in the text is one of the three forms of the past participle that were then current. See (c) "the new form *understanded* (-*stonded*), very common from about 1530 to 1585".

202,391 As with the treatment of the adverb, conjunction, and preposition above, the discussion of the construction of the interjection gives no vernacular meanings for the Latin. For the different cases that are required by interjections, cf. Lily, *Libellus de constructione* (1513), E4ʳ⁻ᵛ, and also Linacre's *Progymnasmata*, e6ᵛ. See Plate 9 (p. 155) for the end of the text on construction.

CARMEN DE MORIBUS

204,1 A copy of this famous poem is contained in Lily's *Epigrammata*; see Appendix IV, 5. It is also included in John Colet's *Aeditio* of 1527, E5ᵛ-E7ʳ. The text of this edition has been printed in Blach (1909), 45: 75–77. The *Carmen de moribus* has also been issued together with later editions of Colet's *Aeditio* and Lily's *Rudimenta grammatices* (cf. *Checklist* 20.3–20.13, 51.5–51.16). The poem was also frequently reprinted in later, seventeenth and eighteenth century, editions of *A Short Introduction of Grammar*. A late eighteen-century prose version in English is given in Adamson (1919), 130–32.

204,9 uocarit: *i.e.* vocaverit.

204,17 attramentum: The double "t" indicates that the preceding "a" is long. For the spelling cf. also *OED*, atrament [ad. L. *atramentum* blacking, ink, f.]. The first example there, from Trevisa's translation of 1398 of Bartholomaeus Anglicus, *De proprietatibus rerum*, xix. xxxiii (1495), 879, reads: "Attrament is made of sote."

206,47 laudabere: *i.e.* laudaberis.

206,55 These lines show the contrast between those grammarians who wrote in medieval Latin, cf. the expressions "*grammaticastros*" (line 55), "*barbara turba*" (line 58), and those who used classical Latin "*turba latina*" (line 62), to whom the author of this poem claimed to belong. The usage of "*grammaticastros*" antedates the earliest recorded examples in R. E. Latham (1999 repr.), *Revised Medieval Latin Word-List from British and Irish Sources*, London, 214, *grammaticaster*, dated 1564, and *c.*1620, with the meaning "ignorant scholar"; and in the *OED*, [ad. med. L. *grammaticaster* "scriba, notarius"], meaning "a petty or inferior grammarian (used in contempt)". The first example is dated there to 1601.

loqui (line 60): This line should end with a comma because the full stop of the original interrupts the construction of the sentence.

206,69 pedibus ue: See also emes ue (line 75): This spelling is typical of this copy of the text. It may be due to the compositor or may have been taken from his copy.

206,72 exprobret (correction of "*exprobet*"): At this point Blach's (1909) edition corrects the text of the *Carmen* which follows Colet's *Aeditio* (1527), to "*improbat*" (p. 76, line 1767), where the original reads "*exprobet*" (E7ʳ). This reading in Colet as well as in the 1542 text is probably a typographical error for "*exprobret*". In his edition Blach makes a large number of changes in spelling, wording and even word order. (E.g. children (Blach (1908), 66: 1)—chyldren (Colet, *Aeditio*, A1ᵛ, line 1); them selfe (Blach (1908), 83: 425)—themselfe (Colet, B3ʳ, line 7); *Circum uicinum* (Blach (1909), 53: 1340)—*Circum uicinos* (Colet, D6ʳ, line 6); I come from my chambre: *edeo* [sic] *a cubiculo* (Blach (1909), 74: 1678–1679)—I come from my chambre *Redeo a cubiculo* (Lily, *Rudimenta grammatices* (1527), E5ʳ, lines 25–26); *Et quaecunque nobis reddis* (Blach (1909), 75, line 1736)—*Et quaecunque mihi reddis* (*Carmen de moribus* (1527), E6ᵛ, line 7); *Est medium uirtus quod tenuisse iuuat* (Blach (1909), 76, line 1743)—*Est uirtus medium quod tenuisse iuuat* (*Carmen de moribus* (1527), E6ᵛ, line 14).

CHRISTIANI HOMINIS INSTITUTUM

210,1 This poem was written by Erasmus at John Colet's request for his newly refounded school of St Paul's. Its first edition entitled *Institutum Christiani hominis carmine pro pueris. ab Erasmo compositum*, was published by Thierry Martens at Louvain in September 1514, in combination with Cato's *Distichs*, a collection of moral precepts in hexameter couplets put together in the second or third century, as well as various other moralizing works. The collection was entitled *Opuscula aliquot Erasmo Roterodamo castigatore*. See *CWE*, vol. 85, Introduction, xxv–xxvi. For a bibliographical description see Nijhoff-Kronenberg 534. This text has also been edited in *CWE*, vol. 85, no. 49: 92–107, with an English translation by C. H. Miller; with notes in vol. 86, no. 49: 505–509. On the publishing history of this poem see *CWE*, vol. 3, Ep. 298, p. 2, Introduction. A modern edition (with variants cited from editions up to 1518) is given by C. Reedijk (ed.) (1956). *The Poems of Desiderius Erasmus*. Leiden, no. 94: 307–13. Another modern edition of the text, as revised by Erasmus and printed at his request by Matthias Schürer in Strasburg in October 1515, is given in Ernst-Wilhelm Kohls (1971). *Der Katechismus des Erasmus von Rotterdam (1512/1513)*, in *Evangelische Katechismen der Reformationszeit*. Gütersloh, 21–26.

Ad Galatas 5. | Valet in Christo fides quæ per dilectionem operatur (lines 2 and 3): The text starts with the motto of the chapter to the Galatians (5,1–28). Colet's English text "The artycles of the fayth" preceding his *Aeditio* (1527) also begins with this motto (A2ʳ).

212,48 The order of The Seven Sacraments in this text varies from that of earlier editions. Here matrimony is listed in the first place, followed by baptism, confirmation, etc., whereas the sacrament of orders is discussed only in sixth place, followed by extreme unction. In the editions printed by Martens (1514) (ed. Reedijk (1956)), also in *CWE*, vol. 85, *Poems*, and Schürer (1515) (ed. Kohls (1971)), orders is listed as the first sacrament, followed by matrimony, baptism, confirmation, Holy Eucharist, penance, and extreme unction. The same sequence is also given in Colet, *The seuen sacraments*, preceding his *Aeditio* (1527), A2ᵛ. In contrast to the earlier editions, the wording of the present text on the sacrament of orders has also been revised. Cf. *CWE*, vol. 85, which reads: "*Ordine nanque sacro confertur sacra potestas | Ut fungare ministeriis CHRISTO auspice sanctis*", p. 96. On the revision of the sequence of the sacraments after the Reformation, see J. J. Scarisbrick (1997), *Henry VIII*, 410–18; on Erasmus's position towards religious life cf. McConica (1965), 22.

214,77 munisterijs: (Cf. "*ministeriis*" in the previous note). This word represents a cryptogram, an expression carrying a hidden meaning. The holy sacraments are *mysteria* (secrets) as well as *ministeria* (services) of the Church. But they can also be understood as *munera* (gifts) for the priests, a common usage which includes a criticism of the Catholic Church for taking money from the people for the sacraments (e.g. confession, marriage, etc.). See Franz Blatt (1928), 'Ministerium—Mysterium', 80–81.

216,133 fœdum ue, nocens ue: For this spelling see Commentary: *Carmen de Moribus*, p. 253, note to verse 69.

218,183 Hoc Fac Et Vives: Luke 10,28 is Christ's command with which the text ends. This postcript is also given at the end of Colet's *Aeditio* on A3ᵛ.

218,184 This edition of *An Introduction of the Eyght Partes of Speche* was printed by Thomas Berthelet at the sign of the Lucrece—the sign where he had his premises near the conduit in Fleet Street, from 1524 to 1546. His device, which occupies the whole page of I5ᵛ, shows Lucretia in flowing robes, within an architectural frame, stabbing herself. See McKerrow 80; *STC²*, vol. 3: 18–19, 237, 257; also *ODNB*, vol. 5: 480–81.

Cum priuilegio ad imprimendum solum (line 187): Under the terms of King Henry VIII's proclamation of 16 November 1538, the printers of English language books were obliged to submit their copy first to "some of his gracis priuie counsayle, or other suche as his highnes shall appoynte" to obtain a licence for printing, that may then be indicated by the words "Cum priuilegio regali". However, they were further obliged to add the words "ad imprimendum solum" to any such statement to clarify the limited extent and nature of the privilege. Henry granted various commercially advantageous privileges to different printers for specified texts for specified periods. A monopoly on printing the authorized grammar was a very valuable asset for Berthelet. Cf. W. W. Greg (1966). 'Ad imprimendum solum', 409–11. A version of this proclamation is given in Hughes and Larkin, vol. 1, no. 186: 270–76, at 271–72. See also Heinze (1976), 137–38, and Neville (1990), 198–99.

APPENDIX I

STRUCTURE AND CONTENTS OF *AN INTRODUCTION OF THE EIGHTE PARTES OF SPECHE AND THE CONCORDES OF LATYNE SPECHE*

The numbers in brackets refer to the page and line number of the opening line of each item.

An Introduction of the eighte partes of speche.

The four declinable and the four indeclinable parts of speech (161,5)

Noun: (161,7)
Definition (161,8)
Noun substantive and noun adjective (161,11)
Proper and common noun (161,21)
Number (singular and plural) (161,25)
Case (six cases) (162,28)
Articles (*hic, hęc, hoc*) (162,45)
Gender (seven genders) (162,53)
Declension of nouns (five declensions) (163,67)
Declension of adjectives (165,153)
Comparison (three degrees) (166,191)

Pronoun: (167,223)
Definition (167,224)
Fifteen pronouns and their compounds (167,226)
Primitives also called demonstratives (167,230)
Relatives (167,233)
Derivatives (167,235)
Accidents (five accidents) (167,237)
Declension (four declensions) (167,239)
Person (three persons) (169,318)

Verb: (169,325)
Definition (169,326)
Personal and impersonal verb (169,328)
Gender of personal verb (five genders) (169,331)
Mood (six moods) (170,343)
Tense (five tenses) (170,369)
Person (three persons) (171,381)
Conjugation (four conjugations) (171,385)

Identification of the four conjugations by their stem-vowels (171,387)
Main forms of the four sample verbs *amare, docere, legere,* and *audire* (171,392)
Conjugation of the four verbs (forms of the same person of each verb are grouped together) in the six moods and five tenses in the active voice (171,398)
Gerunds (verbal nouns) (174,526)
Supines (175,531)
Present participle (175,536)
Future participle (175,541)
Conjugation of the substantive verb *esse* in the six moods and five tenses (175,547)
Main forms of the four sample verbs *amare, docere, legere,* and *audire* in the passive voice (177,604)
Conjugation of the four verbs in the six moods and five tenses in the passive voice (forms of the same person of each verb are grouped together) (177,608)
Past participle (180,734)
Future participle (180,736)
Main forms of *posse, velle, nolle, malle, edere, fieri, ferre,* and *ferri* (180,739)
Conjugation of these auxiliary verbs and main verbs in the six moods and five tenses (forms of the same person are grouped together) (181,753)
Exceptions: *eo* and *queo* (184,884)
Formation of tenses (184,888)
Declension of impersonal verbs (184,896)

Participle: (184,900)
Definition (184,901)
Tense (four tenses) (184,904)
Form and formation of present participle (185,906)
Meaning and formation of the future participle in –*rus* (185,910)
Form and formation of the past participle (185,913)
Meaning and formation of the future participle in –*dus* (185,917)
Formation of the present participle and future participle in -*rus* from active verb and neuter verb (185,923)
Formation of past participle and future participle in -*dus* from passive verb (185,926)
Formation of present participle, past participle and future participle in -*rus* from deponent verb (185,929)
Formation of participle in -*dus*, if deponent verb takes accusative case (185,931)
Formation of four participles from common verb (185,934)
Declension of present participle with three articles (185,936)
Declension of participles of other tenses like adjectives (185,938)

Adverb: (185,940)
Definition (185,941)
Adverbs of time, place, number, order, asking and doubting, etc. (185,943)
Comparison of adverbs (186,967)

Conjunction: (186,969)
Definition (186,970)
Conjugations copulative, disjunctive, etc. (186,972)

Preposition: (187,984)
Definition (187,985)
Prepositions with accusative case (187,987)
Prepositions with ablative case (187,1003)
Prepositions with accusative or ablative case (187,1016)

Interjection: (188,1027)
Definition (188,1028)
Different kinds of interjections (188,1030)

The Concordes of latyne speche.

Three concords: (192,3)
First concord between nominative case and verb (192,3)
Second concord between substantive and adjective (192,4)
Third concord between antecedent and relative (192,5)
Identification of the principal verb (192,7)
Identification of the nominative case to the verb (192,12)
Position of the nominative case to the verb in questions (192,15)

First concord: (192,18)
Agreement of personal verb with its nominative case in number and person (192,19)
Hierarchy of persons (192,22)
Form of the verb following two nominative cases singular with copulative conjunction (192,24)
Form of the verb coming between two nominative cases of different numbers (192,30)

Second concord: (192,35)
Identification of substantive (192,36)
Agreement of adjective and substantive in case, gender, and number (193,38)
Joining of participles and pronouns with substantives (193,41)
Hierarchy of genders (193,44)
Substantives singular with a copulative conjunction take adjective plural (193,46)

Third concord: (193,50)
Identification of the antecedent (193,51)
Agreement of relative with its antecedent in gender, number, and person (193,54)
Difference between English 'that' used as relative pronoun and as a conjunction (193,56)
Construction of the antecedent singular with copulative conjunction (193,62)
Neuter gender for substantives or antecedents denoting things (193,65)

The relative case: (193,72)
Relative case used as nominative case to the verb (193,73)
Nominative case between relative and verb (194,77)
Relative between two substantives of different gender (194,80)
Interrogative pronouns and infinites (194,84)

Construction of nouns substantive: (194,87)
Construction of two nouns substantive with different meanings (194,88)
Construction of two nouns substantive belonging to one thing (194,92)
Construction of *res* with adjective (194,95)
Construction of adjective in neuter gender used as substantive (194,98)
Construction of expressions of praise or dispraise of a thing (194,102)
Construction of *opus* and *usus* (194,105)

Construction of adjectives: (194,108)
The genitive case (194,109)
Adjectives expressing desire, knowledge, etc., with genitive case (194,110)
Partitive nouns, certain interrogatives with genitive case (195,115)
Questions and the following answers in the same case and tense (195,120)
Nouns of the comparative and superlative degree put partitively with genitive case (195,127)
Nouns of the comparative degree with 'than' or 'by' with ablative case (195,131)

The dative case (195,134)
Adjectives signifying profit, likeness, etc., with dative case (195,135)
Nouns of the passive signification in -*bilis* and participles in -*dus* with dative case (195,140)

The accusative case (195,143)
The 'measure of length', etc., after adjectives with accusative case (195,144)

The ablative case (196,149)
Adjectives signifying fullness, emptiness, etc., with ablative case (196,150)
The adjectives *dignus, indignus*, etc., with ablative case (196,156)

Construction of the pronoun: (196,159)
Primitive pronouns with genitive case (196,160)
Genitive case after distributives, partitives, etc. (196,163)

Construction of the verb: (196,166)
Sum, forem, fio, etc., with nominative case before and after them (196,168)

The genitive case (196,174)
Auxiliary verb *sum* signifying possession, etc., with genitive case (196,175)
Exceptions (196,177)
Verbs signifying esteem or regard with genitive case (196,179)
Verbs of accusing, condemning, etc., with genitive or ablative case with or without preposition (196,181)

The dative case (197,193)
Verbs construed with 'to', or 'for' with dative case (197,194)
Sum with its compounds, etc., with dative case (197,210)

The accusative case (197,218)
Transitive verbs with accusative case of the sufferer (197,219)
Neuter verbs with accusative case (197,222)
Verbs of asking, teaching, and arraying [*here*: to equip sb.; to arm] take two accusative
    cases (197,224)

The ablative case (198,227)
Verbs construed with ablative of the instrument or of the cause (198,228)
The word signifying price after verbs with ablative case (198,231)
Verbs signifying plenty or scarceness, etc., with ablative case (198,236)
Verbs signifying receivyng, distance, etc., with ablative case (198,241)
Verbs of comparison or exceeding with ablative case (198,245)
Absolute ablative (198,248)

Construction of passives: (198,255)
Passive verb with ablative and preposition or dative case (198,256)
Gerunds (verbal nouns) (198,260)
Case of gerunds or supines (198,261)
Gerund in -*di* (199,264)
Gerund in -*do* (199,271)
Gerund in -*dum* (199,282)

Supines (199,292)
First supine with active signification after verbs and participles signifying moving to a place
    (199,293)
Second supine with passive signification after adjectives (199,296)
Nouns signifying time take the ablative case (200,303)
Nouns signifying space between places with accusative case (200,308)
Nouns appellative or names of great places used with preposition (200,312)
Impersonal verbs (200,330)
'It' as a sign of the impersonal verb (200,331)
Impersonal verbs with dative case (201,335)
Impersonal verbs with accusative case (201,338)
Impersonal verbs of the passive voice with ablative case (201,342)
Neuter verb changed into impersonal verb (201,345)

Participle: (201,347)
Cases followed by participles (201,348)
The four ways participles are changed into nouns (201,350)
Participles changed into nouns with genitive case (201,360)
Participles with active signification with accusative case (201,362)

Adverb: (201,365)
Adverbs of quantity, time, and place with genitive case (201,366)
Adverbs with dative case (201,368)
Datives used adverbially (201,370)
Adverbs with accusative case (201,372)
Prepositions changed into adverbs (201,374)

Conjunction: (202,376)
Copulative and disjunctive conjunctions between the same cases (202,377)
Copulative and disjunctive conjunctions between different cases (202,379)
Copulative and disjunctive conjunctions joining the same moods and tenses (202,381)

Preposition: (202,384)
Preposition 'in' not expressed but understood with ablative case (202,385)
Compound verb with case of the preposition that it is compounded with (202,388)

Interjection: (202,390)
Interjection with nominative, dative, accusative, and vocative cases (202,391)

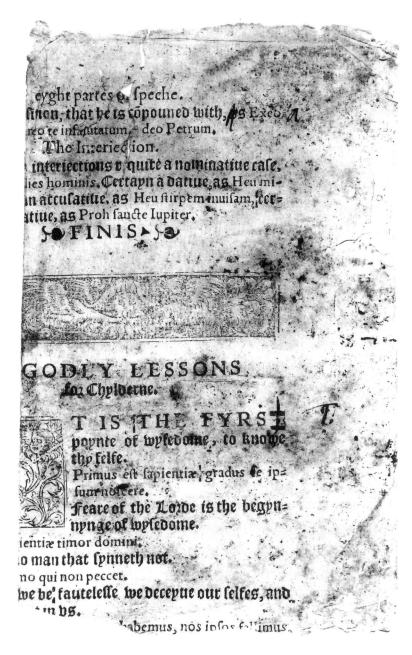

eyght partes o. speche.
...tion, that he is copouneo with, as Exeo
...reo te infatutatum, deo Petrum.

The Interiection.

...interiections r quite a nominatiue case,
...lies hominis. Certayn a datiue, as Heu mi=
...n accusatiue, as Heu stirpem inuisam, cer=
...atiue, as Proh sancte Iupiter.

FINIS

GODLY LESSONS
for Chylderne.

T IS THE FYRST
poynte of wysedome, to knowe
thy selfe.
Primus est sapientiæ gradus se ip=
sum noscere.

Feare of the Lorde is the begyn=
nynge of wysedome.
...ientiæ timor domini.
...o man that synneth not.
no qui non peccet.
...we be fauteleffe we deceyue our selfes, and
...in vs.
...habemus, nos infos fallimus.

Plate 10. Fragment of a proof leaf of *An Introduction Of The Eyght Partes Of speche*. [London: Thomas Berthelet, *c*.1540]. (Bodl. Lib., Vet.A1.a.4(1).)

Appendix II

THE OXFORD PROOF LEAF

This fragment of *An Introduction of the eyght partes of speche, and the Construction of the same*, attributed to William Lily [London: Thomas Berthelet, *c*.1540.] is part of a quarto leaf of a proof of an edition of which there is no recorded copy. It is printed on paper, on one side of the sheet only with some off-setting on the verso, and it contains two manuscript proof corrections in ink. This unique single leaf fragment is recorded under STC^2 15610.6 following the entry for the *Introduction* of 1542. Its location is Bodl. Lib., Vet.A1 a.4(1).[1] Considering the very small number of schoolbooks which has come down to us from the Tudor period, this proof is of great interest, since survivals of this kind of material are of considerable rarity. It offers a view into the production methods used in Berthelet's printing house and, moreover, it shows a stage of production of a particular text. The text of the proof sheet may be several removes away from the published text of which there is no record.[2]

A comparison of the text of the proof leaf (Plate 10) with the 1542 text, which represents the first extant copy of the text as issued from Berthelet's printing house, is necessarily restricted to the same passages in the two books (Plate 7, p. 153, and Plate 9, p. 155), which show corresponding portions of the 1542 text.

Contents of a proof leaf of an edition of the *Introduction* dated *c*.1540:

In what follows the missing parts of the text in the description are taken from the 1542 copy, placed within angle brackets, and are represented by a different fount.

[Running-title [1ʳ]:] eyght partes o<f> speche. | [Begins, lines 1–2:] <**of the prepo**>sition, that he is cōpouned with, as *Exeo* | <*domo.* **Præte**>*reo te insalutatum.* <*A*>*deo Petrum.* | [lines 3–6:] The Interiec<t>ion. | <**C Certayne**> interiections r<e>quire a nominatiue case, | <**as** *O festus d*>*ies hominis.* Certayn a datiue, as *Heu mi-*|<*hi.* **Certaine a**>n accusatiue, as *Heu stirpem inuisam,* cer=| [Ends, lines 7–8:] <**tayne a voc**>atiue, as *Proh sancte Iupiter.* | [In the centre: leaf type orn.] *FINIS* [triangular orn. and leaf type orn.]

[Greg, *Ornament I*, state TBᵇ, 210 (= Beale 16)] |

[Heading, lines 9–10:] *GODLY LESSONS* | for Chylderne. | [Begins, lines 11–13:] *Iʳ T IS THE FYRST* | poynte of wysedome, to knowe | thy selfe. | [Lines 14–20:] *Primus est sapientiæ gradus se ip=*|*sum noscere.* | Feare of the Lorde is the begyn=|nynge of wysedome. | <*Initium sap*>*ientiæ timor domini.* | <**There is n**>o man that synneth not. | <*Non est hom*>*o qui non peccet.* | [Ends, lines 21–23:] <**If we saye**> we be fautelesse we deceyue our selfes, and | <**truthe is not in**> vs. | <*Si dixerimus peccatum non ha*>*bemus, nos i*<*psos fall*>*imus.*

¹ The BL has a photographic reproduction of this proof leaf at 1881.d.22.(10).

² In a manuscript note, dated 26 July 1971, which accompanies the fragment, the late David M. Rogers, of the Bodl. Lib., Oxford, wrote: "This proof leaf is also Thomas Berthelet's work, and seems to represent an even earlier edition, of about 1540."

4°: [?A–H⁴|⁶].

Single unperfected proof leaf without signature or pagination, possibly H3ʳ.

Typography, material, and other physical features:

Horizontal chain-lines. Chain-line spacing *c*.23 to 25 mm. No watermark. The left part of the leaf is torn away (about 21 mm), resulting in the loss of the left margin and part of between eight and thirteen lines of text; of the last line of text present only a few words remain. The lower margin, several lines of text and any signature or catchword from the lower part of the leaf are missing, with the result that only twenty-three mostly incomplete lines of text, excluding the running-title, are extant. The leaf starts with the running-title and eight lines which represent the end of the treatise on *The Concordes of latyne speche*. A decorative rectangular ornament is followed by the heading for *Godly Lessons for Chylderne* with thirteen lines of text, of which six are incomplete.

The following types are used:
Textura 95b (Greg 1) (e.g. line 1: that he is compouned with);
Roman 109 (Greg 7) (e.g. line 9: *GODLY LESSONS*);
Roman 90b (Greg 12) (e.g. line 2: *te insalutatum Adeo Petrum*).

The proof shows the same types and initial *I* (only half of which is preserved) as used in the 1542 edition. The manuscript corrections indicate and correct typographical errors. They are as follows: The passage in line 1 of the original reads: *ss Exeo* for *as Exeo*. The correction consists of a stroke through the first *s* in the text, and the correct letter *a* is given in the margin. The second correction mark occurs in line 11 where a composing error affecting the *T* of *FYRST* has been crossed through by a vertical stroke, with *T* written in the margin. There are four other corrections on this page indicating 'add space'.

Provenance:

The fragment shows signs of having been used as binder's waste, but unfortunately its provenance is unknown.

Bibliographical References:

Within *STC²* 15610.6 (with incorrect shelfmark); *BLC*, vol. 160: 69; Moore, 72; Alston, vol. 15, within no. 495 (with incorrect shelfmark); within *ESTC* S120457.

What does seem most interesting and the most important point about the proof, apart from its actual existence, is the textual variation to the 1542 edition. The proof has the *Godly Lessons* after the final section on *The Interiection* (without the last sentence) from *The Concordes*, whereas the 1542 edition (and apparently *STC²* 15610.7, 15610.8, and 15610.9 (= Appendix III, 4.1, 6.0, and 7.1)) has them after the section *Of an Interiection* from the *Introduction*, before the section on *The Concordes* (Plate 9, p. 155). Does this suggest some editorial prevarication over the proper order for the text that was perhaps not finalized at the time? Or is it evidence of sloppy typesetting from copy by Berthelet's compositors? Is this a possible reason for it not having been published? Assuming the overall text, of which the proof is a part, was similar to the 1542 edition, then the proof leaf would probably have been H3ʳ, with the text finishing on H4ᵛ.

EDITIONS OF THE LATIN GRAMMAR ATTRIBUTED TO WILLIAM LILY, 1540–1603

The following chronological listing of editions of 'Lily's Latin Grammar' is intended as a survey and means of identifying the individual copies that have come down to us from the Tudor period. It aims to provide a record of the earliest extant editions that were available when this grammar first appeared with the imprimatur of Henry VIII as the only grammar to be used in the teaching of Latin and which continued thus to the end of Queen Elizabeth's reign in 1603. At about this time it not only became the subject of some criticism from certain grammarians, but also became the object of competitive commercial interest amongst printers keen to share in its lucrative market. An accurate comprehensive printed listing of all the extant editions and variants is not available.[1] What we have is the list of editions given in *STC²* from 1540 to 1638 (nos. 15610.5–15633.8), adding a number of additional works based on 'Lily', or influenced to some degree by it, the continuation provided by Wing, vol. 2, covering editions from 1641 to 1700 (nos. L2254–L2304D) with some shorter versions and a synopsis of 'Lily', and Alston's vols. 15 and 16, listing editions, edited versions, and other related works from 1540 to 1800 under various authorial or title headings.[2]

The present list records in detail all the known extant copies of editions of 'Lily's Grammar' in publicly accessible libraries, starting from the earliest extant copy dated 1540, to a copy dated 1602. Other copies of these editions and copies representing other editions may possibly survive elsewhere. It becomes apparent that the English and the Latin part of 'Lily's Grammar' had an independent existence. The two parts were not invariably intended to appear as a single volume and therefore, for any given edition of one part, there need not have been a corresponding edition of the other part. It may be that the youngest students were provided with the English part only and the older boys with the Latin part only.

Appendix III describes bibliographically independent items separately, but they are listed and numbered in such a way that the physical relationships remain evident. It provides, for each edition, the titles of the grammar in English (part 1) and the grammar in Latin (part 2) with information about format, collation, and other bibliographical features, the present location of copies (with information about their physical state), the microfilm reel number and item, and published references to them. The dates are those appearing in the originals (in the imprint, colophon, or elsewhere); supplied dates have been taken from the *ESTC*. Those copies located in the British Library, London, in Cambridge University Library, in the Bodleian

---

[1] A chronological bibliographical index and census of copies of all known editions of all the grammatical works associated with Lily, including *Absolutissimus de octo orationis partium constructione libellus*, *Rudimenta grammatices*, *De generibus nominum*, *Brevissima Institutio*, and *A Short Introduction of Grammar*, as well as derivative works and commentaries, compiled by David Mackenzie, will, in due course, be deposited in The Walker Library of St Paul's School, where it may be available to interested researchers.

[2] Cf. p. 2 above, footnote 4.

Library, Oxford, and in Nottingham University Library, and also in the college libraries of Cambridge and Oxford have been examined personally. Information about other copies has been provided or verified by librarians and, where relevant, has been checked against images from *EEBO*. The transcription of the titles preserves the spelling and punctuation of the originals, except that only the first capital letter of the beginning of a word has been preserved and abbreviations have been expanded silently. Angle brackets indicate letters which are legible only in part or missing completely; obvious printers' errors are indicated by [*sic*]. I have modernized or translated the printer's imprint and have excluded the imprint information from the title-page transcriptions.

1.0 [Edition of the Latin part]

[Title-page, A1ʳ:] *Institutio Compendiaria Totius Grammaticae, Quam Et Eruditissimus atque idem illustrissimus Rex noster hoc nomine euulgari iussit, ut non alia quam hæc una per totam Angliam pueris prælegeretur.*

London: Thomas Berthelet, 1540.
4°: A⁶ B–T⁴ V⁶.
Title enclosed within title-page border McK&F 19.
Leaves 24, 77, and 78 misnumbered 42, 78, and 80 respectively.

BL, C.21.b.4.(3). Printed on vellum. The dates both on the title-page and in the colophon have been altered in ink facsimile from M.D.XL. to M.D.XL.II. H3 (leaf 27) mis-bound before H2 (leaf 26) and I3 (leaf 31) mis-bound before I2 (leaf 30).
Bound with *Alphabetum Latino Anglicum* (*STC²* 19.2) and *An Introduction Of The Eyght Partes Of speche* (= no. 3.0 below).
London, Lambeth Palace Library, 1540.5 (formerly MS 1368). Printed on vellum.

Maitland, *List*, 207, Note DD, 385–86 (BL copy) and Note DD, 385–92 (Lambeth copy); Maitland, *Index*, 61 (Lambeth copy); Nichols (1857), vol. 1: xxa–xxb, cccxlii; *BM Catalogue*, vol. 2: 883, 954 (BL copy); *STC²* 15610.5; *BLC*, vol. 159: 102 (BL copy); Alston-Hill, 71 (BL copy); Sharpe 2103; Alston, vol. 15, no. 494; *ESTC* S2394 (BL copy) and S2184 (Lambeth copy). Microfilm: UMI, *EEB*, reel 1845: 1c (BL copy); reel 1797: 36 (Lambeth copy).

2.0 [Another edition of the English part—the Oxford proof leaf]

[Title-page, ?A1ʳ. No copy recorded.] [? *An Introduction Of The Eyght Partes Of speche, and the Construction of the same.*]

[London: Thomas Berthelet, *c*.1540.]
4°: [?A–H⁴ I⁶]

Bodl. Lib., Vet.A1.a.4(1). Single unperfected proof leaf without signature or pagination, possibly H3ʳ.
Within *STC²* 15610.6 (with incorrect shelfmark); *BLC*, vol. 160: 69; Moore, 72; Alston, vol. 15, within no. 495 (with incorrect shelfmark); within *ESTC* S120457.
Photographic reproduction of the original: BL, 1881.d.22.(10). See Appendix II and Plate 10.

3.0 [Edition of the English part]

[Title-page, A1ʳ:] *An Introduction Of The Eyght Partes Of speche, and the Construction of the same, compiled and sette forthe by the commaundement of our most gracious souerayne lorde the king.*

London: Thomas Berthelet, 1542.
4°: A–H⁴ I⁶ (I6 blank).
Title enclosed within title-page border McK&F 19.

BL, C.21.b.4.(2). Printed on vellum.
Bound with *Alphabetum Latino Anglicum* (*STC²* 19.2) and *Institutio Compendiaria Totius Grammaticae* (= no. 1.0 above).
BM Catalogue, vol. 2: 883, 954; Kennedy 2491; *STC* 15605; *STC²* 15610.6 (with incorrect collation; corrected in the *Addenda and Corrigenda*, vol. 3: 285); *BLC*, vol. 160: 69; Alston-Hill, 72; Alston, vol. 15, no. 495; *ESTC* S120457. (For further references see p. 146 above).
Microfilm: UMI, *EEB*, reel 59: 06; reel 1845: 1b. See Plate 1, Frontispiece.

4.0 [Another edition of the English and Latin parts]

4.1 [Title-page of the English part, A1ʳ:] *An Introduction Of The Eyght Partes Of speche, and the Construction of the same compyled and sette forth by the commaundement of our most gracious souerayne lorde the kyng.*

London: Thomas Berthelet, 1543.
4°: A–H⁴ I⁶ (I6, ?blank).
Title enclosed within title-page border McK&F 19.

4.2 [Title-page of the Latin part, A1ʳ:] *Institutio Compendiaria Totius Grammaticae, Quam Et Eruditissimus atque idem illustrissimus Rex noster hoc nomine euulgari iussit, ut non alia quam hæc una per totam Angliam pueris prælegeretur.*

London: Thomas Berthelet, 1543.
4°: A–X⁴.
Title enclosed within title-page border McK&F 19.
University of Illinois at Urbana-Champaign Library, 475 L62s 1543. (Wanting I6 in the English part.).
Quaritch Catalogue 436, item 1022; Quaritch Catalogue 464, item 174 (with a reproduction of the title-page of the Latin part); *STC²* 15610.7; Alston, vol. 15, no. 496; *ESTC* S1112.
Microfilm: UMI, *EEB*, reel 1729: 17a; reel 1729: 17b (only Latin part).

5.0 [Another edition of the Latin part]

[Title-page, A1ʳ:] *Institutio Compendiaria Totius Grammaticae, Quam Et Eruditissimus atque idem illustrissimus Rex noster hoc nomine euulgari iussit, ut non alia quam hæc una per totam Angliam pueris prælegeretur.*

· London: Thomas Berthelet, 1543.
8°: A–N⁸ O⁴.

San Marino, California, Henry E. Huntington Library, RB 82392. MS notes. Bound with *An Introduction Of the Eyght Partes Of Speche*, 1544; = no. 6.0 below.
Britwell Handlist, 590; *STC²* 15610.8; Alston, vol. 15, no. 497; *ESTC* S109437.
Microfilm: UMI, *EEB*, reel 520: 04; 1835: 29. (Both microfilms only have the title-page of the Latin part.)

6.0 [Another edition of the English part]

[Title-page, A1ʳ:] *An Introduction Of The Eyght Partes Of Speche and the Construction of the same, compyled and set forthe by the commaundement of our most gracious soueraygne lorde the kyng.*

London: Thomas Berthelet, 1544.
8°: A–F⁸ G⁴.

San Marino, California, Henry E. Huntington Library, RB 82392. Bound with *Institutio Compendiaria Totius Grammaticae*; = no. 5.0 above. For references that apply to both nos. 5.0 and 6.0, see no. 5.0 above.
Britwell Handlist has a reproduction of the title-page of this part facing page 590.
Microfilm: UMI, *EEB*, reel 520: 04; 1835: 29.

7.0 [Another edition of the English and Latin parts]

7.1 [Title-page of the English part, A1ʳ:] *An introduction of the eight partes of speeche, and the Construction of the same, compiled and sette forthe by the commaundement of our moste gracious soueraigne lorde the kyng.*

London: Thomas Berthelet, 1546.
4°: A–I⁴.
Title enclosed within title-page border McK&F 50.

7.2 [Title-page of the Latin part, A1ʳ:] *Institutio compendiaria totius grammaticæ, quam eruditissimus atque idem illustrissimus rex noster hoc nomine euulgari iussit, ut non alia quam hæc una per totam Angliam pueris prælegatur.*

London: Thomas Berthelet, 1546.
4°: A–V⁴ (R3 mis-signed K3).
Title enclosed within title-page border McK&F 50.

Glasgow, University Library, Sp Coll Hunterian Bv.3.26.
Ferguson, 222; *STC²* 15610.9; Alston, vol. 15, no. 498 (with incorrect format); *ESTC* S93472.
Microfilm: UMI, *EEB*, reel 2137: 11.

8.0 [Another edition of the English part]

[Title-page, a1ʳ:] *A Shorte Introduction Of Grammar, generally to be vsed in the Kynges Maiesties dominions, for the bryngynge vp of all those that entende to atteyne the knowlege of the Latine tongue.*

[London: Reyner Wolfe.] 1548.
4°: a⁴ [?b–e⁸]
Title enclosed within title-page border McK&F 66.

London, Lambeth Palace Library, Fragment, no. 70.
The two pairs of conjugate quarto leaves of an otherwise unrecorded edition, with continuous text, signed 'a.ii' on the second leaf, are typographically almost identical to no. 9.1 below.
Maitland, *List*, no. 484: 426–27; Maitland, *Index*, 49; Kennedy 2493; *STC²* 15610.10; Alston, vol. 15, no. 499 (with incorrect format and number of leaves); *ESTC* S2185.
Microfilm: UMI, *EEB*, reel 1797: 37.
Repr. Lily and Colet (1548/49) (= *EL* 262 (1970), Appendix II); sig. a1ᵛ ed. Blach 1909), 45: 89–90; excerpt of a2ʳ⁻ᵛ ed. Baldwin (1944), vol. 1: 180.

9.0 [Another edition of the English and Latin parts]

9.1 [Another edn.] [Title-page of the English part, A1ʳ:] *A Shorte Introduc tion* [sic] *Of Grammar, generally to be vsed in the Kynges Maiesties dominions, for the bryngynge vp of all those that entende to atteyne the knowlege of the Latine tongue.*

London: Reyner Wolfe, 1549.
4°: A–D⁸ E⁴.
Title enclosed within title-page border McK&F 66.

9.2 [Title-page of the Latin part, A1ʳ:] *Breuissima Institutio seu Ratio Grammatices Cogno-scendæ, ad omnium puerorum, vtilitatem præscripta, quam solam Regia Maiestas in omnibus scholis profitendam præcipit.*

London: Reyner Wolfe, 1549.
4°: A–K⁸.
Title enclosed within title-page border McK&F 66.

Bodl. Lib., 4° M.22.Art.BS. (Lacks A4.5 of the English part and K1–4 of the Latin part).
STC² (= *STC*) 15611 (with incorrect citations of missing leaves); *Halkett and Laing* S191; Vancil (1993), 150; *HEL* (2000), II, no. 3601; Alston, vol. 15, no. 500 (with incorrect format and citations of missing leaves); *ESTC* S104797.
Microfilm: UMI, *EEB*, reel 85: 10.
English part repr. in Lily and Colet (1548/49) (= *EL* 262 (1970)); for the sigs. A4.5 wanting in the English part of this copy, sigs. a4.5 of the English part (= no.12.1.a below, Oxford copy) are given as Appendix I; sigs. A2ʳ–A3ʳ of the English part ed. Görlach (1993), Text 3: 218–19; see also Görlach, 409–10.

10.0 [Another edition of the Latin part]

[Title-page of the Latin part, ?A1ʳ:] *Breuissima Institutio seu Ratio Grammatices Cogno-scendæ, ad omnium puerorum vtilitatem præscripta, quam solam Regia Maiestas in omnibus scholis profitendam præcipit.*

London: [Reyner Wolfe] 1553.
4°: [?A–K⁸].
Title enclosed within title-page border McK&F 66.

BL, Harl. 5974(14). Title-leaf only.
Wolf, 229; *STC²* 15611.3; Alston, vol. 15, no. 501 (with incorrect format and wrongly indicating an inferred place of printing); *ESTC* S125708.
Microfilm: UMI, *EEB, Tract Supplement*, reel E3: 2[13], item Harl. 5974(14).[3]

11.0 [Another edition of the English and Latin parts]

11.1.a [Title-page of the English part, a1ʳ:] *A Short Introduction Of Grammar Generallie To Be Vsed. Compiled And Set Forth, For The Bringyng VF [sic] Of All Those That Intend To Attaine The In o wlege [sic] Of The Latin Tongue.*
11.1.b [Head-title, d3ᵛ:] *Desiderii Erasmi, . . . de Ratione studii.*
11.1.c [Head-title, e1ʳ:] *Omnium Nominum in Regulis Generum.*
11.1.d [Head-title, f7ᵛ:] *De Modo Repetendae Lectionis.*

[Geneva: Conrad Badius] 1557.
8°: a–c⁸ d⁴ e–f⁸.

---

[3] *EEBO* lists, under Lily, William (*EEB, Tract Supplement* / E4:1[4b]), a fragment with Wolfe's device dated 1553 at the BL (Harl. 5927(8)), incorrectly described as "Possibly from William Lily, *A shorte introduction of grammar generally to be vsed . . .*, 1553". This fragment is from another, so far unidentified, work.

11.2.a [Title-page of the Latin part, A1^r:] *Breuissima Institutio, seu ratio Grammatices Cogno-scendae, Ad Omnium Puerorum Vtilitatem Praescripta: Quam Solam Regia Maiestas In Omnibus Scholis Profitendam Praecipit.*

11.2.b [Head-title, E4^r:] *De Modo Repetendae Lectionis.*

11.2.c [Head-title, E5^r:] *De Constructione octo partium.*

[Geneva: Conrad Badius] 1557.
8°: A–H^8.

CUL, Aa*.6.13 (F). Lacks sigs. e–f of the English part.
BL, C.107.c.29. Misbound, with sigs. e–f of the English part occurring after H8 of the Latin part.

Britwell Handlist, 590; Sayle 6316; *STC^2* 15611.7; *BLC*, vol. 160: 69; Alston, vol. 15, no. 502; *ESTC* S125077.
Microfilm: UMI, *EEB*, reel 1995: 11.

12.0 [Another edition of the English and Latin parts]

12.1.a [Title-page of the English part, a1^r:] *A Short Introduction Of Grammar Generallie To Be Vsed. Compiled And Set Forth, For The Bringyng Vp Of All Those That Intend To Attaine The Kn o wlege [sic] Of The Latin Tongue.*

12.1.b [Head-title, d3^v:] *Desiderii Erasmi, . . . de Ratione studii.*

[Geneva: Conrad Badius] 1557.
8°: a–c^8 d^4.

12.2.a [Title-page of the Latin part, A1^r:] *Breuissima Institutio, seu ratio Grammatices Cogno-scendae, Ad Omnium Puerorum Vtilitatem Praescripta: Quam Solam Regia Maiestas In Omnibus Scholis Profitendam Praecipit.*

12.2.b [Head-title, E4^r:] *De Modo Repetendae Lectionis.*

12.2.c [Head-title, E5^r:] *De Constructione octo partium.*

[Geneva: Conrad Badius] 1557.
8°: A–H^8.

CUL, Aa*.11.12 (F).
Bodl. Lib., 8° I.18.Art.BS.
University of Illinois at Urbana-Champaign Library, 475 L62s 1557.
Washington, D.C., Folger Shakespeare Library, Folger STC 15612, Copy 2 (lacking H8).
Sayle 6316; *STC^2* 15612; Alston, vol. 15, no. 503; *ESTC* S106921.
Microfilm: UMI, *EEB*, reel 443: 08. (*EEBO* incorrectly states that the Bodl. Lib. copy of this edition is incomplete, lacking the Latin part.) Sigs. a4.5 of the English part, missing from the 1549 Oxford copy (= no. 9.1 above), repr. in Lily and Colet (1548/49) (= *EL* 262 (1970), Appendix I).

13.0 [Another edition of the English and Latin parts]

13.1.a [Title-page of the English part, a1^r:] *A Short Introduction Of Grammar Generallie To Be Vsed. Compiled And Set Forth, For The Bringyng Vp Of All Those That Intend To Attaine The Knowlege Of The Latin Tongue.*

13.1.b [Head-title, d3^v:] *Desiderii Erasmi, . . . de Ratione studii.*

[Geneva: Conrad Badius] 1557 (1 March).
8°: a–c⁸ d⁴.

At the end of *De Ratione studii* on d4ʳ there are five lines in italic beginning "*Liberi, obedite Parentibus ac Pr<e>ceptoribus vestris in Domino*" in place of the "*Pulcherrimæ ac tutissimæ*" text of two lines in roman occurring in nos. 11.1 and 12.1. at this point and also on d3ʳ.

13.2.a [Title-page of the Latin part, A1ʳ:] *Breuissima Institutio, seu ratio Grammatices Cognoscendae, Ad Omnium Puerorum Vtilitatem Praescripta: Quam Solam Regia Maiestas In Omnibus Scholis Profitendam Praecipit.*
13.2.b [Head-title, E4ʳ:] *De Modo Repetendae Lectionis.*
13.2.c [Head-title, E5ʳ:] *De Constructione octo partium.*

[Geneva: Conrad Badius] 1557.
8°: A-H⁸.

Ripon Cathedral Library, XVII.A.3. Latin part only. On long-term deposit at Leeds University Library. This copy of the *Breuissima Institutio* is bound in an original vellum wrapper and was evidently issued independently of the English part. It is, however, from the same edition as the Huntington and Folger copies.
San Marino, California, Henry E. Huntington Library, RB 82394. The Huntington copy, like the Folger copy, does not have sigs. e–f of the English part, as found in no. 11.1 above.
Washington, D.C., Folger Shakespeare Library, Folger STC 15612, Copy 1.
STC² 15613; Shaw L959; Alston, vol. 15, no. 504 (with UMI, *EEB* number for the 1577 copy, = no. 28.0 below); *ESTC* S109455.
Microfilm: UMI, *EEB*, reel 379: 15.

14.0 [Another edition of the English and Latin parts]

14.1 [Title-page of the English part, A1ʳ:] *A Shorte Introduction Of Grammar, generally to be vsed.* [*sic*] *compiled and sette forth, for the bringyng vp of all those that intende to attaine the knowledge of the Latine tongue.*

London: Reyner Wolfe, 1558.
4°: A–C⁸ D⁶.
Title enclosed within title-page border McK&F 161.

14.2 [Title-page of the Latin part, A1ʳ:] *Breuissima Institutio Seu Ratio Grammatices Cognoscendę, ad omnium puerorum vtilitatem præscripta, quam solam Regia Maiestas in omnibus scholis profitendam pręcipit.*

London: Reyner Wolfe, 1558.
4°: A–I⁸.
Title enclosed within title-page border McK&F 161.

Cambridge, Pembroke College, 11.5.9.
STC² 15613.3; Alston, vol. 15, no. 505 (with incorrect format); *ESTC* S2186.
Microfilm: UMI, *EEB*, reel 1797: 38.

15.0 [Another ed. of the English and Latin parts.]

15.1 [Title-page of the English part, A1ʳ:] *A Shorte Introduction Of Grammar, generally to be vsed.* [*sic*] *compiled and sette forth, for the bringing vp of all those that intende to attaine the knoweledge of the Latine tongue.*

London: Reyner Wolfe, 1560.
4°: A–C^8 D^6.

15.2 [Title-page of the Latin part, A1^r:] *Brevissima.* [*sic*] *Institutio Seu Ratio Grammatices Cognoscendę, ad omnium puerorum utilitatem pręscripta, quam solam Regia Maiestas in omnibus scholis profitendam præcipit.*

London: Reyner Wolfe [?1560].
4°: A–I^8.

Cambridge, Clare College, B^1.2.21(1). Lower half of A4 of the English part missing; colophon on D6^v. Latin part wanting I8. The leaves in gathering B of the Latin part are misbound in the following order: 3, 2, 1, 4, 5, 8, 7, 6. With *STC^2* 15621.3 bound at the end; = no. 30.0 below. *STC^2* 15613.5; Alston, vol. 15, no. 506 (with incorrect format); *ESTC* S93473.

16.0 [Another edition of the English and Latin parts]

16.1 [Title-page of the English part, ?A1^r. No copy recorded.] [? *A Shorte Introduction of Grammar, generally to be vsed.*]

London: Reyner Wolfe, 1564.
4°: A–C^8 D^6.

16.2 [Title-page of the Latin part, A1^r:] *Breuissima Institutio Seu Ratio Grammatices cognoscendæ, ad omnium puerorum vtilitatem præscripta, quam solam Regia Maiestas in omnibus Scholis profitendam præcipit.*

London: Reyner Wolfe, 1564.
4°: A–I^8.
Title enclosed within title-page border McK&F 66.

Washington, D.C., Folger Shakespeare Library, Folger STC 15613.8. Leaf A1 of the English part and leaves I7.8 of the Latin part wanting.
STC^2 15613.7; Alston, vol. 15, no. 507 (with incorrect format); *ESTC* S93474.
Microfilm: UMI, *EEB*, reel 2223: 06.

17.0 [Another edition of the English part]

[Title-page, ?A1^r. No copy recorded.] [? *A Shorte Introduction of Grammar, generally to be vsed.*]

London: Reyner Wolfe, 1566.
4°: A–D^8. (Colophon on D8^v).

Bodl. Lib., 4° A.17.Art.BS. (Wanting A1.8). Bound after the Latin part, no. 18.0 below. *STC^2* (= *STC*) 15614; Alston, vol. 15, no. 508 (with incorrect format); *ESTC* S106926.

Microfilm: UMI, *EEB*, reel 443: 09.
English part ed. Blach (1908; 1909), 44: 65–117; 45: 51–80. (A1 and A8 of this part in Blach's edition were taken from no. 25.1 below.)

18.0 [Title-page, A1^r:] *Breuissima Institutio Seu Ratio Grammatices cognoscendæ, ad omnium puerorum vtilitatem præscripta, quam solam Regia Maiestas in omnibus Scholis profitendam præcipit.*

London: Reyner Wolfe, 1567.
4°: A–H⁸ ?I⁶.
Title enclosed within title-page border McK&F 124.

Bodl. Lib., 4° A.17.Art.BS. (Wanting F1–3, H1,2 and all after H6). Bound before the English part, no. 17.0. For references that apply to both nos. 17.0 and 18.0 see no. 17.0 above.

19.0 [Another edition of the English and Latin parts]

19.1 [Title-page of the English part, A1ʳ:] *A Shorte Introduction Of Grammar generally to be vsed: compiled and set forth, for the bringing vp of all those that intende to attaine the knowledge of the Latine tongue.*

London: Reyner Wolfe, 1567.
4°: A–D⁸.
Title enclosed within title-page border McK&F 124.

19.2 [Title-page of the Latin part, A1ʳ:] *Breuissima Institutio Seu Ratio Grammatices cogno-scende, ad omnium puerorum vtilitatem præscripta, quam solam Regia Maiestas in omnibus Scholis profitendam præcipit.*

London: Reyner Wolfe, 1567.
4°: A–H⁸ I⁶.
Title enclosed within title-page border McK&F 124.

Washington, D.C., Folger Shakespeare Library, Folger STC 15614.2.
STC² 15614.2; Alston, vol. 15, no. 509 (with incorrect format); *ESTC* S93475.
Microfilm: UMI, *EEB*, reel 2121: 07.
English and Latin parts repr. in Lily, *Shorte Introduction* (1567). Title-page of the English part reproduced in *CWE*, vol. 24: 450.

20.0 [Another edition of the English and Latin parts]

20.1 [Title-page of the English part, A1ʳ:] *A Short Introduction Of Grammar Generallie To Be Vsed: Compiled and sette forth, for the bringing vp of all those that intend to attaine the knowledge of the Latin tongue.*

London: Reyner Wolfe, 1567.
8°: A–B⁸ c⁸ d⁴.

20.2 [Title-page of the Latin part, A1ʳ:] *Breuissima institutio, seu ratio grammatices cogno-scendæ, Ad omnium puerorum vtilitatem pręscripta: quam solam Regia Maiestas in omnibus Scholis profitendam præcipit.*

London: Reyner Wolfe, 1567.
8°: A–G⁸ [?H⁸].

Aberystwyth, National Library of Wales, STC 15614.4. (Wanting all after G8).
STC° 15614.4 (with incorrect collation); Alston, vol. 15, no. 510 (with collation as in *STC*); *ESTC* S93476.
Microfilm: UMI, *EEB*, reel 2148: 01.

21.0 [Another edition of the English and Latin parts]

21.1 [Title-page of the English part, A1ʳ:] *A Shorte Introduction Of Grammar generally to be vsed: compiled and set forth, for the bringing vp of all those that intende to attaine the knowledge of the Latine tongue.*

London: Reyner Wolfe, 1568.
4°: A–D⁸.
Title enclosed within title-page border McK&F 124.

21.2 [Title-page of the Latin part, A1ʳ:] *Breuissima Institutio Seu Ratio Grammatices cognoscende, ad omnium puerorum vtilitatem præscripta, quam solam Regia Maiestas in omnibus Scholis profitendam præcipit.*

London: Reyner Wolfe, 1568.
4°: A–H⁸ I⁶.
Title enclosed within title-page border McK&F 124.

Washington, D.C., Folger Shakespeare Library, Folger STC 15614.3.⁴
Halliwell-Phillipps (1880). 'Lily's Grammar'. Note to Lupton's article in *Notes and Queries*, 6ᵗʰ ser., 2: 462; Kennedy 2498; *STC²* 15614.6; Alston, vol. 15, no. 511 (with incorrect format); *ESTC* S93477.
Microfilm: UMI, *EEB*, reel 2294: 81.

22.0 [Another edition of the Latin part]

[Title-page of the Latin part, A1ʳ:] *Brevissima Institutio Seu Ratio Grammatices cognoscendę, ad omnium puerorum utilitatem pręscripta, quam solam Regia Maiestas in omnibus Scholis profitendam præcipit.*

London: Reyner Wolfe, 1569.
8°: .⁸A–L⁸ M¹⁰. (Preceded by *Index Festorum Mobilium* and Calendar. Issued with *Omnium Nominum in Regulis* and Erasmus's *De Modo Repetendae Lectionis*.)
Title enclosed within title-page border McK&F 120.

Nottingham, University Library, Briggs Collection LT109.PA/L4. Interleaved copy with manuscript notes.
STC² 15614.8; Alston, vol. 15, no. 512; *ESTC* S93478.

23.0 [Another edition of the English and Latin parts]⁵

23.1 [Title-page of the English part, A1ʳ:] *A Shorte Introduction Of Grammar, generally to be vsed, compiled and sette forth, for the bringyng vp of all those that intende to attaine the knowledge of the Latine tongue.*

[Holland? *c*.1570.]
4°: A–C⁸ D⁴.

---

⁴ Leaves G4.5 of the Latin part, listed in *STC²* 15614.6 as being at Illinois University Library (formerly in the possession of T. W. Baldwin), are untraceable at Illinois. Their present location is unknown.

⁵ The 1570 edition listed at *STC²* 15614.9 and Alston, vol. 15, no. 513, have been omitted here. See David Mackenzie (2005), 'A Ghostly Lily?', *The Library*, 7ᵗʰ ser., vol. 6: 423–24.

23.2.a [Title-page of the Latin part, A1ʳ:] *Breuissima Institutio Seu Ratio Grammatices Cognoscendae, Ad Omnium puerorum vtilitatem præscripta, quam solam Regia Maiestas in omnibus scholis profitendam præcipit.*
23.2.b [Head-title, ²A1ʳ:] *Nominum In Regulis Generum Contentorum, Tum Heteroclitorum, ac verborum interpretatio aliqua.*

[Holland? *c*.1570.]
4°: A–H⁸ I⁴ ²A–B⁴.

CUL, Aa*.5.60 (E).
Sayle 756; *STC²* (= *STC*) 15615; Alston, vol. 15, no. 514 (with incorrect format); *ESTC* S100279.
Microfilm: UMI, *EEB*, reel 1354: 02.

24.0 [Another edition of the Latin part]⁶

[Title-page, ?A1ʳ. No copy recorded.] [?*Breuissima Institutio Seu Ratio Grammatices cognoscendæ,*]

[London: Reyner Wolfe, ?1570.]
4°: [?A–H⁸ I⁶]

Bodl. Lib., Douce Fragm. e.42 (19). Conjugate leaves 14.5 only, signed I.iiii and I.v.
Not listed in *STC²*, Alston, or *ESTC*.

25.0 [Another ed. of the English and Latin parts.]

25.1 [Title-page of the English part, A1ʳ:] *A Shorte Introduction Of Grammar, generally to bee vsed: compiled and set forthe, for the bringinge vp of all those that intende to attayne the knowledge of the Latine tongue.*

London: Reyner Wolfe, 1572.
4°: A–D⁸.
Title enclosed within title-page border McK&F 124.

25.2.a [Title-page of the Latin part, A1ʳ:] *Breuissima Institutio Seu Ratio Grammatices cognoscendę, ad omnium puerorum vtilitatem præscripta, quam solam Regia Maiestas in omnibus Scholis profitendam præcipit.*
25.2.b [Head-title, H3ᵛ:] *Desiderii Erasmi . . . de ratione studij.*
25.2.c [Head-title, H4ᵛ:] *De Modo Repetendae Lectionis.*
25.2.d [Head-title, H5ᵛ:] *Magister Discipulos ad studia literarum cohortans.*
25.2.e [Head-title, H6ᵛ:] *Omnium Nominum In Regulis.*

London: Reyner Wolfe. 1573. (Colophon on I6ᵛ dated 1572.)
4°: A–H⁸ I⁶
Title enclosed within title-page border McK&F 124.

---

⁶ The date of this edition has been inferred from the state of the woodcut initial Q beginning the section *De ultimis syllabis*. I should like to thank Dr Georgianna Ziegler, Folger Shakespeare Library, Washington DC, for comparing the copies of 'Lily's Grammar' in their possession with this fragment.

Bodl. Lib., 4° G.12.Art.BS. (Lower right edges of B7,8 torn away with loss of some text).
STC² (= *STC*) 15616; Alston, vol. 15, no. 515 (with incorrect format); *ESTC* S106930.
Microfilm: UMI, *EEB*, reel 443: 10.
A1 and A8 of the English part of this edition were included in Blach's edition (1908), 44: 65–117
(= no. 17.0 above).

26.0 [Another edition of the English and Latin parts]

This is the first extant edition of the two parts issued together with a single signature sequence.

26.a [Title-page of the English part, A1ʳ:] ·A· *Shorte Introduction Of Grammar, generallye to be
vsed: Compyled and set forth, for the bringyng vp of all those that intende to attaine the
knowledge of the Latine tongue.*[7]
26.b [Section-title of the Latin part, E7ʳ:] *Breuissima Institutio Seu Ratio Grammatices cognoscendæ, ad omnium puerorum vtilitatem perscripta* [*sic*], *quam solam Regia Maiestas in
omnibus Scholis profitendam præcipit.*
26.c [Head-title, Q1ʳ:] *Omnium Nominum in Regulis.*

London: Assignes of Francis Flower, 1574.
8°: A–R⁸. Woodcut and date, 1574, on R7ᵛ. ?R8 blank.[8]
Titles to 26.a and 26.b enclosed within title-page border McK&F 143.

Bodl. Lib., 8° L.14.Art.Seld. (Wanting R8, ?blank).
STC² (= *STC*) 15617; Alston, vol. 15, no. 516; *ESTC* S106723.
Microfilm: UMI, *EEB*, reel 474: 07.

27.0 [Another edition of the English and Latin parts]

27.1 [Title-page of the English part, ?A1ʳ. No copy recorded.] [? *A Shorte Introduction of
Grammar, generally to be vsed:*]

[London: Assignes of Francis Flower, ?1575.]
4°: [?A–D⁸].

27.2.a [Title-page of the Latin part, A1ʳ:] *Breuissima Institutio Seu Ratio Grammatices cognoscendæ, ad omnium puerorum vtilitatem præscripta, quam solam Regia Maiestas in omnibus
Scholis profitendam præcipit.*
27.2.b [Head-title, H2ʳ] *Desiderii Erasmi, . . . De ratione studij.*
27.2.c [Head-title, H3ʳ:] *De Modo Repetendæ Lectionis . . . Erasmo Authore.*
27.2.d [Head-title, H3ᵛ:] *Magister Discipulos ad studia literarum cohortans.*
27.2.e [Head-title, I1ʳ:] *Omnium Nominum In Regulis.*

---

[7] The first line of the title to the English part of this edition is an open face xylographic
block, with two stops at either side of the 'A' and a digraph 'TE' in '*Shorte*'. This block was also
used in the titles of the English parts of nos. 29.a, 34.0, and 36.0. Another version of this
open face xylographic block using swash letters occurs in no. 32.a.

[8] The woodcut on R7ᵛ is the first recorded appearance of a design by Hans Holbein the
Younger, sometimes referred to as the Tree of Knowledge cut. Variations of it continued to
be included in many editions of 'Lily's Grammar' down to the nineteenth century. This first
version is described and illustrated in Ruth Samson Luborsky and Elizabeth Morley Ingram
(1998), *A Guide to English Illustrated Books, 1536–1603*, 2 vols, Tempe, Ariz., vol. 1: 504–506, and
vol. 2, illustration 128, with notes of its subsequent appearance to 1602. The attribution on
Holbein is based on Arthur M. Hind (1952), *Engraving in England in the Sixteenth and Seventeenth
Centuries*, Vol. 1: *The Tudor Period*, Cambridge, 5.

London: Assignes of Francis Flower, 1575.
4°: A–G⁸ H⁴ I⁸.
Title enclosed within title-page border McK&F 152.

CUL, Syn.7.57.84. Wanting all except quire C of the English part and wanting E6 of the Latin part. (With blank leaves inserted in the Latin part. The first is before E1, the last is before G3; there is none between E8 and F1. All are blank except the recto of the leaf before E2, which is filled by a manuscript note in a different hand from the marginalia in the rest of the volume.) *STC²* (= *STC*) 15618; Alston, vol. 15, no. 517 (with incorrect format); *ESTC* S112694.
Microfilm: UMI, *EEB*, reel 1632: 14.

28.0 [Another edition of the Engl.ish and Latin parts]

28.a [Title-page of the English part, A1ʳ:] *A Shorte Introduction Of Grammar, generally to be vsed: Compyled and set forth, for the bringing vp of all those that intende to attayne the knowledge of the Latine tongue.*
28.b [Section-title of the Latin part, ?D8ʳ. No copy recorded.] [? *Breuissima Institutio Seu Ratio Grammatices cognoscendæ,*]
28.c [Head title, L6ᵛ:] *Desiderii Erasmi . . . De ratione studij.*
28.d [Head title, L7ᵛ:] *De Modo Repetendæ . . . Erasmo Authore.*

London: Assignes of Francis Flower, 1577.
4°: A–L⁸.
Title of the English part enclosed within title-page border McK&F 152.

BL, 1568/3703. Wanting D7,8 (the latter being the section-title to the Latin part); A1.8 are mutilated.
BM Catalogue, vol. 2: 931–32, 954; Kennedy 2503; *STC²* (= *STC*) 15620;⁹ *BLC*, vol. 160: 69; Alston, vol. 15, no. 518 (also with incorrect format); *ESTC* S109926.
Microfilm: UMI, *EEB*, reel 736: 14.

29.0 [Another edition of the English and Latin parts]

29.a [Title-page of the English part, A1ʳ:] *·A· Shorte Introduction Of Grammar, generallie to be vsed: Compiled and set forth, for the bringing vp of all those that intende to attaine the knowledge of the Latine tongue.*
29.b [Section-title of the Latin part, E7ʳ:] *Breuissima Institutio Seu Ratio Grammatices cogno-scendæ, ad omnium puerorum vtilitatem perscripta [sic], quam solam Regia Maiestas in omnibus Scholis profitendam præcipit.*
29.c [Head-title, Q1ʳ:] *Omnium Nominum In Regulis.*

London: Assignes of Francis Flower, 1584.
8°: A–R⁸ (R8? blank).
Titles of the English and Latin parts enclosed within title-page border McK&F 143.

San Marino, California, Henry E. Huntington Library, RB 62210. Wanting R8.
STC² (= *STC*) 15621; Alston, vol. 15, no. 519; *ESTC* S109466.
Microfilm: UMI, *EEB*, reel 263: 07.

---

⁹ The fragment located in New College, Oxford, and listed as *STC²* 15620, Alston, vol. 15, no. 518, and *ESTC* S109926 is actually another copy of no. 38.0 below.

30.0 [Another edition of the English and Latin parts]

30.a [Title-page of the English part, ?A1^r. No copy recorded.] [? *A Shorte Introduction of Grammar, generallie to be vsed:*]

30.b [Section-title of the Latin part, ?E7^r. No copy recorded.] [? *Breuissima Institutio Seu Ratio Grammatices cognoscendæ,*]

30.c [Head-title, Q1^r:] *Omnium Nominum In Regulis.*

[?London: Assignes of Francis Flower] 1585.

8°: [?A–P^8] Q–R^8 (?R8 blank). Dated on R7^v.

Cambridge, Clare College, B^1.2.21(2). Wanting all before Q1 and R8. Bound with no. 15.0 above.

STC^2 15621.3 (incorrectly stating this copy bound with *STC^2* 15613.7 = no. 16.0 above); *ESTC* S93479.

31.0 [Another edition of the English and Latin parts]

31.a [Title-page of the English part, ?A1^r. No copy recorded.] [? *A Short Introduction of Grammar, generally to be vsed:*]

31.b [Section-title of the Latin part, E7^r:] *Breuissima Institutio Seu R atio* [sic] *Grammatices cognoscendæ, ad omnium puerorum vtilitatem perscripta* [sic]*, quam solam Regia Maiestas in omnibus Scholis profitendam præcipit.*

31.c [Head-title, Q1^r:] *Omnium Nominum In Regulis.*

London: Assignes of Francis Flower, 1585 (R6^v dated 1590).

8°: A–R^8. (?R8 blank.)

Section-title of the Latin part enclosed within title-page border McK&F 202.

BL, Ames I.451. Section-title-leaf of the Latin part only.

Washington D.C., Folger Shakespeare Library, Folger STC 15622.2 Part 2. Wanting A1–E6, R7,8.[10] (Bound with the English part dated 1590 (*STC^2* 15622.3; = no. 35.0 below).

STC^2 15621.5 (with incorrect signature reference and final date); Alston, vol. 15, no. 520; *ESTC* S124916.

Microfilm: UMI, *EEB*, reel 2025: 15.

32.0 [Another edition of the English and Latin parts]

32.a [Title-page of the English part, A1^r:] *A Short Introduction of Grammar, generally to be vsed: Compiled and set foorth, for the bringing vp of all those that intend to attain the knowledge of the Latine tongue.*[11]

32.b [Section-title of the Latin part, E4^r:] *Breuissima Institutio Seu Ratio Grammatices cognoscendæ, ad omnium puerorum vtilitatem perscripta* [sic]*, quam solam Regia Maiestas in omnibus Scholis profitendam præcipit.*

32.c [Head-title, O3^r:] *Omnium Nominum in Regulis.*

---

[10] Pending further bibliographical research, these fragments, which, it has been suggested, may actually originate from more than one edition, have here been listed as elements of a single edition, following current published bibliographical information.

[11] The words "*A SHORT*" of the title-page of the English part are apparently composed of one or two xylographic blocks in open-face swash letter. The "*A*" may be separate from "*SHORT*" or both could be a single block. Either way, it is quite different in style from the other block used in no. 26.a with stops either side of the "*A*" and with the digraph "*TE*".

London: [Thomas Dawson for] Assignes of Francis Flower, 1585.
8°: A–P⁸.
The tree of knowledge cut is on P8ᵛ with the date 1586 below.
Titles of the English and Latin parts enclosed within title-page border McK&F 202.

London, St Paul's School. The volume has five leaves of binder's waste, one at the front and four at the back, of *STC²* 20589.5.
STC² 15621.7; Alston, vol. 15, no. 521; *ESTC* S93480.

33.0 [Another edition of the Latin part]

33.a [Title-page, A1ʳ:] *Breuissima Institutio Seu Ratio Grammatices cognoscendæ, ad omnium puerorum vtilitatem præscripta, quam solam Regia Maiestas in omnibus Scholis profitendam præcipit.*
33.b [H2ʳ:] *Desiderii Erasmi, . . . De ratione studij.*
33.c [H3ʳ:] *De Modo Repetendae.*
33.d [I1ʳ:] *Omnium Nominum in Regulis.*

London: Assignes of Francis Flower, 1587. (Last leaf dated 1578.)
4°: A–G⁸ H⁴ I⁸.
Title enclosed within title-page border McK&F 152.

(The outer sheet of quire I, the beginning and end of *Omnium Nominum in Regulis, i.e.* leaves 1, 2, 7, and 8, of which the first two are signed M.j. and M.ij., and which has the date 1578 on leaf 8, appears to be from a hitherto unrecorded edition of the English and Latin parts in a single signature sequence, similar to the 1577 edition, as no. 28.0 above. The first leaf of the inner sheet is correctly signed I.3.)
Bodl. Lib., Douce L 185. (Interleaved, and with an inserted leaf, signed I3, from another work. Bound with no. 34.0).
Eton College Library, DDi.12.37. (Latin part only, bound with an unrecorded 1591/1592 edition of the English part (= no. 36.0 below)).
Halliwell, 81; *STC²* (= *STC*) 15622; Quarrie 143; Alston, vol. 15, no. 522 (with incorrect format); *ESTC* S106727.
Microfilm: UMI, *EEB*, reel 474: 08.

34.0 [Another edition of the English part]

[Title-page, A1ʳ:] *A· Shorte Introduction of Grammar, generally to be vsed: Compiled and set forth, for the bringing vp of all those that intend to attaine the knowledge of the Latine tongue.*

London: Assignes of Francis Flower, 1588. (D7ᵛ dated 1589.)
4°: A–D⁸. (Wanting D8, ?blank, ?colophon.)
Title enclosed within title-page border McK&F 152.

Bodl. Lib., Douce L 185. (Interleaved. Bound with no. 33.0.)
Halliwell, 81; *STC²* (= *STC*) 15622; Alston, vol. 15, no. 522 (with incorrect format); *ESTC* S106727.[12]
Microfilm: UMI, *EEB*, reel 474: 08.

---

[12] Halliwell, STC², Alston, and *ESTC* all incorrectly treat nos. 33.0 and 34.0 as a single entity, apparently based on the assumption—made prior to the appearance of the Eton College Library copy of no. 33.0—that the hitherto unique Bodl. Lib. volume represented the form in which these editions invariably appeared.

35.0 [Another edition of the English and Latin parts]

35.a [Title-page of the English part, A1^r:] *A Short Introduction of Grammar, generally to be vsed: Compiled and set foorth for the bringing vp of all tho se* [sic] *that intend to attain to the knowledge of the Latine tongue.*

35.b [Section-title of the Latin part, ?E7^r. No copy recorded.] [? *Breuissima Institutio Seu Ratio Grammatices cognoscendæ,*]

35.c [Head-title, ?Q1^r. No copy recorded.] [? *Omnium Nominum in Regulis.*]

London: Assignes of Francis Flower, 1590.
8°: A–E^8 [?F–R^8].
Title enclosed within title-page border McK&F 202.

Washington, D.C., Folger Shakespeare Library, Folger STC 15622.2 Part 1. (Leaf A1 mounted, wanting all after E6. MS notes. Bound with the Latin part dated 1585, *STC^2* 15621.5; = no. 31.0 above).
STC^2 15622.3; Alston, vol. 15, no. 523; *ESTC* S93481.
Microfilm: UMI, *EEB*, reel 2137: 12.

36.0 [Another ed. of the English part]

[Title-page, A1^r:] ·A· *Shorte Introduction Of Grammar, generally to be vsed: Compiled and set forth, for the bringing vp of all those that intend to attaine the knowledge of the Latine tongue*

London: Assignes of Francis Flower, 1591. (D7^v dated 1592; colophon on D8^r; further woodcut on D8^v.)
4°: A–D^8.
Title enclosed within title-page border McK&F 152.

Eton College Library, DDi.12.37. (Bound with a copy of *STC^2* 15622 = no. 33.0 above.)
Quarrie 143; Not listed in *STC^2*, Alston, or *ESTC*.

37.0 [Another edition of the English and Latin parts]

37.a [Title-page of the English part, ?A1^r. No copy recorded.] [? *A Short Introduction of Grammar, generally to be vsed:*]

37.b [Section-title of the Latin part, E7^r:] *Breuissima Institutio Seu Ratio Grammatices cognoscendæ, ad omnium puerorum vtilitatem perscripta* [sic], *quam solam Regia Maiestas in omnibus Scholis profitendam præcipit.*

37.c [Head-title, Q1^r:] *Omnium Nominum in Regulis.*

London: Assignes of Francis Flower, 1592.
8°: A–R^8 (R6^v with woodcut and date 1594 below, R7,8 ?blank).
Title of the Latin part enclosed within title-page border McK&F 202.

Oxford, Christ Church, f.9.55. (Wanting title-leaf A1 and R7,8 ?blank.)
STC^2 15622.7; Alston, vol. 15, no. 524 (with incorrect date of title-page to part 2); *ESTC* S124561 (with incorrect format).
Microfilm: UMI, *EEB*, reel 1967: 07.

38.0 [Another edition of the English part]

[Title-page of the English part, A1^r:] *A Shorte Introduction of Grammar, Generally to be vsed: Compiled and set foorth, for the bringing vp of all those that intend to attaine the knowledge of the Latin tongue.*

London: Assignes of Francis Flower, 1593.
4°: [?A–D⁸].

London, Westminster Abbey, P.2.36. (Leaves A1,2,7,8 in duplicate, used as binder's waste in, and subsequently removed from, a copy of the works of Demosthenes, Paris, 1570. (Adams D265–67; Renouard, *Imprimeurs*, vol. 3, no. 628.))
Oxford, New College, BT3.251.9. (Leaves A1,2,7,8, C1,2,7,8, used as binder's waste in a copy of Joannes Paulus Pernumia, *Philosophia naturalis ordine*, Patavia, 1570 (YY.46.7) (Adams P713)).[13]
STC² 15622.8; Alston, vol. 15, no. 525 (with incorrect format); *ESTC* S96048.

39.0 [Another edition of the Latin part]

39.1 [Title-page, A1ʳ:] *Breuissima Institutio Seu Ratio Grammatices cognoscendæ, ad omnium puerorum vtilitatem præscripta, quam solam Regia Maiestas in omnibus Scholis profitendam præcipit.*
39.2 [Head-title, K7ᵛ:] *Desiderii Erasmi, . . . De ratione studij.*
39.3 [Head-title, L1ʳ:] *De Modo Repetendae Lectionis.*
39.4 [Head-title, L2ʳ:] *Magister Discipulos ad studia cohortans.*
39.5 [Head-title, L3ᵛ:] *Omnium Nominum in Regulis.*

London: [Thomas Dawson for] Assignes of Francis Flower, 1596.
8°: A–K⁸ L⁴ M⁸ N⁴. (F2 signed E2.)
Title enclosed within title-page border McK&F 217.

Cambridge, King's College, M.71.5².
BL, Harl. 5974(75) (Title-leaf only).
BL, Huth 108 (2).
Oxford, Corpus Christi College, delta 17.8.
Oxford, St John's College, HB4/3.b.3.16. (Lower part of E1, most of E2 and lower fore-edge of G1 wanting.)
Washington, D.C., Folger Shakespeare Library, Folger STC 15623 (2 copies).
Wolf, 231; *STC²* (= *STC*) 15623; *BLC*, vol. 159: 102, also vol. 160: 69; Alston, vol. 15, no. 526 and plate CXXIX (with a reproduction of the title-page); *ESTC* S101414.
Microfilm: UMI, *EEB*, reel 995: 01. Microfilm of Harley leaf: UMI, *EEB, Tract Supplement*; reel E3: 2, item Harl. 5974(75).
Sigs. A3ᵛ–A4ᵛ of BL, Huth 108 (2), ed. Harry Morgan Ayres (1926). *Speculum* 1: 441–42.

40.0 [Another edition of the English part]

[Title-page, A1ʳ:] *A Short Introduction Of Grammar generally to be vsed: Compiled and set foorth for the bringing vp of all those that intend to attaine to the knowledge of the Latine tongue.*

---

[13] The New College fragment is listed erroneously as *STC²* 15620 (= no. 28.0 above), where it is said: "There is a frag. of an unidentified 4° ed. at Oxford, New College, with this imprint, but the date is cropt." This fragment (without being described as such) is also recorded in *ESTC* under the number for 28.0.

London: [Thomas Dawson for] Assignes of John Battersby, 1597.
8°: A–E⁸.
Title enclosed within title-page border McK&F 217.

Cambridge, King's College, M.71.5¹.
BL, Huth 108 (1).
Oxford, Corpus Christi College, delta 17.8.
Oxford, St John's College, HB4/3.b.3.16. (Wanting leaves A1, A2, and part of B7, B8).
Washington, D.C., Folger Shakespeare Library, Folger STC 15623 (2 copies, copy 2 with leaves A1 and A2 frayed.)
Wolf, 231; *STC²* (= *STC*) 15623; *BLC*, vol. 159: 102, also vol. 160: 69; Alston, vol. 15, no. 526. *ESTC* S101414.
Microfilm: UMI, *EEB*, reel 995: 01.

41.0 [Another ed. of the English and Latin parts]

41.a [Title-page of the English part, A1ʳ:] *A Short Introduction of Grammar, generally to be vsed: Compiled and set foorth, for the bringing vp of all those that intend to attain to the knowledge of the Latine tongue.*
41.b [Section-title of the Latin part, E7ʳ:] *Brevissima Institutio Seu Ratio Grammatices cognoscendæ, ad omnium puerorum vtilitatem perscripta* [sic], *quamsolam* [sic] *Regia Maiestas in omnibus Scholis profitendam præcipit.*
41.c [Head-title, Q1ʳ:] *Omnium nominum in regulis.*

London: [Thomas Dawson for] Assignes of John Battersby, 1599.
8°: A–R⁸. (R8, ?blank; colophon on R7ʳ.)
Titles of the English and Latin parts enclosed within title-page border McK&F 202.

CUL, Syn.8.59.101. Fragment of the upper portions of leaves A2, A3, A6 and A7 of the English part only.¹⁴
University of Illinois at Urbana-Champaign Library, 475 L62s 1599. (Wanting R8, ?blank.)
Sayle 6794; *STC* 15605a; *STC²* 15623.5; Quaritch Catalogue 464, item 175; Alston, vol. 15, no. 527; *ESTC* S108017.
Microfilm: UMI, *EEB*, reel 517: 09 (refers to the CUL leaves, not to the Illinois copy).
Title-page of the Latin part is reproduced in Baldwin (1944), vol. 1, frontispiece.

42.0 [Another edition of the English part]

[Title-page, A1ʳ:] *A Short Introduction Of Grammar generally to be vsed: Compiled and set fo<o>rth for the bringing vp of all those that intend to attaine to the knowledge of the Latine tongue*

London: [Thomas Dawson for] Assignes of John Battersby, 1599.
8°: A–E⁸.
Title enclosed within title-page border McK&F 217.

---

¹⁴ The EEBO reference refers to the CUL leaves, not to the Illinois copy. I should like to thank Professor Alvan Bregman, Illinois University Library, for comparing the images in EEBO for the fragment of *STC²* 15623.5 located in CUL with the 1599 Illinois copy with the shelfmark 475 L62s 1599.

BL, 1568/3786. (Bound with a copy of the Latin part of the 1602 edition; = no. 43.2 below.)

BL, Harl. 5974(98), fragment, leaf A2 (with MS annotations on both sides).

BM Catalogue, vol. 2: 932, 954; *STC²* (= *STC*) 15624; *BLC*, vol. 160: 69; Alston, vol. 15, no. 528; *ESTC* S101413.

Microfilm: UMI, *EEB*, reel 995: 02. Microfilm of Harley leaf: UMI, *EEB, Tract Supplement*, reel E3: 2[91], item Harl. 5974(98).

43.0 [Another edition of the English and Latin parts]

43.1 [Title-page of the English part, A1ʳ:] *A Short Introduction Of Grammar generally to be vsed: Compiled and set fo<o>rth for the bringing vp of a<l>l those that intend to attaine to the knowledge of the Latine tongue.*

London: Assignes of John Battersby, 1602.

8°: A–E⁸.

Title enclosed within title-page border McK&F 217.

43.2 [Title-page of the Latin part, A1ʳ:] *Breuissima Institutio Seu Ratio Grammatices cogno-scendæ, ad omnium puerorum vtilitatem præscripta, quam solam Regia Maiestas in omnibus Scholis pro<f>itendam præcipit.*

London: [Thomas Dawson for] Assignes of John Battersby, 1602.

8°: A–K⁸ L⁴ M⁸ N⁴.

Title enclosed within title-page border McK&F 217.

BL, 1568/3786. (Latin part only, bound with a copy of the English 1599 edition; = no. 42.0 above.)

Bodl. Lib., 8° Z.66.Art.BS.

CUL, Rel.d.61.2° (Latin part only). (Sig. B is bound 2, 1, 4, 3, 6, 5, 8, 7.) (Bound with a 1606 edition of the English part; = *STC²* 15625.)[15]

Eton College Library, S.B.1602.

BM Catalogue, vol. 2: 932; Sayle 7307; *STC²* 15624.5; *BLC*, 160: 69; Alston, vol. 15, no. 529 (not noting that the CUL copy is incomplete; with incorrect microfilm reference to *STC²* 15611.7; = no. 11.0 above); *ESTC* S125078.

Microfilm: UMI, *EEB*, reel 1995: 12.

---

[15] The copy listed in *STC²* and Alston as being in the Devonshire Collection at Chatsworth was apparently sold at auction by Christie's in 1981 or 1982, but not separately catalogued. Its present location is unknown.

Appendix IV

WORKS BY, OR ATTRIBUTED TO, WILLIAM LILY

The following list provides information about copies of the first extant editions of major works by William Lily and other works connected with his name. No attempt has been made to identify and list all extant single texts by Lily, for example scattered pieces such as verses on title-pages, verse epitaphs, commendatory poems, or commentaries on other grammarians' works. The copies noted are those located in libraries of Great Britain and America, and in the Bavarian State Library, Munich. There may well be, and in the case of Thomas More's and William Lily's epigrams there are, other copies of the same editions in existence elsewhere. For the copies listed below, details including their title or heading, collation, place of printing, printer, present location, bibliographical references, and, as far as available, notices of modern editions are provided. The transcriptions of the titles preserve only the first capital of words in upper case, abbreviations are expanded silently, but otherwise original spelling is retained. The works are arranged chronologically according to the date of the first extant edition.

1 William Lily, *Libellus de constructione*

[Title-page, A1ʳ:] *Libellus de constructione Octo partium orationis.* [Revised by Desiderius Erasmus.][1]
London: Richard Pynson, 1513.
4°: A–D⁶ E⁴.

Bodl. Lib., 4° C.23.Art.BS.
Bodleian Library Exhibition Catalogue 74; *STC* 5544 and 10497; *STC²* 15601.3; Johnston 107; Trapp-Schulte Herbrüggen 15; Sharpe 2103; *HEL* (1998), I, no. 1248; *ESTC* S111399.
Microfilm: UMI, *EEB*, reel 61: 38; 96: 18.
See Erasmus and Lily (1513), *Libellus de constructione*, ed. M. Cytowska (1973), in *Opera Omnia Desiderii Erasmi Roterodami*. Amsterdam, vol. I,4: 119–43. [Text based on the later revised edn., Basle: John Froben, August 1515.][2]

---

[1] On the authorship of this grammar see Colet's prefatory letter to Lily dated 1513 on A1ᵛ of this copy where it does not become clear whether Lily compiled this text. Erasmus's letter, included in the 1515 edition which is entitled *Absolutissimus de octo orationis partium constructione libellus* (Bodl. Lib., 4° E 6(4) Art.Seld., a2ʳ), however, says that it was Lily's work which Colet had asked him to compile; see *CWE*, vol. 3, Ep. 341: 146–47. Cf. also Knight (1823), *The Life of Dr. John Colet*, Cambridge, 128–30. In his treatise *De Erudienda Iuventute* (1526), Leonard Cox also attributes this grammar to William Lily. See Breeze and Glomski (eds.) (1991), *Humanistica Lovaniensia*. 40: 141 and 143 (English translation).
[2] See Cytowska's (1973) edition, Introduction, 105–17.

2 William Lily, *Rudimenta grammatices*

[Title-page, A1ʳ:] *Guilelmi Lilii Angli Rudimenta. Parvulorum Lilii nuper Impressa et correcta.*[3]
[York: Ursyn Mylner, 1516?]
4°: A⁴ B² (B2 mis-signed Biii).

Bodl. Lib., 4° Rawlinson 206(3).
Bodleian Library Exhibition Catalogue 75; *STC²* 15609.3; Trapp-Schulte Herbrüggen 15; Sharpe 2103; *Checklist* 51.1; Alston, vol. 15, no. 402; *ESTC* S103871.
Microfilm: UMI, *EEB*, reel 1995: 10.

3 Thomas More and William Lily, *Progymnasmata*

[Title, x4ʳ:] *Progymnasmata Thomae Mori, Et Guilielmi Lilii Sodalium.*
[Published together with More's *Epigrams* and the 3ʳᵈ edn. of his *Vtopia.*]
[Title-page, x1ʳ:] *Epigrammata Clarissimi Disertissimique Viri Thomae Mori Britanni, Pleraque E Graecis Versa.*
[General title-page, a1ʳ:] *De Optimo Reipublicæ Statu Deque noua insula Vtopia libellus uere aureus, nec minus salutaris quàm festiuus, clarissimi disertissimi'que uiri Thomae Mori inclytæ ciuitatis Londinensis ciuis et Vicecomitis. Epigrammata clarissimi disertissimi'que uiri Thomae Mori, pleraque è Græcis uersa. Epigrammata. Desiderii Erasmi Roterodami.*
Basle: John Froben, March 1518.
4°: a–s⁴ t–u⁶ x–z⁴, A–I⁴ K⁶ L–T⁴ V⁶ (pp. 1–164, 165–356).
(The text of the *Progymnasmata* by More and Lily runs from sigs. x4ʳ–y4ʳ (pp. 171–79).)

Cambridge, King's College (2 copies). J.46.7 (this copy lacks the *Epigrammata. Desiderii Erasmi Roterodami*, sigs. L–T⁴ V⁶), and Keynes Ec7.3.16.
Cambridge, Trinity College, III.4.89 (3). (This copy also finishes at K6.)
BL, G.2398.(1).
London, Lambeth Palace Library, **MX 811 518. (This copy also finishes at K6.)
Manchester, John Rylands University Library, 17704.
Munich, Bavarian State Library, SB Rar.1862.
Bodl. Lib., Mar. 891. (This copy wants gatherings y and H.)
Maitland, *List*, no. 337:151; Heckethorn 90; Isaac, *Index*, 14177; Gibson 3; Davies 303; Adams M1756; Shaaber M222; *BLC*, vol. 324: 231; Smith 3; *VD* 16, vol. 14, M 6294; Sharpe 2103.
See Thomas More, *The Complete Works*, Vol. 3, Part II: *Latin Poems*, ed. and trans. Miller, Bradner *et al.* (1984), 78–95, nos. 1–18. (Text based on the later revised edition, Basle: John Froben, 1520.)

4 William Lily, *Antibossicon*

[Title-page, [a]1ʳ:] *Antibossicon.* [In verse.]
London: Richard Pynson, 1521.
4°: [a]⁴ b–f⁴ (f4ᵛ blank).

BL, C.70.e.16.(1) (imperfect, wanting d1 which is supplied in photocopy from the Bodl. Lib. copy).
London, Lambeth Palace Library, 1521.4.

---

[3] The earliest extant copy of this Latin syntax in English when published together with John Colet's *Aeditio* is that of the 1527 edition where it is entitled *Guillelmi Lilij Angli Rudimenta.* See *Checklist* 51.3 and 20.1.

Bodl. Lib., 4° F.33 (2) Art. (The text in this copy is followed by *Antibossicon Guilielmi Hormani ad Guilielmum Lilium.* [etc.] (sigs. g⁸ h⁴).)
Cambridge, Corpus Christi College, SP.105(2).
Cambridge, St John's College, A.2.14(2).
University of Illinois at Urbana-Champaign Library, Uncat. Horman, William. *Antibossicon . . .* Londini, 1521.
San Marino, California, Henry Huntington Library (2 copies), RB 61554.
Washington D.C., Folger Shakespeare Library, Folger STC 15606.
BM Catalogue, vol. 2: 954; *STC²* (= *STC*) 15606; Johnston 156; *BLC*, vol. 192: 288; Sharpe 2103; *ESTC* S106235.
Microfilm: UMI, *EEB*, reel 85: 08.

5 William Lily, *Epigrammata*

[Title-page, a1ʳ:] *Epigrammata Guilelmi Lilii. Angli.* [In verse.]
[London: Wynkyn de Worde, 1522.]⁴
4°: a⁴.

London, Lambeth Palace Library, 1521.4.
Dublin, Trinity College, DD.hh.56 no. 4.
This book contains the following items:
Praecepta Morum [or: *Carmen de moribus*]⁵ [*c.*1510]. Sigs. a1ᵛ– a3ʳ.
Diuo Carolo Imperatori semper Augusto Guilielmi Lilii Acclamatio [*Acclamatio Caroli V Germani imperatoris*].⁶ Sigs. a3ʳ–a4ᵛ.
De Rege Castelle Philippo, Nauiganti in Hispaniam. Guilielmi Lilii Carmen [*c.*1506].⁷ Sig. a4ᵛ.
Maitland, *List*, no. 408: 415–16; Maitland, *Index*, 68; *STC²* 15606.5; Sharpe 2103; *ESTC* S120457.
Microfilm: UMI, *EEB*, reel 1797: 35.

---

⁴ See Carlson (1993). 'Printers' Needs: Wynkyn de Worde's Piracy of William Lily's *Epigrammata* in 1522', in Carlson (1993), 123–41, and note 1: 231–32, where the date of printing is also discussed; and Pamela Ayres Neville (1990), *Richard Pynson, King's Printer (1506–1529)*, London, 249.

⁵ Items of the *Epigrammata* had been available separately in some form before this book was printed by Wynkyn de Worde. On the *Carmen de moribus* see pp. 81–82 above. A copy of this poem is found in the 1527 edn. containing John Colet's *Aeditio* and William Lily's *Rudimenta grammatices* (*Checklist* 20.1, 51.3), E5ᵛ–E7ʳ.

⁶ This item, containing a series of seven related poems and the motto '*Carolus, Henricus, Viuant*', praising Henry VIII and Charles V, was written in 1522, probably in May, for use in the public celebrations that greeted the emperor's entry into the City of London. See Sydney Anglo (1969), *Spectacle, Pageantry, and Early Tudor Policy*, Oxford, 187–202; also C. R. Baskervill (1936), 'William Lily's Verse for the Entry of Charles V into London', *The Huntington Library Bulletin* 9: 1–14, at 1–8. The first of these poems was printed by Baskervill, 10. It is also found, with variations, in BL, MS Harley 540, fol. 57ʳ (printed by Baskervill, 6). MS Harley 540, fols. 57ʳ–59ʳ, written by John Stow in the reign of Elizabeth I, preserves thirteen other poems by Lily: epitaphs for John Colet, Henry VII's queen, Elizabeth of York, the Bishop of Lincoln, William Atwater, Thomas Lupset, Lily's wife Agnes, also two exchanges with Polydore Vergil, Latin verse translations of epigrams from the Greek Anthology not otherwise attested, an encomium of Cardinal Thomas Wolsey, and others. See also Neville (1990), 168, footnote 219; and Gilbert Tournoy (1988), 'La Poésie de William Lily pour le Diptyque de Quentin Metsijs', *Moreana* 25, no. 97: 63–66.

⁷ The final item consists of verses on the storm which brought Philip the Handsome, Duke of Burgundy, accidentally to England and blew the eagle weather-vane off St Paul's Cathedral on 15 January 1506. For a manuscript version see BL, MS Harley 540, fol. 59ʳ.

6 William Lily, Epigrams in Latin and English. Selections

[Title-page, a1^r:] *Of the tryumphe/ and the verses that Charles themperour/ and the most myghty redouted kyng of England/ Henry the .viii. were saluted with/ passyng through London.*
[A translation of the verses in honour of Charles V on his entry into London on 6 June 1522.]
[London]: Richard Pynson, [1522.][8]
4°: a^6.

San Marino, California, Henry E. Huntington Library, RB 56691.
STC 5017; *STC²* 15606.7; Johnston 168; Sharpe 2103; *ESTC* S104955.
Microfilm: UMI, *EEB*, reel 132: 12.
Ed. Baskervill (1936), no. 9: 8–14; BL, MS Harley 540, 57^r (*Acclamatio*).

7 Lucius Coelius Lactantius, *Carmen*

[Title-page, a1^r:] *L. Lactantii Firmiani Carmen. De passione dominica. De resurrectione. De Phenice. Guilielmi Lilii In laudem uirginis deiparę carmen eruditum. Ab Erasmo Institutum christiani hominis feliciter ędutum.*
[London: Richard Pynson, 1522?]
4°: a–[?]^4, imperfect.

BL, 847.h.1. Imperfect; lacks all after b4. (Lily's and Erasmus's works are listed on the title-page, but the texts themselves are missing.)

BM Catalogue, vol. 2: 920–21; *STC²* (= *STC*) 15118; Johnston 169; *BLC*, vol. 182: 28; *ESTC* S120690.
Microfilm: UMI, *EEB*, reel 70: 13.

8 William Lily, *De generibus nominum*

[Title-page, A1^r:] *Guilielmi Lilii Grammatici et poëtæ eximij, Paulinæ scholæ olim moderatoris, De generibus nominum, Ac uerborum præteritis et supinis Regulæ pueris apprime utiles. Opus Recognitum et adauctum cum Nominum ac Verborum interpretamentis, per Ioannem Rituissi* [sic] *Scholæ Paulinæ præceptori* [sic]. [c.1510] [Ed. J. Rightwise. In verse.]
Antwerp: Michael Hillenius, 1525.
8°: A–C^8 D^4.

BL, G. 7476.
Lily, *Shorte Introduction* (1567), vii; Njhoff-Kronenberg 1373; *BM STC* (*Netherlands*), 118; Shaaber L103; *BLC*, vol. 192: 288; Sharpe 2103.[9]

---

[8] For an edition of these epigrams see C. R. Baskervill (1936), 8–14. Cf. Carlson (1993), 127, and note 8: 232–33; also Neville, 127–28, 249.

[9] The *BM Catalogue*, vol. 2: 954, *STC* 15607, and *BLC*, vol. 192: 288, list another, quarto edition of this grammar printed in [1520?] (BL, 625.d.11.). This is the *De generibus nominum*, [Southwark, Peter Treveris, 1528?]. 4°: A–E^4, wanting E4, ?blank. *STC²* 15607; Sharpe 2103; *ESTC* S104793. Microfilm: UMI, *EEB*, reel 85:09. It seems very probably to have been printed by Treveris, but it seems unlikely that he printed this as early as 1520. The date [1528?] in *STC²* may have been based on the information for the printer. On Peter Treveris (*fl.* 1525–1532) see *STC²*, vol. 3: 171.

9 *Institutio.* Attributed to William Lily

[Title-page, A1ʳ:] *Institutio Compendiaria Totius Grammaticae, Quam Et Eruditissimus atque idem illustrissimus Rex noster hoc nomine euulgari iussit, ut non alia quam hæc una per totam Angliam pueris prælegeretur.*
London: Thomas Berthelet, 1540.
For bibliographical details see Appendix III, 1.0 (2 copies).

10 *Introduction.* Attributed to William Lily

[Title-page, A1ʳ:] *An Introduction Of The Eyght Partes Of speche, and the Construction of the same, compiled and sette forthe by the commaundement of our most gracious souerayne lorde the king.*
London: Thomas Berthelet, 1542.
For bibliographical details see pp. 140–46 above, also Appendix III, 3.0.
See also proof leaf of [*An Introduction of the Eyght Partes of Speche*].
[London: Thomas Berthelet, *c.*1540].
For bibliographical details see p. 77 above, Appendix II, and Appendix III, 2.0.

11 Lorenzo Gualtieri (Lorenzo Spirito) [*Il libro delle sorti.* English.][10]

[Title, A1ʳ:] *The booke of Fortune.*
[Made in Italian. A translation by William Lily? Partly in verse, with woodcuts.]
London: For Edward Wright, 1618. (Entered the Stationers' Register to William Powell, 6 February 1560).
2°: A⁸ B¹² C–E⁸ F⁶.

BL, C.144.e.10.
STC² (= *STC*) 3306; *BLC*, vol. 310: 147; *ESTC* S116406.
Microfilm: UMI, *EEB*, reel 1299: 05.

---

[10] See Elizabeth Edmondston (1965), 'Unfamiliar Libraries IX: Sion College', *The Book Collector* 14: 165–77, at 177, and Plates V and VI; also Hubertus Schulte Herbrüggen (1967), 'Sir Thomas Mores Fortuna-Verse', in H. Meller and H.-J. Zimmermann (eds.), *Lebende Antike. Symposion für Rudolf Sühnel*, Berlin, 155–72, especially 162–65, and 171–72.

DEFINITIONS OF THE PARTS OF SPEECH IN
LATIN GRAMMARS IN ENGLISH
(INCLUDING SOME LATIN GRAMMARS IN LATIN)

This appendix aims to provide the reader with the definitions of the parts of speech used in the tradition of grammar writing in English. It lists definitions of the parts of speech that are contained in Latin grammars written in English, starting from the *Introduction*, 1542, and going back as far as *c*.1400, the period to which the first extant Latin grammatical manuscript in English can be dated. The appendix also includes the definitions given in Ælfric's *Grammar* (*c*.995) and Latin grammars that had influenced the grammar attributed to Lily and those throughout the tradition. The definitions listed here also include definitions of the parts of speech given in those sections of grammars that deal with declension separately. These definitions reflect the tradition of the authorized grammar and, at the same time, they shed light on the variety of ways in which pupils had to define the parts of speech. For the printed grammars the definitions are usually taken from the earliest extant and complete edition. However, unique fragmentary copies are also included. The different versions of school texts that were compiled by a specific grammarian or schoolmaster, or that can be attributed to one, are arranged in groups, such as those by Thomas Linacre, whose grammars are followed by John Colet's *Aeditio*, both of which exhibit parallels to the 1542 *Introduction*. Those grammars by, or attributed to, John Stanbridge are also kept together, as well as those by John Vaus and the Scottish Donatus that were intended for use in Scotland. Otherwise the texts are arranged in reverse chronological order. The order of the parts of speech in this appendix follows that employed in the 1542 *Introduction*.

Definitions of the noun:

A NOVVNE IS the name of a thyng that maye bee seen, felt, heard or vnderstand. As the name of my hande in latine is *Manus*.The name of an howse, is *Domus*.The name of goodnesse is *Bonitas*. (*Introduction*, 1542. BL, C.21.b.4.(2), A4ʳ–F2ʳ [the parts of speech], at A4ʳ (present edition, 161, 8–10).)

A nowne is the name of a thynge that is. and may be seen/ felte/ herde/ or vnderstande. As the name of my hande in latyn is *.Manus*. the name of a hous is *.Domus*. the name of goodnes is *.Bonitas*. (John Colet, *Aeditio*, 1527. EL, 298 (1971), A6ʳ–D7ʳ [the parts of speech], at A6ʳ; *Checklist* 20.1.)

Of them [the parts of speech] that be declined, these .iij. nowne, pronowne, and participle be declined with gendre, case, and nombre. [*etc.*] Of nownes some be declined this wyse. The masculine gendre the nominatiue singular poeta, the genitiue poetæ, [*etc.*] (Thomas Linacre, *Rudimenta grammatices*, [1525?]. EL, 312 (1971), A2ʳ–F1ʳ [*Rudimenta declinationum*], at A2ʳ).
A Nowne is: that betokeneth a thynge without any difference of tyme, and is declined with case. (*Ibid.*, F1ʳ–G1ᵛ [*Rudimenta definitionum*], at F1ʳ; *Checklist* 55.1.)

Of the mouable. nowne. pronowne and participle. ben declined with gendre. case and nombre. [etc.]. Of nownes: som be declined this wyse. The masculyne gendre the nominatyfe case and singuler nombre poeta. the genityfe poete [etc.]. (Thomas Linacre, *Progymnasmata grammatices vulgaria*, [1512.]. BL, G.7569, A2ʳ–b5ᵛ [on declension], at A2ʳ.)

A Nowne is: that betokeneth a thynge wyth oute ony dyfference of tyme or person. and is declyned with case. (*Ibid.*, b5ᵛ–c4ʳ [definitions of the parts of speech], at b5ᵛ; *Checklist* 54.1.)

Quhat is ane nowne? ane part of orisone/ with cais. betakenand body or thing: propirly or comonly. propirly. as, how? as/ Roma, rome. tybris, the watir of tibyr: comonly as how? as vrbs ane towne, flumen ane flude: (John Vaus, 1531. *Rudimenta puerorum in artem grammaticam.* Aberdeen, University Library, AUL Λ Vaur 2, cc8ʳ–ee4ʳ [*de partium orationis interpretatione lingua vernacula*], at cc8ʳ; *Checklist* 56.1.)

(Preceptor) How know yow a nowne substantiue (Discipulus) for he may stonde by him self with[1] owt help of an other worde: and is declined with one article/ as hic magister or with two at the most as hic et hec conuiua. (*Donate and accidence for children*, 1515. Bodl. Lib., Arch. A e.19, A2ʳ–C3ʳ, at A2ʳ; *Checklist* 19.1.)

Where of .iiii. be declyned and mouable/ as Nowne/ Pronowne: Verbe: and particyple. [etc.]. Of these .iiii. partes mouable/ thre be declyned with case/ as Nowne: Pronowne. and Partycyple. [etc.]. Fyue thynges be expedient to the declynynge of a nowne. Artycle. Case: Gendre. Nombre: and Declenson. (John Holt, *Lac puerorum*, [1508.]. BL, C.33.b.47, A3ʳ–C8ʳ [on declension], at A3ʳ.)

A Nowne betokeneth a thynge without ony difference of tyme. Also the name of all þat I may see fele or perceyue by ony of my fyue wytes/ is a nowne. (*Ibid.*, C8ʳ–E2ʳ [definitions of the parts of speech], at C8ʳ; *Checklist* 53.2.)

Of the whyche .viii. partyes .iiii. be declyned. Nowne. pronowne and Particyple with case. [etc.]. That other betokneth the thynge/ doynge suffrynge or beynge. as nowne and pronowne. But nowne of hymselfe betokeneth a certeyne thynge comynly or properly. [A2ʳ]. How knowest a nowne substantyue? for he may stonde by hymself without helpe of another word. and is declyned with one article or .ii. at the most. as hic magister. hic et hec sacerdos. [A4ᵛ]. (*Informatio puerorum*, [1499?]. Cambridge, Magdalene College, Pepysian Library, PL 1305(3), A2ʳ–B3ʳ, D2ᵛ–D3ᵛ; *Checklist* 17.1.)

How knowe ye a nowne? For he ys a parte of reason declinyd wyth case. And the name of euery thynge that may be felte/ sene/ herde/ or vndurstande ys yn laten a nowne propre or appellatyue. ([*Abridged version of the Accidence, with other extracts*], 1534. CUL, Syn.8.53.74, A2ʳ–C8ᵛ, at A2ʳ; *Checklist* 16.35.)

How knowe yow a nowne? for he is a part of reson declined with case. and the name of euery thynge that may be felt. sene. hard or vnderstonde. is in latyne a nowne propur or appellatyue. (John Stanbridge, *Accidence*, [1505?]. Bodl. Lib., 4°A 18(2) Art.BS, A1ʳ–C6ᵛ, at A2ʳ; *Checklist* 16.1.)

How knowe ye a nowne/ for al þat I may fele see here or vnderstand þat bereth þe name of a thyng is a nowne. (*Short Accidence*, attributed to John Stanbridge [1495?]. San Marino, California, Henry E. Huntington Library, RB 152101, A1 and A4, at A1ʳ (*Early Printed Editions*, Text I, 226, 11–13; *Checklist* 15.1.)

---

[1] wth

How knowest a nown for al maner thyng þat a man may see fele. Here. or vnderstonde þat berith þe name of a thynge is a nowne. (*Long Accidence*, attributed to John Stanbridge [1495.]. Bodl. Lib., Douce D 238(2), A1ʳ–B6ᵛ, at A1ʳ (*Early Printed Editions*, Text A, 152, 11–13; *Checklist* 14.1).)

How knowyst a nowne? A nowne ys all maner of thyng þat y may see, fele or hondyll or beryth þe name of a thyng, þe name þerof ys a nowne. (*c.*1492–1494. Bodl. Lib., MS Douce 103, fols. 53ʳ–57aʳ (Thomson, *Edition*, Text K, 56, 12–14; *Checklist* 12).)

How knowest a nowne? Of euery thing that is in this world or out of this world the name is a nowne, as 'man', 'angel', 'vertue', etcetera. Whad maner of speche 'a man'? A nowne. Whiso? For hit berith the name of a thing that is in this world. 'Hevyn': whad maner of speche? A nowne. Whi so? For hit beryth the name of a thing that is out of this world. (S. xv³ᐟ⁴. Worcester, Cathedral Library, MS F.123, fol. 99ᵛ (Thomson, *Edition*, Text M, 63, 13–19; *Checklist* 11).)

How know ȝe a nown? For all þat I may see or fele or know þat beryth þe name of a thyng is a nown, as *homo* for 'a man', *corpus* for 'a body', *anima* for 'a sowle' and all so lyke. (S. xv³ᐟ⁴. BL, MS Add. 12,195, fol. 66ʳ (Thomson, *Edition*, Text E, 44, 11–14; *Checklist* 10).)

Howe know þu a nown? For all þat I may see, here, fele or vndirstande þat beryth þe name of a thyng is a nown. (S. xv². BL, MS Add. 37,075, fols. 1ʳ–6ᵛ (Thomson, *Edition*, Text F, 45, 11–12; *Checklist* 9).)

How knowist thow a nowne? For all thyng that I may se or fele or vndirstond that bereth the name of a thyng the name therof ys a nowne. (1444–1483. Bodl. Lib., MS Rawlinson D. 328, fols. 119ʳ, 120ʳ, 121ʳ, 122ʳ, 123ʳ, 124ʳ–125ʳ, 126ʳ (Thomson, *Edition*, Text L, 61, 27–29; *Checklist* 8).)

Qwerby knowyst a nown? For al thyng þat may be seen, herd oþer felt or beryth þe name of a thyng is a nown. (S. xvᵐᵉᵈ. Cambridge, St John's College, MS F.26(163), fols. 1ʳ–12ʳ. (Thomson, *Edition*, Text C, 17, 11–12; *Checklist* 7).)

How knowe ȝe a noun? For þe Laten of eny þyng ys a noun. (S. xvᵐᵉᵈ. Aberystwyth, NLW, MS Peniarth 356B, fols. 163ʳ, 165ʳ–167ᵛ. (Thomson, *Edition*, Text B, 9, 10; *Checklist* 6).)

How knos þu a nowne? For all þat I may fele, here or se þat berys þe name of a thyng, þe name þerof ys a nowne. (S. xvᵐᵉᵈ. Aberystwyth, NLW, MS Peniarth 356B, fols. 54ᵛ–57ᵛ and 48ʳ (Thomson, *Edition*, Text A, 1, 11–12; *Checklist* 5).)

How knowst a nown? A party of resun þat is clynud wit cas or wit articul & betokuns body or þyng be name. Body as how? As *homo, animal, lignum, lapis.* Þing as how? As *virtus, sciencia.* (1420s. Oxford, Lincoln College, MS Lat. 130, fols. 7ʳ–9ᵛ. On long-term deposit in Bodl. Lib. (Bland, 148, [2–8]; *Checklist* 4).)

How knowyste a noun substantyf? A party of reson that betokenyth substaunce wyth qualite and is declined wyth case and article; and so the name of euery thyng in the world is a noun substantyf. [. . .] How knowyst a noun substantyf? Euery word that is declined wyth on article or to atte moste, as *hic magister, hic et hec sacerdos.* (S. xv¹. Cambridge, Trinity College, MS O.5.4, fols. 4ᵛ–6ᵛ (Thomson, *Edition*, Text D, 32, 8–11, 12–14; *Checklist* 2).)

Nomen est pars orationis, quę rem significat sine ulla temporis aut personæ differentia. (*Institutio Compendiaria Totius Grammaticae*, 1540. Attributed to William Lily. BL, C.21.b.4.(3), at C1ʳ; Appendix III, 1.0.)

Nomen est pars orationis: que vnicuique subiectorum corporum/ seu rerum communem/ vel propriam qualitatem distribuit. (Joannes Sulpitius Verulanus, *Opus insigne grammaticum*, 1494. JRUL, 19691, at a3ᵛ.)

Quid est nomen? Est pars orationis cum casu corpus aut rem proprie communiterue significans. Unde dicitur nomen. Nomen dicitur quasi notamen quod hoc notemus vniuscuiusque substantie qualitatem. uel a greco quod est onoma. (Nicolaus Perottus, *Rudimenta grammatices*, 1486. CUL, Inc.5.F.2.8 [3287], at a3ᵛ.)

NOMEN is nama, mid ðâm wê nemnað ealle ðing ǽgðer gê synderlîce gê gemǽnelîce. synderlîce be âgenum naman: *Eadgarus, Adelwoldus*; gemǽnelîce: *rex* cyning, *episcopus* bisceop. (Ælfric, *Praefatio de partibus orationis*, in *Grammatik und Glossar* (Zupitza, 8, 8–11).) on ðisum eahta dǽlum synd ðâ mǽstan and ðâ mihtigostan NOMEN ET VERBUM, þæt is, nama and word. mid ðâm naman wê nemnað ealle ðing and mid ðâm worde wê sprecað be eallum ðingum. (Ælfric, *Grammatik und Glossar* (Zupitza, 11, 8–11).)

Nomen est pars orationis, quae unicuique subiectorum corporum seu rerum communem vel propriam qualitatem distribuit. (Priscian, *Institutiones grammaticae* (*GL* II, 56, 29–57, 1).)

Nomen est pars orationis cum casu corpus aut rem proprie communiterue significans, proprie ut Roma Tiberis, communiter ut urbs flumen. (Donatus, *Ars maior* (Holtz, 614, 2–3; *GL* IV, 373, 2–3).)

Nomen quid est? Pars orationis cum casu corpus aut rem proprie communiterue significans. (Donatus, *Ars minor* (Holtz, 585, 7–8; *GL* IV, 355, 5–6).)

Definitions of the pronoun:

A Pronowne is a parte of speche, muche lyke a nowne, whiche is vsed in shewyng or rehersyng. (*Introduction*, 1542. BL, C.21.b.4.(2), A4ʳ–F2ʳ [the parts of speech], at B4ᵛ (present edition, 167, 224–25.)

A Pronowne is moche lyke a nowne/ and in reason standeth for a nowne. (John Colet, *Aeditio*, 1527. *EL*, 298 (1971), A6ʳ–D7ʳ [the parts of speech], at B3ʳ; *Checklist* 20.1.)

Of pronownes, some be primitiues: as ego, tu, sui, ille, iste, hic, is, ipse. Al other be deriuatiues. (Thomas Linacre, *Rudimenta grammatices*, [1525?]. *EL*,312 (1971), A2ʳ–F1ʳ [*Rudimenta declinationum*], at A4ᵛ.)
A Pronowne is a parte of speche declined with case, whiche signifieth a thynge without any difference of tyme, and euer with a certayne difference of person. Otherwyse. whiche signifieth a thyng, as shewed rehersed or had with some difference of persone, and therfore some be called relatiues, some demonstratiues, and some possessiues. (*Ibid.*, F1ʳ–G1ᵛ [*Rudimenta definitionum*], at F3ᵛ; *Checklist* 55.1.)

Of pronownes: some be primitiues. as ego. tu. sui. ille. iste. hic. is. ipse. All other be deriuatyues. (Thomas Linacre, *Progymnasmata grammatices vulgaria*, [1512.]. BL, G.7569, A2ʳ–b5ᵛ [on declension], at A4ʳ.)
A pronowne is a part of spech declinyd with case. which sygnyfieth a thing with out any dyfference of tyme. and euer with certeyne difference of parson. (*Ibid.*, b5ᵛ–c4ʳ [definitions of the parts of speech], at c1ᵛ; *Checklist* 54.1.)

Quhat is ane pronowne? Ane part of orisone quhilk is put for ane nowne and may al maist als mekil as ane nowne and sumtyme resauis certane persone. (John Vaus, *Rudimenta puerorum in artem grammaticam*, 1531. Aberdeen, University Library, AUL ∧ Vau r 2, cc8ʳ–ee4ʳ [de partium orationis interpretatione lingua vernacula], at dd3ᵛ; *Checklist* 56.1.)

(Preceptor) How know you a pronowne (Discipulus) for he is a parte of reson declined with case put for a nowne and receyueth certen parsone. (*Donate and accidence for children*, 1515. Bodl. Lib., Arch. A e.19, A2ʳ–C3ʳ, at B1ʳ; *Checklist* 19.1.)

Here be .xv. pronownes besyde theyr compoundes/ as Ego: tu: sui: ille: ipse: iste: hic and is: meus: tuus: suus: noster: vester. nostras: and vestras. Of the whiche .viii. be primatyues/ as Ego tu sui etc. and .vii. deriuatyues/ as meus tuus suus etc. (John Holt, *Lac puerorum*, [1508.]. BL, C.33.b.47, A3ʳ–C8ʳ [on declension], at B1ᵛ.)

A pronowne is a parte of speche þe whiche is sette for a propre name of a man/ or ony thynge els and receyueth certayne nombre and certayne persone. (*Ibid.*, C8ʳ–E2ʳ [definitions of the parts of speech], at D2ʳ⁻ᵛ; *Checklist* 53.2.)

That other betokneth the thynge/ doynge suffrynge or beynge. as nowne and pronowne. [*etc.*]. Pronowne betokeneth a certeyne thyng not of hymself: but by the way of shewyng or reportyng. [A2ʳ]. How knowest a Nowne or pronowne primityfe? For he is not formed of any other worde: As this Nowne Mons. and these .viii. pronownes Ego. Tu. Sui. Ille. Ipse. Iste. Hic and Is. [A2ʳ⁻ᵛ] (*Informatio puerorum*, [1499?]. Cambridge, Magdalene College, Pepysian Library, PL 1305(3), A2ʳ–B3ʳ, D2ᵛ–D3ᵛ; *Checklist* 17.1.)

How knowe ye a Pronowne? For he is a parte of reason put for a nowne/ and betokeneth no certayne thynge of hym selfe but by the way of shewynge or rehersynge. ([*Abridged version of the Accidence, with other extracts*], 1534. CUL, Syn.8.53.74, A2ʳ–C8ᵛ, at A5ᵛ; *Checklist* 16.35.)

How knowe you a pronowne? For he is a part of reson put for a nowne: and betokenys no certeyn thynge of hymselfe. but by the waye of showynge or rehersynge. (John Stanbridge, *Accidence*, [1505?]. Bodl. Lib., 4° A 18(2) Art. BS, A1ʳ–C6ᵛ, at A5ᵛ; *Checklist* 16.1.)

How know ye a pronown for he is sette for a propre nown and somtyme receyueth þe certein persones. (*Short Accidence*, attributed to John Stanbridge [*c.*1505.]. CUL, Syn.5.50.2², fols. 2 and 3, at [2]ʳ (*Early Printed Editions*, Text K, 229, 17–18; *Checklist* 15.2).)

How knowest thou a pronowne. For he is a parte of reason declyned with case. that is set for a propre name and betokeneth as moche as a propre name of a man· and other while receyueth certeyn person and certeyn nombre. (*Long Accidence*, attributed to John Stanbridge [1495.]. Bodl. Lib., Douce D 238(2), A1ʳ–B6ᵛ, at A6ᵛ (*Early Printed Editions*, Text A, 157, 315–18; *Checklist* 14.1).)

How knowyst a pronowne? For he ys a parte of speche declynyd wᵗ case þe wyche ys seyt for a propur name of a man and resewyth to hym certeyn personys. (*c.*1492–1494. Bodl. Lib., MS Douce 103, fols. 53ʳ–57aʳ (Thomson, *Edition*, Text K, 57, 90–92; *Checklist* 12).)

How know ye a pronown? For he is sett for a propir nown and sumtyme receuyth certeyn person. (S. xv². BL, MS Add.37,075, fols. 1ʳ–6ᵛ. (Thomson, *Edition*, Text F, 46, 80–81; *Checklist* 9).)

Qwerby knowyst a pronown? For he is set for a nown and signyfyith neer a moche as a nown, and oþer qwyle receyuyth certeyne person. (S. xvᵐᵉᵈ. Cambridge, St John's College, MS F.26 (163), fols. 1ʳ–12ʳ (Thomson, *Edition*, Text C, 21, 198–200; *Checklist* 7).)

How know ȝe a pronowne? A pronoun is a maner of speche declyned wᵗ case, þe whiche is sette for a propur noun and receyuethe certeyn person. (S. xvᵐᵉᵈ. Aberystwyth, NLW, MS Peniarth 356B, fols. 163ʳ, 165ʳ–167ᵛ (Thomson, *Edition*, Text B, 10, 71–73; *Checklist* 6).)

How knos þu a pronown? A pronowne ys a party of spech þe wych ys set for a mon and resayuys certayn person and certen nowmbyr. (S. xv^med. Aberystwyth, NLW, MS Peniarth 356B, fols. 54^v–57^v and 48^r (Thomson, *Edition*, Text A, 3, 120–22; *Checklist* 5).)

How knowest a pronoun? A party of reson declynyd, the whych is sette for a propre name and reseueth certayn person. (S. xv^1. Cambridge, Trinity College, MS O.5.4, fols. 4^v–6^v (Thomson, *Edition*, Text D, 36, 198–99; *Checklist* 2).)

Pronomen est pars orationis, qua, in demonstranda, aut repetenda re aliqua, utimur. (*Institutio Compendiaria Totius Grammaticae*, 1540. Attributed to William Lily. BL, C.21.b.4.(3), at G2^r; Appendix III, 1.0.)

Pronomen est pars orationis: que pro nomine proprio vniuscuiusque rei accipitur: personasque finitas recipit. (Joannes Sulpitius Verulanus, *Opus insigne grammaticum*, 1494. JRUL, 19691, at a5^v.)

Quid est pronomen? Est pars orationis declinabilis que pro nomine proprio vniuscuiusque accipitur personasque finitas recipit. (Nicolaus Perottus, *Rudimenta grammatices*, 1486. CUL, Inc.5.F.2.8 [3287], at d8^v–e1^r.)

PRONOMEN is đæs naman speljend, sê spelađ þone naman, þæt đû ne đurfe tuwa hine nemnan. gif đû cwest nû: hwâ lǽrde đê?, þonne cweđe ic: Dûnstân. hwâ hâdode đê? hê mê hâdode: þonne stent se hê on his naman stede and spelađ hine. eft, gif đû âxast: *quis hoc fecit?* hwâ dyde đis?, þonne cwest đû: *ego hoc feci* ic dyde đis: þonne stent se ic on đînes naman stede; *tu* đû; *ille* sê. (Ælfric, *Praefatio de partibus orationis*, in *Grammatik und Glossar*, Zupitza, 8, 11–17; 9, 1–2.)
PRONOMEN EST PARS ORATIONIS, QVAE PRO NOMINE PROPRIO VNIVSCVIVSQVE ACCIPITVR PERSONASQVE FINITAS RECIPIT. PRONOMEN ys naman speljend, ân dǽl lêdensprǽce, sê byđ underfangen for âgenum naman, and hê underfêhđ hâdas mid fulre gewissunge. (Ælfric, *Grammatik und Glossar*, Zupitza, 92, 2–6.)

Pronomen est pars orationis, quae pro nomine proprio uniuscuiusque accipitur personasque finitas recipit. (Priscian, *Institutiones grammaticae* (*GL* II, 577, 2–3).)

Pronomen est pars orationis, quae pro nomine posita tantundem paene significat personamque interdum recipit. (Donatus, *Ars maior*; Holtz, 629, 2–3; *GL* IV, 379, 23–24.)

Pronomen quid est? Pars orationis, quae pro nomine posita tantundem paene significat personamque interdum recipit. (Donatus, *Ars minor*; Holtz, 588, 2–3; *GL* IV, 357, 2–3.)

Definitions of the verb:

A VERBE is a parte of speche, declyned with mode and tense, betokenyng to do, as *Amo*, I loue: to suffer, as *Amor*, I am loued: or to be, as *Sum*, I am. (*Introduction*, 1542. BL, C.21.b.4.(2), A4^r–F2^r [the parts of speech], at C2^r; present edition, 169, 326–27.)

A Verbe is a specyall parte of speche that cometh in euery perfyt reason/ and in eueri sentence. And it is a worde that eyther betokeneth beynge of a thynge/ as *Sum*, I am: or doynge of a thynge/ as *Amo*, I loue: or sufferynge of a thynge/ as *Amor*, I am loued. (John Colet, *Aeditio*, 1527. *EL*, 298 (1971), A6^r–D7^r [the parts of speech], at B5^r; *Checklist* 20.1.)

The uerbe is declined with modes, tenses, persons, and nombres. (Thomas Linacre, *Rudimenta grammatices* [1525?]. *EL*, 312 (1971), A2^r–F1^r [*Rudimenta declinationum*], at B2^v.)

A Verbe is a part of speche declined with mode and tense, and betokeneth to be, to do, or to suffre, with some difference of tyme, as sum, eram, amo amabam, amor amabar. (*Ibid.*, F1^r–G1^v [*Rudimenta definitionum*], at F4^r; *Checklist* 55.1.)

The verbe is declyned: with modes. tens. persons and nowmbres. (Thomas Linacre, *Progymnasmata grammatices vulgaria*, [1512.]. BL, G.7569, A2^r–b5^v [on declension], at A4^v.)

A Verbe is a parte of speche: declyned wyth mode and tens. and betokeneth to be. to doo. or to suffre. with some dyfference of tyme. as sum. eram amo. bam. Amor. bar. (*Ibid.*, b5^v–c4^r [definitions of the parts of speech], at c2^v; *Checklist* 54.1.)

Quhat is ane verbe? ane part of orison declinand with mode tyme and persone: without cais, betakynnand doing or suffering or baith or ellis nouthir: doyng as how? as amo i lwf. suffering as how? as amor i am lwfit? baith as how? as criminor i blame or i am blamyt/ nouthir as how? as sum i am, sto i stand, sedeo i syt. (John Vaus, *Rudimenta puerorum in artem grammaticam*, 1531. Aberdeen, University Library, AUL Λ Vau r 2, cc8^r–ee4^r [*de partium orationis interpretatione lingua vernacula*], at dd5^v; *Checklist* 56.1.)

(Preceptor) How know you a verbe (Discipulus) for he ys declyned with mode and tens with owt case and article and betokeneth to do/ suffre/ or to be. (*Donate and accidence for children*, 1515. Bodl. Lib., Arch. A e.19, A2^r–C3^r, at B1^v; *Checklist* 19.1.)

Verbe is declyned with coniugacion/ mode/ tense/ nombre/ and persone. (John Holt, *Lac puerorum*, [1508.]. BL, C.33.b.47, A3^r–C8^r [on declension], at B3^r.)

A verbe betokeneth a thynge with some token of tyme/ as I loue I loued. I haue loued. Also he betokeneth to do/ suffre/ or to be. as pugno/ vapulo sum. (*Ibid.*, C8^r–E2^r [definitions of the parts of speech], at D2^v; *Checklist* 53.2.)

How many of these be necessary to make a perfyte reason? ii. at the lest/ wherof that oon/ betokeneth to doo or to suffre or to be/ as verbe. [A2^r]. How knowest a verbe? For he is a parte of reson declyned with mode and tense: wyth noumbre and person without case and article. and betokeneth to do/ suffre or to be. [A6^v]. (*Informatio puerorum*, [1499?]. Magdalene College, Pepysian Library, PL 1305(3), A2^r–B3^r, D2^v–D3^v; *Checklist* 17.1.)

How knowe ye a Verbe? For he is declyned wyth mode and tens/ wythowt case and artycle/ and betokeneth to do or to suffer or to be. ([*Abridged version of the Accidence, with other extracts*], 1534. CUL, Syn.8.53.74, A2^r–C8^v, at A8^r; *Checklist* 16.35.)

Howe knowe you a verbe? For he is declyned with mode and tens withoute case and article. And betokenyth to do or to suffyr or to be. (John Stanbridge, *Accidence* [1505?]. Bodl. Lib., 4° A 18(2) Art.BS, A1^r–C6^v, at B1^v; *Checklist* 16.1.)

How know ie a verbe for he is declyned with mode tens without case or artycle and be tokeneth too do or to suffre or to be. (*Short Accidence*, attributed to John Stanbridge [*c*.1505.]. CUL, Syn.5.50.2^2, fols. 2 and 3, at [2]^v; *Early Printed Editions*, Text K, 230, 53–55; *Checklist* 15.2.)

How knowest an Verbe. For he is a parte of reason declyned with mode and tense without case or article. and betokeneth to doo to suffre or to be. (*Long Accidence*, attributed to John Stanbridge [1495.]. Bodl. Lib., Douce D 238(2), A1^r–B6^v, at A7^v; *Early Printed Editions*, Text A, 158, 376–78; *Checklist* 14.1.)

How knowyst a verbe? For he ys a party of speche declyned w^t mode, tyme and coniugacion, w^{t}owte case or artycle, betokynyng 'to do', or sufferyng or 'to be'. (*c*.1492–1494. Bodl. Lib., MS Douce 103, fols. 53^r–57a^r; Thomson, *Edition*, Text K, 58, 114–16; *Checklist* 12.)

How know ye a verbe? For he is declyned w^t mode and tens w^{t}owt case and articull, and betokenyth 'to do' or 'to suffyr' or 'to be'. (S. xv^2. BL, MS Add. 37,075, fols. 1^r–6^v; Thomson, *Edition*, Text F, 47, 123–25; *Checklist* 9.)

Qwerby knowyst a verbe? For it is declyned w^t moodd and tens and persone and betokenyth 'to do' or 'to suffyr' or 'to be'. (S. xv^{med}. Cambridge, St John's College, MS F.26(163), fols. 1^r–12^r; Thomson, *Edition*, Text C, 24, 356–58; *Checklist* 7.)

How know ȝe a verbe? A verbe ys maner of spech þe whiche is declyned w^t mod and tens w^{t}owte case and article and betokeneth 'to do' or 'to suffer'. (S. xv^{med}. Aberystwyth, NLW, MS Peniarth 356B, fols. 163^r, 165^r–67^v; Thomson, *Edition*, Text B, 12, 152–54; *Checklist* 6.)

How knos þu a verbe? A party of spech þat ys declynet w^t mod and tens, w^{t}out case or articull, and betokyns 'to do' or 'to suffur' or 'to be'. (S. xv^{med}. Aberystwyth, NLW, MS Peniarth 356B, fols. 54^v–57^v and 48^r; Thomson, *Edition*, Text A, 4, 165–67; *Checklist* 5.)

Wat ys a verbe? A party of resun þat ys clynud wit mod & wit tens & betokuns doyng or suffuryng. (1420s. Oxford, Lincoln College, MS Lat. 130, fols. 7^r–9^v. On long-term deposit in Bodl. Lib.; Bland, 157 [3–5]; *Checklist* 4.)

How knowest a verbe? A party of reson that bytokenyth doyng or suffryng and is declined wyth moode and tyme w^{t}oute case, as 'I love the for I am loued of the', *Amo te quia amor a te*. (S. xv^1. Cambridge, Trinity College, MS O.5.4, fols. 4^v–6^v; Thomson, *Edition*, Text D, 38, 291–94; *Checklist* 2.)

Verbum est pars orationis, quæ modis et temporibus inflexa, esse aliquid, agereue, aut pati significat, ut Sum, Moueo, Moueor. (*Institutio Compendiaria Totius Grammaticae*, 1540. Attributed to William Lily. BL, C.21.b.4.(3), at H1^r; Appendix III, 1.0.)

Verbum est pars orationis cum temporibus/ et modis sine casu agendi/ vel patiendi significatiuum. (Joannes Sulpitius Verulanus, *Opus insigne grammaticum*, 1494. JRUL, 19691, at a4^v.)

Verbum quid est? est pars orationis declinabilis cum modis et temporibus sine casu agendi uel patiendi significatiua. Unde dicitur uerbum? a uerberatu aeris quod proferendo aer uerberatur licet enim hoc accidat omnibus partibus orationis tamen precipue in hac dictione quasi proprium eius accipitur quia hac frequentius utimur in omni oratione. (Nicolaus Perottus, *Rudimenta grammatices*, 1486. CUL, Inc.5.F.2.8 [3287], at b6^v.)

VERBVM is word, and word getâcnað weorc oððe ðrôwunge oððe geþafunge. weorc byð, þonne ðû cwest: *aro* ic erige; *uerbero* ic swinge. þrôwung byð, þonne ðû cwyst: *uerberor* ic eom beswungen; *ligor* ic eom gebunden. geðafung byþ, ðonne ðû cwyst; *amor* ic eom gelufod; *doceor* ic eom gelǽred. (Ælfric, *Praefatio de partibus orationis*, in *Grammatik und Glossar*, Zupitza, 9, 2–8.)

VERBVM EST PARS ORATIONIS CVM TEMPORE ET PERSONA SINE CASV AVT AGERE ALIQVID AVT PATI AVT NEVTRVM SIGNIFICANS, VERBVM ys word, ân dǽl lêdensprǽce mid tîde and hâde bûtan case getâcnjende oððe sum ðing tô dônne oððe sum ðing tô þrôwigenne oððe nâðor. (Ælfric, *Grammatik und Glossar*, Zupitza, 119, 6–11.)

Verbum est pars orationis cum temporibus et modis, sine casu, agendi vel patiendi significativum. (Priscian, *Institutiones grammaticae*; GL II, 369, 2–3.)

Verbum est pars orationis cum tempore et persona sine casu aut agere aliquid aut pati aut neutrum significans. (Donatus, *Ars maior*; Holtz, 632, 5–6; *GL* IV, 381, 13–14.)

Verbum quid est? Pars orationis cum tempore et persona sine casu aut agere aliquid aut pati aut neutrum significans. (Donatus, *Ars minor*; Holtz, 591, 6–7; *GL* IV, 359, 4–5.)

Definitions of the participle:

A PARTICIPLE is a parte of speche, deriued of a verbe, and taketh part of a nowne as gendre and case, parte of a verbe, as tense and signification: and parte of bothe, as number and figure. (*Introduction*, 1542. BL, C.21.b.4.(2), A4ʳ–F2ʳ [the parts of speech], at E3ᵛ; present edition, 184, 901–903.)

A Participle cometh deryued of a verbe and hath in sygnificacyon moche the maner of his verbe thath he cometh of and is declyned with case as a nowne. (John Colet, *Aeditio*, 1527. *EL*, 298 (1971), A6ʳ–D7ʳ [the parts of speech], at D3ʳ; *Checklist* 20.1.)

Participles endynge in ans or in ens be declined ofter the thyrd declination of nownes: as amans, tis. legens, tis. (Thomas Linacre, *Rudimenta grammatices* [1525?]. *EL*, 312 (1971), A2ʳ–F1ʳ [*Rudimenta declinationum*], at E4ʳ.)
A Participle is a part of speche declined with case whiche signifieth a dede with some difference of tyme, and is in the actiue voyce other present or future: as amans amaturus. And in the passiue voyce of the preter and future: as amatus amandus. (*Ibid.*, F1ʳ–G1ᵛ [*Rudimenta definitionum*], at G1ʳ; *Checklist* 55.1.)

Participles endyng in ans or in ens be declyned after the fyrste declynation of nownes as amans tis. legens tis [*etc.*]. (Thomas Linacre, *Progymnasmata grammatices vulgaria*, [1512.]. BL, G.7569, A2ʳ–b5ᵛ [on declension], at b4ᵛ.)
A particyple is a part of spech declyned with case which sygnyfieth a dede wyth some difference of tyme. in the actyue voyce other present or future. as amans amaturus. and in the passyue voyce of the preter and future and oftyme the present. as amatus amandus. (*Ibid.*, b5ᵛ–c4ʳ [definitions of the parts of speech], at c3ᵛ; *Checklist* 54.1.)

Quhat is ane participile? ane part of orisone declinand witht cais. part takand fra ane nowne part fra ane verbe and part fra baith that ane and that othir. (John Vaus, *Rudimenta puerorum in artem grammaticam*, 1531. Aberdeen, University Library, AUL ∧ Vau r 2, cc8ʳ–ee4ʳ [*de partium orationis interpretatione lingua vernacula*], at dd8ʳ; *Checklist* 56.1.)

(Preceptor) [How] know you a participle (Discipulus) for he is a parte of reson declined with case and article that taketh parte of a verbe/ as tyme and signification: and parte of a nown as gendre and case with declination. (*Donate and accidence for children*, 1515. Bodl. Lib., Arch. A e.19, A2ʳ–C3ʳ, at C2ʳ; *Checklist* 19.1.)

A particyple hath gendre and case as hath a nowne tyme and sygnificacyon as hath a verbe/ nombre and fygure as they haue bothe. (John Holt, *Lac puerorum*, [1508.]. BL, C.33.b.47, A3ʳ–C8ʳ [on declension], at C6ʳ.)
A Participle is a parte of speche declyned with case þe whiche taketh parte of a nowne/ parte of a verbe/ and parte of bothe. He taketh of a nowne gendre and case/ of a verbe tyme and significacyon/ of both nombre and fygure. (*Ibid.*, C8ʳ–E2ʳ [definitions of the parts of speech], at E1ʳ; *Checklist* 53.2.)

How knowest a participle? for he is a parte of reason declyned with case and article: and taketh parte of Nowne: parte of Verbe. what of nowne? Gendre noumbre and case. what of verbe? Tyme significacyon and fygure. (*Informatio puerorum*, [1499?]. Cambridge, Magdalene College, Pepysian Library, PL 1305(3), A2ʳ–B3ʳ, D2ᵛ–D3ᵛ, at B2ᵛ; *Checklist* 17.1.)

How know ye a Partycyple? For he ys a part of reason declyned wyth case/ and taketh parte of a nowne and parte of a verbe. What taketh he of a nowne? Case/ gendre and nombre.

What of a verbe? Tens/ signification and fygure. ([*Abridged version of the Accidence, with other extracts*], 1534. CUL, Syn.8.53.74, A2ʳ–C8ᵛ, at C4ᵛ; *Checklist* 16.35.)

Howe knowe you a participul? For he is a part of reson declyned with case. and takys part of a nowne and parte of a verbe. (John Stanbridge, *Accidence* [1505?]. Bodl. Lib., 4° A 18(2) Art. BS, A1ʳ–C6ᵛ, at C2ʳ; *Checklist* 16.1.)

How know ye a partyciple for he taketh parte of a nown parte of a verbe part of both. (*Short Accidence*, attributed to John Stanbridge [c.1505.]. CUL, Syn.5.50.2², fols. 2 and 3, at [3]ᵛ; *Early Printed Editions*, Text K, 231, 105–106; *Checklist* 15.2.)

How knowest a participle. For he is an parte of reason declyned with case þat takith parte of a Nowne. parte of Verbe. parte of both. (*Long Accidence*, attributed to John Stanbridge [1495.]. Bodl. Lib., Douce D 238(2), A1ʳ–B6ᵛ, at B2ʳ; *Early Printed Editions*, Text A, 161, 503–505; *Checklist* 14.1.)

How knowyst a partycypull? For he ys a party of spech declynyd wᵗ case and takyth parte of a nowne, party of a verbe, and party of both two. (c.1492–1494. Bodl. Lib., MS Douce 103, fols. 53ʳ–57aʳ; Thomson, *Edition*, Text K, 59, 168–70; *Checklist* 12.)

How know ye a participill? For he takyth parte off a nown, parte of uerbe, parte of bothe. (S. xv². BL, MS Add. 37,075, fols. 1ʳ–6ᵛ; Thomson, *Edition*, Text F, 48, 186–87; *Checklist* 9.)

Qwerby knowyst a participyl? For he takyth part of nown, part of verbe and part of bothe. Qwat takyth he of nown? Gendyr and case. Qwat of þe verbe? Tyme and significacyon. And qwat of bothe? Nowmbyr and fygure.² (S. xvᵐᵉᵈ. Cambridge, St John's College, MS F.26 (163), fols. 1ʳ–12ʳ; Thomson, *Edition*, Text C, 28, 492–95; *Checklist* 7.)

How knos þu a partycypul? A party of spech þat ys declynet wᵗ case and articull and betokyns 'to do' or 'to suffyr' or 'to be' as a verbe. (S. xvᵐᵉᵈ. Aberystwyth, NLW, MS Peniarth 356B, fols. 54ᵛ–57ᵛ and 48ʳ; Thomson, *Edition*, Text A, 6, 239–41; *Checklist* 5.)

How knowyste a partyciple? A party of reson that is declined and bytokenyth doyng or suffryng wyth case and tyme wythoute mode. (S. xv¹. Cambridge, Trinity College, MS O.5.4, fols. 4ᵛ–6ᵛ; Thomson, *Edition*, Text D, 41, 440–42; *Checklist* 2.)

Participium est pars orationis inflexa casu: quę a nomine genera et casus, a uerbo tempora et significationes. Ab utroque Numerum et Figuram, uelut precario accipit. (*Institutio Compendiaria Totius Grammaticae*, 1540. Attributed to William Lily. BL, C.21.b.4.(3), at K4ʳ; Appendix III, 1.0.)

Participium est pars orationis: que pro verbo accipitur: ex quo deriuatur: et genus/ et casum habet ad similitudinem nominis: et accidentia a verbo absque discretione personarum/ et modorum. (Joannes Sulpitius Verulanus, *Opus insigne grammaticum*, 1494. JRUL, 19691, at a5ᵛ.)

Participium quid est? est pars orationis declinabilis que pro uerbo ponitur ex quo deriuatur genus et casum habens ad similitudinem nominis. Quare dicitur participium? quia partem capit a nomine/ partem a uerbo. (Nicolaus Perottus, *Rudimenta grammatices*, 1486. CUL, Inc.5.F.2.8 [3287], at d7ʳ.)

PARTICIPIVM ys dǽl nimend. hê nymđ ânne dǽl of naman and ôđerne of worde. of naman hê nymđ CASVS, þæt is, declinunge, and of worde hê nymđ tîde and getâcnunge. of him bâm

---

² Thomson, *Edition*, Text C, 28, 495 reads 'persone' at this point.

hê nymđ getel and hiw. *amans* lufjende cymđ of đâm worde *amo* ic lufige: þonne nymđ hê of đâm naman him ealle đâ syx CASVS: NOMINATIVVM, GENITIVVM, DATIVVM, ACCVS-SATIVVM, VOCATIVVM, ABLATIVVM; ET PLVRALITER and menigfealdlîce. đes PARTICIPIVM is đrêora cynna: *hic amans uir* þes lufjenda wer; *haec amans femina* þis lufjende wîf; *hoc amans mancipium* þes lufjende þêowa man; ET CETERA. (Ælfric, *Praefatio de partibus orationis*, in *Grammatik und Glossar*, Zupitza, 9, 18–21; 10, 1–7.)

PARTICIPIVM EST PARS ORATIONIS PARTEM CAPIENS NOMINIS PARTEMQVE VERBI. þes part mæg bêon gehâten dælnimend, forþan đe hê nimđ of naman cynn and CASVS, and of worde hê nimđ tîde and getâcnunga: of him bâm hê nimđ getel and gefêgednysse. (Ælfric, *Grammatik und Glossar*, Zupitza, 242, 10–14.)

Participium est igitur pars orationis, quae pro verbo accipitur, ex quo et derivatur naturaliter, genus et casum habens ad similitudinem nominis et accidentia verbo absque discretione personarum et modorum. (Priscian, *Institutiones grammaticae*; GL II, 552, 18–20.)

Participium est pars orationis, dicta quod partem capiat nominis partemque uerbi. Recipit enim a nomine genera et casus, a uerbo tempora et significationes, ab utroque numerum et figuram. (Donatus, *Ars maior*, Holtz, 644, 2–4; GL IV, 387, 18–20.)

Participium quid est? Pars orationis partem capiens nominis, partem uerbi; nominis genera et casus, uerbi tempora et significationes, utriusque numerum et figuram. (Donatus, *Ars minor*, Holtz, 597, 5–6; GL IV, 363, 13–15.)

Definitions of the adverb:

AN ADVERBE is a parte of speche, ioyned to the verbes to declare his sygnification. (*Introduction*, 1542. BL, C.21.b.4.(2), A4ʳ–F2ʳ [the parts of speech], at E4ʳ; present edition, 185, 941–42.)

An aduerbe is a parte that accompanyeth the verbe and declared the maner and the circunstans of the doynge or of þe suffryng of the verbe: as sayenge *.Amo*, I loue. (John Colet, *Aeditio*, 1527. *EL*, 298 (1971), A6ʳ–D7ʳ [the parts of speech], at D5ʳ; *Checklist* 20.1.)

Aduerbes, some be of tyme: as hodie, cras, heri, [*etc*.]. (Thomas Linacre, *Rudimenta grammatices*, [1525?]. *EL*, 312 (1971), A2ʳ–F1ʳ [*Rudimenta declinationum*], at E4ᵛ.)
An aduerbe is a part vndeclined that determineth or limytteth the signification of the uerbe, as adiectiues do of propres or appellatiues: as bene facis, male facis, clare legis, non legis. (*Ibid.*, F1ʳ–G1ᵛ [*Rudimenta definitionum*], at G1ʳ⁻ᵛ; *Checklist* 55.1.)

Aduerbys some be of tyme as hodie. cras. heri. [*etc*.]. (Thomas Linacre, *Progymnasmata grammatices vulgaria* [1512.]. BL, G.7569, A2ʳ–b5ᵛ [on declension], at b4ᵛ.)
A aduerbe is a part vndeclyned that determyth or limytyth the signyfication of the verbe. as adiectyues doo of propres or appellatyues. as bene facis male facis. clare legis. non legis. (*Ibid.*, b5ᵛ–c4ʳ [definitions of the parts of speech], at c3ᵛ; *Checklist* 54.1.)

Quhat is ane aduerbe? ane part of orisone ondeclinabil. the quhilk is cassin to ane verbe: and declaris and fulfillis the significatione of the verbe that it is cassin to. (John Vaus, *Rudimenta puerorum in artem grammaticam*, 1531. Aberdeen, University Library, AUL Λ Vau r 2, cc8ʳ–ee4ʳ [*de partium orationis interpretatione lingua vernacula*], at dd7ᵛ; *Checklist* 56.1.)

(Preceptor) How know you an aduerbe (Discipulus) for he is a parte of reson vndeclined/ set commonly ny to the verbe/ to fulfil and shew his signification. (*Donate and accidence for children*, 1515. Bodl. Lib., Arch. A e.19, A2ʳ–C3ʳ, at C2ʳ; *Checklist* 19.1.)

There be many significacyons of aduerbes/ some be of tyme/ as quando. heri. [*etc.*]. (John Holt, *Lac puerorum*, [1508.]. BL, C.33.b.47, A3ʳ–C8ʳ [on declension], at C6ᵛ.)

An aduerbe is sette to the verbe to fulfyll and declare the significacyon of the verbe. (*Ibid.*, C8ʳ–E2ʳ [definitions of the parts of speech], at E1ᵛ; *Checklist* 53.2.)

How knowest an aduerbe? for he is a parte of reason vndeclyned declaring for the more parte the circumstaunce or doyng/ sufferyng or beyng/ whether it be verbe or particyple gerundyfes or supyn. And not only this/ but also oft tyme declareth the signyficacyon of adiectyfes. and may be construed with all cases. (*Informatio puerorum*, [1499?]. Cambridge, Magdalene College, Pepysian Library, PL 1305(3), A2ʳ–B3ʳ, D2ᵛ–D3ᵛ, at D3ʳ; *Checklist* 17.1.)

How knowe ye an Aduerbe? For he ys a parte of reason vndeclyned that ys ioyned to verbes/ partycyples/ gerundyues and supynes and sometyme to other partes/ to declare fulfyll mynesshe or chaunge the sygnifycatyon of them. ([*Abridged version of the Accidence, with other extracts*], 1534. CUL, Syn.8.53.74, A2ʳ–C8ᵛ, at C6ᵛ; *Checklist* 16.35.)

Howe knowe you an aduerbe? For he is a part of reson vndeclyned that is ioyned to verbys participuls gerundyues and supyns. to declare and fulfyll the sygnificacion of them. (John Stanbridge, *Accidence* [1505?]. Bodl. Lib., 4° A 18(2) Art.BS, A1ʳ–C6ᵛ, at C3ᵛ; *Checklist* 16.1.)

How know ye an aduerbe. for he is sette nexte of verbe for to declare and fulfyll þe sygnifycation of the verbe. (*Short Accidence*, attributed to John Stanbridge [*c.*1505.]. CUL, Syn.5.50.2², fols. 2 and 3, at [3]ᵛ; *Early Printed Editions*, Text K, 230, 98–99; *Checklist* 15.2.)

How knowest an Aduerbe. For he is a parte of reason vndeclyned· that stondith next the verbe to declare and fulfill the significacion of the verbe. (*Long Accidence*, attributed to John Stanbridge [1495.]. Bodl. Lib., Douce D 238(2), A1ʳ–B6ᵛ, at B2ʳ; *Early Printed Editions*, Text A, 160, 490–92; *Checklist* 14.1.)

How knowyst an aduerbe? For he ys a party of spech vnndeclynyd, the wych ys caste to a uerbe and makyth playne and fulfyllyth syngnyfycacion of the verbe. (*c.*1492–1494. Bodl. Lib., MS Douce 103, fols. 53ʳ–57aʳ; Thomson, *Edition*, Text K, 59, 165–67; *Checklist* 12.)

How know ye an aduerbe? For he is set nere þe uerbe and declarith his significacion. (S. xv². BL, MS Add. 37,075, fols. 1ʳ–6ᵛ; Thomson, *Edition*, Text F, 48, 180–81; *Checklist* 9.)

Qwerby knowyst an aduerbe? For he is cast to a verbe and fulfyllyth þe significacyon of þe verbe. (S. xvᵐᵉᵈ. Cambridge, St John's College, MS F.26(163), fols. 1ʳ–12ʳ; Thomson, *Edition*, Text C, 27, 482–83; *Checklist* 7.)

How knos þu aduerbe? A party of spech þat ys vndeclynyt, þe wych ys cast to a verbe to declare and fulfyll þe sygnificacion of þe verbe. (S. xvᵐᵉᵈ. Aberystwyth, NLW, MS Peniarth 356B, fols. 54ᵛ–57ᵛ and 48ʳ; Thomson, *Edition*, Text A, 6, 226–28; *Checklist* 5.)

How knowyste an aduerbe? A party of reson that is not declinyd and is y-sette wyth the verbe and declareth the significacion of the verbe. (S. xv¹. Cambridge, Trinity College, MS O.5.4, fols. 4ᵛ–6ᵛ; Thomson, *Edition*, Text D, 39, 381–82; 40, 383; *Checklist* 2.)

Aduerbium est pars orationis non flexa, quæ adiecta uerbo, sensum eius perficit atque explanat. Explanat enim interdum, sicut nomen, ut, Homo egregie impudens. Ne parum sis leno. Aliquoties ut aduerbium, ut, Parum honeste se gerit. (*Institutio Compendiaria Totius Grammaticae*, 1540. Attributed to William Lily. BL, C.21.b.4.(3), at L2ʳ; Appendix III, 1.0.)

Aduerbium est pars orationis indeclinabilis: que adiecta verbo significationem eius explanat: atque implet. (Joannes Sulpitius Verulanus, *Opus insigne grammaticum*, 1494. JRUL, 19691, at a6ᵛ.)

Quid est aduerbium? est pars orationis indeclinabilis que adiecta uerbo significationem eius explanat atque implet. Quare dicitur aduerbium quia stat ad uerbum hoc est iuxta uerbum. (Nicolaus Perottus, *Rudimenta grammatices*, 1486. CUL, Inc.5.F.2.8 [3287], at e3ᵛ.)

ADVERBIVM is wordes gefêra, forðan ðe hê næfð nâne fulfremednysse, bûton hê mid ðâm worde bêo. word gefyld his âgene getâcnunge mid fullum andgyte. þonne ðû cwyst: *scribo* ic wrîte, þonne byð ðær full andgyt. ADVERBIVM is *bene* wel. hêr nys nâ ful andgyt, bûton ðû cweðe word ðâr tô: *bene scribo* wel ic wrîte; *bene scribis* wel ðû wrîtst; *bene scribit* wel hê wrît; ET PLVRALITER and menigfealdlîce: *male legimus* yfele wê rædað; *melius legitis* bet gê rædað; *optime legunt* sêlost hî rædað; ET CETERA. (Ælfric, *Praefatio de partibus orationis*, in *Grammatik und Glossar*, Zupitza, 9, 8–18.)

ADVERBIVM EST PARS ORATIONIS INDECLINABILIS, CVIVS SIGNIFICATIO VERBIS ADICI-TUR; ADVERBIVM is ân dæl lêdensprǽce undeclinigendlîc, and his getâcnung byð tô wordum geðêod. ADVERBIVM mæg bêon gecweden wordes gefêra, forðan ðe hê byð ǽfre tô wordum geðêod and næfð full andgit, bûton hê mid worde bêo. *sapienter* wîslîce is ADVERBIVM. ic cweðe nû swutelîcor: *sapienter loquor* wîslîce ic sprece; *feliciter facis* gesǽlelîce ðû dêst; *humiliter precatur* êadmôdlîce hê bit. (Ælfric, *Grammatik und Glossar*, Zupitza, 222, 13–14; 223, 1–7.)

Adverbium est pars orationis indeclinabilis, cuius significatio verbis adicitur. hoc enim perfi-cit adverbium verbis additum, quod adiectiva nomina appellativis nominibus adiuncta, ut 'prudens homo prudenter agit, felix vir feliciter vivit'. (Priscian, *Institutiones grammaticae*; GL III, 60, 2–5.)

Aduerbium est pars orationis, quae adiecta uerbo significationem eius explanat atque inplet, ut iam faciam uel non faciam. (Donatus, *Ars maior*; Holtz, 640, 2–3; *GL* IV, 385, 11–12.)

Aduerbium quid est? Pars orationis, quae adiecta uerbo significationem eius explanat atque inplet. (Donatus, *Ars minor*; Holtz, 595, 25–26; *GL* IV, 362, 15–16.)

Definitions of the conjunction:

A CONIVNCTION is a parte of speche, that ioynethe woordes, and sentences together. (*Introduction*, 1542. BL, C.21.b.4.(2), A4ʳ–F2ʳ [the parts of speech], at F1ʳ; present edition, 186, 970–71.)

A Coniunccyon is that byndeth wordes and sentences togyder. (John Colet, *Aeditio*, 1527. EL, 298 (1971), A6ʳ–D7ʳ [the parts of speech], at D5ᵛ; *Checklist* 20.1.)

Of coniunctions, Some be copulatiues: as et, que, atque, ac, quoque, etiam, nec, neque. [*etc*.]. (Thomas Linacre, *Rudimenta grammatices* [1525?]. EL, 298 (1971), A2ʳ–F1ʳ [*Rudimenta declinationum*], at F1ʳ.)
A coniunction is a part vndeclined, that knytteth and ordreth sentences to gyther. (*Ibid*., F1ʳ–G1ᵛ [*Rudimenta definitionum*], at G1ᵛ; *Checklist* 55.1.)

Of coniunctions some be copulatyues. as et. que. atque. ac quoque. etiam. nec. neque. [*etc*.]. (Thomas Linacre, *Progymnasmata grammatices vulgaria* [1512.]. London, BL, G.7569, A2ʳ–b5ᵛ [on declension], at b5ᵛ.)
A coniunction ys a part vndeclynyd that knyttyth and ordryth sentencys to gydre and some tyme wordys. (*Ibid*., b5ᵛ–c4ʳ [definitions of the parts of speech], at c3ᵛ–c4ʳ; *Checklist* 54.1.)

Quhat is ane coniunctione? Ane part of orisone ondeclinabile: quhilk coniunys and ordires dictionis orisonis and sentencis: dictionis as how? as socrates et plato: orisonis as paris amat et hector pugnat. Sentencis as how? as socrates currit ergo mouetur. (John Vaus, *Rudimenta puerorum in artem grammaticam*, 1531. Aberdeen, University Library, AUL Λ Vau r 2, cc8ʳ–ee4ʳ [*de partium orationis interpretatione lingua vernacula*], at ee2ʳ; *Checklist* 56.1.)

Qwhat is a coniunctione a part of oresone þe quilk knitis ordour and sentens. (Donatus, *Ars minor*. A version in Scots, *c*.1507?. Aberdeen, University Library, Λ³ Vau r 1, one leaf only, 1ᵛ; *Checklist* 18.1.)

(Preceptor) How know you a Coniunction (Discipulus) for he is a parte of resone vndeclined that ioyneth and ordreth wordes and sentences. (*Donate and accidence for children*, 1515. Bodl. Lib., Arch. A e.19, A2ʳ–C3ʳ, at C2ᵛ; *Checklist* 19.1.)

Of coniunctions. Some be Copulatyues/ as et atque [*etc*.]. (John Holt, *Lac puerorum*, [1508.]. BL, C.33.b.47, A3ʳ–C8ʳ [on declension], at C7ᵛ.)
A Coniunction byndeth or Joyneth wordes to gyder in ordre or in sentence. (*Ibid.*, C8ʳ–E2ʳ [definitions of the parts of speech], at E2ʳ; *Checklist* 53.2.)

How knowest a Coniunctyon? For he is a parte of reason vndeclyned that byndeth or ioyneth wordes or sentense to geder. (*Informatio puerorum*, [1499?]. Cambridge, Magdalene College, Pepysian Library, PL 1305(3), A2ʳ–B3ʳ, D2ᵛ–D3ᵛ, at D3ʳ; *Checklist* 17.1.)

How knowe ye a Coniunctyon? For he ys a parte of reson vndeclyned/ that ioyneth wordes or sentenses to gyder. ([*Abridged version of the Accidence, with other extracts*], 1534. CUL, Syn.8.53.74, A2ʳ–C8ᵛ, at C7ʳ; *Checklist* 16.35.)

Howe knowe yow a coniunction? For he is a parte of reason vndeclyned. that ioyneth wordys or sentens togyder. (John Stanbridge, *Accidence*, [1505?]. Bodl. Lib., 4° A 18(2) Art.BS, A1ʳ–C6ᵛ, at C4ᵛ; *Checklist* 16.1.)

How know ye a coniunccion/ for he Ioyneth other partes of reason togyder in ordre. (*Short Accidence*, attributed to John Stanbridge [1495?]. San Marino, California, Henry E. Huntington Library, RB 152101, A1 and A4, at A4ʳ; *Early Printed Editions*, Text I, 227, 72–73; *Checklist* 15.1.)

How knowest a Coniunction. For he is a parte of reason vndeclynede that byndeth or ioyneth wordes or sentences togydre in ordre. (*Long Accidence*, attributed to John Stanbridge [1495.]. Bodl. Lib., Douce D 238(2), A1ʳ–B6ᵛ, at B3ᵛ; *Early Printed Editions*, Text A, 162, 579–81; *Checklist* 14.1.)

How knowyst a coniunccion? For he ys a party of speche vndeclynyd, the wych cowpullyth or dyscowpulyth all othere partes of speche yn ordur. (*c*.1492–1494. Bodl. Lib., MS Douce 103, fols. 53ʳ–57aʳ; Thomson, *Edition*, Text K, 60, 200–202; *Checklist* 12.)

How know ye a coniunccion? For he joynyth odyr partis of reson togedyr in ordyr. (S. xv². BL, MS Add. 37,075, fols. 1ʳ–6ᵛ; Thomson, *Edition*, Text F, 49, 216–17; *Checklist* 9.)

Qwerby knowyst a coniunccyon? For it joyneth or disioyneth oþer partys of reson and ordeynyth in hem perfyth sentence. (S. xvᵐᵉᵈ. Cambridge, St John's College, MS F.26(163), fols. 1ʳ–12ʳ; Thomson, *Edition*, Text C, 29, 571–73; *Checklist* 7.)

How knos a coniunccion? A party of spech þat ys vndeclynet and ionys oþer partys of spechys togedyr. (S. xvᵐᵉᵈ. Aberystwyth, NLW, MS Peniarth 356B, fols. 54ᵛ–57ᵛ and 48ʳ; Thomson, *Edition*, Text A, 7, 304–305; *Checklist* 5.)

How knowest a coniunccion? A party of reson that is not declynyd and wole joyne tweyne nomynatyf case in rewarde of a verbe, other ellys twey verbes in reward of a nominatyf case.

(S. xv¹. Cambridge, Trinity College, MS O.5.4, fols. 4ᵛ–6ᵛ; Thomson, *Edition*, Text D, 42, 491–93; *Checklist* 2.)

Coniunctio est pars orationis, quę sententiarum clausulas apte connectit. (*Institutio Compendiaria Totius Grammaticae*, 1540. Attributed to William Lily. BL, C.21.b.4.(3.), at M1ᵛ; Appendix III, 1.0.)

Coniunctio est pars orationis indeclinabilis coniunctiua aliarum partium orationis. (Joannes Sulpitius Verulanus, *Opus insigne grammaticum*, 1494. JRUL, 19691, at a6ᵛ.)

Quid est coniunctio? Est pars orationis indeclinabilis adnectans ordinansque sentenciam. (Nicolaus Perottus, *Rudimenta grammatices*, 1486. CUL, Inc.5.F.2.8 [3287], at e4ʳ.)

CONIVNCTIO is gedêodnys odđe fêging. þes dǣl ne mæg nâht þurh hine sylfne, ac hê gefêgđ tôgædere ǣgđer gê naman gê word. gif đû befrinst: *quis equitat in ciuitatem?* hwâ rît intô đâm port?, đonne cweđ hê: *rex et episcopus* se cyningc and se bisceop. se *et*, þæt is, and, 7, is CONIVNCTIO: *ego et tu* ic and đû. word hê gefêgđ þus: *stat et loquitur* hê stent and sprycđ; ET CETERA. (Ælfric, *Praefatio de partibus orationis*, in *Grammatik und Glossar*, Zupitza, 10, 8–15.)

CONIVNCTIO EST PARS ORATIONIS INDECLINABILIS ADNECTENS ORDINANSQVE SENTENTIAM. CONIVNCTIO mæg bêon gecweden geþêodnys. sê is ân dǣl lêdensprǣce undeclinigendlîc gefæstnjende and endebyrdigende ǣlcne cwyde. swâswâ lîm gefæstnađ fel tô sumum brede, swâ getîgđ sêo CONIVNCTIO þâ word tôgædere. þes dǣl gefæstnađ and gefrætwađ lêdensprǣce and hwîlon tôscǣt and hwîlon geendebyrt. *pius et fortis fuit Dauid rex* ârfæst and strang wæs David cyning: se *et* is CONIVNCTIO, þæt is on englisc and. *ego et tu* ic and đû, *nos et uos* wê and gê wyllađ ân. nû þû miht gehŷran, hû þes dǣl tîgđ þâ word tôgædere. nǣfđ þes dǣl nâne mihte nê nân andgit, gif hê âna stent, ac on endebyrdnysse lêdensprǣce hê gelîmađ þâ word, nê hê ne biđ nâht on englisc âwend bûtan ôđrum wordum. (Ælfric, *Grammatik und Glossar*, Zupitza, 257, 16–17; 258, 1–13.)

Coniunctio est pars orationis indeclinabilis, coniunctiva aliarum partium orationis, quibus consignificat, vim vel ordinationem demonstrans. (Priscian, *Institutiones grammaticae*; GL III, 93, 2–3.)

Coniunctio est pars orationis adnectens ordinansque sententiam. (Donatus, *Ars maior*, Holtz, 646, 14; *GL* IV, 388, 28.)

Coniunctio quid est? Pars orationis adnectens ordinansque sententiam. (Donatus, *Ars minor*, Holtz, 599, 13; *GL* IV, 364, 33.)

Definitions of the preposition:

A PREPOSITION is a parte of speche moste commonly sette before other partes in apposition, as *Ad patrem*, or in composition, as *Indoctus*. (*Introduction*, 1542. BL, C.21.b.4.(2), A4ʳ–F2ʳ [the parts of speech], at F1ʳ; present edition, 187, 985–86.)

A Preposicyon is a parte of speche put before other wordes: other ioyneth to the wordes in compoundes: as *Indoctus*, or a soundre from þe wordes: as *Coram deo*, determining them to the accusatyf case/ or to þe ablatyf case/ or to bothe. (John Colet, *Aeditio*, 1527. *EL*, 298 (1971), A6ʳ–D7ʳ [the parts of speech], at D5ᵛ; *Checklist* 20.1.)

Prepositions be these ad, apud, ante, aduersus or aduersum, [*etc.*]. (Thomas Linacre, *Rudimenta grammatices* [1525?]. *EL*, 312 (1971), A2ʳ–F1ʳ [*Rudimenta declinationum*], at E4ʳ.)

A preposition is a part of speche vndeclined, whiche signifieth circumstaunce or hauyour of a thynge in place, ordre, or cause: as in, post, propter. (*Ibid.*, F1ʳ–G1ᵛ [*Rudimenta definitionum*], at G1ʳ; *Checklist* 55.1.)

Prepositions be these ad. apud. ante. aduersus. or sum. [*etc.*]. (Thomas Linacre, *Progymnasmata grammatices vulgaria* [1512.]. BL, G.7569, A2ʳ–b5ᵛ [on declension], at b4ᵛ.)
A preposytion is a part of spech vndeclyned which sygnyfieth respecte or hauyour of a thyng in place. ordre. or cause. as in. post. propter. (*Ibid.*, b5ᵛ–c4ʳ [definitions of the parts of speech], at c3ᵛ; *Checklist* 54.1.)

Quhat is ane prepositione? ane part of orison ondeclinabil quhilk is put befoir vthir partis off orisone and eikis and chang or makis les the significatione of thame. Eikis as quhow? as facio perficio, fero perfero. Changis as quhow? as equus iniquus makis les as quhow? as rideo subrideo: tristis subtristis. (John Vaus, *Rudimenta puerorum in artem grammaticam*, 1531. Aberdeen, University Library, AUL Λ Vau r 2, cc8ʳ–ee4ʳ [*de partium orationis interpretatione lingua vernacula*], at ee2ᵛ; *Checklist* 56.1.)

(Preceptor) How know you a preposicion (Discipulus) for he is a parte of spech vndeclined: commonly set before other partes of reson bothe in apposicion and composicion. (*Donate and accidence for children*, 1515. Bodl. Lib., Arch. A e.19, A2ʳ–C3ʳ, at C2ᵛ; *Checklist* 19.1.)

Of preposicyon separable there ben thre sortes. (John Holt, *Lac puerorum*, [1508.]. BL, C.33.b.47, A3ʳ–C8ʳ [on declension], at C7ʳ.)
A Preposicyon is sette before all other partes of speche in apposicyon or in composicyon. (*Ibid.*, C8ʳ–E2ʳ [definitions of the parts of speech], at E1ᵛ; *Checklist* 53.2.)

How knowest a preposicion? for he is a parte of reason vndeclyned: most comynly set before other parties of reason/ both in apposycion and in composycion. (*Informatio puerorum*, [1499?]. Cambridge, Magdalene College, Pepysian Library, PL 1305(3), A2ʳ–B3ʳ, D2ᵛ–D3ᵛ, at D2ᵛ; *Checklist* 17.1.)

How knowe ye a preposicyon? For he ys a parte of reason vndeclyned most communely set before other partes of reason in apposicyon and in composicyon. ([*Abridged version of the Accidence, with other extracts*], 1534. CUL, Syn.8.53.74, A2ʳ–C8ᵛ, at C7ᵛ; *Checklist* 16.35.)

Howe know you a preposicion? For he is a part of reson vndeclyned moste commynly set before all other partys of reason in apposicion or in composicion. (John Stanbridge, *Accidence*, [1505?]. Bodl. Lib., 4° A 18(2) Art. BS, A1ʳ–C6ᵛ, at C5ʳ⁻ᵛ; *Checklist* 16.1.)

How knowe ye a preposicion/ for he is set byfore other partes of reason in preposicion or in composicion. (*Short Accidence*, attributed to John Stanbrige [1495?]. San Marino, California, Henry E. Huntington Library, RB 152101, A1 and A4, at A4ᵛ; *Early Printed Editions*, Text I, 227, 82–83; *Checklist* 15.1.)

How knowest a Preposicion. For he is a parte of reason vndeclyned. that is set before al other partes of reason in apposicion or composicion. (*Long Accidence*, attributed to John Stanbridge [1495.]. Bodl. Lib., Douce D 238(2), A1ʳ–B6ᵛ, at B4ʳ; *Early Printed Editions*, Text A, 162, 601–603; *Checklist* 14.1.)

How knowyst a preposicion? For he ys a party of speche vndeclynyd the wych ys set before or be-endyth yn apocycyon or yn compocycyon, and odur wyle seruyth to accusatyf case and odur wyle to ablatyf case and odur wyle to both too. (*c.*1492–1494. Bodl. Lib., MS Douce 103, fols. 53ʳ–57aʳ; Thomson, *Edition*, Text K, 60, 203–206; *Checklist* 12.)

How know ye a preposicion? For he is sett byfore oþer partys of reson in apposicion or in composicion. (S. xv². BL, MS Add. 37,075, fols. 1ʳ–6ᵛ; Thomson, *Edition*, Text F, 49, 227–28; *Checklist* 9.)

Qwerby knowyst a preposicyon? For he is set beforn oþer partys of reson and seruyth to certeyn case. (S. xvᵐᵉᵈ. Cambridge, St John's College, MS F.26(163), fols. 1ʳ–12ʳ; Thomson, *Edition*, Text C, 30, 590a-591; *Checklist* 7.)

How knos þu a preposicion? A party of spech þe wech ys vndeclynet and ys set before oþer partys of spechys togedyr in apposicion and composicion. (S. xvᵐᵉᵈ. Aberystwyth, NLW, MS Peniarth 356B, fols. 54ᵛ–57ᵛ and 48ʳ; Thomson, *Edition*, Text A, 7, 310–12; *Checklist* 5.)

How knowest a preposicion? A party of reson that is not declinyd and seruith to accusatyf case and ablatyf. (S. xv¹. Cambridge, Trinity College, MS 0.5.4, fols. 4ᵛ–6ᵛ. (Thomson, *Edition*, Text D, 42, 520–21; *Checklist* 2.)

Praepositio est pars orationis indeclinabilis, quæ alijs orationis partibus uel compositione, uel appositione præponitur. Appositione, ut Christus sedet ad dexteram patris. Compositione, ut Adactum iuramentum adhibendum admonuit. Quædam prępositiones postponi inueniuntur, ut

$$\left.\begin{array}{l}\text{Cum} \\ \text{Tenus} \\ \text{Versus} \\ \text{Vsque}\end{array}\right\} \text{ut} \left\{\begin{array}{l}\text{Quibuscum} \\ \text{Pube tenus} \\ \text{Angliam uersus} \\ \text{Ad occidentem usque}\end{array}\right.$$

(*Institutio Compendiaria Totius Grammaticae*, 1540. Attributed to William Lily. BL, C.21.b.4.(3), at M3ᵛ; Appendix III, 1.0.)

Prepositio est pars orationis indeclinabilis: que preponitur alijs partibus orationis per appositionem: vt coram deo. per compositionem: vt impius. (Joannes Sulpitius Verulanus, *Opus insigne grammaticum*, 1494. JRUL, 19691, at a6ʳ.)

Quid est prepositio? Est pars orationis indeclinabilis que alijs partibus orationis in appositione uel compositione preponitur. (Nicolaus Perottus, *Rudimenta grammatices*, 1486. CUL, Inc.5.F.2.8 [3287], at e3ʳ.)

PRAEPOSITIO is foresetnyss. sê byđ geđêod naman and worde and stent æfre on foreweardan. *ab illo homine* fram đâm men: hêr is se *ab* PRAEPOSITIO. *apud regem sum* ic eom mid đâm cyninge: hêr is se *apud* PRAEPOSITIO. *ad regem equito* ic rîde tô cyninge, ET CETERA. (Ælfric, *Praefatio de partibus orationis*, in *Grammatik und Glossar*, Zupitza, 10, 15–20.)

PRAEPOSITIO EST PARS ORATIONIS INDECLINABILIS. PRAEPOSITIO mæg bêon gecweden on englisc foresetnys, forđan đe hê stent æfre on foreweardan, swâ hwær swâ hê byđ, bêo hê gefêged tô ôđrum worde, ne bêo hê. hwîlon hê geêacnađ and gefyld þæra worda andgit, đe hê tô cymđ, and hwîlon hê âwent heora getâcnunge and hwîlon wanađ. *celsus* is hêalîc. dô đær tô PRAEPOSITIO *ex*, þonne byđ hit *excelsus* swŷđe hêalîc: hêr hê gefyld þæt andgit. *iustus* is rihtwîs. dô đær tô PRAEPOSITIO *in*, þonne byđ hit *iniustus* unrihtwîs: hêr hê âwent þæt andgit. *rideo* ic hliche. dô đær tô PRAEPOSITIO *sub*, þonne byđ hit *subrideo* ic smercige: hêr hê gewanađ þæt andgit and swâ gehwær. (Ælfric, *Grammatik und Glossar*, Zupitza, 267, 14–17; 268, 1–9.)

Est igitur praepositio pars orationis indeclinabilis, quae praeponitur aliis partibus vel appositione vel compositione. (Priscian, *Institutiones grammaticae*; *GL* III, 24, 13–14.)

Praepositio est pars orationis, quae praeposita aliis partibus orationis significationem earum aut conplet aut mutat aut minuit. (Donatus, *Ars maior*; Holtz, 648, 4–5; *GL* IV, 389, 19–20.)

Praepositio quid est? Pars orationis, quae praeposita aliis partibus orationis significationem earum aut conplet aut mutat aut minuit. (Donatus, *Ars minor*; Holtz, 600, 8–9; *GL* IV, 365, 10–11.)

Definitions of the interjection:

AN INTERIECTION is a parte of speche, which betokeneth a passion of the mynde, vnder an vnperfect voyce. (*Introduction*, 1542. BL, C.21.b.4.(2), A4ʳ–F2ʳ [the parts of speech], at F2ʳ; present edition, 188, 1028–29.)

An interieccyon is a sounde or a voyce that brasteth out in speche betokenynge the affeccyon of the mynde. (John Colet, *Aeditio*, 1527. *EL*, 298 (1971), A6ʳ–D7ʳ [the parts of speech], at D6ᵛ; *Checklist* 20.1.)

Interiections, Some be of sorowe: as hei, heu, o, ah, ueh. [*etc.*]. (Thomas Linacre, *Rudimenta grammatices* [1525?]. *EL*, 312 (1971), A2ʳ–F1ʳ [*Rudimenta declinationum*], at F1ʳ.)

An interiection is a part vndeclined, the whiche vnder a rude and vnparfet voyce betokeneth some passion of the mynde: as sorowe, drede, indignation, or maruelynge. (*Ibid.*, F1ʳ–G1ᵛ [*Rudimenta definitionum*], at G1ᵛ; *Checklist* 55.1.)

Interiections some be of sorowe as hei. heu. o. ah. veh. [*etc.*]. (Thomas Linacre, *Progymnasmata grammatices vulgaria* [1512.]. BL, G.7569, A2ʳ–b5ᵛ [on declension], at b5ʳ.)
A interiecction ys a part vndeclynyd the which vndre a rude voyce betokeneth some passyon of þe mynde. as sorowe drede indygnation or merueling. (*Ibid.*, b5ᵛ–c4ʳ [definitions of the parts of speech], at c3ᵛ; *Checklist* 54.1.)

Quhat is ane interiectione? ane part of orisone ondeclinabill the quhilk betakynnis the affek off the mynd onder ane vnknawin voce. (John Vaus, *Rudimenta puerorum in artem grammaticam*, 1531. Aberdeen, University Library, AUL Λ Vau r 2, cc8ʳ–ee4ʳ [*de partium orationis interpretatione lingua vernacula*], at ee3ᵛ; *Checklist* 56.1.)

(Preceptor) How know you an Interiection (Discipulus) for he is a parte of reson vndeclyned that sheweth thaffect of the mynde/ the worde being vnperfect. (*Donate and accidence for children*, 1515. Bodl. Lib., Arch. A e.19, A2ʳ–C3ʳ, at C3ʳ; *Checklist* 19.1.)

Of interiections. Some be Of Joye/ as eya euge [*etc.*]. (John Holt, *Lac puerorum*, [1508.]. BL, C.33.b.47, A3ʳ–C8ʳ [on declension], at C7ᵛ.)
An Interieccyon betokeneth passyon of the soule with an vnperfyte voyce or noyse/ as haha tehe/ out/ alas/ and well a waye etc. (*Ibid.*, C8ʳ–E2ʳ [definitions of the parts of speech], at E2ʳ; *Checklist* 53.2.)

Interiectyon [*etc.*] which is a parte of reason vndeclyned much lyke an aduerbe. and betokenyth passyon of mannys soule/ that is to say/ ioy. sorow. drede. indignacion or meruelyng. and that with an inordynat voyce. as Proh dolor. for the nominatif case. Hei mihi. for the datyf. Heu me miserum. for the accusatife. O nox illa que tenebras attulisti. for the vocatyf. (*Informatio puerorum* [1499?]. Cambridge, Magdalene College, Pepysian Library, PL 1305(3), A2ʳ–B3ʳ, D2ᵛ–D3ᵛ, at D3ʳ; *Checklist* 17.1.)

How knowe yow an Interiectyon? For he ys a part of reason vndeclyned that showyth the affexyon of mans mynd/ wyth an vnperfect voyce for ioye serowe wondre drede or indignatyon. et cetera. ([*Abridged version of the Accidence, with other extracts*], 1534. CUL, Syn.8.53.74, A2ʳ–C8ᵛ, at C8ʳ; *Checklist* 16.35.)

Howe knowe you an Interiection? For he is a part of reson vndeclyned that betokenyth passion of a mannys soule with an imperfit voice. for ioy sorowe wondyr drede et cetera. (John Stanbridge, *Accidence* [1505?]. Bodl. Lib., 4° A 18(2) Art.BS, A1ʳ–C6ᵛ, at C6ʳ; *Checklist* 16.1.)

How know ye an Interieccion/ for it betokeneth the affecte of the mynde vnder an vnperfyte voyce/ as Ioye wo wonder Indygnacion. (*Short Accidence*, attributed to John Stanbridge [1495?]. San Marino, California, Henry E. Huntington Library, RB 152101, A1 and A4, at A4ᵛ; *Early Printed Editions*, Text I, 227, 92–94; *Checklist* 15.1.)

How knowest an Interiection. For he is a parte of reason vndeclyned. þat betokeneth passion of a mannys soule with an vnperfyte voyce with Ioye. sorowe. wondre. drede or Indignacion as/ Hate/ hey/ fy/ alas/ weleaway. so howe out out. and other lyke. (*Long Accidence*, attributed to John Stanbridge [1495.]. Bodl. Lib., Douce D 238(2), A1ʳ–B6ᵛ, at B4ᵛ; *Early Printed Editions*, Text A, 163, 637–41; *Checklist* 14.1.)

How knowyst an interieccyon? For he ys a party of speke vndeclynyd the wych shewᵗ a monnys wyll wᵗ a vnperfytt voyce, as wondur, drede or merwell. (*c*.1492–1494. Bodl. Lib., MS Douce 103, fols. 53ʳ–57aʳ; Thomson, *Edition*, Text K, 60, 207–209; *Checklist* 12.)

How know ye an interieccion? For he betokenyth passion of a mannys soule vndyr an vnperfite voyce, as of joy, woo, wondyr, drede or indignacion. (S. xv². BL, MS Add. 37,075, fols. 1ʳ–6ᵛ; Thomson, *Edition*, Text F, 49, 238–40; *Checklist* 9.)

Qwerby knowyst an interieccyon? For it lyth among oþer partys of reson and betokenyth passyon of sowle wᵗ an vnperfyth voyis, and betokenyth joye or sorow or dred or wunderyng or indignacyon, as 'aha', 'alas', 'welawey', 'out out', 'owgh', 'so howgh', and soch oþer. (S. xvᵐᵉᵈ. Cambridge, St John's College, MS F. 26(163), fols. 1ʳ–12ʳ; Thomson, *Edition*, Text C, 30, 612–16; *Checklist* 7.)

How know ʒe an interieccion? An interieccion ys a party of speche vndeclyned þat betokeneth passion of soule wᵗ an vnperfete voys. (S. xvᵐᵉᵈ. Aberystwyth, NLW, MS Peniarth 356B, fols. 163ʳ, 165ʳ–67ᵛ; Thomson, *Edition*, Text B, 14, 261–63; *Checklist* 6.)

How knos þu an interieccion? A party of spech þat ys vndeclynet þe wech betokyns passion of a monus sole wᵗ a imperfyt voyse, as 'fy', 'out', 'alas' and 'waylaway'. (S. xvᵐᵉᵈ. Aberystwyth, NLW, MS Peniarth 356B, fols. 54ᵛ–57ᵛ and 48ʳ; Thomson, *Edition*, Text A, 8, 324–26; *Checklist* 5.)

How knowyste an interieccion? A party of reson that bytokenyth talente of a mannys thouʒte and is not declinyd, as 'fy', 'hay'. (S. xv¹. Cambridge, Trinity College, MS O.5.4, fols. 4ᵛ–6ᵛ; Thomson, *Edition*, Text D, 43, 530–32; *Checklist* 2.)

Interiectio est pars orationis quæ sub incondita uoce animi affectum demonstrat. (*Institutio Compendiaria Totius Grammaticae*, 1540. Attributed to William Lily. BL, C.21.b.4.(3), at N1ᵛ; Appendix III, 1.0.)

Interiectio est pars orationis indeclinabilis: que mentis affectum significans: interiacet alijs partibus orationis. (Joannes Sulpitius Verulanus, *Opus insigne grammaticum*, 1494. JRUL, 19691, at a6ᵛ.)

Quid est interiectio? Est pars orationis indeclinabilis voce incognita mentis affectum significans. Quare dicitur interiectio? Quia interiacet alijs partibus orationis. Cur greci interiectionem inter aduerbia ponunt? Quoniam hec quoque uel adiungitur uerbis ut si dicam pape quid video. uel uerba ei subaudiuntur ut si dicam pape etiam si non addatur miror habet in se eius uerbi significationem. (Nicolaus Perottus, *Rudimenta grammatices*, 1486. CUL, Inc.5.F.2.8 [3287], at e4ʳ.)

INTERIECTIO is betwuxâworpennyss. se dæl lîð betwux ôðrum wordum and geswutelað þæs môdes styrunge. *heu* geswutelað môdes sârnysse: *heu mihi* wâmmê. *pape* geswutelað wundrunge, *atat* geswutelað ôgan, *racha* geswutelað æbylignysse, ET CETERA. (Ælfric, *Praefatio de partibus orationis*, in *Grammatik und Glossar*, Zupitza, 10, 20; 11, 1–5.)
INTERIECTIO EST PARS ORATIONIS SIGNIFICANS MENTIS AFFECTVM VOCE INCONDITA, INTERIECTIO is ân dæl lêdensprǽce getâcnjende þæs môdes gewilnunge mid ungesceapenre stemne. INTERIECTIO mæg bêon gecweden betwuxâlegednys on englisc, forþan ðe hê lîð betwux wordum and geopenað þæs môdes styrunge mid behŷddre stemne. (Ælfric, *Grammatik und Glossar*, Zupitza, 277, 15–17; 278, 1–4.)

Interiectio tamen non solum quem dicunt Graeci σχετλιασμόν significat, sed etiam voces, quae cuiuscumque passionis animi pulsu per exclamationem intericiuntur. habent igitur diversas significationes: gaudii, ut 'euax'; doloris, ut 'ei'. (Priscian, *Institutiones grammaticae*, GL III, 90, 12–15.)

Interiectio est pars orationis interiecta aliis partibus orationis ad exprimendos animi adfectus: aut metuentis, ut ei; aut optantis, ut o; aut dolentis, ut heu; aut laetantis, ut euax. (Donatus, *Ars maior*, Holtz, 652, 5–7; *GL* IV, 391, 26–28.)

Interiectio quid est? Pars orationis significans mentis affectum uoce incondita. (Donatus, *Ars minor*, Holtz, 602, 2; *GL* IV, 366, 13–14.)

BIBLIOGRAPHY

Primary works

MANUSCRIPTS

Aberystwyth, National Library of Wales:
MS 423D (John Anwykyll. *Vulgaria*, fols. 21^v-31^r. Written by Edward of Chirk (1480s)).

London, British Library:
MS Add. 6212 (Dr Ward's Memoranda and Correspondence: Letters from Rev. Thomas Birch. 'Remarks upon Professor Ward's Edition of Lily's Grammar'. 21. Sept. 1731 (fols. 9^{r-v}), and 5 Oct. 1732 (11^{r-v})).
MS Add. 6218 (Dr Ward's Memoranda and Correspondence: 'Memoranda, Collections, Fragments, etc., Relating to Different Editions of Lily's Latin Grammar', in *Notes on Greek and Latin Grammar*, fols. 3^r-14^v).
MS Add. 6274 (*Statuta Paulinæ Scholæ. John Colet's Statutes for St Paul's School*. Mid-sixteenth century, fols. 1^r-11^v).
MS Add. 11,360 (*A Manuscript Catalogue of the Library of the Rev. C.M. Cracherode, Bequeathed by him to the British Museum. In his Own Handwriting* [1790?]).
MS Add. 37,075 (*Nominale*, fols. 276^r-303^v. 2nd half of the fifteenth century).
MS Add. 47,611 (*Notebook Kept by [the Rev. Clayton Mordaunt Cracherode] as an Elected Trustee of the British Museum, from 11 June 1784 until 10 Dec. 1796*).
MS Add. 59,740 (*Cracherode Library: Catalogue of the Library of the Rev. Clayton Mordaunt Cracherode, c. 1800*).
MS Harley 540 ('Lily's Epigrams', in *Stowe's Historical Collections*, vol. 4, fols. 7^r-59^r).
MS King's 387 (*Bibliothecæ Cracherodianæ Catalogus*. [A Transcript by Samuel Ayscough of the Rev. Clayton Mordaunt Cracherode's Own Catalogue, with Additions. 19 May 1800]).
MS Lansdowne 808 (*One of John Bagford's Volumes of his Collections of Materials for a General History of Printing*, fols. 67^r-68^v).
MS Lansdowne 949 (Vol. XV of *Bishop Kennett's Collections: Containing a Copy of the Statutes for St Paul's School, London*, fols. 1^v-10^r).
MS Lansdowne 979 (Vol. XLV of *Bishop Kennett's Collections: Consisting of Biographical Memoranda from A.D. 1521 to A.D. 1540*, fol. 32^r).
MS Royal 19,400 (*Autograph Letters of Reformers and Martyrs, 1536-1569*. Letter no. 92, by Richard Cox, 3 Maij 1566, G3^r).

The National Archives (formerly: Public Record Office):
TNA, PROB/11/21 (The two copies of William Lily's will. Fol. 4, pages 24^v-25^r, and fol. 8, pages 61^v-62^r).

Oxford, Bodleian Library:
MS Auct. F.3.9. (John of Cornwall. *Speculum gramaticale*. Dated 1346 in the colophon, pp. 1–180; Thomas Hanney, *Memoriale iuniorum*, pp. 189–340).

Oxford, Magdalen College:
MCA, CP8/49 (*Bursary Book*, vol. 1).
MCA, EL/1 (*Ledger A*).

PRINTED TEXTS

Ælfric. *Ælfric's Colloquy*. Ed. G. N. Garmonsway (1978). 2nd rev. edn. Exeter: University of Exeter. (Exeter Medieval English Texts). (1st edn. London: Methuen's Old English Library, 1939.)

Ælfric. *Aelfrics Grammatik und Glossar. Text und Varianten*. Ed. Julius Zupitza (1880). Berlin. Vierte, unveränderte Auflage mit einer Einleitung von Helmut Gneuss. Hildesheim: Weidmannsche Verlagsbuchhandlung, 2003.

Ælfric. *Ælfric's Prefaces*. Ed. Jonathan Wilcox (1994). Durham Medieval Texts. 9. New Elvet, Durham: Department of English Studies; corrected repr. 1996.

Ælfric Bata. *Anglo-Saxon Conversations. The Colloquies of Ælfric Bata*. Ed. Scott Gwara. Trans. with an Introduction by David W. Porter (1997). Woodbridge, Suffolk, and Rochester, New York: The Boydell Press.

Alexander de Villa Dei. *Das Doctrinale des Alexander de Villa-Dei*. Ed. Dietrich Reichling (1893). Monumenta Germaniae paedagogica, xii. Berlin: Hofmann; repr. New York: Franklin, 1974. (Research and Source Works Series. Studies in the History of Education, 11.)

Alphabetum Latino Anglicum (1543). London: Thomas Berthelet. (BL, C.21.b.4.(1).)

Anglo-Saxon and Old English Vocabularies. Ed. Thomas Wright (1884). 2 vols. 2nd edn. Ed. and collated by Richard Paul Wülcker. London; repr. of the 2nd edn. Darmstadt: Wissenschaftliche Buchgesellschaft, 1968. (1st ed. London, 1857.)

Bale, John (*c*.1549–1557). *Index Britanniae Scriptorum. John Bale's Index of British and Other Writers*. Ed. Reginald Lane Poole and Mary Bateson (Oxford, 1902) (Anecdota Oxoniensia, 4,9). (Bodl. Lib., MS Selden Supra 64, fols. x–y). Repr. with a new Introduction by Caroline Brett and James P. Carley. Cambridge: Brewer, 1990.

Bale, John (1557–1559). *Scriptorum Illustrium Maioris Brytanniae Catalogus*. 2 vols. Basle; repr. Westmead, Farnborough, Hants.: Gregg, 1971.

Biblia Sacra iuxta Vulgatam Versionem. Ed. Robert Weber *et al.* (1969). 2 Bde. Stuttgart: Württembergische Bibelanstalt. (3rd corrected repr. 1983.)

Bloxam, John Rouse (1853–1885). *A Register of the Presidents, Fellows, Demics [. . .] and Other Members of Saint Mary Magdalen College in the University of Oxford*. 8 vols. Oxford: Parker.

Bridges, John (1791). *The History and Antiquities of Northamptonshire*. Compiled from the Manuscript Collections. 2 vols. Oxford: Payne.

Bullokar, William (1580). *Booke at Large* and *Bref Grammar for English* (1586). Facsimile Reproductions with an Introduction by Diane Bornstein (1977). Delmar, New York: Scholars' Facsimiles and Reprints.

Bullokar, William (1580–1581). *A Short Introduction or Guiding*, in *The Works of William Bullokar*. Vol. I. Ed. B. Danielsson and R. C. Alston (1966). Leeds: The University of Leeds. School of English.

Bullokar, William (1586). 'Bref Grammar for English', in Max Plessow (ed.) (1906), *Geschichte der Fabeldichtung in England bis zu John Gay* (1726). Palaestra 52. Berlin: Mayer und Müller, 331–85, 386–88.

Bullokar, William (1586). *Pamphlet for Grammar*, in J. R. Turner (ed.) (1980), *The Works of William Bullokar*. Vol. II. Leeds: The University of Leeds. School of English. (Leeds Texts and Monographs, *New Series 1*.)

Camden, William (1610). *Britannia. Britain, or a Chorographicall Description of the Most Flourishing Kingdomes, England, Scotland, and Ireland*. [. . .]. Written first in Latine by William Camden. Translated newly into English by Philemon Holland. London: George Bishop and John Norton. (BL, Maps C.7.b.2.)

Certayne Briefe Rules of the regiment or construction of the eyght partes of speche, in englishe and latine (1537). London: Thomas Berthelet. (Bodl. Lib., Douce G.359.)

Colet, John (1527). *Aeditio*. Antwerp: Christopher van Ruremond?, A6^r–D6^v. [A facsimile ed.] (= *EL*, 298 (1971)). Menston: The Scolar Press.

Colet, John (1527). *Aeditio*, in S. Blach (ed.) (1908; 1909), 'Shakespeares Latein-grammatik', *Jahrbuch der Deutschen Shakespeare-Gesellschaft* 44: 65–117; 45: 51–80.

Colet, John, and William Lily (1529). *Rudimenta grammatices et Docendi methodus*. [Southwark]: Peter Treveris. (BL, C.40.c.39.)

A Companion to Arber. Being a Calendar of Documents in Edward Arber's Transcript of the Registers of the Company of Stationers of London, 1554–1640; with Text and Calendar of Supplementary Documents. Ed. W. W. Greg (1967). Oxford: Clarendon Press.

Concilia Magnae Britanniae et Hiberniae, a Synodo Verolamiensi A.D. CCCCXLVI. ad Londinensem A.D. MDCCXVII. Ed. David Wilkins (1737). 4 vols. London: Gosling; repr. Bruxelles: Culture et Civilisation, 1964.

Cox, Leonard (1526). *De Erudienda Iuventute*, in Andrew Breeze and Jacqueline Glomski (eds.) (1991). 'An Early British Treatise upon Education: Leonard Cox's *De Erudienda Iuventute*'. With Translation and Introduction. *Humanistica Lovaniensia* 40: 112–67.

Documentary Annals of the Reformed Church of England; Being a Collection of Injunctions, Declarations, Orders, Articles of Inquiry, etc., from the Year 1546 to the Year 1716. Ed. Edward Cardwell (1844). Oxford: Oxford University Press. (A new edn. in 2 vols., Ridgewood, New Jersey, USA: The Gregg Press, 1966.)

Dodd, Charles (pseud.) [Hugh Tootell] (1737–1742). *The Church History of England, from the Year 1500, to the Year 1688. Chiefly with Regard to Catholicks*. 3 vols. Brussels: [Bowyer]; repr. Westmead, Farnborough, Hants.: Gregg, 1970.

'Die Donat- und Kalender-Type. Nachtrag und Übersicht'. Ed. Paul Schwenke (1903). *Veröffentlichungen der Gutenberg-Gesellschaft* 2: 35–49.

Donate and accidence for children (1515). Paris: Philippe de Coblencz. (Oxford: Bodleian Library, Arch.A e.19.)

Donatus, Aelius. *Ars maior*, in Louis Holtz (ed.) (1981), *Donat et la Tradition de l'Enseignement Grammatical. Étude sur l'Ars Donati et sa Diffusion (IVe–IXe Siècle) et Édition Critique*. Paris: CNRS. (Documents, Études et Répertoires [35]), 603–74. (Also in *GL* 4, 367–402.)

Donatus, Aelius. *Ars minor*, in Louis Holtz (ed.) (1981), *Donat et la Tradition de l'Enseignement Grammatical. Étude sur l'Ars Donati et sa Diffusion (IVe–IXe Siècle) et Édition Critique*. Paris: CNRS. (Documents, Études et Répertoires [35]), 585–602. (Also in *GL* 4, 355–66.)

Donatus, Aelius. *The Ars Minor of Donatus. For One Thousand Years the Leading Textbook of Grammar*. Trans. Wayland Johnson Chase (1926). University of Wisconsin Studies in the Social Sciences and History, no. 11. Madison, Wisconsin: University of Wisconsin, Introduction 1–26, text and English trans. 28–55; Trans. repr. in Peter H. Salus (ed.) (1969). *On Language. Plato to von Humboldt*. New York: Holt, Rinehart and Winston, 92–103.

Donatus, Aelius (*c*.1507?). *Ars minor*. A Version in Scots. [Scotland? Printer of the Aberdeen Donatus]. (Aberdeen, University Library, Λ^3 Vau r 1.)

Dorne, John. 'Day-Book of John Dorne, Bookseller in Oxford, A.D. 1520'. Ed. F. Madan (1885), in C. R. L. Fletcher (ed.), *Collectanea* I. Part III. OHS. Oxford: Clarendon Press, 71–177.

Dorne, John. 'Supplementary Notes to *Collectanea* I. Part III, Day-Book of John Dorne, Bookseller in Oxford, 1520'. Ed. F. Madan (1890), in M. Burrows (ed.), *Collectanea* II. OHS. Oxford: Clarendon Press, 453–78. (This article largely incorporates Henry Bradshaw (1886). 'Half-Century of Notes on the Day-Book of John Dorne'. Repr. (1889), in *Collected Papers of Henry Bradshaw*. Cambridge, 421–51.) (See Bradshaw, Henry.)

Early Printed Editions of the Long Accidence and Short Accidence Grammars. Ed. Hedwig Gwosdek (1991). Anglistische Forschungen 213. Heidelberg: Winter.

An Edition of the Middle English Grammatical Texts. Ed. David Thomson (1984). Garland Medieval Texts. 8. New York and London: Garland.

Educational Charters and Documents, 598 to 1909. Ed. Arthur F. Leach (1911). Cambridge: Cambridge University Press; repr. New York: Ams Press, 1971.

Elyot, Thomas (1531). *The Boke Named the Gouernour*. Ed. Henry Herbert Stephen Croft (1880). 2 vols. London: Kegan Paul.

Elyot, Thomas (1539). *The Castel Of Helthe, Gathered, and made by syr Thomas Elyot knight*. London: Thomas Berthelet. (London, Lambeth Palace Library, 1539.3.)

Elyot, Thomas (1539). *The Castel Of Helth Gathered And Made By Syr Thomas Elyot knyghte*. London: Thomas Berthelet. (BL, C.54.a.18.)

Elyot, Thomas (1541). *The Castel Of Helth Corrected And in some places augmented*. London: Thomas Berthelet. (BL, C.112.b.23.)

Elyot, Thomas (1541). *The Castel Of Helth Corrected And in some places augmented*. London: Thomas Berthelet. (Bodl. Lib., Tanner 272(1).)

Elyot, Thomas (1541). *The Castell of Helth corrected and in some places augmented*. London: Thomas Berthelet. (BL, G.10333.)

Elyot, Thomas (1547). *The Castel of Helth Corrected And In Some places augmented*. London: Thomas Berthelet. (BL, C.124.aaa.13.)

Erasmus, Desiderius. *Der Katechismus des Erasmus von Rotterdam* (1512/1513), in *Evangelische Katechismen der Reformationszeit vor und neben Martin Luthers Kleinem Katechismus*. Ed. Ernst-Wilhelm Kohls (1971). Gütersloh: Mohn, 21–26. (Texte zur Kirchen- und Theologiegeschichte, Heft 16.)

Erasmus, Desiderius (1514). *Institutum Christiani hominis carmine pro pueris. ab Erasmo compositum, in Opuscula aliquot Erasmo Roterodamo castigatore et interprete*. Louvain: Thierry Martens. (The Hague, Royal Library, 228 E 80.)

Erasmus, Desiderius. *Opus Epistolarum Des. Erasmi Roterodami. Denuo recognitum et auctum*. Ed. P. S. Allen (1906–1958). 12 vols. Oxford: Clarendon.

Erasmus, Desiderius. *The Poems of Desiderius Erasmus*. Ed. C. Reedijk (1956). Leiden: Brill.

Erasmus, Desiderius (1974–). *Collected Works of Erasmus*. Toronto: University of Toronto Press. (*The Correspondence*, vols. 1–13. Annotated by James K. McConica; *Literary and Educational Writings*, vols. 23–24. Ed. Craig R. Thompson; Poems of Erasmus, vols. 85–86. Ed. and annotated by Harry Vredeveld.)

Erasmus, Desiderius, and William Lily (1515). *Libellus de constructione octo partium orationis*, in *Opera Omnia Desiderii Erasmi Roterodami*. Ed. M. Cytowska (1973). Vol. I,4. Amsterdam: North-Holland Publishing Company, 119–43.

Évrard de Béthune. *Eberhardi Bethuniensis Graecismus*. Ed. Johannes Wrobel (1887). Corpus grammaticorum medii aevi, i. Breslau: Koebner; repr. Hildesheim: Olms, 1987.

Excerptiones de Prisciano: The Source for Ælfric's Latin–Old English Grammar. Ed. David W. Porter (2002). Anglo-Saxon Texts, 4. Woodbridge: Brewer.

A Fifteenth Century School Book. From a Manuscript in the British Museum (MS. Arundel 249). Ed. William Nelson (1956). Oxford: Clarendon Press.

Garrett Godfrey's Accounts, c.1527–1533. Ed. Elisabeth Leedham-Green, D. E. Rhodes, and F. H. Stubbings (1992). Cambridge: Cambridge Bibliographical Society.

Grammatici Latini. Ed. Heinrich Keil (1855–1880). 8 vols. Leipzig: Teubner; repr. Hildesheim: Olms, 1961, 1981.

Hayne, Thomas (1640). *Grammatices Latinæ compendium, Anno 1637*. London: Edward Griffin for Andrew Hebb. (Bodl. Lib., Wood.42.[2].)

Higden, Ranulf. *Polychronicon Ranulphi Higden Monachi Cestrensis; Together with the English Translations of John Trevisa and of an Unknown Writer of the Fifteenth Century*. Ed. Churchill Babington and J. R. Lumby (1865–1886). Rolls Series, 41. 9 vols. London: Longman.

Historical Manuscripts Commission (HMC) (1874). Fourth Report, Part I. Report and Appendix. London: Eyre and Spottiswoode.

Historical Manuscripts Commission (HMC) (1884). Ninth Report, Part II. Appendix and Index. London: Eyre and Spottiswoode.

Holt, John [1508]. *Lac puerorum*. London: Wynkyn de Worde. (London, British Library, C.33.b.47.)

Horman, William (1519). *Vulgaria*. London: Richard Pynson. Facsimile Edition (1975). The English Experience, no. 745. Amsterdam: Norwood.

Informatio puerorum [1499?]. London: Richard Pynson. (Cambridge, Magdalene College, Pepysian Library, PL 1305(3).)

Johannes de Garlandia. *Compendium gramatice. Auf der Grundlage aller bekannten Handschriften*. Ed. Thomas Haye (1995). *Ordo. Studien zur Literatur und Gesellschaft des Mittelalters und der frühen Neuzeit*, Bd. 5. Köln, Weimar, Wien: Böhlau.

John of Genoa (1286). *Summa grammaticalis quae vocatur Catholicon*. Printed ed.: Joannes Balbus (1460). *Catholicon*. Mainz: [Johannes Gutenberg?]; repr. Westmead, Farnborough, Hants.: Gregg, 1971.

'Letters of the Oxford *Dictatores*'. Ed. H. G. Richardson, in H. E. Salter, W. A. Pantin, and H. G. Richardson (eds.) (1942), *Formularies Which Bear on the History of Oxford, c.1204–1420*. Vol. II. OHS, New Ser. V: 329–450.

Lily, George (1548). 'Virorum aliquot in Britannia, qui nostro seculo eruditione, et doctrina clari, memorabilesque fuerunt, elogia', in Paolo Giovio. *Descriptio Britanniae, Scotiae, Hyberniae, et Orchadum*. Venice: Michael Tramezinus, 45^r–54^v. (BL,598.d.11.(1).)

Lily, William (1513). *Libellus de constructione Octo partium orationis* [Anon. Ed. D. Erasmus]. London: Richard Pynson. (Bodl. Lib., 4° C.23.Art.BS.)

Lily, William (1515). *Absolutissimus de octo orationis partium constructione libellus*. Paris: Nicolas Crespin. (Bodl. Lib. 4° E 6(4) Art.Seld.)

Lily, William [1516?]. *Guilelmi Lilii Angli Rudimenta Parvulorum Lilii Nuper Impressa et correcta*. [York: Ursyn Mylner]. (Bodl. Lib., 4° Rawlinson 206(3).)

Lily, William (1521). *Antibossicon*. London: Richard Pynson. (BL, C.70.e.16.(1).)

Lily, William [1522]. *Epigrammata Guilelmi Lilii Angli*. [London: Wynkyn de Worde]. (Dublin, Trinity College, DD.hh.56 no. 4.)

Lily, William [1522]. 'Of the tryumphe and the verses that Charles themperour & the most myghty redouted kyng of England Henry the .VIII. were saluted with passyng through London', in 'William Lily's Verse for the Entry of Charles V into London'. Ed. C. R. Baskervill (1936). *The Huntington. Library Bulletin* 9: 8–14.

Lily, William (1525). *De generibus nominum, Ac verborum praeteritis et supinis Regulae*. Antwerp: Michael Hillenius. (BL, G.7476.)

Lily, William (1527). *Rudimenta grammatices*, in John Colet (1527). *Aeditio*. Antwerp: Christopher van Ruremond?, D7^r-E5^v. [A facsimile ed.]. (= *EL*, 298 (1971).)

Lily, William [c.1540]. [*An Introduction of the Eyght Partes of Speche, and the Construction of the Same*,] attributed to William Lily. [London: Thomas Berthelet]. (Bodl. Lib., Vet.A1.a.4(1).)

Lily, William [c.1540]. [*An Introduction of the Eyght Partes of Speche, and the Construction of the Same*,] attributed to William Lily. [London: Thomas Berthelet]. A photographic reproduction of a proof-sheet of *An Introduction of the eyght partes of speche* [1952]. (BL, 1881.d.22.(10.).)

Lily, William (1540). *Institutio Compendiaria Totius Grammaticae*. Attributed to William Lily. London: Thomas Berthelet. (London, Lambeth Palace Library, 1540.5.)

Lily, William (1540). *Institutio Compendiaria Totius Grammaticae*. Attributed to William Lily. London: Thomas Berthelet. (BL, C.21.b.4.(3).)

Lily, William (1566). *A Shorte Introduction of Grammar*, in S. Blach (ed.) (1908; 1909), 'Shakespeares Lateingrammatik'. *Jahrbuch der Deutschen Shakespeare-Gesellschaft* 44: 65–117; 45: 51–80.

Lily, William (1567). *A Shorte Introduction of Grammar*. [A facsimile ed.]. With an Introduction by Vincent J. Flynn (1945). Delmar, New York: Scholars' Facsimiles and Reprints; repr. 1977.

Lily, William (1739). *A Short Introduction of Grammar, generally to be used*. Ed. J. W. [John Ward]. 3 parts. London: S. Buckley and T. Longman. (BL, 1607/6049(1).)

Lily, William (1752). *A Short Introduction of Grammar, generally to be used*. Ed. John Ward. 3 parts. London: S. Buckley and T. Longman. (BL, 1568/3357(1).)

Lily, William, and John Colet (1549). *A Short Introduction of Grammar*. [A facsimile ed.]. (= *EL*, 262 (1970).) Menston: The Scolar Press.

Lily, William, and Thomas More (1518). *Progymnasmata Thomae Mori et Guilielmi Lilii sodalium*, in C. H. Miller *et al*. (eds.) (1984), *The Complete Works of St. Thomas More*. Vol. 3, Part II: *Latin Poems*. New Haven and London: Yale University Press, 78–95 and 321–26.

Linacre, Thomas [1512]. *Progymnasmata grammatices vulgaria*. London: John Rastell. (BL, G.7569.)

Linacre, Thomas [1525?]. *Rudimenta grammatices*. [A facsimile ed.]. (= *EL*, 312 (1971).) Menston: The Scolar Press.

The Loeb Classical Library (1912–). Ed. T. E. Page *et al.* London: Heinemann; repr. Cambridge, MA: Harvard University Press. (Cicero. *On Ends* [*De finibus*], vol. 40; *On Friendship* [*De amicitia*], vol. 154; *Letters to Friends* [*Ad familiares*], vol. 216N. Horace. *Odes and Epodes*, vol. 33. Ovid. *Tristia*, vol. 151. Plato. *The Republic*, vols. 123, 164, 237, 276. Sallust. *The War with Catiline*, vol. 116. Terence. *The Woman of Andros* [*Andria*]; *The Eunuch*, vol. 22N. Virgil. *Eclogues*; *Georgics*, vol. 63N.)

More, Thomas (1518, March). *Utopia. Epigrammata, etc.* Basle: Johann Froben. (BL, G.2398.(1.).)

More, Thomas. *The Correspondence of Sir Thomas More*. Ed. Elizabeth Frances Rogers (1947). Princeton: Princeton University Press.

More, Thomas. *The Complete Works of St. Thomas More*. Vol. 3, Part II: *Latin Poems*. Eds. C. H. Miller, L. Bradner, C. A. Lynch, and R. P. Oliver (1984). New Haven and London: Yale University Press.

Mulcaster, Richard (1581). *Positions Concerning the Training Up of Children*. Ed. William Barker (1994). Toronto: University of Toronto Press.

Mulcaster, Richard (1582). *Mulcaster's Elementarie*. Ed. E. T. Campagnac (1925). With an Introduction. Tudor and Stuart Library. Oxford: Clarendon Press.

Pace, Richard (1517). *De Fructu Qui Ex Doctrina Percipitur* (*The Benefit of a Liberal Education*). Ed. and trans. Frank Manley and Richard S. Sylvester (1967). The Renaissance Society of America, Renaissance Text Series, II. New York: Ungar Publishing.

Palsgrave, John (1540). *The Comedy of Acolastus. Translated from the Latin of Fullonius*. Ed. P. L. Carver (1937). EETS, OS, 202. London: Oxford University Press.

Perottus, Nicolaus [1486.]. *Rudimenta grammatices*. [Louvain:] Aegidius van der Heerstraten. (CUL, Inc.5.F.2.8 [3287].)

Petrus Helias. *Summa super Priscianum*. Ed. Leo Reilly (1993). 2 vols. Studies and Texts, 113. Toronto: Pontifical Institute of Mediaeval Studies.

Petrus Hispanus (non-papa). *Summa 'Absoluta Cuiuslibet'*. Ed. Corneille Henri Kneepkens (1987). *Het Iudicium Constructionis. Het Leerstuk van de Constructio in de 2de Helft van de 12de Eeuw*. Deel IV. Nijmwegen: Ingenium Publishers.

Petrus de Isolella. *Compendium grammatice*. Ed. Charles Fierville (1886). *Une Grammaire Latine Inédite du XIIIᵉ Siècle. Extraite des Manuscrits No 465 de Laon et No 15462 (Fonds Latin) de La Bibliothèque Nationale*. Paris: Imprimerie Nationale.

Pits, John (1619). *Relationum Historicarum de Rebus Anglicis*. Paris: Rolinum Thierry and Sebastianum Cramoisy; repr. Westmead, Farnborough, Hants.: Gregg, 1969.

Plinius, Secundus (1496). *C. Plynius Secundus De Naturali Hystoria diligentissime Castigatus*. Brescia: Angelus and Jacobus Britannicus. (BL, IC.31152.)

Priscian. *Institutiones grammaticae*. Ed. Martin Hertz, in *Grammatici Latini*. Ed. Heinrich Keil (1855–1859). Vols. II and III. Leipzig: Teubner; repr. Hildesheim: Olms, 1961,1981. (= *GL* II: 1–597; *GL* III: 1–377.)

Records of the Court of the Stationers' Company. Vol. 1: *1576 to 1602 ~ from Register B*. Ed. W. W. Greg and E. Boswell (1930). London: The Bibliographical Society.

Records of the Court of the Stationers' Company. Vol. 2: *1602 to 1640*. Ed. William A. Jackson (1957). London: The Bibliographical Society.

The Register of John Morton, Archbishop of Canterbury, 1486–1500. Ed. Christopher Harper-Bill (1987–2000). 3 vols. The Canterbury and York Society, vols. 75, 78, 89. Woodbridge, Suffolk: The Boydell Press.

Rhenanus, Beatus. *Briefwechsel des Beatus Rhenanus.* Ed. Adalbert Horawitz und Karl Hartfelder (1886). Leipzig: Teubner; repr. Nieuwkoop: de Graaf, 1966.

Rotuli parliamentorum, ut et petitiones et placita in parliamento [1278–1503]. Ed. John Strachey (1767–1777). 6 vols. London.

Stanbridge, John [1495] *Long Accidence.* Attributed to John Stanbridge, in H. Gwosdek (ed.) (1991), *Early Printed Editions of the Long Accidence and Short Accidence Grammars.* Anglistische Forschungen 213. Heidelberg: Winter, 152–64.

Stanbridge, John [1495?]. *Short Accidence.* Attributed to John Stanbridge, in H. Gwosdek (ed.) (1991), *Early Printed Editions of the Long Accidence and Short Accidence Grammars.* Anglistische Forschungen 213. Heidelberg: Winter, 226–28.

Stanbridge, John [1496]. *Long Parvula.* Attributed to John Stanbridge [London]: Richard Pynson. (Cambridge: Magdalene College, Pepysian Library, PL 1305(4).)

Stanbridge, John [1496?]. *Parvula.* Attributed to John Stanbridge [Westminster: Wynkyn de Worde]. (Bodl. Lib., Douce D 238(3).)

Stanbridge, John [1505?]. *Accidence.* London: Richard Pynson. (Bodl. Lib., 4°A 18(2)Art.BS.)

Stanbridge, John [*c.*1505]. *Short Accidence.* Attributed to John Stanbridge, in H. Gwosdek (ed.) (1991). *Early Printed Editions of the Long Accidence and Short Accidence Grammars.* Anglistische Forschungen 213. Heidelberg: Winter, 229–31.

Stanbridge, John [1507?]. *Parvulorum institutio ex stanbrigiana collectione.* London: Wynkyn de Worde. (Cambridge, King's College, M.28.43².)

Stanbridge, John (1519). *The Vulgaria of John Stanbridge and the Vulgaria of Robert Whittinton* (1520). Ed. Beatrice White (1932 for 1931). EETS, OS, 187. London: Kegan Paul; repr. New York: Kraus Reprint, 1971.

Stanbridge, John (1534). *Abridged Version of the Accidence, with other extracts.* Antwerp: Martin de Keyser. (CUL, Syn.8.53.74.)

Stapleton, Thomas (1588). 'Vita et Illustre Martyrium Thomæ Mori, Angliæ Quondam Supremi Cancellarii', in T. Stapleton. *Tres Thomae.* [. . .]. *D. Thomæ Mori Angliæ quondam Cancellarij Vita.* Douai: John Bogard.

Stapleton, Thomas. *The Life and Illustrious Martyrdom of Sir Thomas More by Thomas Stapleton.* Ed. E. E. Reynolds (1966). Trans. Philip E. Hallett. London: Burns and Oates. (Trans. first published 1928.)

The Statutes of the Realm, from Magna Carta to the End of the Reign of Queen Anne. From Original Records [etc.] (1101–1713). Ed. Sir T. Edlyn Tomlins *et al.* (1810–1828). 12 vols. London: Record Commission.

Strype, John (1822). *Ecclesiastical Memorials Relating Chiefly to Religion and the Reformation of it,* [. . .]. 3 vols. Oxford: Clarendon Press.

Sulpitius Verulanus, Joannes (1494). *Opus insigne grammaticum.* London: Richard Pynson. (JRUL, 19691.)

Synodalia. A Collection of Articles of Religion, Canons, and Proceedings of Convocations in the Province of Canterbury, from the Year 1547 to the Year 1717. Ed. Edward Cardwell (1842). 2 vols. Oxford: Oxford University Press; repr. Westmead, Farnborough, Hants.: Gregg, 1966.

Tanner, Thomas (1748). *Bibliotheca Britannico-Hibernica: Sive, de Scriptoribus, qui in Anglia, Scotia, et Hibernia ad Saeculi XVII Initium Floruerunt*. London: Bowyer.

Tavelegus, David (1547). *Progymnasmata Graecae Grammatices Authore Davido Tavelego Medico*. Antwerp: Joannes Loëus. (BL, C.28.a.14.)

Thurot, Charles (1869). *Extraits de Divers Manuscrits Latins Pour Servir à L'Histoire des Doctrines Grammaticales au Moyen Âge*. Paris: Imprimerie Impériale; repr. Frankfurt am Main: Minerva, 1964.

Tractate zur Unterweisung in der Anglo-Normannischen Briefschreibekunst nebst Mitteilungen aus den zugehörigen Musterbriefen. Ed. Wilhelm Uerkvitz (1898). D.Phil. Dissertation. Greifswald: Kunike.

A Transcript of the Registers of the Company of Stationers of London, 1554–1640 A.D. Ed. Edward Arber (1875–1894). 5 vols. London: Privately printed.

Tudor Royal Proclamations. Ed. Paul L. Hughes and James F. Larkin (1964–1969). 3 vols. New Haven and London: Yale University Press.

Vaus, John (1531). *Rudimenta puerorum in artem grammaticam*. [Paris]: Jodocus Badius Ascensius. (Aberdeen, University Library, AUL Λ Vau r 2.)

Vergil, Polydore (1534). *Polydori Vergilii Vrbinatis Anglicae Historiae Libri XXVI*. Basle: John Bebel. (BL, G.4762.)

Vergil, Polydore. *The Anglica Historia of Polydore Vergil A.D. 1485–1537*. Ed. with a Trans. by Denys Hay (1950). Camden Series. Vol. LXXIV. London: Offices of the Royal Historical Society.

The Victoria History of the Counties of England (VCH). Ed. Herbert Arthur Doubleday and William Page (1900–). *A History of Hampshire and the Isle of Wight*. Ed. William Page (1903). Vol. 15,2. London: Constable; repr. Folkestone, Kent: Dawsons of Pall Mall, 1973.

The Victoria History of the Counties of England (VCH). Ed. Herbert Arthur Doubleday and William Page (1900–). *A History of Lancaster*. Ed. William Farrer and J. Brownbill (1908). Vol. 18,2. London: Constable; repr. Folkestone, Kent: Dawsons Pall Mall, 1991.

The Victoria History of the Counties of England (VCH). Ed. Herbert Arthur Doubleday and William Page (1900–). *A History of Suffolk*. Ed. William Page (1907). Vol. 34,2. London: repr. Folkestone, Kent: Dawsons of Pall Mall, 1975.

The Victoria History of the Counties of England (VCH). Ed. Herbert Arthur Doubleday and William Page (1900–). *A History of Sussex*. Ed. William Page (1907). Vol. 36,2. London: Constable; repr. Folkestone, Kent: Dawsons of Pall Mall, 1973.

Visitation Articles and Injunctions of the Period of the Reformation, 1536–1575. Ed. Walter Howard Frere and William McClure Kennedy (1910). 3 vols. London: Longmans, Green. (Alcuin Club Collections, 14–16.)

Wolsey, Thomas (1529). *Methodus*, in John Colet and William Lily. *Rudimenta grammatices et Docendi methodus*. [Southwark]: Peter Treveris. (BL, C.40.c.39, A3^r–A4^v.)

Wood, Anthony à (1813–1820). *Athenæ Oxonienses. An Exact History of all the Writers and Bishops who have had their Education in the University of Oxford. To which are Added The Fasti or Annals of the Said University*. A New Edition with Additions, and a Continuation by Philip Bliss. 4 vols. London: Rivington; repr. New York: Johnson Reprint Corporation, 1967. (The Sources of Science, No. 55.)

Wright, Thomas (1852). 'Rules of the Free School at Saffron Walden, in Essex, in the Reign of Henry VIII', *Archaeologia* 34: 37–41.

Secondary works

Adams, H. M. (1967). 'Catalogue of Books Printed on the Continent of Europe, 1501–1600', in *Cambridge Libraries*. 2 vols. Cambridge: Cambridge University Press; repr. Mansfield Centre, Conn.: Fine, 2000.

Adamson, John William (1919). *A Short History of Education*. Cambridge: Cambridge University Press.

Allen, C. G. (1954). 'The Sources of "Lily's Latin Grammar": A Review of the Facts and Some Further Suggestions', *The Library*, 5th ser., 9: 85–100.

Allen, C. G. (1959). 'Certayne Briefe Rules and "Lily's Latin Grammar"', *The Library*, 5th ser., 14: 49–53.

Alston, R. C. (1965–). *A Bibliography of the English Language from the Invention of Printing to the Year 1800*. 20 vols. Leeds: Arnold. (Vol. 21 in preparation.) (A Corrected Reprint of Volumes I–X. Reproduced from the Author's Annotated Copy with Corrections and Additions to 1973. Ilkley: Janus Press, 1974.)

Alston, R. C. (1966). 'Bibliography and Historical Linguistics', *The Library*, 5th ser., 21: 181–91.

Alston, R. C. (ed.) (1967–1972). *English Linguistics, 1500–1800. A Collection of Facsimile Reprints*. 365 vols. Menston: The Scolar Press.

Alston, R. C. (1999). 'What Mad Pursuit?' *The Henry Sweet Society Bulletin* 32: 25–30.

Alston, R. C., and Brad Sabin Hill (1996). *Books Printed on Vellum in the Collections of The British Library*. London: The British Library.

Ames, Joseph [No year]. [*A Collection of 7425 Title Pages of Books Printed in England, Scotland and Ireland Before the Year 1749, Brought Together By Joseph Ames, and Arranged Originally in Three, Now in Six Volumes*]. 6 vols. [No Place]. (BL, Ames. 1–6.)

Ames, Joseph (1749). *Typographical Antiquities: Being an Historical Account of Printing in England*. London: Faden.

Anglo, Sydney (1969). *Spectacle, Pageantry, and Early Tudor Policy*. Oxford: Clarendon Press.

[Anon.] (1907). 'Eton and Winchester in 1530', *Etoniana* 9: 131–36.

[Anon.] (1911). 'An Eton Curriculum of 1528', *Etoniana* 12: 190–92.

Arnold, Ivor D. O. (1937). 'Thomas Sampson and the *Orthographia Gallica*', *Medium Aevum* 6: 193–209.

Ax, Wolfram (2001). 'Lorenzo Valla (1407–1457), *Elegantiarum linguae Latinae libri sex* (1449)', in W. Ax (ed.), *Von Eleganz und Barbarei. Lateinische Grammatik und Stilistik in Renaissance und Barock*. Wolfenbütteler Forschungen, Bd. 95. Mainz: Harrassowitz, 29–57.

Ayres, Harry Morgan (1926). 'A Note on the School Pronunciation of Latin in England', *Speculum* 1: 440–43.

Baldwin, T. W. (1943). *William Shakspere's Petty School*. Urbana: University of Illinois Press.

Baldwin, T. W. (1944). *William Shakspere's Small Latine and Lesse Greeke*. 2 vols. Urbana: University of Illinois Press.

Baratin, Marc (1998). 'Donat', in *HEL*, vol. 1, no. 1205: 40–42.

Baratin, Marc (2005). 'Priscianus Caesariensis (5./6. Jahrhundert n. Chr.)', in W. Ax (ed.), *Lateinische Lehrer Europas. Fünfzehn Portraits von Varro bis Erasmus von Rotterdam*. Köln, Weimar, Wien: Böhlau, 247–72.

Barber, Charles (1997). *Early Modern English*. 2nd edn. Edinburgh: Edinburgh University Press; repr. 2001. (1st edn. London: Deutsch, 1976.)

Baskervill, C. R. (1936). 'William Lily's Verse for the Entry of Charles V into London', *The Huntington Library Bulletin* 9: 1–14.

Baugh, Albert C., and Thomas Cable (2002). *A History of the English Language*. 5th edn. London: Routledge. (1st edn. New York: D. Appleton-Century Company, 1935.)

Bautz, Friedrich Wilhelm (Hrsg.) (1975–2010). *Biographisch-Bibliographisches Kirchenlexikon*. Fortgeführt von Traugott Bautz. 32 Bde. Hamm, Westfalen: Bautz. (Also digital version.)

Beale, Joseph Henry (1926). *A Bibliography of Early English Law Books. The Ames Foundation*. Cambridge, MA: Harvard University Press. (Supplement (1943). Compiled by Robert Bowie Anderson); repr. Buffalo, N.Y.: Dennis 1966.

Berndt, Rolf (1965). 'The Linguistic Situation in England from the Norman Conquest to the Loss of Normandy (1066–1204)', in R. Lass (ed.) (1969), *Approaches to English Historical Linguistics. An Anthology*. New York: Holt, Rinehart and Winston, 369–91. (Orig. publ. in *Philologica Pragensia*. 8 (1965), 145–63.)

Bezner, Frank (2005). 'Lorenzo Valla (1407–1457)', in W. Ax (ed.), *Lateinische Lehrer Europas Fünfzehn Portraits von Varro bis Erasmus von Rotterdam*. Köln, Weimar, Wien: Böhlau, 353–89.

Bietenholz, Peter G., and Thomas B. Deutscher (eds.) (1985–1987). *Contemporaries of Erasmus. A Biographical Register of the Renaissance and Reformation*. 3 vols. Toronto: University of Toronto Press.

Birrell, T. A. (1987). *English Monarchs and Their Books: From Henry VII to Charles II*. Panizzi Lectures 1986. London: The British Library.

Blach, S. (ed.) (1908; 1909). 'Shakespeares Lateingrammatik', *Jahrbuch der Deutschen Shakespeare-Gesellschaft* 44: 65–117; 45: 51–100.

Blackwell, Constance (1982). 'Niccolò Perotti in England – Part I: John Anwykyll, Bernard André, John Colet and Luis Vives'. *Res Publica Litterarum* 1: 13–28.

Blagden, Cyprian (1960). *The Stationers' Company. A History, 1403–1959*. London: George Allen and Unwin.

Blake, Norman (1996). *A History of the English Language*. Basingstoke: Macmillan Press.

Bland, Cynthia Renée (1991). *The Teaching of Grammar in Late Medieval England. An Edition, with Commentary, of Oxford, Lincoln College, MS Lat. 130*. East Lansing: Colleagues Press.

Blatt, Franz (1928). 'Ministerium—Mysterium', *Archivum Latinitatis Medii Aevi* 4: 80–81.

Bloomfield, B. C., and Karen Potts (eds.) (1997). *A Directory of Rare Book and Special Collections in the United Kingdom and the Republic of Ireland*. 2nd edn. London: Library Association Publishing. (1st edn. 1985.)

Bodleian Library Exhibition Catalogue. Bodleian Library Records. Unpublished Papers for Erasmus and his Friends (1969).

Botfield, Beriah (1855–1856). *Bibliotheca Membranacea Britannica, or Notices of Early English Books Printed upon Vellum*. London: Philobiblon Society. Bibliographical and Historical Miscellanies. Vol. 2, no. 4: 1–28.

Bradshaw, Henry (1886). 'A Half-Century of Notes on the Day-Book of John Dorne, Bookseller in Oxford, A.D. 1520, as edited by F. Madan for the Oxford Historical Society'. Repr. (1889), in *Collected Papers of Henry Bradshaw*.

Cambridge: Cambridge University Press, 421–51. (See 'Day-Book of John Dorne; Supplementary Notes'. Ed. F. Madan (1890).)

The British Library General Catalogue of Printed Books to 1975 (1979–1988). 360 vols. and 6 Supplements. London: Bingley and Saur.

Brodie, Alexander H. (1974). 'Anwykyll's Vulgaria. A Pre-Erasmian Textbook', *Neuphilologische Mitteilungen* 75: 416–27.

Brousseau, Christine (2009). 'Evrard of Béthune', in *Lexicon Grammaticorum*, vol. 1: 443–44.

Bühler, Curt F. (1960). *The Fifteenth-Century Book: The Scribes, the Printers, the Decorators*. Philadelphia: University of Pennsylvania Press.

Bullen, George, and Gregory W. Eccles (1884). *Catalogue of Books in the Library of the British Museum Printed in England, Scotland, and Ireland, and of Books in English Printed Abroad, to the Year 1640*. 3 vols. London: The Trustees of the British Museum.

Bullough, Donald A. (1991). 'The Educational Tradition in England from Alfred to Ælfric: Teaching *utriusque linguae*', in D. A. Bullough. *Carolingian Renewal: Sources and Heritage*. Manchester: Manchester University Press, 297–334. (Orig. publ. in *XIXa Settimana di Studio del Centro italiano di studi sull 'alto medioevo: La Scuola nell 'Occidente Latino dell 'Alto Medioevo*. Spoleto, 1972, 453–94.)

Burrows, Montagu (1890). 'Linacre's Catalogue of Books Belonging to William Grocyn in 1520 Together with his Accounts as Executor Followed by a Memoir of William Grocyn', in M. Burrows (ed.), *Collectanea*. 2nd ser. Oxford: OHS. Part V, 317–80.

Bursill-Hall, G. L. (1976). 'Johannes de Garlandia – Forgotten Grammarian and the Manuscript Tradition', *Historiographia Linguistica* 3: 155–77.

Bursill-Hall, G. L. (1977). 'Teaching Grammars of the Middle Ages. Notes on the Manuscript Tradition', *Historiographia Linguistica* 4: 1–29.

Carlson, David R. (1992). 'The "Grammarians' War" 1519–1521, Humanist Careerism in Early Tudor England, and Printing', *Medievalia et Humanistica*, New Ser., 18: 157–81.

Carlson, David R. (1993). *English Humanist Books. Writers and Patrons, Manuscript and Print, 1475–1525*. Toronto: University of Toronto Press; repr. in paperback, 1995.

Catalogue of Books Printed in the XVth Century Now in the British Museum [British Library] (1908–2007). 13 vols. Vols. 1–10, 12. London: British Museum, 1908–1985; vols. 1–8 repr. 1963. *Catalogue of Books Printed in the XVth Century now in the British Library*. Vols. 11, 13. 't Goy-Houten: Hes & de Graaf, 2004, 2007.

Charlton, Kenneth (1965). *Education in Renaissance England*. London: Routledge.

Christie-Miller, Sydney Richardson (1933). *The Britwell Handlist, or Short-Title Catalogue of the Principal Volumes from the Time of Caxton to the Year 1800 Formerly in the Library of Britwell Court, Buckinghamshire*. 2 vols. London: Bernard Quaritch.

Clanchy, M. T. (1993). *From Memory to Written Record. England 1066–1307*. 2nd edn. Oxford: Blackwell Publishers. (1st edn. 1979.)

Clarke, M. L. (1978). 'The Education of a Prince in the Sixteenth Century: Edward VI and James VI and I', *History of Education* 7,1: 7–19.

Colombat, Bernard (1998a). 'Erasme, Didier, [and] Lily[e], William', in *HEL*, vol. 1, no. 1248: 86–88.

Colombat, Bernard (1998b). 'Perotti, Niccolò', in *HEL*, vol. 1, no. 1243: 78–80.

Colombat, Bernard (1998c). 'Sulpitius, Johannes Antonius—Verulanus', in *HEL*, vol. 1, no. 1244: 80–81.

Colombat, Bernard, and Carole Gascard (1998). 'Despautère, Jean', in *HEL*, vol. 1, no. 1247: 84–86.

Colombat, Bernard, and Elisabeth Lazcano (1998, 2000). *Corpus Représentatif des Grammaires et des Traditions Linguistiques*. 2 vols. (= Histoire Épistémologie Langage. Hors-sér. nos. 2–3.) Paris: SHESL. (Also digital version.)

Copinger, W. A. (1895-1902). *Supplement to Hain's Repertorium Bibliographicum*. 2 parts (part 2 in two vols.). London: Sotheran and Co.; repr. Milan: Görlich, 1950.

Daub, Susanne (2005). 'Johannes de Garlandia (*c*.1195 after 1258). Von der Wortkunde bis zur Poetik—Bücher für den Universitätsunterricht in Paris', in W. Ax (ed.), *Lateinische Lehrer Europas. Fünfzehn Portraits von Varro bis Erasmus von Rotterdam*. Köln, Weimar, Wien: Böhlau, 331–52.

Davies, Hugh W. (1962). *Catalogue of a Collection of Early German Books in the Library of C. Fairfax Murray*. 2 vols. London: The Holland Press.

Davies, Martin (gen. ed.) (1998). *The Illustrated Incunabula Short Title Catalogue on CD-ROM*. 2nd edn. Reading: Primary Source Media in Association with the British Library.

Davis, Adina (1974). 'Portrait of a Bibliophile XVIII: Clayton Mordaunt Cracherode I, II', *The Book Collector* 23: 339–54, 489–505.

Davis, Virginia (1993). *William Waynflete. Bishop and Educationalist*. Studies in the History of Medieval Religion, 6. Woodbridge, Suffolk: The Boydell Press.

De Clercq, Jan, Pierre Swiggers, and Toon Van Hal (2009). 'Despauterius, Joannes', in *Lexicon Grammaticorum*, vol. 1: 372–73.

Dibdin, Thomas Frognall (ed.) (1810–1819). *Typographical Antiquities or The History of Printing in England, Scotland, and Ireland.* [. . .]. *Begun by the Late Joseph Ames* [. . .] *Considerably Augmented by William Herbert* [. . .] *and Now Greatly Enlarged*. 4 vols. London: Miller; repr. Bristol: Thoemmes Press, 1996.

Dibdin, Thomas Frognall (1817). *The Bibliographical Decameron, or Ten Days Pleasant Discourse Upon Illuminated Manuscripts and Subjects Connected with Early Engraving, Typography, and Bibliography*. 3 vols. London: Bulmer.

Dibdin, Thomas Frognall (1825). *The Library Companion, or the Young Man's Guide and the Old Man's Comfort in the Choice of a Library*. 2nd edn. London: Harding.

Dobson, E. J. (1968). *English Pronunciation, 1500–1700*. 2 vols. 2nd edn. Oxford: Clarendon Press. (1st edn. 1957.)

Dons, Ute (2004). *Descriptive Adequacy of Early Modern English Grammars*. Topics in English Linguistics 47. Berlin and New York: Mouton de Gruyter.

Dowling, Maria (1986). *Humanism in the Age of Henry VIII*. London: Croom Helm.

Duff, E. Gordon (1902). 'English Printing on Vellum to the End of the Year 1600', *Publications of the Bibliographical Society of Lancashire* 1: 1–20.

Duff, E. Gordon (1905). *A Century of the English Book Trade. Short Notices of all Printers, Stationers, Book-Binders* [. . .] *from the Issue of the First Dated Book in 1457 to the Incorporation of the Company of Stationers in 1557*. London: The Bibliographical Society; repr. in paperback, Cambridge: Cambridge University Press, 2011.

Duff, E. Gordon et al. (1895–1913). *Handlists of Books Printed by London Printers, 1501–1556*. Parts 1–4. London: Bibliographical Society.

Dugdale, William (1818). *The History of Saint Paul's Cathedral in London*. 3rd edn. London: Lackington. (1st edn. 1658.)

Edmondston, Elizabeth (1965). 'Unfamiliar Libraries IX: Sion College', *The Book Collector* 14: 165–77. (Repr. Nendeln/Liechtenstein: Kraus Reprint, 1969.)

Eggs, Ekkehard (1996). 'Grammatik', in *HWRh*, vol. 3, cols. 1030–1112.

Elton, G. R. (1960). 'Henry VIII's Act of Proclamations', *The English Historical Review* 75, no. 294: 208–22.

Elton, G. R. (1965). Review Article of Tudor Proclamations. Vol. I: *The Early Tudors, 1485-1553*. Ed. Paul L. Hughes and James F. Larkin (1964). New Haven and London: Yale University Press, in *The Historical Journal* vol. 8, no. 2: 266–71.

Emden, A. B. (1957-1959). *A Biographical Register of the University of Oxford to A.D. 1500*. 3 vols. Oxford: Clarendon Press; repr. 1989.

Emden, A. B. (1961). 'Additions and Corrections. Supplemental Lists Nos. 1 and 2', *Bodleian Library Record* 6, no. 6: 668–88; (1964), 7, no. 3: 149–64.

Emden, A. B. (1963). *A Biographical Register of the University of Cambridge to 1500*. Cambridge: Cambridge University Press.

Emden, A. B. (1974). *A Biographical Register of the University of Oxford, A.D. 1501 to 1540*. Oxford: Clarendon Press.

Enkvist, Nils Erik (1975). 'English in Latin Guise. A Note on Some Renaissance Textbooks', *Historiographia Linguistica* 2: 283–98.

Ferguson, Mungo (1930). *The Printed Books in the Library of the Hunterian Museum of the University of Glasgow. A Catalogue*. Glasgow: Jackson.

Feuillerat, Albert (1910). *John Lyly. Contribution à l'Histoire de la Renaissance en Angleterre*. Cambridge: Cambridge University Press.

Fisher, Payne (1684). *The Tombs, Monuments, etc., Visible in S. Paul's Cathedral (and S. Faith's beneath it) Previous to its Destruction by Fire A.D. 1666*. Ed. G. Blacker Morgan. London; repr. privately, 1885.

Flynn, Vincent Joseph (1938). 'William Lily and the English Hospice'. Repr. from: *The Venerabile. Conducted by the Past and Present Students of the Venerabile English College, Rome*, vol. 9, no. 1. Exeter: Catholic Records Press, 1–8.

Flynn, Vincent Joseph (1938-1939). 'Englishmen in Rome during the Renaissance', *Modern Philology* 36: 121–38.

Flynn, Vincent Joseph (1943). 'The Grammatical Writings of William Lily, ?1468-?1523', *The Papers of the Bibliographical Society of America* 37: 85–113.

Foot, Mirjam M. (1978-1983). *A Collection of Bookbindings. The Henry Davis Gift*. 2 vols. London: The British Library.

Foster, Joseph (1891-1892). *Alumni Oxonienses: The Members of the University of Oxford, 1500-1714*. 4 vols. Early Series. London: Parker; repr. Nendeln/Liechtenstein: Kraus Reprint, 1968.

Fox-Davies, A. C. (1909). *A Complete Guide to Heraldry*. Rev. and annotated by J. P. Brooke-Little. London, 1909; repr. with revisions, London: Nelson and Sons, 1969.

Franzen, Christine (1991). *The Tremulous Hand of Worcester. A Study of Old English in the Thirteenth Century*. Oxford: Clarendon Press.

Fridén, Georg (1948). *Studies on the Tenses of the English Verb from Chaucer to Shakespeare with Special Reference to the Late Sixteenth Century*. Inaugural Dissertation. Uppsala: Almqvist.

Funke, Otto (1938). 'William Bullokars Bref Grammar For English (1586)', *Anglia* 62, N. F. 50: 116–37.

Funke, Otto (1941). *Die Frühzeit der Englischen Grammatik*. Schriften der Literarischen Gesellschaft Bern, IV. Bern: Lang.

Gardiner, Robert Barlow (ed.) (1884–1906). *The Admission Registers of St Paul's School, from 1748 to 1876; from 1876 to 1905*. 2 vols. London: Bell.

Gensini, Stefano (2009). 'Valla, Lorenzo', in *Lexicon Grammaticorum*, vol. 2: 1552–53.

Gibson, Margaret, rev. Corneille Henri Kneepkens (2009). 'Petrus Helias', in *Lexicon Grammaticorum*, vol. 2: 1158.

Gibson, M. T., and S. P. Hall (eds.). (1982–1985). 'R. W. Hunt, The History of Grammar in the Middle Ages. Additions and Corrections', *Bodleian Library Record* 11: 9–19.

Gibson, R. W. (1961). *St. Thomas More: A Preliminary Bibliography of His Works and of Moreana to the Year 1750*. New Haven and London: Yale University Press.

Gildersleeve, B. L., and Gonzalez Lodge (1894). *Gildersleeve's Latin Grammar*. 3rd edn., rev. and enl. Boston: Heath.

Gleason, John B. (1989). *John Colet*. Berkeley, Los Angeles: University of California Press.

Glei, Reinhold F. (2005). 'Alexander de Villa Dei (*c*.1170–1250), *Doctrinale*', in W. Ax (ed.), *Lateinische Lehrer Europas. Fünfzehn Portraits von Varro bis Erasmus von Rotterdam*. Köln, Weimar, Wien: Böhlau, 291–312.

Görlach, Manfred (1991). *Introduction to Early Modern English*. Cambridge: Cambridge University Press; repr. 1993. (Orig. publ. in German as *Einführung ins Frühneuenglische*. Heidelberg: Quelle and Meyer, 1978.)

Gneuss, Helmut (1996). *English Language Scholarship. A Survey and Bibliography from the Beginnings to the End of the Nineteenth Century*. Medieval and Renaissance Texts and Studies, 125. Binghamton, New York: Center for Medieval and Early Renaissance Studies.

Gneuss, Helmut (2001). *Handlist of Anglo-Saxon Manuscripts. A List of Manuscripts and Manuscript Fragments Written or Owned in England up to 1100*. Medieval and Renaissance Texts and Studies, 241. Tempe, Arizona: Arizona Center for Medieval and Renaissance Studies. (Addenda and Corrigenda (2003), in *Anglo-Saxon England*, 32: 293–305.)

Gneuss, Helmut (2002). 'Ælfrics Grammatik und Glossar: Sprachwissenschaft um die Jahrtausendwende in England', in W. Hüllen and Friederike Klippel (eds.), *Heilige und Profane Sprachen. Die Anfänge des Fremdsprachenunterrichts im Westlichen Europa*. Wolfenbütteler Forschungen, 98. Wiesbaden: Harrassowitz, 77–92.

Gneuss, Helmut (2003). 'The Study of Language in Anglo-Saxon England', in D. Scragg (ed.), *Textual and Material Culture in Anglo-Saxon England*. Thomas Northcote Toller and the Toller Memorial Lectures. Cambridge: Brewer, 75–105. (Publications of the Manchester Centre for Anglo-Saxon Studies, vol. 1.) (Orig. publ. in Gneuss (1996). *Language and History in Early England*. Aldershot, Hants.: Variorum, 3–32.)

Gneuss, Helmut (2005). 'The First Edition of the Source of Ælfric's Grammar', *Anglia* 223 (2005), 246–59. (Review article on *Exerptiones de Prisciano: The Source for Ælfric's Latin–Old English Grammar*. Ed. David W. Porter (2002). Anglo-Saxon Texts 4. Woodbridge: Brewer.)

Gneuss, Helmut (2009). *Ælfric of Eynsham. His Life, Times, and Writings*. Old English Newsletter Subsidia, 34. Kalamazoo: Medieval Institute Publications, Western Michigan University.

Godden, Malcolm R. (1999). 'Ælfric of Eynsham', in M. Lapidge *et al.* (eds.), *The Blackwell Encyclopaedia of Anglo-Saxon England*. Oxford: Blackwell Publishers; repr. in paperback, 2001.

Goff, Frederick R. (ed.) (1964). *Incunabula in American Libraries. A Third Census of Fifteenth-Century Books Recorded in North American Collections*. New York. (Supplement. New York, 1972. Additional Material and Corrections. 1973. Repr. from the Annotated Copy of the Original Edition. Millwood, New York: Kraus Reprint 1989.)

Gray, G. J. (1893). *A General Index to Hazlitt's Handbook and his Bibliographical Collections (1867–1889)*. Ed. W. Carew Hazlitt. London: Quaritch.

Greg, W. W. (1904–1906). 'Notes on the Types, Borders, etc., Used by Thomas Berthelet', *Transactions of the Bibliographical Society* 8: 187–220.

Greg, W. W. (1966). 'Ad Imprimendum Solum', in W. W. Greg (1966), *Collected Papers*. Ed. J. C. Maxwell. Oxford: Clarendon Press, 406–12.

Griffiths, Antony (1996). 'The Reverend Clayton Mordaunt Cracherode (1730–99)', in A. Griffiths (ed.), *Landmarks in Print Collecting. Connoisseurs and Donors at the British Museum since 1753*. London: British Museum Press for the Trustees of the British Museum.

Griffiths, Jane (2002). 'The Grammarian as "Poeta" and "Vates": Self-Presentation in the *Antibossicon*', in Toon van Houdt *et al.* (eds.), *Self-Presentation and Social Identification: The Rhetoric and Pragmatics of Letter Writing in Early Modern Times*. Supplementa Humanistica Lovaniensia XVIII. Leuven: Leuven University Press, 317–35.

Grondeux, Anne (1998). 'Évrard de Béthune', in HEL, vol. 1, no. 1230: 64–66.

Gruber, J. *et al.* (1989). 'Grammatik, grammatische Literatur', in *Lexikon des Mittelalters* (1980–1999). Eds. Liselotte Lutz *et al.* 10 vols. Munich and Zurich: Artemis, vol. IV, cols. 1637–43.

Gwosdek, Hedwig (1994). 'Elementarunterricht', in HWRh, vol. 2 (Bie-Eul), cols. 1004–13.

Gwosdek, Hedwig (1999). 'The First English Grammars of St Paul's School, London, in Their Grammatical Tradition', *The Henry Sweet Society Bulletin* 33: 5–22.

Gwosdek, Hedwig (2000). *A Checklist of Middle English Grammatical Manuscripts and Early Printed Grammars, c. 1400–1540*. The Henry Sweet Society Studies in the History of Linguistics 6. Münster: Nodus Publikationen.

Gwosdek, Hedwig (2004). 'Whittington, Robert (or Whittinton: *c*.1480-*c*.1553)', in R. B. Todd (ed.), *The Dictionary of British Classicists, 1500–1960*. 3 vols. Bristol: Thoemmes Press, vol. 3: 1058–59.

Gwosdek, Hedwig (2009). 'Lily, William', in *Lexicon Grammaticorum*, vol. 2: 912–14.

Hain, Ludwig (1826–1838). *Repertorium Bibliographicum, in quo Libri Omnes ab Arte Typographica Inventa Usque ad Annum MD. Typis Expressi Ordine Alphabetico* [. . .], *Recensentur*. 2 vols. (in 2 parts each). Stuttgart: Cotta; repr. with additional vols. Milan: Görlich, 1966.

Halliwell, J. O. (1860). *A Hand-List of the Early English Literature Preserved in the Douce Collection in the Bodleian Library*. London.

Halliwell-Phillipps, J. O. (1880). 'Lily's Grammar'. Note to J. H. Lupton's article, in *Notes and Queries* 6th ser., 2: 441–42, 461–62.

Harris, P. R. (1998). *A History of the British Museum Library, 1753–1973*. London: The British Library.

Hay, Denys (1975). 'England and the Humanities in the Fifteenth Century', in H. A. Oberman and Thomas A. Brady, Jr. (eds.), *Itinerarium Italicum. The Profile of the Italian Renaissance in the Mirror of its European Transformations. Dedicated to Paul Oskar Kristeller on the Occasion of his 70th Birthday*. Studies in Medieval and Reformation Thought. Vol. XIV. Leiden: Brill, 305–67.

Hazlitt, W. Carew (1867). *Handbook to the Popular, Poetical, and Dramatic Literature of Great Britain, from the Invention of Printing to the Restoration*. London: Russell Smith.

Hazlitt, W. Carew (1903). *Bibliographical Collections and Notes on Early English Literature Made During the Years 1893–1903*. London; repr. New York: Franklin, 1961. (Burt Franklin: Bibliography and Reference series # 26.)

Heckethorn, Charles William (1897). *The Printers of Basle in the XV and XVI Centuries. Their Biographies, Printed Books and Devices*. London: Unwin Brothers.

Heinze, R. W. (1976). *The Proclamations of the Tudor Kings*. Cambridge: Cambridge University Press.

Herbert, William (ed.) (1785–1790). *Typographical Antiquities or an Historical Account of the Origin and Progress of Printing in Great Britain and Ireland. Begun by the Late Joseph Ames*. 3 vols. London: Payne and Son.

Herendeen, W. H. (1988). 'Coletus Redivivus: John Colet—Patron or Reformer?', *Renaissance and Reformation*, New Series 12: 163–88.

Hind, Arthur M. (1952–1964). *Engraving in England in the Sixteenth and Seventeenth Centuries. A Descriptive Catalogue with Introductions*. 3 vols. Vol. 3 by Arthur M. Hind *et al.* Cambridge: Cambridge University Press.

Hoffmann, Ann (1977). *Lives of the Tudor Age, 1485–1603*. London: Osprey Publishing.

Holtz, Louis (2005). 'Aelius Donatus (um die Mitte des 4. Jahrhunderts n. Chr.)', in W. Ax (ed.), *Lateinische Lehrer Europas. Fünfzehn Portraits von Varro bis Erasmus von Rotterdam*. Köln, Weimar, Wien: Böhlau, 109–31.

Honan, Park (1998). *Shakespeare. A Life*. Oxford: Oxford University Press.

Hooper, Katy (1994). 'David Tolley. Physician (M.A., B.M.): Probate Inventory. 1558', in R. J. Fehrenbach and E. S. Leedham-Green (eds.), *Private Libraries in Renaissance England. A Collection and Catalogue of Tudor and Early Stuart Book-Lists*. Vol. 3, PLRE 67–86. Medieval and Renaissance Texts and Studies, vol. 117. Marlborough: Matthew Publications, 36–44.

Horden, John (ed.) (1980). *Halkett and Laing: A Dictionary of Anonymous and Pseudonymous Publications in the English Language, 1475–1640*. 3rd rev. and enl. edn. Vol. 1. Harlow and London: Longman.

Hughes, Paul L., and James F. Larkin (eds.) (1964–1969). *Tudor Royal Proclamations*. 3 vols. Vol. I (1964): *The Early Tudors, 1485–1553*. New Haven and London: Yale University Press.

Hüllen, Werner (1999). *English Dictionaries 800–1700. The Topical Tradition*. Oxford: Clarendon Press.

Hüllen, Werner (2002). 'Three Properties of Early European Language Teaching and Learning', in W. Hüllen und F. Klippel (eds.), *Heilige und Profane Sprachen*.

Die Anfänge des Fremdsprachenunterrichts im Westlichen Europa. Wolfenbütteler Forschungen, 98. Wiesbaden: Harrassowitz, 211–20.

Hunt, Arnold (1997). 'Book Trade Patents, 1603–1640', in Arnold Hunt *et al.* (eds.), *The Book Trade and its Customers, 1450–1900*. Historical Essays for Robin Myers. New Castle, Delaware: Oak Knoll Press, 27–54.

Hunt, R. W. (1980*a*). 'Studies on Priscian in the Eleventh and Twelfth Centuries I. Petrus Helias and his Predecessors', in G. L. Bursill-Hall (ed.), *The History of Grammar in the Middle Ages: Collected Papers*. Amsterdam Studies in the Theory and History of Linguistic Science III. Studies in the History of Linguistics. 5. Amsterdam: Benjamins, 1–38. (Orig. publ. in *Mediaeval and Renaissance Studies*. The Warburg Institute, London. 1 (1941–1943), 194–231.)

Hunt, R. W. (1980*b*). 'Hugutio and Petrus Helias', in G. L. Bursill-Hall (ed.), *The History of Grammar in the Middle Ages: Collected Papers*. Amsterdam Studies in the Theory and History of Linguistic Science III. Studies in the History of Linguistics. 5. Amsterdam: Benjamins, 145–49. (Orig. publ. in *Mediaeval and Renaissance Studies*. The Warburg Institute, London. 2 (1950), 174–78.)

Hunt, R. W. (1980*c*). 'Oxford Grammar Masters in the Middle Ages', in G. L. Bursill-Hall (ed.), *The History of Grammar in the Middle Ages: Collected Papers*. Amsterdam Studies in the Theory and History of Linguistic Science III. Studies in the History of Linguistics. 5. Amsterdam: Benjamins, 167–97. (Orig. publ. in *Oxford Studies Presented to Daniel Callus*. OHS, new ser., 16 (1964), 163–93.)

Hunt, R. W. (1980*d*). '*Absoluta*. The *Summa* of Petrus Hispanus on Priscianus Minor', in G. L. Bursill-Hall (ed.), *The History of Grammar in the Middle Ages: Collected Papers*. Amsterdam Studies in the Theory and History of Linguistic Science III. Studies in the History of Linguistics. 5. Amsterdam: Benjamins, 95–116. (Orig. publ. in *Historiographia Linguistica*. 2 (1975), 1–23.)

Hunt, Tony (1991). *Teaching and Learning Latin in Thirteenth-Century England*. 3 vols. Cambridge: Brewer.

Huntsman, Jeffrey F. (1983). 'Grammar', in D. L. Wagner (ed.), *The Seven Liberal Arts in the Middle Ages*. Bloomington: Indiana University Press, 58–95.

Hurt, James (1972). *Ælfric*. Twayne's English Authors Series, 131. New York: Twayne Publishers.

Isaac, Frank (1930, 1932). *English and Scottish Printing Types, 1501–1535, 1508–1541. 1535–1558, 1552–1558*. Facsimiles and Illustrations, No. II and III. Printed for the Bibliographical Society. Oxford: Oxford University Press.

Isaac, Frank (1936). *English Printers' Types of the Sixteenth Century*. London: Oxford University Press.

Isaac, Frank (1938). *An Index to the Early Printed Books in the British Museum*. Part II. *1501-1520*. Section II: *Italy*. Section III: *Switzerland and Eastern Europe*. London: Bernard Quaritch.

Jayne, Sears (1995). *Plato in Renaissance England*. Archives Internationales d'Histoire des Idées, 141. Dordrecht: Kluwer Academic Publishers.

Jensen, Kristian, rev. Hedwig Gwosdek (2009). 'Linacre, Thomas', in *Lexicon Grammaticorum*, vol. 2: 914–15.

Jones, Richard Foster (1953). *The Triumph of the English Language: A Survey of Opinions Concerning the Vernacular from the Introduction of Printing to the Restauration* London: Oxford University Press; repr. Stanford: Stanford University Press, 1974.

Kalivoda, Gregor (1996). 'Grammatikunterricht', in *HWRh*, vol. 3, cols. 1112–74.

Kastovsky, Dieter (2010). 'Translation Techniques in the Terminology of Ælfric's *Grammar*: Semantic Loans, Loan Translations and Word-Formation', in Merja Kytö, John Scahill, and Harumi Tanabe (eds.), *Language Change and Variation from Old English to Late Modern English. A Festschrift for Minoji Akimoto*. Bern, Berlin: Lang, 163–74.

Keiser, George R. (1998). *Works of Science and Information. A Manual of the Writings in Middle English, 1050–1500*. (1967–2005). 11 vols. Ed. J. Burke Severs (vols. 1–2); Albert E. Hartung (vols. 3–10); Peter G. Beidler (vol. 11). New Haven, Conn.: The Connecticut Academy of Arts and Sciences, vol. 10, chapter 10, II: 3714–26, 3936–52.

Kennedy, Arthur G. (1927). *A Bibliography of Writings on the English Language from the Beginning of Printing to the End of 1922*. Cambridge, MA; repr. Freeport, New York: Books for Libraries Press, 1973.

Ker, N. R. (1957). *Catalogue of Manuscripts Containing Anglo-Saxon*. Oxford: Clarendon Press; repr. 1990.

Kneepkens, Corneille Henri (2009). 'Petrus Hispanus (non papa)', in *Lexicon Grammaticorum*, vol. 2: 1158.

Knight, Samuel (1724). *The Life of Dr. John Colet, Dean of S. Paul's in the Reigns of K. Henry VII. and Henry VIII. and Founder of S. Paul's School*. London: Downing.

Kohnen, Thomas (2001). 'Creating Counterparts of Latin: The Implicit Vernacular Tradition in Late Middle English and Early Modern English Grammars and Textbooks', in Hannes Kniffka (ed.), *Indigenous Grammar Across Cultures*. Frankfurt am Main: Lang, 507–42.

Kornexl, Lucia (2003). 'From Ælfric to John of Cornwall: Evidence for Vernacular Grammar Teaching in Pre- and Post-Conquest England', in L. Kornexl and U. Lenker (eds.), *Bookmarks from the Past. Studies in Early English Language and Literature in Honour of Helmut Gneuss*. Frankfurt am Main: Lang, 229–59.

Kornexl, Lucia (2004). '"For Englisch was it neuere": Grammatical Metalanguage in Medieval England', in L. Moessner and C. M. Schmidt (eds.), *Anglistentag 2004. Aachen. Proceedings*. Trier: Wissenschaftlicher Verlag, 77–87.

Kurath, Hans, Robert E. Lewis, and Sherman M. Kuhn (eds.) (1952–2001). *Middle English Dictionary*. 12 vols. plus print plan and bibliography (2 vols.). 1st edn. Ann Arbor: University of Michigan Press. (2nd edn. digital version.)

Latham, Robert (1978). *Catalogue of the Pepys Library at Magdalene College, Cambridge*. Vol. I: Printed Books. Compiled by N. A. Smith. Cambridge: Brewer.

Latham, R. E. (1965). *Revised Medieval Latin Word-List from British and Irish Sources*. London: Oxford University Press; repr. 1999.

Law, Vivien (1990). 'The History of Morphology: Expression of a Change in Consciousness', in W. Hüllen (ed.), *Understanding the Historiography of Linguistics. Problems and Projects. Symposium at Essen, 23–25 November 1989*. Münster: Nodus Publikationen, 61–74.

Law, Vivien (1997). 'Ælfric's *Excerptiones de Arte Grammatica Anglice*', in V. Law. *Grammar and Grammarians in the Early Middle Ages*. Longman Linguistics Library. London: Longman, 200–223. (Orig. publ. in *Histoire Épistémologie Langage* 9 (1987), 47–71.)

Law, Vivien (2003). *The History of Linguistics in Europe. From Plato to 1600*. Cambridge: Cambridge University Press.

Law, Vivien, rev. Louis Holtz (2009). 'Ælfric', in *Lexicon Grammaticorum*, vol. 1: 14–15.

Leedham-Green, E. S. (1992). 'Bishop Richard Cox', in R. J. Fehrenbach and E. S. Leedham-Green (eds.), *Private Libraries in Renaissance England. A Collection and Catalogue of Tudor and Early Stuart Book-Lists*. Vol. 1, *PLRE* 1–4. Medieval and Renaissance Texts and Studies, vol. 87. Marlborough: Matthew Publications, 3–39.

Legge, M. Dominica (1939). 'William of Kingsmill – a Fifteenth-Century Teacher of French in Oxford', in *Studies in French Language and Mediaeval Literature Presented to Professor Mildred K. Pope*. Publications of the University of Manchester. 268. Manchester: Manchester University Press, 241–46.

Lendinara, Patrizia (1999). 'The *Colloquy* of Ælfric and the *Colloquy* of Ælfric Bata', in P. Lendinara. *Anglo-Saxon Glosses and Glossaries*. Aldershot, Hampshire: Ashgate Publishing, 207–87. (Variorum Collected Studies Series, CS622.)

Lepschy, Giulio (ed.) (1994). *History of Linguistics*. Vol. 2: *Classical and Medieval Linguistics*. London and New York: Longman. (English Translation of *Storia della Linguistica*. Bologna: il Mulino, 1990.) (Longman Linguistics Library.)

Leroux C., and G. Scheurweghs (1962). 'The Influence of the Latin Grammar of William Lily on the Early English Grammarians in the Netherlands (II)'. *Leuvense Bijdragen* 51: 124–28.

Lewis, Charlton T., and Charles Short (1969). *A Latin Dictionary*. Rev., enl., and in great part rewritten. Oxford: Clarendon Press. (1st edn. 1879.)

Lowndes, William Thomas (1834). *The Bibliographer's Manual of English Literature, Containing an Account of Rare, Curious, and Useful Books*. 4 vols. London: Pickering. New Edition, revised, corrected and enlarged by Henry G. Bohn. 6 vols. London: Bohn, 1864.

Luborsky, Ruth Samson, and Elizabeth Morley Ingram (1998). *A Guide to English Illustrated Books, 1536–1603*. 2 vols. Tempe, Ariz.: Arizona Center for Medieval and Renaissance Studies. (Medieval and Renaissance Texts and Studies, vol. 166.)

Lupton, J. H. (1880). 'Lily's Grammar', *Notes and Queries*, 6th ser., 2: 441–42, 461–62.

Lupton, J. H. (1890). 'The Tudor Exhibition', *The Pauline* 8, no. 40: 69–72.

Lupton, J. H. (1909). *A Life of John Colet, D.D.* 2nd edn. London: Bell; repr. Hamden, Conn.: The Shoe String Press, 1961. (1st edn. 1887.)

Mace, Nancy A. (1993). 'The History of the Grammar Patent, 1547–1620', *The Papers of the Bibliographical Society of America* 87: 419–36.

Mackenzie, David (2005). 'A Ghostly Lily?', *The Library*, 7th ser., vol. 6: 423–24.

Macray, W. D. (1894–1915). *A Register of the Members of St Mary Magdalen College, Oxford. From the Foundation of the College*. New ser. 8 vols. London: Frowde et al.

Maitland, S. R. (1843). *A List of Some of the Early Printed Books in the Archiepiscopal Library at Lambeth*. London.

Maitland, S. R. (1845). *An Index of Such English Books, Printed Before the Year MDC as are Now in the Archiepiscopal Library at Lambeth*. London: Rivington.

Malone, Edward A., and Michele Valery Ronnick (2004). 'Lily, William (*c*.1468–1522)', in R. B. Todd (ed.), *The Dictionary of British Classicists, 1500–1960*. 3 vols. Bristol: Thoemmes Press, vol. 2: 579–81.

Matthew, H. C. G., and Brian Harrison (eds.) (2004). *Oxford Dictionary of National Biography. From the Earliest Times to the Year 2000*. 61 vols., plus 1st supplement 2009. Oxford: Oxford University Press. (Also digital version.)

Maxwell-Lyte, H. C. (1899). *A History of Eton College (1440–1898)*. 3rd. edn., rev. throughout and greatly enl. London: Macmillan. (1st edn. London, 1875.)

McConica, James Kelsey (1965). *English Humanists and Reformation Politics under Henry VIII and Edward VI*. Oxford: Clarendon Press.

McDonnell, Michael F. J. (1909). *A History of St Paul's School*. London: Chapman and Hall.

McDonnell, Michael F. J. (1959). *The Annals of St Paul's School*. London: Privately Printed for the Governors.

McDonnell, Michael F. J. (1977). *The Registers of St Paul's School, 1509–1748*. London: Privately Printed for the Governors.

McKerrow, Ronald B. (ed.). (1910). *A Dictionary of Printers and Booksellers in England, Scotland and Ireland, and of Foreign Printers of English Books, 1557–1640*. London; repr. London: Bibliographical Society, 1968.

McKerrow, Ronald B. (1913). *Printers' and Publishers' Devices in England and Scotland, 1485–1640*. Bibliographical Society, Illustrated Monographs, no. 16. London; repr. London: Bibliographical Society, 1949.

McKerrow, R. B., and F. S. Ferguson (1932 (for 1931)). *Title-Page Borders Used in England and Scotland, 1485–1640*. Bibliographical Society, Illustrated Monographs, no. 21. London: Bibliographical Society.

McKitterick, David (2005). '"Not in STC": Opportunities and Challenges in the ESTC', *The Library*, 7th ser., vol. 6: 178–94.

Mead, A. H. (1990). *A Miraculous Draught of Fishes: A History of St Paul's School*. London: James and James.

Michael, Ian (1970). *English Grammatical Categories and the Tradition to 1800*. Cambridge: Cambridge University Press; repr. in paperback 2010.

Michael, Ian (1993). *Early Textbooks of English. A Guide*. Reading: Colloquium on Textbooks, Schools and Society.

Miller, William E. (1963). 'Double Translation in English Humanistic Education', *Studies in the Renaissance* 10: 163–74.

Miner, John N. (1990). *The Grammar Schools of Medieval England. A. F. Leach in Historiographical Perspective*. Montreal and Kingston: McGill-Queen's University Press.

Moessner, Lilo (2000). 'Word-Formation in Early Modern English Grammars', in B. Reitz and Sigrid Rieuwerts (eds.), *Anglistentag 1999. Mainz. Proceedings*. Trier: Wissenschaftlicher Verlag, 21–34.

Moore, J. K. (1992). *Primary Materials Relating to Copy and Print in English Books of the Sixteenth and Seventeenth Centuries*. Occasional Publication, no. 24. Oxford Bibliographical Society. Oxford: Bodleian Library.

Munby, A. N. L., and Lenore Coral (eds.) (1977). *British Book Sale Catalogues, 1676–1800*. A Union List. London: Mansell.

Murphy, James J. (1980). 'The Teaching of Latin as a Second Language in the 12th Century', *Historiographia Linguistica* 7: 159–75.

Murray, James A. H., H. Bradley, W. A. Craigie, and C. T. Onions (eds.) (1933). *The Oxford English Dictionary*. Oxford. 2nd edn., 22 vols., prepared by J. A. Simpson and E. S. C. Weiner. Oxford: Clarendon Press, 1989. (3rd edn. in preparation, digital version.)

The National Union Catalog. Pre-1956 Imprints (1968–1981). 754 vols. London and Chicago: Mansell.

Nelson, William (1952). 'The Teaching of English in Tudor Grammar Schools', *Studies in Philology* 49: 119–43.

Nichols, John (1812–1815). *Literary Anecdotes of the Eighteenth Century; Comprizing Biographical Memoirs of W. Bowyer, and Many of His Learned Friends.* 9 vols. London: Nichols, Son, and Bentley. (1ˢᵗ edn. 1782.)

Nichols, John Gough (ed.) (1857). *Literary Remains of King Edward the Sixth. Edited from his Autograph Manuscripts with Historical Notes, and a Biographical Memoir.* 2 vols. London: Roxburghe Library; repr. New York: Burt Franklin, 1957. (Burt Franklin Research and Source Works, 51.)

Nichols, John Gough (1858). 'The Latin Grammar Issued by Royal Authority in 1540', *Notes and Queries*, 2ⁿᵈ ser., 6, no. 149: 368.

Nijhoff, W., and Kronenberg, M. E. (1923–1971). *Nederlandsche Bibliographie van 1500 tot 1540.* 3 vols. The Hague: Martinus Nijhoff.

Nugent, Elizabeth M. (ed.) (1956). *The Thought and Culture of the English Renaissance. An Anthology of Tudor Prose, 1481–1555.* Cambridge: Cambridge University Press.

Orme, Nicholas (1973). *English Schools in the Middle Ages.* London and New York: Methuen.

Orme, Nicholas (1989*a*). 'Early School Note-Books', in N. Orme. *Education and Society in Medieval and Renaissance England.* London: Hambledon Press, 73–86. (Orig. publ. in *The Yale University Library Gazette* 40 (1985), 47–57.)

Orme, Nicholas (1989*b*). 'An Early-Tudor Oxford Schoolbook', in N. Orme. *Education and Society in Medieval and Renaissance England.* London: Hambledon Press, 123–52. (Orig. publ. in *Renaissance Quarterly* 34 (1981), 11–39.)

Orme, Nicholas (1989*c*). 'A Grammatical Miscellany from Bristol and Wiltshire', in N. Orme. *Education and Society in Medieval and Renaissance England.* London: Hambledon Press, 87–112. (Orig. publ. in *Traditio* 38 (1982), 301–26.)

Orme, Nicholas (1989*d*). 'A School Note-Book from Barlinch Priory', in N. Orme. *Education and Society in Medieval and Renaissance England.* London: Hambledon Press, 113–21. (Orig. publ. in *Somerset Archaeology and Natural History* 128 (1984), 55–63.)

Orme, Nicholas (1989*e*). 'Schools and Society from the Twelfth Century to the Reformation', in Orme. *Education and Society in Medieval and Renaissance England.* London: Hambledon Press, 1–22.

Orme, Nicholas (1998). *Education in Early Tudor England. Magdalen College Oxford and Its School, 1480–1540.* Magdalen College Occasional Paper 4. Oxford: Magdalen College.

Orme, Nicholas (1999). 'Schools and School-books', in Lotte Hellinga and J. B. Trapp (eds.), *The Cambridge History of the Book in Britain.* Vol. III: 1400–1557. Cambridge: Cambridge University Press, 449–69.

Orme, Nicholas (2006). *Medieval Schools. From Roman Britain to Renaissance England.* New Haven and London: Yale University Press.

Padley, George Arthur (1976). *Grammatical Theory in Western Europe, 1500–1700.* Vol. 1: *The Latin Tradition.* Cambridge: Cambridge University Press.

Padley, George Arthur (1985, 1988). *Grammatical Theory in Western Europe, 1500–1700. Trends in Vernacular Grammar I, II.* Cambridge: Cambridge University Press.

Paetow, Louis John (1910). *The Arts Course at Medieval Universities with Special Reference to Grammar and Rhetoric.* University of Illinois Studies, vol. 3, no. 7. Urbana-Champaign: University Press.

Pafort, Eloise (1946). 'A Group of Early Tudor School-Books', *The Library*, 4th ser., 26, no. 4: 227–61.

Parks, George B. (1954). *The English Traveler to Italy.* Vol. I: *The Middle Ages (to 1525).* *Storia e Letteratura. Raccolta di Studi e Testi*, 46. Roma: Edizioni di Storia e Letteratura.

Pàroli, Teresa (1968). 'Indice della Terminologia Grammaticale di Aelfric', *Annali dell'Istituto Orientale di Napoli, Sezione Linguistica* 8: 113–38.

Percival, W. Keith (1986). 'Renaissance Linguistics: The Old and the New', in T. Bynon and F. R. Palmer (eds.), *Studies in the History of Western Linguistics in Honour of R. H. Robins*. Cambridge: Cambridge University Press, 56–68.

Petrilli, Raffaella (2009). 'Donatus, Aelius', in *Lexicon Grammaticorum*, vol. 1: 396–97.

Picciotto, Cyril M. (1939). *St. Paul's School.* London and Glasgow: Blackie and Son.

Poldauf, Ivan (1948). *On the History of Some Problems of English Grammar Before 1800.* Prague Studies in English. Prague: Faculty of Philosophy of Charles University.

Pollard, A. W., and G. R. Redgrave (1926). *A Short-Title Catalogue of Books Printed in England, Scotland, and Ireland and of English Books Printed Abroad, 1475–1640*, 1st edn. London: Bibliographical Society.

Pollard, A. W., and G. R. Redgrave (1976–1991). *A Short-Title Catalogue of Books Printed in England, Scotland, and Ireland and of English Books Printed Abroad, 1475–1640.* 2nd edn., rev. and enl. Begun by W. A. Jackson and F. S. Ferguson. Completed by Katharine F. Pantzer. 3 vols. London: Bibliographical Society.

Quaritch, Bernard, Ltd. (1930). *A Catalogue of Books in English History and Literature from the Earliest Times to the End of the Seventeenth Century (No. 436).* London: Quaritch.

Quaritch, Bernard, Ltd. (1932). *A Catalogue of Rare and Valuable Early Schoolbooks (No. 464).* London: Quaritch.

Quarrie, Paul (1990). *Treasures of Eton College Library. 550 Years of Collecting.* Ed. Michael F. Robinson. New York: The Pierpont Morgan Library.

Renouard, Philippe (1964–1995). *Imprimeurs et Libraires Parisiens du XVIe Siècle.* *Ouvrage Publié d'après les Manuscrits de Philippe Renouard.* 5 vols., 4 supplements. Paris: Bibliothèque Nationale. (Histoire générale de Paris: Collection de documents.)

Reynolds, Suzanne, rev. Anne Grondeux (2009). 'Giovanni Balbi', in *Lexicon Grammaticorum*, vol. 1: 540–41.

Richardson, H. G. (1939). 'An Oxford Teacher of the Fifteenth Century', *Bulletin of the John Rylands University Library of Manchester* 23: 436–57.

Richardson, H. G. (1941). 'Business Training in Medieval Oxford', *American Historical Review* 46: 259–80.

Richter, Michael (1979). *Sprache und Gesellschaft im Mittelalter. Untersuchungen zur Mündlichen Kommunikation in England von der Mitte des Elften bis zum Beginn des Vierzehnten Jahrhunderts.* Monographien zur Geschichte des Mittelalters, Bd. 18. Stuttgart: Hiersemann.

Rissanen, Matti (1999). 'Syntax', in R. Lass (ed.), *The Cambridge History of the English Language.* Vol. III, 1476–1776. Cambridge: Cambridge University Press, 187–331, 684–701.

Robins, Robert Henry (1997). *A Short History of Linguistics.* 4th edn. Longman Linguistics Library. London and New York: Longman. (1st edn. 1967.)

Robins, Robert Henry (1998a). 'The Evolution of English Grammar Books Since the Renaissance', in V. Law (ed.), *Texts and Contexts. Selected Papers on the History of Linguistics*. Münster: Nodus Publikationen, 113–28. (The Henry Sweet Society Studies in the History of Linguistics 5). (Orig. publ. in G. Leitner (ed.) (1986). *The English Reference Grammar*. Linguistische Arbeiten, vol. 172. Tübingen: Niemeyer, 292–306.)

Robins, Robert Henry (1998b). 'William Bullokar's *Bref Grammar for English*: Text and Context', in V. Law (ed.), *Texts and Contexts. Selected Papers on the History of Linguistics*. Münster: Nodus Publikationen, 169–84. (The Henry Sweet Society Studies in the History of Linguistics 5). (Orig. publ. in G. Blaicher and B. Glaser (eds.) (1994), *Anglistentag 1993. Eichstätt. Proceedings*. Tübingen: Niemeyer, 19–31.)

Rosier, Irène (1998a). 'Alexandre de Villedieu', in *HEL*, vol. 1, no. 1229: 63–64.

Rosier, Irène (1998b). 'Johannes de Balbis', in *HEL*, vol. 1, no. 1236: 72–73.

Rosier, Irène (1998c). 'Pierre Helie', in *HEL*, vol. 1, no. 1228: 62–63.

Rosier, Irène, and Vivien Law (1998). 'Ælfric', in *HEL*, vol. 1, no. 1226: 59–60.

Rosier-Catach, Irène (2009). 'Petrus de Isolella', in *Lexicon Grammaticorum*, vol. 2: 1157–58.

Rothwell, William (1983). 'Language and Government in Medieval England', *Zeitschrift für Französische Sprache und Literatur* 93: 258–70.

Sachs, C. E. A. (1858). 'Studien zur Geschichte der englischen Grammatik', *Archiv für das Studium der Neueren Sprachen* 23: 406–14. (Repr. London: Johnson Reprint Corporation, 1967.)

Salmon, Vivian (1989). 'John Rastell and the Normalization of Early Sixteenth-Century Orthography', in L. E. Breivik *et al.* (eds.), *Essays on English Language in Honour of Bertil Sundby. Studia Anglistica Norvegica*, 4. Oslo: Novus, 289–301.

Salmon, Vivian (1999). 'Orthography and Punctuation', in R. M. Hogg (ed.), *The Cambridge History of the English Language*. Vol. III: 1476–1776. Ed. Roger Lass. Cambridge: Cambridge University Press, 13–55, 670–76.

Sauer, Hans (1997). 'Knowledge of Old English in the Middle English Period?', in R. Hickey and Stanisław Puppel (eds.), *Language History and Linguistic Modelling. A Festschrift for Jacek Fisiak on his 60th Birthday*. 2 vols. Trends in Linguistics. Studies and Monographs, 101. Berlin and New York: Mouton de Gruyter, vol. 1: 791–814.

Sayle, Charles E. (1900–1907). *Early English Printed Books in the University Library Cambridge (1475–1640)*. 4 vols. Cambridge; repr. New York: Johnson Reprint, 1971.

Sayle, Charles E. (1913–1915). 'Reynold Wolfe', *Transactions of the Bibliographical Society* 13, 171–92.

Scarisbrick, J. J. (1997). *Henry VIII*. New Haven and London: Yale University Press. (1st edn. 1968.)

Scheurweghs, G. (1961). 'The Influence of the Latin Grammar of William Lily on the Early English Grammarians in the Netherlands (I)', *Leuvense Bijdragen* 50: 140–51.

Schmidt, Gabriela (2007). '"The variety of teaching is divers": Pluralisierung der Autoritäten und die versuchte Etablierung von "Uniformität" im englischen Lateinunterricht unter Heinrich VIII', *Mitteilungen des Sonderforschungsbereichs 573, Pluralisierung und Autorität der Frühen Neuzeit* 2007/2, 43–53. Available at:

<http://www.sfb-frueheneuzeit.uni-muenchen.de/mitteilungen/M2–2007/ pluralisierung.pdf>

Schmitt, Wolfgang O. (1969). 'Die Ianua (Donatus)—ein Beitrag zur Lateinischen Schulgrammatik des Mittelalters und der Renaissance', *Beiträge zur Inkunabelkunde*. Dritte Folge, 4. Berlin: Akademie Verlag, 43–80.

Schulte Herbrüggen, Hubertus (1967). 'Sir Thomas Mores Fortuna-Verse. Ein Beitrag zur Lösung einiger Probleme', in H. Meller and H.-J. Zimmermann (eds.), *Lebende Antike. Symposion für Rudolf Sühnel*. Berlin: Erich Schmidt Verlag, 155–72.

Shaaber, M. A. (1975). *Check-list of Works of British Authors Printed Abroad, in Languages Other Than English, to 1641*. New York: The Bibliographical Society of America.

Sharpe, Richard (1997). *A Handlist of the Latin Writers of Great Britain and Ireland Before 1540*. Turnhout: Brepols. (Publications of the Journal of Medieval Latin, vol. 1.)

Shaw, David J. (1984–1998). *The Cathedral Libraries Catalogue. Books Printed Before 1701 in the Libraries of the Anglican Cathedrals of England and Wales*. 2 vols. (Vol. 2 in 2 parts). London: The British Library and the Bibliographical Society.

Short, Ian (1980). 'On Bilingualism in Anglo-Norman England', *Romance Philology* 33: 467–79.

Short-Title Catalogue of Books Printed in the Netherlands and Belgium and of Dutch and Flemish Books Printed in Other Countries from 1470 to 1600 Now in the British Museum (1965). London: Trustees of the British Museum.

Simon, Joan (1966). *Education and Society in Tudor England*. Cambridge: Cambridge University Press. (Repr. in paperback, 1979.)

Smith, Constance (1981). 'An Updating of R. W. Gibson's "St. Thomas More": A Preliminary Bibliography', *Sixteenth Century Bibliography* 20. St Louis: Center for Reformation Research.

Smith, William G., and Frank P. Wilson (1970). *The Oxford Dictionary of English Proverbs*. With an Introduction by Joanna Wilson. 3rd rev. edn. Oxford: Clarendon Press; repr. 1984. (1st edn. 1935.)

Stammerjohann, Harro (gen. ed.) (2009). *Lexicon Grammaticorum. A Bio-Bibliographical Companion to the History of Linguistics*. 2nd edn., rev. and enl. 2 vols. Tübingen: Niemeyer. (1st edn. 1996.)

Stanier, Robert Spenser (1958). *Magdalen School. A History of Magdalen College School, Oxford*. 2nd edn. Oxford: Blackwell. (1st edn., OHS, New Ser., vol. iii. Oxford: Clarendon Press, 1940.)

Stephen, Leslie, and Sidney Lee (eds.) (1908–1909). *The Dictionary of National Biography*. 22 vols. and its supplements. London: Oxford University Press. (Reissue of the 1st edn. 1885–1900, 63 vols. and 3 supplementary vols.)

Stewart, Mary Beth (1937–1938). 'William Lily's Contribution to Classical Study', *The Classical Journal* 33: 217–25.

Stray, Christopher (1989). 'Paradigms of Social Order: the Politics of Latin Grammar in 19th-Century England', *The Henry Sweet Society Newsletter* 13: 13–24.

Stray, Christopher (1994). '"Paradigms Regained": Towards a Historical Sociology of the Textbook', *Journal of Curriculum Studies* 26: 1–29.

Stray, Christopher (ed.) (1995). *Grinders and Grammars. A Victorian Controversy*. Reading: The Textbook Colloquium.

Stray, Christopher (1996). 'Primers, Publishing, and Politics: The Classical Textbooks of Benjamin Hall Kennedy', *The Papers of the Bibliographical Society of America* 90: 451–74.

Tavoni, Mirko (1998). 'Renaissance Linguistics', in G. Lepschy (ed.), *History of Linguistics*. Vol. 3: *Renaissance and Early Modern Linguistics*. London and New York: Longman, 1–108. (English Translation of *Storia della Linguistica*. Bologna: il Mulino, 1992.) (Longman Linguistics Library.)

Thomson, David (1979). *A Descriptive Catalogue of Middle English Grammatical Texts*. New York and London: Garland.

Thomson, David (1980). 'Grammar in English in the Late Middle Ages', in A. C. de la Mare and B. C. Barker-Benfield (eds.), *Manuscripts at Oxford: An Exhibition in Memory of Richard William Hunt (1908–1979)*. Oxford: Bodleian Library, 79–82.

Thomson, David (1982). 'Cistercians and Schools in Late Medieval Wales', *Cambridge Medieval Celtic Studies* 3: 76–81.

Thomson, David (1983). 'The Oxford Grammar Masters Revisited', *Mediaeval Studies* 45: 298–310.

Tilley, Morris Palmer (1950). *A Dictionary of the Proverbs in England in the Sixteenth and Seventeenth Centuries*. Ann Arbor: University of Michigan Press; repr. 1966.

Todd, Robert B. (ed.). (2004). *The Dictionary of British Classicists*. 3 vols. Bristol: Thoemmes Continuum.

Tournoy, Gilbert (1988). 'La Poésie de William Lily pour le Diptyque de Quentin Metsijs', *Moreana* 25, no. 97: 63–66.

Trapp, J. B. (1991). *Erasmus, Colet and More: The Early Tudor Humanists and Their Books*. The Panizzi Lectures 1990. London: The British Library.

Trapp, J. B., and H. Schulte Herbrüggen (1978). *'The King's Good Servant'. Sir Thomas More 1477/8–1535*. Catalogue of the Exhibition at the National Portrait Gallery, London, from 25 November 1977 to 12 March 1978. London: National Portrait Gallery.

Tuck, J. P. (1951). 'The Latin Grammar, attributed to William Lily', *The Durham Research Review. Institute of Education, University of Durham* 2: 33–39.

Tuck, J. P. (1956). 'The Beginnings of English Studies in the Sixteenth Century', *The Durham Research Review. Institute of Education, University of Durham* 7: 65–73.

Ueding, Gert (ed.) (1992–2011). *Historisches Wörterbuch der Rhetorik*. 10 vols. Tübingen: Niemeyer.

University Microfilms International (1938–). *Early English Books, 1475–1640. Selected from A. W. Pollard and G. R. Redgrave's Short-Title Catalogue of Books Printed in England [. . .]*. 2nd edn. W. A. Jackson, F. S. Ferguson, and K. F. Pantzer. Ann Arbor, Michigan: ProQuest Information and Learning.

Urban, Sylvanus (1756). 'List of Deaths for the Year 1756', *Gentleman's Magazine* 26: 499–500.

Vancil, David E. (1993). *Catalog of Dictionaries, Word Books, and Philological Texts, 1400–1900: Inventory of the Cordell Collection, Indiana State University*. Westport, Conn.: Greenwood Press.

Venn, John, and J. A. Venn (1922–1927). *Alumni Cantabrigienses. A Biographical List of All Known Students, Graduates and Holders of Office at the University of Cambridge, from the Earliest Times to 1900. Part I: From the Earliest Times to 1751*. 4 vols. Cambridge: Cambridge University Press; repr. Nendeln/Liechtenstein: Kraus Reprint, 1974–1976.

Verrac, Monique (2000a). 'Colet, John, [and] Lily, William', in *HEL*, vol. 2, no. 3601: 93–95.

Verrac, Monique (2000b). 'William Bullokar', in *HEL*, vol. 2, no. 3603: 97–100.

Verzeichnis der im deutschen Sprachbereich erschienenen Drucke des XVI. Jahrhunderts. (VD 16) (1983–2000). Herausgegeben von der Bayerischen Staatsbibliothek in München in Verbindung mit der Herzog August Bibliothek in Wolfenbüttel. 25 Bde. Stuttgart: Hiersemann.

Vorlat, Emma (1975). *The Development of English Grammatical Theory, 1586–1737, with Special Reference to the Theory of Parts of Speech.* Leuven: Leuven University Press.

Vorlat, Emma (2009). 'Bullokar, William', in *Lexicon Grammaticorum*, vol. 1: 227–28.

Walmsley, John (2004). 'Latein als Objektsprache, Englisch als Metasprache in Spätmittelalterlichen Grammatischen Texten', in G. Haßler and G. Volkmann (eds.), *History of Linguistics in Texts and Concepts.* 2 vols. Münster: Nodus Publikationen, vol. 2: 455–67.

Walther, Hans (1982–1986). *Proverbia Sententiaeque Latinitatis Medii Ac Recentioris Aevi.* Nova series. Ed. Paul Gerhard Schmidt. 3 Bde. Carmina Medii Aevi Posterioris Latina II/7–9. Göttingen: Vandenhoeck und Ruprecht.

Watanabe, Shoichi (1958). *Studien zur Abhängigkeit der Frühneuenglischen Grammatiken von den Mittelalterlichen Lateingrammatiken.* Münster: Kramer.

Watson, Foster (1908). *The English Grammar Schools to 1660. Their Curriculum and Practice.* Cambridge: Cambridge University Press; repr. London: Cass, 1968.

Weiss, Robert (1967). *Humanism in England During the Fifteenth Century.* 3rd edn. Oxford: Blackwell. (1st edn. 1941.)

Whiting, Bartlett Jere (1968). *Proverbs, Sentences, and Proverbial Phrases from English Writings Mainly Before 1500.* Cambridge, MA: Harvard University Press.

Williams, Edna Rees (1958). 'Ælfric's Grammatical Terminology', *PMLA* 73, no. 5: 453–62.

Williams, R. R. (1940). *Religion and the English Vernacular. A Historical Study, Concentrating upon the Years 1526-53.* London: Society for Promoting Christian Knowledge.

Wing, Donald (1972–1998). *Short-Title Catalogue of Books Printed in England, Scotland, Ireland, Wales, and British America and of English Books Printed in Other Countries, 1641-1700.* 2nd edn., rev. and enl. 4 vols. New York: The Modern Language Association of America. (1st edn. 1945-1951.)

Wolf, Melvin H. (1974). *Catalogue and Indexes to the Title-Pages of English Printed Books Preserved in the British Library's Bagford Collection.* London: British Museum Publications for the British Library Board.

Woolfson, Jonathan (1998). *Padua and the Tudors: English Students in Italy, 1485–1603.* Toronto, Buffalo: University of Toronto Press.

Zachrisson, R. E. (1927). *The English Pronunciation at Shakespeare's Time as Taught by William Bullokar with Word-Lists from all his Works.* Uppsala, Sweden; repr. New York: Ams Press, 1970.

UNPUBLISHED WORKS

Berndt, Rolf (1963). *Die Sprachsituation in England während der ersten dreieinhalb Jahrhunderte nach der normannischen Eroberung. Behauptung und Durchsetzung des Englischen gegenüber dem Französischen.* Habilitationsschrift (Summary). Philosophische Fakultät der Universität Rostock.

Butler, Marilyn Sandidge (1981). *An Edition of the Early Middle English Copy of Ælfric's 'Grammar' and 'Glossary' in Worcester Cathedral MS F.174.* Ph.D. Dissertation. The Pennsylvania State University.

Flynn, Vincent Joseph (1939). *The Life and Works of William Lily, the Grammarian.* D.Phil. Thesis. The University of Chicago. Chicago, Illinois.

Grant Ferguson, Meraud (2001). *A Study of English Book-Trade Privileges during the Reign of Henry VIII.* D.Phil. Thesis. The University of Oxford.

Hirsh, Edward L. (1935). *The Life and Works of George Lily.* Ph.D. Dissertation. New Haven, Conn.

Johnston, Stanley Howard, Jr. (1977). *A Study of the Career and Literary Publications of Richard Pynson.* Ph.D. Dissertation. The University of Western Ontario. London, Ontario.

Neville, Pamela Ayers (1990). *Richard Pynson, King's Printer (1506–1529): Printing and Propaganda in Early Tudor England.* Ph.D. Dissertation. Warburg Institute, University of London.

Thomson, David (1977). *A Study of the Middle English Treatises on Grammar.* 3 vols. D.Phil. Thesis. The University of Oxford.

INDEX

Forenames precede surnames before 1200, and follow them afterwards.

A Short Introduction to the Latin Tongue, see Eton Latin Grammar, The

A Shorte Introduction of Grammar, see An Introduction of the eyght partes of speche, and the Construction of the same

Absolutissimus de octo orationis partium constructione libellus, see Libellus de constructione

Act of Supremacy 223

Ad Pubem Anglicam. Hexasticon, see An Introduction of the eyght partes of speche, and the Construction of the same

Aeditio, see Colet, John

Ælfric Bata, grammarian 38

Ælfric of Eynsham, grammarian 31–35, 37, 40–41, 48

   Colloquy 33, 37–39, 57

   Glossary 32–33, 37–38, 40

   Grammar 29, 32–40, 48, 135, 138, 289, 292, 294, 296, 299, 301, 303, 305, 308

Æsop, *Fables* 71–73

Æthelwold, Bishop of Winchester 32, 35

Alexander de Villa Dei, author of *Doctrinale* 52–54, 57, 62

Alphabetum Latino Anglicum 25, 75–76, 140, 146, 266–67

Altera pro docilitate pietatis 76

Ames, Joseph, bibliographer 25, 145–46, 221

Amor Dei, Amor Sui, Amor Proximi 82

An Introduction of the eyght partes of speche, and the Construction of the same 9, 16, 25, 76, 85–86, 121, 132, 140–41, 148, 254, 263, 266–83, 288

   Ad Pubem Anglicam. Hexasticon 76, 78, 224

   An Introduction of the eighte partes of speche [text on accidence] 76, 141, 151, 256

   Carmen de moribus, see Lily, William

   Christiani Hominis Institutum, see Erasmus

   Concordes of latyne speche, The 76, 80, 141, 256, 258, 264

   Godly Lessons for Chyldren 76, 78–80, 104, 141, 221, 242, 263–64

   Royal Proclamation by Henry VIII, The [text] 8–10, 16, 23–24, 26, 76–77, 84, 86, 110, 122, 150, 221–22, 242

   To the Reder 16, 76–77, 86, 110, 141, 221–22, 226

Anglo-Norman 40–43

Antibossicon, see Lily, William

Anwykyll, John, schoolmaster 63–65, 68, 89, 116

Authorized Version of the Bible (1611) 124

Ave Maria, The 28, 70, 75

Badius, Conrad, printer 269–71

Banbury School, Oxfordshire 118–19

Bartholomaeus Anglicus, friar 252

Battersby, John, printer 4–5, 282–83

Berthelet, Thomas, King's Printer 3, 9, 75, 77–78, 84, 105, 140, 142, 144–45, 148, 220–21, 224, 254–55, 263–64, 266–68, 288

Bible 79, 124, 242, 248

Birch, Thomas 14

Black Death 1, 45

Bollifant, Edmund, alias Carpenter, printer 129

Book of Common Prayer 8

Booke of Fortune, The, see Gualtieri, Lorenzo Spirito, author

Breuissima Institutio seu Ratio Grammatices Cognoscendæ, see Institutio Compendiaria Totius Grammaticæ

Britannicus, Angelus and Jacobus, printers 91

Bullokar, William, author of *Pamphlet for Grammar* 30, 109, 123, 125, 128–39

Burby, Cuthbert, printer 4

Caesar, Gaius Iulius, Commentaries 73

Camden, William, antiquary and headmaster 95

Canterbury, The province of 118

Convocation 119–20

Carmen de moribus, see Lily, William

Cato, *Distichs* 57, 70–73, 253

Caxton, William, printer and author 59, 61

Certayne Briefe Rules of the regiment or construction of the eyght partes of speche 26, 105–106, 244–51

Chaucer, Geoffrey, poet 44
Christiani Hominis Institutum, see Erasmus
Cicero, author 66, 71–73, 79, 245–47, 249
Clement, John, physician 94
Colet, John 2, 16–20, 26, 63, 68, 82–83, 90, 92–95, 117, 226, 253, 284, 286
  Aeditio 6, 17–22, 24, 26, 72–74, 80–83, 88, 93, 100–104, 107, 110, 117–19, 149, 223, 225–36, 238–41, 252–54, 285–86, 289, 292, 294, 297, 299, 301, 303, 306
  Cathechyzon 82
  Statuta Paulinæ Scholæ 72, 83, 91, 93, 117
columnar format, columns, see tabular form, tables
Concordes of latyne speche, The, see An Introduction of the eyght partes of speche
Constitutions and Canons Ecclesiastical (1571), see Episcopal Injunctions
construe, to 80, 104
Convocatio prælatorum (1604), see Episcopal Injunctions
Cornwall, John of, schoolmaster, author of Speculum gramaticale 45–49
Cox, Leonard, schoolmaster 61–62, 118, 284
Cox, Richard, bishop, tutor to Edward VI 71, 86–87, 143, 247
Cracherode, Clayton Mordaunt, book collector 145
Creed, The 28, 70, 75, 82
Cromwell, Thomas, Lord Chancellor of England 84
Cuckfield Grammar School, Sussex 48, 69–70

Dawson, Thomas, printer 4, 5, 279, 281–83
De generibus nominum, see Lily, William
Despauterius, Joannes (Joannes de Spouter), grammarian 71
Dibdin, Thomas Frognall, bibliographer 25, 146, 221
dictamen, treatises on 56
Donate and accidence for children 290, 293, 295, 297, 299, 302, 304, 306
Donatus, Aelius, grammarian
  Ars maior 50–51, 240, 292, 294, 296, 299, 301, 303, 306, 308
  Ars minor 33, 50–51, 53, 56, 58, 80, 104, 112, 226, 228, 230, 240, 292, 294, 296, 299, 301, 303, 306, 308
  Ars minor. A version in Scots 289, 302
  Donet 50–51, 240
Dorne, John, bookseller in Oxford 7, 59, 79
double translation 104
Dunstan, Archbishop of Canterbury 32, 34, 294

Edward III, King of England, Statute of Pleading 44

Edward VI, King of England 3, 9–12, 16, 75, 146, 223, 226
  Injunction (1548) 9–10
Edward, Duke of Somerset 9
Elementary Latin Grammar (1847) 15
Elizabeth I, Queen of England 3–4, 10–13, 223, 265, 286
  Injunction (1560) 10
Elyot, Sir Thomas, author of The Castel of Helth 85–86, 125–26
English Hospice in Rome, The 90
English Primer (authorized in 1545) 7–8, 122
'Englishes, Englysshe' 79–80, 105, 244
Epigrammata Guilielmi Lilii Angli, see Lily, William
Epigrams in Latin and English, see Lily, William
Episcopal Injunctions 11
Erasmus 2, 70, 74, 82, 93, 124, 254, 284, 287
  Christiani Hominis Institutum 76–78, 82–83, 108, 253
  Copia verborum 70–71
  De Modo Repetendae Lectionis 269–71, 274–77, 279, 281
  De Ratione studii 269–71, 275–77, 279, 281
  Epigrammata Desiderii Erasmi Roterodami 285
  Libellus de constructione 6–7, 18, 71, 93, 106–107, 244, 248–52, 284
Eton College 14, 55, 74, 86, 91, 112, 121
  statutes 56
  timetables 48, 69, 70–72, 74
Eton Latin Grammar, The 14–16
Évrard de Béthune, grammarian, author of Graecismus 52, 54, 62
Excerptiones de Prisciano 34, 235
Exeter City Grammar School 56

Farnaby, Thomas, grammar master 14
Fitzroy, Henry, Duke of Richmond and Somerset 84
Flower, Francis, printer, assignes of 3–5, 276–81
Froben, John, printer 94, 284–85
Fullonius, William, schoolmaster 84

Gawain-Poet 44
Genoa, John of (Joannes de Balbis Januensis), author of the Catholicon 53
George III, King of England 224
Godfrey, Garrett 7, 79
Godly Lessons for Chyldren, see An Introduction of the eyght partes of speche
Golden rule 75
Gower, John, poet 44
Grammar patent 3, 5
'Grammarians' War' 91
Grocyn, William, Greek scholar 89, 91
Gualtieri, Lorenzo Spirito, author 288

Hanney, Thomas, grammarian 53
Hart, John, orthoepist 125
Hayne, Thomas, schoolmaster 86
Hazlitt, William Carew, bibliographer 25, 146
Henry IV, King of England 224
Henry VI, King of England 55
Henry VII, King of England 95, 286
Henry VIII, King of England 3, 9, 19, 73, 75, 84, 86, 90, 94–95, 110, 119–20, 222–23, 255, 286
    authorization of the *Grammar* 1, 6–7, 10–11, 22, 85–86, 99, 108, 111, 122–23, 221, 265
    Royal Proclamation by Henry VIII, see An Introduction of the eyght partes of speche, and the Construction of the same
Herbert, William, bibliographer 25, 145–46, 220–21
Higden, Ranulf, historian 45
Hillenius, Hochstratanus (Hillen), Michael, printer 287
Holbein, Hans, the younger, artist 220, 276
Holt, John, grammarian, author of *Lac puerorum* 228, 232, 235–36, 240, 243, 245–46, 290, 293, 295, 297, 300, 302, 304, 306
Horace, poet 70–71, 73, 95, 247
Horman, William, grammar master 79, 91, 286
Hornby, James John, headmaster 15
House of Lords, *Calendar* (10 July 1641) 14
Hunt, Thomas, printer 64

Informatio puerorum 290, 293, 295, 297, 300, 302, 304, 306
Institutio Compendiaria Totius Grammaticæ 8, 16, 19, 25, 76, 120, 140, 145, 266–68, 288, 291, 294, 296, 298, 300, 303, 305, 307
    Ad Lectorem 76
    De Etymologia 76
    De Grammatica et eius partibus. De Orthographia 76
    De Prosodia 77
    Errata Insigniora 76
    Syntaxis. De Constructione Octo Partium 76–77
    Totius Angliae Ludimagistris Ac Grammaticae Praeceptoribus 8, 76
Ipswich Grammar School 70, 72–74, 82, 119
    Rudimenta grammatices et Docendi methodus 72–74, 82, 119

James I, King of England 5
John of Garland, grammarian, author of *Compendium gramatice* 52–53

Kendall, John, administrator 90
Kennedy, Benjamin Hall, headmaster 15

Kennedy, Marion Grace and Julia 15
King Edward VI School, Stratford-upon-Avon 12
King's Bookseller and Stationer, *see* Wolfe, Reyner
Kingsmill, William, teacher 45

Lactantius, Lucius Caecilius Firmianus, poet 287
Laetus, Julius Pomponius, scholar 90
Langland, William, poet 44
Latin English alphabet 75
Latin grammar
    grammatical terminology 33, 35, 37, 48, 103, 115, 127
    humanist grammar 15, 63–66, 118, 121
    monolingual grammar 29, 127
    speculative grammar 31, 51
    uniform grammar 8–9, 12, 84, 118–122, 221, 223
    written in verse 52–54
Latins, *latinitates* 56–57, 70–72, 79
law, canon and civil, study of 28–29
Leland, John, antiquary 94
Leylond, John, grammarian 49–50, 53, 55, 65, 111–12
    Accedence MSS 49–51, 53, 112–14, 225–27, 229–31, 233, 236, 238, 240, 243, 291, 293–96, 298, 300, 302–305, 307
    Comparacio MSS 49, 59
    Formula MSS 49, 246–48
    Informacio MSS 49, 65, 113–14, 244–45, 249
    Other MSS 49, 243, 245
Libellus de constructione octo partium orationis, see Lily, William, *see also* Erasmus
Lily, Agnes, Lily's wife 90, 92, 286
Lily, Dionysia, Lily's daughter 90, 92
Lily, George, Lily's son, canon of St Paul's 89–90, 92
Lily, Peter, Lily's son 90
Lily, William 7, 16, 18–19, 22, 68, 74, 81, 88–98, 100, 284, 286
    Antibossicon 91, 285
    Booke of Fortune, The, see Gualtieri, Lorenzo Spirito
    Carmen de moribus 18, 73–74, 76–78, 81–83, 88, 96, 108, 142, 252–54, 286
    De generibus nominum 18, 71–73, 265, 287
    Epigrammata Guilielmi Lilii Angli 81, 252, 286
    Epigrams in Latin and English. Selections 287
    Libellus de constructione 6–7, 18, 71, 93, 106–107, 244, 248–52, 265, 284
    Rudimenta grammatices 6, 18–24, 72–74, 82, 88, 93, 104–105, 119, 243–46, 251–53, 265, 285–86
Lily, William and Sir Thomas More
    Progymnasmata Thomae Mori et Guilielmi Lilii sodalium 93–94, 284–85

Linacre, Thomas, grammarian
   Progymnasmata grammatices vulgaria 6, 103,
      107, 232, 237, 240, 243, 246–52, 290, 292,
      295, 297, 299, 301, 304, 306
   Rudimenta grammatices 6, 103, 107, 232,
      236–37, 240, 243, 246–52, 289, 292, 294,
      297, 299, 301, 303, 306
Loëus, Joannes, printer 87
London
   Christ's Hospital 86
   Gresham College, *see* Ward, John,
      professor of rhetoric
   Merchant Taylors' School 12, 86
   place of printing 6, 26, 129, 140, 220–21,
      263, 266–69, 271–88
   St Anthony's School 56
   St Paul's School 12, 18, 48, 63, 68, 72–74,
      81–83, 90–91, 93, 95–96, 100, 104,
      117–18, 253, 265, 279
   Westminster School 14, 95
Lord's Prayer, The, *Pater Noster* 28, 70, 75
Lowndes, William Thomas, bibliographer
   25
Lucian (of Samosata), poet 72
Lupset, Thomas, scholar 94, 286
Lyly (Lily), John, playwright 92

Manchester Grammar School, Statutes
   (1 April 1525) 118
Martens, Thierry, printer 253–54
Mary, Princess, sister of Henry VIII, Queen of
   France 84
Mary, Queen of England 4, 10, 132, 134,
   223
   Injunction (1558) 10–11
Maynwaring, Arthur, politician 146
medicine, study of 7, 28, 123
Mercers' Company 91
mnemonic verses 65–67
More, Sir Thomas, statesman 90, 92–93, 95,
   284
   *Progymnasmata Thomae Mori et Guilielmi Lilii
      sodalium*, *see* Lily, William and Sir
      Thomas More
Mosellanus, Petrus (Peter Schade),
   grammarian 71
Mulcaster, Richard, schoolmaster and
   author 12–13, 126
Mylner, Ursyn, printer 285

New Learning 63–64, 66, 68, 108, 111, 116
New Testament 124
Newcome, Henry, schoolmaster 146
Nominale 56, 58, 68
Norton, Bonham, printer 5
Norton, John, printer 5

Omnis donatio bona 76
Omnium Nominum in Regulis 269, 274–82

Oratio ad Deum pro timore pio 76
Oswald, Bishop of Worcester and
   Archbishop of York 32
Ovid, poet 70, 72–73, 244
Oxford
   Cardinal College, now Christ Church 72,
      119
   Christ Church, Hall 96
   Magdalen College 64, 89, 116
   Magdalen College School 59–60, 63–65,
      68, 72, 89, 116, 119
   Merton College 46
   New College 55, 65
   Oxford dictatores 45
   place of printing 56, 64, 116
   St Mary's Hall 87
   University of 45–46
Oxford proof leaf 77, 80, 242, 262–64, 266

Pace, Richard, ambassador 94
Palsgrave, John, teacher and scholar of
   languages 83–85
parse, to 80, 104, 130, 133, 244
Paul's Accidence, *see* Aeditio
Payne, Roger, bookbinder 145
Pencrich, Richard, schoolmaster 46
Pernumia, Joannes Paulus, author 281
Perottus, Nicolaus, grammarian, author of
      Rudimenta grammatices 7, 63, 65, 117,
      292, 294, 296, 298, 301, 303, 305, 308
Petrus de Hispanus, grammarian 52
Petrus de Isolella, grammarian 53
Petrus Helias, grammarian 51–52
Pirckheimer, Willibald, humanist writer 94
Plato, philosopher 222
Pliny (Plinius), author 65, 91
Powell, William, printer 288
presentation copy 75–76
primer 2
Printers of the University of Cambridge 5
Priscian, author of *Institutiones grammaticae*
      33–34, 51, 225, 229, 234–35, 240, 292,
      294, 296, 299, 301, 303, 305, 308
Privy Council decree (April 16th, 1629) 5
Progymnasmata grammatices vulgaria, *see*
      Linacre, Thomas, grammarian
*Progymnasmata Thomae Mori et Guilielmi Lilii
      sodalium*, *see* Lily, William and Sir
      Thomas More
Psalter, The 70
Public School Latin Primer, The 15
Public Schools Act (1868) 15
Pynson, Richard, printer 3, 66, 93, 284–85,
   287

quadrivium, *see* Seven Liberal Arts, The
Queen's Printer, *see* Reynell, Sir Carew
question-and-answer form, catechetical
      form 50, 53, 62, 105, 107, 113–14, 240

Rastell, John, printer 125
Reformation in England 69, 73, 82, 111, 122, 124, 254
Revised Latin Primer, The 15
Reynell, Sir Carew, gentleman pensioner of Queen Elizabeth 4
Rhenanus, Beatus, humanist writer 94
Rightwise, John, grammar master 91–92, 95, 287
Rood, Theodoric, printer 59, 64, 116
Royal Articles, The 11
royal committee, group of experts 8, 86, 88, 99, 104, 108, 110, 223–24
Royal injunctions 9–12
Rudimenta grammatices [Lily], *see* Lily, William
Rudimenta grammatices [Linacre], *see* Linacre, Thomas, grammarian

Saffron Walden Grammar School, Essex 48, 69, 71
Sallust, author 66, 70–73
Sampson, Thomas, teacher 45
Scarbot, Andrew, grammar master 116
Schürer, Matthias, printer 254
Seneca, author 65
Seven Liberal Arts, The 28
Seven Sacraments, The 82, 213, 254
Shakespeare, William 12, 18
Shrewsbury School 15
Skelton, John, poet 91
Smith, Sir Thomas, orthoepist 125
St Albans School 56
Stanbridge, John, grammarian 6–7, 60, 64–65, 68, 116, 119
   Abridged version of the Accidence, with other extracts 290, 293, 295, 298, 300, 302, 304, 307
   Accidence 101–102, 229–30, 232–37, 239–40, 243, 290, 293, 295, 298, 300, 302, 304, 307
   Accidence, a version of the 59, 61, 70–72
   Long Accidence 26, 59–61, 243, 291, 293, 295, 298, 300, 302, 304, 307
   Long Parvula 59–60, 65, 105, 116, 244
   Parvula 60, 70, 72, 105, 244
   Parvulorum institutio, Institutiones parvulorum 66–67, 71, 105, 116, 244
   Short Accidence 60–61, 243, 290, 293, 295, 298, 300, 302, 304, 307
   Sum es fui 59, 70, 236
   Vocabula 68–72
   Vulgaria Stanbrigiana 68
Stapleton, Thomas, theologian 95
Stationers' Company 4–5
Statute of Proclamations (31 Henry VIII, c. 8.) 77
Stockwood, John, grammar master 13
Sulpitius Verulanus, Joannes, grammarian 7, 72, 90, 117

Opus insigne grammaticum 72, 292, 294, 296, 298, 300, 303, 305, 307
Quos decet in mensa 70–71

tabular form, tables 67, 103, 141, 237–38, 241, 248
Talley (Tavelegus), David, classical scholar, author of *Progymnasmata Graecae Grammatices* 87–88
Ten Commandments, The 70, 75, 82
Terence, author 64–66, 70–73, 79, 244, 251
textbook, definition of 1–2
theology, study of 28
Therfore what so euer ye wyll that men shulde do to you, see Golden Rule
Tonbridge School, Kent 13
'Tremulous Hand of Worcester' 40
Treveris, Peter, printer at Southwark 73, 82, 119, 287
Trevisa, John, translator 45, 252
trivium, *see* Seven Liberal Arts, The

uniformity in religious worship 8, 122

Valla, Laurentius, grammarian, author of *Elegantiae* 73
Vaus, John, grammarian 289–90, 292, 295, 297, 299, 302, 304, 306
Verbale 56
Vergil, Polydore, author 95, 286
Virgil, poet 66, 70–72, 247
Visitation Articles and Articles of Enquiry 11
Vocabula 68–69
Vulgaria 56–57, 64, 68–69, 79, 116

Ward, John, professor of rhetoric 14, 86, 145–46
Waynflete, William, bishop 63–64, 116
White, Edward, printer 4–5
Whittington, Robert, grammarian 6–7, 69–70, 72, 91
William the Conqueror 41
Winchester College, Winchester 55, 65, 71–72, 112, 121
   timetable 7, 48, 69, 71–72
Wolfe, Reyner (Reginald), printer 3, 9–10, 268–69, 271–75
Wolsey, Thomas, cardinal 72–74, 119, 286
   Rudimenta grammatices et Docendi methodus Methodus, see Ipswich Grammar School
Worde, Wynkyn de, printer 7, 61, 68, 286
Wright, Edward, bookseller 288
Wyclif, John, translator of the Bible 44, 124
Wycliffites, followers of John Wyclif 124
Wyer, John, printer 220
Wykeham, William, bishop 55, 65

Year Books 44